INTRODUCTION TO COMPUTERS USING THE IBM PC

INTRODUCTION TO COMPUTERS USING THE IBM PC

STEVEN L. MANDELL
Bowling Green State University

WEST PUBLISHING COMPANY
St. Paul New York Los Angeles San Francisco

COPYRIGHT © 1985 By WEST PUBLISHING COMPANY
50 West Kellogg Boulevard
P.O. Box 43526
St. Paul, MN 55165

Printed in the United States of America

Library of Congress Cataloging in Publication Data

Mandell, Steven L.
Introduction to Computers Using the IBM PC.

Includes index.
1. Computers. 2. IBM PC Personal Computer. I. Title.
QA76.M27478 1985 001.64 85-8977
ISBN 0-314-85267-0

Cover Photo: Fran Heyl Associates. Photo by Dan McCoy. Airbrushing by Taly Design.
Composition: Parkwood Composition Service, Inc.
Copy Editor: JoAnn Naplos

Frontmatter Photo Credits

Chapter 1 Courtesy of Paradyne Corporation, **Chapter 2** Woodfin & Camp Associates, Photo by Sepp Seitz, **Chapter 3** Courtesy of Commodore, **Chapter 4** Courtesy of Commodore, **Chapter 5** Courtesy of Radio Shack, a Division of Tandy Corporation, **Chapter 6** Courtesy of RB Robot Corporation, **Chapter 7** Courtesy of Bell Laboratories, **Chapter 8** Courtesy of Consolidated Rail Corporation, **Chapter 9** © Copyright, The Exploratorium, Ed Tannenbaum, **Chapter 10** Woodfin & Camp Associates, Photo by Don Hentich, **Chapter 11** Courtesy of IBM, **Chapter 12** Courtesy of DATAPRODUCTS Corporation, **Chapter 13** © Copyright Phillip A. Harrington, **Chapter 14** Courtesy of Bell Laboratories, **Chapter 15** Courtesy of Sperry-Univac Corporation, **Chapter 16** Courtesy of The Naval Photographic Center, Naval District Washington, Washington, D.C., **Chapter 17** Courtesy of Auto-trol Technology Corporation.

Part and Chapter Opening Photos

Part I Courtesy of Westinghouse Electric Corporation—Industry Electronics Division, **Chapter 1** Courtesy of Producer—Robert Abel; Director/Designer—Randy Roberts; Production Company Producer—Robert Abel; Technical Director—Richard Hollander; Cameraman—John Nelson; Editor—Rick Ross; Model Photography—Tom Barron, Tony Meininger, **Chapter 2** Photo courtesy of 3M, **Chapter 3** Courtesy of Autodesk Incorporated, **Chapter 4** Courtesy of Radio Shack, a division of Tandy Corporation, **Chapter 5** Photo by Norma Morris, **Chapter 6** Courtesy of RCA, **Part II** Courtesy of Evans & Sutherland and Mechanical Dynamics, Inc., **Chapter 7** Courtesy of Pelham and Friends Photography, **Chapter 8** Courtesy of Woodfin Camp & Associates, **Chapter 9** Courtesy of Apple Computer, Inc., **Chapter 10** Courtesy of Apple Computer, Inc., **Chapter II** Dennis Wasserman, Columbus College of Art and Design, Computer Graphics, **Part III** Courtesy of International Business Machines Corporation, **Chapter 12** Courtesy of International Business Machines Corporation, **Chapter 13** Photo courtesy of Hewlett-Packard, **Chapter 14** Courtesy of International Business Machines Corporation, **Chapter 15** Courtesy of Robert Abel and Associates, **Chapter 16** Photo courtesy of Hewlett-Packard, **Chapter 17** Photo provided by Delta Air Lines.

Intext Photo Credits

Fig. 1–1 Courtesy of NASA, **Fig. 1–2** Courtesy of The Coca-Cola Company, **Fig. 1–3** Courtesy of International Business Machines Corporation, **Fig. 1–4** Courtesy of International Business Machines Corporation, **Fig. 1–5** Courtesy of International Business Machines Corporation, **Fig. 1–6** Courtesy of International Business Machines Corporation, **Fig. 1–7** Crown Copyright, Science Museum, London, **Fig. 1–8** Courtesy of International Business Machines Corporation, **Fig. 1–9** Courtesy of International Business Machines Corporation, **Fig. 1–10** Courtesy of International Business Machines Corporation, **Fig. 1–11** Courtesy of Cruft Photo Lab, Harvard University—photographed by Paul H. Donaldson, **Fig. 1–12** Courtesy of Sperry Corporation, **Fig. 1–13** Courtesy of Sperry Corporation, **Fig. 1–14** Courtesy of International Business Machines Corporation, **Fig. 1–15** Courtesy of International Business Machines Corporation, **Fig. 1–16** Courtesy of NCR, Dayton, Ohio, **Fig. 1–17** Photo courtesy of Digital Equipment Corporation, **Fig. 1–18** Courtesy of Radio Shack, a division of Tandy Corporation, **Fig. 2–4** Courtesy of Microsci, **Fig. 2–5** Courtesy of AT&T Bell Laboratories, **Fig. 2–6** Courtesy of Intel Corporation, **Fig. 2–8** Photo courtesy of Boise Cascade Corporation, **Fig. 2–11** Courtesy of Dysan Corporation, **Fig. 2–13** Courtesy of Control Data Corporation, **Fig. 2–14** Courtesy of Verbatim Corporation, **Fig. 2–15** Courtesy of International Business Machines Corporation, **Fig. 2–18** Photo by Norma Morris, **Fig. 2–19** Photo courtesy of Wang Laboratories, Inc., **Fig. 2–24** Courtesy of Interstate Voice Products, **Fig. 2–25** Courtesy of International Business Machines Corporation, **Fig. 2–26** Courtesy of Dataproducts, **Fig. 2–28** Courtesy of Dataproducts, **Fig. 2–32** Courtesy of Datagraphix, Inc., **Fig. 2–33** Courtesy of Hewlett-Packard Company, **Fig. 2–34** Courtesy of Anderson-Jacobson, **Fig. 2–35** Courtesy of NCR, **Fig. 2–36** Courtesy of Hewlett-Packard Company, **Fig. 2–37** Photo courtesy of Armstrong flooring, **Fig. 2–38** Courtesy of Lockheed-California Company, **Fig. 2–39** Courtesy of The Computer Colorworks, **Fig. 2–40** Courtesy of Apple Computer, Inc., **Fig. 3–1** Courtesy of TRW Inc., **Fig. 3–7** Courtesy of Zenith Data Systems, **Fig. 3–16** Courtesy of Texas Instruments, **Fig. 4–1** Courtesy of Apple Computer, Inc., **Fig. 4–2** Courtesy of Radio Shack, a division of Tandy Corporation, **Fig. 4–3** Reproduced with permission of AT&T Corporate Archive, **Fig. 4–4** Courtesy of Sperry Corporation, **Fig. 4–5** Photo by Norma Morris, **Fig. 4–6** Photo courtesy of Hewlett-Packard Company, **Fig. 4–7** Courtesy of Radio Shack, a division of Tandy Corporation, **Fig. 4–8** Courtesy of Apple Com-

Credits are continued following the index.

CONTENTS IN BRIEF

CONTENTS

CHAPTER **5**

COMPUTERS' IMPACT ON SOCIETY
123

CHAPTER **8**

DATA MANAGER

199

CHAPTER **9**

GRAPHICS AND OTHER SOFTWARE PACKAGES

247

PREFACE

In the last few years there has been an explosion in the number of students taking introductory courses on computers. The content of these courses is undergoing constant rethinking and revision. Based upon my discussions with college educators around the country, I began to witness a new trend emerging. Students were gaining an increased awareness of the usefulness of computers through personal implementation of application packages. A word-processing program is considered an essential tool for any student while spreadsheets, file managers, and graphics are increasing significantly in importance. My goal then became to combine computer concepts, application packages, and BASIC programming in a single textbook. The design of this approach is unique because software is integrated directly into the learning experience. However, the material is flexible enough to utilize other software packages. Two years of very hard work with my publisher and programmers have resulted in the book and disks you hold in your hands. Three versions of this text are currently available: Apple (II family), IBM* (PC DOS and MS DOS), and TRS-80 (III and IV).

In structuring the material to be included in these books, I worked closely with both my introductory students at Bowling Green State University and faculty members in other departments teaching computer fundamentals. Our computer labs were filled with students using different prototypes of the software on different machines. The enthusiasm of the students kept me pressing ahead through the lengthy development process.

I was unable to revise any of the existing applications packages to fit my instructional criteria. It was necessary to have software that was user friendly but also would give the appearance of the widely used sophisticated packages. The ultimate result was the need to create a new word processor, (WestWord™) file manager, (WestFile™) spreadsheet, (WestCalc™) and graphics package (WestGraph™) that would satisfy our requirements. After fully operational software packages were developed, we backed down into the instructional subset that is presented in this book. An even smaller subset has been subjected to extensive field testing in conjunction with my original textbook—*Computers and Data Processing: Concepts and Applications,* Third Edition.

*IBM, IBM PC, and IBM PCjr are trademarks of International Business Machines Corporation.

Whenever I am teaching BASIC programming to students, the line outside my office door never seems to diminish. Many of the questions indicate that additional examples and alternate presentations of the material would have provided a satisfactory result. Therefore, I created a BASIC tutorial program (WestTutor™) that presents the same material found in the text in a totally different manner with all new examples. Implementation of this software greatly reduced the number of students seeking assistance and raised test scores. Once again the positive student response to my efforts kept the project alive.

This book has been divided into three sections. The first part focuses on fundamental computer concepts. Through the use of full color and graphics, I believe that this section is one of the most visually appealing presentations of computer concepts. In the second section, applications software comes alive for the student. A friendly introduction to the generic fundamentals of these programs coupled with extensive descriptions, screens, and exercises permits the student to actually master these packages. BASIC programming is presented in the final section of the textbook. The principal instructions required to create a useable program are presented along with numerous examples.

The basic pedagogical format found in this book is designed to aid student comprehension of the material. Chapter outlines are presented to provide a framework for the student. Learning Checks are included throughout all of the chapters to permit immediate feedback on comprehension. Summary Points permit the student to review the material. Questions, Hands-on Exercises, and Programming Exercises afford the student an opportunity to display mastering of the material in a supportive fashion.

I was very fortunate to have had several outstanding college educators serve as reviewers for this project. It is very difficult to express my thanks for their help and aid in shaping this project. Without the professional efforts of the following individuals, this book would not be nearly as effective a teaching vehicle:

Wilbur P. Dershimer
Seminole Community College, Florida

J. Pat Fenton
West Valley College, California

Robert S. Fritz
American River College, California

Pat Hart
Custom Software Unlimited, California

John M. Peavler
Software Consultant, Idaho

Leonard Presby
William Paterson College of New Jersey

Steve W. Wong
Merritt College, California

Wayne M. Zage
Purdue University, Indiana

Supplementary Educational Material

A complete instructor resource package has been designed to reduce administrative efforts. The classroom support for each chapter of the first section includes a detailed Lecture Outline, Answers to Review Questions, and Additional Questions. For the Packaged Software section, Answers to Exercises in the Text and Additional Exercises (with answers) are included to supplement the West Publishing Company Instructional Diskettes. The BASIC Programming section includes Answers to Programming Exercises in the Text and a minimum of fifteen Additional Programming Exercises per chapter, for a combined total of over 140 programming exercises in the text and the Instructor's Manual. All programs are accompanied by a flowchart and an actual printout of the program. A Test Bank with over 800 multiple choice questions is also included in the Instructor's Manual. Answers to the questions follow each chapter test.

There are over fifty Transparency Masters provided in the Instructor's Manual. Transparency Masters of the computer display screens shown in the Packaged Software section aid in the discussion of the WestFile™, WestGraph™, WestWord™, and WestCalc™ diskettes. Masters of sample programs and flowcharts aid in the discussion of BASIC programming.

Educational versions of a word processor (WestWord™), electronic spreadsheet (WestCalc™), file manager (WestFile™), graphics package (WestGraph™) are provided on diskettes. Each educational program corresponds to a chapter in Section II of the text, Packaged Software, so the student can gain hands-on experience while learning about microcomputers and applications software. These instructional packages will acquaint students with the basic concepts of commercial software packages in a simple, easy-to-follow format.

WestTutor™ is a computer-assisted instruction package to be used to support Section III, BASIC Programming. Instructions are provided at the bottom of each screen to direct the student through the tutorial. At the end of a section, check-point questions are included to test the student's understanding of the material. The student reads each question and selects an answer. The program then indicates whether the correct answer was chosen and gives an explanation of why the answer is correct.

Acknowledgments

Numerous corporations and government agencies provided the color photographs found in this book. Many professionals provided the assistance required for completion of a textbook of this magnitude: Kim Girnus, Karen McKee, Rick Rabb, Phil Robb, Bob Szymanski, and Russ Thompson on packaged software; Sue Baumann and Mike Costarellq on BASIC; Shannan Benschoter, Linda Cupp, and Meredith Flynn on manuscript preparation. A special note of appreciation goes to Laura Bores for her helpful suggestions and valuable contributions to the student material.

The design of the book is a tribute to the many talents and great patience of John Orr. The production of the book is a credit to Sharon Walrath.

Norma Morris gave her heart and soul to this project in addition to her organization and editing skills. One final acknowledgment goes to my publisher and valued friend, Clyde Perlee, Jr. If it were not for his constant encouragement, this project would never have been completed.

Steven L. Mandell

INTRODUCTION TO COMPUTERS USING THE IBM PC

PART I

COMPUTER LITERACY

CHAPTER 1

COMPUTERS IN THE WORLD AROUND US

Chapter Outline

INTRODUCTION

Twenty-five years ago, talk of computers centered on how they could be used in business, science, and technology. One could easily list the areas where computers were being used, because their use was quite limited. Today, it would not be so easy to make such a list. In fact, it might be easier to list the areas where computers are *not* being used. The reality is that computers have entered almost every aspect of the average American's life.

Think of the many household items that use some type of computer. Televisions, video recorders, stereos, ovens, and even coffee makers are computer-controlled. Computerized phones can store and dial up to a hundred telephone numbers. A simple voice command such as "Phone Mom" will instruct the machine to dial your mother's number.

In many American households, the home video game craze of the late 1970s has given way to the personal computer craze. In 1984, an estimated 10 percent of American households had personal computers. Home computer use goes far beyond budgeting tasks like checkbook balancing and tax preparation. For example, computers can simplify meal planning by developing menus, making up shopping lists, and suggesting dishes that use only the ingredients you have on hand! Electrical appliances, lawn sprinklers, and burglar alarm systems can be controlled by personal computers.

Our cars contain computer devices that control the functions of the engine and act as miniature service stations, checking to make sure everything is in proper working condition. In some large cities, computers monitor and direct traffic flow on highways, helping to prevent bottlenecks, especially during rush hour.

In the workplace, computerization has made bookkeeping, financial analysis, and manufacturing processes, among other functions, faster and more efficient. Presidents of companies use small computers to help them make decisions. Word processors, minicomputers and microcomputers, robots, and telecommunication systems are all examples of computer technology that is becoming common in everyday work.

The list of other tasks that are made easier by computers is almost endless. Computers are used in medical research to test new drugs, in science to predict the weather, in music to synthesize and reproduce sounds, in art to produce pictures of near-photographic quality, and in education to help students learn basic skills. Moviegoers may notice an increased sophistication in special effects, thanks to computer scene simulation. Even the farmer of the 1980s benefits from computer use in bookkeeping, maintaining animal health records, and devising economical feed programs.

Computer
A general-purpose machine with applications limited by the creativity of the humans who use it.

These examples demonstrate the dramatic effects computers have on all of us, every day. Chapter 1 discusses additional examples of how computers are used in society and provides introductory material to start you on the road to understanding the machine we call the **computer.**

COMPUTERS IN SOCIETY

The Earth and Beyond

One interesting use of computers involves the space shuttle flights (see Figure 1–1). The shuttle computers have nearly total control of the shuttle

Figure 1–1 COMPUTER DISPLAY SCREENS IN SPACE SHUTTLE
Many computer devices appear in this "fish-eye" lens view of the flight deck of the Space Shuttle Orbiter 102 Columbia. The three cathode ray tubes (CRTs) display data and information for the crew.

from just before the launch until just before landing. Even when they are not in total control, the computers interpret the actions of the pilot and send the signals that command the shuttle.

On board each shuttle are five computers. Four of them work together to operate the shuttle. These four main computers process the same data. All four must agree for the systems they control to operate normally. If one computer doesn't agree, it is turned off, and the other three operate the shuttle. If one of the three remaining computers disagrees, it too will be shut off, with the remaining two left to make the decisions. If the remaining two computers disagree, both are turned off, and the fifth computer is turned on to make the final decision.

We can appreciate the importance of the shuttle computers when we see the amount of data that must be processed. During the first shuttle flight, which lasted just over fifty-four hours, the computers processed 324 billion instructions. Such instructions must be executed very quickly. During some parts of the flights, the computers perform 325,000 operations each second. With this amount of on-board computer power, today's shuttle flights can be handled by only four ground controllers; the earlier Apollo flights used hundreds of controllers.

Computers also are used in space for other applications. The dozens of satellites orbiting Earth are controlled by computers. These computers handle communications, track weather, and gather geographic data, among other jobs. Satellites gather data in the form of photographs, television images, or infrared photos. This data is sent to Earth stations that house computer systems into which the data is entered. The computers process the data into forms usable by geographers, meteorologists, or military personnel. For example, U.S. military satellites can sense the testing, deployment, or launching of nuclear weapons. They can also detect the location of nuclear weapon production plants anywhere around the world.

Although most satellites perform satisfactorily in orbit, sometimes problems arise with the satellites or their computers. Recently, a satellite that had been in space only a short time veered out of its orbit. A program error had caused the computer to execute its instructions in an incorrect order and turn the satellite in the wrong direction.

Daily Encounters

The business world has come to depend on computers for its daily operations. The types of computers businesses use vary from computers that fill large rooms to very small computers that sit on individual desks.

Some organizations have used computers merely to simplify their accounting activities. In other organizations, computers enhance decision making. For instance, computers can calculate sales forecasts using any number of variables or combinations of variables. A computer can quickly check the effects on sales by manipulating variables such as price, inventory level, advertising dollars spent, or coupons offered. Before computers were available to businesses, tasks like sales forecasting had to be kept simple because of limits on people's time and capabilities. Today, the computer's high speed and high memory capacity help produce better sales forecasts and perform more complex calculations.

Furthermore, the use of computers has greatly reduced the number of errors in various business calculations. Clerks sometimes transpose figures or make mistakes in manual addition or subtraction. Modern computers are so reliable that they almost never make these kinds of errors.

Most businesses lend themselves to computerization. Historically, the types of jobs most easily computerized have been routine, repetitive jobs. These simple tasks can be performed by a computer quickly and accurately. A good example is the preparation of a company's payroll. The preparer first must find each employee's gross pay by multiplying the pay rate by the number of hours worked, then must subtract taxes and other deductions from gross pay to arrive at net pay. This process must be repeated for each employee. When given a set of instructions, the computer can figure payrolls quickly with little error.

On the other hand, the decision-making aspects of a business are not easily computerized. These processes are not routine and are hard to define, making it difficult to write specific instructions for the computer. Many businesses are now computerizing risk analysis, one important aspect in business decision making. Risk analysis determines if a business investment will be profitable. The largest users of computerized risk analysis to date have been oil companies and utilities. Utility companies generally use the analysis to determine locations for nuclear power stations, while oil companies use it to place offshore oil-drilling rigs.

Many businesses link their computers by communication lines so that several computers may share data and programs. Connecting computers eliminates the need to duplicate the data stored by each computer. The data is more easily kept up-to-date, because all changes made to the data on any computer are immediately accessible by the other computers.

In many cases, telephone wires link the computers. Recently, the use of fiber optic cables has improved transmission. For example, communications in the financial district of Miami are carried on pulses of light sent over the hair-thin glass fibers. These communication lines transmit voice and data. With glass fibers, the data transmissions are quicker and more accurate than with conventional lines.

Just as computers improve business people's performance, they improve the services offered to consumers. Computers affect the way many businesses, from banks to restaurants to grocery stores, deal with their customers.

Shopping is a popular activity, and large shopping malls cater to this popularity. But many malls are confusing because of their size and the complex layout of their stores. Now the confusion has been lessened in some shopping malls around the country by computers that act as electronic directories. Mall shoppers can use the computers to locate restaurants, restrooms, and even stores offering sales. This type of system could also be used in airports, museums, and hotels.

Figure 1–2 TALKING VENDING MACHINE *Customers get a "thank you" when they purchase Coke from the "talking vendor." Maybe it's harder to kick a machine that says nice things!*

Even vending machines have been computerized. An example is the Coca-Cola Company's talking vending machine in Figure 1–2. As is often the case with novelties, this one seems to be paying off. The machine greets customers, asks them for more money if they haven't deposited enough, tells them if the soft drink they have selected is sold out, and at the end of the transaction cheerily invites them to "come again." Between customers, the machine plays music. Bottlers who use the new dispenser report "tremendous" increases in sales.

Imagine the kitchen in a popular restaurant during its busiest lunch hour—waitresses scurrying around, picking up customer orders, and cooks shouting among themselves. This scene might describe a normal restaurant kitchen but not one that uses a computerized ordering system. Just such a system improves the service at the American Cafe, a restaurant on Capitol Hill in Washington, D.C.

At the American Cafe, waitresses enter orders at a computer keyboard terminal. The orders are flashed on a video screen for the chefs in the kitchen. The system eliminates order slips, lost orders, misinterpretations of waitresses' handwriting, and wasted trips to the kitchen to check on orders. Since all orders are entered on the computer, the restaurant manager can easily obtain information about what the most popular menu items are, what inventory levels are for each stock item, and how much money each waitress brings in, hour by hour. Information of this sort saves time and helps the manager control the restaurant better.

Schools are joining businesses and homes as frequent computer users. **Computer-assisted instruction (CAI)** is an increasingly popular way to use computers as educational tools (see Figure 1–3). When students use computers to help them build basic skills in math, science, and grammar, they can work at their own paces and receive immediate feedback. Because the computer constantly monitors a student's progress, the student can spend more time on trouble areas without delay in feedback. The use of

Computer-assisted instruction (CAI)
Direct interaction between a student and a computer acting as an instructor.

Figure 1–3 COMPUTER-ASSISTED INSTRUCTION
Computer-assisted instruction is becoming more popular in the United States. Although much CAI is oriented toward reinforcing basic skills, new CAI software simulates real-life events and teaches thinking skills in addition to memory skills.

CAI in the classroom also gives the teacher more time to spend with students individually. Another advantage is that students become familiar with the uses and benefits of computers.

One example of CAI is a computerized study course available to help students prepare to take the Scholastic Aptitude Test (SAT). This course has a question mode and a test mode. The question mode helps the student prepare for the test by explaining why answers are correct or incorrect and by suggesting problem-solving strategies. The test mode offers timed practice exams. After taking the practice exam, the student receives scores, including the number of correct and incorrect answers, a scaled SAT score, and the percentage of correct answers in each skill area.

The computer can also be an effective spelling teacher. Help sessions and spelling quizzes are provided for the student's use. At the end of a quiz, the student is shown the correct spelling of all misspelled words. Any words the student has misspelled are presented first in the next quiz to give the student another chance to learn the correct spelling. At the end of a session, a bar chart is displayed on the screen to show the results of the quizzes.

Computers can also help school administrators. Simulating bus loads, maintaining schedules, monitoring material lending, and generating library catalogs are a few of their many uses. By computerizing these tasks, administrators and teachers free themselves from some administrative tasks and gain more time to work with students.

Computers After Hours

Computers play important roles in sports and entertainment, too. For example, computers deserve some recognition for helping the U.S. ski team win three gold and two silver medals during the 1984 Winter Olympics. Computers helped the team in three ways: administration of business matters, education and entertainment for athletes, and development of training and sports medicine programs. The computer helped to develop special diets and training schedules for each skier according to individual physical characteristics and type of racing. The team's sports medicine program used the computer as an aid in evaluating each athlete's physical and psychological profile. Individualized counseling programs were set up to help the athletes perform better on the slopes.

In many sports, computers keep statistics on teams and players that would be quite time-consuming to calculate manually. For example, using basketball data such as points scored, minutes played, and rebounds made, the computer can calculate points per minute, rebounds per minute, and many other statistics for each player. This type of information can be used to evaluate a player's overall performance or to compare one player with another or with team averages.

Real sports players form the basis for some new video games for home computers. One game pits Larry Bird of the Boston Celtics against Julius Erving of the Philadelphia 76'ers in a nonstop game of one-on-one basketball. Video-game matchups between sports figures in baseball and tennis are being planned. An earlier computerized contest called "The Greatest Game Never Played" pitted National League baseball stars like Hank Aaron against Babe Ruth and other American Leaguers. An Apple computer selected the two teams from real statistics and then projected how they would fare against each other.

A new twist in home computer games is interactive fiction, which is much like a murder mystery or a science-fiction thriller. However, the player controls the action and makes all the decisions, using imagination and ingenuity to solve mysteries or fulfill fantasy adventures. Each game has many endings but only one ultimate solution. The player moves through the game while the computer program advances the plot. This interaction between the player's moves and the program permits an almost limitless number of variations. Computer games like this allow people to become super sleuths or cosmic warriors right in their own living rooms.

The use of computers has become such an everyday part of our lives that it is easy to forget that only forty-five years ago most people had barely heard of computers. Computer technology has advanced rapidly since the completion of ENIAC, the first electronic computer put to large-scale use, in the 1940s.

HISTORY OF THE COMPUTER

Early Developments

True electronic computers entered the technological revolution only about forty-five years ago. But they are linked to a long line of calculating devices that began in prehistoric times when shepherds tied knots in pieces of string to keep count of their herds.

Abacus
An early calculating device on which rows of beads on wires are used to perform mathematical operations.

A better place to begin studying the evolution of computers would probably be after prehistoric times, with the invention of the **abacus,** one of the earliest known computational devices. An abacus consists of several wires or posts, each strung with seven beads, as shown in Figure 1–4. The abacus user performs additions and subtractions by moving the beads on the wires.

Mechanical calculator
A calculator in which numbers are manipulated through a series of gears.

Pascal, Blaise
A French mathematician credited with developing the first mechanical calculator in 1642.

Leibnitz, Gottfried von
A German mathematician who developed a device that added, subtracted, multiplied, divided, and calculated square roots.

The invention of the first **mechanical calculator** is credited to **Blaise Pascal,** a French mathematician and physicist, in 1642. The calculator, shown in Figure 1–5, was operated by gears, much as a car's mileage odometer is. Pascal's calculator was only capable of adding and subtracting. Then, around 1690, **Gottfried von Leibnitz,** a German mathematician, used Pascal's ideas to create a device that could add, subtract, multiply, divide, and calculate square roots (see Figure 1–6).

Jacquard, Joseph
A Frenchman who used punched cards to alter weaving loom settings without human intervention.

In these early machines, the gears had to be reset by the user for each separate operation. One of the first signs of automation came in France's weaving industry during the early 1800s, when **Joseph Jacquard** developed a loom controlled by a series of punched cards (see Figure 1–7). Each card, made of cardboard, contained a coded instruction in its pattern of holes. As the cards passed over a series of rods, the rods "read" the holes and translated the codes into different colors and weave patterns. These punched cards are recognized as the forerunners of computer programs because they affected what the machine did without changing the machine in any way.

Babbage, Charles
The father of computers; designed the difference engine and the analytical engine.

Difference engine
A machine developed by Charles Babbage in 1822 to compute logarithm tables.

In the early 1800s, the English inventor **Charles Babbage** designed and built an experimental model of a device called the **difference engine** (see

Figure 1–4 THE ABACUS
The invention of the abacus is often credited to the Chinese. Abacuses like the one pictured are still used in places such as Shanghai.

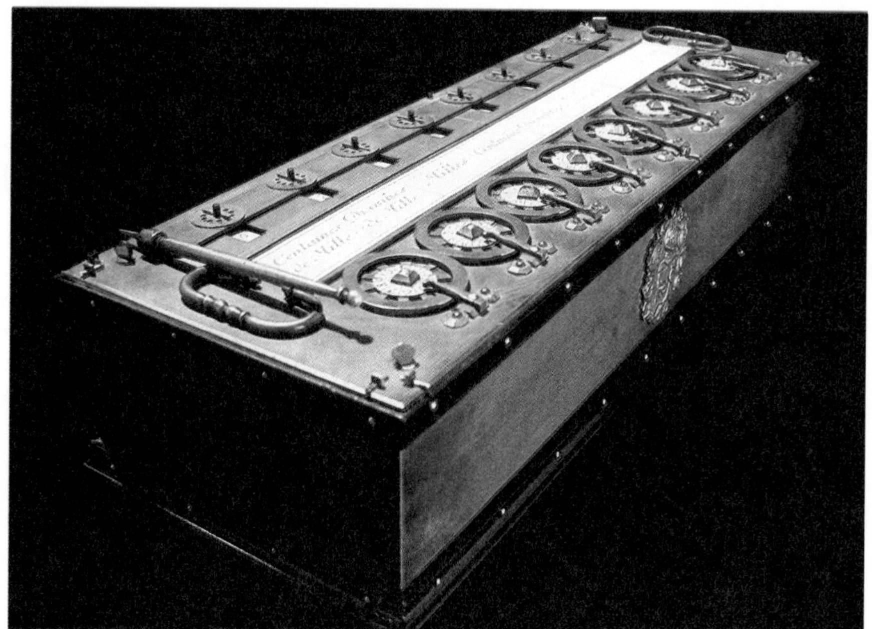

Figure 1–5 PASCAL'S MECHANICAL CALCULATOR
Pascal got the idea for his invention when he was helping his father prepare tax reports for government officials in Paris. However, clerks and bookkeepers never used his invention because they were afraid they would lose their jobs to the machines.

Figure 1–8). It was designed to calculate logarithm tables without human intervention. Unfortunately, when Babbage tried to make a larger version of the difference engine, he found that manufacturers could not produce parts precise enough to meet the machine's requirements.

Later, Babbage worked on a new model he called the **analytical engine;** it could add, subtract, multiply, and divide according to instructions coded in punched holes on cards. The results were to be kept in a memory unit called the "store." Although Babbage died before he could build the analytical engine, his son used his notes and drawings to build a working model of the machine. Because of his inventions, Babbage is known as the father of computers.

The idea of using punched cards for putting data and instructions into the machine was adopted in the 1880s by **Herman Hollerith** and employees of the U.S. Census Bureau, who developed machines that sorted and stored census data on cards (see Figure 1–9). Hollerith designed a card about the size of a dollar bill with eighty columns and twelve rows onto which coded data could be recorded as punched holes. A machine then

Figure 1–7 JACQUARD'S LOOM
In Jacquard's loom, a string of cards passed over a group of rods. The rods were attached to the colored threads used in the weaving pattern. The holes in the cards determined which of the rods pulled the threads down at a given time.

Analytical engine
An invention by Charles Babbage that incorporated several ideas used in computers today, such as memory and punched cards.

Hollerith, Herman
An American who designed a machine to read data from punched cards.

Figure 1–6 LEIBNITZ'S MACHINE
Fifty years passed between Pascal's invention and Leibnitz's machine. Machines developed during these fifty years could not do much more than Pascal's machine.

Figure 1–8 BABBAGE'S DIFFERENCE ENGINE Babbage's model of the difference engine worked very well, so he received a grant from the British government to build a full-scale version. But Babbage could not build the precision parts for his machine, and the grant was withdrawn after much money had been wasted.

read the data from the cards. Despite a population increase of three million between 1880 and 1890, the time needed to process the census data was reduced from seven and a half years in 1880 to two and a half years in 1890, thanks to Hollerith's machines.

During the late 1920s and early 1930s, accounting machines evolved that could perform extensive record-keeping functions by using many punched cards. Although they handled America's business data-processing load well into the 1950s, these machines were limited in speed, size, and versatility because they relied on moving mechanical parts (see Figure 1–10).

A major step toward the development of the modern computer came in 1944 when **Howard Aiken,** a professor of mathematics at Harvard University, designed a machine called the Mark I. The **Mark I,** shown in Figure 1–11, was the first **automatic calculator.** It used electromagnetic relays and mechanical counters instead of mechanical gears to perform arithmetic operations. With this shift to electricity, a new way to instruct the machine was needed. On mechanical devices, the gears could be positioned (by hand or punched card) to represent different numbers. But the electric currents that operated the Mark I had only two states—on and off—to represent numbers. Therefore, a computer "language" based on the **binary number system,** which uses groups of 1s and 0s to represent on and off, had to be used with the Mark I. This computer language is called **machine language** because the computer can directly interpret the instructions.

Two years after the development of the Mark I, the first digital electronic calculator computer put to large-scale use was completed at the University of Pennsylvania. This machine was called the **ENIAC,** short for Electronic Numerical Integrator and Calculator (see Figure 1–12). A **digital computer** operates on binary digits to perform arithmetic processes such as addition.

The ENIAC could multiply two ten-digit numbers in 3/1,000 of a second,

Aiken, Howard
Harvard University professor who designed the Mark I, the first automatic calculator.

Mark I
The first automatic calculator; used electromagnetic relays and mechanical counters instead of mechanical gears to perform arithmetic operations.

Automatic calculator
A device that used electromagnetic relays and mechanical counters to handle numbers.

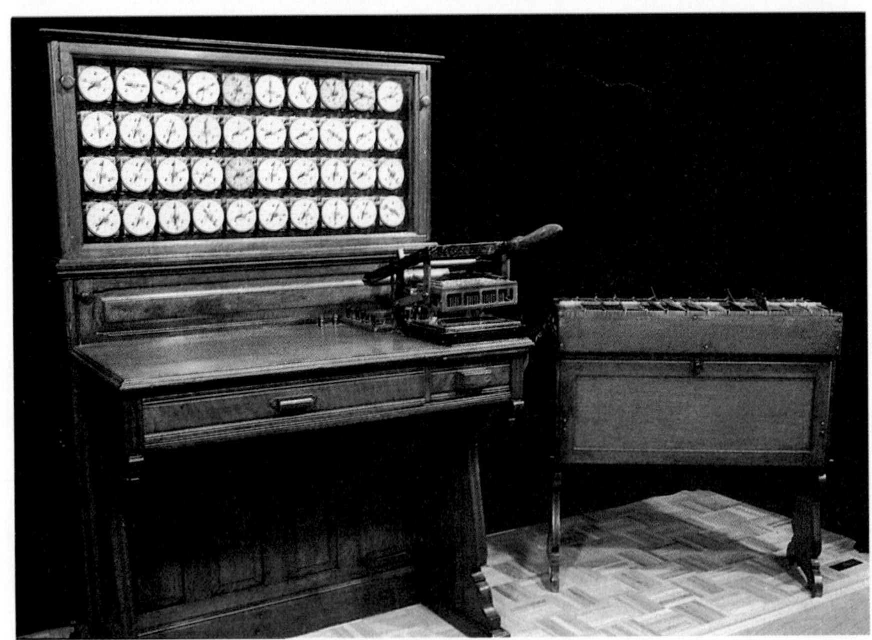

Figure 1–9 HOLLERITH'S CENSUS MACHINE After Hollerith proved that his machine could be successful, he founded the Tabulating Machine Company to produce punched-card equipment to sell to business and government. Later, his company became International Business Machines Corporation (IBM).

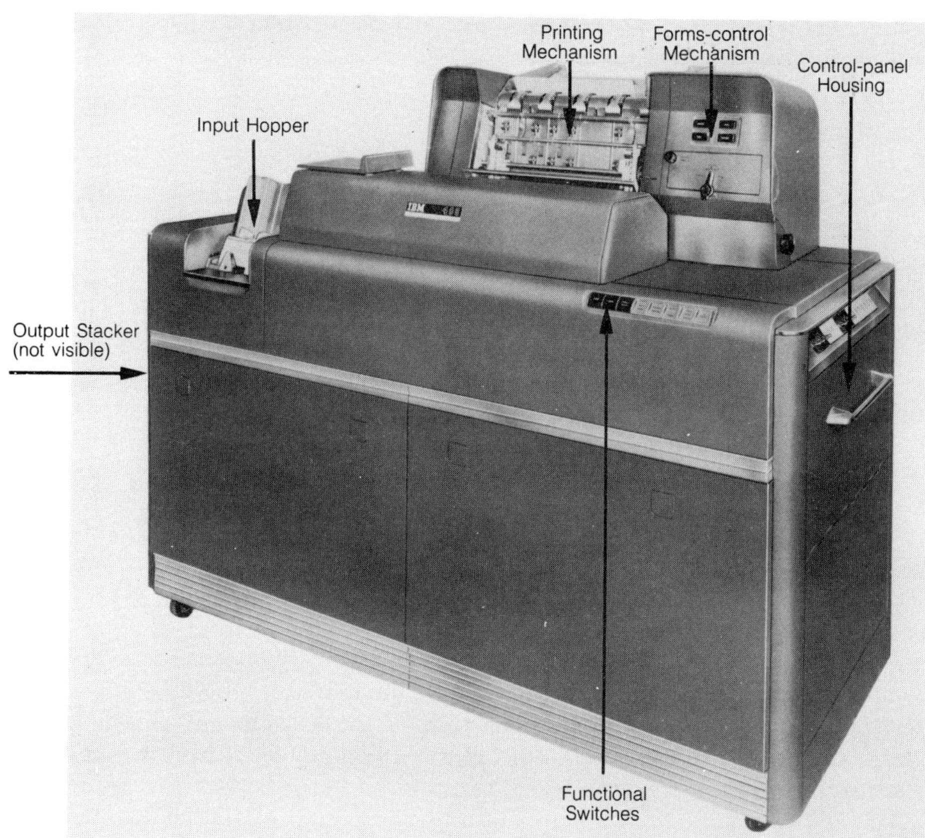

Figure 1–10 ACCOUNTING MACHINE Accounting machines developed in the late 1920s and early 1930s could read data from punched cards, perform calculations, rearrange data, and print results in varied formats.

Binary number system
The number system that uses the digits 1 and 0.

Machine language
A language based on 0s and 1s; the only set of instructions a computer can execute directly.

ENIAC
Electronic Numerical Integrator and Calculator; the first electronic computer put to large-scale practical use.

Figure 1–11 THE MARK I Howard Aiken wanted to develop a general-purpose accounting machine that could be used by scientists as well as business people. After Aiken had already begun work on his large machine, he read the works of Charles Babbage and was surprised to see how closely his ideas paralleled those of Babbage.

Digital computer
The type of computer that operates on binary digits and relies on counting for its operations.

Figure 1–12 THE ENIAC
J. P. Eckert, shown here, developed the ENIAC with John Mauchly. The machine was supposed to calculate tables to help the U.S. Army aim weapons with more accuracy, but it was not completed until after World War II ended.

compared with about 3 seconds required by the Mark I. At the time it was developed, the ENIAC seemed so fast that scientists estimated that just seven computers like it could handle all the calculations the world would ever need.

The ENIAC was huge. It weighed 30 tons and contained 18,000 vacuum tubes. It was 10 feet high, 100 feet long, and covered 1,500 square feet of floor space. Because the ENIAC had no internal "memory," instructions had to be fed into it by the use of combinations of switches that were moved manually. Each switch represented either a 0 or a 1.

Stored-program computer
A computer that stores instructions in memory in order to process data at its own speed without human intervention.

In the mid-1940s, a mathematician, John von Neumann, proposed a way to store instructions inside computers. This would free the computer to work at its own speed without being slowed by the need to be rewired for each program. Von Neumann's principles led to the development of the **stored-program computer.** The first computer in the United States to have internal memory and use stored-program instructions was known as the **EDVAC** (Electronic Discrete Variable Automatic Computer).

EDVAC
Electronic Discrete Variable Automatic Computer; an early stored-program computer.

With the development of the EDVAC, the computer became a useful scientific and business tool. The EDVAC could operate without human intervention, depending only upon stored instructions. This development marked the beginning of the modern computer era. Since then, many refinements in computers' speed, size, and cost have been made. The many advancements in computer technology are divided into four time periods called generations.

First-Generation Computers

First-generation computers
Computers developed in the period 1951–1958; used vacuum tubes.

The **first generation** of computers lasted from 1951 until 1958. This era began with the sale of the first commercial electronic computer to the U.S.

Census Bureau. This machine, called the **UNIVAC I** (see Figure 1–13), was the first computer designed for business data-processing applications.

First-generation computers were large, costly to buy, expensive to power, and often unreliable because of their delicacy and complexity. Their internal operations were controlled through the use of vacuum tubes. These tubes were fairly large, and they generated so much heat that special air-conditioning had to be installed to handle it.

It was during this period that **symbolic languages** were developed. Symbolic languages use symbols made up of letters and numbers to stand for the 0s and 1s of machine language. For example, ADD may stand for addition. Computer instructions written in symbolic languages were easier for people to use than machine language. But symbolic language had to be translated into machine code before the computer could follow the instructions.

The machine code was stored as magnetized spots on the outer surface of a cylinder-shaped device called a **magnetic drum,** which rotated at high speeds as the symbolic code was being translated. The magnetic drum was used to store data internally.

Second-Generation Computers

The **second generation** of computers (see Figure 1–14) spanned the years from 1959 through 1964. It was during this time that the technology race really began.

The most notable change was that **transistors** replaced vacuum tubes. As a result, computers became much smaller, faster, and more reliable. They also became more efficient because they generated less heat and required less power to operate.

Also at this time, **magnetic cores** replaced magnetic drums as storage

UNIVAC I
UNIVersal Automatic Computer; the first commercial electronic computer; became available in 1951.

Symbolic languages
Languages that use symbols to represent instructions; must be translated into machine language before being executed by the computer.

Magnetic drum
A cylinder with a magnetic outer surface on which data can be stored by the magnetizing of specific positions.

Second-generation computers
Computers developed in the period 1959–1964; used transistors; were smaller and faster and had larger storage capacity than first-generation computers.

Transistor
A type of electronic circuitry that controls current flow without the use of a vacuum.

Magnetic core
A type of computer memory; doughnut-shaped rings strung on wires and magnetized to represent an "on" or "off" condition.

Figure 1–13 A FIRST-GENERATION COMPUTER The UNIVAC I, like the ENIAC, was a creation of Eckert and Mauchly. It used vacuum tubes, punched cards, symbolic language, and magnetic drums, all typical features of first-generation computers.

Figure 1–14 A SECOND-GENERATION COMPUTER
This IBM 7070 demonstrates the use of magnetic tapes for secondary storage. The reels of tape were mounted on tape drives. Magnetic tapes largely replaced punched cards. A 2,400-foot reel of tape can store as much data as 400,000 punched cards.

media. A magnetic core—a small doughnut-shaped ring—is placed at the intersection of a vertical and a horizontal wire. When currents are run through the wires, these magnetic cores become charged. Many cores strung together hold the stored data.

Next, second-generation computers were given **auxiliary storage,** sometimes called **external** or **secondary storage.** Data was stored outside the computer on either **magnetic tapes** or **magnetic disks.** The use of auxiliary storage ended the limitation on how much data the computer could store and reduced the use of punched cards. Using magnetic tapes for input and output operations increased the speed of the computer.

Finally, improvements were made in the symbolic programming languages. New languages were more like English than the earlier ones, making programming the computer much easier.

Auxiliary storage
Storage outside the computer; also known as external or secondary storage.

Magnetic tape
A storage medium consisting of a narrow strip of material upon which spots are magnetized to represent data.

Magnetic disk
A storage medium consisting of a platter made of metal or flexible plastic and coated with magnetic recording material.

Third-Generation Computers

The **third generation** of computers lasted from 1965 through 1970. During this time, technology continued to improve and computers became even smaller, while their memory capacities became larger (see Figure 1–15).

The third generation is marked chiefly by the development of **integrated circuits,** which replaced transistors. With integrated circuits, hundreds of electrical components could be included on one silicon chip less than one-eighth-inch square. Third-generation computers like the one shown in Figure 1–16 could handle many applications, such as inventory control, scheduling of labor and materials, and bank credit-card billing.

A number of other developments characterized this period. **Minicomputers** were introduced, for example (see Figure 1–17). These machines had many of the same capabilities as large computers; but they were much smaller, had less storage space, and cost less. Another development was

Third-generation computers
Computers developed in the period 1965–1970; featured integrated circuits, reduced size, lower costs, and increased speed and reliability.

Integrated circuits
Electronic circuits etched on a small silicon chip less than one-eighth-inch square.

Minicomputer
A computer with the components of a full-size system but with a smaller memory.

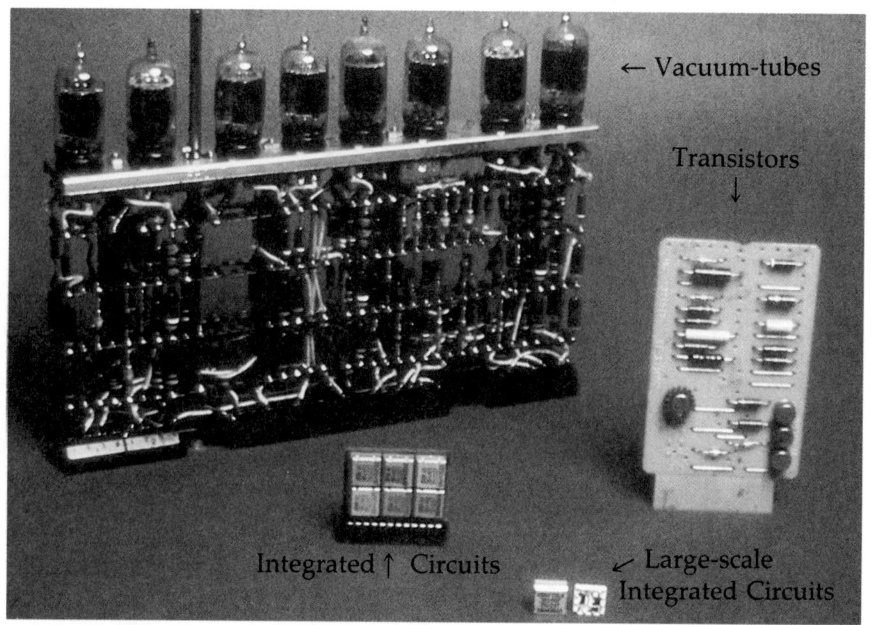

Figure 1–15 FOUR GENERATIONS OF COMPUTER COMPONENTS
Early vacuum tubes often burned out—perhaps once every seven to fifteen minutes. Each successive generation of components was more reliable. Today's silicon chips are very reliable, in part because of the high degree of quality control in their manufacture.

the use of **remote terminals,** input/output devices that are electronically linked to a main computer but located at some distance from it. A popular innovation was the introduction of families of computers that could support as many as forty different external devices, such as printers and remote

Remote terminal
A terminal placed at a location distant from the central computer.

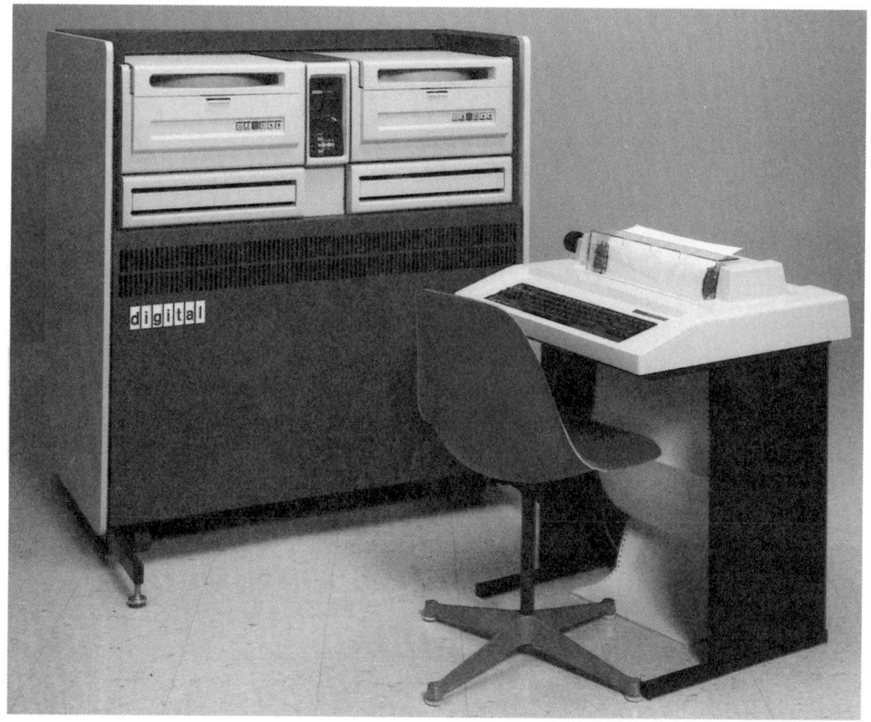

Figure 1–16 A THIRD-GENERATION COMPUTER SYSTEM
This NCR V-8600 computer system mirrored the features of the third-generation families of computers. If a company needed more memory, the investment in software was not wasted. A larger computer of the same family could be bought that would run the same programs.

Figure 1–17 A THIRD-GENERATION MINICOMPUTER This DEC PDP 11/60 minicomputer was produced by Digital Equipment Corporation, which introduced the first commercially successful minicomputers in 1965. Minicomputers became a huge success with medium-sized and small businesses, which could not afford the more expensive large computers.

terminals. Each computer in the family contained a different main storage capacity. A company could easily move up to a machine with more storage while continuing to use the same external devices.

Fourth-generation computers
Computers developed in the period 1971–present, the era of large-scale integrated circuits and microprocessors.

Fourth-Generation Computers

Large-scale integration (LSI)
The process of packing thousands of electronic circuits onto a single silicon chip.

The period for the **fourth generation** of computers is given as 1971 to the present. Although we are clearly in the fourth generation, the dividing line between the third and fourth generations is not as well defined as the dividing lines marking the first three generations.

Microprocessor
The central processing unit of a microcomputer; fits on a small silicon chip.

Microcomputer
A very small computer; sometimes a single-function computer.

Very-large-scale integration (VLSI)
Integrated circuits on a silicon chip, packed even more densely than with LSI.

Chip circuitry has become increasingly miniaturized in fourth-generation machines. **Large-scale integration (LSI)** circuits, featuring thousands of electronic components on a single silicon chip, became common during the 1970s. From LSI technology came the **microprocessor,** the small "computer on a chip" that controls microwave ovens, sewing machines, thermostats, and certain functions in automobiles. Microprocessor chips can manage the functions of the computer, perform calculations, and control other devices just as large computers can. The combination of the microprocessor and other densely packed chips used for storage and input/output operations forms a **microcomputer** (see Figure 1–18). Modern microcomputers have more power than the large computers of earlier generations.

LSI has already progressed into **VLSI (very-large-scale integration),** which means even more capabilities in even smaller packages. Table 1–1 summarizes the generations of computers and their features.

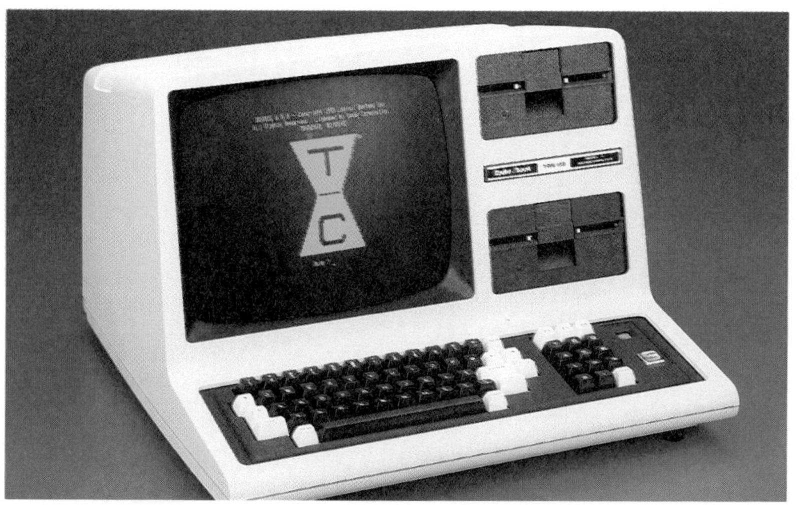

Figure 1–18 MICROCOMPUTER
This TRS-80 Model IV is an example of a microcomputer with keyboard, screen, and disk drives all in one unit. Other types of microcomputers can be attached to regular television screens or have separate monitors that contain the screens.

Table 1–1 GENERATIONS OF COMPUTER DEVELOPMENT
Many features characterized computer development in each generation. This table outlines several not mentioned in the text.

PERIOD	COMPUTER SYSTEM CHARACTERISTICS
First Generation 1951–1958	Vacuum tubes in electronic circuits Magnetic drum as primary internal storage medium Limited main storage capacity Slow input/output; punched-card orientation Heat and maintenance problems Applications: payroll processing and record keeping Examples: IBM 650; UNIVAC I
Second Generation 1959–1964	Transistors for internal operations Magnetic core as primary internal storage medium Increased main storage capacity Faster input/output; tape orientation High-level programming languages (COBOL, FORTRAN) Great reduction in size and heat generation Increased speed and reliability Batch-oriented applications: billing, payroll processing, updating inventory files Examples: IBM 1401; Honeywell 200; CDC 1604
Third Generation 1965–1970	Integrated circuits Magnetic core and solid-state main storage More flexibility with input/output; disk orientation Smaller size and better performance and reliability Emergence of minicomputers Remote processing through communication Applications: airline reservation system, market forecasting, credit-card billing Examples: IBM System/360; NCR 395; Burroughs B5500; DEC PDP-11 Series (minicomputers)
Fourth Generation 1971–?	Large-scale integration Increased storage capacity and speed Greater versatility of input/output devices Introduction of microprocessors and microcomputers Applications: mathematical modeling and simulation, electronic funds transfer, computer-aided instruction, home computers Examples: IBM 3033; Burroughs B7700; HP 3000 (minicomputer); Apple II; IBM PC (microcomputers)

LEARNING CHECK

1. Many of the jobs that are easily computerized are
   a. decision-making tasks.
   b. routine and repetitive.
   c. hard to define.
   d. used in risk analysis.
2. A name for the use of computers in the classroom is ________.
3. The first automated device was a ________ that read punched cards for instructions.
4. Which inventor is known as the father of computers?
5. The Mark I, an automatic calculator, was the first machine to use electric currents to represent data and instructions. Since on and off are the two states of electricity, the language for this machine was based on the ____ (three words).
6. The EDVAC is remembered as one of the first machines to use the _____ concept.
7. What characterized second- and third-generation computers in the same way that vacuum tubes characterized first-generation computers?

ANSWERS: 1. b. 2. computer-assisted instruction. 3. loom. 4. Charles Babbage. 5. binary number system. 6. stored-program. 7. transistors and integrated circuits.

TODAY'S COMPUTERS AND HOW THEY WORK

Many people think of computers as machines with human or even mysticalpowers. In reality, computers do not possess these qualities. Computers cannot think or perform tasks on their own. They must be given step-by-step instructions for any tasks they perform.

Computers can carry out only three basic functions:

- They can add, subtract, multiply, and divide.
- They can make comparisons. They can compare two values to see if they are equal or if one value is greater or less than the other. These values may be either numeric or alphabetic.
- They can store and retrieve information.

Instruction set
The basic set of instructions built into a computer that tells it what to do.

The manufacturer builds into the computer a basic set of instructions—an **instruction set**—that performs these three tasks. By working with the instruction set, people can direct the computer to perform these tasks.

Data Processing

The computer's three basic functions allow it to process data much as a person does—by collecting and manipulating data to reach some desired objective. When such processing is performed by computers, it is called **electronic data processing (EDP),** known simply as data processing.

All data processing involves converting raw facts into arrangements of information upon which decisions can be based. Although the terms *data* and *information* may sometimes be used to mean the same thing, in the computer world they are distinctly different. **Data** is raw, unorganized facts. **Information,** on the other hand, is made up of facts that have been organized in a usable and meaningful way (see Figure 1–19). Information must

Electronic data processing (EDP)
Data processing performed by electronic devices such as computers rather than by manual or mechanical means.

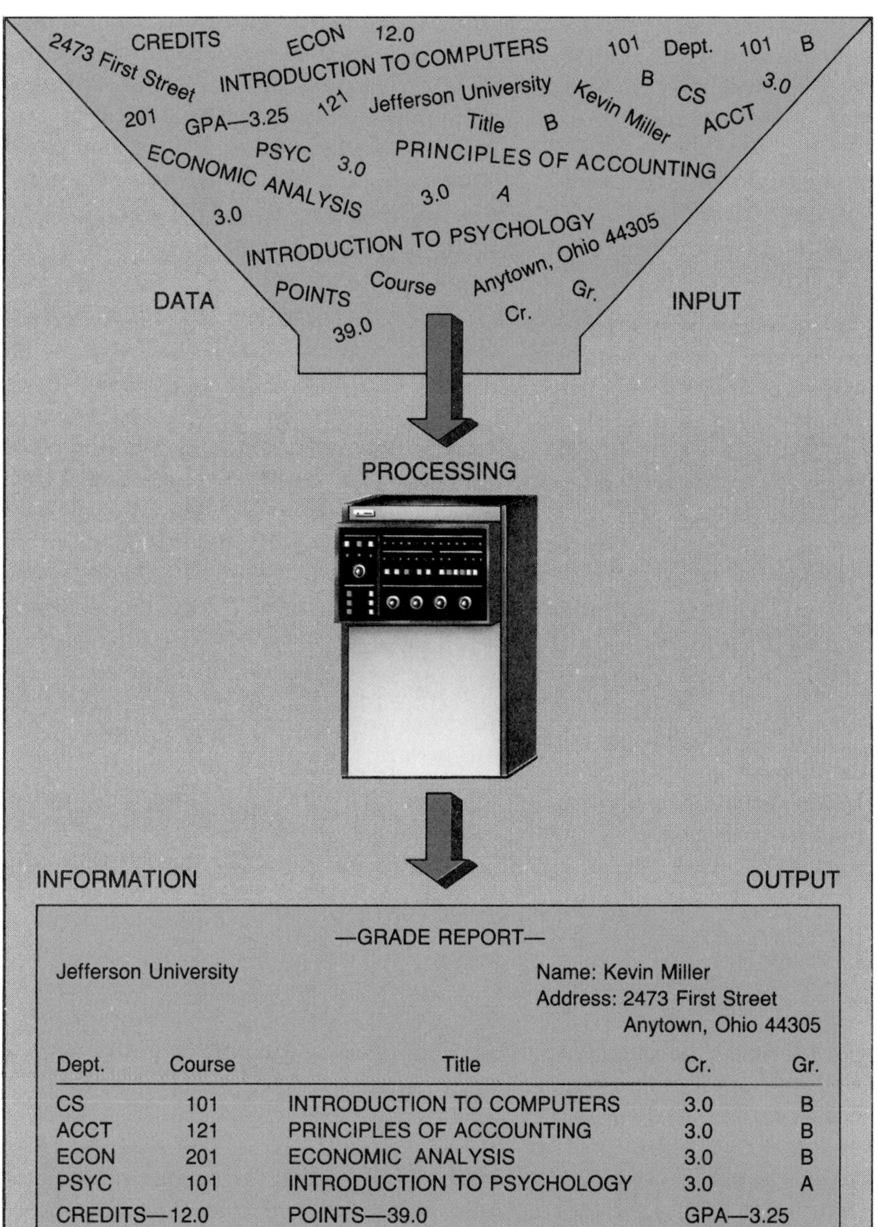

Figure 1–19 DATA VERSUS INFORMATION
A jumble of data—the raw, unorganized facts—becomes a grade report summary when it is processed into meaningful information by the computer.

Data
Raw, unorganized facts.

Information
Data that has been processed so that it is meaningful.

be accurate, complete, timely, and relevant and must be delivered to the right person at the right place if it is to be useful.

Input
Data submitted to the computer for processing.

Processing
The producing of output or information from the input or data.

Output
The information that comes from the computer as a result of processing.

Computers deal with data in a logical and unchanging three-part sequence: input, processing, and output. **Input** involves gathering the relevant data, translating it into a form the computer can understand, and submitting it to the computer. **Processing** is the computer's handling and arranging of the data. Finally, **output** involves producing results that will be understandable and meaningful to the user. These three steps are required for all types of data processing. Figure 1–20 shows the data flow.

Input, the first part of the data flow, is divided into three steps. First, data must be collected. Second, the data must be checked for accuracy, completeness, and relevance. Careful checking is essential. If the data submitted to the computer is incorrect, all the results will be useless. Third, the data must be coded so that it can be read by the computer.

Depending on what the user requests, the processing portion of the data flow may include classifying, sorting, calculating, summarizing, or storing of data. Classifying means organizing the raw facts according to characteristics that make sense to the user. The students at a college may be classified as freshmen, sophomores, juniors, and seniors, for example. The next step may be sorting, which involves putting data into a sequence to make processing easier. If the students in the senior class are sorted alphabetically by last names, the processing can be speeded up. A calculation may be needed to determine each student's grade point average or the number of hours earned toward graduation. Summarizing is used to reduce large amounts of data to a clear and brief form. For instance, a school principal may be interested in a summary naming students who make the honor roll each term or who are involved in athletics. Finally, storing data is an important part of processing; it ensures that the data will be readily available for later processing or retrieval.

Output, the last part in the data flow is, like input, a three-step process. The first step involves retrieving the processed information from the computer's storage devices. The second step involves converting the information from the form used to store it into a form the user can understand. The final step involves communicating that information to those who need it, when they need it. Usually, this is done through a terminal display or a printed copy.

The Incredible Power of the Computer

The modern computer gets most of its power from its amazing speed, accuracy, and memory. Since computers are so fast, their speed is measured in fractions of a second. Today's computers can complete computations in a few **nanoseconds,** or billionths of a second.

Nanosecond
One-billionth of a second.

Computers are accurate because their electronic circuits are reliable. Once an electric path is determined, electricity will follow the same path each time it is used. Remember, however, that even though the internal circuits that make up the computer are accurate, the output can still be

Figure 1–20 FLOW OF DATA Data is classified, sorted, calculated, summarized, and/or stored during the processing stage of the data-processing flow. Some hardware can act as both input and output devices and media.

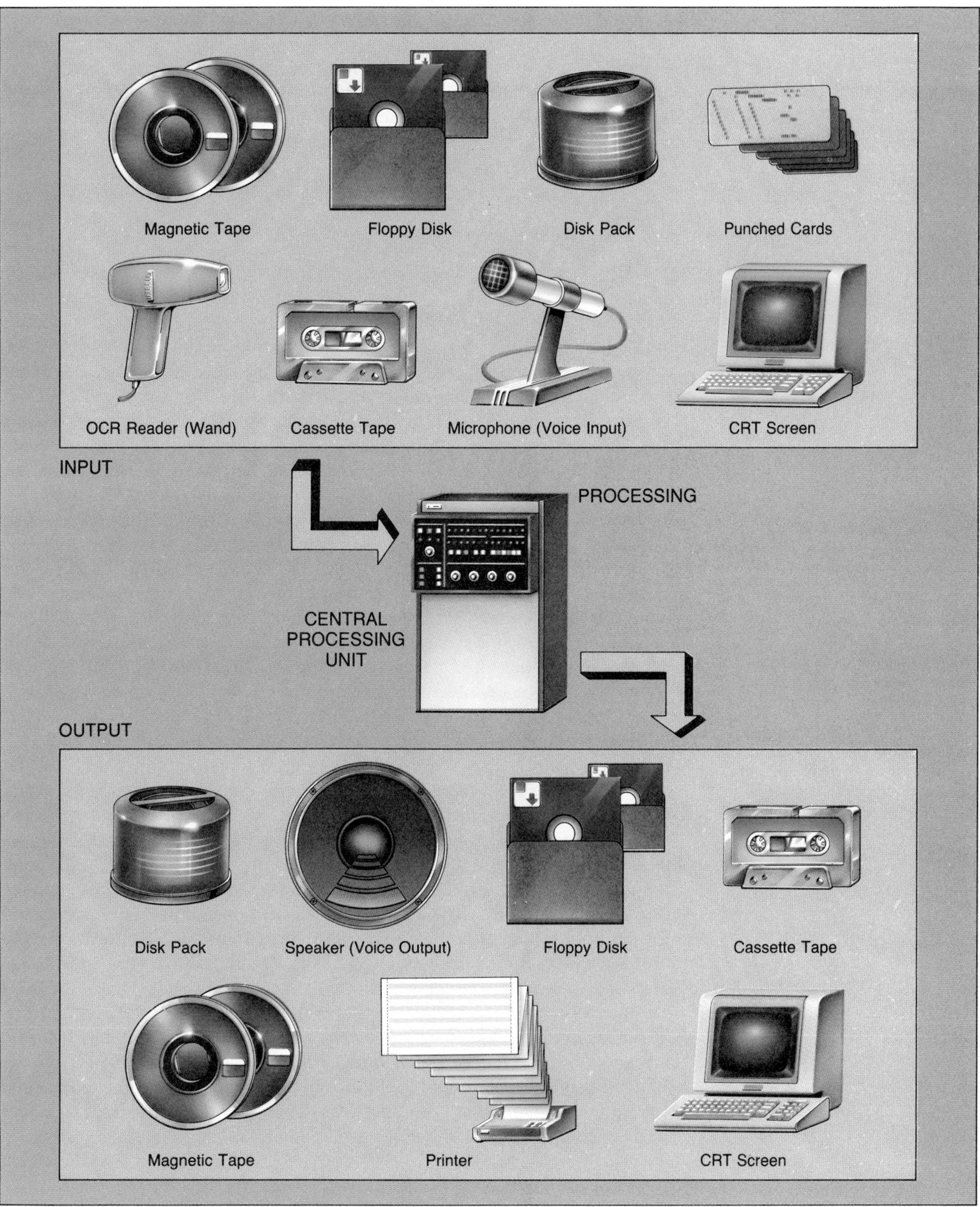

incorrect. If the data or the instructions given to the computer are incorrect, the output from the computer will be incorrect, too.

Memory
The part of the computer that provides the ability to store data.

Computers have large memory capacities, both internal and external. Computers can store data in and retrieve it from **memory** at incredible speeds. Data can be stored in a computer in a fraction of the space used by paper files to store the same data. Further, the computer can retrieve the data in a fraction of the time it takes to find data in paper files.

Hardware and Software

Hardware
The physical devices that make up a computer system.

Modern computers' power depends on both equipment and instructions, usually classified as hardware and software. The **hardware** is the physical equipment that makes up the computer system. Hardware devices are the parts of the computer that can be touched; they include the central processing unit, input devices, output devices, and storage devices.

The hardware of a personal computer (a microcomputer) consists of the TV-like screen and the typewriter keyboard, sometimes combined with a printer. At a department store, the wand the clerk uses to record the price of an item is a form of input hardware. Other hardware includes punched cards, magnetic tapes, and floppy disks. The machines that use cards, tapes, or disks to input data—such as card readers and tape or disk drives—are also hardware. Chapter 2 discusses hardware in more detail.

Software
Programs used to direct the computer in solving problems and overseeing operations.

Program
A series of step-by-step instructions that provides a problem solution and tells the computer exactly what to do.

Programmer
The person who writes the step-by-step instructions that tell the computer what to do.

Software is the instructions that operate the computer—that is, the **programs.** Software is developed by people called **programmers.** They write the instructions that tell the computer what to do.

Some software is permanently installed inside the computer to direct the computer's basic functions. For example, permanent software tells the computer how to add and subtract numbers or how to calculate a square root. This software cannot be changed.

Other software is introduced to the computer on media such as magnetic tapes and disks. This software tells the computer how to process specific data. It must be used together with the permanent software already inside the computer. For example, a programmer may write a program that figures students' grade point averages (GPA). Because the computer already has permanent software that tells it how to add and perform other arithmetic functions, the GPA program does not have to include those instructions. But software like the GPA program, unlike the permanent software inside the computer, can be changed. So, if a new method for figuring GPA is required, the original program can be changed accordingly. Software is discussed again in Chapter 3.

Firmware
Software programs put in hardware form.

A concept that merges hardware and software places software programs in hardware form. The result is called **firmware.** Firmware can take the form of a densely-packed chip or a cartridge that is inserted in a slot on the computer. Since schools seldom change their method for calculating GPA, they could permanently install a GPA software program as firmware in their computers.

Types of Computers: Analog and Digital

There are two types of computers: analog and digital. Digital computers, such as the Mark I and the ENIAC, operate on the basis of two states of electricity; either the electricity is flowing (on) or it is not flowing (off). These two states can be represented by **binary digits,** with 1 representing on and 0 representing off. The binary digits, or **bits,** are grouped together to represent numbers and letters.

Bit
Short for BInary digiT; a digit position in a binary number.

Analog computers measure and display continuous physical or electrical conditions such as pressure, temperature, voltage, and volume. Gasoline pumps, for instance, use an analog device to measure the volume of gasoline that has been pumped and, at the same time, display the appropriate price. This book will not discuss analog computers but will focus on digital computers.

Analog computer
A computer that measures continuous physical or electrical conditions.

The Central Processing Unit

The **central processing unit (CPU),** sometimes called the **mainframe,** is the "brain" of the computer. It is composed of three units: (1) the control unit; (2) the arithmetic/logic unit (ALU); and (3) the primary storage unit (see Figure 1–21).

Central processing unit (CPU)
The "brain" of the computer; it interprets and executes instructions and communicates with input/output and storage devices.

As its name implies, the **control unit** controls the activities in the CPU. The unit does not process or store any data but directs the operations of the other parts of the computer. Instructions given to the computer by the user are interpreted by the control unit, which sends out signals to circuits to execute the instructions. The appropriate input devices are instructed to send the necessary data to the computer. The control unit also keeps track of which parts of the program have already been executed and which

Mainframe
The central processing unit (CPU); the "brain" of the computer system.

Control unit
The section of the CPU that coordinates the execution of program segments.

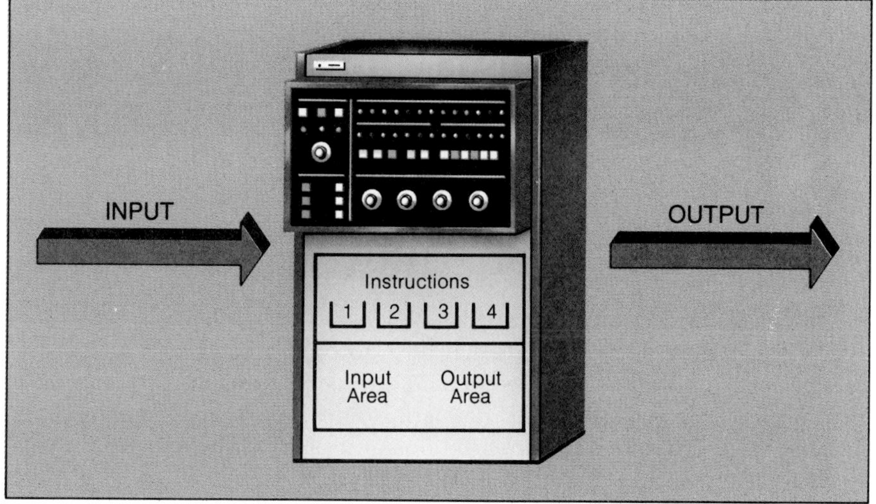

Figure 1–21 THE COMPUTER AND ITS PARTS
The central processing unit (CPU) consists of the three parts shown here. In many of today's computers, the primary storage unit is part of the computer but resides on chips other than the one that holds the CPU.

ones must still be done. Finally, it controls the execution of specific instructions, collects the output, and sends the output to the designated output device—for example, a display screen.

Arithmetic/logic unit (ALU)
The section of the CPU that performs mathematical computations and logic operations.

The **arithmetic/logic unit (ALU)** performs arithmetic computations and logical operations. Logical operations involve making comparisons and then doing something based on the result. A comparison you might make is "If today is Friday, then I will pick up my paycheck and go to the bank; if not, I won't." This isn't exactly the type of logic statement with which a computer would work, but the idea is the same. The computer would work with a logic statement like this: "If this is the end of the input data, then make the calculations and print the results; if not, read more input data." Arithmetic and logic statements are the only type of instructions the ALU can execute. But almost everything we want the computer to do is either an arithmetic or logic problem. The only major exceptions to this are when the computer reads the input and prints the output.

Primary storage unit
The section of the CPU that holds instructions, data, and intermediate and final results during processing.

The **primary storage unit** (or main storage unit) is the computer's internal memory. It is actually part of the internal hardware and is necessary for the computer to function. Primary storage holds instructions, data, and the intermediate and final results of processing. When instructions are entered into the computer, the control unit sends them to primary storage. The control unit then retrieves one item at a time from primary storage to interpret and process. Results from processing the instructions are also put into primary storage until the control unit causes the results to be transferred to an output device, such as a printer or display screen, or to an external storage medium.

Stored-Program Concept

As discussed earlier, a program is a series of instructions written by a programmer to direct the computer to perform a given task. It is the primary storage unit that allows modern computers to store programs or portions of programs. The **stored-program concept** refers to the storing of a program's instructions and data in memory. Holding these instructions in storage allows the computer to call upon them instantly and so to operate at top speed.

Stored-program concept
The idea of storing instructions in computer memory in electronic form so the computer can process data without human intervention.

Instructions are entered into the computer by way of punched cards, tapes, disks, or keyboards. The computer is then free to act on these instructions at its own pace. In earlier computers, the instructions were either plugged into the computer in preprogrammed, unchangeable circuitry or read into the computer one step at a time, with each step executed as it was entered. This was a slow process, mainly because the human operators had to change the instructions manually.

When instructions or data are placed into computer memory, primary storage acts much as a tape recorder. The instructions and data remain there until new instructions and data are stored over them. Therefore, it is possible to execute the same instructions and process the same data over and over again until a change is made.

WHAT THE FUTURE WILL BRING

Artificial intelligence
An area of study that seeks to develop techniques to use computers to solve problems that appear to require imagination, intuition, or intelligence.

Some people believe we are entering a fifth generation of computers. This generation will explore the use of **artificial intelligence,** which is the ability of computers to reason and think like humans to solve problems requiring imagination, intuition, and intelligence. A significant characteristic of the fifth-generation computer will be its ability to help program itself. A computer of this generation will listen when its human user talks and will then do what it has been told. It will be able to program the instructions necessary to accomplish the task. It will also be able to ask questions if it does not understand. It will sort through large volumes of data to find and use only what pertains to the problem at hand. In addition, it will be able to translate documents from one language to another.

Artificial intelligence is an exciting and controversial subject. The concept includes such topics as robotics, voice-recognition systems, and decision making.

Robotics is the science of designing and building robots. Industrial robots consist usually of mechanical arms operated by computer "brains." Robots are most commonly used in factories, but their uses are expanding. A more detailed discussion on robotics is included in Chapter 6.

A new product in the artificial intelligence market is a voice-recognition system that can be used with microcomputers. This new system, once available only for large computers, will recognize the words and phrases that the user teaches it.

To recognize words and phrases, the computer codes the user's spoken words into digital patterns and matches these patterns with words previously entered into memory. The computer then follows the instructions in its memory that match the recognized words. Computers that can follow spoken instructions are much easier to use in some circumstances. For example, voice-recognition systems are extremely useful for handicapped people or in jobs where the users' hands must be busy with something else.

Currently, attempts are being made to program computers to simulate the decision-making process of humans. Researchers would like to enable computers to exhibit the common sense of humans. Computers could then compare alternatives and think through problems that have not been already defined.

How far will artificial intelligence technology advance? Many research efforts are aimed at developing computer programs that perform tasks such as thinking, reasoning, making logical decisions, and remembering past experiences. Technical developments in this field are moving rapidly.

Practical applications for artificial intelligence seem endless. Intelligent computers could read books, newspapers, journals, and magazines and prepare summaries. They could search libraries for facts pertaining to a decision that must be made and suggest courses of action and probable consequences.

Besides artificial intelligence, research is continuing into other computer-related areas. New methods of producing chips and memory devices are being studied. Proposals have been made to manufacture computer chips in the relatively dust-free environment of space. Cleanliness would mean better quality control and fewer defective chips.

Biochips
Minute computer chips assembled from organic molecules or genetically engineered proteins.

The possibility of building biochip computers has been considered in recent years. **Biochips** would replace the silicon chips in today's computers with organic molecules or genetically engineered proteins. Biochips would offer several advantages. They would increase the densities of the computing elements and perform tasks not even possible with silicon chips. They would also be capable of reproducing themselves. Although much research has been done on biochips, their use remains theoretical.

Judging from a preview of the future, it seems that the main limitation on computer applications is the imagination and ingenuity of the humans who use them.

LEARNING CHECK

1. The three functions today's computers can perform include all of the following except
   a. adding, subtracting, multiplying, and dividing.
   b. making comparisons.
   c. programming themselves.
   d. storing and retrieving information.
2. In terms of the computer, what is the difference between data and information?
3. The portion of the data flow in which information is retrieved from the computer's storage devices and communicated to the users is ________.
4. Computer terms for equipment and instructions are ________ and ________.
5. The three units that comprise the central processing unit (CPU) are the ________, the ________, and the ________.
6. Two technologies that will be explored in the future are
   a. the stored-program concept and artificial intelligence.
   b. artificial intelligence and biochips.
   c. biochips and weightlessness.
   d. practical applications and libraries.

ANSWERS: 1. c. 2. Data is raw, unorganized facts while information is data that has been organized into a usable and meaningful form. 3. output. 4. hardware and software. 5. control unit, arithmetic/logic unit, primary storage unit. 6. b.

SUMMARY POINTS

- Computers are extremely versatile and they affect almost all areas of life—our education, work, and leisure activities.

- Major developments in calculating devices include the abacus, Pascal's and Leibnitz's calculating machines, and Babbage's difference engine.
- The first "programmable" machine was a weaving loom. The same punched-card principle was used later by Hollerith in processing census data.
- The Mark I was the first automatic calculator, and it introduced the use of machine language.
- ENIAC was the first electronic computer put to large-scale practical use, but it had no internal memory. A later machine, EDVAC, used internal memory and stored-program instructions.
- First-generation computers used vacuum tubes to control operations. These machines were large and unreliable, and generated much heat.
- Second-generation computers used transistors to control operations. Transistors are smaller, more reliable, and faster than vacuum tubes.
- Third-generation computers used integrated circuits to control operations. Integrated circuits are smaller, faster, and more reliable than transistors.
- Fourth-generation computers use large-scale integration (LSI) and continue to become smaller, faster, and less costly.
- There are two types of computers—analog and digital.
- Computers use a stored-program concept: data and instructions are stored in internal memory.
- The central processing unit consists of the control unit, arithmetic/logic unit, and primary storage unit.
- Computers can perform three basic functions. They can (1) add, subtract, multiply, and divide; (2) make comparisons; and (3) store and retrieve information.
- Data is the raw facts submitted to the computer; information is the organized output after processing.
- Electronic data processing (EDP) is the manipulation of data by a computer.
- Input is data submitted to the computer. Processing refers to the steps the computer takes to arrange the data. Output is the usable information that results from processing.
- The input stage involves collecting, checking, and coding the data to prepare it for the computer.
- Computer processing involves classifying, sorting, calculating, summarizing, and storing the data.
- The output stage involves retrieving the information from the computer's storage, converting it to a form the user can understand, and communicating it to the user.
- Computers get most of their power from three features: speed, accuracy, and memory.
- Computers are made up of hardware and software. Hardware is the physical components, which include the central processing unit, input and output devices, and storage devices. Software is the instructions that operate the computer, the programs.
- The stored-program concept refers to the storage of instructions in the computer's memory in electronic form so the computer can process data at its own speed without human intervention.

- A current topic in computer science is artificial intelligence, which refers to attempts to give computers the ability to reason and think like humans.
- Biochips, in theory, could replace today's silicon chips with organic molecules or genetically engineered proteins.

REVIEW QUESTIONS

1. Explain what is included in computer-assisted instruction (CAI).
2. How are computers important in the space shuttle program?
3. Why were Charles Babbage and his engines important to the development of computers?
4. What was the name of the first automatic calculator? Explain how the binary number system is significant to its development.
5. What was the first computer sold commercially, and for what was it used?
6. What were some of the characteristics of the first-generation computer?
7. What technology replaced the vacuum tube, and what advantages did it offer?
8. Explain the difference between analog and digital computers.
9. What steps are included in the processing stage of the data flow?
10. Explain the stored-program concept.

3M
OPTICAL STORAGE DISK
SIDE 1

CHAPTER 2

HARDWARE

Chapter Outline

INTRODUCTION

Computer hardware consists of the physical devices that comprise the computer itself, the input and output devices, and the storage media. Hardware, then, includes the parts of the computer that are tangible.

This chapter discusses the variety of hardware available for both large and small computers. It also examines the form in which the computer represents and sends data.

STORAGE

Computers derive much power from the amount of data they can store. You may remember that some storage is inside the computer and is often called primary storage. Data in primary storage can be accessed quickly. Other storage is located outside the computer on auxiliary storage media. When data and instructions are needed from secondary storage media, the computer can transfer all or portions of the required material to primary storage. How does the computer find the right material? How does it get the data? How does it ensure that the data is accurate? This section answers these questions and others as it examines storage and retrieval of data from hardware devices.

Storage Locations and Addresses

When the CPU stores programs, input, data, and output, it does not store them randomly. It uses a systematic method to assign a location to each data item and instruction. Each location has an address so that the CPU can find the item or instruction when it needs to. To process data, the CPU must first locate each relevant instruction and piece of data.

Computer storage can be compared with a large array of mailboxes. Each mailbox is a specific location with its own number and address. Each can hold one item of information. Since each location in storage has a different address, stored-program instructions can locate particular items by giving their addresses.

Variable
A meaningful symbolic name assigned by a programmer to a storage location in the computer.

Suppose, for instance, the computer is instructed to calculate an employee's salary by subtracting the total tax to be withheld from the gross pay. Let's say that TOTAL TAX is stored at Mailbox 101 and has a value of $50 and that GROSS PAY is stored at Mailbox 108 and has a value of $260, as shown in Figure 2–1. The calculation is made when the computer is told to subtract the contents of Mailbox 101 (TOTAL TAX) from the contents of Mailbox 108 (GROSS PAY). TOTAL TAX and GROSS PAY are examples of **variables,** which are symbolic names. The values for these variables are $50 and $260. The programmer only has to tell the computer to subtract TOTAL TAX from GROSS PAY and the computer concludes that it should subtract the value in Mailbox 101 from the value in Mailbox 108. The term *variable* is used because while the variable name (the storage address) itself does not change, the data stored at that location may vary. The values of TOTAL TAX and GROSS PAY, for example, are likely to change with each employee. The addresses of TOTAL TAX and GROSS PAY will not.

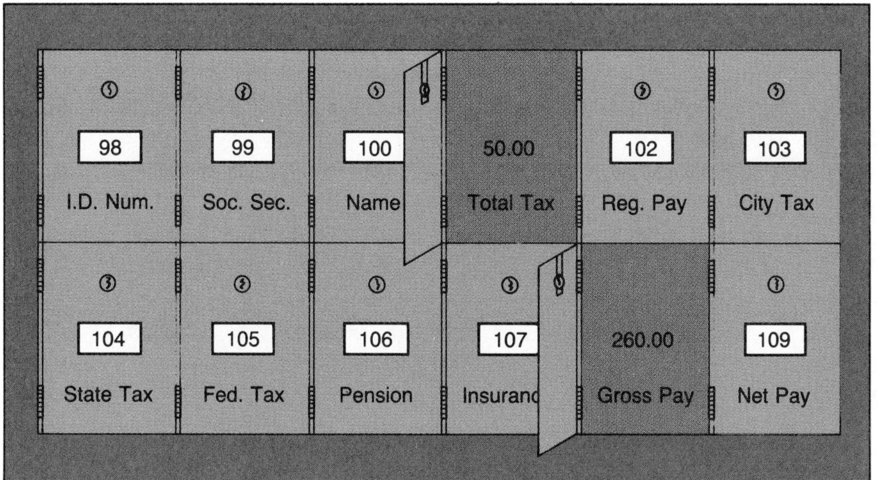

Figure 2–1 MAILBOX REPRESENTATION OF STORAGE Computers must locate data quickly and efficiently to be able to meet the user's needs.

Primary Storage

As you know, primary storage consists of all storage that is considered part of the CPU, or the main computer. (Secondary storage, which is separate from the CPU, is discussed later in the chapter.) Older primary storage units are composed of magnetic cores. Each core can store one binary digit, or bit (more on bits later in the chapter). Magnetic core storage is based on the principle that when electricity flows through a wire, a magnetic field is created. The direction of the magnetic field, which depends on the direction in which the electric current flows, determines which binary state a core represents. A clockwise flow of current produces an "on" condition (represented in binary code by a 1), and a counterclockwise flow produces an "off" condition (represented by a 0), as shown in Figure 2–2. Recall from Chapter 1 that computers only recognize machine language, which uses combinations of 0s and 1s.

In the storage unit, many cores are strung on a screen, or plane, of intersecting wires. If enough electricity were sent down a wire to magnetize a core, all the cores on that wire would be magnetized. To keep that from happening, the computer uses half-currents. When half the needed amount

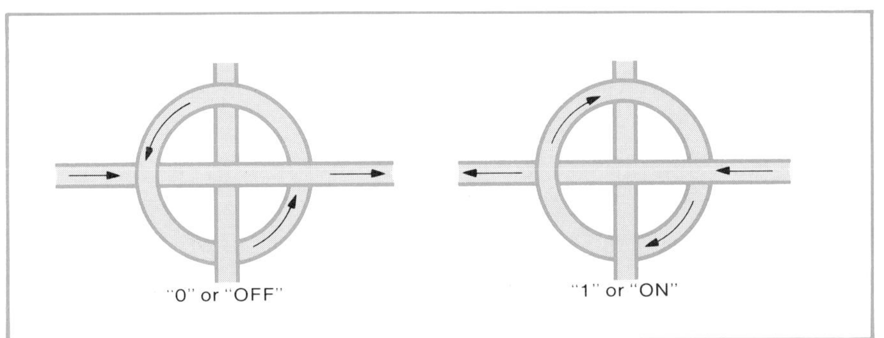

Figure 2–2 MAGNETIZING A CORE The direction of the current through the wires determines the direction of magnetization. The wires and cores are fitted on a large frame. Many frames are needed to provide adequate memory.

Figure 2–3 SELECTING A CORE
The half-currents traveling down the two wires will magnetize only one core.

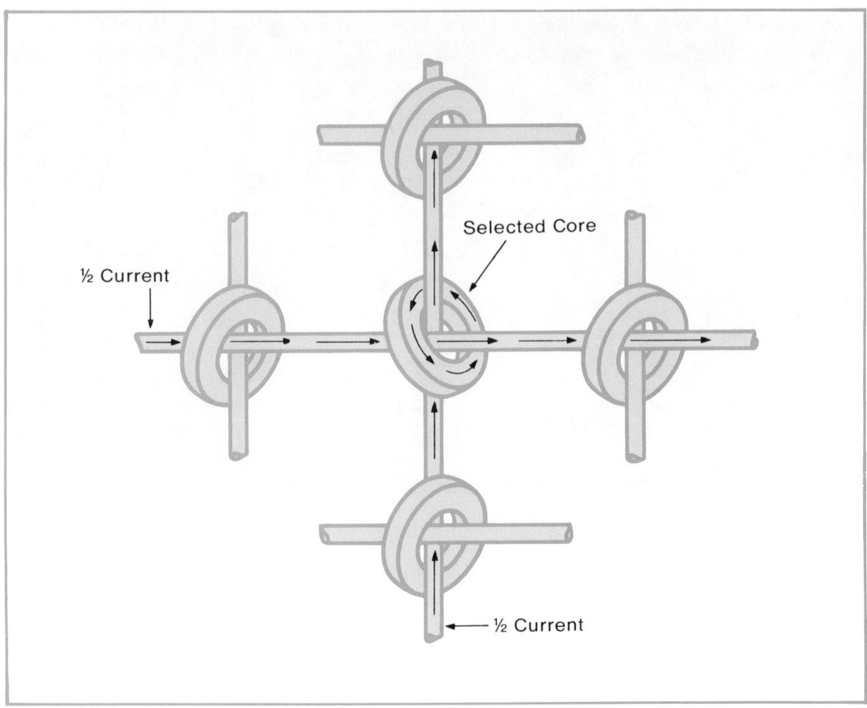

Semiconductor
A transistor used as a type of primary storage medium; it stores data in bit cells located on silicon chips.

New developments have led to the use of **semiconductors** in primary storage units and to a decline in the use of core memory. Semiconductor memory consists of a miniature circuitry on a silicon chip. One silicon chip the size of a single core can store as much data as thousands of cores (Figure 2–4). Semiconductor memory also allows much faster data retrieval than core memory.

Figure 2–4 CARD OF MEMORY CHIPS Many microcomputers allow the user to add more memory by plugging in an extra card. This card of memory chips is inserted in the disk drive slot and provides storage similar to that provided by disks. Data retrieval from such chips is fifty times faster than data retrieval from floppy disks. (Disks are discussed later in the chapter.)

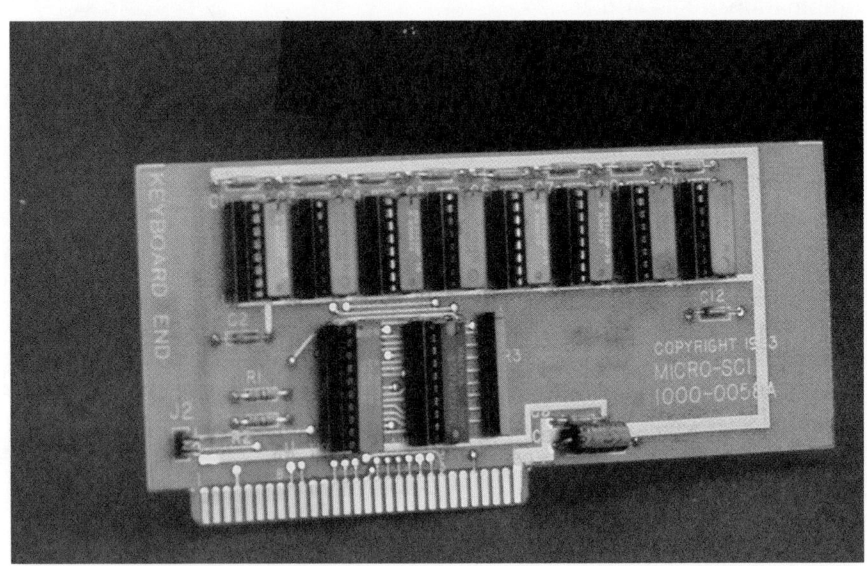

Semiconductors store data in locations called **bit cells,** which are in either an on or an off state. As in cores, on corresponds in binary code with a 1; off, with a 0.

One advantage of core memory over semiconductor memory is that core memory retains its contents even without electrical power. Semiconductor memory, which relies on currents rather than magnetic charges, loses its contents in the event of a power failure.

Another type of memory device, called **bubble memory,** is being considered as an alternative for use in primary storage, as well as secondary storage. Bubble memory uses magnetized spots, or bubbles, on a thin film of semiconductor material (Figure 2–5). These bubbles keep their magnetism indefinitely. Bubble memory chips can hold more data in a smaller area than either cores or semiconductors, but production difficulties and high costs have so far limited their use.

Figure 2–5 BUBBLE MEMORY
This bubble memory section is magnified 1,500 times.

Read-Only Memory (ROM) and Random-Access Memory (RAM)

Read-only memory (ROM) is a type of memory that is **hard wired,** which means that its instructions are built into the hardware and cannot be changed or deleted by stored-program instructions. The only way to change the contents of ROM is to alter the physical construction of the circuits.

Read-only memory holds operating systems, compilers to translate high-level languages to machine languages, and instructions for commonly used functions such as calculating square roots and evaluating exponents. Such instructions can be built into either the hardware or the software. Building them into the hardware provides the advantages of speed and reliability, since the operations are part of the computer circuitry.

The sequences of instructions built into ROM to carry out its functions are called **microprograms.** Microprograms are usually supplied by the computer manufacturer and cannot be altered by the users.

One version of ROM that can be programmed especially for the user is called **programmable read-only memory (PROM).** Once programmed, however, it cannot be changed. PROM gives the user the advantages of ROM plus the flexibility to meet special needs. However, mistakes programmed into a PROM unit cannot be corrected.

To overcome this problem, **erasable programmable read-only memory (EPROM)** has been developed. EPROM can be erased through certain processes such as bathing the chip in ultraviolet light. The chip then can be reprogrammed (Figure 2–6).

Random-access memory (RAM) is the major type of memory used in primary storage. RAM stores program instructions or data for use in solving particular problems. The program instructions or data that have been stored in RAM can be accessed (read) over and over again without destroying them. RAM is also reusable, that is, new program instructions or data may be stored (written) over existing ones. Semiconductor RAM, unlike ROM, is not permanent, meaning that when the power is turned off, everything stored in RAM is erased. By adding more RAM chips, a user can increase the computer's memory capacity.

Bit cells
Storage locations in semiconductors.

Bubble memory
A memory device in which data is represented by magnetized spots (or bubbles) on a thin film of semiconductor material.

Read-only memory (ROM)
Memory containing items that cannot be deleted or changed by stored-program instructions.

Hard wired
Memory devices that cannot be changed or deleted by other stored-program instructions.

Microprogram
A sequence of instructions wired into read-only memory, used to tailor a system to meet the user's processing requirements.

Figure 2–6 AN EPROM CHIP
This EPROM chip is ready to be mounted in a plastic carrier with pins that allow it to be plugged into a circuitry board.

Registers

Register
An internal computer component used for temporary storage of instructions or data.

Registers are temporary storage areas for instructions and data. Even though they are located in the CPU, they are not addressed or even considered part of primary storage. Registers can receive information, hold it, and transfer it very quickly as directed by the control unit.

A register works something like a pocket calculator. The person using the calculator acts as the control unit by transferring numbers from a piece of paper to the display of the calculator. The paper can be compared to the primary storage unit of the CPU. The calculation is performed in the calculator (arithmetic/logic unit) and the number is transferred to the display (register). The person (control unit) then transfers the answer to a sheet of paper (primary storage).

Accumulator
A register that gathers results of computations.

Storage register
A register that holds information coming from or going to the primary storage unit.

Instruction register
A register where each instruction is stored until decoded by the control unit.

Address register
A register that holds the address of a location containing a data item called for by an instruction.

General-purpose register
A register that can be used as an accumulator or an address register.

The types of registers are named for their functions. An **accumulator** is a register that holds the results of computations, such as the sum of a list of numbers. A **storage register** holds information being sent to or taken from the primary storage unit. An **instruction register** holds instructions until they are decoded by the control unit. When an instruction calls for data, the address of the data item is held in the **address register.** Finally, **general-purpose registers** can be used for both arithmetic and addressing functions.

The computer uses registers in all the calculations and manipulations it performs. However, the user of the computer never consciously works with registers unless programming in assembly language (more on assembly language in Chapter 4).

Secondary Storage

In many instances, the amount of instructions and data to be stored by a computer is much greater than the capacity of primary storage. The data and instructions can be stored in auxiliary, or secondary, storage, which is not part of the CPU.

Secondary storage devices are connected to the CPU by electrical lines. The computer can retrieve data from secondary storage as the data is needed for processing. Once the processing is completed, the data and results can be sent back to secondary storage.

The most common types of secondary storage media are magnetic tapes and magnetic disks. Punched cards, mass storage, magnetic drums, floppy disks, and cassette tapes are also used. (Figure 2–7 shows some of these media.) Secondary storage is much cheaper than primary storage, but it also is many times slower.

Magnetic Tape. A **magnetic tape** is a continuous strip of plastic coated with a magnetizable material, usually iron oxide, wound onto a reel. It is similar to the tape used in reel-to-reel stereo recorders. Normally, tapes are one-half-inch wide and are wound in lengths of 2,400 feet.

Magnetic tape
A storage medium consisting of a narrow strip of material upon which spots are magnetized to represent data.

Data is stored on magnetic tape through magnetization of small spots of the iron oxide coating. Although these spots can be read by the computer, they are invisible to the human eye. Large volumes of information can be stored on a single tape. As many as 1,600 characters per inch are common, and some tapes can store 6,250 characters per inch. A 2,400-foot reel of tape can store as much data as 400,000 punched cards.

When a program calls for the information contained on a magnetic tape, the tape is mounted onto a **tape drive** (Figure 2–8). The drive has a read/write head (Figure 2–9) that creates or reads the bits as the tape moves past the head. When it is reading, the head detects the magnetized areas and converts them into electrical pulses to send to the CPU. When writing, the head magnetizes the appropriate spots on the tape while erasing any previously stored data.

Tape drive
A device used to read from or write to magnetic tape.

Cassette Tape. For small computers that do not need large amounts of secondary storage, **tape cassettes** are sometimes used. Tape cassettes look like those used in audio recording—and some can be used that way—but those meant for storing data are made of high-quality, high-density digital recording tape.

Tape cassette
A sequential storage medium using high-density digital recording tape to record data in small computer systems.

The low cost of tape cassettes has made them an economical storage medium for home computers. They can be used with a regular cassette player, are easy to store, and are easy to keep secure, since they can be removed and kept in a safe place.

Magnetic Disk. The **magnetic disk** is a metal platter, usually fourteen inches in diameter, coated on both sides with a magnetizable material. A magnetic disk resembles a phonograph record, but it has smooth surfaces instead of a record's characteristic grooves. Data is stored in a set of concentric circles. Each circle is called a **track.** One track never touches another, as Figure 2–10 shows. A typical disk has two hundred tracks on each surface.

Magnetic disk
A storage medium consisting of a platter made of metal or plastic and coated with a magnetic recording material.

Track
One of a series of concentric circles on the surface of a magnetic disk.

Figure 2–7 SECONDARY STORAGE FOR A COMPUTER SYSTEM Instructions or data from secondary storage media are entered into the primary storage unit of a computer, either as a whole or in portions, to be processed.

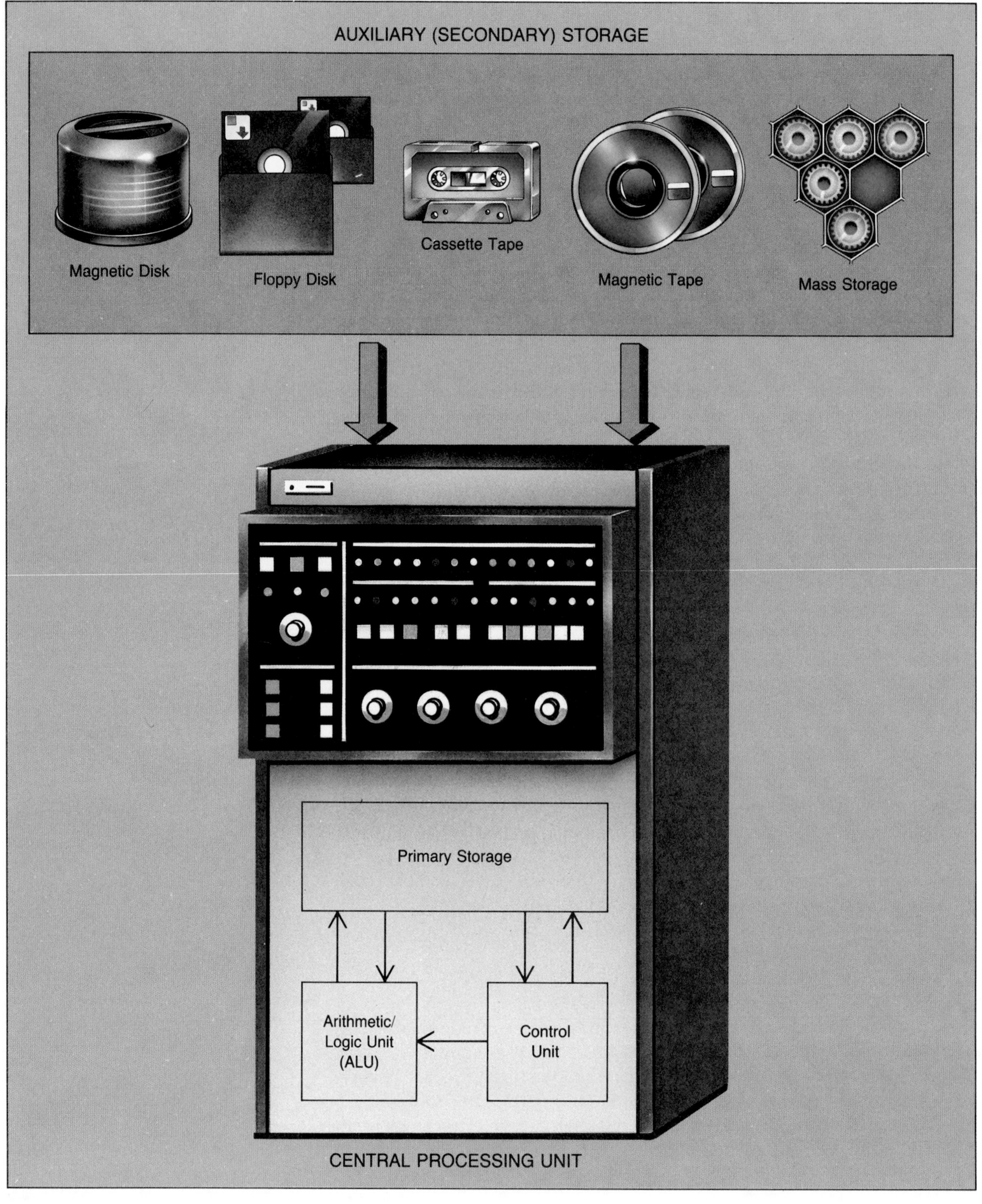

Figure 2–8 MAGNETIC TAPE DRIVE A computer operator mounts tapes on tape drives and pushes the proper buttons for entry of stored data into the computer. Magnetic tape is an inexpensive medium for data storage, but data must be accessed sequentially.

Usually several disks are mounted on a center shaft to form a **disk pack** (Figure 2–11). The individual disks are spaced on the shaft to allow room for a read/write head to move between them. The disk pack in Figure 2–12 has eleven disks and provides twenty usable recording surfaces. The extreme top and bottom surfaces are not used for storing data because they are likely to become scratched or nicked. A disk pack may contain six to eleven disks.

A disk pack must be positioned in a **disk drive** for the data it contains to be processed. The disk drive rotates all disks in unison at speeds of 40 to 3,600 revolutions per second. In some models the disk packs can be removed (Figure 2–13); in others they are permanently mounted on the disk drive.

Disk drive
Machine used to rotate magnetic disks during data transmission.

Disk pack
A stack of magnetic disks mounted on a center shaft.

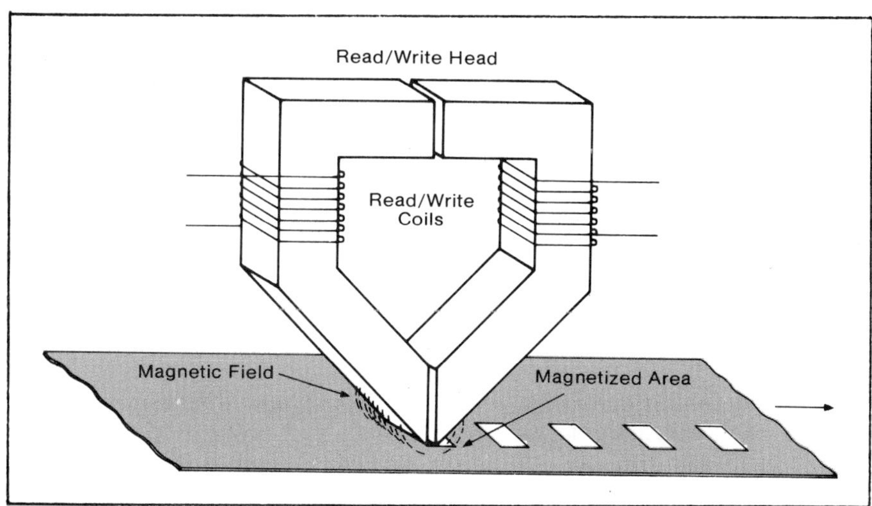

Figure 2–9 RECORDING ON MAGNETIC TAPE
The read/write head contains read/write coils that determine which operation will take place. A magnetic field is created to either write data or detect data.

Figure 2–10 TOP VIEW OF DISK SURFACE Data is written onto a disk in concentric circles—circles that do not touch each other. In contrast, the track on a phonograph record is a continuous path that spirals toward the center of the platter.

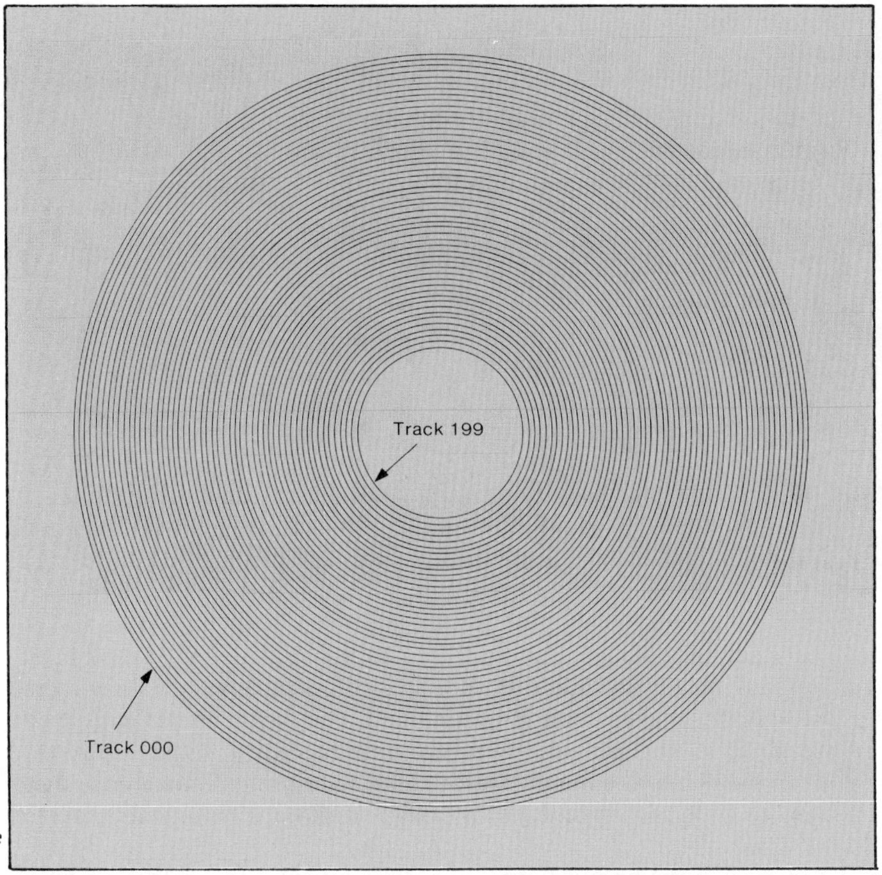

Track 199

Track 000

Access mechanism
The device that positions the read/write head of a direct-access storage device over a particular track.

Floppy disk
Low-cost, random access data storage device, made of plastic.

As noted earlier, data on a disk is read or written by read/write heads positioned between the disks. Most disk units have one read/write head for each recording surface. All the heads are permanently connected to an **access mechanism.** Some disk units have a read/write head for each track on each disk. Access time is much shorter with this type of disk unit, since the access mechanism does not need to move from track to track. Such units are very expensive, however.

Figure 2–11 DISK PACK Disk packs like the one pictured are primarily used with mainframe computers and minicomputers. However, manufacturers of microcomputers now offer hard disks and hard disk drives as well as disk pack units that contain the disks and the drive.

Floppy Disk. The **floppy disk** (also called diskette or flexible disk) was introduced in 1973 to replace punched cards for data entry. But it can also store programs and data files. These disks are made of plastic and coated with an oxide substance and are available in two standard sizes—eight inches and five and one-quarter inches in diameter. Recently, a new three-inch microdisk was introduced. (Figure 2–14 shows some floppy disks.) Because they are inexpensive, the disks are very popular for use with minicomputer systems, point-of-sale terminals, and personal computers. They are reusable, are easy to store, weigh less than two ounces each, and can be mailed safely. Because floppy disks can be removed from the systems that use them, they provide the system with added security.

A typical floppy disk can store as much as three thousand punched cards and the storage capacity is rapidly increasing. Their capacity extends

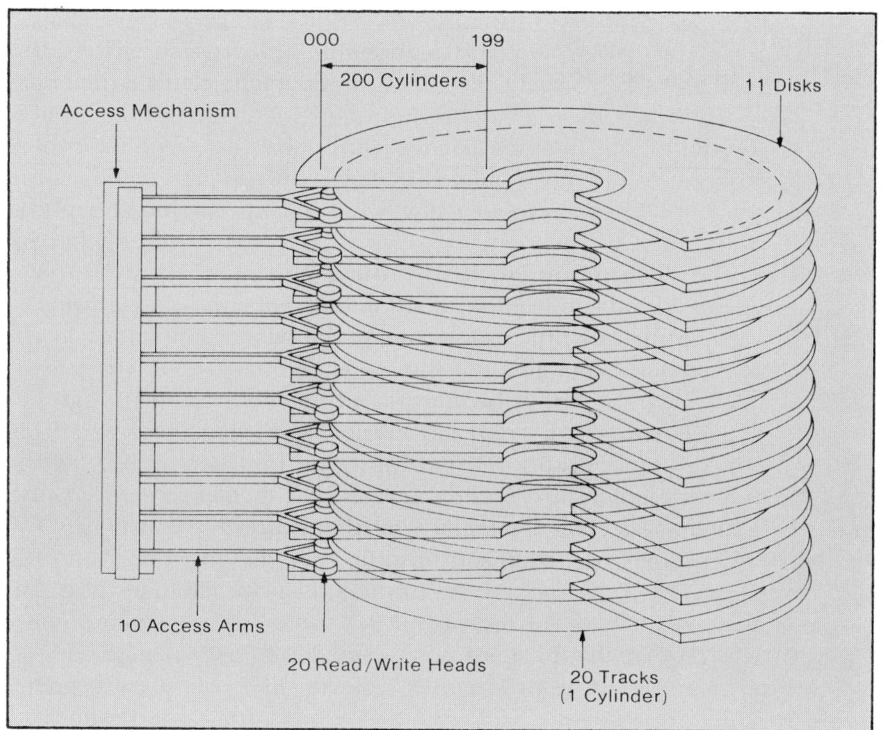

Figure 2–12 DISK PACKS SHOWING READ/WRITE HEADS Data on disks in disk packs is arranged in cylinders, because of the concentric tracks on each disk. The access arms move the read/write heads to the proper cylinder before an exact location is found.

from 100 K to 1 megabyte on the five-and-a-quarter-inch disks and 125 K to 1.2 megabytes on the eight-inch disks. K is an abbreviation for kilobyte, which stands for 1,024 bytes in computer terminology, while a megabyte is one million bytes. A **byte** generally represents one character, such as a letter or a number.

Byte
A string of bits that represents one character.

Figure 2–13 REMOVABLE DISK PACKS Computer operators are mounting removable disk packs in their disk storage units. Disks must be kept clean and free of scratches so that the data will retain integrity.

Figure 2–14 FLOPPY DISKS
Floppy disks have typically come in two sizes, eight inches and five and one-quarter inches in diameter. A newer size of disk is about three inches in diameter. These microdisks are usually encased in hard plastic, while the floppy disks are protected by flexible jackets.

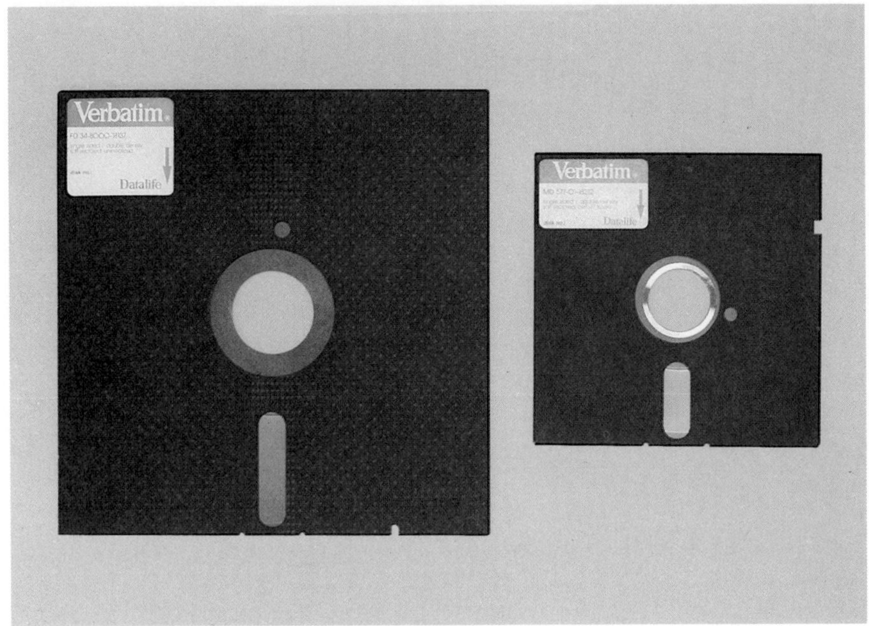

Magnetic drum
A cylinder with a magnetic outer surface on which data can be stored when specific positions are magnetized.

Magnetic Drum. The **magnetic drum** is a cylinder-shaped device, coated with a material that can be magnetized, that rotates at high speeds. Data is stored on tracks that go around the drum. Read/write heads similar to those used with magnetic disks are positioned above the tracks. Today, use of magnetic drums has diminished. However, the drums are still used in areas where the storage device must withstand movement and vibration and access to data must be very quick—for example, in the guidance systems of modern missiles.

Mass storage device
A device that allows relatively fast access to large amounts of data at a low cost.

Cartridge tape
A mass storage medium that uses high-density tapes.

Mass Storage. Using primary storage is very fast but also very expensive. Even disk storage can be expensive when very large amounts of data must be stored and accessed. To meet the need for less expensive storage, system designers have developed **mass storage devices.** These devices allow reasonably rapid access to data, although the time is still much slower than that of primary storage or magnetic disk. Large files, backup files, and seldom-used files can be placed in mass storage at a relatively low cost.

One type of mass storage uses **cartridge tapes** as the storage medium. The cartridges are similar to cassette tapes in design. One high-density tape can store as much data as a thousand tape reels but takes only one-tenth the storage space. Mounting of the cartridges is controlled by the computer system (Figure 2–15) rather than by a human operator, making it faster than traditional operator-controlled methods.

Sequential access
Retrieval in which stored records must be read, one after another, in a fixed sequence, until the needed data is located; common of magnetic tapes.

Access Methods

Access methods are the ways in which data is retrieved from storage. The simplest method is **sequential access.** With this method, all the data must be read in order from the beginning until the desired record is found. Sequential access is similar to the way songs are stored on a cassette tape. To find a particular song, you must run the tape forward on "play" until the portion of tape with the desired song is reached. Similarly, if a computer using sequential access is searching for data on a certain employee, it must start at the beginning of the **file.** (A file is a collection of all of the **records** kept on a certain subject, such as employee records in a personnel file.) By reading through the file one record at a time, the computer will eventually find the desired record. When the correct record has been found, the computer will read it to find the desired data. Data retrieval from magnetic tape is sequential.

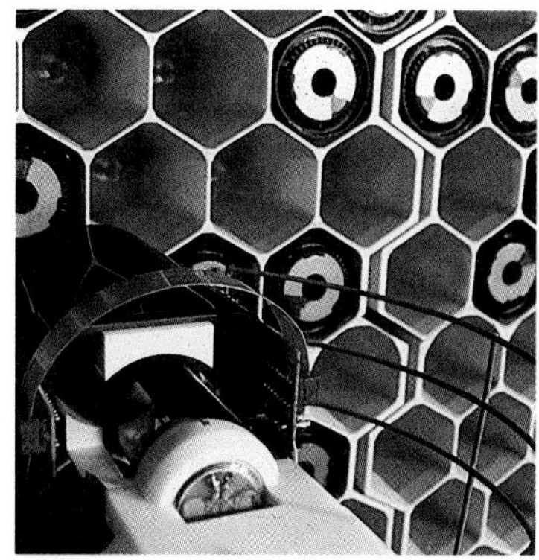

Figure 2–15 MASS STORAGE
A mechanical arm removes a cartridge from its cell when the data stored on it is needed for processing. Because these data cartridges are stored in slots resembling a honeycomb, this type of storage is sometimes called honeycomb mass storage.

Sequential-access processing takes time. Consider a file with 10,000 employee records. If an inquiry is made about an employee whose record is number 9,000, the computer will have to read through 8,999 other records before reaching the correct one. A faster method of locating data would be for the computer to go directly to the correct record, as people do when they use a filing cabinet. A secretary, for example, can find information about an employee named Smith much more quickly by going directly to the drawer marked S, than by searching all drawers from the beginning.

Computers can use an access method that goes directly to the correct record, or close to it, and reads the data starting from that point. This type of data retrieval is called **direct access.** By using direct access to retrieve data, the computer can find a record much more quickly than with sequential access. Direct access is used with magnetic disks and magnetic drums.

File
A collection of related records.

Record
A collection of data items that relate to a single unit.

Direct access
Retrieval in which stored data can be found in any order, at random; common of magnetic disks.

Types of Processing

The ways a computer can process data are similar to the ways it can access data. **Batch processing** occurs when the program instructions and all the data are collected and entered into the computer at one time by the operator. The computer then carries out the processing without interruption from the programmer or the user. With this type of processing, no input is accepted after the batch of data and instructions has been submitted for processing.

On-line processing takes place when the user is in direct communication with the computer. Processing occurs as input data is submitted; data need not be submitted in a batch. On-line processing is commonly used with **interactive programs,** which ask the user questions as part of their execution. For example, interactive programs and on-line processing are used for airline ticket reservation systems. The ticket agent first requests from the computer a list of all the flights from, say, Cleveland to San Francisco on a certain date. After the agent selects one flight, the program asks questions about the preferred class and so on. Each request is processed immediately after the data item has been entered, and the ticket agent knows immediately if seats are available.

Certain tasks are more suited to each type of processing system. Batch processing is more practical for applications that involve the processing of large volumes of data, such as payroll preparation. On-line processing is

Batch processing
Processing in which the entire program is executed at once; all instructions and data are submitted at one time.

On-line processing
Processing that allows the user to interact with the computer during program execution.

Interactive program
A program that allows the user to enter data during execution.

used when the answers to questions will affect later questions, input, and output.

Storage Integrity

Storage integrity refers to the correctness and accuracy of stored data. Obviously, this is important; if the data is incorrect, the results of processing or inquiry into the data will be useless.

Storage integrity can be maintained in several ways. First, the data entered into the system must be correct. Second, the data already stored must be maintained in a way that keeps it from being altered or lost. Any updates or changes to the data must be accurate. Third, a system of backup files must be kept to ensure that data is not lost. For instance, data may be destroyed if a disk drive stops functioning properly. If the user has a backup copy of the data, the system can be returned to normal operation quickly. Making a backup file involves copying files from one storage medium to another and storing the copy at another location.

A final consideration is data security. This has become even more important recently with the use of telecommunications. Computers may be connected by normal telephone lines to other computers hundreds of miles away. Using telephone lines opens up the data to access by unauthorized users. These users can alter or destroy data and can sometimes gain access to top-secret information. A company's data is a valuable asset. Its destruction or alteration can cost the company much money and can even force it into bankruptcy. Thus, some type of security system must be used to prevent unauthorized access to stored data.

Trends in Storage Media

Innovations in computer storage seem to be aimed at making improvements in three areas: speed, capacity, and cost.

The speed of the computer is limited by the speed of the electricity passing through the circuits. Major increases in speed have been made simply by decreasing the size of the circuitry, which means that the electricity flowing through the circuits has less distance to travel.

A relatively new development is the Josephson Junction, which works by super-cooling the circuitry. The metals used in the circuits are cooled to absolute zero, the temperature at which molecules stop moving. This causes the metals to lose their resistance to the flow of electricity. Therefore, the electronic pulses can be conducted at a speed much higher than ever before. Josephson Junction devices are in the experimental stage.

The storage capacity of the computer is being increased dramatically as more storage capability is packed into smaller and smaller spaces. By using very-large-scale integration (VLSI), researchers have packed more circuitry onto a single chip. However, engineers began to experience difficulty designing smaller and smaller chips containing more and more circuits. New developments that use computers themselves to assist in the design of VLSI chips are helping to overcome this limiting factor. The result is chips that contain even greater storage capacity.

During the 1970s, bubble memory appeared to be a revolutionary replacement for existing primary and secondary storage media. It was faster and more reliable than disks. However, bubble memory cost too much to warrant widespread use, and it did not become popular, as it had been expected to. Today, the use of bubble memory is increasing as some companies are building bubble memory into portable computers and microcomputers.

Laser technology permits massive quantities of data to be stored at greatly reduced costs. A laser storage system can store nearly 128 billion characters of data at about one-tenth the cost of standard magnetic media.

In a laser system, data is recorded by a laser beam that forms patterns on the surface of a polyester disk coated with a thin layer of rhodium metal. To read data from this sheet, the laser reflects light off the surface, reconstructing the data into a stream of digits the computer recognizes. Unlike some other storage devices, this system will not lose data in a power failure.

LEARNING CHECK

1. The computer must know the ________ of the locations of data or instructions.
2. Semiconductor primary storage retains its contents even without electrical power. (True or false?)
3. A type of storage that is hard wired and cannot be changed by stored-program instructions is
   a. random-access memory.
   b. primary storage.
   c. registers.
   d. read-only memory.
4. Types of secondary storage media include all of the following except
   a. magnetic tape.
   b. diskettes.
   c. tape drives.
   d. cartridge tapes.
5. Data is retrieved from disks by the sequential-access method. (True or false?)
6. Interactive programs require ________ processing.
7. Methods that help ensure storage integrity include all of the following except
   a. accurate data.
   b. backup files.
   c. use of telephone lines for transmission.
   d. accurate data maintenance.

ANSWERS: 1. addresses. 2. false. 3. d. 4. c. 5. false. 6. on-line. 7. c.

MACHINE LANGUAGE AND DATA REPRESENTATION

Machine language
A language based on 0s and 1s; the only language a computer can understand directly.

When data is entered to a computer through an input device such as a terminal keyboard, it is not in a form the computer can interpret. Computers cannot understand the complex symbols that humans use. They recognize only a code composed of 0s and 1s, known as **machine language.** Before the computer can execute the English-like statements of most programming languages, the statements must be translated by special programs into machine language. Machine language may use binary code or one of several other codes based upon it.

Binary Representation

Binary number system
The number system that uses the digits 0 and 1 and has a base of 2.

Binary representation
The use of binary numbers to represent data.

Since data is represented in the computer by the electrical states of its circuitry—on and off—data representation is easily accomplished by using the **binary number system.** In the binary system, as you know, there are only two digits, 1 and 0, which represent on and off. Using binary numbers to represent data is called **binary representation.**

The binary system is similar to the decimal number system (base 10) we use every day. For example, the decimal number 8,703 can be analyzed like this:

8703

$$
\begin{aligned}
3 \times 10^0 &= 3 \times 1 &= 3\\
0 \times 10^1 &= 0 \times 10 &= 0\\
7 \times 10^2 &= 7 \times 100 &= 700\\
8 \times 10^3 &= 8 \times 1000 &= \underline{8000}\\
& & 8703
\end{aligned}
$$

Each position represents a certain power of the base 10, as shown in Figure 2–16. The digits farther to the left in a decimal number represent larger powers than the digits to the right. This same principle is true for binary representation, also shown in Figure 2–16. The difference is that in

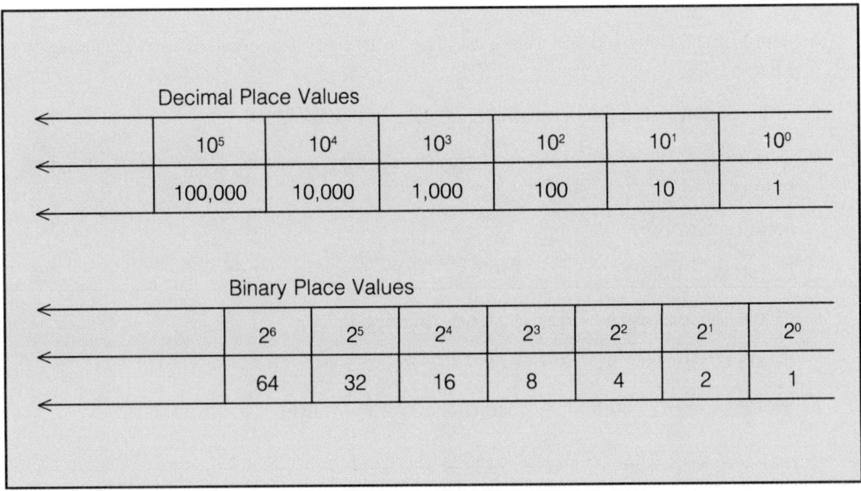

Decimal Place Values
10^5 10^4 10^3 10^2 10^1 10^0
100,000 10,000 1,000 100 10 1
Binary Place Values
2^6 2^5 2^4 2^3 2^2 2^1 2^0
64 32 16 8 4 2 1

Figure 2–16 DECIMAL PLACE VALUES AND BINARY PLACE VALUES
The place values in both the decimal system and the binary system are indicated by superscript numbers. They indicate the power of the number and are sometimes referred to as exponents. To obtain the power, multiply the number by itself as many times as the exponent indicates. For example, $2^3 = 2 \times 2 \times 2$, or 8. Therefore, 2^3 is the same as the eights' place.

binary representation, each position in the number represents a power of the base 2. For example, consider the decimal number 19. In binary code, the value equivalent to 19 is written as follows:

```
10011
||||└──────────────── 1 × 2^0 = 1 × 1  =  1
|||└───────────────── 1 × 2^1 = 1 × 2  =  2
||└────────────────── 0 × 2^2 = 0 × 4  =  0
|└─────────────────── 0 × 2^3 = 0 × 8  =  0
└──────────────────── 1 × 2^4 = 1 × 16 = 16
                                         19
```

As indicated in the example above, the binary system uses combinations of 0s and 1s to represent various values. A 0 indicates the absence of a specific power of 2, and a 1 indicates the presence of a specific power of 2. Each of these binary digits is called a **bit.**

Bit
Short for BInary digiT; a digit position in a binary number.

Computer Codes

Using binary numbers can become complex, especially with large numbers, so many computers use coding schemes other than simple binary notation to represent numbers. One basic coding scheme is called the **four-bit binary coded decimal (BCD)** system. Instead of using one long string of 0s and 1s to represent a decimal number, each decimal digit is represented by a distinct group of four binary bits. For example, the decimal number 152 is represented by three groups of four bits, with one group for the 1, one group for the 5, and one group for the 2. The decimal number 152 is represented in binary and in BCD as follows:

Four-bit binary coded decimal (BCD) System
A four-bit binary digit computer code used to represent decimal numbers.

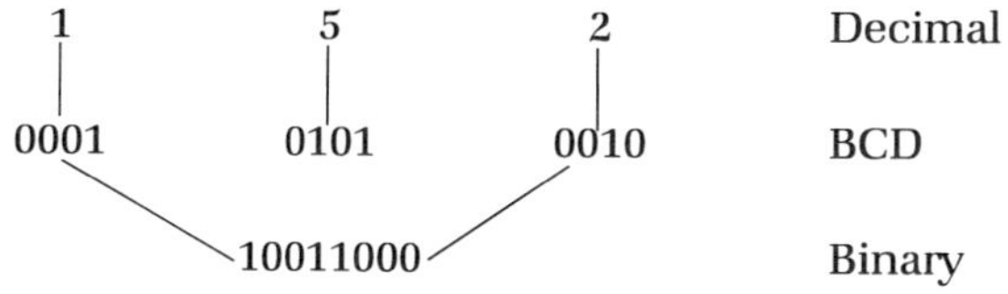

1	5	2	Decimal
0001	0101	0010	BCD
	10011000		Binary

Another method of data representation is known as **Extended Binary Coded Decimal Interchange Code (EBCDIC).** This eight-bit code is used to represent upper- and lower-case letters and additional special characters, as well as the digits 0 through 9, as shown in Table 2–1.

Extended Binary Coded Decimal Interchange Code (EBCDIC)
An eight-bit binary code used to represent numbers and characters.

The **American Standard Code for Information Interchange (ASCII)** is yet another code designed for representing numbers, letters, and special characters. This seven-bit code was developed by several computer manufacturers working together to create a standard code that would be common among various computers. However, some machines had already been designed to operate on eight-bit code patterns. The problem was solved by creation of an eight-bit version of ASCII, called ASCII-8.

American Standard Code for Information Interchange (ASCII)
A standard seven-bit binary code used for information interchange among data processing systems and associated equipment.

Table 2–1 EBCDIC REPRESENTATION
Just like a secret code, the EBCDIC representation puts letters and numbers into computer-readable form.

CHARACTER	EBCDIC BIT CONFIGURATION	CHARACTER	EBCDIC BIT CONFIGURATION
A	1100 0001	S	1110 0010
B	1100 0010	T	1110 0011
C	1100 0011	U	1110 0100
D	1100 0100	V	1110 0101
E	1100 0101	W	1110 0110
F	1100 0110	X	1110 0111
G	1100 0111	Y	1110 1000
H	1100 1000	Z	1110 1001
I	1100 1001	0	1111 0000
J	1101 0001	1	1111 0001
K	1101 0010	2	1111 0010
L	1101 0011	3	1111 0011
M	1101 0100	4	1111 0100
N	1101 0101	5	1111 0101
O	1101 0110	6	1111 0110
P	1101 0111	7	1111 0111
Q	1101 1000	8	1111 1000
R	1101 1001	9	1111 1001

Code Checking

Computers do not always function without errors. When errors occur, they must be detected immediately to keep the data from being changed.

Most computers include an extra bit at each storage location to check for certain kinds of internal errors. This extra bit is called a **parity bit.**

Parity bit
A bit added to detect incorrect transmission of data; it conducts internal checks to determine whether the correct number of bits are present.

Computers can be set to either odd parity or even parity. If a computer is set for odd parity, each character is represented by an odd number of 1 bits. The parity bit is set to 0 if the number of 1 bits in the character is already odd. If the number of 1 bits is even, the parity bit is set to 1, making the total number of 1 bits odd. With even parity, the parity bit is set to either 0 or 1 so that the total number of 1 bits is even.

When the computer checks each character for errors, it checks for the proper number of 1 bits. For example, a computer set for even parity will check for an even number of 1 bits and will detect an error in any character having an odd number of 1 bits.

If an error is detected, the computer may try to redo the read or write operation in which the error occurred. If the error remains, the computer will inform the operator. The computer cannot correct these errors; it can only detect them.

Check digit
An additional bit determined by performance of some calculation on the code; used to catch input errors.

A **check digit** works similar to a parity bit. The difference is that while the parity check is an internal operation, performed in the computer's circuits, a check digit is used in program instructions to catch input errors. The check digit is determined by some mathematical calculations on the code, specified by the programmer. The resulting digit becomes part of the code. Credit cards, banking cards, and employee ID cards generally use check digits. For example, assume that calculations performed on the employee number 93976 resulted in the check digit 4. The computer could tell when an operator mistakenly entered 93996 instead of 93976 because the calculations on the digits would not result in 4, the check digit.

LEARNING CHECK

1. The number system computers can understand imitates the on and off states of electrical current. It is called the ________ number system.
2. ________ is the code of 1s and 0s that represent the on and off states of electrical current.
3. What does the binary number 11010 stand for in decimal system representation?
4. In 1100010 (base 2), the underlined digit stands for the third power of 2, or the ________ place.
5. If 326 were written in four-bit binary coded decimal form, it would look like

   a. 101000110.

   b. 0003 0002 0006.

   c. 101 001 110.

   d. 0011 0010 0110.
6. Two types of checks, one for the computer itself and one for data entry, are carried out by the ________ and the ________.

ANSWERS:
1. binary. 2. Machine language. 3. 26. 4. eights. 5. d. 6. parity bit, check bit.

INPUT DEVICES

Punched Cards

Traditionally, data from documents such as time cards, bills, invoices, and checks was transferred onto punched cards and then read into the computer. Today, many of these documents are punched cards themselves; data is keyed directly onto the cards at their source. A common example is the phone bill. After customers mail in their payments, the bills themselves can be read directly into the computer, saving time and eliminating errors that could result from retyping the data.

The standard punched card has eighty vertical columns and twelve horizontal rows, as shown in Figure 2–17. It is called an eighty-column punched card or a Hollerith card, after its developer, Herman Hollerith. Data is represented by holes punched in a particular column to represent a given character. Each column can hold one letter, number, or special character. The pattern of holes used to represent characters is known as **Hollerith Code.**

Hollerith code
A method of data representation using eight-column punched cards.

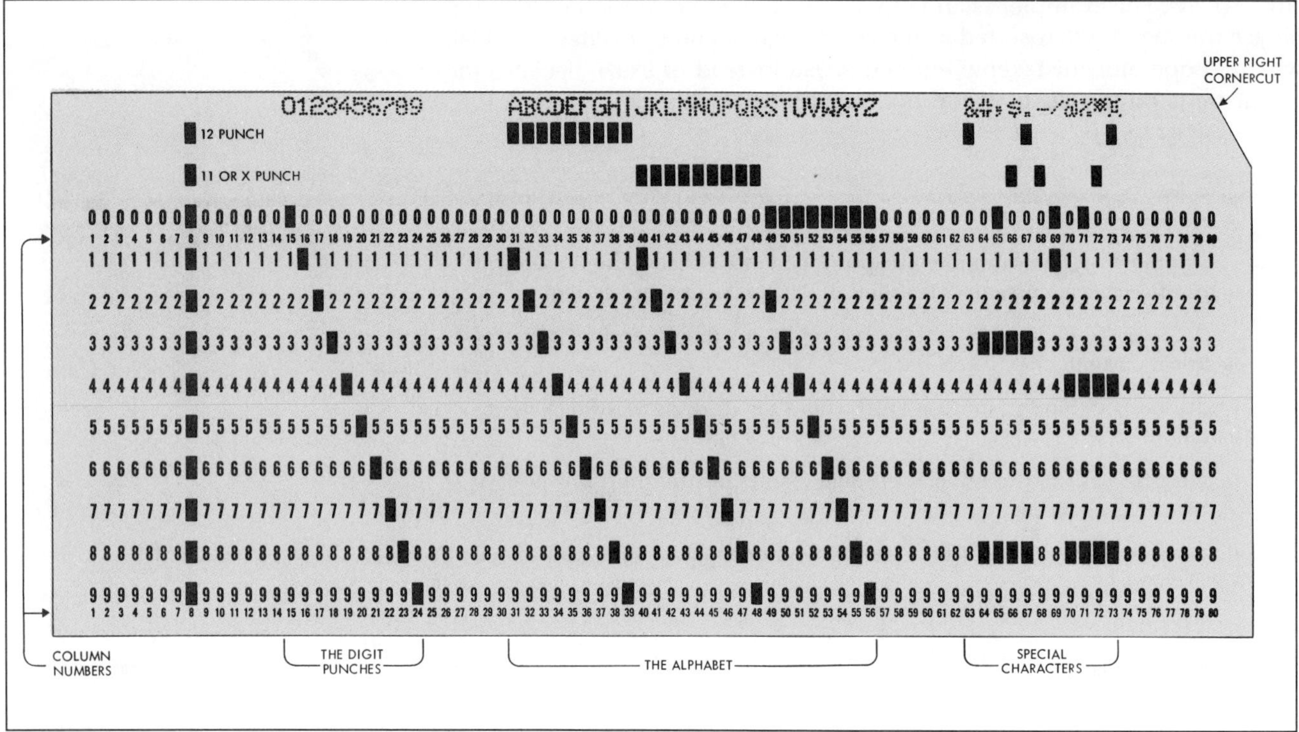

Figure 2–17 EIGHTY-COLUMN PUNCHED CARD This punched card is coded by the placement of the punched holes. Each row and column of places to punch stands for a character. The code commonly used is the Hollerith code.

Figure 2–18 KEYPUNCH Keypunches are used less frequently today, since so much data is stored on magnetic tape or disks. Many keypunch machines allow the operator to verify data before the cards are punched. This decreases waste caused by errors.

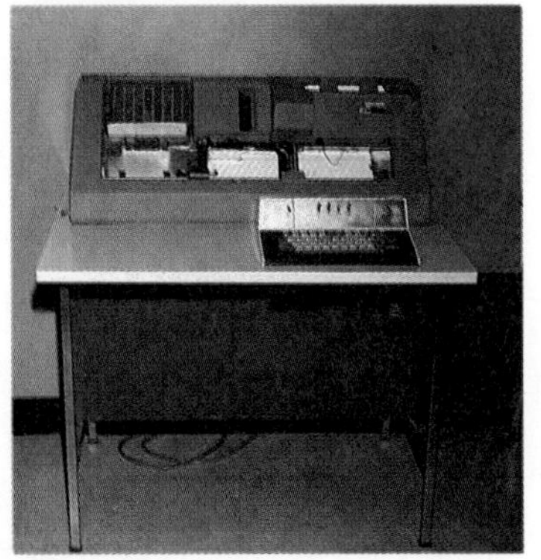

Data is recorded on punched cards with a keypunch (Figure 2–18). The keypunch has a standard keyboard, similar to an ordinary typewriter's. The data is typed on the keyboard by an operator, and the machine punches the correct holes in the card. The machine automatically feeds, positions, and stacks the cards as well.

There are several drawbacks to using punched cards. First, if the data to be input requires more than eighty columns, two or more cards must be used. Second, if a data record requires less than eighty columns, the remaining space on the card is left unused and is thus wasted. Third, if the data on a card needs to be changed, or if a mistake is made, a new card must be keypunched and the old one discarded. Finally, punched-card systems require a lot of mechanical movement, which makes them slow and inefficient.

Key-to-Magnetic-Media Systems

Because of the many limitations of punched cards, other methods to record and enter data have been developed. These methods use magnetic media, such as magnetic tape or magnetic disks. Data is entered through a keyboard—as with the keypunch—but is stored as magnetized spots on the surface of the tape or disk. Because the spots retain their magnetism, the data can be stored and used indefinitely. Unlike punched cards, which cannot be repunched, tape and disks allow the user to replace old data with new data. Tape and disks can also store much more data than cards, in a much smaller space. In addition, data stored on tape or disk can be read into the CPU hundreds of times faster than data stored on cards.

Advances in disk technology, along with the fact that disks are easier to use and require even less storage space than tapes, will eventually result in most key-to-tape systems being replaced by key-to-disk or key-to-diskette systems.

A typical **key-to-disk system** consists of several keyboard terminals, all connected to a minicomputer (see Figure 2–19). The data is entered into the minicomputer, where it is edited by stored programs. If an error is detected, the system interrupts the operator and waits until a correction has been made. The correct data is then stored on the magnetic disk for input into the computer.

Key-to-disk system
Several keying devices connected to a minicomputer and a disk drive.

An increasingly popular data-entry system is the **key-to-diskette system,** which uses a flexible (or floppy) disk instead of a hard disk. The data is entered through a keyboard, displayed on a screen for the operator to check, and then recorded on the diskette. Key-to-tape, key-to-disk, and key-to-diskette systems offer many advantages over punched-card input: they are faster, quieter, and smaller and are reusable. However, they also cost more.

Key-to-diskette system
A keyboard display screen and a flexible disk drive.

Source-Data Automation

Data entry has always been a troublesome area. Data can be processed at high speeds, but the time needed to enter it is significantly greater. This increases the overall processing time.

Traditionally, data has been collected and then, at some later time, converted to computer-readable form and entered into the computer. Another

Figure 2–19 KEY-TO-DISK SYSTEM
Office workers enter data on individual terminals. However, the terminals are linked to a computer that ensures proper storage of the data on disks.

Source-data automation
The process that allows data to be collected in computer-readable form at its source.

approach, called **source-data automation,** collects data already in computer-readable form. By eliminating steps in the data-entry cycle, source-data automation improves the speed, accuracy, and efficiency of data-processing operations. There are several methods of source-data automation, including magnetic-ink character recognition, optical recognition, and voice recognition systems.

Magnetic-ink character recognition (MICR)
A process that allows magnetized characters to be read by a magnetic-ink character reader.

Magnetic-Ink Character Recognition. Magnetic ink contains particles of iron oxide, and characters formed from the ink can be read not only by humans but by computers. A **magnetic-ink character recognition (MICR)** device reads the shape of each character. A major application of magnetic-ink character recognition is in processing bank checks. The magnetic-ink characters are printed along the bottom of the checks, as shown in Figure 2–20. Between 750 and 1,500 checks can be read and sorted by an MICR device per minute.

Optical Recognition. Optical recognition devices read marks or symbols coded on paper and convert them into electrical pulses. These pulses are then transmitted to the CPU or to a storage medium for later processing.

Optical-mark recognition (OMR)
A capability of devices with scanners to convert marks on a page into computer data.

Bar-code reader
A device that reads a bar code by means of reflected light.

Universal product code (UPC)
A code that uses ten pairs of vertical bars to represent the identities of the manufacturer and the item.

Optical-character recognition (OCR)
A capability of devices with scanners to read characters and convert optical images into electrical signals for the computer.

The simplest method of optical recognition is **optical-mark recognition (OMR).** An optical-mark page reader simply scans a document by means of reflected light and records the presence or absence of marks at specific locations on a page. This data is immediately translated into machine language. One use of OMR is in scoring multiple-choice examinations (Figure 2–21). OMR is also used in inventory control, surveys, questionnaires, and payroll applications. Generally, with OMR up to 2,000 forms can be read and processed in an hour.

Another type of optical recognition uses a **bar-code reader** to read patterns of marks called bar codes (Figure 2–22). Data is represented in a bar code by the widths of the bars and the distance between them. Probably the most familiar bar code is the **Universal Product Code (UPC),** which is used in grocery stores. It consists of ten pairs of vertical bars, which identify both the product and its manufacturer.

Optical-character recognition (OCR) devices can read several different character types, including uppercase and lowercase letters (Figure 2–23). The OCR characters are similar to MICR characters but do not need magnetic ink. The OCR device also relies on reflected light to translate written

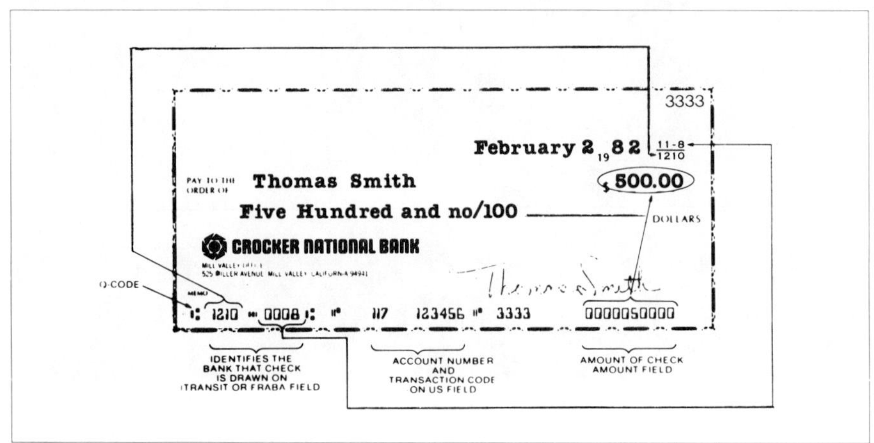

Figure 2–20 MAGNETIC INK CHARACTERS The primary use for magnetic ink characters is on checks. Checks come with some data already entered in magnetic ink. Once a check is written, the bank that cashes it must enter new magnetic ink characters for the amount of the check.

Figure 2–21 OPTICAL-MARK RECOGNITION (OMR) FOR MULTIPLE-CHOICE TEST Marking the boxes correctly with the proper pencil is important because it allows the OMR reader to grade the test correctly.

Name ______________ Student No. ______________

Subject ______________ Teacher ______________

Date ______________ Hour ______________

Scores	
Part 1	
Part 2	
Total	

Directions:
Use a No. 2 pencil to fill in completely the lettered box corresponding to your answer. For example, if you believe the correct answer relates to box c, fill in box c as follows:
Example: a b ▬ d e
To change your answer, erase completely and re-mark.

Error →

Do not mark in this shaded area. It is reserved for the error-indicating function of the Test Scorer.

T F

1–50 a b c d e

Part 1

Rescore

Visual Products Division/3M
St. Paul, Minnesota 55101 Made in USA
FORM NO. 80-882
3M CAT. NO. 78-6969-0351-3

Number Correct

L-2S

Feed →

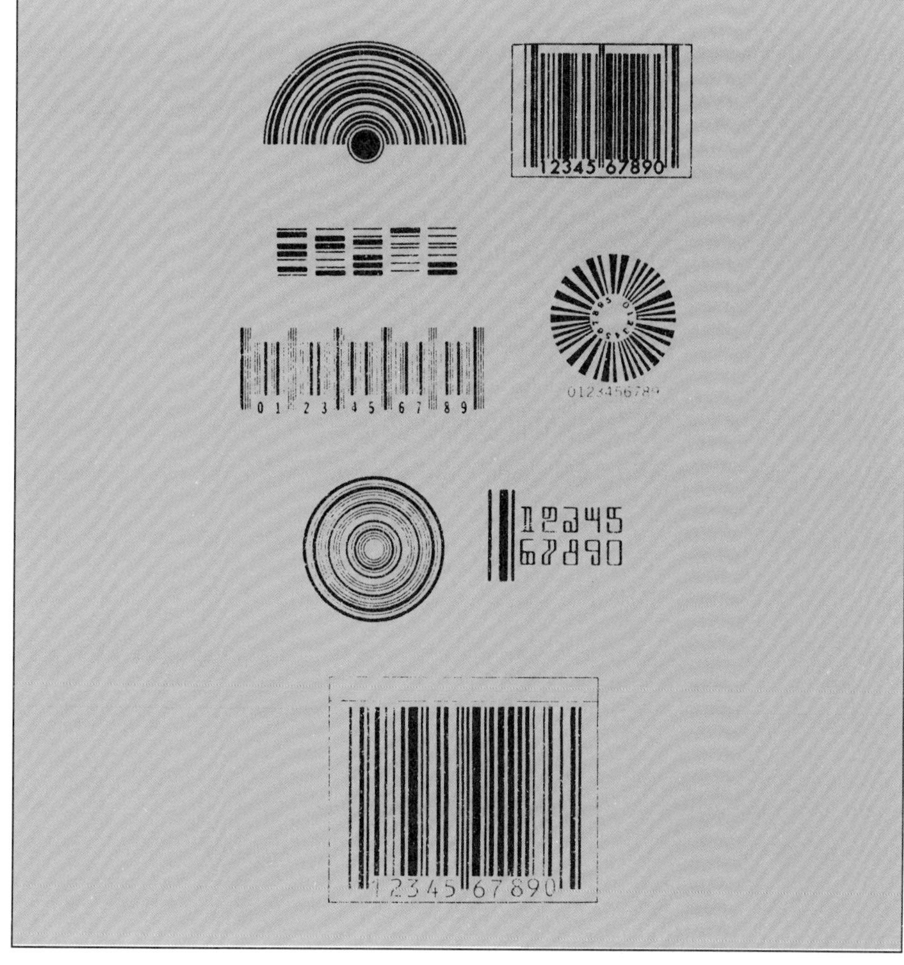

Figure 2–22 TYPES OF BAR CODES (LEFT)
The most common bar code is the Universal Product Code. Have you seen any of the other codes shown here?

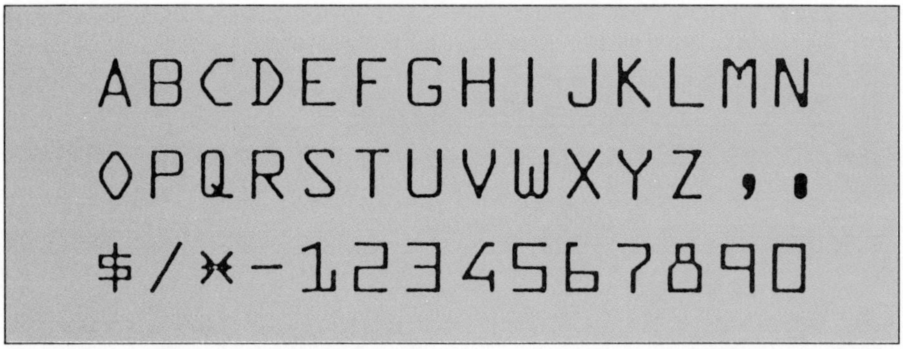

Figure 2–23 OCR CHARACTERS
OCR characters are specially shaped so that an OCR reader can properly detect them. Specially designed characters of one style form a font. A font is a style of type.

ABCDEFGHIJKLMN
OPQRSTUVWXYZ,.
$/*-1234567890

data into machine-readable form. Some of the most advanced OCR readers can even read handwritten characters. Optical-character recognition has been used extensively in mail sorting, credit card billing, utility billing, and inventory control.

Voice-recognition system
A system in which the user can "train" the computer to understand his or her voice and vocabulary.

Voice Recognition. **Voice-recognition systems** (Figure 2–24) rely on the computer's having been "trained" to understand the user's voice. Recognition is very limited, so the user is restricted to the few patterns the computer has been programmed to acknowledge. Current voice-recognition modules can recognize up to a hundred words and phrases. Since data can be entered in natural spoken language, greater accuracy in data entry is obtained.

LEARNING CHECK

1. A typical key-to-disk system consists of several keyboard terminals, a minicomputer, and magnetic tape drives. (True or false?)
2. Source-data automation
   a. saves time and makes data collection more accurate.
   b. makes data entry a troublesome area for data processing.
   c. collects data about an event in batch form.
   d. collects historical data.
3. An MICR device reads the ______ of each character.
4. The Universal Product Code is an example of what kind of code?
5. Voice-recognition systems can help to ensure the ______ of data.

ANSWERS: 1. false. 2. a. 3. shape. 4. bar code. 5. accuracy.

OUTPUT DEVICES

Once the data has been entered into the computer, it is processed and then presented as output. The output may, for example, appear as **soft**

copy on a CRT screen, or it may be printed as **hard copy,** a permanent printed copy. The type of output best suited to the user's needs determines the output device used.

Printers

Computer printers print processed data in a form that humans can read. To produce a copy, the printer (Figure 2–25) must first receive electronic signals from the central processing unit. In an **impact printer,** these signals activate print elements that strike the paper with the ribbon to make the impression. In the newer **nonimpact printers,** the signal activates heat, laser, or photographic actions to form the letters, numbers, and special characters. Table 2–2 shows the print speeds of impact and nonimpact printers.

Impact Printers. Impact printers come in a variety of shapes and sizes. Some print one character at a time, others print one line at a time. Printer-keyboard, dot matrix, and daisy wheel printers are the three principal character-at-a-time devices. Line-at-a-time devices include print wheel printers, chain printers, and drum printers.

- *Printer-Keyboards.* The **printer-keyboard** (Figure 2–26) is similar to an office typewriter except that a stored program, rather than a person, controls all instructions, such as spacing, carriage returns, and printing of characters. The CPU sends these instructions directly to the printer. The keyboard allows an operator to communicate with the computer to enter data or instructions.
- *Dot Matrix Printers.* **Dot matrix printers** (also called wire matrix printers) print characters as formations of dots, much as a football or basketball scoreboard does. The matrix is a rectangle composed of pins. Combinations

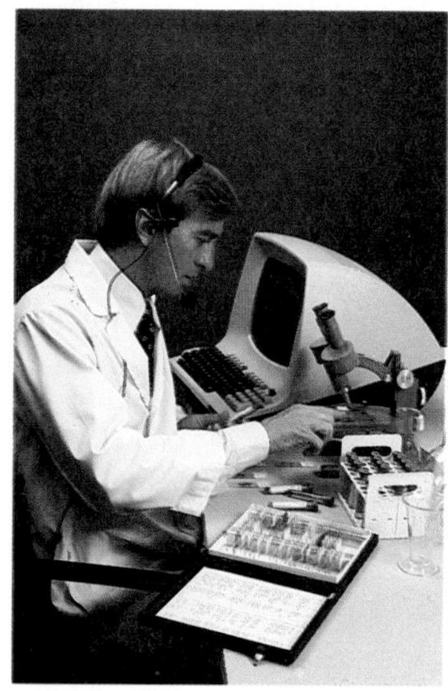

Figure 2–24 VOICE-RECOGNITION TERMINAL
This lab technician is using a terminal made by Interstate Electronics for voice data entry. This technique replaces keyboard entry and leaves the user's hands free for other tasks.

Soft copy
Output displayed on a CRT screen; not a permanent record, as hard copy is.

Impact printer
A printer that physically presses print elements together with the ribbon and paper to make the impression.

Nonimpact printer
A printer that uses heat, laser technology, or photographic techniques to make impressions; the print element never touches the paper.

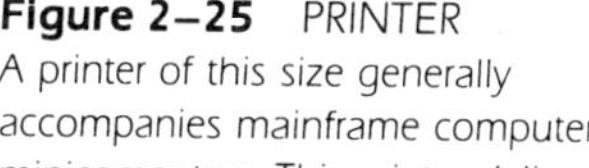

Figure 2–25 PRINTER
A printer of this size generally accompanies mainframe computers or minicomputers. This printer delivers the familiar computer printout sheets on paper containing green and white bars.

Table 2–2 PRINTER TYPES AND SPEEDS

PRINTER TYPE	APPROXIMATE PRINTING CAPABILITY
IMPACT PRINTERS	
Character-at-a-Time:	
Printer-keyboard	15 characters per second
Daisy wheel	50 characters per second
Dot-matrix (Wire-matrix)	120 characters per second
Line-at-a-Time:	
Print wheel	150 lines per minute
Print chain	2,000 lines per minute
Print drum	2,000 lines per minute
NONIMPACT PRINTERS	
Ink jet	200 characters per second
Xerographic	4,000 lines per minute
Electrothermal	5,000 lines per minute
Electrostatic	5,000 lines per minute
Laser	21,000 lines per minute

of pins are activated to represent various numbers, letters, and special characters (see Figure 2–27). Dot matrix printers can ordinarily print up to 120 characters per second.

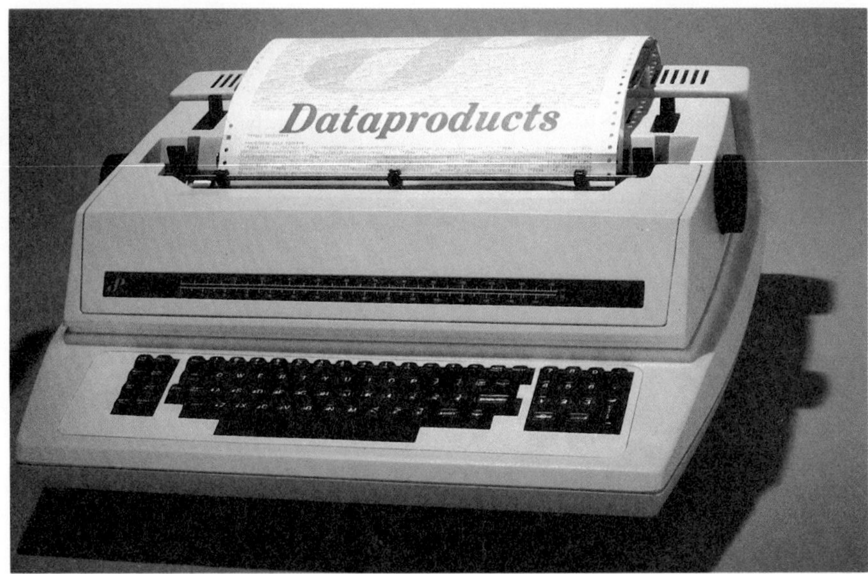

Figure 2–26 PRINTER-KEYBOARD
This Dataproducts terminal prints at fifty characters per second, a relatively slow rate.

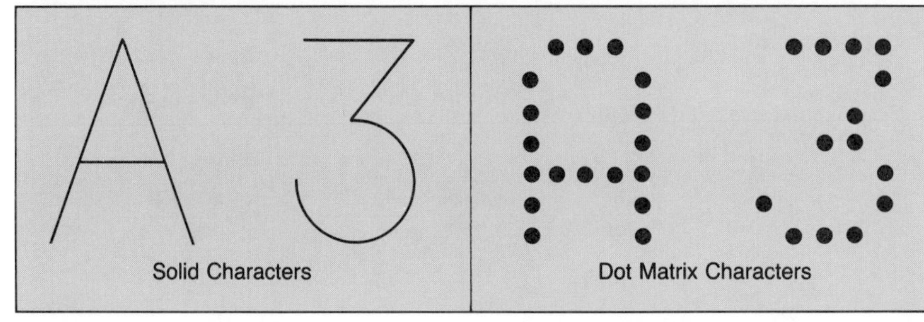

Figure 2–27 SOLID VERSUS DOT MATRIX CHARACTERS
Solid-font characters are characters that are completely filled in. A typewriter will deliver a solid-font character. Dot matrix characters are produced in formations of dots. The more dots in a dot matrix element, the more solid the character will look. At one time, dot matrix printouts were considered only rough draft quality. Today, some printers produce dot matrix output that looks almost like solid-font output.

● *Daisy Wheel Printers.* **Daisy wheel printers** also resemble office typewriters. The daisy wheel—the font, or type, carrier—has a set of spokes, each with a single character at the tip (see Figure 2–28). The wheel rotates to bring the desired character into position and is then struck by a hammer to form an image on paper. Daisy wheels come in several type styles. This printer offers high-quality type and is often used with word processors to produce typewriter-quality output. It can print up to 50 characters per second.

Daisy wheel printer
A character-at-a-time impact printer with removable daisy wheels (print wheels); produces letter-quality type.

● *Print Wheel Printers.* A **print wheel printer** usually has 80, 120, or 132 print wheels, one for each of the print locations on the line. Each print wheel contains forty-eight characters—the alphabet, numbers, and some special characters—and rotates until the character called for moves into the right print position on the current print line (see Figure 2–29). When all the wheels are in their correct positions, a hammer drives the paper against the wheels and an entire line of output is printed. Print wheel printers can print about 150 lines per minute (a comparatively slow output).

Print wheel printer
A line-at-a-time impact printer that has one print wheel for each print position on a line.

● *Chain Printers.* A **chain printer's** character set is assembled on a chain that moves horizontally past all print positions (see Figure 2–30). There is one print hammer for each column on the paper. Characters are printed when hammers press the paper against an inked ribbon, which, in turn, presses against the right characters on the print chain. Type styles can be changed easily on chain printers. Some of these devices can print up to 2,000 lines per minute.

Chain printer
A line-at-a-time impact printer, its character set is assembled on a chain that moves horizontally past all print positions.

● *Drum Printers.* A **drum printer** uses a metal cylinder with rows of characters engraved (raised) across its surface. Each band on the drum contains the complete character set and corresponds to one print position on the line (see Figure 2–31). As the drum turns, all characters move past the print

Drum printer
A line-at-a-time printer that consists of a metal cylinder with rows of characters engraved across its surface.

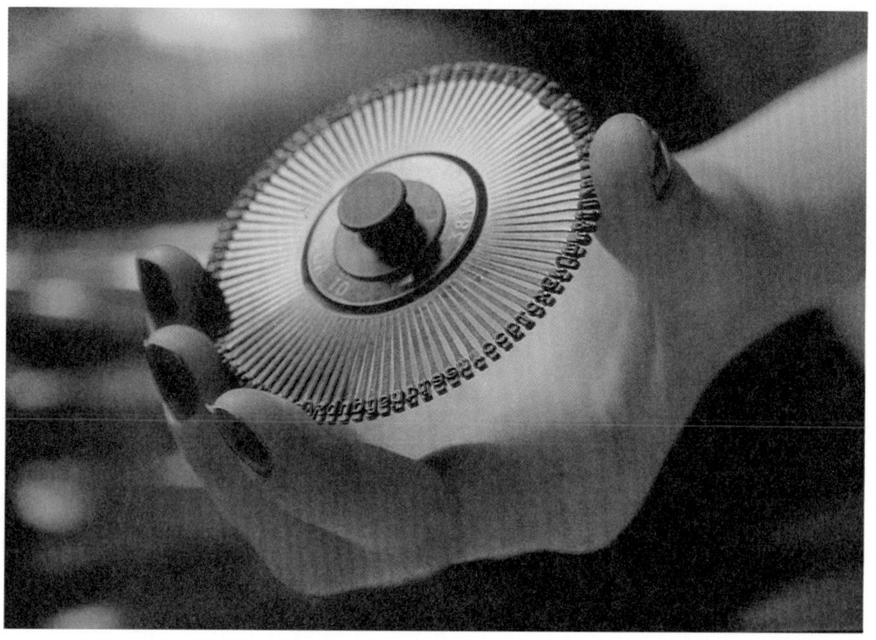

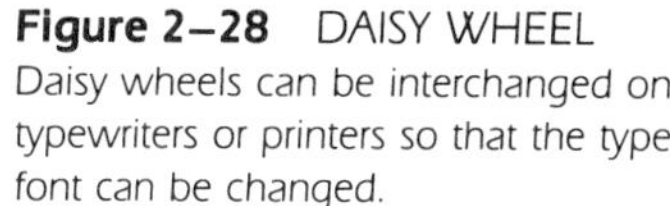

Figure 2–28 DAISY WHEEL
Daisy wheels can be interchanged on typewriters or printers so that the type font can be changed.

Figure 2–29 PRINT WHEEL
This is just one of the 80, 120, or 132 print wheels that are positioned in a print wheel printer. All the wheels rotate to the proper position before the hammers strike the elements, paper, and ribbon together.

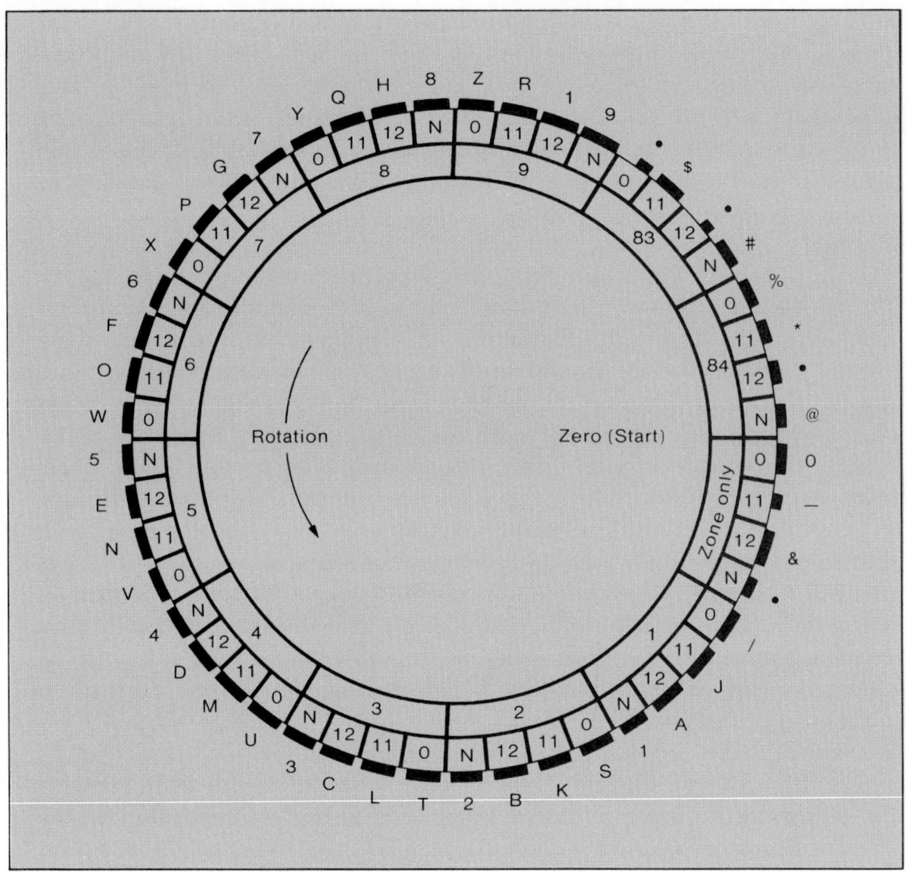

Figure 2–30 PRINT ELEMENT OF CHAIN PRINTER
In a chain printer, type rides on a track.

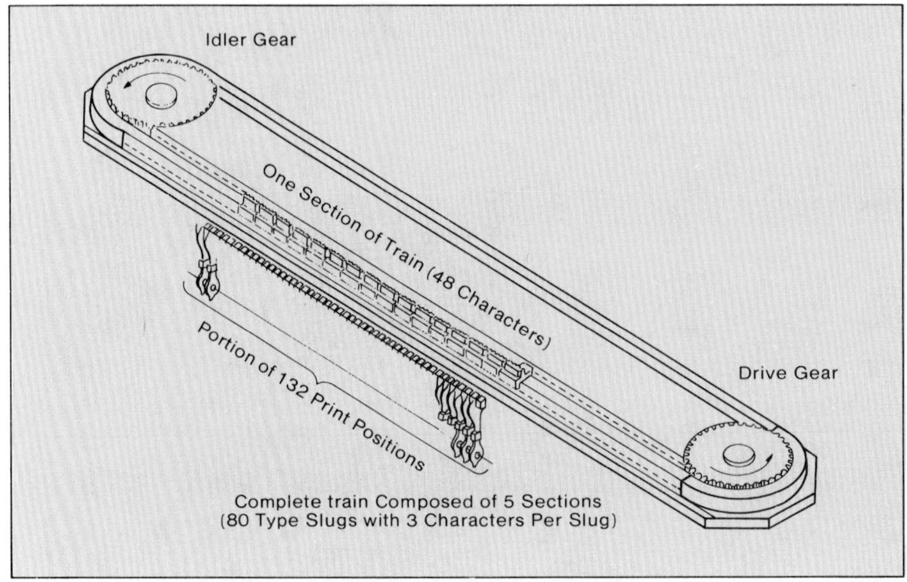

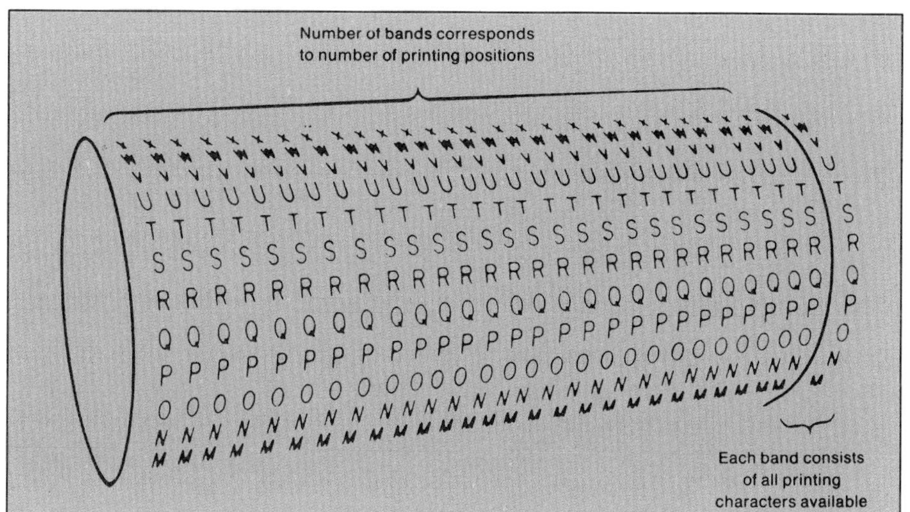
Number of bands corresponds
to number of printing positions
Each band consists
of all printing
characters available

Figure 2–31 PRINT DRUM
Print drums are used less frequently today as they are replaced by line printers with newer technologies.

position. A hammer presses the paper against an inked ribbon and the drum when the appropriate characters are in place. One line is printed for each revolution of the drum, since all characters reach the print position during each revolution. Some drum printers can print 2,000 lines a minute.

Nonimpact printers

- *Electrostatic Printers.* An **electrostatic printer** forms images of characters on special paper, using a dot matrix of electrically charged wires or pins. The paper is moved through a solution containing ink particles that have an electrical charge opposite that of the image. The ink particles stick to each charged image on the paper and form the characters.

Electrostatic printer
A nonimpact printer that forms an image of a character on special paper using a dot matrix of charged wires or pins.

- *Electrothermal Printers.* **Electrothermal printers** generate characters by using heat and heat-sensitive paper. Rods in a matrix are heated. As the ends of the selected rods touch the heat-sensitive paper, they create images. Both the electrothermal printer and the electrostatic printer are quiet in operation, and some can print up to 5,000 lines per minute.

Electrothermal printer
A nonimpact printer that uses heat in the print element to create characters on heat-sensitive paper.

- *Ink Jet Printers.* In an **ink jet printer,** a nozzle shoots a stream of charged ink toward the paper. Before reaching the paper, the ink passes through an electrical field that arranges the charged particles into characters at a rate of up to 200 characters a second.

Ink jet printer
A nonimpact printer that uses a stream of charged ink to form characters.

- *Laser Printers.* **Laser printers** combine laser beams and electrophotographic technology to create images (see Figure 2–32). A beam of light is focused through a rotating disk containing a full set of characters. The character image is projected onto a piece of film or photographic paper, and the print or negative is developed and "fixed" like an ordinary photograph. Since the output is high quality, the process is often used to print books. Laser printers produce up to 21,000 lines a minute.

Laser printer
A type of nonimpact printer that combines laser beams and electrophotographic technology to form images on paper.

- *Xerographic Printers.* **Xerographic printers** use printing methods like those used in common photocopying machines. For example, Xerox, the

Xerographic printer
A nonimpact printer that uses printing methods similar to those used in common xerographic copying machines.

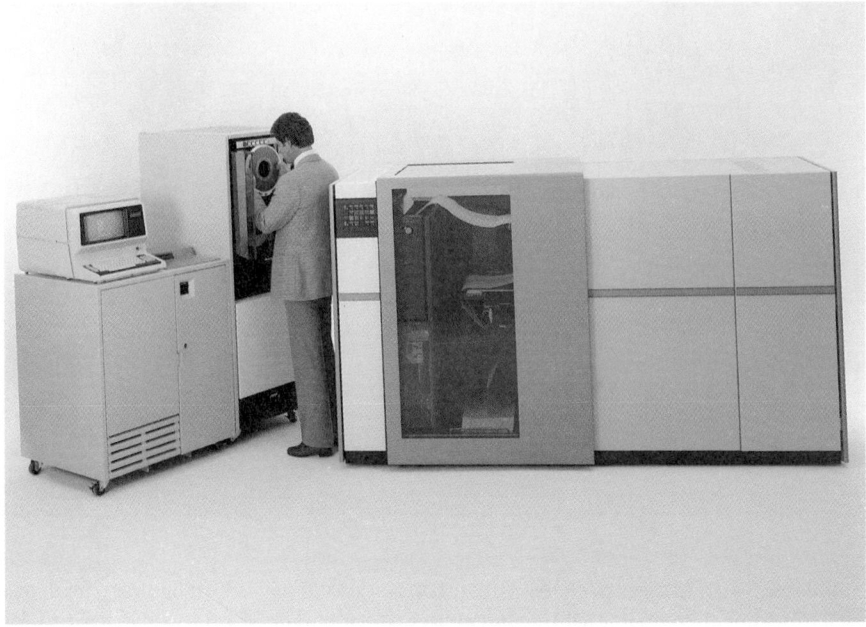

Figure 2–32 LASER PRINTER
This laser printer, made by Datagraphix, Inc., operates at speeds up to 21,000 lines per minute. Much smaller laser printers are now available for microcomputer users.

pioneer in this type of printing, has one model that prints on single, standard-size sheets of plain paper rather than on the continuous form paper normally used. This eliminates the need to separate the perforated pages from one another and allows for the use of better-quality paper. Xerographic printers can produce 4,000 lines a minute.

Printing systems now being introduced combine many features of the printing process into one machine, including stacking, routing, hole punching, blanking out of proprietary information, and perforating. Some printers produce both text and form designs on plain paper, eliminating the need for preprinted forms.

Plotter
A special printer used to print graphic images such as charts, graphs, and pictures.

Plotters

A **plotter** produces hard copies of graphic images: lines, curves, complex shapes, bar charts, graphs, organizational charts, engineering drawings, maps, trend lines, supply and demand curves, and other useful graphics. Figure 2–33 shows one type of plotter. Plotters are composed of pens, a movable carriage, sometimes a drum, and a holder for chart paper. The pens and/or paper can move up and down and back and forth, allowing for very detailed drawing. Some plotters can make drawings in up to eight different colors.

Figure 2–33 PLOTTER
This is a flatbed plotter. The paper lies flat under a bar that holds the pens. Some plotters are called drum plotters, because the paper rolls out on a cylinder while the graphic design is being plotted.

Computer Output Microfilm

Sometimes large amounts of information must be printed and stored for future reference. Printing the output on conventional-size paper would quickly create both a storage problem and an access problem. An alternative to conventional printing is offered by **computer output microfilm (COM).** Here, photographed images are produced in miniature by the computer. Sometimes the output is first recorded on magnetic tape and then transferred to thirty-five-millimeter microfilm rolls or to four-by-six-inch microfiche cards.

Computer output microfilm (COM)
Miniature photographic images of output produced on microfilm rather than on paper.

A COM system can store graphics as well as characters, and records at a rate of twenty-five to fifty times traditional printing speeds. It costs relatively little to produce additional microfilm copies.

Terminals

A terminal cannot be classified simply as an input or an output device, because it can be used for both functions. A **terminal** is a device through which data can leave or enter a computer. Remote terminals are located at a distance from the central computer which processes the data. In most cases, input and output are transmitted to and from the computer through communication channels such as telephone lines.

Terminal
A device through which data can leave or enter a computer.

Touch-Tone Terminals. **Touch-tone terminals** such as the one shown in Figure 2–34 are remote terminals used with ordinary telephone lines. Data is entered through special keyboards. There are several types of touch-tone devices. Some can read magnetic strips on plastic cards, such as credit cards. Others can be used with audio-response units that give the user a verbal response rather than a printed or displayed one. For example, if a bank teller enters a customer's account number to check the account status, the computer can verbally report over the telephone how much money is in that account.

Touch-tone terminal
A remote terminal that uses telephone lines to pass data from a special keyboard to the computer.

Figure 2–34 TOUCH-TONE TERMINAL This device, made by Anderson Jacobsen, combines voice and data communication.

Figure 2–35 POINT-OF-SALE TERMINAL WITH FIXED SCANNER A clerk checks out a customer by passing the merchandise over a scanner, which reads product information from a code printed on the product.

Point-of-Sale Terminals. **Point-of-sale (POS) terminals** are remote terminals that function as traditional cash registers and at the same time collect sales data. These devices have a keyboard for data entry, a panel to display the price, a cash drawer, and a printer that provides a cash receipt. POS terminals are commonly used in retail businesses. Figure 2–35 shows a typical supermarket terminal.

Visual Display Terminals. **Visual display terminals** display data instantly on cathode ray tubes (CRTs) or other types of screens (see Figure 2–36). Visual display terminals are faster than printers (they display up to 10,000 characters a second), and quieter. The soft copy is well suited to those who need information immediately but who do not need to keep a permanent record of it. Often, a user checks data as it appears on the screen during the data entry process.

Graphic Display Devices. **Graphic display devices** show output on a video screen (see Figure 2–37). Such devices are particularly useful to designers and engineers, because the screen can display graphs, charts, and drawings with complex curves and shapes. Some of these terminals, such as the one in Figure 2–38, are coupled with a **light pen,** which enables the user to modify the graphics on the screen by "drawing" with the pen's light-sensitive tip.

Figure 2–36 VISUAL DISPLAY TERMINAL Visual display terminals may provide amber, blue, green, or white characters on a black or grey background.

Point-of-sale (POS) terminal
A terminal that serves as a cash register but can also send sales and inventory data to a central computer.

Visual display terminal
A television-like screen used to display soft-copy output; sometimes called a CRT (cathode ray tube).

Graphic display device
A special visual display terminal used to display graphic images.

Light pen
A pen-shaped object with a photoelectric cell at its end; used to draw lines on a visual display screen.

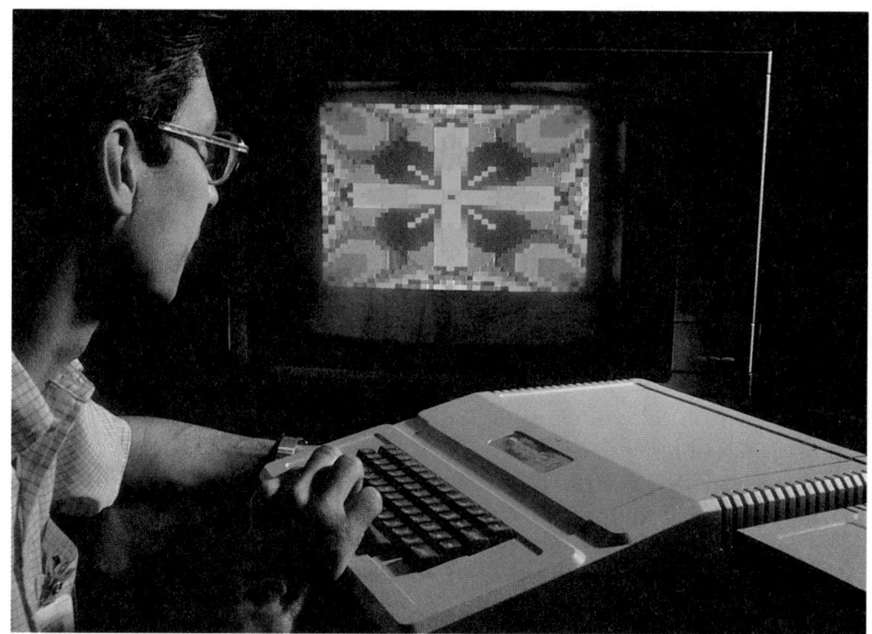

Figure 2–37 GRAPHIC DISPLAY DEVICE The clarity of graphics on a graphic display screen depends on the number of pixels (picture elements) that are addressed. The greater the number of pixels on a screen, the higher the resolution, or clarity, of the graphics. Resolution can be controlled by both the screen and the software.

Figure 2–38 GRAPHIC DISPLAY DEVICE WITH LIGHT PEN An engineer can use a light pen to produce a graphic design. The light pen can help change a small detail or enlarge a section.

Intelligent terminal
A terminal that can be programmed to perform functions such as editing of data, data conversion, and controlling of other terminals.

Intelligent Terminals. **Intelligent terminals** are remote terminals that can be programmed by stored instructions. Although they have the same type of components found in full-size computers, intelligent terminals have limited storage space and are sometimes limited in the instructions they can carry out. Most of these terminals have a visual display and/or a printer attached. They are useful for editing data before transmission to a central computer. The use of intelligent terminals will continue to grow as their cost continues to decrease.

SPECIAL INPUT/OUTPUT DEVICES

Graphics tablet
A flat, board-like surface that, when drawn on, transfers the image to a computer screen.

Spatial digitizer
An input device that can graphically reconstruct a three-dimensional object on the computer display screen.

Touch screen
A computer screen that can detect the point at which it is touched by the user; it allows the user to bypass the keyboard.

Mouse
A desk-top input device that controls cursor movement, allowing the user to bypass the keyboard.

Several special input/output devices are gaining popularity. These devices, which include graphics tablets, spatial digitizers, touch screens, and "mouse" systems, are used primarily with microcomputers.

Graphics tablets are flat, board-like surfaces directly connected to a computer CRT screen. The user draws on the tablet using a pencil-like device, and the resulting image appears on the screen with colors, textures, and patterns (see Figure 2–39).

Three-dimensional graphics can be created on the display screen by use of a **spatial digitizer.** With a spatial digitizer the user can enter the *X*, *Y*, and *Z* coordinates of any three-dimensional object by tracing the object with the digitizer's arm or pointer. The precise measurements are taken electronically, and the object is reconstructed graphically on the screen.

A **touch screen** looks like a normal computer screen, but it can detect a touch by the user and can identify the point at which the user actually touches the screen. The touch screen is especially useful when the user has a list of alternatives from which to choose. When the user touches the desired alternative, the computer registers the choice made and continues processing accordingly.

The **mouse** is a hand-movable input device that controls the position

Figure 2–39 GRAPHICS TABLET
A graphics tablet allows the user to bypass the keyboard and enter data from a flat pad.

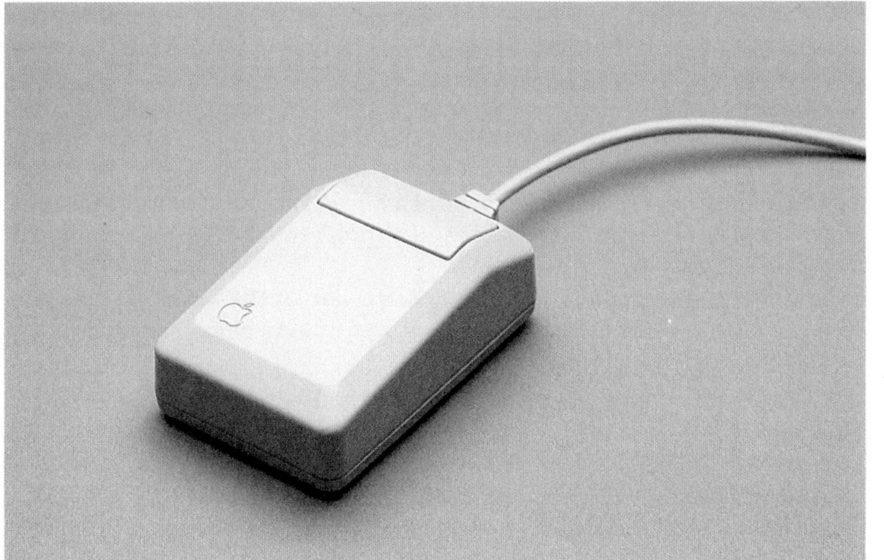

Figure 2–40 MOUSE
Some microcomputers allow a mouse to enter data. The mouse is similar to the tracker balls used in video games, except the roller is in the belly of the mouse. The user slides the mouse around on the desk, and a cursor on the screen moves according to the movements on the desk. A click of the button on the mouse commands the computer.

of the cursor on the screen (see Figure 2–40). (The **cursor** is the mark on the display screen that indicates the current location at which data will be entered.) The mouse is connected to the computer by an input cord. When the mouse is rolled on a flat surface, it sends electronic signals through the cord to the computer to move the cursor on the screen quickly and easily.

Cursor
A mark on the display screen that shows the current location for data entry.

All these special devices allow the user to bypass the keyboard. Thus, the computer system becomes more **user-friendly**—easier for the user to use and understand.

User-friendly
Describes software or hardware that is easy for people to use and understand.

LEARNING CHECK

1. If output appears on a CRT screen, rather than on a printed page, it is referred to as ________.
2. A printer does not have to be an impact printer to use the dot matrix method of forming letters. (True or false?)
3. All the following are nonimpact printers except the
   a. ink jet printer.
   b. laser printer.
   c. drum printer.
   d. xerographic printer.
4. Computer output microfilm (COM) solves the problem of ________.
5. The mouse allows the user to control the ________ without using the keyboard.

ANSWERS: 1. soft copy. 2. true. 3. c. 4. storage (or access). 5. cursor.

SUMMARY POINTS

- Primary storage units often use semiconductor memory, which consists of miniature circuitry on a silicon chip.
- Locations in the primary storage unit are used to store instructions and data, and are identified by their addresses.
- Read-only memory (ROM) is hard wired by the manufacturer to perform specific functions. Some types of ROM can be programmed by the user (PROM) and others can be erased and reprogrammed by use of special procedures (EPROM).
- Random-access memory (RAM) chips are one of the basic memory devices used by the CPU. The addition of more RAM chips can increase a computer's memory capacity.
- Registers are temporary holding areas for instructions and data. They are located in the CPU but are not considered part of the primary storage unit. Types of registers include accumulators, storage registers, instruction registers, general-purpose registers, and address registers.
- Secondary storage is located outside the CPU; it is used to supplement primary storage.
- Sequential-access storage devices must be read from and written to sequentially—that is, from the beginning and in order. Common sequential-access devices are magnetic tapes and tape cassettes.
- Direct-access storage devices allow the user to gain access to data at any point without reading from the beginning. Common direct-access storage devices are magnetic disks and floppy disks.
- A computer can process data in two ways. With batch processing, all data and instructions are entered into the computer at one time, and processing takes place without interruption. On-line processing allows the user to enter data during processing.
- Interactive programs ask the user questions as a part of execution. They are commonly used during on-line processing.
- Mass storage devices are used to store files that are very large, are infrequently used, or are backups (copies of files). Mass storage provides slower access to data than primary storage or magnetic disks but is relatively inexpensive. A common mass storage medium is cartridge tape.
- Machine language is based on electrical states, often represented by the binary system, and is the only language the computer understands.
- Because the computer understands only machine language, codes have been devised to represent data to the computer. The primary code is binary, which uses base 2.
- A bit is a digit position in a binary number.
- A parity bit is used for internal error-checking. A check digit is used to catch certain input errors.
- Punched cards contain data represented by holes made by a keypunch machine.
- Key-to-magnetic-media systems consist of typewriter-like keyboards that enter data magnetically onto magnetic tapes, magnetic disks, or floppy disks.
- Source-data automation allows data to be collected in computer-readable form at its source and as it occurs. Common devices are magnetic-ink

character recognition (MICR) devices, optical-mark recognition (OMR) devices, bar-code readers, optical-character recognition (OCR) devices, and voice recognition systems.

- Impact printers create their images by pressing print elements against the paper to create an impression. Common impact printers are printer-keyboards, dot matrix printers, daisy wheel printers, print wheel printers, chain printers, and drum printers.
- Nonimpact printers create their images in a variety of ways, but the print element never touches the paper. Common nonimpact printers are electrostatic printers, electrothermal printers, ink jet printers, laser printers, and xerographic printers.
- Plotters are special printers used to produce graphic images such as lines, curves, and complex shapes.
- Computer output microfilm (COM) is hard-copy output produced on microfilm rather than paper.
- A terminal is a device through which data can leave or enter a computer. There are touch-tone terminals, point-of-sale terminals, visual display terminals, graphic display devices, and intelligent terminals.
- Special input/output devices include graphics tablets, spatial digitizers, touch screens, and mouse systems.

REVIEW QUESTIONS

1. Explain how the CPU stores programs, input, data, and output.
2. Explain the differences among ROM, PROM, and EPROM.
3. What are registers used for? Name the different types of registers.
4. What is secondary storage and why is it used?
5. What is sequential access?
6. Name the only language a computer can understand and explain how it works.
7. What is a check digit used for?
8. What is source-data automation?
9. Explain the difference between impact and nonimpact printers.
10. Name five types of terminals.

Layer 1 Fill Ortho Snap Table

CHAPTER 3

SOFTWARE

Chapter Outline

INTRODUCTION

Without software, computers would be almost worthless. Software commands computers to perform the tasks people want them to perform. This chapter discusses the types of software, the programming process, and the programming languages that help people communicate with computers.

PROGRAMS AND OPERATING SYSTEMS

System program
Instructions written to coordinate the operation of computer circuitry and to help the computer run quickly and efficiently.

Application program
A sequence of instructions written to solve a specific problem.

Programs

There are two basic types of computer programs: system programs and application programs. **System programs** control the operations of the computer hardware and directly affect the way the computer works. They simplify the use of the hardware and help the computer run quickly and efficiently. System programs are written for specific computer models and cannot be used on different machines without being changed. These programs are usually provided by the computer manufacturer or by a specialized programming company.

Application programs solve particular problems for the computer user. They are written to perform specific jobs. These programs can be either written by the user or purchased from a special software company (see Figure 3–1). When the programs are written in an English-like language, they can usually be used on different machines with only minor changes.

Operating Systems

In the early days of computers, the basic computer operations were monitored by human operators. The operators entered the programs as needed and ran the input and output devices. Compared with the machines, the

Figure 3–1 A COMPUTER PROGRAMMER
A programmer works at a computer center in Hilheim, West Germany. The opportunities available to skilled programmers are truly international.

operators were very slow; so they caused delays in processing. To move closer to getting maximum efficiency from computers, operating systems were developed. An **operating system** is a collection of programs the computer uses to manage its own operations, eliminating the need for constant monitoring by human operators. Since these programs operate at computer speeds and control the system, they are classified as system programs.

Each program in the operating system performs certain tasks, with all the programs working together as a team to run the computer efficiently. The operating system programs are stored in an auxiliary storage area known as the **system residence device,** which stores only system programs. From there, the programs can be quickly loaded into primary storage as they are needed.

The operating system is made up of two types of programs: control programs and processing programs. **Control programs** monitor system operations and perform such tasks as input/output, scheduling, and communicating with the computer operator or programmer. The **supervisor program** (also known as the monitor or executive) is the major part of the operating system. It coordinates the activities of the system's other parts. When the computer is turned on, the supervisor is the first program to be transferred into primary storage from the system residence device. The electronic supervisor schedules input/output operations and allocates resources to various input/output devices. It also sends messages to the human computer operator to indicate the status of particular jobs, error conditions, and so on.

Processing progams, the second type of operating system program, are executed under the supervision of control programs and are used by the programmer to simplify program preparation. The principle processing programs include language translators, library programs, and utility programs.

A **language translator program** (compiler, assembler, or interpreter) translates programs written in English-like programming languages into machine language instructions of 0s and 1s. A **librarian program** maintains a list of programs in auxiliary storage and contains instructions for adding and deleting programs. **Utility programs** perform specialized functions, such as transferring data from tape to tape, tape to disk, card to tape, or tape to printer (see Figure 3–2).

Operating system
A collection of programs designed to permit a computer system to manage itself.

System residence device
An auxiliary storage device (disk, tape, or drum) in which operating system programs are stored and from which they are loaded into main storage.

Control program
A set of instructions, usually part of an operating system, that helps control the operations and management of a computer system.

Supervisor program
The major part of the operating system; it coordinates the activities of the system's other parts.

Processing program
A routine, usually part of the operating system, used to simplify program preparation and execution.

Language translator program
A program that translates programs written in English-like programming languages into machine language instructions of 0s and 1s.

Utility program
A subsystem of the operating system that can perform specialized, repeatedly used functions.

LOGIC DESIGN

Basic Logic Patterns

Writing instructions for computers is not as difficult as you may think. The major consideration is to follow certain rules so that the computer can execute the instructions you give it. Actually, all computer instructions are based on only four basic logic patterns: simple sequence, selection, loop, and branch (see Figure 3–3).

Simple sequence logic involves the computer's performing one instruction after another in order. If a computer is given three instructions that

Simple sequence
A program logic pattern in which one statement, or instruction, after another is executed in the sequence in which it is stored.

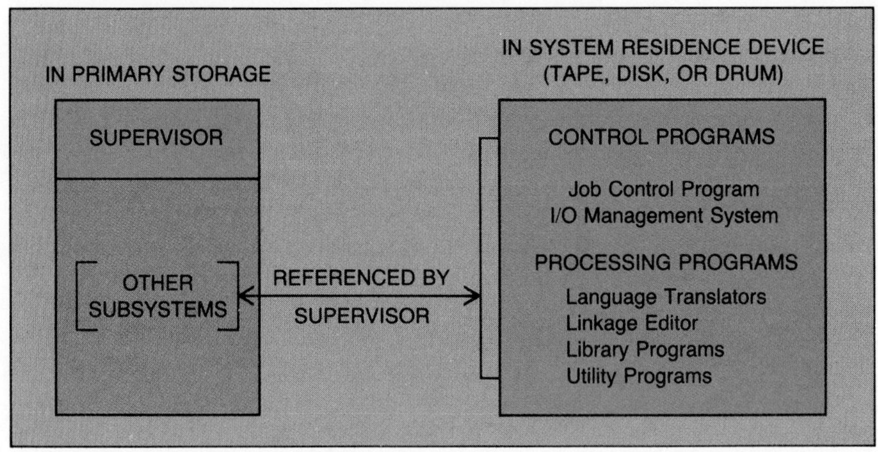

Figure 3–2 OPERATING SYSTEM
The supervisor program of the operating system is transferred to primary storage from the system residence device and remains there for the processing period. Other subsystems in the system residence device are called by the supervisor program when needed.

are numbered 1, 2, and 3, it will execute instruction 1 first, instruction 2 second, and instruction 3 third. This is the logic pattern most often used. In fact, the computer assumes that all instructions are to be done in this order unless it is told otherwise.

Selection
A program logic pattern in which the computer makes a choice between two paths.

With the **selection** pattern, the computer must choose between two or more items. Each choice is based on one of the three comparisons a computer can make: equal to, less than, or greater than. When complex selections must be made, several of these comparisons are made in a sequence.

For an example of the selection logic pattern, consider how a bank's computer processes a savings account withdrawal. First, the computer subtracts the amount of the withdrawal from the balance in the savings account. Then, it compares the resulting balance with zero. If the resulting balance is less than zero, the computer would not process the withdrawal or give you the money. If the resulting balance is greater than or equal to zero, the computer would process the withdrawal and give you the money. All selection logic patterns work basically in the same way. The computer compares two items and then selects a response based on the result of the comparison.

Loop
A program logic pattern in which the computer repeatedly executes a series of instructions as long as specified conditions are met.

The **loop** pattern causes an interruption in the normal sequence of processing and allows the computer to loop back to a set of previous instructions. The computer then carries out these instructions again according to the simple sequence pattern. This allows the computer to execute the same instruction any number of times. For example, if a certain set of instructions in a payroll program is to be carried out for each of 500 employees, the computer can loop through these instructions 500 times. Instructing the computer to loop allows the programmer to avoid writing out the instructions in simple sequence 500 times.

Branch
Program logic pattern that allows the computer to bypass (branch around) instructions and alter the normal flow of execution.

The **branch** pattern lets the computer skip over some instructions instead of executing them. Branching is used most effectively with selection or looping. This way, based on a certain comparison, the computer could branch ahead, loop back, or continue with the simple sequence.

The use of branching has several drawbacks. Jumping from one instruction to another uses more computer time than executing consecutive in-

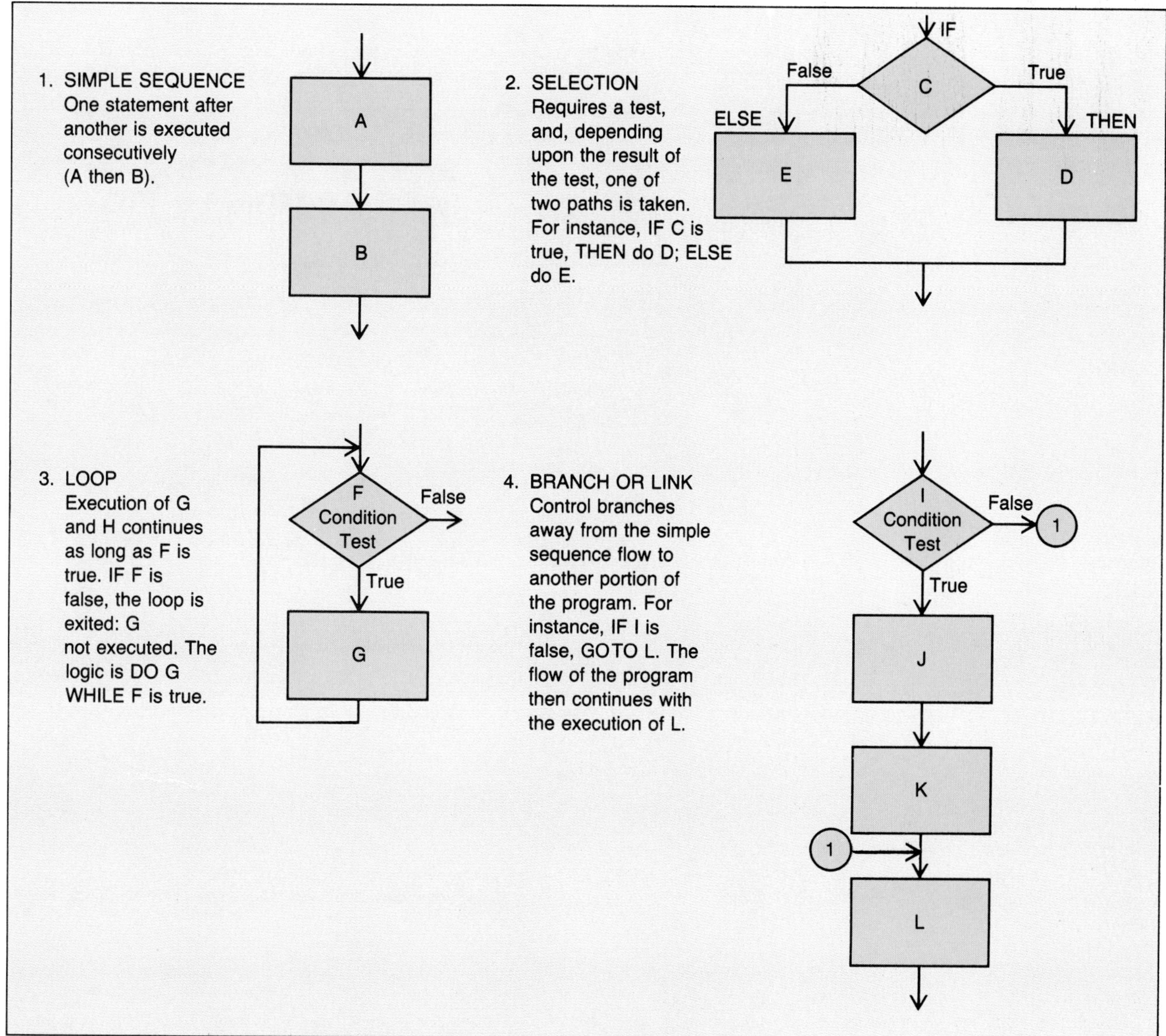

1. SIMPLE SEQUENCE
One statement after another is executed consecutively (A then B).
A
B
2. SELECTION
Requires a test, and, depending upon the result of the test, one of two paths is taken. For instance, IF C is true, THEN do D; ELSE do E.
IF
C
False
True
ELSE
THEN
E
D
3. LOOP
Execution of G and H continues as long as F is true. IF F is false, the loop is exited: G not executed. The logic is DO G WHILE F is true.
F
Condition
Test
False
True
G
4. BRANCH OR LINK
Control branches away from the simple sequence flow to another portion of the program. For instance, IF I is false, GOTO L. The flow of the program then continues with the execution of L.
I
Condition
Test
False
1
True
J
K
1
L

Figure 3–3 FOUR PROGRAM LOGIC PATTERNS Flowcharts demonstrate the logic patterns. Most programming languages use the first three patterns. BASIC commonly uses the GOTO statement, which is a form of branch.

structions. Also, because the normal order of instructions is not followed, it is difficult for other programmers to follow the flow of the instructions.

Flowcharts

The solution to a problem should be well thought out before a program is written. Even after the programmer has prepared a solution, the actual programming can still be difficult. Several programming tools have been designed to simplify the programming process. One of these is the **flowchart,** sometimes called a block diagram or a logic diagram. A flowchart

Flowchart
A graphic representation of the processing performed in a program.

Figure 3–4 FLOWCHART SYMBOLS Creating a flowchart can be easy when just a few of the flowchart symbols are used.

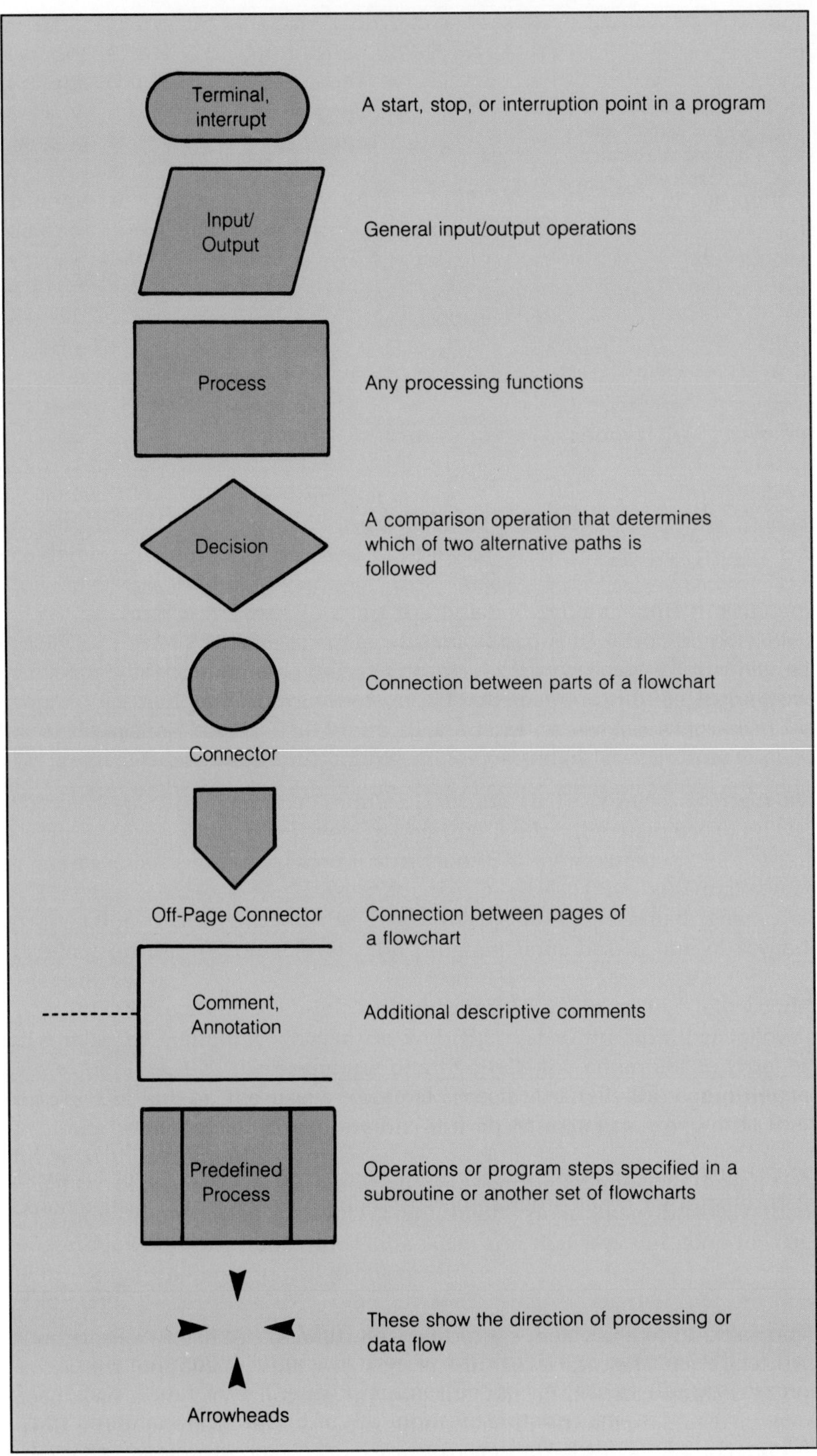

Terminal, interrupt
A start, stop, or interruption point in a program
Input/ Output
General input/output operations
Process
Any processing functions
Decision
A comparison operation that determines which of two alternative paths is followed
Connector
Connection between parts of a flowchart
Off-Page Connector
Connection between pages of a flowchart
Comment, Annotation
Additional descriptive comments
Predefined Process
Operations or program steps specified in a subroutine or another set of flowcharts
Arrowheads
These show the direction of processing or data flow

uses easily recognized symbols to represent the type of processing to be done in a program (see Figure 3–4). These symbols are arranged from top to bottom, using the four basic logic patterns, in the same logical sequence as the program statements (instructions) will appear.

The symbol represents a start, stop, or interruption in a program. The symbol shows a process step such as addition, subtraction, multiplication, or division. Most of the data manipulation performed in a program is represented by the process symbol. The symbol represents a comparison, or decision—a program statement that directs the computer to compare two or more values. In a decision step the computer can take either of two paths, one if the comparison is true, the other if it is false. Finally, the symbol shows that the program requires either input or output of data. The programmer arranges all these symbols in a sequence to design a flowchart. Figure 3–5 shows a grocery bill calculation

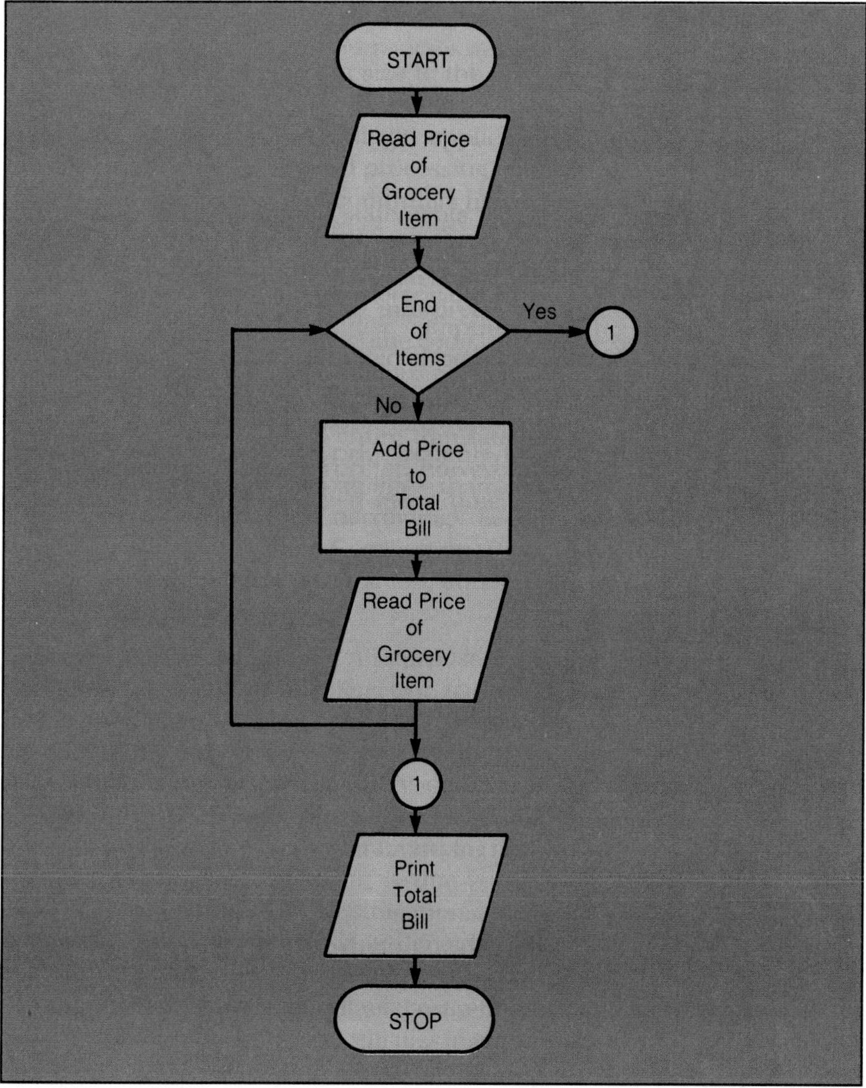

Figure 3–5 EXAMPLE OF A FLOWCHART Can you think of the kind of question that prompted the building of this flowchart?

in flowchart form. The symbols are arranged from top to bottom and from left to right. Lines connect the symbols and arrows indicate the flow of logic from statement to statement. Finally, the instructions written in the symbols give a general description of each step needed to solve the problem.

Pseudocode

Pseudocode
A brief set of instructions written in sentence form, in the same sequence as the program statements.

Another programming tool is **pseudocode,** a brief set of instructions written in sentence form. The sentences are arranged in the order in which the program statements will eventually appear. By using pseudocode, the programmer can focus on the steps required to solve a problem, rather than on how to use the computer language. When the pseudocode is completed it can be easily translated into computer language. Each pseudocode statement should translate into one program statement.

Figure 3–6 shows a pseudocode for the grocery bill flowchart in Figure 3–5. The pseudocode statements express the basic logic patterns and match the flowchart statements.

Structured Programming

Structured programming
A top-down modular approach to programming that emphasizes dividing a program into logical sections.

Using flowcharts and pseudocode makes it easier for a programmer such as the one in Figure 3–7 to write structured programs. **Structured programming** divides a program into logical sections in order to reduce testing time, increase programmers' productivity, and make the program clear and easy to follow.

Structured programming encourages well-thought-out program logic. It uses three of the four available logic patterns: simple sequence, selection, and loop. Branching should be used only under special conditions.

Proper program
A program using the structured programming approach, with only one entrance and one exit.

A basic concept of structured programming is the construction of programs in modules, with each module an independent segment that performs only one function. The modules should be small to make programming and detecting and correcting errors easier. Each module should have only one entry point and one exit point. This allows a programmer to easily follow the flow of instructions, which progresses from top to bottom. When the modular approach is used, the one-entry/one-exit guideline is easier to incorporate into the program. A program that has only one entrance and one exit is called a **proper program.**

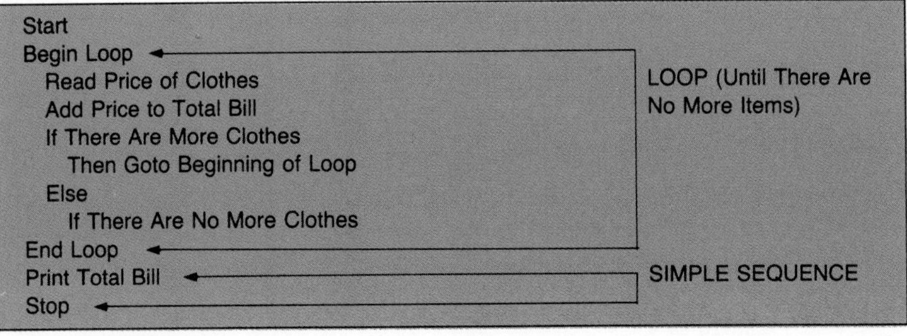

Start
Begin Loop
Read Price of Clothes
Add Price to Total Bill
If There Are More Clothes
Then Goto Beginning of Loop
Else
If There Are No More Clothes
End Loop
Print Total Bill
Stop
LOOP (Until There Are No More Items)
SIMPLE SEQUENCE

Figure 3–6 EXAMPLE OF PSEUDOCODE A pseudocode is something like a list of things to do. The list is in a logical order of occurrence and identifies the tasks in short phrases.

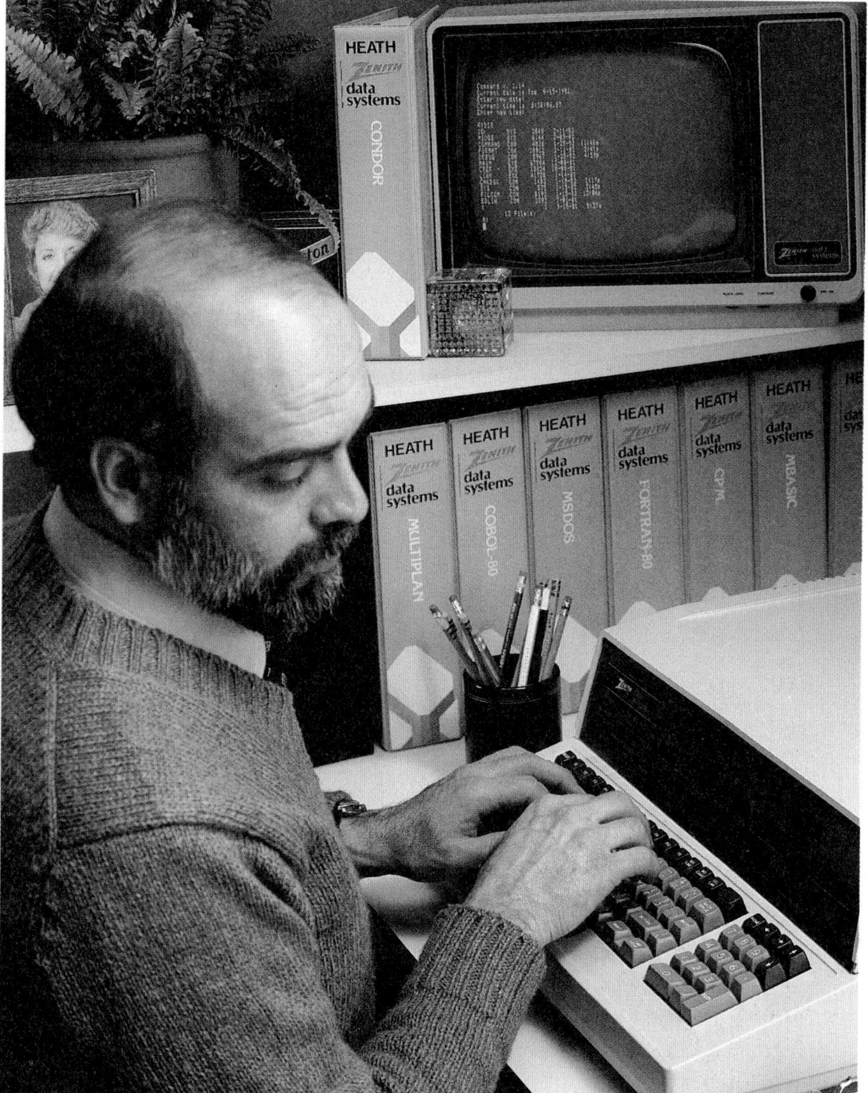

Figure 3–7 SOLVING PROBLEMS
This computer user may use flowcharts, pseudocode, or even structured programming techniques to help solve problems.

THE PROGRAMMING PROCESS

Solving problems by using the computer and a set of step-by-step instructions is referred to as programming. People often associate programming with coding. **Coding** is expressing the problem solution in a particular programming language, but it is only one part of programming.

In order to arrive at the instructions needed to solve a problem, the programmer must follow four steps, known as the programming process. These steps are:

1. Defining the problem.
2. Designing a solution.
3. Coding the program.
4. Compiling, testing, and debugging the program.

Coding
The process of expressing a problem solution in a programming language.

LEARNING CHECK

1. The kinds of programs used to solve particular problems for the computer user are called ________ programs.
2. An operating system is

   a. a collection of programs that help the computer manage its own operations.

   b. a collection of programs that are useful for particular tasks such as preparing payrolls.

   c. the same as a supervisor program.

   d. a system residence device.
3. The two categories of operating system programs are ________ programs and ________ programs.
4. The branch pattern of logic can be used effectively with the loop pattern of logic. (True or false?)
5. What are two ways to design a solution before actually beginning to program in a specific programming language?
6. One characteristic of ________ programming is the use of modules.

ANSWERS:
1. application. 2. a. 3. control, processing. 4. true. 5. using flowcharts and pseudocodes. 6. structured.

Defining the Problem

The first part of problem solving with the computer is built on the answers to a number of questions. Who needs information? What information is needed? What data is needed to yield the information, and where can it be found? Will the data have to be accumulated in a certain order? In what form must the data be entered into the computer once it has been gathered? In what form will the output be most useful to the intended users?

Designing a Solution

Once the problem has been analyzed, the programmer can begin designing the computer-assisted solution. Since even the most advanced computer is rigidly limited in the logical patterns it can apply to a problem, the design will require considerable creativity from the programmer.

By using flowcharts and pseudocodes, the programmer can, at this point, concentrate on how to solve the problem in a creative way rather than on how to write the program in a computer language. These tools make it simpler to convert the program instructions into a computer language. Not only do flowcharts and pseudocodes boost programmers' creativity, but they also allow programmers to make more efficient use of their time.

Coding the Program

Coding is translating the problem solution into a programming language. The language used will depend on what the program is expected to do and what facilities are available to the programmer. We will not discuss the actual coding of a program, because that would require referring to a particular programming language. However, there are general rules that should be followed to ensure that the program is well written.

Getting the right answer or response is one requirement of a well-written program, but not the only one. The right answer may be obtained in various ways. But one program can be better than another. The programmer should strive for these qualities in a program:

- Ease of reading and understanding. The program should be written so that another programmer will quickly be able to see what is happening.
- Reliability. The program should consistently produce the right output.
- Workability under all conditions. Even when internal logic is correct, incorrect or inappropriate data may cause the output to be incorrect or inappropriate. Programs should include some tests that make acceptance of incorrect or inappropriate data less likely.
- Ease of modification and updating. The use of structured programming makes modification and updating easier, because a change in one module does not require a change in others.
- Portability—that is, ability to be used on other computers without modification.

Compiling, Debugging, and Testing the Program

Before the coded program can be executed, it must be translated into machine language. This is done by a language translator program (more on compilers and interpreters later). Once the program has been translated, the first thing the programmer will probably notice is some error messages. This does not mean that the programmer has poor coding skills. Rather, it exemplifies Murphy's first law of programming: A program seldom works the first time. It must be debugged.

The term **debugging** came into use in the summer of 1945, when scientists were working on one of the earliest computers, the Mark II. The computer had stopped for no apparent reason, and the programmers were trying to figure out what was wrong with it. They finally discovered that a moth was caught in one of the relays. They removed the bug and the computer worked fine. Since then, computer scientists have used the term debugging to refer to removing any type of error or malfunction from a computer's hardware or software.

Debugging
Removing any type of error or malfunction from a computer's hardware or software.

Testing is the final step in writing a good program. It begins once everything else has been finished and the program appears to be working fine. When the programmer tests the program, an attempt should be made to test every possibility. The programmer should test each possible input, including incorrect input, to see how the program reacts. Testing will never prove that the program will work in all situations for all input, but it will decrease the chances that it won't.

LEVELS OF LANGUAGES

Computers will do what they are told, but they must be told what to do in special programming languages. As computers have evolved in sophistication, so have the programming languages they use. There are three levels of language: machine language, assembly language, and high-level language. Each level has special characteristics.

Machine Language

Machine language, you may remember, is the code that designates the on/off electrical states in a computer. Old as the computer itself, this language is expressed as combinations of 0s and 1s. This is the only language the computer can recognize and respond to. Each type of computer has its own machine language, which is not transferrable to another type of computer. Each instruction in machine language must state not just the operation required, but also the storage locations of the data items. Since these requirements—plus the nature of the language itself—make machine-language programming very complex, tedious, and time consuming, other languages have been developed.

Assembly Language

Assembly language
A symbolic programming language that uses convenient abbreviations (mnemonics) rather than groupings of 0s and 1s.

Assembly language is a little easier to use and understand than machine language. With it, programmers must still specify both operations and storage locations. But the 0 and 1 groupings of machine language used to specify machine operations are replaced by convenient symbols and abbreviations. For example, STO may stand for store and TRA for transfer. Nonetheless, programming in assembly language remains a complex task.

High-Level Languages

High-level language
English-like language coding scheme that is procedure-, problem-, and user-oriented.

High-level languages provide an easy way to program computers. Such languages are designed so that a programmer's attention can focus on the problem itself, rather than on the details of computer operations. Many high-level languages are English-like and use common mathematical terms and symbols. These features reduce the time and effort needed to write a program and make programs easier to correct or modify.

High-level languages least resemble the 0 and 1 combinations of machine language. Figure 3–8 shows the difference between a simple statement in BASIC, a high-level language, and its equivalent in machine language. Although one assembly language statement is generally equivalent to one machine language statement, a single high-level language statement can represent many machine language statements. Because of this, it may take five or six machine-level instructions to carry out one BASIC statement.

```
(a) HIGH-LEVEL LANGUAGE (APPLE-SOFT BASIC)
100  C = A + B
(b) MACHINE LANGUAGE (MOS-TECH 6502 MACHINE LANGUAGE)
1010  0000  0000  0000  0000  1101
1010  1101  0000  1110  0000  1101
0111  1001  0110  0000  0000  1100
1101  1000
1000  1101  0011  1111  0000  1100
```

Figure 3–8 ONE BASIC STATEMENT AND CORRESPONDING MACHINE LANGUAGE INSTRUCTIONS These program segments demonstrate that one BASIC statement is sufficient for an instruction, while several machine language lines are necessary.

Language Translation

Assembly and high-level languages cannot be executed directly by computers. The set of instructions written by the programmer, the **source program,** must be converted into machine-executable form by a language translator program. The resulting translation, known as the **object program,** is the same as a program originally written in machine language.

The translator program for assembly language is called an **assembler program,** and a high-level language translator is called either an **interpreter** or a **compiler** program. Translator programs are designed for specific machines and languages. A compiler that translates a program written in FORTRAN into a machine language program, for example, cannot translate COBOL statements. Figure 3–9 illustrates the different levels of language.

During the translation process, the object program is generated, and the programmer receives a notice if any errors are detected. Such errors are usually violations of the rules of a particular programming language. These are called **syntax errors.** For example, an error warning will be generated if language keywords such as WRITE or COMPUTE are misspelled. The error-message listing may give the number of each statement in error and may also describe the nature of the errors (see Figure 3–10). The object program is ready for execution only after all errors have been corrected. Several attempts at error correction may be needed.

Source program
A sequence of instructions written by the programmer in either assembly language or a high-level language.

Object program
A sequence of machine-executable instructions converted from source-program statements by a language translator program.

Assembler program
A language translator program used to convert assembly language into machine language.

Compiler
A language translator program used for high-level languages such as FORTRAN or COBOL; translates source-program statements into machine-executable code.

Syntax error
Error that violates the rules of a programming language.

PROGRAMMING LANGUAGES

A programming language may be placed into one of three categories, depending on its purpose. **Machine-oriented languages** permit the most efficient use of the computer; the instructions are already in machine-readable form, so no computer time is wasted translating them. **Procedure-oriented languages** concentrate on the various processing steps in a particular application and are designed to make it easier for the programmer to direct the computer to perform these steps. **Problem-oriented languages** are designed to solve processing requirements with minimal programming effort. They allow the user to focus on the desired results rather than on the individual steps needed to get the results.

Procedure-oriented language
A programming language designed to solve processing requirements with a minimal amount of programming effort.

Problem-oriented language
A programming language designed to solve specific kinds of problems, allowing the user to focus on desired results.

Machine-Oriented Languages

Machine Language. As you know, machine language is the only language the computer can recognize and respond to. A programmer using machine

Figure 3–9 LANGUAGE LEVELS Assembly language and high-level languages must be translated into machine language before the computer can understand the instructions or data.

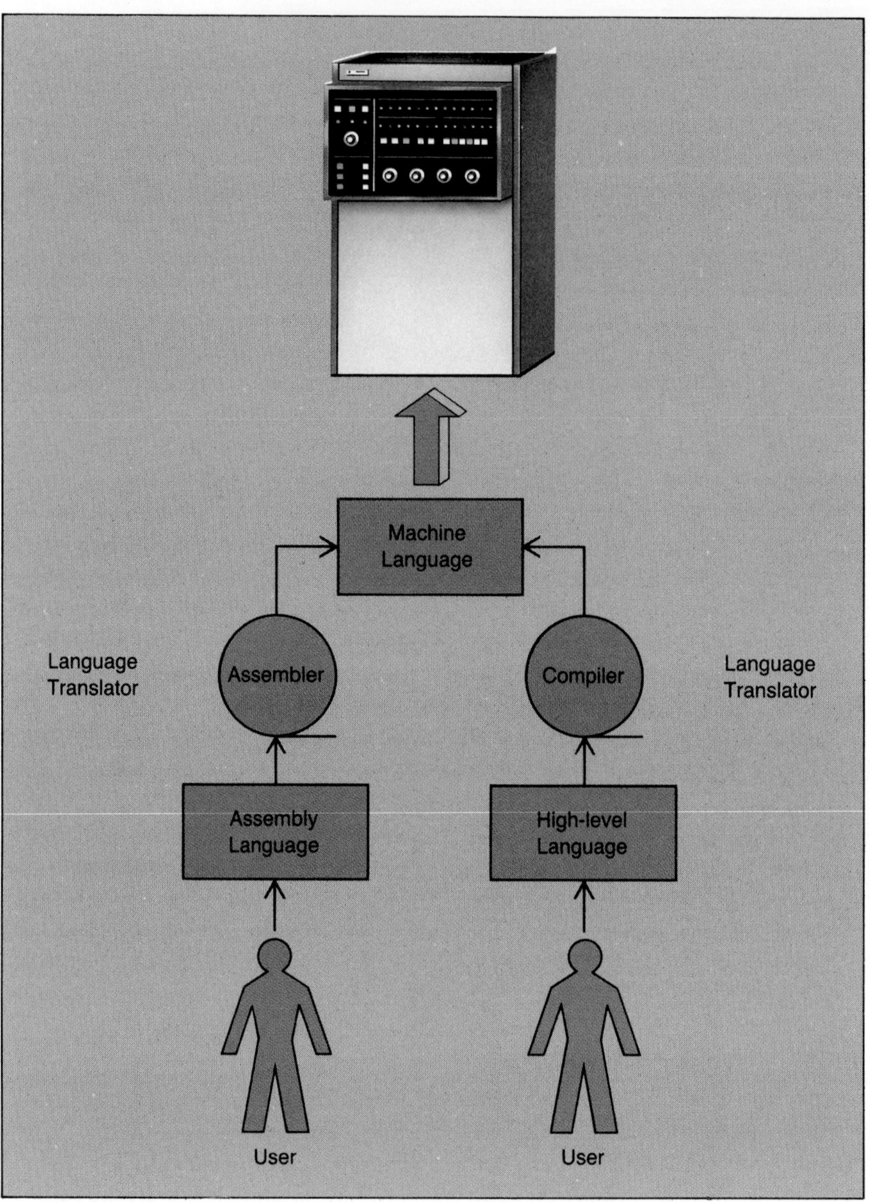

Figure 3–10 COMPILER-DETECTED ERRORS When the user receives coded messages to identify the type of error that was made, he or she may not have to search as deeply for programming problems.

Statement Number	Error Message
2061	Invalid or no program heading
2399	Identifier already declared
2480	Identifier not declared
2491	Illegal symbol
2601	Type conflict of operands
2621	Minus sign not preceded by a space. Assume space.

language must specify absolutely everything to the computer—which means that the programmer must know exactly how the computer works. Actual numerical addresses of storage locations must be specified for instructions and data, requiring the programmer to have knowledge of every switch and register (the temporary storage areas for holding data and instructions).

Assembly Language. To lessen the disadvantages of working with machine language, programmers developed assembly languages. In these, the programmer uses symbolic names—or **mnemonics**—to specify machine operations. Mnemonics are English-like abbreviations for the machine language instructions. Table 3–1 shows some common arithmetic operations coded in an assembly language and in the binary code of machine language.

Mnemonics
Symbolic names (memory aids) used to represent machine operation in symbolic languages such as assembly language and high-level programming languages.

The mnemonic codes for assembly language instructions differ depending on the type and model of computer. Thus, assembly language programs, like machine language programs, can be written only by persons who know the internal operation of the specific computer. Figure 3–11 shows a program to calculate student grades in assembly language.

Procedure-Oriented Languages

FORTRAN. **FORTRAN** (FORmula TRANslator) is the oldest high-level programming language. It was introduced in the mid-1950s when most programs were written in either assembly or machine language. The goal was to develop a programming language that resembled English but that could be translated into machine language by the computer.

FORTRAN
FORmula TRANslator; a programming language used primarily in performing mathematical or scientific operations.

When FORTRAN was first released, the computer was used mainly by engineers, scientists, and mathematicians. Naturally, FORTRAN was designed to meet their needs, a purpose that has remained unchanged.

Early FORTRAN compilers contained many errors and inefficiencies. To compound the difficulties, several manufacturers offered variations of FORTRAN that could be used only with their own brands of computers. For these reasons, the American National Standards Institute (ANSI) decided to develop a standardized FORTRAN. In 1966, two versions were standardized: ANSI FORTRAN and Basic FORTRAN. A more recent version, FORTRAN 77, which supports structured programming, has made the language

OPERATION	ASSEMBLY-LANGUAGE MNEMONIC CODE	TYPICAL BINARY CODE
Add memory to register	A	01011010
Store accumulator in memory	STA	01001001
Compare memory locations	CLC	11010101
Branch on carry clear	BCC	00110010
Load from memory into register	L	01011000
Multiply register by memory	M	01011100
Compare register to memory	CPY	10010111
Subtract memory from accumulator	SBC	10110011

Table 3–1 ASSEMBLY LANGUAGE MNEMONIC CODES
These examples compare assembly language mnemonic (or symbolic) codes with binary coding. Learning the symbols is less confusing than keeping track of hundreds of 1s and 0s.

Figure 3–11 STUDENT GRADES PROGRAM IN ASSEMBLY LANGUAGE The actual assembly language consists of mnemonics. The rest of the program is for the benefit of the user.

```
* THIS PROGRAM CALCULATES THE AVERAGE OF THREE TEST SCORES FOR FIVE
* STUDENTS AND ASSIGNS A LETTER GRADE
         BALR  12,0           SET UP BASE REGISTER
         USING *,12
         LA    3,5            LOAD REGISTER 3 WITH A 5
         XPRNT HEADER,27      PRINT HEADING
         XPRNT PRTOUT-1,31    PRINT BLANK LINE
LOOP     XREAD NAME,30        READ IN DATA CARD
         XDECI 4,TEST1        CONVERT TEST1 TO BINARY AND PUT IN REG 4
         XDECI 5,TEST2        CONVERT TEST2 TO BINARY AND PUT IN REG 5
         XDECI 6,TEST3        CONVERT TEST3 TO BINARY AND PUT IN REG 6
         AR    5,4            ADD CONTENTS OF REG 4 TO REG 5
         AR    5,6            ADD CONTENTS OF REG 6 TO REG 5
         SR    4,4            ZERO OUT REG 4
         L     6,=F'3'        LOAD REG 6 WITH CONSTANT 3
         DR    4,6            DIVIDE CONTENTS OF REG 4 BY REG 6
         MVC   PRTOUT(15),NAME  MOVE NAME TO PRINT AREA
         C     5,=F'90'       COMPARE AVERAGE IN REG 5 TO 90
         BM    B              IF MINUS (AVERAGE < 90) BRANCH TO B
         MVI   PRTOUT+23,C'A'  MOVE LETTER GRADE A TO PRINT AREA
         B     PRINT          BRANCH TO PRINT
B        C     5,=F'80'       COMPARE AVERAGE TO 80
         BM    C              IF AVERAGE < 80 BRANCH TO C
         MVI   PRTOUT+23,C'B'   MOVE LETTER GRADE B TO PRINT AREA
         B     PRINT          BRANCH TO PRINT
C        C     5,=F'70'       COMPARE AVERAGE TO 70
         BM    D              IF AVERAGE < 70 BRANCH TO D
         MVI   PRTOUT+23,C'C'  MOVE LETTER GRADE C TO PRINT AREA
         B     PRINT          BRANCH TO PRINT
D        C     5,=F'60'       COMPARE AVERAGE TO 60
         BM    F              IF AVERAGE < 60 BRANCH TO F
         MVI   PRTOUT+23,C'D'  MOVE LETTER GRADE D TO PRINT AREA
         B     PRINT          BRANCH TO PRINT
F        MVI   PRTOUT+23,C'F'  MOVE LETTER GRADE F TO PRINT AREA
PRINT    XPRNT PRTOUT-1,31    PRINT NAME AND GRADE
         BCT   3,LOOP         BRANCH BACK TO READ AGAIN
         BR    14             STOP
* DECLARE VARIABLES
HEADER   DC    C'1 STUDENT NAME        GRADE'
NAME     DS    CL15
TEST1    DS    CL5
TEST2    DS    CL5
TEST3    DS    CL5
         DC    C' '
PRTOUT   DC    CL30' '
         END
               =F'3'
               =F'90'
               =F'80'
               =F'70'
               =F'60'


 STUDENT NAME       GRADE

JOANN WEISS           A
TOM FARR              D
ANN BLASS             B
BOB WILLS             F
JANIS MAYS            C
```

more useful. Figure 3–12 shows the program to calculate student grades written in FORTRAN.

COBOL. **COBOL** (COmmon Business-Oriented Language) is a frequently used business programming language. The first commercial versions of COBOL appeared in 1960. One of the objectives in designing COBOL was to establish a language that was machine-independent, one that could easily be used on any computer. In 1968, ANSI published guidelines for a standardized version of COBOL that became known as ANSI COBOL. Since COBOL is standardized, companies can purchase new computer equipment with little or no rewriting of existing COBOL programs.

COBOL's disadvantages are it tends to be wordy and its computational capabilities are limited. This makes it unsuitable for scientific applications. Figure 3–13 shows the student grade program written in COBOL.

COBOL
COmmon Business-Oriented Language; a business programming language.

PL/1
Programming Language 1; a general-purpose programming language used in both business and scientific applications.

PL/1. **PL/1** (Programming Language 1) was developed as a procedure-oriented language suited for both scientific and business applications. With increased use of management science techniques—such as linear programming and regression analysis—business programmers discovered the

Figure 3–12 STUDENT GRADES PROGRAM IN FORTRAN FORTRAN is a procedure-oriented language that has extraordinary mathematical capabilities. It is most useful in situations where complex arithmetic calculations are needed.

```
C THIS PROGRAM CALCULATES THE AVERAGE OF THREE TEST SCORES FOR FIVE
C STUDENTS AND ASSIGNS A LETTER GRADE
      INTEGER TEST1, TEST2, TEST3, I
      REAL  AVG
      CHARACTER  NAME*15, GRADE
      WRITE (6,100)
 100  FORMAT ('1',1X,'STUDENT NAME',7X,'GRADE')
      WRITE (6,200)
 200  FORMAT (' ')
      DO 500 I = 1, 5
      READ (5,300) NAME, TEST1, TEST2, TEST3
 300  FORMAT (A15,3I3)
      AVG = (TEST1 + TEST2 + TEST3) / 3.0
      IF (AVG .GE. 90) GRADE = 'A'
      IF ((AVG .GE. 80) .AND. (AVG .LT. 90)) GRADE = 'B'
      IF ((AVG .GE. 70) .AND. (AVG .LT. 80)) GRADE = 'C'
      IF ((AVG .GE. 60) .AND. (AVG .LT. 70)) GRADE = 'D'
      IF (AVG .LT. 60) GRADE = 'F'
      WRITE (6,400) NAME, GRADE
 400  FORMAT (1X,A15,7X,A1)
 500  CONTINUE
      STOP
      END


 STUDENT NAME        GRADE

JOANN WEISS            A
TOM FARR               D
ANN BLASS              B
BOB WILLS              F
JANIS MAYS             C
```

Figure 3–13 STUDENT GRADES PROGRAM IN COBOL
Designers of COBOL wanted to make the language resemble English so that a program written in COBOL would be easy to understand. Today, well-written COBOL programs tend to be self-explanatory.

```
IDENTIFICATION DIVISION.
PROGRAM-ID. GRADES.

ENVIRONMENT DIVISION.
CONFIGURATION SECTION.
SOURCE-COMPUTER.   IBM-370.
OBJECT-COMPUTER.   IBM-370.
INPUT-OUTPUT SECTION.
FILE-CONTROL.
    SELECT CARD-FILE ASSIGN TO UR-S-SYSIN.
    SELECT PRINT-FILE ASSIGN TO UR-S-OUTPUT.

DATA DIVISION.
FILE SECTION.
FD  CARD-FILE
    LABEL RECORDS ARE OMITTED
    RECORD CONTAINS 80 CHARACTERS
    DATA RECORD IS GRADE-CARD.
01  GRADE-CARD.
    02  STUDENT-NAME  PIC A(15).
    02  TESTONE       PIC 999.
    02  TESTTWO       PIC 999.
    02  TESTTHREE     PIC 999.
    02  FILLER        PIC X(56).
FD  PRINT-FILE
    LABEL RECORDS ARE OMITTED
    RECORD CONTAINS 132 CHARACTERS
    DATA RECORD IS PRINT-REC.
01  PRINT-REC.
    02  OUT-LINE      PIC X(132).
WORKING-STORAGE SECTION.
77  TEST-TOTAL        PIC 999.
77  AVERAGE           PIC 999V99.
77  HEADING1          PIC X(32) VALUE
                      ' STUDENT NAME       LETTER GRADE'.
77  BLANK-LINE        PIC X(132) VALUE SPACES.
01  LINE-FORM.
    02  NAME          PIC A(15).
    02  FILLER        PIC X(11).
    02  LETTER        PIC X.
```

need for a language with greater computational capabilities than COBOL. Similarly, scientific programmers needed a language with greater file-handling ability than FORTRAN. PL/1 combines COBOL and FORTRAN features.

PL/1 is a powerful language because it is flexible, supporting many options and applications. All the languages discussed previously require strict coding rules. PL/1, in contrast, is a free-form language with very few coding restrictions. It can be used by both beginning and expert programmers, and it easily supports structured programming.

Because PL/1 is such a powerful language, its compiler requires a large amount of storage, which prevents it from being used in smaller computers. However, as minicomputers and microcomputers become more powerful, subsets of PL/1 may become workable. Figure 3–14 shows the student grades program written in PL/C, which is a subset of PL/1.

```
PROCEDURE DIVISION.
BEGIN.
    DISPLAY HEADING1.
    DISPLAY BLANK-LINE.
    OPEN INPUT CARD-FILE,
         OUTPUT PRINT-FILE.
    PERFORM WORK-LOOP 5 TIMES.
    PERFORM FINISH.
WORK-LOOP.
    READ CARD-FILE
      AT END PERFORM FINISH.
    ADD TESTONE, TESTTWO, TESTTHREE GIVING TEST-TOTAL.
    DIVIDE TEST-TOTAL BY 3 GIVING AVERAGE.
    IF (AVERAGE IS GREATER THAN 90 OR EQUAL TO 90) THEN
      MOVE 'A' TO LETTER
    ELSE IF (AVERAGE IS GREATER THAN 80 OR EQUAL TO 80) THEN
      MOVE 'B' TO LETTER
    ELSE IF (AVERAGE IS GREATER THAN 70 OR EQUAL TO 70) THEN
      MOVE 'C' TO LETTER
    ELSE IF (AVERAGE IS GREATER THAN 60 OR EQUAL TO 60) THEN
      MOVE 'D' TO LETTER
    ELSE MOVE 'F' TO LETTER.
    MOVE STUDENT-NAME TO NAME.
    WRITE PRINT-REC FROM LINE-FORM AFTER ADVANCING 1 LINES.
FINISH.
    CLOSE CARD-FILE,
          PRINT-FILE.
    STOP RUN.




 STUDENT NAME          GRADE

JOANN WEISS              A
TOM FARR                 D
ANN BLASS                B
BOB WILLS                F
JANIS MAYS               C
```

Figure 3–13 (Continued)

Problem-Oriented Languages

RPG. **RPG** (Report Program Generator) is a problem-oriented language that was designed to produce business reports. Essentially, a programmer using RPG must describe the kind of report desired but need not specify much of the logic involved. Acting on the description, a generator program can build a program to produce the report. Little programming skill is needed.

RPG
Report Program Generator; a problem-oriented programming language designed to produce business reports.

Instead of coding statements, the programmer completes specification forms, such as those shown in Figure 3–15. All files to be used by RPG must be defined once through the specification forms. After the files have been defined, the programmer has only to enter the operations to be performed and the content and format of the desired output. The entries on the RPG forms are entered into the computer, and the RPG generator program then builds an object program, which the computer executes.

```
GRADE:  PROCEDURE OPTIONS (MAIN);
/* THIS PROGRAM CALCULATES THE AVERAGE OF THREE TEST SCORES FOR FIVE */
/* STUDENTS AND ASSIGNS A LETTER GRADE                               */
DECLARE (NAME) CHARACTER(15);
DECLARE (LETTER) CHARACTER(1);
DECLARE (TEST1, TEST2, TEST3, I) FIXED DECIMAL(3);
DECLARE (DUMMY) CHARACTER(56);
DECLARE (AVERAGE) FIXED DECIMAL(5,2);
PUT PAGE LIST (' STUDENT NAME       LETTER GRADE');
PUT SKIP;
DO I=1 TO 5;
  GET EDIT (NAME, TEST1, TEST2, TEST3) (A(15), F(3), F(3), F(3));
  GET EDIT (DUMMY) (A(56));
  AVERAGE = (TEST1 + TEST2 + TEST3) / 3.0;
  IF AVERAGE >= 90 THEN LETTER = 'A';
    ELSE IF AVERAGE >= 80 THEN LETTER = 'B';
      ELSE IF AVERAGE >= 70 THEN LETTER = 'C';
        ELSE IF AVERAGE >= 60 THEN LETTER = 'D';
          ELSE LETTER = 'F';
  PUT SKIP EDIT (NAME, '           ', LETTER) (A(15), A(11), A(1));
END;  /* DO */;
END;


 STUDENT NAME        GRADE

JOANN WEISS            A
TOM FARR               D
ANN BLASS              B
BOB WILLS              F
JANIS MAYS             C
```

Figure 3–14 STUDENT GRADES PROGRAM IN PL/C PL/C is less wordy than COBOL and is well suited for short programming projects.

Because RPG requires little main storage space, it is one of the primary languages of small computers and minicomputers. But it has shortcomings, among them a limited computational capability and a lack of standardization. RPG programs written for one computer may require major changes to be used on another computer.

Logo
An educational, problem-oriented programming language that is easy for children to learn yet is powerful enough to be used for complicated programming tasks.

Logo. **Logo** is an educational programming language. Although it was designed especially for children, Logo is powerful and flexible enough to be used for some very complicated programming tasks (see Figure 3–16).

Logo is based on the use of graphics. The central figure of Logo is a "turtle," the cursor, which is initially positioned in the middle of the computer screen. The user makes the turtle move on the screen by directing it to take "turtle steps." As the turtle moves, it leaves "turtle tracks," which form lines on the screen.

By moving the turtle around the screen with the commands of the language, the programmer can draw shapes. These shapes can be stored for later use, or they can be changed to shapes of increasing complexity.

Although the main strength of Logo is turtle graphics, the language has much more than graphics to offer. Most versions of Logo allow the user to do simple arithmetic, and some versions perform sophisticated math func-

Figure 3–15 RPG SPECIFICATION FORMS A programmer using RPG completes forms similar to these and then defines files. Then operations, content, and format of the desired output are entered. Finally the items written on the forms are entered into the computer.

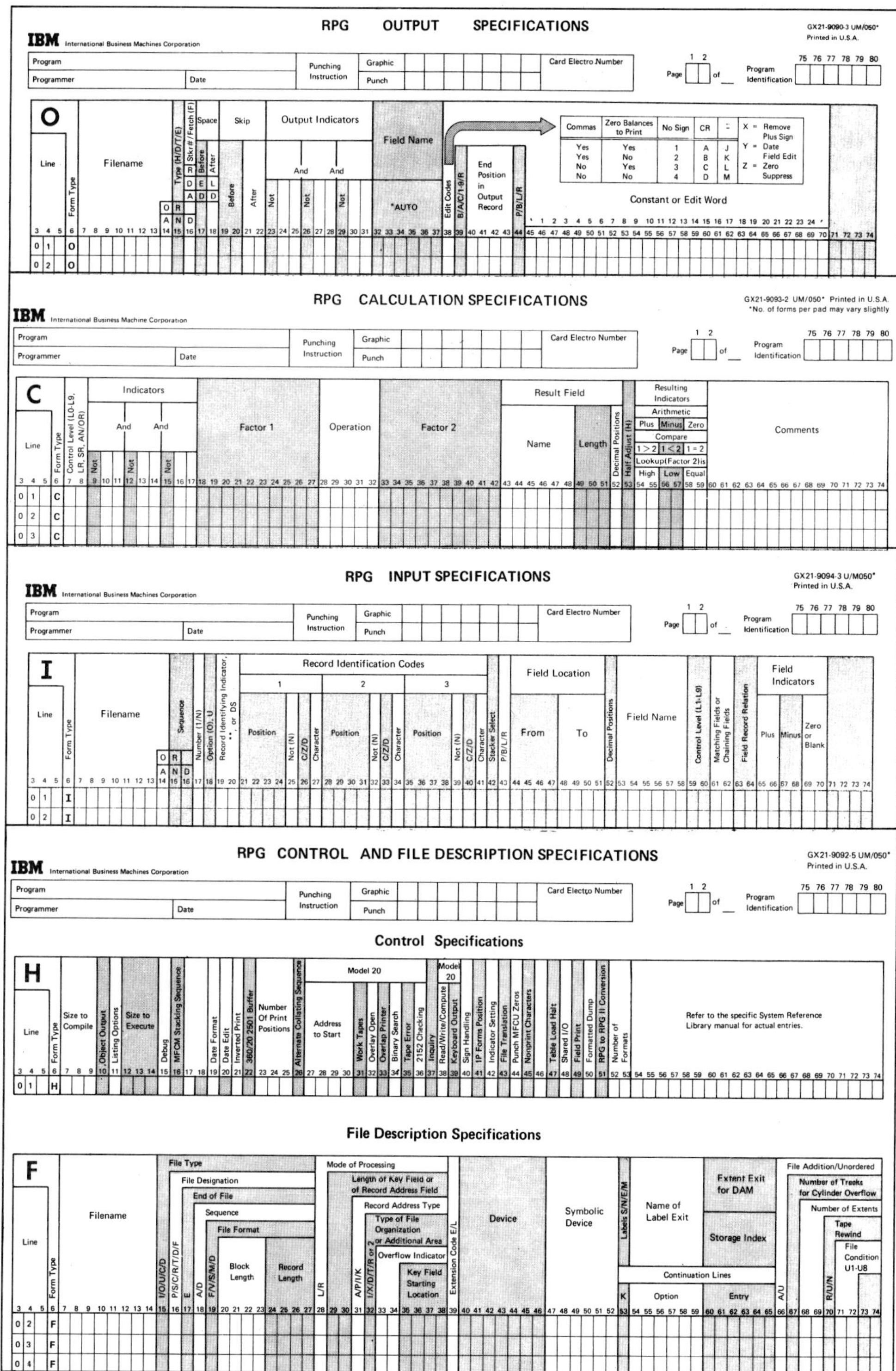

IBM International Business Machines Corporation

RPG OUTPUT SPECIFICATIONS

GX21-9090-3 UM/050* Printed in U.S.A.

Program | Programmer | Date | Punching Instruction | Graphic | Punch | Card Electro Number | Page of | Program Identification

O | Line | Form Type | Filename | Type (H/D/T/E) | Stacker Select/Fetch (F) | Space | Before | After | Skip | Before | After | Output Indicators | And | And | Not | Not | Not | Field Name | *AUTO | Edit Codes | Blank After (B) | End Position in Output Record | P/B/L/R | Constant or Edit Word

Commas	Zero Balances to Print	No Sign	CR	–	X = Remove Plus Sign
Yes	Yes	1	A	J	Y = Date Field Edit
Yes	No	2	B	K	Z = Zero Suppress
No	Yes	3	C	L	
No	No	4	D	M	

IBM International Business Machine Corporation

RPG CALCULATION SPECIFICATIONS

GX21-9093-2 UM/050* Printed in U.S.A. *No. of forms per pad may vary slightly

Program | Programmer | Date | Punching Instruction | Graphic | Punch | Card Electro Number | Page of | Program Identification

C | Line | Form Type | Control Level (L0-L9, LR, SR, AN/OR) | Indicators | And | And | Not | Not | Not | Factor 1 | Operation | Factor 2 | Result Field | Name | Length | Decimal Positions | Half Adjust (H) | Resulting Indicators | Arithmetic | Plus | Minus | Zero | Compare | 1 > 2 | 1 < 2 | 1 = 2 | Lookup(Factor 2)is | High | Low | Equal | Comments

IBM International Business Machines Corporation

RPG INPUT SPECIFICATIONS

GX21-9094-3 U/M050* Printed in U.S.A.

Program | Programmer | Date | Punching Instruction | Graphic | Punch | Card Electro Number | Page of | Program Identification

I | Line | Form Type | Filename | Sequence | Number (1/N) | Option (O), U | Record Identifying Indicator, **, or DS | Record Identification Codes | 1 | 2 | 3 | Position | Not (N) | C/Z/D | Character | Stacker Select | P/B/L/R | Field Location | From | To | Decimal Positions | Field Name | Control Level (L1-L9) | Matching Fields or Chaining Fields | Field Record Relation | Field Indicators | Plus | Minus | Zero or Blank

IBM International Business Machines Corporation

RPG CONTROL AND FILE DESCRIPTION SPECIFICATIONS

GX21-9092-5 UM/050* Printed in U.S.A.

Program | Programmer | Date | Punching Instruction | Graphic | Punch | Card Electro Number | Page of | Program Identification

Control Specifications

H | Line | Form Type | Size to Compile | Object Output | Listing Options | Size to Execute | Debug | MFCM Stacking Sequence | Date Format | Date Edit | Inverted Print | 360/20 2501 Buffer | Number Of Print Positions | Alternate Collating Sequence | Model 20 | Address to Start | Work Tapes | Overlay Open | Overlay Printer | Binary Search | Tape Error | 2152 Checking | Model 20 | Inquiry | Read/Write/Compute | Keyboard Output | Sign Handling | 1P Forms Position | Indicator Setting | File Translation | Punch MFCU Zeros | Nonprint Characters | Table Load Halt | Shared I/O | Field Print | Formatted Dump | RPG to RPG II Conversion | Number of Formats

Refer to the specific System Reference Library manual for actual entries.

File Description Specifications

F | Line | Form Type | Filename | File Type | File Designation | End of File | Sequence | File Format | I/O/U/C/D | P/S/C/R/T/D/F | E | A/D | F/V/S/M/D | Block Length | Record Length | Mode of Processing | Length of Key Field or of Record Address Field | Record Address Type | Type of File Organization or Additional Area | Overflow Indicator | Key Field Starting Location | L/R | A/P/I/K | I/X/D/T/R or 2 | Extension Code E/L | Device | Symbolic Device | Labels S/N/E/M | Name of Label Exit | Extent Exit for DAM | Storage Index | Continuation Lines | K | Option | Entry | A/U | File Addition/Unordered | Number of Tracks for Cylinder Overflow | Number of Extents | Tape Rewind | File Condition U1-U8 | R/U/N

Figure 3–16 LOGO IN THE CLASSROOM Texas Instruments was the first computer manufacturer to make the children's programming language Logo available to consumers.

tions such as trigonometry and logarithms. List processing—the ability to operate on numbers, letters, words, and sentences—is another feature on most versions of Logo.

PILOT
Programmed Inquiry, Learning, Or Teaching; an easy-to-learn , problem-oriented programming language used mostly for designing computer-aided instruction (CAI) programs.

PILOT. **PILOT** (Programmed Inquiry, Learning, Or Teaching) was originally designed to introduce computers to children. Today, the main use of PILOT is in designing computer-aided instruction (CAI) programs.

PILOT was especially designed for use in drills, tests, and dialogues. Information is presented to the user and questions are asked. Then, depending on the response given, the program branches to one of several alternatives.

In PILOT programs, each line must begin with a one- or two-letter code that tells the computer what to do with the rest of the line that follows. For example, a T at the beginning of a line tells the computer to type, or display the line on the user's terminal screen. A C tells the computer to compute a mathematical expression, and an M matches any words that follow with user input.

PILOT is very easy to learn and allows even the beginner to design CAI programs. The drawbacks of PILOT are that its programs run slower than programs written in some other languages and that it is not good for use with complex computational problems.

Interactive program
A program that permits the user to enter data during execution.

Interactive Programming Languages. Interactive programming languages are problem-oriented languages used in **interactive programs,** which use immediate input from the programmer or user to direct the processing. The computer can respond to the input instantaneously.

Several interactive languages use an interpreter rather than a compiler

Table 3–2 COMPARISON OF PROGRAMMING LANGUAGES

FEATURE	ASSEMBLY LANGUAGE	FORTRAN	COBOL	PL/I	RPG	LOGO	PILOT	BASIC	PASCAL	APL
Strong math capabilities	X	X		X		X		X	X	X
Good character manipulation capabilities	X		X	X		X	X	X	X	X
English-like			X	X		X	X	X	X	
Available on many computers	X	X	X		X	X	X	X	X	
Highly efficient	X					X				
Standardized		X	X	X			X	X		
Requires large amount of storage			X	X		X				X
Good interactive capability						X	X	X	X	X
Procedure oriented		X	X	X		X		X	X	X
Problem oriented					X		X			
Machine dependent	X									

to translate source program statements to object program code. Unlike a compiler, which translates an entire program into an object code before executing it, an interpreter evaluates and translates program statements one instruction at a time. The interpreter takes one source program instruction, translates it into machine code, and then executes it. It then takes the next instruction, translates it, executes it, and so on. An interpreter can save space because the interpreter program itself can be quite small. The need to store the program's entire translated object code in the computer is also eliminated. The interpreter, however, can be inefficient, since program statements that are used many times must be translated each time they are executed.

Described below are three interactive programming languages—BASIC, Pascal, and APL.

● ***BASIC.*** **BASIC** (Beginner's All-Purpose Symbolic Instruction Code) was developed at Dartmouth College for use with time-sharing systems. The language is easy to learn and can be used by people with little or no programming experience. Beginners can learn to write fairly complex BASIC programs in a matter of hours.

BASIC
Beginner's All-Purpose Symbolic Instruction Code; a programming language used for interactive problem solving, often used by people who are not professional programmers.

Although it was originally intended for instructional use at the college level, many companies now use BASIC for their data-processing needs. The increase in popularity of BASIC is duc partly to its simplicity and variety of uses. Finally, the use of BASIC is increasing because of its ability to work well with microcomputers, which are rapidly growing in popularity. Figure 3–17 shows the student grades program written in BASIC.

● ***Pascal.*** **Pascal** is named after the French philosopher and mathematician, Blaise Pascal, inventor of the first mechanical adding machine. Niklaus Wirth, a Swiss computer scientist, developed Pascal between 1968 and 1970.

Pascal
A programming language named after the French mathematician Blaise Pascal; developed to teach programming techniques to students.

```
10 REM THIS PROGRAM CALCULATES THE AVERAGE OF THREE TEST SCORES
20 REM FOR FIVE STUDENTS AND ASSIGNS A LETTER GRADE
25 PRINT
26 PRINT
30 PRINT "STUDENT NAME      GRADE"
35 PRINT "------------      -----"
36 PRINT
40 FOR I = 1 TO 5
50   READ STUDENT$,TEST1,TEST2,TEST3
60   LET A = (TEST1 + TEST2 + TEST3) / 3
70   IF A < 90 THEN 100
80   LET G$ = "A"
90   GOTO 200
100  IF A < 80 THEN 130
110  LET G$ = "B"
120  GOTO 200
130  IF A < 70 THEN 160
140  LET G$ = "C"
150  GOTO 200
160  IF A < 60 THEN 190
170  LET G$ = "D"
180  GOTO 200
190  LET G$ = "F"
200  PRINT STUDENT$;TAB(18);G$
210 NEXT I
220 DATA JOANN WEISS,83,96,91,TOMM FARR,61,78,69
230 DATA ANN BLASS,93,82,87,BOB WILLS,43,56,62
240 DATA JANIS MAYS,73,84,71
999 END
```

```
STUDENT NAME      GRADE
------------      -----

JOANN WEISS         A
TOMM FARR           D
ANN BLASS           B
BOB WILLS           F
JANIS MAYS          C
```

Figure 3–17 STUDENT GRADES PROGRAM IN BASIC Computer manufacturers offer many versions of BASIC. This BASIC program may need to be changed before it can be run on another system.

APL
A Programming Language; a terminal-oriented, symbolic programming language especially suitable for interactive problem-solving.

The first Pascal compiler became available in 1971. Like BASIC, Pascal was developed to teach programming concepts to students. But it is rapidly finding acceptance in business and scientific applications.

The language is relatively easy to learn, like BASIC, yet it is powerful, like PL/1. Unlike PL/1, however, Pascal is available on microcomputers, where it seems to be a good alternative to BASIC.

Probably the major drawback to Pascal is that it is not yet standardized. Moreover, some critics say that Pascal has poor input/output capabilities. Figure 3–18 shows the student grades program in Pascal.

● **APL** (A Programming Language) was conceived in 1962 by Kenneth Iverson and described in his book of the same name. APL became available to the public through IBM in 1968. Many businesses now use it as their main

```
PROGRAM GRADES;
VAR
  NAME:STRING;
  TEST1,TEST2,TEST3,I:INTEGER;
  AVERAGE:REAL;
  GRADE:CHAR;
BEGIN
  FOR I := 1 TO 3 DO
    BEGIN
      WRITELN('ENTER STUDENT NAME');
      READLN(NAME);
      WRITELN('ENTER SCORES FOR TESTS 1,2,AND 3');
      READLN(TEST1,TEST2,TEST3);
      AVERAGE := (TEST1 + TEST2 + TEST3) / 3;
      IF AVERAGE < 90 THEN
        IF AVERAGE < 80 THEN
          IF AVERAGE < 70 THEN
            IF AVERAGE > 60 THEN
              GRADE := 'D'
            ELSE GRADE := 'F'
          ELSE GRADE := 'C'
        ELSE GRADE := 'B'
      ELSE GRADE := 'A';
      WRITELN;
      WRITELN;
      WRITELN;
      WRITELN('STUDENT NAME      LETTER GRADE');
      WRITELN(NAME:11,GRADE:10);
      WRITELN;
      WRITELN;
      END;
  END.


ENTER STUDENT NAME
JOANN WEISS
ENTER SCORES FOR TESTS 1,2,AND 3
83 96 91



STUDENT NAME      LETTER GRADE
JOANN WEISS          A


ENTER STUDENT NAME
TOMM FARR
ENTER SCORES FOR TESTS 1,2,AND 3
61 78 69



STUDENT NAME      LETTER GRADE
  TOMM FARR          D


ENTER STUDENT NAME
JANIS MAYS
ENTER SCORES FOR TESTS 1,2,AND 3
73 84 71



STUDENT NAME      LETTER GRADE
 JANIS MAYS          C
```

Figure 3–18 STUDENT GRADES PROGRAM IN PASCAL
Many high schools may begin to offer courses in Pascal so that students will be prepared to take advanced placement tests in computer science. Pascal is the language chosen for the tests.

Figure 3–19 APL CODING
APL coding looks more difficult than coding in the other high-level languages.

APL CODING	ENGLISH TRANSLATION
A + B	A plus B
A←25	A = 25
A⌊B	Finds the smaller of A and B
V1←2 5 11 17	Creates a vector of 4 components and assigns the vector to V1
⌈/V1	Finds the maximum value in the vector V1

LEARNING CHECK

1. Which of the following is not a step in the programming process?
   a. Defining the problem.
   b. Coding the program.
   c. Getting the right answer.
   d. Debugging the program.
2. Name two characteristics of a good program besides getting the right answer.
3. Assembly language is a(n) ________ -oriented language.
4. A source program becomes an object program through a language translator. Name the three kinds of language translating programs.
5. Name two interactive programming languages.

ANSWERS:
1. c. 2. ease of reading and understanding, reliability, workability under all conditions, ease of modification and updating, portability. 3. machine. 4. compiler, interpreter, assembler. 5. BASIC, Pascal, APL.

programming language. It functions best when used for interactive processing through a terminal.

A programmer can use APL in two modes: execution and definition. In the execution mode, the terminal can be used like a desk calculator. An instruction is keyed in on one line, and the response is shown immediately on the following line. In the definition mode, a series of instructions is entered into the memory, and the entire program is executed on command from the programmer. Its two-mode capability makes APL unlike any of the other high-level programming languages discussed so far.

APL can be used to perform some very complex operations with minimal coding (see Figure 3–19). Its lack of formal restrictions on input and output and its free-form style make it a very powerful language.

This language has a few disadvantages as well. It is difficult to read, requires a special keyboard, and is unsuitable for handling large data files. It also requires a large storage space for its compiler. In addition, no detailed explanation of the language is available. Figure 3–20 shows an APL keyboard, and Figure 3–21 illustrates an interactive APL session. Table 3–2 on page 95 compares all the languages discussed in this chapter.

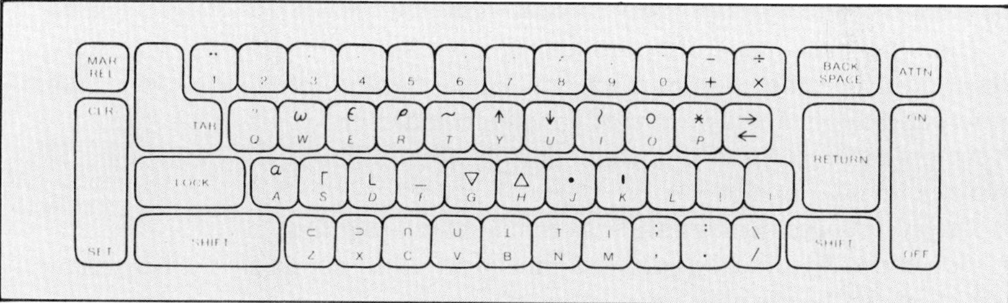

Figure 3–20 APL KEYBOARD
The APL keyboard indicates the various symbols used for programming in this language.

Figure 3–21 INTERACTIVE APL SESSION For the student grades program used in previous examples, a programmer would be prompted to enter the data.

```
        ∇GRADE[⎕]∇
     ∇  GRADE
[1]     ⍝ THIS PROGRAM CALCULATES THE AVERAGE OF THREE TEST SCORES
[2]     ⍝ FOR THREE STUDENTS AND ASSIGNS A LETTER GRADE
[3]      I←0
[4]     LOOP:I←I+1
[5]      →(I>3)/OUT
[6]      ' '
[7]      'ENTER STUDENT NAME:
[8]      NAME←⍞
[9]      'ENTER SCORES FOR TEST 1,2,AND 3:
[10]     SCORES←⎕
[11]     AVG←(+/SCORES)÷3
[12]     →(AVG≥90)/A
[13]     →(AVG≥80)/B
[14]     →(AVG≥70)/C
[15]     →(AVG≥60)/D
[16]     →(AVG<60)/F
[17]    A:'GRADE:  A'
[18]     →LOOP
[19]    B:'GRADE:  B'
[20]     →LOOP
[21]    C:'GRADE:  C'
[22]     →LOOP
[23]    D:'GRADE:  D'
[24]     →LOOP
[25]    F:'GRADE:  F'
[26]     →LOOP
[27]    OUT:
     ∇
        GRADE

ENTER STUDENT NAME:
JOANN WEISS
ENTER SCORES FOR TEST 1,2,AND 3:
⎕:
        83 96 91
GRADE:  A
```

SUMMARY POINTS

- There are two types of computer programs: system programs and application programs. System programs control the operations of the computer, and application programs solve particular problems.
- An operating system is a collection of programs the computer uses to manage its own operations.
- The system residence device stores system programs.
- Flowcharts, structured programming, and pseudocode are tools used by programmers to simplify the writing of programs.
- The programming process involves four important steps: (1) defining the problem, (2) designing a solution, (3) coding the program, and (4) compiling, testing, and debugging the program.
- There are three levels of computer language: (1) machine language, (2) assembly language, and (3) high-level language. High-level languages are the most English-like and the most widely used.
- Before the programmer's source program can be executed, it must be translated into a machine-readable object program by a language translator program. There are three types of language translators. Assembler programs (used to translate assembly language programs) and compiler programs (used to translate high-level languages) translate the entire program at once. An interpreter translates one instruction at a time rather than the entire program at once.
- Machine-oriented languages make the most efficient use of the computer. Procedure-oriented languages concentrate on the various processing steps needed to perform the task at hand. Problem-oriented languages help programmers solve processing requirements with minimal programming effort by focusing on results, rather than on the steps necessary to get the results.
- The most commonly used procedure-oriented languages are COBOL, used for business applications; FORTRAN, used for scientific applications; and PL/1, used for both business and scientific applications.
- The most commonly used problem-oriented language is RPG.
- Interactive programming languages are used for programs that accept immediate input from the programmer or the user during program execution. Such languages include BASIC, Pascal, and APL.

REVIEW QUESTIONS

1. Name the two types of programs that comprise the operating system and explain the function of each.
2. What is the purpose of a problem-oriented language?
3. What is the purpose of a procedure-oriented language?
4. Name the four basic logic patterns.
5. What is pseudocode?
6. How does structured programming make changing and updating a program easier?
7. What are the steps used in the programming process to help a programmer develop the instructions needed to solve a problem?
8. How are an assembler, an interpreter, and a compiler different?
9. What is an object program?
10. How are interactive programming languages used?

TRS-80 Model II TRSDOS version 1.2 December 31, 1979.
(c)(p) 1979 TANDY CORPORATION. All rights reserved.
Unauthorized reproduction of this software is prohibited
and is in violation of United States copyright laws.
ENTER DATE (MM/DD/YYYY)
Radio Shack
TRS-80
MODEL II
MICRO
COMPUTER
POWER
RESET

CHAPTER 4

MICROCOMPUTERS AND COMPUTER SYSTEMS

Chapter Outline

INTRODUCTION

Microprocessor
The central processing unit of a microcomputer; fits on a small silicon chip.

During its short history, computer technology has experienced rapid growth in all areas. Today there are many different types of computers from which to choose, from very large systems to **microprocessors** used for a single purpose—for example, monitoring fuel flow in an automobile. Along with advances in computers have come improvements in software. Computer users have many alternatives to consider today when deciding which software to use. They may also choose among various levels of service and support available for computers and computer software.

Even with the high level of technology that already exists in the computer world, new developments are occurring at a fast pace. These developments are primarily aimed at expanding the computer's capabilities, decreasing its size, and making it easier to use.

MICROCOMPUTERS

Microcomputer
The smallest type of computer; differs from larger computers in capability, price, and size.

How Microcomputers Evolved

Microcomputers, the small computers that have become almost as common in the average American home as stereo systems, have only been around since about 1974 (see Figure 4–1). In ten short years, consumers have found uses for microcomputers in offices, homes, laboratories, and schools. Computer stores have sprung up in large cities and small towns alike to meet the demand for these computers (see Figure 4–2).

The first microcomputers appeared when hobbyists became fascinated with computer technology. Computer hobbyists began building their own personal computers from scratch or from kits in basements, garages, and bedrooms. When manufacturers realized the potential market for personal computers, they began to develop microcomputer systems geared toward personal use.

Figure 4–1 MICROCOMPUTERS
Microcomputers, the least expensive category of computers, are general-purpose machines used in many applications in homes, offices, and schools.

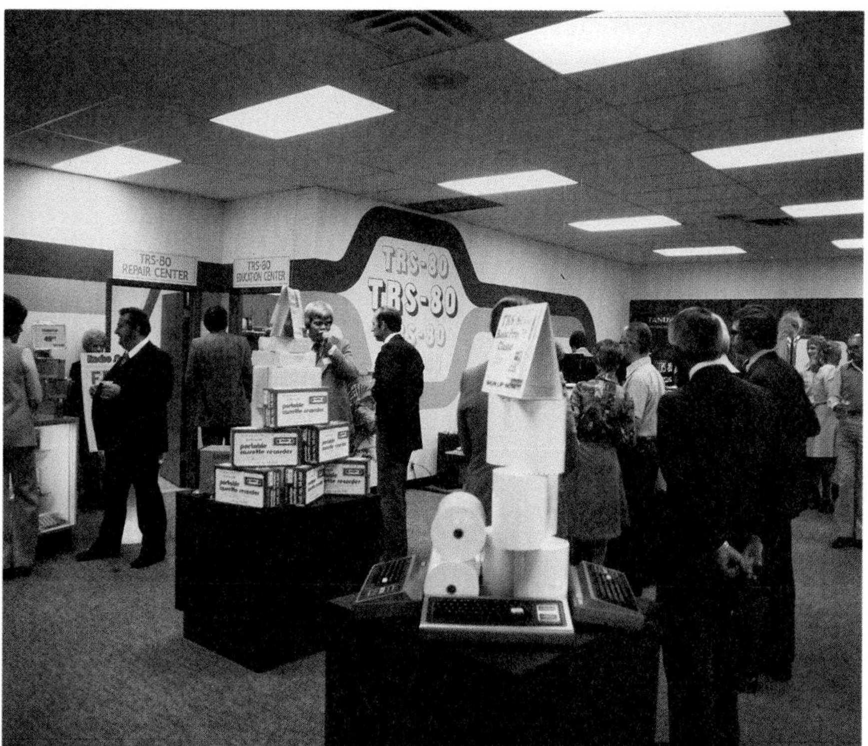

Figure 4–2 COMPUTER STORES
The Computer Center at Radio Shack (a division of Tandy Corporation) bustles with activity. Microcomputer users buy a great deal of hardware and software to give their systems greater capabilities. This has created a demand for computer stores in all areas.

The personal computer was first marketed commercially in 1975, when the Altair 8800 computer was introduced. This early microcomputer was preassembled and came with simple programs to perform simple jobs such as balancing a checkbook or playing a game of backgammon.

Today, companies such as IBM, DEC, Apple, Radio Shack, Wang, and Hewlett-Packard have entered the microcomputer market, and competition is stiff. Manufacturers have responded by lowering prices and staging expensive advertising campaigns to try to capture the interest of the consumer. That competition may be partially responsible for the amazing advances made in microcomputer technology in recent years.

How Microcomputers Differ From Other Computers

Microcomputers differ from larger computers (minicomputers, mainframes, and supercomputers) in capability, price, and size. But the capabilities of microcomputers are expanding rapidly, and there is no longer a clear distinction between the capabilities of microcomputers and those of the next class of computers, minicomputers. Microcomputers are even being used in place of larger computers (mainframes) by some companies. Therefore, microcomputers can most easily be distinguished by their price and size.

Microcomputers are the smallest computers. They usually can sit on a desktop. Microcomputers get their power from microprocessors that contain an arithmetic/logic unit and the control capability for memory and input/output access. The CPU performs similar functions in larger computers. However, whereas the CPU for large computers contains many chips, the microprocessor is a single silicon chip about the size of a nail head (see Figure 4–3).

Peripherals
Auxiliary computer equipment such as printers, disk drives, and storage devices.

Because a microcomputer's power comes from only one chip, it lacks the speed and some of the capabilities of larger computers. It also has less internal memory. But a microcomputer can be connected to **peripherals**—auxiliary computer equipment such as storage devices, printers, and disk drives. With peripherals, a microcomputer can be used for many highly sophisticated tasks.

The major advantage of microcomputers is cost. Because their operating systems are less complex than those of larger computers, they are not as expensive to build. Microcomputer prices range from about a hundred dollars to about ten thousand dollars.

The prefix *micro*, then, should be thought of more in terms of size and cost than capability. Microcomputers are very powerful for their size. Today's microcomputers can equal the power of earlier room-sized computers. Although they still cannot perform as many complex functions as large computers available today, advances in microcomputer technology are giving them more speed, more memory, and more software.

How Microcomputers Are Used

Uses for microcomputers have expanded as the computers themselves have acquired more features. Microcomputers can be used as typewriters, cal-

Figure 4–3 MICROPROCESSOR
This microprocessor from Bell Labs has as much processing power as some minicomputers.

Figure 4–4 MICROCOMPUTERS TO AID IN DECISION MAKING
This executive analyzes information at his desk. Having a microcomputer in the office is not only convenient but speeds up the flow of information within an organization.

culators, accounting systems, record keepers, and telecommunications instruments. They can also act as easels, tutors, and toys.

In business, microcomputers are used for ordering, controlling inventory, bookkeeping, processing payroll, and many other tasks. Executives are putting microcomputers in their offices so they can have access to the information they need when making decisions (see Figure 4–4).

Microcomputers also serve a wide variety of uses in homes. Even persons with little or no programming experience can use microcomputers to balance checkbooks, store recipes, prepare budgets, and play games. With flashy graphics and joysticks, a home microcomputer can become a personal video game arcade. Some people have even connected household appliances to their computers. For example, computers can turn lights on and off, control heating and air conditioning, and run the lawn sprinkler.

Recently, experiments in banking and shopping at home by computer have been conducted and considered successful. At first, most people resisted the changes created by such systems. Once people saw the systems could work, however, the advantages became clear. For example, shopping and banking at home saves time and money by eliminating the need to drive around town to banks and stores. The temptation to buy on impulse is also lessened because people are not tempted by displays of products they do not need, as they might be if they walked through the stores.

In schools, microcomputers are used to instruct students and perform administrative jobs. They can help students understand subjects such as math, science, and English by offering individualized instruction (see Figure 4–5), and they can help administrators perform such tasks as ordering supplies, processing payrolls, and keeping enrollment records.

Microcomputers can also make hobbies more enjoyable. For example, special programs written for music buffs make it easy to create, edit, store, and play musical compositions, all on the computer. Other programs help

Figure 4–5 MICROCOMPUTERS IN THE SCHOOL Even these six-year-olds can enjoy using microcomputers in school. Increasingly, students' orientation to computers begins in their first years.

coin and stamp collectors catalog their collections. These are just a few of the programs geared toward the interests of hobbyists.

Chapter 5 discusses more of the many uses of minicomputers in society. Later chapters explain in detail word processing, spreadsheet, data manager, and graphics software packages for microcomputers.

Distributed processing
A system in which several microcomputers located in various locations are linked together by cables to form a network.

An important development triggered by the use of microcomputers is **distributed processing.** A distributed processing system is a series of microcomputers linked by communication lines so that processing can be done at different locations.

Historically, organizations used large computers in a central location for all their processing needs. As the main computer became overloaded, users began to add microcomputers at the points where processing was required, reducing the workload on the large central computer. For example, microcomputers located at a manufacturing company's factories around the country could handle inquiries and produce reports for each plant manager. The need for one large computer to process the information for all the factories would be reduced. Because the microcomputers would be linked by communication lines, executives at company headquarters still would have access to each factory's reports.

The Smallest Microcomputers

The smallest microcomputers available are portables. Portables are light enough to be carried and do not need an external source of power. They are powered by batteries, either rechargeable or replaceable. Portables usually need some form of direct-access mass storage medium, such as floppy disks.

Portables can be divided further by size into briefcase-sized, notebook-sized, and handheld. The Hewlett-Packard 110 is briefcase-sized and is

Figure 4–6 HEWLETT-PACKARD 110 PORTABLE COMPUTER
This computer can easily fit in a briefcase, which makes it easy to carry on business trips.

noted for being much faster than other portables (see Figure 4–6). Radio Shack's Model 100 is notebook-sized and is used mostly for word processing (see Figure 4–7).

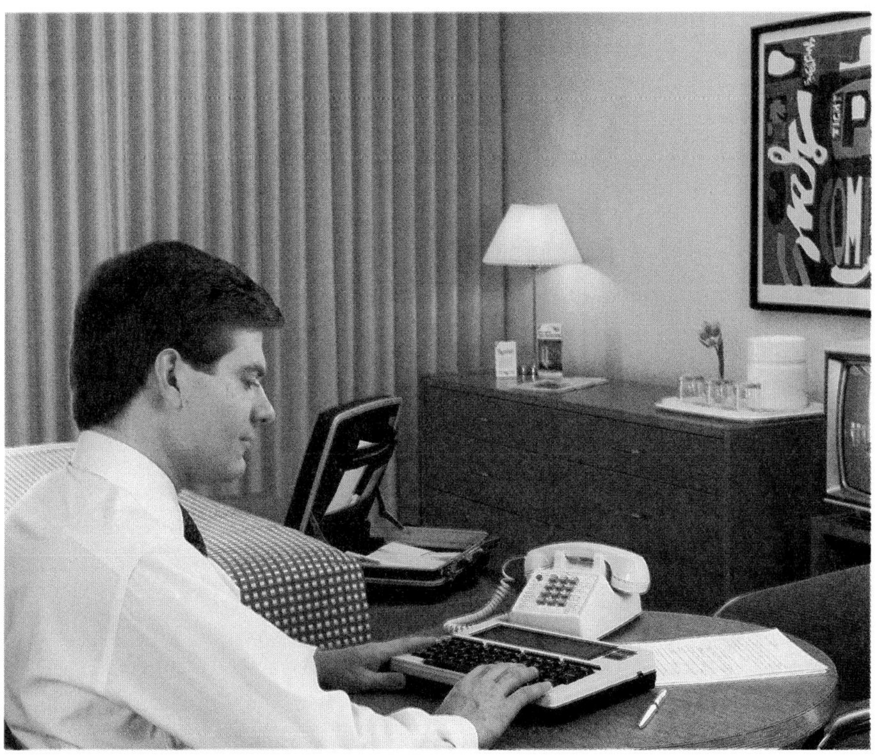

Figure 4–7 RADIO SHACK MODEL 100 PORTABLE COMPUTER
This lower-priced portable is used mostly for special functions such as word processing.

Portables should be distinguished from another class of small microcomputers, the transportables. Transportables are generally larger than portables but still small enough to be carried. They are different from portables because they require an external power source. Even though it weighs only seven and a half pounds, the Apple IIc shown in Figure 4–8 is a transportable, because it does not contain its own power source.

Some portables are capable of almost as much as small desk-top microcomputers, and their prices reflect it. They range in price from around three thousand dollars to around five thousand dollars. Other portables are dedicated to certain functions and carry a much lower price tag, from around eight hundred dollars to around two thousand dollars.

Three technologies are responsible for the sophistication of portables. Microprocessors give portables the power of a full-sized computer in a single chip. Flat display panels allow portables to be slim and therefore easy to carry. Finally, battery power frees portables from dependency on external power sources.

So far, portables have been found to be especially useful for reporters and businesspeople. A reporter can, for example, cover a presidential news conference two thousand miles from the newspaper's headquarters, write the story with the help of a word-processing package on a portable computer, and use a **modem** to send the finished product over the phone, ready for printing. Businesspeople who travel frequently also find portables useful. Salespeople can use them to develop sales or status reports to send back to the main office. They can record information on the spot while it is fresh in their minds. The hours they spend on airplanes now can be productive if they work on portable microcomputers as they travel. Also, time spent in the office summing up data after a sales trip can be reduced.

Modem
An inexpensive piece of electronic equipment that lets the computer use telephone lines to send information to other computers and receive information from them.

Figure 4–8 APPLE IIc
The Apple IIc is a transportable microcomputer that requires an external power source and a separate display. It weighs only seven and a half pounds.

Figure 4–9 MINICOMPUTER
Minicomputers appeared in the early 1970s and were designed for specialized applications. They are typically used in engineering, industrial automation, and word processing.

OTHER COMPUTER SYSTEMS

Minicomputers

Minicomputer
The second smallest type of computer; has the components of a full-size system but less capability.

The computer ranking next in size to the microcomputer is the **minicomputer** (see Figure 4–9). These machines were developed in the early 1970s and were designed for specialized applications such as engineering, industrial automation, and word processing. Minicomputer development has progressed rapidly, and minicomputers now have much greater capabilities than before.

One reason for the popularity of minicomputers is their flexibility. They can be plugged into standard electrical outlets and do not require special air-conditioned rooms like larger computers. Further, minicomputer systems may consist of any number of peripherals connected by communication lines. This flexibility allows users to expand their minicomputer systems simply by adding more hardware.

Minicomputers range in price roughly from $15,000 to $250,000. They have greater processing capabilities than most microcomputers (but remember, the distinction is narrowing). Leading minicomputer manufacturers are Digital Equipment Corporation (DEC), Hewlett-Packard, Data General, Honeywell, General Automation, and Texas Instruments.

Mainframes

Mainframe
A large central computer system; mainframes are very sophisticated and are used in many applications.

Mainframe computers like the one shown in Figure 4–10 are large, sophisticated systems that can process enormous amounts of data at very high speeds, hold millions of characters in primary storage, and support many input, output, and auxiliary devices. In size and power, they are second only to supercomputers. Mainframes are more expensive than microcomputers or minicomputers, ranging in price from about $200,000 to over $1,000,000.

Mainframes are used by organizations that process a great deal of data. Examples of mainframe users are large businesses, hospitals, and universities. The demand for these large systems is diminishing because the trend in the computer industry today is away from a large central computer to distributed systems that use smaller computers in numerous locations.

Figure 4–10 MAINFRAME Mainframes are used primarily by businesses, hospitals, universities, and banks that process a great deal of data.

Further, most companies that need mainframes already have them. Many mainframe manufacturers, in order to remain competitive, have started to make minicomputers and microcomputers. Major competitors in the mainframe market are IBM, Burroughs, Honeywell, Univac, National Cash Register (NCR), Control Data Corporation (CDC), and Amdahl.

Figure 4–11 CRAY-1 SUPERCOMPUTER The Cray-1, the first supercomputer, was developed in 1977 and is one of less than a hundred supercomputer systems in use worldwide. Applications requiring the capabilities of supercomputers include meteorology, aerodynamics, seismology, and nuclear physics.

Supercomputers

Supercomputers, also called maxicomputers, are the largest, fastest, and most powerful computer systems available. In fact, a supercomputer can perform at least ten million instructions per second.

These systems are also very expensive, and their costs are justified in very few cases. Supercomputers can cost as much as ten to fifteen million dollars. To justify costs this high, a corporation must be very large and must need to process millions of instructions very quickly or maintain large data bases. Today, supercomputers are used mainly in the scientific areas of weather forecasting, nuclear weapons development, and energy supply and conservation.

An example of a supercomputer is the Cray-1, developed by Cray Research, Inc., and shown in Figure 4–11. The Cray-1 was the first supercomputer developed and is one of approximately seventy supercomputer systems in use worldwide. Even with the price of computer hardware decreasing, supercomputer software costs remain high, and it is not likely that many users will purchase supercomputers.

Supercomputer
Also called a maxicomputer; the fastest, most powerful computer system available; performs at least ten million instructions per second.

LEARNING CHECK

1. A single silicon chip that gives microcomputers their power is the ________.
2. What is the main reason for microcomputers' success in the home market?
3. There is a clear difference between the capabilities of microcomputers and minicomputers. (True or false?)
4. What are the characteristics of portable microcomputers?
5. The largest, fastest computer systems are called ________.

ANSWERS:

1. microprocessor. 2. Their cost is relatively low. 3. false. 4. They are light enough to be carried and require no external power source. 5. supercomputers or maxicomputers.

LOCAL-AREA NETWORKS

Microcomputers can be integrated to form **local-area networks (LANs),** which allow computers in the same general locale to communicate with each other. Most networks operate within one office building or link nearby buildings. The microcomputers are usually linked by cable and are usually within a thousand feet of each other (see Figure 4–12).

The main advantage of LANs is that they enable users at different terminals to share files and programs. Work stations gain more capabilities—in word and data processing, information retrieval, and communication, for example—without the duplication of equipment, data bases, and activities.

Local-area network (LAN)
A system that links microcomputers in adjacent offices and buildings for intercompany communication.

Local-area networks also involve a few disadvantages. The most significant is that computer brands are not always compatible. Some computer models cannot be used with other brands or models without additional

Figure 4–12 LOCAL-AREA NETWORK Local-area networks will continue to gain popularity because of the explosion in microcomputer use. Portable microcomputers with LAN capability may represent the wave of the future.

equipment, which drives up the cost of the LAN. However, as technology advances, compatibility between computers should improve. More and more companies may need LANs in coming years to remain competitive.

SOFTWARE CONSIDERATIONS

Computer systems are a major expense. It is true that as technology surges ahead in computer systems development, hardware prices continue to go down. Software costs, however, continue to go up, driving overall data-processing costs to higher and higher levels. Before purchasing a computer, then, a company should consider how it will obtain software.

Acquiring Software

Software can be developed in-house by employees of the organization, or it can be purchased from a software firm (software house). Software and consulting firms develop information systems for businesses. They specialize in either system software or application software, which are often sold together in packages to accomplish specific processing objectives. There are advantages and disadvantages to developing software in-house and to buying it.

By developing the software in-house, the company can ensure that its specific needs and wants will be met. Reports, forms, and files can be designed to meet exact specifications. In contrast, programs purchased from software firms are general and may have to be tailored to fit the needs of the organization.

Although general programs purchased from software firms may need tailoring, they can be purchased at a fraction of the cost of developing in-house programs. This is because maintaining the staff of analysts and programmers needed to develop software in-house is very costly. Finally, purchased programs can be ready for use in a short time. In-house programs can take months or even years to complete.

The increased use of microcomputers has caused a huge increase in software sales. Many microcomputer users do not have the time, money, or expertise needed to produce programs; so the only way for them to get software is to purchase it from software houses. These firms usually offer a wide variety of packages, from computer games to household programs to business programs. Many firms periodically update their software packages to contain the latest developments requested by users. Other firms develop specialized software packages for clients on a contractual basis. Such software is written by the firm's programmers to meet the specific needs of the client.

Using Service Bureaus and Time-Sharing Companies

Alternatives to purchasing computer hardware and software are offered by **service bureaus** and **time-sharing companies.** These facilities allow computer users to take advantage of the sophistication of a large computer system without incurring all its costs. They also provide computer services to companies who do not need twenty-four-hour-a-day processing.

Service bureau
A computer facility that provides data-processing services to users who do not have their own computer systems.

Time-sharing company
A computer facility that rents computer time to users who have purchased input/output devices, which they link to the computer with some type of communication lines.

Growth in the time-sharing industry is primarily due to advances in data-communication equipment. Time-sharing customers usually purchase input/output devices, which are linked to the computers of the time-sharing company by communication lines, such as regular telephone lines. The customer pays for the amount of CPU time used in processing. Storage space on magnetic tapes and disks also can be rented. A disadvantage of using time-sharing services is that it becomes very expensive as the user's data-processing needs increase. The more computer time needed, the greater the monthly costs.

Service bureaus also provide data-processing services. Some bureaus perform all data-processing activities for small firms. Others specialize in providing temporary personnel to key in data or to program. Many specialize in providing services for a particular industry, such as oil companies or savings and loan associations.

One service bureau, McDonnell Douglas Automation Company (McAUTO), maintains the largest computer center in the world. In an average week McAUTO services approximately three thousand customers and processes over thirty thousand jobs. The McAUTO computer center contains sixteen thousand terminals connected to thirteen large-scale computers.

PACKAGED SOFTWARE

So far not much has been said about the software packages that give microcomputers their amazing power. Software packages are available that perform many of the functions the average personal computer user wants. Ready-made programs for business, home management, education, and games can be purchased for microcomputers. Later chapters of this book give a detailed explanation of various software packages, including their uses, features, and hardware requirements.

Software packages can be either stand-alone or integrated. A stand-alone package performs only one function, such as payroll, inventory, home budgeting, word processing, or graphics. Until recently, stand-alone packages were the only type available.

Now integrated software packages are gaining popularity. An integrated package offers two or more functions that work together. An example is a package that combines graphics capabilities with a spreadsheet. Together, these applications can produce management reports that contain charts and graphs as part of the text.

Integrated packages can be more useful than a collection of stand-alone packages if they meet certain requirements. First, an integrated package should contain several parts that are normally separate application programs. Next, data should be easily shared by all the parts. Finally, the package should use a common command set. With a common command set, the same keys are used to do the same tasks for all applications in the package. This makes the package easier to use.

A drawback of integrated software packages is users need different things from software, and some users may not find a package that meets their specific needs. When a user does find a package that seems suitable, the user must check which function in the package is dominant. If a word processor with the capability to perform some spreadsheet analysis is needed, word processing should be the main function of the package.

One of the most popular integrated packages at this time is *Symphony* by Lotus. Built around a spreadsheet, the package also offers word-processing, data base, communication, and graphics functions. For needs revolving around word processing, *PeachText 5000* by PeachTree Software is useful. Integrated packages will become even more useful as more packages are developed to meet special needs.

System analyst
A specialist who evaluates the goals, priorities, organization, and needs of a business to develop an efficient method for conducting operations.

System analysis
A detailed, step-by-step investigation of a system aimed at determining what must be done and how best to do it.

SYSTEM ANALYSIS AND MANAGEMENT INFORMATION SYSTEMS

Sometimes a business employs the services of a **system analyst** to help choose the computer system that will best meet the needs of the organization. The analyst goes through a process called **system analysis** to come up with suggestions about the total system. System analysis is a detailed, step-by-step investigation of a system aimed at determining what needs to be done and how best to do it. Some of the factors a system analyst might consider are what type of hardware is needed, whether to develop software in-house or purchase it, whether to use a time-sharing arrangement or a service bureau, and even what specific personnel may be needed. The combination of these factors make up a firm's computer system.

The system analyst may also evaluate a firm's goals, priorities, and general requirements and make suggestions about the kinds of information that could be helpful to its managers. This process is part of establishing a **management information system (MIS),** which uses computers to help managers make better decisions. An MIS differs from a simple data-processing system. Simple data processing is used primarily to collect and manipulate data to produce reports, but the purpose of an MIS is to provide managers with useful information that specifically supports their decision-making tasks. To be useful, the MIS must provide information to the appropriate manager at the right time.

Management information system (MIS)
A system that extends computer use beyond routine reporting into the area of management decision making.

OTHER CONSIDERATIONS

Service and Support

The service and support available for hardware and software are important factors in the choice of a computer system.

Service refers to repair and maintenance of the computer hardware. Computer equipment is generally reliable, but it does need repair occasionally. In a business, it is important that repairs be made quickly so that processing is not interrupted for long.

There are many different service contracts available to owners of computer equipment. These contracts vary in the amount of service offered and in price and should be weighed against the importance of keeping the computer equipment operating correctly. If the system must be kept running with little or no **downtime** (time the computer is not working), a full-service contract may be necessary. This contract will provide routine maintenance on a weekly basis, as well as prompt repair of any malfunctions. If the company can tolerate some downtime, less expensive contracts may be chosen. For instance, a contract may be selected that provides no routine maintenance but provides repair when problems occur.

Downtime
The time when a computer is not working.

Support usually refers to maintenance of software. When a user purchases software, the software company should agree to correct errors and problems. This is especially important since, as time goes on, previously unnoticed errors may emerge. Without the support of the software vendor, it can be very difficult—even impossible—for a programmer to find the cause of a problem in a program. Many purchased programs do not come with a copy of the source code, the program code that is readable by humans. If the programs are to be maintained in-house, a copy of the source code is needed.

Legal Considerations

Owners of computer systems must be concerned with computer crime and legal liability. There is no single definition of computer crime, but generally it involves crime committed by use of a computer. This can include fraud, theft, and many forms of deceit. Because computer crimes are often associated with professional or salaried workers, they are classified as white-collar crimes.

One of the many types of computer crime is financial crime. This type involves such schemes as producing multiple checks, transferring money to false accounts, and juggling confidential information. Although it is not the most common type of computer crime, financial crime results in the greatest monetary loss.

Another type of computer crime is the theft of computer services, which involves the unauthorized use of computer facilities. Such thefts include occasions when a politician uses a city computer to conduct campaign mailings, when an employee uses the company computer after working hours, or when a young person gains access to a company's computer for fun.

Two somewhat different types of crime cause the loss of the computer itself. First is the outright theft of computer equipment. Because of the continued miniaturization of computer equipment, theft has become easier. Second is the sabotage, or physical destruction, of computer equipment, which can be carried out by former employees or people from rival companies.

Another important concern today is the theft of software. This problem has increased with the widespread use of microcomputers. There are companies that make unauthorized copies of software and sell them. With so many computers in use, there is a large market for this stolen software. Another problem for software companies occurs when one person buys a program, makes copies, and gives them to friends. This drastically reduces the market for software and thus, the profitability of software companies is also reduced.

Many times companies do not report computer crimes because they fear bad publicity. This is especially true with banks and other financial institutions. Executives in such organizations often prefer not to let the public learn that someone was able to defraud their company. They believe people would lose confidence in the company and stop using its services.

The profile of the average computer criminal is interesting. Often the person is young, male, ambitious, and technically competent, with an impressive educational background. He may come from any level of employees, including technicians, programmers, managers, and high-ranking executives. This person would seem to be a promising employee because of his impressive background. But the damage he can cause makes him a very dangerous employee.

Companies that use computers must take into account many legal considerations besides computer crime. A major concern today is privacy. Modern computers store large amounts of data about individuals, and some of this data could be embarrassing or harmful if revealed. If an individual's privacy is invaded, the result may be an expensive and time-consuming lawsuit against the company that stored or used the personal information. In one instance, the records of two separate individuals were confused and later combined, causing serious credit problems for one individual. After a long court battle, the company involved was fined ten thousand dollars plus court costs for negligence and failure to exercise reasonable care in programming its computer.

When establishing and maintaining a computer system, then, a company must consider the issues of legal liability and computer crime. An overlooked or neglected area may leave an opening for theft or fraud or for lawsuits involving invasion of privacy or even negligence. To protect against these occurrences, good planning and proper control, including a well-thought-out security system, must be made part of the computer system. Chapter 6 discusses computer crime and legal liability in more detail.

TRENDS

This chapter introduced the four basic sizes of computers—supercomputers, mainframes, minicomputers, and microcomputers. Keep in mind that the distinctions among these classifications are becoming less clear-cut.

According to some computer experts, today's trends indicate that most computers will someday be the size of microcomputers. Microcomputers now offer such features as hard-disk storage and multi-user capabilities, which once were associated only with mainframes; and microcomputers continue to grow more powerful. At the same time, large computers are getting smaller. The future may bring a drastic decrease in the use of mainframes. They may someday be practical only for very large companies or for organizations that require extremely sophisticated calculating capabilities.

An exciting area growing in popularity is **telecommunications**—the combined use of communication facilities, such as telephone lines, and computers. Almost any computer can be connected to the phone system by use of communications software and a modem. With this hookup, any computer system from a small personal computer to a large mainframe can gain access to a growing world of information and services.

Telecommunications
The combined use of communications facilities, such as telephone lines, and a computer.

Hundreds of telecommunications services are available to personal computer users. They can shop and bank, can call up stock quotes, financial news, and movie reviews, and can even have access to an electronic encyclopedia. Telecommunications systems also make available special information tailored to the needs of professionals such as doctors, lawyers, scientists, and accountants.

Businesses can use telecommunications for **teleconferencing** and **telecommuting.** Teleconferencing saves time and travel expenses by allowing executives in one city to be heard, and sometimes seen, by executives in other cities without leaving their offices. Electronic and/or image-producing means are used in this form of telecommunications. Telecommuting uses computer hookups between offices and homes to allow employees to work

Teleconferencing
A way to hold cross-country conferences by electronic and/or image-producing means.

Telecommuting
A way to use computer hookups between offices and homes to allow employees to work at home.

at home. Employees need not take the time and trouble to travel to work, while the company need not provide them with work space at the office.

LEARNING CHECK

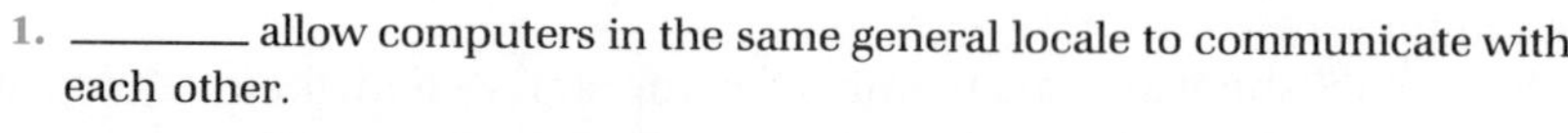

1. ______ allow computers in the same general locale to communicate with each other.
2. Software that is developed ______ is more likely to meet the exact needs and wants of an organization.
3. Which method of software development is less costly, and why?
4. A(n) ______ software package performs only one function.
5. A detailed, step-by-step investigation of a system aimed at determining what must be done and how best to do it is called ______.

ANSWERS:

1. Local-area networks. 2. in-house. 3. Purchasing software is less costly, because the company that purchases its software need not maintain a staff of programmers and analysts. 4. stand-alone. 5. system analysis.

SUMMARY POINTS

- Microcomputers, the smallest computers, are used extensively in businesses and in homes for many different tasks.
- The heart of the microcomputer is the microprocessor, which functions similarly to the CPU of a large computer.
- Microcomputers differ from other computers in capability, size, and price. Microcomputer capabilities are expanding rapidly, and therefore distinctions based on capability are becoming less clear.
- Distributed processing uses several microcomputers linked by communication lines so that processing can be done at different locations.
- Portable computers, the smallest microcomputers, are characterized by their light weight and by the fact that they do not need an external power source.
- Transportable computers are still light enough to carry, but they require an external power source.
- Minicomputers are the second smallest computers. They generally have greater capabilities than microcomputers.
- Mainframes are used by organizations that process a great deal of data. They can process data at very high speeds, hold millions of characters in primary storage, and support many input, output, and auxiliary devices.
- Supercomputers are the most sophisticated computer systems available. They perform at least ten million instructions per second.
- Local area networks (LANs) allow microcomputers in the same general locale to communicate with each other.
- Many firms specialize in developing software to sell to computer users who do not want to develop software in-house.

- A computer user can gain access to a large computer system without purchasing one by using service bureaus or time-sharing companies.
- Software packages can be stand-alone or integrated. A stand-alone package performs only one function, but an integrated software package offers two or more functions that work together and share data.
- The job of a system analyst is to help an organization choose the computer system that will best meet its needs.
- The purpose of a management information system is to help managers make decisions by providing them with useful information pertaining to the specific task at hand.
- Besides hardware and software, many other factors such as service, support, crime, and legal liability, must be considered when a computer system is designed.
- The primary trend in computer systems is that microcomputers will be used by an increasing number of people and will replace traditional mainframes in more and more companies.

REVIEW QUESTIONS

1. Explain the differences between a microcomputer and a minicomputer.
2. What is distributed processing?
3. What is a microprocessor?
4. What are some of the uses of microcomputers today?
5. What advantages and disadvantages are involved in purchasing software rather than developing it in-house?
6. What is time sharing?
7. What is a service bureau?
8. Why do companies employ the services of system analysts?
9. Why are modems important to telecommunications?
10. Describe telecommuting.

CHAPTER 5

COMPUTERS' IMPACT ON SOCIETY

Chapter Outline

Introduction
Computers at Home
Dedicated Systems
General-Purpose Computers
Information Networks
New Developments
Learning Check
Computers in Art and Entertainment
Computers in the Arts
Computers in Sports and Leisure Activities
Office Automation
Word Processing
Communication
Information Retrieval
Computers in Science
Performing Mathematical Calculations
Simulating and Modeling
Controlling Laboratory Instruments and Devices
Learning Check
Computers in Medicine
Computer-Assisted Diagnosis
Life-Support Systems
Information Storage and Retrieval
Restoring and Monitoring the Human Body
Computers in Business
Computers in Finance
Computers in Management
Computers in Sales
Computers in Publishing
Computers in Manufacturing
Learning Check
Computers in Government
Simulation and Modeling
Data Bases
Other Computer Applications
Computers in Education
Computer Literacy
Educational Software
Learning Check
Summary Points
Review Questions

INTRODUCTION

Computers are everywhere around us, influencing what we do. Consider several examples. At one time, mail took many days or even weeks to travel across the United States. Today, with the help of computers, mail can be sent electronically in a matter of hours and sometimes in even less time than that. Many tedious jobs are made easier by the computer. As will be seen in Chapter 8, a typist using word-processing software can be much more productive than when doing the jobs the old ways. Even in sports, the computer can make scheduling league games a relatively simple task. Whether in art, entertainment, science, medicine, business, government, education, or the home, computers are playing an important and ever-increasing role, as we shall see in this chapter.

COMPUTERS AT HOME

Since personal computers have become popular for home use, two distinct attitudes toward them have emerged. The first is enthusiasm. Computer enthusiasts thoroughly enjoy using their personal computers and can't wait to find other uses for them. The other attitude—aversion—is displayed by people who fear more than dislike the machine and are unwilling to adjust to the fact that computers are a very real part of their daily lives.

The number of computer enthusiasts is growing, especially as appealing new models of computers are introduced that are smaller, less expensive, and easier to use. Once a person buys a computer, the computer's success will be decided by how well it meets the purchaser's expectations. This brings us to the question of what exactly we can expect from a home computer.

Dedicated Systems

Dedicated computer
A computer that has a specific function determined by its hardware.

A microcomputer can be dedicated to one particular job, or several microcomputers together can be used to handle many of a home's mechanical functions. A **dedicated computer's** specific function is determined by its hardware. In Arizona, a computer-controlled house has been built as a showcase of automated systems. Called *Ahwatukee* (a Crow Indian word meaning "house of dreams"), this house is described as the state of the art in technology, ecology, and sociology. Visitors come by the thousands each month to view the house.

Ahwatukee has five microcomputers that run five separate systems. The environmental control system monitors heating, cooling, and the opening and closing of windows and doors. Sensors in the security system are on the alert for intruders or fire. As people move through the house, the electrical switching system senses their movement and automatically adjusts the lights. An energy management system assures the cost-efficient use of electricity. Finally, an information storage and retrieval system is included for personal and home business needs.

Of course, not all dedicated computers in the home operate on such a grand scale. Microprocessors are often built into appliances like sewing

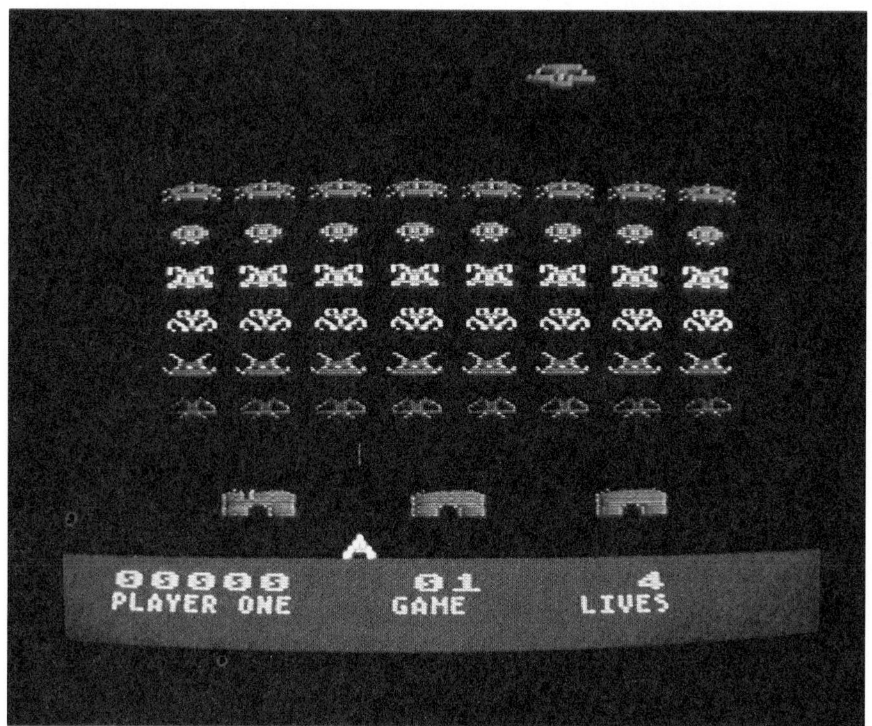

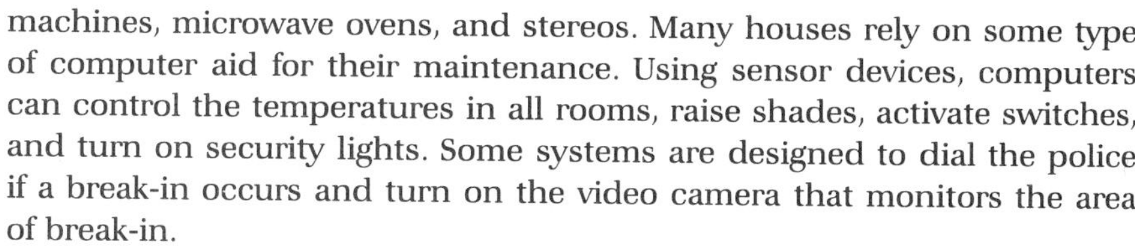

Figure 5–1 HOME VIDEO GAMES
Video games may not be only for fun. Some people claim video games build skills such as inductive thinking, spatial orientation, and the ability to deal with a number of interacting variables.

machines, microwave ovens, and stereos. Many houses rely on some type of computer aid for their maintenance. Using sensor devices, computers can control the temperatures in all rooms, raise shades, activate switches, and turn on security lights. Some systems are designed to dial the police if a break-in occurs and turn on the video camera that monitors the area of break-in.

The video game machine is probably the most popular dedicated computer in homes today (see Figure 5–1). Systems offered by companies such as Atari, Intellivision, and ColecoVision are designed only to play games. Although technically these game systems are computers, few can be used for other purposes. Most of the systems use **joysticks,** not keyboards, to control what happens on the CRT screen. However, some game companies are developing and selling add-on equipment to turn an electronic game machine into a general-purpose computer.

Joystick
A piece of equipment to control the cursor or object movement on the CRT screen.

General-Purpose Computers

In 1983 alone about five million home computers were sold, double the number sold in 1982. The prices of personal computers have dropped considerably since they first came on the market, because many manufacturers have been caught up in price wars in attempts to gain larger shares of the market. Sales, promotions, and rebates also contribute to the decrease in prices.

Beginning computer users who want to try their hand at computing can pick up an inexpensive model like the VIC-20 or the Timex-Sinclair for less than a hundred dollars. For around a thousand dollars, a sophisticated home computer such as the Apple IIe or the IBM PCjr can be purchased that will meet most of the average user's needs. The experienced user who needs a home computer to manage a small business can expect to spend between three and ten thousand dollars, which is still quite reasonable considering the usefulness of the system. In choosing the computer, the potential owner should consider what tasks it should handle. Since the tasks a computer can perform are largely determined by its software, let us take a look at some of the software currently available for general-purpose microcomputers.

Games. You swoop down in a helicopter to rescue wounded soldiers, being careful to pick up enough before taking off. Then you rush back to the 4077th to perform surgery—removing shrapnel from the patients. Have you been hired as an extra on the television show "M*A*S*H"? No, you are playing a video game on your home computer. Other games have been adapted from movies and TV shows and even from rock groups. The first rock 'n' roll video game is Journey Escape, which takes its name from the popular group Journey.

Video game software was the most common type of software purchased for home computers in 1983. In that year alone, 75 million home video game cartridges were bought by U.S. consumers, up from 60 million in 1982. However, the market for this software may have become glutted. Some industry forecasters believe that annual sales of game cartridges have peaked and will slowly drop.

Educational games are gaining popularity, particularly with younger people and parents. Today's educational software offers games that are fun, visually attractive, thought-provoking, and nonviolent. For instance, Discovery Games, developed by Children's Television Workshop and Apple Computer, introduce children to the basics of computer use: loading disks, choosing from a menu, operating the RETURN key, and so on. Other useful skills like counting, word recognition, typing, and elementary logic and reasoning are enhanced, as well as creativity and imagination.

Budgeting, Finance, and Record Keeping. For adults, one of the most useful functions of a home computer is to control the budget and checkbook, and much software designed for this purpose is available to buy. Software is available, too, for keeping all the lists and files that help run a household. Addresses, phone numbers, lists of insured possessions, charge card numbers, recipes, Christmas card and birthday records, investment information—all can be stored by computer.

Hobbies. Many programs geared toward the special interests of hobbyists are available. Such software comes in a range of prices, depending upon how deeply involved you are in the hobby and how much you'd like the program to do. For example, hardware and software are available for most personal computers that allow a music buff to experiment with music synthesis. Coin and stamp collectors can buy programs that will record their inventories and produce investment and tax reports on their collection. Computers are also used to control model trains and airplanes.

Educational Instruction. Computers can also help children and adults learn about a wide variety of subjects—math, foreign languages, speed reading, air navigation, typing, and geography, to name a few. Educational software can take the form of either a game, as shown in Figure 5–2, or a tutorial. In either case, the computer instructs, questions, and corrects responses. With these types of computer-assisted instruction (CAI), students can decide when they want a lesson—no appointments with teachers, and no getting ready to go to class.

In 1984, the National Education Corporation (NEC) began offering a system called EdNET, which lets personal computer owners study at home. Over forty courses are available to independent-study participants. Students can correspond with instructional specialists as well as take tests via their home computers. Another company, TeleLearning Systems of San Francisco, makes over two hundred courses available to home computer users.

Information Networks

One advantage of owning a computer is being able to keep up with the changing world without leaving home. Personal computers can be connected by a communication network system to a large computer that functions as a huge information center. Thus, research data once available only at the local public or university library can now be accessed at home.

Two of the largest in-home information network systems are CompuServe in Columbus, Ohio, and The Source in McLean, Virginia. For a fee, these

Figure 5–2 EDUCATIONAL GAMES
Many parents breath a sigh of relief when their children play educational computer games instead of watching TV. Children can be actively involved with computers; watching TV is a passive pastime.

on-line services bring a vast store of information to the home computer user's fingertips: video versions of major newspapers, stock market reports, airline and hotel reservation services, sports news, movie and book reviews, gourmet recipes, foreign language drills, and home buying and selling information, to name just a few (see Figure 5–3). Complete encyclopedias can be found on certain information networks. The main advantage of an electronic encyclopedia is that it is always kept up-to-date. On-line services enable customers to access the types of **data bases** described above and many more. (The term *data base,* as used here, refers to a cluster of data related to certain topics or organized to meet the needs of a special group of users. The data is centrally organized so it can be accessed by users.) Computerized banking and shopping services also use some type of network along with a personal computer.

On-line service
A company that sells access to information in its data bases and other services to computer users.

Data base
A group of data related to certain topics or organized to meet the needs of a special group of users.

The overall result of networking is that many routine activities can now be done at home faster and more easily than the conventional way. Further, the up-to-date information that networking provides is a valuable advantage to people such as researchers, businesspersons, and private investors.

New Developments

As computers have become more common in American homes, new developments have made them more versatile, easier to use, and easier to fix. Some of these developments are the "mouse," home robots, and hardware diagnostic tools.

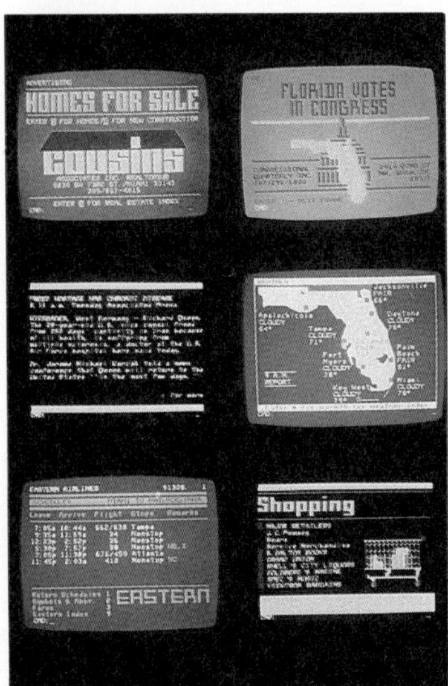

Figure 5–3 INFORMATION NETWORK MENU SCREEN
With a subscription to an information network, personal computer users have the world at their fingertips. These women are checking the week's best-selling fiction books.

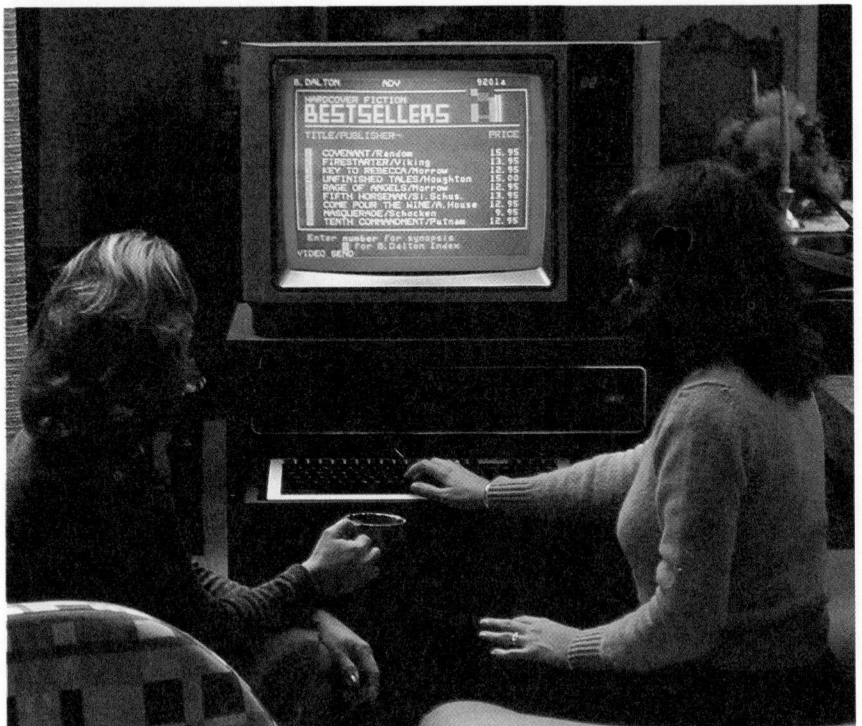

The mouse, shown in Figure 5–4, is a desktop input device. By remembering where the mouse was and sensing how it has been moved on a flat surface, the computer can tell the cursor on the screen to move in the corresponding direction. Using the mouse simplifies input and makes computers easier to use. For this reason the mouse is being used in many new computers, such as Apple's Lisa and Macintosh.

Figure 5–4 DESKTOP MOUSE
The mouse was invented in 1964 but has only recently become popular as an input device for personal computers.

Robots are beginning to make their way into the homes of many Americans. Currently, there are between ten thousand and fifteen thousand personal robots in U.S. homes. These machines are not fantasy robots like *Star Wars'* C-3PO and R2-D2 that can do almost as much as a human. What they *can* do is navigate around a room, pick up and carry objects, talk, sing, tell jokes, and act as watchdogs (see Figure 5–5). But remember that a robot must be programmed to do these things. Although robots have a long way to go before they are household fixtures, they probably will be useful in the home, just as they are in the factory.

Hardware diagnostic tools help the user figure out what to do when the computer fails to work as it should—as it invariably will, sooner or later. Most new operators panic first (thinking they broke the machine) and seek help second. However, the first order of business should be finding out where the problem lies. Hardware diagnostic tools are programs that help identify the problem. One of these, Diagnostics II, can determine if the problem is in the memory, microprocessor, disk drive, terminal, or printer. Finding an appropriate solution is then easier.

Hardware diagnostic tools
Programs that help identify problems with computer hardware.

LEARNING CHECK

1. A dedicated computer's specific function is determined by its ________.
2. Name some general types of software a home computer owner can buy.
3. When the computer instructs, questions, and corrects a user's responses, it is being used for ________.
4. An information network offers free access to information to home computer users. (True or false?)
5. The ________ is a desktop input device that moves the cursor around on the screen.

ANSWERS:

1. hardware. 2. software for games; budgeting, finance, and record keeping; hobbies; and educational instruction. 3. computer-assisted instruction. 4. false. 5. mouse.

COMPUTERS IN ART AND ENTERTAINMENT

As computers find more uses in the home, they also are emerging in the areas of art, entertainment, and leisure. Some of the computer features being used in these activities are word processing, sound production, and graphics. A trip to the theater, museum, or sports arena will yield examples of some of these uses. Other examples are brought to our homes, through

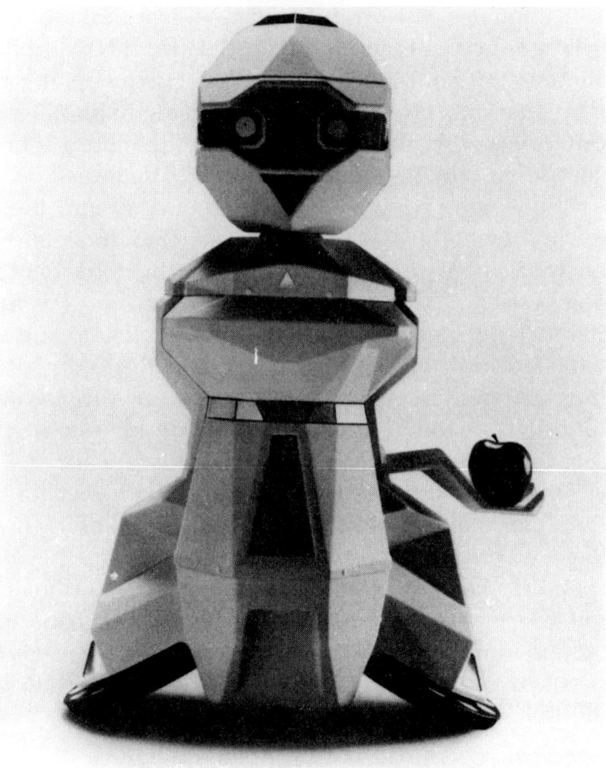

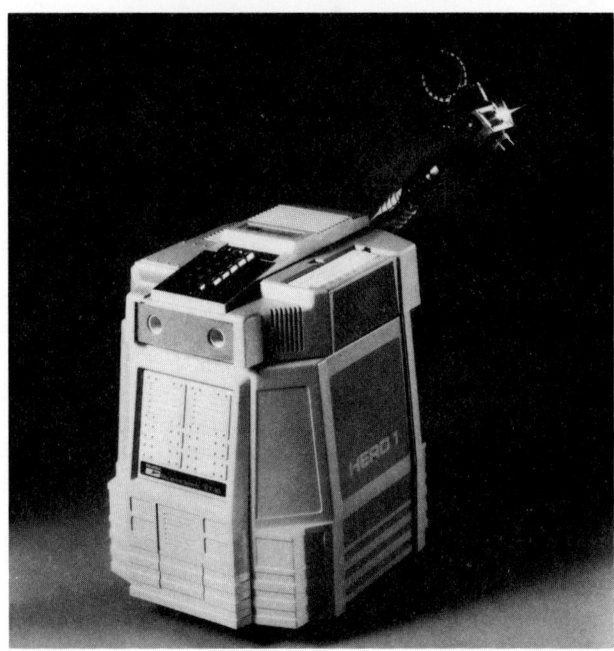

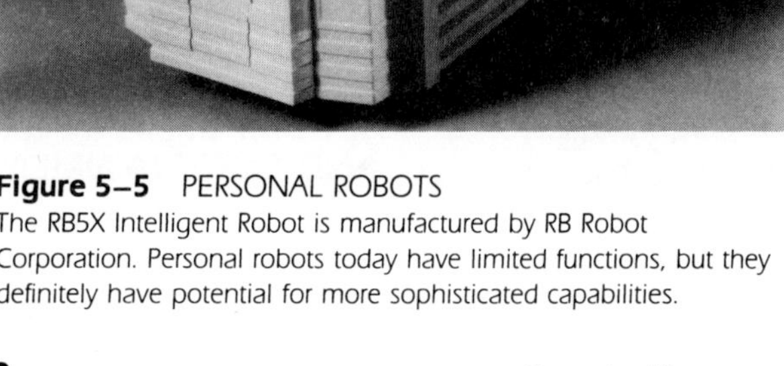

Figure 5–5 PERSONAL ROBOTS
The RB5X Intelligent Robot is manufactured by RB Robot Corporation. Personal robots today have limited functions, but they definitely have potential for more sophisticated capabilities.

television and radio. Most of us do not directly interact with the computers used to produce a work of art, a music composition, or a motion picture. We simply enjoy the effects made possible by them. Let's look at some examples.

Computers in the Arts

Computers have many applications in the arts—in graphics, music, literature, architecture, dance, and drama, for example. Computers control stage lighting, simulate music, and help artists create portraits and dazzling pictures. Word processors simplify the writing of everything from novels to newsletters.

Capturing the Movements of Dance. One fascinating use of computer graphics is to help choreographers develop dance notation—dance steps graphically displayed and explained in a written shorthand. Traditionally, no permanent record is kept of how a ballet such as *The Nutcracker* should be performed. A form of notation does exist for recording dance steps and techniques, but using it is very time-consuming. As many as six hours may be needed to hand-record one minute of dance. Filming and videotaping have been used to capture a dance, but these methods are unsatisfactory. The camera can capture only one angle, and sometimes lighting restricts what is actually filmed.

Coming to the rescue, however, are new computer graphic systems, now in their early stages of use. These systems record a dance by analyzing dancers' movements and translating the information into animated human figures displayed on a CRT screen. The computerized version becomes a permanent record of the dance.

Broadway's Computer Debut: A Chorus Line. In 1976, computers made their way to Broadway in the hit musical *A Chorus Line.* A Tony Award was given to the show's lighting director, Tharon Musser, whose company used a computer lighting system called Light Palette. Since that time, other Broadway presentations have employed computer-controlled lighting (see Figure 5–6). House lights and footlights, particularly, are controlled by the computer. Moving spotlights are still handled by electricians.

Computers and Music. The eerie rhythms of the new wave group A Flock of Seagulls, the funky rhythms of jazz keyboardist Herbie Hancock, the hypnotic sound track of *Chariots of Fire*—all are examples of how computers have changed mainstream pop music. Computerized instruments have revolutionized how music is made, how it sounds, and who can make it—professionals and amateurs alike.

Computer music systems can produce strange and wonderful sounds and store complex sequences of music for later playback (see Figure 5–7). A musician can play parts of a song into the computer, edit and mix them electronically, have the computer convert the sounds to notes, and finally, receive a printed copy of the song.

Figure 5–6 COMPUTER-CONTROLLED LIGHTING
Strand Century's Light Palette Control Console allows complex lighting changes to be programmed in advance and played back exactly as recorded or changed for live performances. Here the Light Palette and its operator control the lighting of a concert at Universal Amphitheatre in Los Angeles.

Computer music systems are efficient for radio and television commercials and movie and television sound tracks. First, computers can eliminate the need to hire musicians and rent recording studios. Second, computers can store music so it can be played for the client at any time. Changes can be made and stored as many times as necessary. Computers helped produce music for Kentucky Fried Chicken and Dr. Pepper commercials, and the theme song for the television show "St. Elsewhere" was recorded by only two men and a computer!

Computer Screens as Artists' Canvases. An exciting new medium for artists is the computer screen used with graphics tablets and light pens. An artist can use the computer in a variety of ways to create drawings, colorful

Figure 5–7 COMPUTERIZED MUSIC SYSTEMS Computer music systems are ideal for the home market because they are small, flexible, and low in cost. Some predict they will replace organs and pianos in the home.

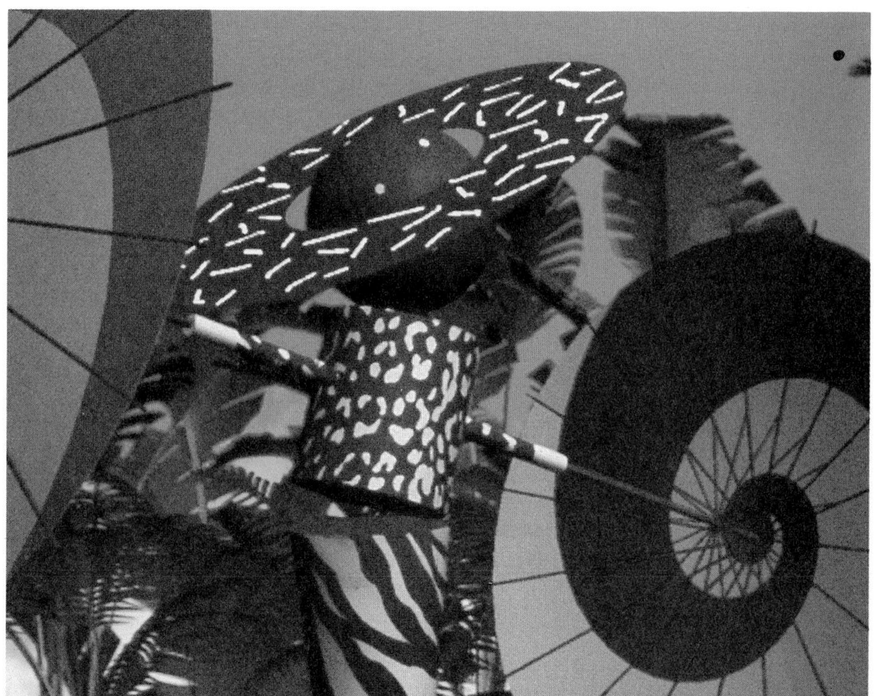

Figure 5–8 PROGRAMMED ART High Fidelity, computer animation produced by Robert Abel and Associates, shows a geometric figure dancing with umbrellas. Red and white two-dimensional textures were mapped onto the three-dimensional geometric shapes for a stylistic effect.

pictures and graphics, landscapes, or even portraits. Some artists with a good knowledge of programming create art by writing programs that generate complex patterns (see Figure 5–8). Other computer artists create pictures by drawing with a stylus on a graphics tablet. Corresponding images are represented on a CRT screen or printed out as a hard copy (see Figure 5–9).

One of the leading microcomputer artists in the United States today is Saul Bernstein. Bernstein began his art career in the early 1960s and started dabbling in computerized art in 1978. He has since gained nationwide recognition and has won an Emmy for his efforts in computerized animation. Using a stylus on a graphics tablet much as he used a paintbrush on canvas, Bernstein has created wonderful images and portraits. He was commissioned by Hewlett-Packard to produce portraits of England's Queen Elizabeth and Prince Charles. The computer portraits were so accurate the Queen thought they had been produced photographically. Other artists have also created computer art with much success (see Figure 5–10, for example).

Designing with Computer Graphics. Design specialists have recently begun using computer graphics in their art. For example, two New York firms—a design firm and a company specializing in animation and still images—combined their efforts to reconstruct a silver-plated fruit bowl designed in 1906 by the Austrian architect Josef Hoffmann. Using computer graphics, designers reconstructed the bowl, known as Rosenschale, from a single photograph, the only existing record of how thc bowl looked.

Figure 5–9 COMPUTER ARTIST
Here a Hewlett-Packard 2730A is used by a computer artist.

Figure 5–10 COMPUTER PORTRAIT

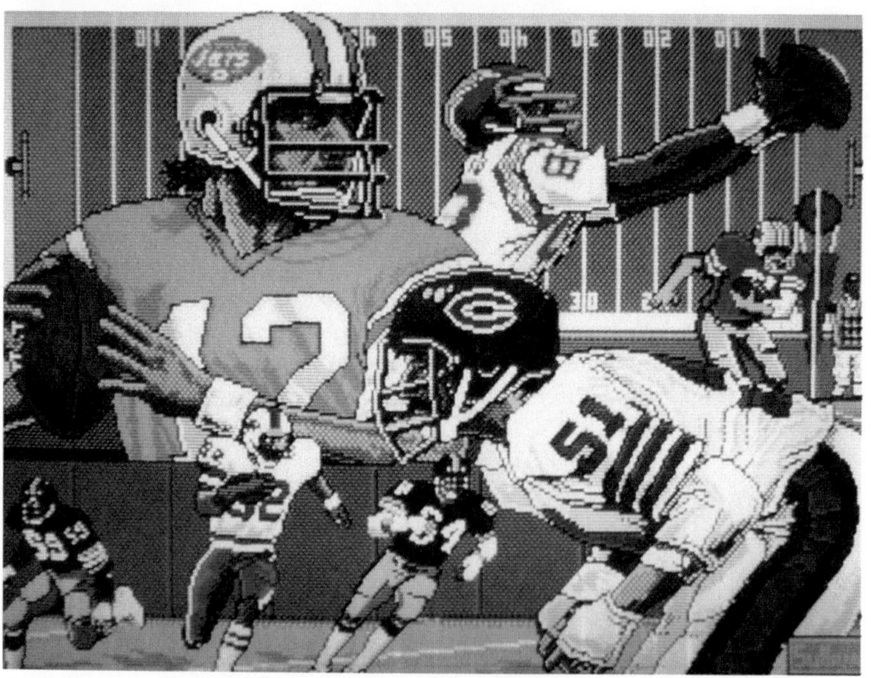

Three-dimensional reconstruction begins with analysis of a two-dimensional picture of an object. In the case of the Rosenschale, selected points from the bowl's photograph were given to the computer. These points were used to create an image on the screen. When the image was rotated, designers could study the bowl's shape by comparing each image with the original photograph. After making several models, they were able to produce an amazingly accurate replica of the Rosenschale.

Architectural firms and firms that design consumer products will be looking to computer graphics to help them recreate works of the past and complete projects already on the drawing board. There is no doubt that the design community will benefit from computer graphics.

Computers in Sports and Leisure Activities

Computers are widely used in sports and in leisure activities. In sports, the computer is most often used as it was originally intended—to calculate statistics—and is often used in scheduling games as well. Movies and television offer examples of the many ways computers help make leisure pastimes more enjoyable.

Baseball: A New Pitch. The manager of the Chicago White Sox baseball team uses a computer to calculate statistics, and many other teams follow his example. A Texas Ranger statistician has remarked, "Baseball people are definitely seeking out new and more meaningful ways to scientifically analyze the game."

Computers determine batting averages and runs batted in. They also examine how certain pitchers and hitters work together. To keep such statistics up-to-date, teams employ computer operators to record pitch-by-pitch accounts of each game (see Figure 5–11). A computer located elsewhere stores the information, which it receives from the ball park via a telephone hookup.

Baseball teams also use computer-generated graphics to study their performance. For example, computer graphics are used to analyze the paths of all fly balls hit by Chicago White Sox players.

Computers Schedule the Professionals. On New York City's Staten Island, Holly and Henry Stephenson use a microcomputer to schedule professional baseball, basketball, and soccer games. The two have written programs to plan playing schedules for the National and American baseball leagues, the National Basketball Association (NBA), and the outdoor and indoor soccer leagues, a total of 3,565 games for the five leagues.

Not only does the appropriate day for each game have to be scheduled, but also the hour and location. This brings about some problems. The Baltimore Orioles baseball team, for example, must play out of town during the Preakness horse race. Canadian teams demand home games on their national holidays, but prefer the United States for games on the Fourth of

Figure 5–11 COMPUTERIZED BASEBALL STATISTICS
Here an official of The New York Yankees' Baseball Operation Department uses an Apple II computer at Yankee Stadium. During the games, he records every play for later analysis.

July. Each season the baseball leagues play a total of 2,106 games. Developing the program for the baseball leagues alone required eighteen months of work. But once the Stephensons had a workable program, the scheduling for future seasons became much more efficient.

Computers save much work in scheduling basketball games, too. Eddie Gottlieb, former coach and owner of the Philadelphia Warriors, scheduled NBA games before the Stephensons took over the job. Gottlieb spent six months each year scheduling the league's 943 games. The computer makes the job simpler and faster.

Computers in Movie and Television Production. Hollywood, well known as the home of the film industry, is becoming known for its use of computers in movie production—to help with scriptwriting, to create and manipulate sounds, to produce spectacular special effects, and even to allow machine control of camera movement. Computers are used in television as well, in the production of both programs and commercials.

Writing and revising scripts are time-consuming jobs in both movie and television production. A typical script for a television situation comedy, for example, averages thirty pages per half-hour episode. Such a script may go through seven or more revisions. Because of the need to constantly retype

Figure 5–12 COMPUTERS IN MOVIE PRODUCTION
The film industry relies on computers for creating special effects in movies. Computers had an active role both on and off the screen during the making of *War Games.*

the scripts, Hollywood is turning to computerized word processors to help provide the revised scripts quickly.

Another use of computers in the film industry involves the creation of special effects (see Figure 5–12). For example, a supercomputer created astoundingly realistic images of futuristic spacecraft cruising through space, flying over alien landscapes, and engaging in combat for the Lorimar-Universal film *The Last Starfighter.* The realistic details of the computer-generated images—the transparency and reflections of window glass, the shininess of metal, the barely noticeable movement of clouds, the gradual build-up of dirt on the spacecraft after each battle—added to their lifelike quality.

The supercomputer used about a minute per frame to compute the special effects sequences. It then transferred the images to film. For each second of film time, the computer generated twenty-four frames. In all, the twenty-seven minutes of synthesized special effects in *The Last Starfighter* required the computer to produce almost forty thousand separate frames!

OFFICE AUTOMATION

The widespread use of computers began in the workplace—in offices, banks, and factories. People became familiar with computers gradually as they received bills that had been prepared by computers, saw their bank transactions processed, and received personalized form letters that had been prepared with a word processor. Today, most people are comfortably accustomed to the influence of computers on their lives. Probably the area in which computers have brought about the greatest change and now offer the greatest potential for complete automation is the office.

Office automation
The integration of computer and communication technology with traditional manual procedures in the office.

Office automation is a general term for the processes that combine computer and communication technology with the traditional manual procedures of office work. Office automation may be divided into three categories: (1) word processing, (2) communication, and (3) information retrieval.

Word Processing

Word-processing system
A system that allows text material to be entered, corrected, added to or deleted, and printed.

Word processing has led the advancement of office automation and is definitely the best-established technology in the office today (it is discussed in more detail in Chapter 8). Word processing involves manipulation of text data to achieve a desired output (see Figure 5–13). A typical system consists of a keyboard, a visual display device, a storage unit, and a printer. Like data processing, word processing relieves workers of time-consuming and routine tasks, resulting in increased productivity and quality. Depending on how much typing a secretary does, a word-processing system may increase his or her productivity from 25 to 200 percent.

Word processing bypasses some of the difficulties and drawbacks of traditional writing and typing. A word-processing program not only produces finished copy much faster than a typewriter but also produces it in a form that is as readable and attractive as typewritten copy, if a high-

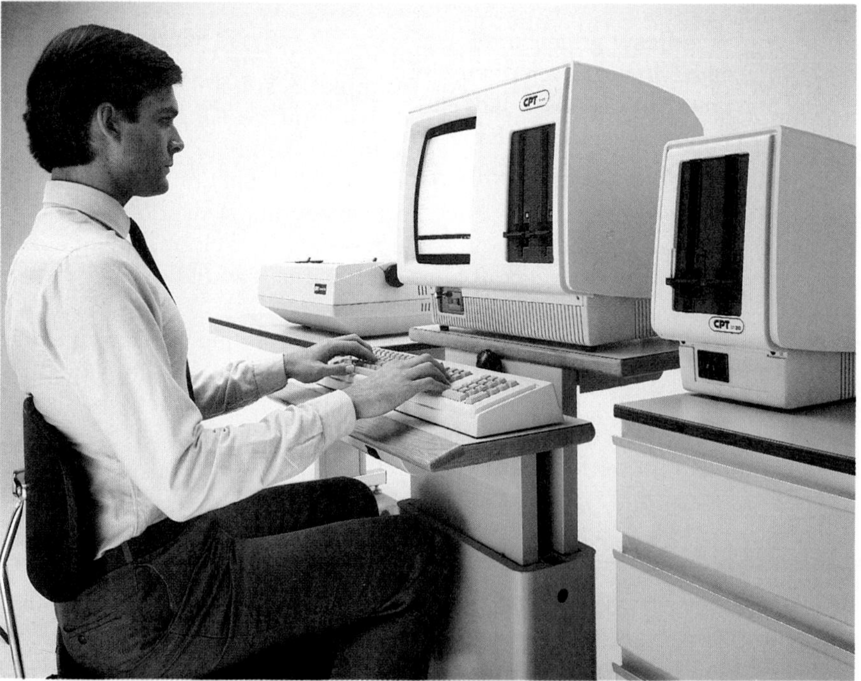

Figure 5–13 WORD-PROCESSING SYSTEM Word processing saves much time in the office by eliminating the need to retype documents and reports every time a revision is made.

quality printer is used. The secretary or other user can edit, rearrange, insert, and delete material—all electronically—and then store the result on tape or disk and/or print it for later use. Each printed copy of the text is an "original." Thus, the output of a reliable word-processing system is of consistently high quality. If numerous form letters must be typed, the secretary has only to type a single letter. By merging the letter with a file containing specific names and addresses an original, yet personalized, letter can be created.

There are other advantages to using a word processor rather than a conventional typewriter. Word processors offer many functions that make text manipulation easy. Standard features include automatic centering, boldfacing, automatic page numbering, automatic alphabetizing, and the ability to search for and find a particular letter, word, or phrase.

In addition to the typical functions of the word processor, some optional software is available. One option, a dictionary, can include up to a million words and is available not only in English but in other languages as well. Misspellings and hyphenation on the copy can be checked by the machine at the rate of one page in ten seconds. Some programs even correct misspelled words after locating them. Special dictionaries with legal and medical terms are also available.

Communication

The exchange of information between workers on different floors, in different buildings, or in different cities and states is an essential and growing part of the business world. Communication in the office can be automated to make the exchange faster and more efficient. The automation can take several forms: electronic mail, voice mail, teleconferencing, and telecommuting. Teleconferencing and telecommuting were mentioned earlier but will be expanded upon here.

Electronic Mail. **Electronic mail,** already used by many businesses in addition to regular mail, may someday replace regular mail. Commercial electronic mail services are offered by the United States Postal Service (E-COM), GTE Telenet (Telemail), and others.

Electronic mail
Messages sent at high speed by telecommunication facilities and placed in a special computer storage area where they can be read.

Used mainly for intercompany communication, electronic mail is messages sent at high speeds using telecommunication facilities. One user of the service can send a message to another user by placing it in a special computer storage area. The receiver can retrieve the message through a terminal by either displaying it or printing it. These two users need not be **on line** (in direct communication with the computer) at the same time. Electronic mail ends the cycle of returning calls only to find that the caller is out.

On line
In direct communication with the computer.

Voice Mail. A variation of electronic mail is **voice mail.** It is computer-based, but the end product is a recorded message, not hard copy. The spoken message is converted by the voice mail system into digital form and stored in the computer's memory. Using a telephone, the receiving party

Voice mail
Messages spoken into a telephone, converted into digital form, stored in memory until recalled, and then reconverted into voice form.

can recall the message and reconvert it into voice form. Several characteristics distinguish voice mail from standard answering machines. Recipients can scan the messages, keep them, or forward them to a third party. Senders can edit their messages. Voice mail also allows for longer messages than answering machines.

Teleconferencing. Teleconferencing brings about two main benefits for managers: reduction in travel time and reduction in travel costs. It may give a corporation a competitive edge by providing its executives with a convenient, fast way to meet (see Figure 5–14). Teleconferencing enables people in different geographical locations to participate in a meeting at the same time. Equipment such as electronic blackboards, which create markings on distant television monitors, and picturephones, which send a person's image and voice to other locations, make teleconferencing possible.

The costs to install and upgrade teleconferencing capabilities are its biggest drawback. For example, Atlantic Richfield Company spent approximately twenty million dollars to upgrade its teleconferencing systems. Few organizations are willing or able to spend that much.

Figure 5–14 TELECONFERENCING The use of teleconferencing is just gaining acceptance. However, some executives don't think they look businesslike on the screen. They worry about such things as disheveled hair or crooked ties.

Telecommuting. Perhaps the most exciting prospect for the automated office involves telecommuting—commuting to the office by computer rather than in person. Some companies are already experimenting with telecommuting. The system has many advantages in areas where office rent is high and mass transit systems or parking facilities are inadequate, and in businesses that do not require frequent face-to-face meetings among office workers. Telecommuting also provides greater flexibility for disabled employees and working parents.

Since it represents a major change from past practices, telecommuting is not widely accepted. Some employees are not sure they have the discipline to work as well at home as they do in friendly office surroundings. Managers fear that employees out of sight may be employees out of control. Thus, telecommuting is likely to appear first at the managerial level and filter down to lower-level employees as its worth is demonstrated.

Salespeople, who are often away from their offices, have been successfully using a kind of telecommuting by taking portable computers and tiny printers along with them on their sales trips. The portable computer can be used to type memos, letters, or reports. In addition, some portable computers have editing capabilities similar to those of a word processor. With a portable computer and a modem, the salesperson can send information over telephone lines back to the office (see Figure 5–15). Once the information has been received at the office, phone messages, edited copy, or other information can be sent back to the salesperson. Other employees can use telecommuting in the same way.

Information Retrieval

Information retrieval—getting stored information to users in a form they can understand—is an important part of office automation. In the past, users often had to look through entire reports to locate information they needed if they were not sure where it was. To avoid this expensive and time-consuming process, they now can use an electronic file management system.

Data-base management and text management systems have been designed to allow users direct access to company information. The information may be in the form of data, text, image, or voice. The user specifies key words and asks the computer to search through large volumes of text and produce lists telling where those words were used.

Information retrieval is not limited to sources or files inside the company. Companies may subscribe to the commercial on-line information services discussed earlier (see Figure 5–16). Access to on-line data bases allows workers to receive the additional information they need very quickly.

COMPUTERS IN SCIENCE

Computers handle a variety of tasks in the broad area of science. Some categories of tasks in which computers can be helpful are in: (1) performing

Figure 5–15 TELECOMMUTING TERMINAL One futurist, Jack M. Nilles, Director of Interdisciplinary Programs at the University of Southern California, estimates that by 1990, 15 to 20 percent of American workers will work from their homes.

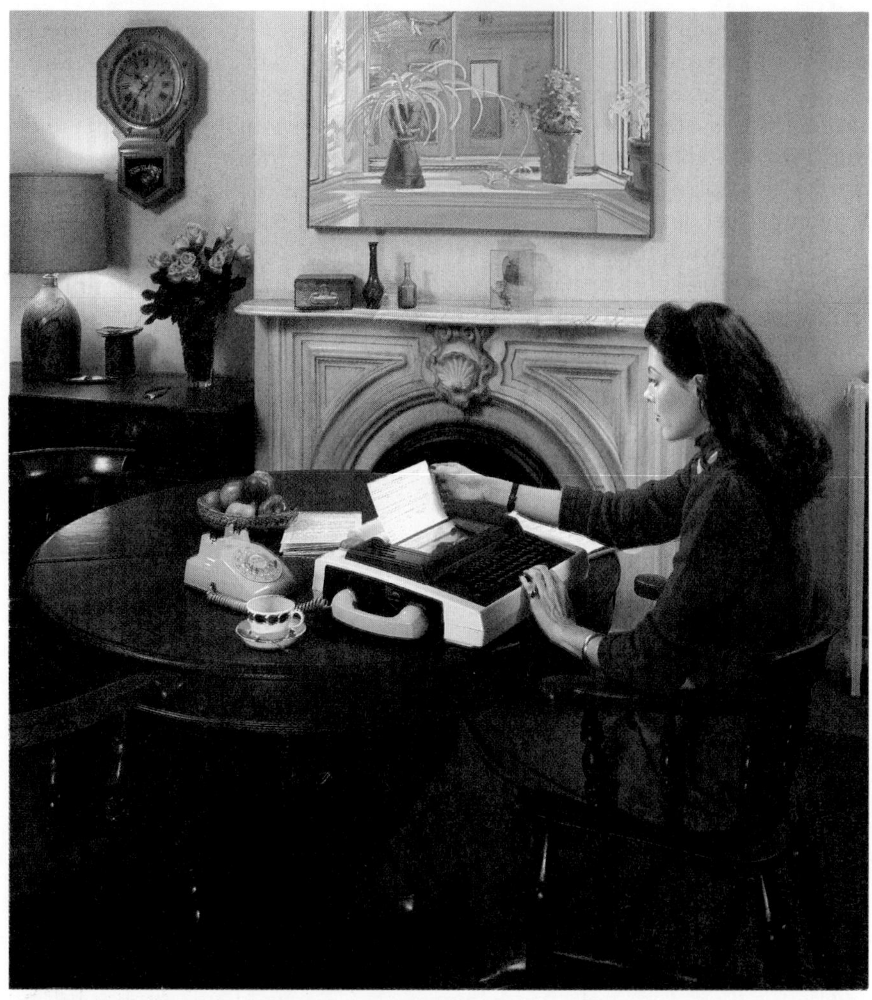

Figure 5–16 ON-LINE INFORMATION SERVICE Office workers access one of the many data bases available from The Source.

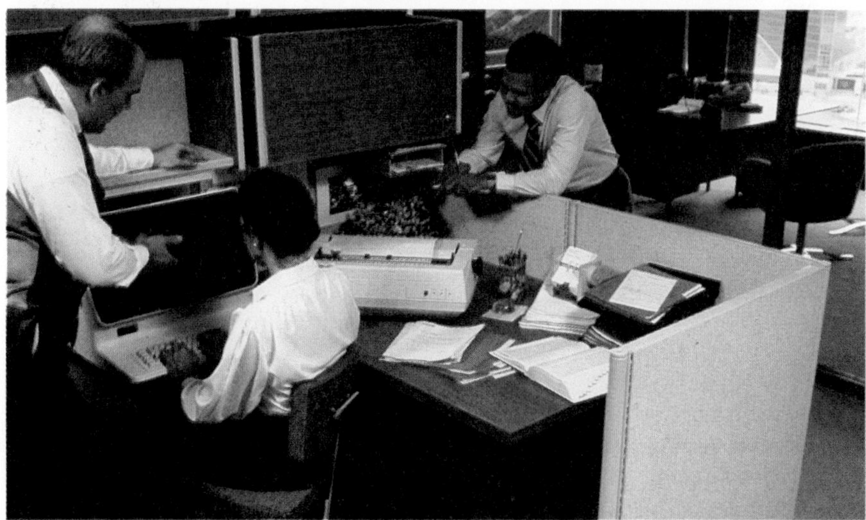

mathematical calculations, (2) simulating and modeling, and (3) controlling laboratory instruments and devices.

Performing Mathematical Calculations

Because of the enormous volume of data that must be stored and processed for some scientific tasks, supercomputers are used to handle the requirements. They process vast amounts of data and produce output in a form that is easy to read and interpret.

An example of computers used to handle large volumes of data is offered by Landsat satellites, which orbit the earth and take pictures. Approximately 30,000 overlapping pictures must be recorded to get a view of the whole earth. The pictures show infrared radiation from the sun that is reflected by the earth. Each of the 30,000 scenes photographed is electronically composed of thirty-two million tiny squares called picture elements, or **pixels.** The wavelengths and intensity of light in a Landsat photograph are measured and changed into digitized electrical impulses. These pulses are stored in magnetic memory. When a ground receiving station is in range, the pictorial data in memory is broadcast into the station. Once received at the station, the data is entered into a computer. Experts reassemble the tiny pixels into photographs that can be interpreted by scientists with the aid of the computer (see Figure 5–17). Scientists observing the pictures can then identify areas of healthy or sick vegetation.

Pixel
One of the many image points comprising a graphic display.

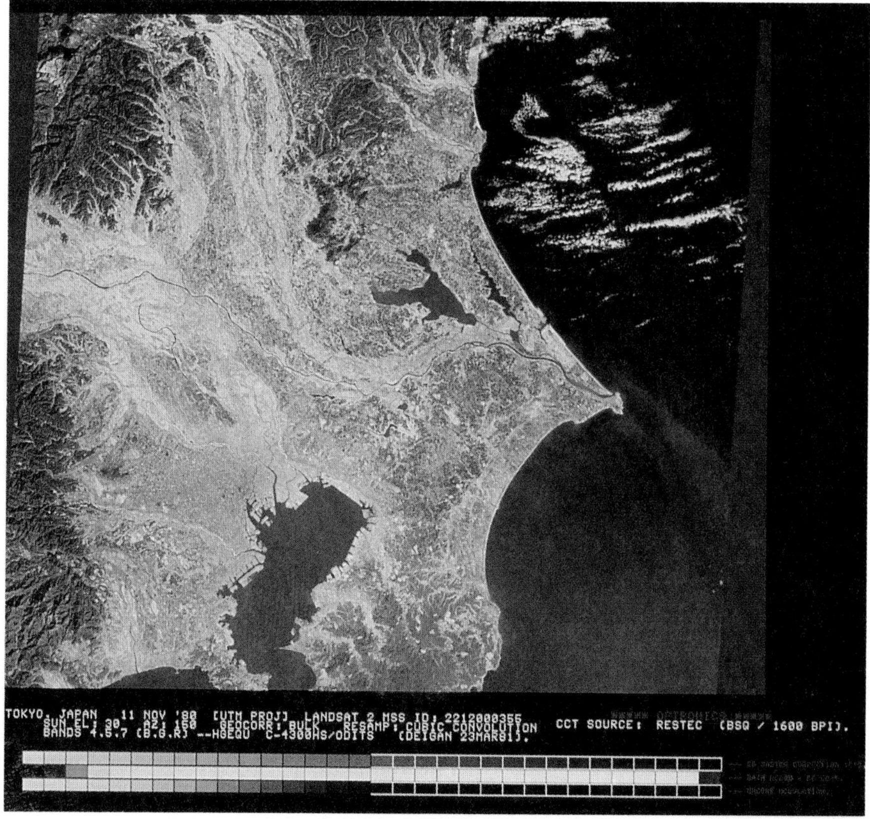

Figure 5–17 LANDSAT
From 570 miles above Tokyo, Japan, this computer-generated Landsat picture defines subtle details in surface geology. Urban areas appear in light blue, Tokyo Bay appears in dark blue, and land under cultivation appears in red.

Real-time system
A system that receives data, processes it, and provides output immediately.

Some scientific tasks require **real-time** mathematical calculations. Real-time refers to the way a computer can process data so fast that it gives immediate feedback. Since real-time computer systems are so quick, they are often used as emergency systems to warn of potential or actual danger. Real-time systems are found in the chemical industry, nuclear power plants, space flight operations, air traffic control, and medicine, all areas in which an immediate alert to problems is crucial.

For example, a crises such as the one at the Three-Mile Island nuclear power plant may be avoided in the future with emergency management systems (see Figure 5–18). One system designed for the chemical industry uses computers to monitor wind velocity and direction, temperature, and toxin levels through chemical sensors located around the plant.

In an emergency, the system supplies instructions and emergency telephone numbers to workers as soon as the problem is discovered. A light pen makes the system easy to use. When a map is displayed on the screen, the user touches the pen to the area where a chemical spill has occurred or uses the pen to answer questions about the spill displayed on the screen. Nearby residents are automatically warned through a prerecorded telephone message. Since the residents are being warned by the computer, the plant personnel are free to work with civil defense people and to mobilize resources within the plant itself.

Simulation
Duplication of the conditions likely to occur when certain variables are changed in a given situation.

Simulating and Modeling

Computers are also used for simulating and modeling. The computer is programmed to consider certain facts (which are stored in memory) and then come to a decision. The computer makes **simulations** by duplicating the conditions likely to occur when certain variables are changed in a given situation. In the chemistry lab, chemical reactions can be simulated on a

Figure 5–18 EMERGENCY MANAGEMENT SYSTEM
The SAFER system (left) is an emergency response system that alerts industrial companies of toxic releases that could pose harm to employees and residents in nearby areas. The display frame (right) shows the essential graphic information helpful in an emergency.

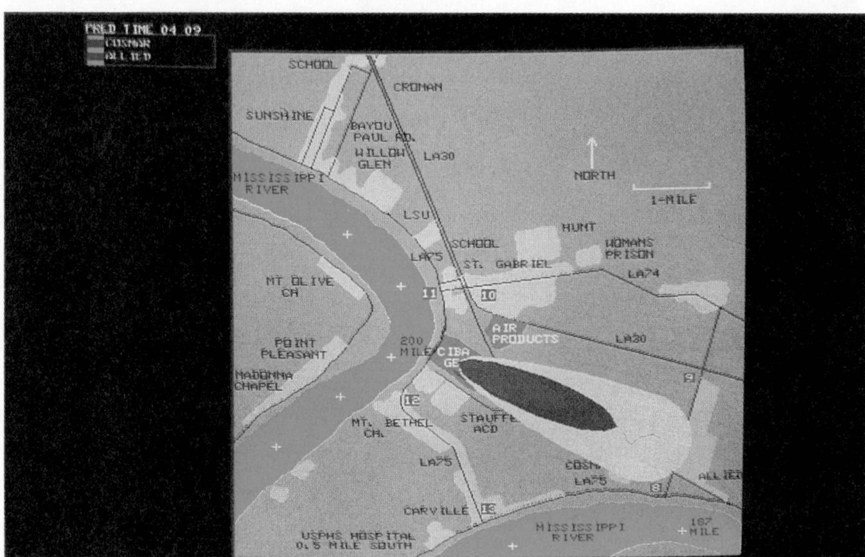

computer. The main advantage of computer simulation is that explosive or otherwise dangerous reactions can be discovered without endangering the chemist or destroying the lab.

In computer **modeling,** the computer constructs a model (or *prototype*) of some object on the video screen. Shapes and sizes can easily be changed to alter the model. Computer models are used in many fields, such as astronomy, ecology engineering, and chemistry. Engineers and designers of airplanes, for example, usually design an aircraft on a computer before building a real model. Many "bugs" can be worked out on the computer, which saves the time and money involved in building model after model.

Modeling
Computer construction of models, or prototypes, on the video screen.

Sometimes simulation and modeling systems are referred to as **expert systems,** because they make decisions using the same information that experts in the field would use. Computer systems programmed to contain the knowledge of geological experts are used to assist oil companies in this way. These systems help oil companies examine geological data and advise them where to drill. Usually, an instrument called a dipmeter has to be dropped down a hole to measure geological conditions. A human specialist then has to read the dipmeter, and these experts are scarce. Computer expert systems can replace the specialist and dipmeter, and have proven to be almost as successful in determining where to drill for oil as the traditional method.

Expert system
Simulation and/or modeling systems that use the information a human expert would to make decisions.

Controlling Laboratory Instruments and Devices

Computers can also control various pieces of laboratory equipment. A program enables the equipment to operate both quickly and "intelligently." The use of computers in this area allows the researcher to spend valuable time conducting other experiments rather than overseeing the instruments.

Computers are used to reduce both the time and cost involved in the study of cells at the California Institute of Technology in Pasadena. DNA is a chemical that carries genetic information in human cells. Strands of DNA used to be synthesized (cloned) using a manual process which took several weeks and sometimes months. This process costs from two to three thousand dollars. A computer can perform the same task in less than a day for only two to three dollars. Since the procedure involves much repetition, the computer can also perform the task with very few mistakes as compared to the manual method.

COMPUTERS IN MEDICINE

Most computer applications in the medical field are found in hospital settings. However, the use of minicomputers and microcomputers is growing quickly in other settings as well—in doctors' offices, in research labs, and in the human body itself. Breakthroughs in medical technology, brought about with the help of computers, are keeping the quality of health care in the United States at an impressive level.

LEARNING CHECK

1. In what three main ways can office work be automated?
2. Electronic mail and teleconferencing are both ways to automate ______ in the office.
3. What does *on line* mean?
4. What type of mathematical task is characterized by immediate feedback?
5. Computer ______ helps work out "bugs" in product designs before actual prototypes are built.

ANSWERS:

1. word processing, communication, and information retrieval. 2. communication. 3. in direct communication with the computer. 4. real-time mathematical calculations. 5. modeling.

Computer-Assisted Diagnosis

Computer-assisted diagnosis *Use of computers to evaluate medical data to show variations from normal.*

Computer-assisted diagnostic techniques are used to evaluate medical data about a patient and compare the results with normal or standard values to reach a diagnosis (see Figure 5–19). Two examples of **computer-assisted diagnosis** used in clinics and hospitals are multiphasic health testing (MPHT) and psychiatric testing.

Multiphasic Health Testing. When a patient goes to a center that conducts multiphasic health testing, he or she is asked to answer questions concerning personal health and family history. These answers are put in a form the computer can read. The results of a battery of tests—such as vision

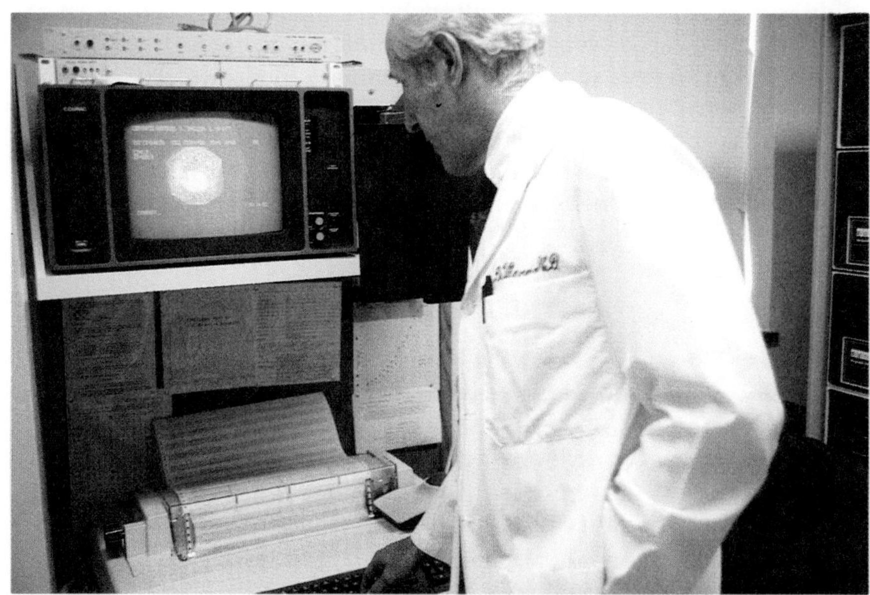

Figure 5–19 COMPUTER-ASSISTED DIAGNOSIS Radiology departments in hospitals are using computers to assist doctors in diagnosis. Here a radiologist reviews a computerized image and a printout of information regarding the image.

and hearing tests, pain tolerance evaluations, chest x-rays, and blood tests—are also computerized. The computer compares the patient's test results against an established "normal limit" or a mean.

The computer then produces printouts of the findings, including any abnormal test results and necessary information from the patient's medical history. The tests can be administered by nurses, and the printouts reviewed by trained physicians. The final results, along with the physician's recommendations or remarks, are sent to the patient's family physician, who can then be consulted by the patient.

Psychiatric Testing. Computers are now being used to help psychiatrists and psychologists in diagnosis. What the computer does is ask the patient questions taken from established psychological tests. (For example: Are you married? Do you drink? Are you depressed?) Depending upon the answer, the computer responds with appropriate follow-up questions. When the test is completed, computer programs analyze the answers and prepare a report to help the therapist understand the patient's problem.

Critics of the use of computers in psychiatry point to a reduction in contact between patient and doctor, misuse by therapists, and the questionable quality of many programs. However, using computers has noticeable benefits as well. One psychologist in Virginia says his patients' bills have been reduced by about 50 percent. He also believes that his clients are more honest with the computer than with him, because they don't feel as if they're being judged.

Life-Support Systems

Only a few years ago, twenty-four-hour nursing care was needed for critically ill patients. Now computers can be used to monitor information about patients in intensive care and coronary care units. Computers monitor physiological variables such as heart rate, temperature, and blood pressure. The computerized monitoring system frees the nurse from constant watch over critically ill patients. The computers provide an immediate alarm if any abnormality occurs, allowing the nurse to react promptly. Typically, information on as many as eight patients can be displayed at the nurse's station.

Information Storage and Retrieval

Doctors and hospitals keep vast amounts of information about many patients. Records of medical history, laboratory tests, doctors' notes, and harmful reactions to drugs are far easier to keep when computers are used. Computers also perform clerical and administrative functions in both hospitals and doctors' offices. Automated patient billing, personnel payroll, and drug inventories are just a few areas in which computers help make administrative operations easier and faster.

Restoring and Monitoring the Human Body

New uses for computers in medicine are emerging daily while older uses are being improved. Originally, artificial pacemakers for humans used transistors to control the heart's beating. But they could only stimulate the heart at a fixed rate of pulse, even though a healthy heart beats at varying rates. Early pacemakers were also heavy—almost seven ounces, which is about three to five times heavier than recent models. Today, programmable pacemakers that use microprocessors enable doctors to program up to thirty separate functions, such as delay between pulses, pulse width, and energy output per pulse. In this way, a pacemaker can be programmed to match each patient's particular heart problems. Some of the more sophisticated pacemakers can even store heart-performance data for retrieval by the physician.

Another use of microcomputers in medicine is to control the movements of artificial limbs. Electrical signals from muscles in an amputee's upper arm, for instance, can generate natural movements in the artificial arm and hand (see Figure 5–20). These new artificial limbs are so sophisticated that they are powerful enough to open jars or crack walnuts yet able to pick up a tomato or a styrofoam cup without crushing it.

Yet another application, still in the experimental stage, is a computerized device called PIMS (Programmable Implantable Medication System). PIMS is a three-inch minicomputer that can be implanted in the body. It is programmed to release measured doses of a drug over time. When drugs are taken orally, once or twice a day, the amount of the drug present in the bloodstream varies over time. By overcoming this variation, PIMS should revolutionize the treatment of chronic illnesses such as diabetes and high blood pressure.

Figure 5–20 ELECTRIC HAND
The first totally electric elbow and hand system was developed by researchers at the University of Utah Center for Biomedical Design. The Otto Bock hand (developed by an orthopedic company in West Germany) is part of the "Utah Arm" prosthesis, which is made for people whose amputation is above the elbow.

COMPUTERS IN BUSINESS

In business, computers have had a greater impact than anywhere else in society. This is due in part to the fact that computers speed operations, reduce mistakes in calculations, and give companies efficient, cost-effective analyses—all important aspects of business. Another major reason for the great impact of computers in business is the domino effect. If Business A speeds up its operations by using computers, then Business B must also computerize to compete. Although there are countless computer applications in business, we will touch on five general areas: (1) finance, (2) management, (3) sales, (4) publishing, and (5) manufacturing.

Computers in Finance

In the past, financial transactions were calculated either by hand or by calculator and recorded with pencil and paper. This method has become obsolete as computers have moved into every area of finance.

General Accounting. General accounting software is a very popular type of business software. In fact, it was the first business software to be offered for use with personal computers. Some of the most common uses of general accounting software in business involve preparation of checks, reports, and forms. Forms, because of their repetitive nature, are well suited to computer processing. Form-oriented accounting packages are responsible for the great number of "personalized" form letters travelling through the U.S. Postal Service. General accounting packages that produce reports keep people informed of everything from grades to monthly gas bills. Checks seem to be the most popular type of output by general accounting programs—at least with those who receive them.

Many accounting programs are designed to perform more than one task. These more sophisticated packages are especially useful to businesses that have computerized most or all of their accounting processes. For example, a department store may have an accounting program that records sales, maintains inventory, and handles billing as well. These types of programs help to eliminate repetition of incoming data and also lessen confusion by performing related tasks at the same time.

Financial Analysis. Today, the most common use of the computer in financial analysis involves the **electronic spreadsheet.** A spreadsheet is a large grid divided into rows and columns. Spreadsheets are used to design budgets, record sales, produce profit-and-loss statements, perform general accounting and bookkeeping, and aid in financial analysis. Although electronic spreadsheets are useful in many areas of business, nowhere are they more helpful than in financial analysis, where forecasts must be made to determine profit margins, sales, and long-term strategies. The reason for the great impact of the electronic spreadsheet in this area is its ability to quickly and accurately answer "What if?" questions. It does this by recalculating all figures when one variable is changed.

Electronic spreadsheet
A large computerized grid divided into rows and columns; used for financial analysis.

For example, if the financial analyst for a clothing manufacturer wants to see how a change in the number of jeans sold would affect the financial status of the company, she could simply enter the projected sales into the computer. Using an electronic spreadsheet, the computer could quickly recalculate all figures that would be affected by the sales figure, such as the cost to manufacture the jeans and the profit. In very little time, the financial analyst could see how profits would go up or down depending on the number of jeans sold. Spreadsheets are discussed in detail in Chapter 9.

Computers in Management

Managers use computers to keep records about employees, customers, suppliers, and business transactions. They also use computers to prepare reports, gather statistics, and send and store correspondence. But the core of business is communication, and computer graphics is becoming an essential part of business communication. In many businesses, computers are used to produce graphs that keep management informed and up-to-date on company statistics, sales records, inventory, and other important data. It is widely agreed that such displays can help managers to make better decisions.

Business graphics have come a long way from the once-standard black line bar graph. Although bar graphs are still used, they have been brightened up. Pie charts, bar graphs, line graphs, and area graphs that are brightly colored and clearly marked can be far more effective in communicating important data than pages upon pages of words and numbers (see Figure 5–21). Executives prefer receiving their information through graphics not only because graphics are attractive but also because they communicate quickly and effectively. Like the engineers and artists who use the computer's graphic capabilities, many executives have come to believe that a picture is worth a thousand words.

Computers in Sales

Businesses use computers in a variety of ways to record sales, update inventories after sales, and make projections based on expected sales. In addition to these standard functions, some computers are also being used to directly serve the customer.

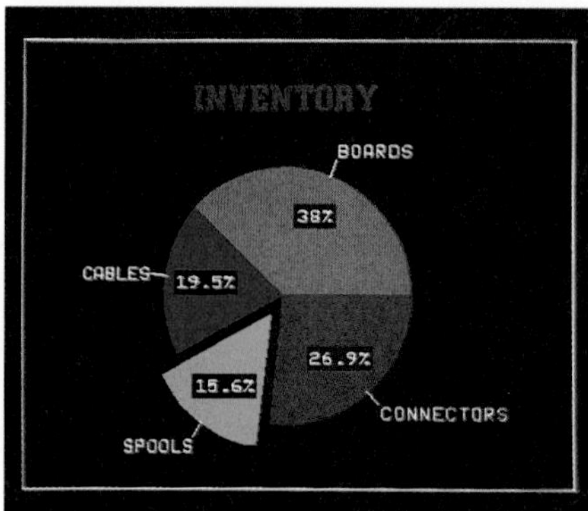

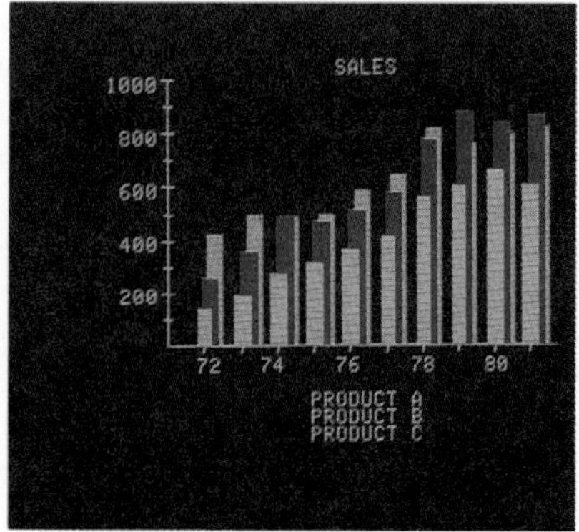

Figure 5–21 BUSINESS GRAPHICS Managers like graphics produced by a computer, such as this pie chart and bar chart, because they summarize information in an easy-to-understand, visual manner.

The Helena Rubenstein cosmetic firm triggered the movement of computers onto the sales floor. The firm introduced computers to help customers in their decisions about perfumes, make-up, and colorings. The effort was very successful and inspired similar applications by other companies.

Computers in Publishing

Almost all businesses require some type of publishing, whether it involves customer information pamphlets, quarterly reports, or entire books. Publishing itself is one of the largest businesses in the United States.

Publishing, consisting of a series of separate operations that end in a final printed product, is a prime candidate for computerization. First, the original manuscript may be written on a word processor. (This is often the case in business, when many people have to approve a document, because many revisions may be required. Word processing makes these updates easier and faster.)

Once the manuscript has been recorded on word-processing equipment, the writer can either transmit the manuscript over phone lines, using a modem, to the publisher's computer or simply mail the floppy disks or tapes. The publishing company can then edit the material on its word processor and send the edited version to the typesetter's computer. Once that computer has typeset the manuscript, it can be printed by a computer-controlled printer, such as a laser printer. The manuscript need never be put on paper until it is actually printed for distribution.

Computers in Manufacturing

Manufacturing, which involves designing and making products, uses computers to become more efficient. It does this in two ways: (1) with special computer-aided design and manufacturing systems (CAD/CAM) and (2) with robotics.

CAD/CAM. Before a product can be produced, it must be designed. The actual design process can be quite time-consuming and costly. **Computer-aided design (CAD)** allows the engineer to design, draft, and analyze a new product idea using computer graphics on a video terminal (see Figure 5–22).

Computer-aided design (CAD)
The use of the computer to help design, draft, and analyze a product; uses computer graphics on a video terminal.

The designer, working with full-color graphics, can easily make changes so the product can be tested before the first prototype is ever built. For example, a CAD system is able to check the designs for poor tolerance between parts and for stress points. This can save a great deal of money by eliminating defective designs before money is spent on building them.

Computer-aided design is often coupled with **computer-aided manufacturing (CAM),** and the combination is known as CAD/CAM. Using CAD/CAM, the engineer can analyze not only the product but also the manufacturing process.

Computer-aided manufacturing (CAM)
The use of the computer to simulate the steps in the manufacturing process.

Robotics. A new class of workers is being called upon to perform undesirable or dangerous work in businesses all over the world. During the

Figure 5–22 CAD
This engineer uses computer-aided design to develop and refine the design of an automobile. Changes can be made in the design before an actual model is built.

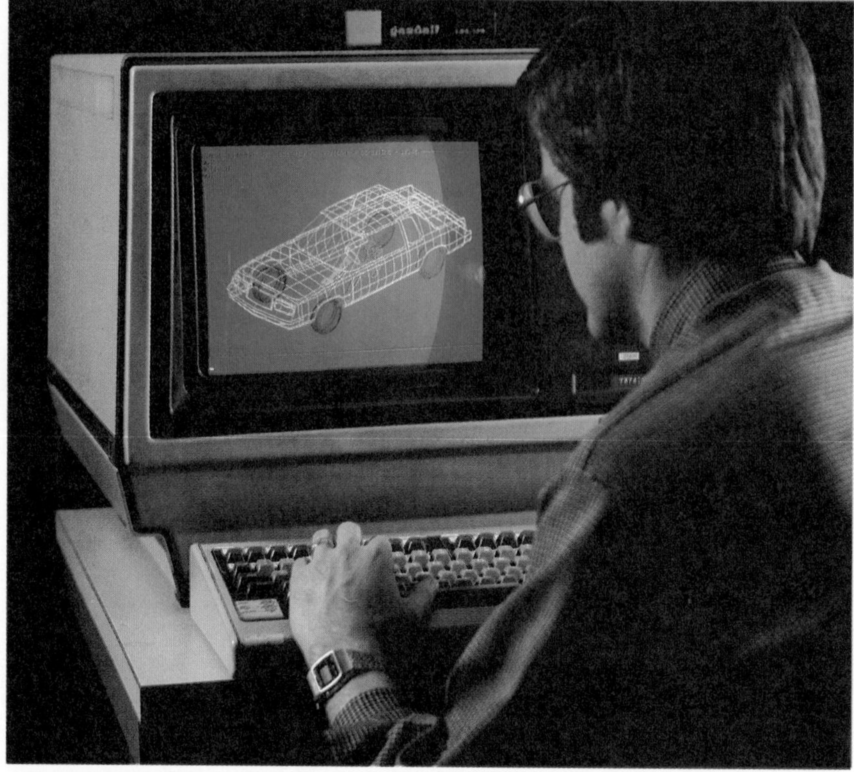

1960s, these workers were assigned simple jobs like spot welding and spray painting. By the 1980s, their duties were much more complex. They began handling nuclear wastes, moving materials, and mining for coal. These are the steel-collar workers, better known as robots.

Robotics
The science dealing with the construction, capabilities, and applications of robots.

Robotics is the science that deals with the construction, capabilities, and applications of robots. Most robots are used to perform tedious, dangerous, or otherwise undesirable work in factories (see Figure 5–23). These industrial robots can work where humans cannot, and do not need protective devices. They never need time off; a typical industrial robot is up and running 97 percent of the time! And the quality of work never suffers. Further, management never has to contend with sick, tired, or bored robots. The machines never complain, go on strike, or ask for higher wages.

Robots are expensive to purchase. However, they can do the work of several or many human laborers; so in the long run, they can save a company quite a lot of money. It is no wonder that the number of industrial robots in the world almost tripled in two years, from 13,700 in 1980 to 31,000 in 1982. By 1990, it is estimated that there will be 330,000 robots in operation around the world.

Some people are afraid that robots may cause mass unemployment. It is true that assembly-line workers sometimes lose their jobs to robots. Many people point out that the use of robots will lead to the need for workers to build, program, maintain, and repair the machines. Still, if robots can take over even those jobs in the future, we may be justified in wondering about the possibility of a "robotized" society.

Figure 5–23 ROBOTICS
Cincinnati Milicron's electricity-driven industrial robot performs a welding operation on stainless steel golf club heads.

LEARNING CHECK

1. Give some reasons why computers have had such a great impact on business.
2. A(n) ________ is used in financial analysis to quickly and accurately answer "What-if?" questions.
3. When computers are used in the publishing industry, the manuscript need not be printed on paper until it is being prepared for final distribution. (True or false?)
4. ________ is often teamed with computer-aided design and referred to as CAD/CAM.
5. Give some reasons why robots are commonly used to perform dangerous jobs.

ANSWERS:

1. Computers speed operations, reduce mistakes, and give efficient, cost-effective analyses. 2. electronic spreadsheet. 3. true. 4. Computer-aided manufacturing. 5. They can work where humans cannot, can perform tasks humans cannot, don't need protective devices, and never tire.

COMPUTERS IN GOVERNMENT

The federal government is the single largest user of computers in the United States. Computers are used by the government to collect and process scientific information. They are also used to gather data on individuals. The two major ways computers are used in government are for simulation and modeling and for data bases.

Simulation and Modeling

Military Applications. Computers have long played an important part in the Department of Defense's weapons development program, doing everything from simulating wars, to designing and testing weapons, to guiding missiles (see Figure 5–24). Both the U.S. Navy and the U.S. Army use computer simulation as a teaching tool. Computer "war games" not only teach tactics, but also provide players with real information, such as real ships' names and data on the accuracy and range of weapons.

The purpose of the Navy's battle simulation game and the Army's nuclear-war simulation is to teach officers to consider both the costs and the benefits of battlefield strategies. It is hoped that the training will prevent unnecessary loss of lives if these officers are confronted with a real-life situation.

National Bureau of Standards Fire Prevention Models. Computer modeling techniques are being tested by the National Bureau of Standards to help with fire prevention. Fire prevention models answer questions about, for example, how quickly a fire spreads, how material burns, and how intense a fire must be before the fire alarm goes off. For maximum effectiveness, the models must include many variables, such as type of furnishings, construction materials used in the building, and chemical makeup of the air. Models can also be used to devise evacuation paths for people in buildings and to aid fire fighters in predicting what areas fire is likely to spread to in a burning building.

National Weather Service Forecasting. Forecasting weather is one of the most interesting applications of computers in government. Huge computers process complex mathematical equations that describe the interaction among many variables, such as air pressure, velocity, humidity, and temperature. Combining this data with mathematical models allows forecasters to predict the weather.

Figure 5–24 WAR SIMULATION
This officer uses the computer to simulate a wartime situation. The display screen represents various situations that might arise in an actual war.

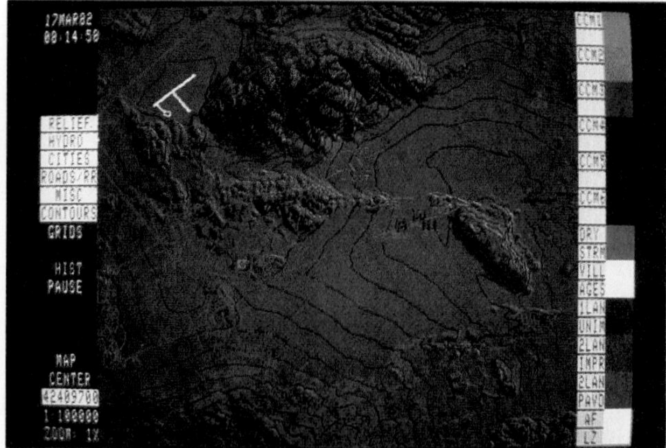

The world's weather information is collected by the National Weather Service in Maryland from a variety of locations: hundreds of data-collection programs (DCPs) placed on buoys, ships, helium-filled balloons, and airplanes; about seventy weather stations; and four satellites. Of the four satellites, two orbit the Earth over the poles to send pictures revealing the movement and shape of clouds. The other two are stationary and photograph the Earth above the equator.

The service's "brain" consists of fourteen computers housed at the meteorological center in Maryland. These computers receive information from some of the DCPs, which beam data up to the two stationary satellites above the equator. The computers also receive information from other DCPs as the information travels from ground station to ground station. The fourteen computers use this incoming data to construct a mathematical description of the atmosphere. These weather reports—two thousand daily—are then sent to local weather offices.

Data Bases

Data bases, large files of information on individuals and documents, are used most frequently by the government. Much of the information in these data bases is acquired from the census returns filed each decade and the income tax returns filed annually. Three of the largest data bases are maintained by the Library of Congress, the Federal Bureau of Investigation, and the Internal Revenue Service.

Library of Congress. The work of the Library of Congress has been radically changed by the computer. The library's storage, retrieval, and printing system now converts library cards into digital images on optical disks developed by Xerox. Under the old system, the library's file cabinets ran the length of a football field. The same information is now stored on about thirty fourteen-inch optical disks. Each disk holds the equivalent of 200,000 cards.

Federal Bureau of Investigation. Another keeper of many, many records is the Federal Bureau of Investigation (FBI). The bureau's master index alone contains nearly five million index cards. To make its records more useful, the FBI has organized several computer data bases and is working toward having all of its five hundred or so offices connected to the data bases by the end of the 1980s.

Internal Revenue Service. Every person living in the United States who earns over a certain amount of money must report to the federal government for tax purposes. In addition, corporations and businesses file annual tax returns. The Internal Revenue Service (IRS) receives millions of tax returns each year. Computers are used by the IRS to monitor these returns and record the information. Without the aid of computers, it would take years to process just one year's worth of returns.

Other Computer Applications

Air Traffic Control. The nation's air traffic control system is expected to become more fully automated over the next decade, at a cost of about $85 billion. This cost includes new computers, advanced radar systems, collision avoidance equipment, and other technological devices. Elements of the ground control system will be built into the plane's cockpit, so the required number of controllers and technicians will drop by about one-third. The display screens currently monitored by two or three controllers will be monitored by one controller with a wider area of air space in his or her control.

Medicaid Payments. After a computer took over payment of federal Medicaid claims in Pennsylvania, the state realized a $12 million savings. The state's 29,000 doctors annually produce around 22 million invoices for the system, which services 1.1 million Medicaid recipients. The savings were achieved by a reduction in the number of erroneous, fraudulent, and duplicate health claims.

Before the state obtained a Univac computer, incoming doctors' bills were paid manually, making it practically impossible to identify duplicate bills. The old system also made it difficult to spot Medicaid recipients who were overusing the system by visiting the doctor too frequently.

COMPUTERS IN EDUCATION

Most people realize that computers will be vital to the adult success of today's youngsters. Parents are demanding from their public schools courses that will prepare their children for this complex technological world (see Figure 5–25).

In addition to teaching about computers, schools often also teach with computers. Computer-assisted instruction (CAI) in the schools is not new. In its traditional format, CAI rarely teaches skills that are new and seldom presents material in an unusual manner. For example, computers are commonly used to drill students on multiplication tables or state capitals. Yet advantages do exist. Each student receives instruction adapted to his or her learning pace, immediate feedback, and motivation from sound and graphics. With a computer as teacher, the teacher-learner relationship is not threatening. The computer is the ultimate in patience and good nature. Even very young children learn to be comfortable with teaching machines. In the long run, this early familiarity with computers may be the most durable lesson for everyone.

Computer Literacy

Computer literacy
Knowledge of how to use computers and understanding of their societal implications.

Not everyone agrees on a definition of **computer literacy,** but most feel that being comfortable using computers to solve problems of both an academic and a personal nature is important. This means that students must at least gain a knowledge of simple programming techniques and the functions of various hardware components.

Many literacy courses are designed so that students also gain an understanding of how computers work, for instance, by examining chips or circuit boards and by taking apart hand calculators, digital watches, and computer games. In this way, students learn to identify the parts of a computer; they can follow the path electricity takes, and they can learn about the practical need for and the use of the binary number system.

To prepare students for adulthood in a highly technical society, literacy courses often examine the effects computers have on society. Knowing the history of computers, their current uses, and projected future trends are all important in understanding how computers are changing our lives.

Educators are also realizing that some form of computer manners must be taught. Students must learn that invading business files, making unauthorized use of communications networks, and pirating software are unethical.

The key to computer literacy is to require students to use computer skills in other classes and in their personal lives. Computer techniques can be taught but also must be reinforced by the entire culture. This means that the traditional practice of providing computer training only to students gifted in math must be replaced. All children, regardless of sex, academic achievement, or the financial resources of the school district, must be provided with computer training. Otherwise, a cultural split between those who can compute and those who cannot will arise. Such a split has already been observed in many high schools and colleges. The math and science departments, but not the humanities departments, have long been using computers. Most colleges are only now beginning to see that computers will affect the lives of all people.

Figure 5–25 COMPUTERS IN THE CLASSROOM Most children are enthusiastic about computer programming courses. Some schools install computers in kindergarten classrooms with great success among students.

Colleges were the first to make extensive educational use of computers—simply because students at this level could come to terms with computers at a time when the machines were still unusual and difficult to operate. Now more and more colleges are requiring students to have their own microcomputers (see Figure).

Learning about computers usually occurs first in classrooms, and not just at secondary and post-secondary levels. Some schools have introduced kindergarteners to computers with good results.

Computer application in education requires that all teachers have computer training. To meet this need, teachers are attending classes and then returning to their schools to lead workshops for other teachers. In many cases, teachers are also learning from their students—situations that, when approached with a good attitude, can be of benefit to both teacher and student.

In the area of computer training, perhaps the hardest fact to accept is that education is never over. Technology has reached no plateau, and no one expects it to reach one soon. Teachers, children, adults, engineers—nearly everyone who wants to stay computer literate—can *never* stop learning.

Educational Software

The quality of the software available for educational purposes is low and many times not even adequate for its intended use. There are two reasons for this. First, educators have felt so much pressure to rush into computer education that they have rarely stopped to look at the situation at hand or think about future needs. They have fought to get the latest equipment and software for the least money and often have found themselves without a well-thought-out plan for using their purchases. Second, most educational software on the market is sadly unimaginative because most software publishers, hurrying to be the first to get their products on the market, neglected software design. Administrators who wanted to get their computers in use had little choice but to purchase these inadequate packages.

It could be said that educational software is only at the first-generation level. However, some new programs have become available recently that make the situation brighter. Educators and software manufacturers alike are finally becoming aware of the need for good educational software and well-planned systems.

Just as television and automobiles changed the daily lives of people the world over, so will computers. We now have a bright beginning for what will be the largest industry in the United States.

LEARNING CHECK

1. Large ________ are maintained by the FBI, IRS, and Library of Congress to keep information about individuals and documents.
2. What advantages does computer-assisted instruction provide?
3. Students who are ________ feel comfortable using computers, are acquainted with programming, and understand simple hardware components.
4. What type of student should be offered computer training?
5. There is a great deal of excellent software available for the educational market. (True or false?)

ANSWERS: 1. data bases. 2. Each student receives instruction geared to his or her learning pace, immediate feedback, and motivation from sound and graphics. 3. computer literate. 4. All students, regardless of sex, academic achievement, or the financial resources of the school district, should receive computer training. 5. false.

SUMMARY POINTS

- Dedicated computer systems can control various mechanical functions in the home. Security and energy conservation are common applications of this sort.
- Many home computers are used for keeping financial records.
- Educational software allows adults and children to learn at home. Some companies provide computerized courses, including tests, for home computer owners.
- Networks and on-line services allow computer users to communicate with other users outside their immediate environment and provide access to large stores of information.

- Office automation combines computers and communication technology to replace or help with manual office procedures. Word processing, communication, and information retrieval are areas in which automation can be applied.
- Automated office communication may use electronic mail, voice mail, teleconferencing, and telecommuting.
- Computer-assisted diagnosis is becoming more common in medicine. A patient's test data is entered into the computer, which compares the results against established normal limits to help make a diagnosis.
- The use of computers in science can be divided into three categories: performing mathematical calculations, simulating and modeling, and controlling laboratory instruments.
- Simulation and modeling systems are sometimes called expert systems because they copy the way human experts approach a problem to find a solution.
- In financial analysis, "What if?" questions are easily answered when electronic spreadsheets are used.
- Computer graphics are often used in business to condense large amounts of data into charts and graphs that are easy to understand. The use of computer graphics helps managers make accurate and timely decisions.
- CAD/CAM systems allow engineers to design, draft, and analyze products and manufacturing processes before building real models.
- Industrial robots, sometimes called steel-collar workers, are used to perform undesirable or dangerous jobs in businesses.
- The federal government is the single largest user of computers in the United States. Government computers are most commonly used for simulation and modeling and for data bases.
- Achieving nationwide computer literacy will require that computer education be available for all young people. All children, and all teachers as well, must be taught to use computers so that a gap does not develop between those who know how to compute and those who do not.

REVIEW QUESTIONS

1. What is a dedicated computer? Give three examples.
2. Name at least four types of software commonly used with general-purpose computers in the home.
3. What is an information network?
4. What sort of information is available to home computer owners who subscribe to CompuServe or The Source?
5. What is a hardware diagnostic tool?
6. Name two different ways computers can be used to produce art.
7. In what ways are computers used to automate office tasks?
8. How do computer-generated business graphs help managers?
9. How does computer-aided design (CAD) save time and money for a company designing new products?
10. In what ways can students be taught to be computer literate?

CHAPTER 6

ISSUES OF CONCERN

Chapter Outline

INTRODUCTION

The impact computers have on our lives goes beyond workplace, classroom, industry, and government. Society is rapidly being changed as computers become commonplace. Many issues have arisen that are both personal and controversial. No clear-cut answers have been found to questions concerning privacy, computer ethics, and computer crime, for example. The next few years should bring about more discussion and legislative action on such issues. Anyone who uses computers or is affected by them should be aware of what these issues involve.

PRIVACY

Computers are the main means by which businesses and government collect and store personal information on credit, employment, taxes, and other aspects of people's lives. Thus, the issue of privacy is an important concern. Since the early 1970s, many people have become worried about the amount of information being gathered about them. As a result, some laws and regulations have been enacted regarding privacy and the use of information about individuals.

Data Bases

Government agencies, banks, credit unions, universities, and many companies keep data banks that contain information about customers, students, employees, and other groups of individuals. Computers have made it easier for organizations to obtain data; so it is tempting for them to acquire more data than they really need. Computers also make it possible to store a great deal of data in one place, and to retrieve it easily. For these reasons it is common for organizations to possess records on individuals that contain much personal information. Many people fear that their privacy is threatened because these records are so easily accessible.

Usually, all data about an individual is stored on one main file. The file can be accessed simply with the person's social security number or some similar identification number. This means that getting into a person's file is, many times, as easy as finding out his or her employee number or social security number. Thus, a real danger involves unauthorized access to records.

The major concerns surrounding the issue of privacy in the age of computerization are the following:

- Too much information about individuals is being collected and stored.
- Information may be inaccurate, incomplete, or out-of-date without the person's being aware of it.
- Sometimes organizations make decisions only on the basis of the contents of computerized records.
- Security of the stored data can be a problem. As indicated above, gaining unauthorized access to a file can sometimes be as easy as finding out a social security number.

In spite of its disadvantages, computerizing data about individuals can reduce costs and increase efficiency for an organization. For example, it is helpful for a bank to know a customer's financial background before granting a loan or for a department store to see a customer's past credit history before giving credit. However, the right balance must be found between an organization's need for information and an individual's right to privacy.

Privacy Legislation

Efforts to protect citizens' privacy have led government, particularly at the federal level, to pass laws and regulations. Most important is the Privacy Act of 1974, which covers information gathered by the federal government. This act, which applies only to federal agencies, provides that:

- Individuals must be able to determine what information about them is being recorded and how it will be used.
- Individuals must be able to correct wrong information.
- Information collected for one purpose should not be used for another without consent of the individual involved.
- Organizations that create, manipulate, use, or divulge personal information must ensure its reliability and take precautions to prevent its misuse.

Some states have adopted laws similar to the federal legislation. Unfortunately, the lawmaking process is slow on this issue, in part because lawsuits over privacy are rare. Since data may be disclosed without the knowledge or consent of the subjects, most people do not know when their privacy has been breached. If they did know, many still would not pursue lawsuits, since they would be making public the very information they wanted protected.

COMPUTER ETHICS

The issue of computer ethics becomes increasingly important as more and more Americans become computer literate. By the year 1990, it is estimated that half the country's labor force will know how to use computers. Any of these people might possibly engage in unethical practices when using computers, both at work and at home. For this reason, instilling some code of computer ethics in everyone who works with computers will be essential.

What exactly is unethical behavior for computer users? There is no clear-cut answer. Think about the following questions and the ethical issues they involve:

- Should an employee be able to use the company computer for personal use?
- Should an employee be able to access the records of other employees?
- Should a company be allowed to add personal information not related to work performance to an employee's computer files?

- Should supervisors keep track of a typist's speed at all times, of how often employees leave their work stations, or of employees' phone calls?
- Is it merely unethical for a person to tap into on-line information networks accessible over phone lines, or is it also a crime?

These questions plus many related ones are the concern of employees, employers, teachers, students, and parents.

One particular problem involves software piracy. Between $200 million and $600 million in sales are lost every year from illegal copying of software. Copying software that has been copyrighted is illegal.

Software is covered by the U.S. Copyright Act of 1976. Although the creator of an original work is considered to possess the copyright from the moment the work is fixed in some concrete medium, he or she gains additional protection by registering the work with the Copyright Office. Registration ensures for the copyright owner the right to bring suit against copyright violations. The creator registers a program by completing Copyright Office registration form TX, paying a ten-dollar fee, and submitting a copy or identifying portion of the program to the Copyright Office.

A copyright notice protects the owner's copyright. In the notice, the symbol ©, the word *copyright*, or the abbreviation *copr.* should appear with the name of the copyright owner and the year of the work's first publication.

What is covered by the copyright? The law makes it illegal to copy a software program except for archival use, which means that one backup copy may be made.

The copyright also protects the object code, the instructions that actually run the computer. These instructions reside in the operating system, applications programs, or ROM (read-only memory). A court precedent set in the case of *Apple vs. Franklin* extended copyright protection to the object code. Apple Computer, Inc., charged the Franklin Computer Corporation with copyright violations for duplicating the operating system programs contained in the Apple II. Apple was granted an injunction to prevent Franklin from selling the Ace 100, the computer which contained the duplicated operating system.

Software vendors have protected their products in other ways besides copyright registration. Many vendors have designed protection codes to make copying disks more difficult. The problem with protecting a disk is that it prevents consumers from making an archival, or backup, copy, which is legal.

Sometimes consumers buy special software that enables them to break the protection codes and make backup copies. Some of these programs include *Locksmith, Nibbles Away,* and *Crack-Shot.* But having access to a code-breaking program increases the temptation to copy disks for friends. It creates one more area in which the user's conscience must rule.

What code of ethics about software would you set for yourself? Would you use a code-breaking disk to make more than one copy? Would you buy a pirated disk, even if you had nothing to do with the copying? Would you make multiple copies of programs in computer magazines? Would you copy from an electronic bulletin board a program that you suspected was pirated? These questions must be addressed if a code of ethics is to be established. The code of ethics will measure behavior against conscience.

The only real solution to the ethics problem is to try to teach ethical behavior to beginning computer students and users, just as business people are taught that it is unethical to accept bribes and doctors are taught that it is unethical to betray a patient's confidence. Both schools and organizations can accept the responsibility of teaching ethics to students and employees. Schools can only try to point out general standards of conduct. But organizations can set definite standards for employees to follow, with penalties to discourage unethical behavior.

CRIME AND SECURITY

Computers can play a role in activities on both sides of the law. They can help prevent and solve crimes, working toward the good of society. Just as easily, however, they can be used for illegal purposes. Persons who commit crimes with the aid of computers can be computer experts armed only with a home computer, programmers writing hidden instructions into programs, or seemingly respectable employees ranging from data-entry clerks to top executives. Computer crimes are difficult to detect, and the laws protecting victims are few. To protect the computer system and the information it stores, organizations and individuals should give serious thought to computer security. Failure to provide adequate security can lead to loss or alteration of data, loss of money, and even the ruin of the system.

Crime Prevention

The FBI maintains a system that keeps track of information on known criminals and on persons considered to be threats to public officials such as the president, vice-president, and visiting heads of state. The FBI's National Crime Information Center is linked to 64,000 federal, state, and local agencies and is one of the most elaborate communication systems in the world (see Figure 6–1).

The Secret Service receives around nine thousand reports a year about people who might pose a threat to public officials. Of these, three hundred to four hundred are considered actually dangerous. By putting the names of persons considered potentially dangerous into the FBI's computer, the Secret Service can find out which persons have criminal records, whether they've been arrested, or whether they're on parole. In addition, local law enforcement officials can quickly find out if a person they have arrested is wanted for committing a crime anywhere else in the country or is suspected of some wrongdoing by the Secret Service.

There is some concern that the FBI is monitoring innocent persons, which may cause harm to their reputations. The controversy exists because determining who poses a potential threat involves very subjective judgment. Factors considered threatening may vary from agent to agent.

Figure 6–1 THE NATIONAL CRIME INFORMATION CENTER
The FBI maintains a central data base of facts about many people and organizations.

Computer-Aided Detection of Crimes

The federal government began using a nationwide computer system in 1984 to track killers who have committed several murders. The five-million-dollar system is similar in operation to the National Crime Information Center's system. It allows police to tap into a clearinghouse of information gathered about murders committed across the nation (see Figure 6–2). Previously, law enforcers had no way to connect crimes committed in different states. Now police can enter details of local killings into the computer at the FBI Training Academy in Virginia. Similarities in crimes committed in different locations can be noted and appropriate actions taken.

In New York City, computers help authorities pinpoint likely targets for arson. Several agencies input data on recent fires along with other information, such as data on landlords who are behind in their taxes and buildings that have been cited for safety violations. Out of this data, the computer produces profiles of the most probable arson targets. City officials can then watch these buildings and tell the owners how to lessen the risk of fire. One advantage of this program is that owners who may think about burning their buildings to collect insurance money know that the city is watching them.

Computer Crime

Law enforcers are not the only people who seek the computer's power. While law enforcers use computers to gather, process, and deliver infor-

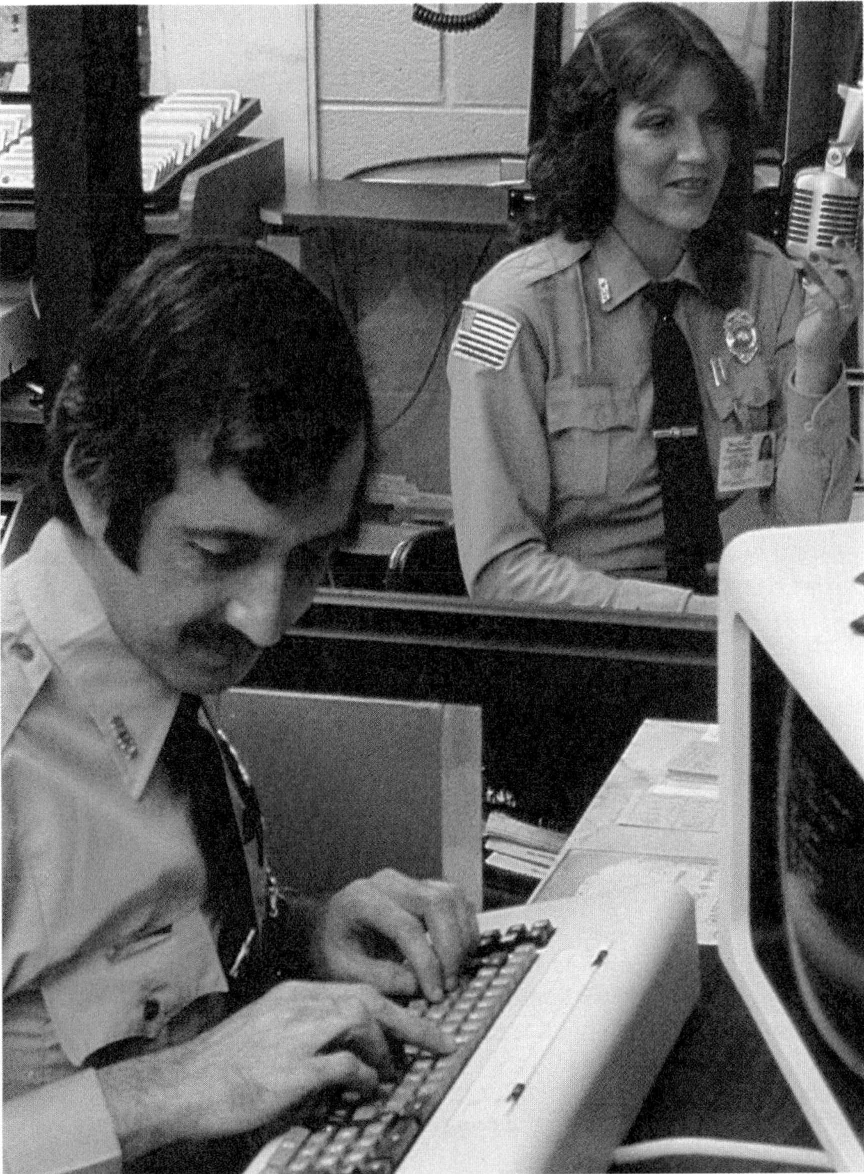

Figure 6–2 COMPUTERS IN LOCAL POLICE WORK
Police in cities and towns use computers to keep track of local criminal activities, as well as to access larger data bases of the FBI and state policing agencies.

mation to help them prevent and detect crimes, law breakers see in computers an opportunity to commit crimes.

In dishonest hands, the computer can become a tool used to steal money or data or to invade someone's privacy. Estimates of losses from computer crime vary greatly. Some experts believe that annual losses range from a hundred million to a billion dollars; others believe the figure should be as high as five billion dollars.

The main reason no one knows exactly how much money is lost because of computer crime is that only a fraction of computer-related crimes are detected. Of the ones detected, only a fraction are reported because many companies fear that the publicity will make them a tempting target for other criminals or that stockholders will panic.

Computer-assisted crimes can take several forms. Probably the most commonly discussed is embezzlement. Computers can be programmed to manipulate payrolls or other financial records. For example, an IBM Corporation employee embezzled $210,000 by depositing customers' checks in his own account, then altering company records by using IBM computers. In another instance, a hospital programmer stole more than $100,000 from his employer by programming the computer to issue checks to phony hospital supply companies.

Stealing data or any valuable computer output is a second form of computer crime. The thief may sell important company information to competitors, as one employee sold his company's customer list for a million dollars. The thief may also try to hold the information for ransom or just use it himself. In 1983, a salesman for a national wine distributor "borrowed" his employer's computerized client list to set up his own company. (He did return the list after the owners threatened to sue.)

Computers can be used to send merchandise and other valuable items to the wrong place. One group of employees stole over $500,000 worth of merchandise from their employer by having the computer send it to the wrong location, where they picked it up and sold it themselves.

A final type of computer crime worth mentioning occurs when frustrated employees, business competitors, or political opponents sabotage a computer system. In New Hampshire, a programmer for a service bureau planted an instruction that would have ordered the company's computer to destroy important records. Luckily, the company found the command, but only by accident.

It is not only trained experts or hardened criminals who crack computer security to tamper with the systems. Students of high-school age (and sometimes even younger) who have become expert computer users routinely challenge themselves by making electronic raids on the computer systems of schools, companies, and government agencies. A group of Milwaukee teenagers who called themselves the "414s," after Milwaukee's area code, used their home computers, connected to phone lines, to snoop through more than sixty computers during the summer of 1983. The FBI finally caught them invading the computer at a nuclear weapons laboratory in New Mexico.

What the 414s brought to light is that no computer system is completely secure. If a group of teenagers with limited resources can tap into the systems of companies and government agencies with ease, what can be done by someone who has very good resources? Because thousands of computers are linked by phone networks, outsiders can gain access to some computers by dialing a local number and typing in the right password on their keyboards. Employees have even easier access; they often know their companies' computers, passwords, and codes. In seven hundred cases of computer crime recorded since 1977, 85 percent involved current or former employees.

Computer security can help prevent computer crimes, or at least make them more difficult to commit. Organizations must take responsibility for providing adequate security measures for their systems to avoid the damages caused by break-in and tampering.

Computer Security

Computer security involves both the system's equipment and the people using it. First, users should be involved in their system's design so that they have some say about how secure they would like it to be. Designers, operators, and users should have proper education and training in the ethics of computer use.

The other aspect of computer security, the equipment, includes devices and programs designed to make the system accessible only to authorized users or to make the data unusable if it does get into the wrong hands. Devices can be installed that use a secret code to scramble data. Only authorized users can get the data in its unscrambled form.

Another security measure requires the user to phone the computer, give a password, and then hang up. If the user and password check out, the computer calls the user back and allows access. This dial-back method ensures that the user is calling from an approved location and that the password corresponds to that location.

A newer method to prevent unauthorized access requires authorized users to pass four tests before access to the computer is granted. The tests ask for (1) something the user knows, such as a password; (2) something the user alone can supply, such as a fingerprint; (3) something the user can do, such as write a signature; and (4) something the user has, such as a magnetic card. Such combinations make it difficult for an intruder to pass all the tests.

Some simple security measures should be followed by any organization that uses a computer system. One is careful screening of all employees who work around computers. This includes programmers, analysts, and data-entry clerks. Another is firing of employees who violate the rules set down for computer use. Security must be taken seriously by everyone involved if it is to be successful.

Computer security cannot be ignored at home, either. Home computers contain significant amounts of valuable personal information that must be protected—confidential financial, medical, and insurance information about family members, for example. Also, more business materials will be kept on home computers as more workers participate in telecommuting. As more home computers become parts of total information networks, protection from unauthorized access will become even more important for home computer users.

Legislation Regarding Computer Crime

The federal government has been slow to pass legislation regarding computer crime because of disagreements about what computer crime is, how often it occurs, and what to do about it. As of mid-1984, twenty-one states had passed their own computer crime laws. Most are related to defining computer crime and setting penalties for it. For example, the Massachusetts state government passed legislation imposing punishments of up to five years in prison and twenty thousand dollars in fines for anyone convicted of damaging computers or software, keeping or destroying software without authorization, entering a computer system with the intent to defraud, or manipulating data to get money, property, or services.

However, just as computer technology changes rapidly, computer laws rapidly become obsolete. Another problem is that some prosecutors do not understand the crimes or the laws, so they hesitate to prosecute cases related to computer crimes. For these reasons and others mentioned earlier, most wrongdoers never are taken to court.

LEARNING CHECK

1. The amount of data collected about a person, the accuracy of the data, and the use of the data are elements in the issue of ________.
2. Computers have made it easy for organizations to ________ data and to store a great deal of data in one place.
3. The Privacy Act of 1974
   a. protects all aspects of privacy.
   b. protects privacy in relation to information gathered by federal agencies.
   c. protects privacy in relation to information gathered by local agencies.
   d. allows individuals to change any data about themselves that they wish.
4. Copyright law protects
   a. privacy.
   b. original creations, such as software.
   c. ethical behavior.
   d. security.
5. Ethics measures ________ against conscience.
6. The federal government has passed much legislation to define and set penalties for computer crimes. (True or false?)

ANSWERS: 1. privacy. 2. obtain. 3. b. 4. b. 5. behavior. 6. false.

INTELLIGENT COMPUTERS: ARE WE READY FOR THEM?

A major effort is being made to develop software that will supply computers with **artificial intelligence (AI),** the ability to think and reason as humans do. The field is not new, and several approaches to artificial intelligence are being investigated. Since there are various theories about exactly how humans think and reason, there are also various ideas about how to develop artificial intelligence in computers.

Expert Systems

Expert systems use what is known about how humans think to build computer programs that imitate the human decision-making process. Data related to a specific problem is stored in the computer. The computer draws upon this data to make decisions just as a human draws upon information stored in the brain. New expert systems are being designed now, and several are already on the market. One of the better-known experimental expert systems, called CADUCEUS, diagnoses medical problems. CADUCEUS contains a store of data on 600 diseases and 2,500 other factors, such as symptoms, laboratory data, and so on. By cross-referencing the two categories, the user can either retrieve information on a certain disease or enter symptoms that can then be linked by the program to a disease. In essence, CADUCEUS incorporates the knowledge of an experienced doctor to generate a diagnosis.

Expert system
Software package designed to imitate how human experts think through a problem to a solution.

Artificial intelligence researchers want to go beyond expert systems, which use only the data submitted and do not exhibit the common sense of humans. Expert systems can only be used for well-defined problems in which the data needed to draw conclusions is easily identified.

Computers with Common Sense: Two Views

In order for artificial intelligence to be truly successful, computers must be able to imitate the way humans think. Humans use more than stored information to think through problems and make decisions. Few problems can be solved without using common sense along with stored information.

So far, no theory about how humans make decisions using common sense has been agreed upon. Even the founders of AI, Marvin Minsky and John McCarthy, disagree. However, both men agree that the basis of common sense depends on the ability to recognize exceptions. For example, the statement, "Birds can fly," is usually true. But there are exceptions. What if the bird is dead, has an injured wing, or is a penguin? Then the statement is no longer true. For a computer to recognize such exceptions, it would have to be programmed to test for every possible exception, which would be quite a task.

Minsky and Roger Shank, the chairman of the computer science department at Yale University, have similar ideas about how to program computers with common sense capabilities. They believe a human has some idea of how a certain situation will progress, based on memories of past experiences. A human tends to associate a new situation with some past experience stored in memory. Computers, then, must be given some way to associate one situation or concept with another but still allow for exceptions (the most difficult part).

Another view, McCarthy's theory, is about assumptions. McCarthy believes that humans assume that a fact is true unless given a reason why it is not true. Therefore, the statement, "Birds can fly," is true unless a reason is given why a particular bird cannot fly. A computer would need to operate in a similar way.

Even though both general theories are valid, no way has yet been found to incorporate either of them in computers. The greatest stumbling block in developing true AI is finding a way to program computers with common sense.

An ethical problem arises from the development of artificial intelligence. If we design a machine that can mimic human thought processes, how will we deal with our creation? Will it truly be only a machine?

To deal with these problems, we may have to change our ideas about humanness. As humans, we have always considered ourselves above other creatures because we are capable of reflective thought—that is, we can think about thinking. How would we deal with machines that fulfilled this definition of being human? If we are going to take part in the creation of intelligent machines, we may need to determine whether we will be willing—or able—to accept the responsibility of being their creators.

COMPUTER MISTAKES: WHO IS RESPONSIBLE?

We have all heard of or experienced computer mistakes. Two questions arise in such situations: (1) Who actually made the mistake? (2) Who is responsible for it?

Computer errors can occur in a number of ways. The most common type of error involves the use of incorrect input. If the wrong data is put into the computer, even though the program does its job correctly, the output will not be correct. (Many computerists refer to this as the "garbage in, garbage out" principle.) Incorrect input can result simply from mistyping data. Gathering the wrong kinds of data or collecting inaccurate data can also result in incorrect input.

Computer errors also occur when a program does not do what it was intended to do. It may be a poorly written program with hidden bugs that cause the output to be inaccurate. Or it may not have been written to include every possible situation. For example, if a program that figures the interest earned on savings accounts does not make allowance for the extra day in each leap year, customers will lose one day's interest.

A third type of error can arise when the computer's capabilities do not match the capabilities called for by the program. If a program demands that all computations be carried out to ten decimal places, then the computer must be able to carry out ten decimal places, or errors will occur. Suppose an engineering program used to design the specifications for miniature electronic parts calls for precision to 1/100,000 of a millimeter. This involves carrying out the calculations to five decimal places. Let's look at how much precision is lost if the computer can only carry out the calculations to three places, or to 1/1,000 of a millimeter.

Suppose one segment of the part (Segment A) measures 0.66594 millimeters; and an adjoining segment (Segment B), 0.83487 millimeters. These segments are fused together, into Segment AB, and the measurement of AB multiplied by 2,700, because that many of the segments will be joined together in the final assembly (see Figure 6–3). If the computer can only carry out the calculations to three decimal places, 4.887 millimeters are lost in the calculations. This is an important loss, since 1/100,000 of a millimeter is significant in the design.

Results if computer could carry out five decimal places:	Results when computer carries out only three decimal places:
0.66594 millimeters (Segment A)	0.665 millimeters (Segment A)
+ 0.83487 millimeters (Segment B)	+ 0.834 millimeters (Segment B)
1.50081 millimeters (Segment AB)	1.499 millimeters (Segment AB)
× 2700.00000 segments	× 2700.000 segments
4052.18700 millimeters	4047.300 millimeters
Difference = 4.887 millimeters	

Figure 6–3 PROGRAMMING ERROR
Problems in output can occur when a program cannot handle the degree of accuracy required for the calculations.

Similar errors can occur when there is some kind of power failure. Even the slightest flicker in the power supply can cause a few bytes of information to be lost or changed. This type of error is extremely hard to detect, but the consequences may be disastrous.

In dealing with mistakes and determining whose fault it is when mistakes are made, little legal guidance exists. Most states have no laws pertaining to computer mistakes. Court decisions are often based on Uniform Commercial Code regulations, which were not drawn up to include computer applications, and rulings have been by no means consistent.

Some court cases have tried to determine who is responsible for computer-related mistakes. One such case involved a stop-payment order on a check. A customer of a large bank ordered the bank to stop payment on a check, which was said to have been written in the amount of $1,844.48. However, the actual amount of the check was $1,844.98. The bank's computer was programmed to stop payment only if every digit on the check matched exactly the numbers on the stop-payment order. In this case, the program noted the fifty cents difference in the amounts and did not stop payment. The judge ruled that the bank was responsible for the $1,844.98, because a human clerk would have considered the difference too slight to be important and would not have issued payment on the check. In essence, the bank's computer program did not do what it was intended to do.

Although computer errors may be fairly obvious, assigning responsibility for them is not. Is the programmer personally responsible for errors written into the program? Or does the company using the program assume responsibility when it purchases the program? Should the typist be held responsible for input errors? Or is it management's responsibility to check the information once it has been processed?

The answers to questions involving responsibility are crucial. Computer errors are far more serious than most people think. Businesses can be destroyed by computer errors. An insurance company survey showed that 90 percent of businesses dependent on computers go out of business after experiencing a major loss of service due to a computer error. Computer errors have also endangered people's health and have ruined reputations. Because of the potential for damage, it is essential that we determine who is responsible for errors.

ROBOTICS AND WORKER DISPLACEMENT

As computer capability grows—through both software and hardware design—jobs that are now done by humans may be reduced in number or eliminated altogether. The fear of being replaced by a computer is always alarming in the short run but needn't be ultimately threatening. What good would having a completely robot-run factory be if consumers cannot afford to buy the products the factory makes because they are out of work. The most lasting effect on society brought about by the computer may be the social reorganization needed to adapt to computer technology and make the best use of it.

As mentioned in Chapter 5, robots can perform many of the functions that humans can. They can operate in dangerous environments, dutifully perform tedious jobs without stopping, and even do some things a single human can't do, such as lift and carry heavy pieces of equipment. However, even now robots' potential is far from being realized. As the "brain" that controls robotic functions becomes more and more like the human brain, the robot will be able to take on new jobs and help with others.

Future robots must be able to recognize objects and then decide what to do with them. Research on sensory recognition is now being explored. The sense of vision can be achieved when a video image is translated into numerical values the computer can understand. Hundreds of thousands of numbers may be needed to enable the robot to "see" a single object. This means that the robot's computer power must be very sophisticated if it is to recognize and interpret many different objects.

An amazing prediction talked about by researchers today is the possibility of robots reproducing themselves. At Fujitsu's robot factory in Japan, robots built a hundred other robots in the factory's first year of operation, with only a hundred human workers supervising and helping! Think of the possibilities for robots in the future. With the proper advances in technology, it may be possible to send a few robots to an uninhabitable planet along with the raw materials to build other robots. These robots could then prepare the planet for the arrival of humans. Such schemes are actually being discussed seriously by NASA.

Talk about the evolution of self-reproducing robots nearly always brings up the question of human versus machine, particularly if these machines have goal-seeking and problem-solving capabilities. If robots ever became threatening, most people would suggest putting them out of operation. But could we do this? Just think how dependent upon computers some parts of our society have already become, and then look ahead to the even more computer-dependent society which is surely coming. Some scientists are predicting the day will arrive when the goals of robots and humans may conflict.

DATA FLOW BETWEEN COUNTRIES: SHOULD IT BE REGULATED?

With the arrival of satellite communications, advanced telecommunications, and networks, data can travel almost anywhere in the world. An issue that has caused international concern in recent years is the flow of data across national borders, commonly called *transborder data flow.* The problem arises because nobody can regulate *where* the information is going or even *what* information is going.

The major users of transborder data flow are large multinational corporations. They use satellites to beam information to their offices and headquarters around the globe instead of sending executives to deliver the information personally. The receiving countries are not too concerned about the loss of travel revenue from these visiting executives. What they are upset about is the loss of software tariffs. For most countries, tariffs, or taxes, must be paid on any tangible goods coming into the country. When software is brought into a country by airplane, by mail, or in someone's briefcase, the company must pay a tariff on it. Now multinational corporations can send million-dollar data-base management systems in and out of countries by satellite without reporting them or paying taxes on them. The tariffs avoided are quite substantial. Countries have no way of knowing what information is coming in by satellite. Even if they could detect it, is intangible information taxable, the same as tangible goods are? At this time, there is little hope of monitoring the flow of data between countries so that the appropriate tariffs can be paid.

A closely related problem involves another kind of tax. Some companies try to avoid paying income taxes by electronically transferring funds between countries. Sweden and Denmark have already enacted strict laws governing transborder data flow to eliminate that practice. The United States has also passed legislation to deal with the problem.

A particularly frightening aspect of transborder data flow is that classified information important to a corporation or a government could be intercepted by competitors or political rivals and used to cause harm. Having information is a method of control in our world economy. For example, finding out which countries are paying the highest prices for commodities—from oil to drugs to wheat—could influence where a company ships those goods. It is even more unsettling to think what might happen if secret government information fell into the wrong hands, without the government even knowing it.

Concerning the regulation of data flow across borders, the multinational corporations ask, "Whose data is it?" So far, the United States has not seriously tried to legislate in this area. However, it may not be possible to remain neutral forever. One thing is certain: as we enter an era in which information means power, we should be aware of where ours is going.

LEARNING CHECK

1. Artificial intelligence is not a new field of study. (True or false?)
2. A type of computer program that attempts to imitate the problem-solving processes of human experts is called an ______ system.
3. Some researchers believe that humans have some preconception about how thinking or dialogue will progress. (True or false?)
4. Name one problem associated with data flow between countries by satellite.

ANSWERS:

1. true. 2. expert. 3. true. 4. the problem of avoidance of tariffs on software; the problem of unauthorized use of top-secret information; the problem of electronic transfer of funds to avoid taxes; the problem of whether something as intangible as data can be treated as a tangible commodity.

SUMMARY POINTS

- Some major concerns about privacy involve the amount of data collected and stored, the accuracy and currency of the information, and the security of stored information.
- The Privacy Act of 1974 is the major piece of federal legislation passed to protect the privacy of the individual.
- Computers aid in crime detection by coordinating the great volumes of data gathered on individuals and crimes.
- Computer crime is a growing concern because it is difficult to detect and because it results in the loss of money and information. There is no doubt that tighter security measures are needed.
- Artificial intelligence is a major research field. Expert systems already display limited intelligence features. Current researchers seeking higher levels of intelligence for computers differ on how knowledge should be stored.
- Robots of the future will have better-developed senses, more powerful "brains," and the capacity to "reproduce."
- The question of who is responsible for computer mistakes is difficult to answer yet very important.
- Transborder data flow is an issue that concerns nations as well as multinational corporations.

REVIEW QUESTIONS

1. What are the major concerns about privacy in relation to computers?
2. What is the major piece of legislation enacted to protect privacy?
3. Name the four most common ways crimes are committed with the aid of computers.
4. What measures can be taken by system owners to reduce illegal or unauthorized computer use?
5. Define artificial intelligence. Describe how an expert system is designed.
6. How are ethics and the issues of privacy and security related?
7. Name the ways in which computer errors occur.
8. What advantages do robots have over human workers?
9. What capabilities may robots have in the future?
10. What is one of the major issues in transborder data flow?

PART II

PACKAGED SOFTWARE

BASIC Reference Card

Introduction to Computers Using The IBM PC ■ Mandell

BASIC Statements

STATEMENT	EXPLANATION	EXAMPLE
DIM	Establishes the dimensions of an array and sets aside the necessary amount of storage	20 DIM A(25)
END	Indicates the end of a program	END
FOR/NEXT	Performs a series of instructions in a loop a given number of times	30 FOR I = 1 TO 5 . . . 70 NEXT I
GOSUB/ RETURN	Branches to a subroutine, then returns to the main program	80 GOSUB 340 . . . 420 RETURN
GOTO	Signals an unconditional transfer of control	15 GOTO 60
IF/THEN/ELSE	Signals a conditional transfer of control	140 IF X = Y THEN PRINT X ELSE GOTO 999
INPUT	Allows data to be entered	40 INPUT J$,A
LET (optional)	Assigns a value to a variable	90 LET X = 23
ON/GOSUB	Signals a conditional transfer of control to a subroutine	90 ON X = Y GOSUB 100,200,300
ON/GOTO	Signals a conditional transfer of control	110 ON J GOTO 40,50,60
OPTION BASE	Declares the minimum value for array subscripts	10 OPTION BASE 1
READ/DATA	Reads data to variables from the data list	90 READ A,B,C 100 DATA 40,50,60
PRINT	Displays or prints output	40 PRINT X
REM	Provides documentation	80 REM LOOP BEGINS
RESTORE	Sets the pointer back to the beginning of the data	180 RESTORE
SPC	Moves the cursor right the specified number of spaces from the last output	240 PRINT SPC(12); "X"
STOP	Terminates program execution and returns to command level	190 STOP
TAB	Moves the cursor horizontally to the right the specified number of spaces from the left margin	180 PRINT TAB(15);"TITLE"
WHILE/WEND	Allows a loop to be executed as long as a condition remains true	240 WHILE A < 10 . . . 320 WEND

Operating System Commands

COMMAND (WHEN IN DOS MODE)	EXPLANATION
DIR	Lists the names of all programs on disk
DISKCOPY source drive: target drive	Copies the entire contents of a disk to another disk
DISKCOMP source drive: target drive	Compares the contents of two files and locates errors
ERASE filename	Removes a file from a disk
FORMAT drive:	Prepares a disk so programs can be stored on it
MODE BW80	Changes the screen width from 40 to 80 columns
MODE BW40	Changes the screen width from 80 to 40 columns
RENAME drive: old filename new filename	Changes the name of a file

COMMAND (WHEN IN BASIC MODE)	EXPLANATION
FILES	Lists the names of all programs on a disk
KILL "drive: filename"	Deletes a file from a disk
LIST	Displays all or part of a program on the screen
LIST, "LPT1"	Prints the complete program currently in main memory
LOAD "drive: program name"	Causes a program stored on disk to be brought back into main memory
NAME "drive: old file name" AS "new file name"	Changes the name of a file
NEW	Clears and prepares main memory for a new program
RUN	Executes a program
SAVE "drive: program name"	Stores a program currently in memory on disk
WIDTH 80	Changes the screen width from 40 to 80 columns
WIDTH 40	Changes the screen width from 80 to 40 columns

Hierarchy of Operations

PRIORITY	OPERATION	EXAMPLE
1	Any operation within parentheses	(4 + 8) * 6 = 72
2	Exponentiation	3 ^ 2 * 2 = 18
3	Multiplication or division	8 + 2 * 5 = 18
4	Addition or subtraction	4 + 12 / 3 = 8

Rules for Variable Names

GENERAL RULES FOR VARIABLE NAMES:	Must start with a letter. May be any combination of letters, numbers, and the period. May be any length, but IBM BASIC will only recognize the first 40 characters. Reserved words may not be used as variable names.
NUMERIC VARIABLE NAMES:	There are three types of numeric variable names: 1. Integer—The last character must be the percent sign (%). 2. Single-precision—The last character may be the exclamation mark (!). If the type of a variable name is not declared, the default is single-precision. These are used to represent numbers with seven digits or less. 3. Double-precision—The last character must be the number sign (#). These are used to represent numbers with 8 or more digits.
STRING VARIABLE NAMES:	The last character must be the dollar sign ($).

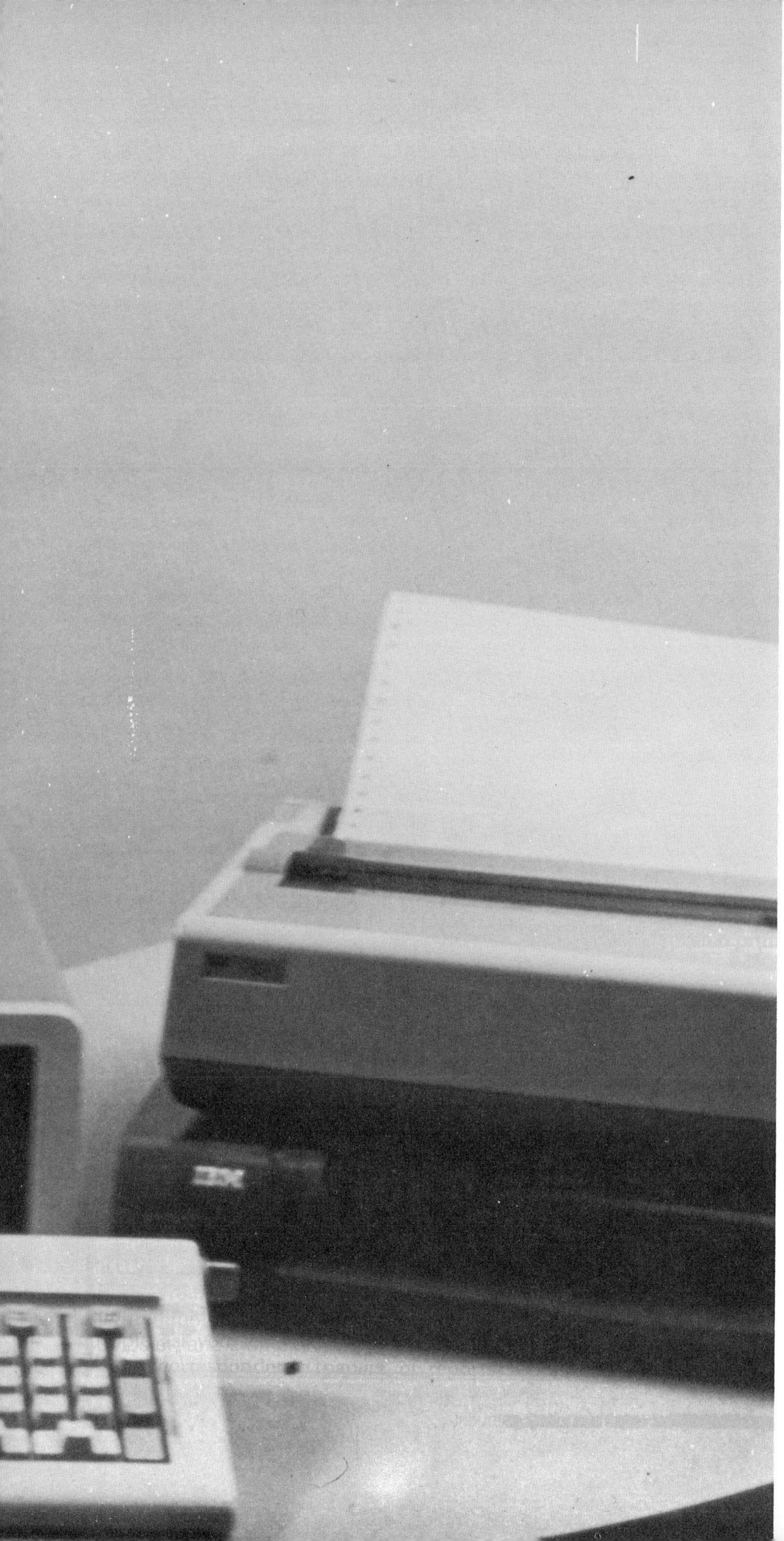

CHAPTER 7

GETTING TO KNOW YOUR IBM PC

Chapter Outline

INTRODUCTION

Welcome to the world of home computing. You have joined the thousands who now work on one of the most versatile and popular home computers. The IBM Personal Computer (IBM PC) and PCjr are capable of running programs, producing high quality graphics, editing text by word processing, writing and playing music, and much more.

This chapter will prepare you to run software packages (programs ready for the user to run) on your IBM PC. Among the wide variety of software packages available for the IBM PC and PCjr, the general types are covered in this book: word processors, spreadsheets, data managers, and graphics packages.

THE IBM PC AND PCjr

The IBM PC and PCjr are similar machines in most respects. The PCjr has less random-access memory than the PC, which prevents some of the software designed for the PC from being used on it. The keyboards also vary slightly, with the PC having 83 keys and the PCjr having 62 keys, as shown in Figure 7–1. The PC keyboard has a numeric keypad on the right side, similar to a calculator's, that can also be used for editing. In addition it has ten function keys, labeled F1 through F10, on the left side. The PCjr does not have the function keys; however, the functions can be performed using the control key <Fn> together with the number keys in the top row of the keyboard.

Figure 7–1 THE IBM PC (BOTTOM) AND PCjr (TOP) KEYBOARDS

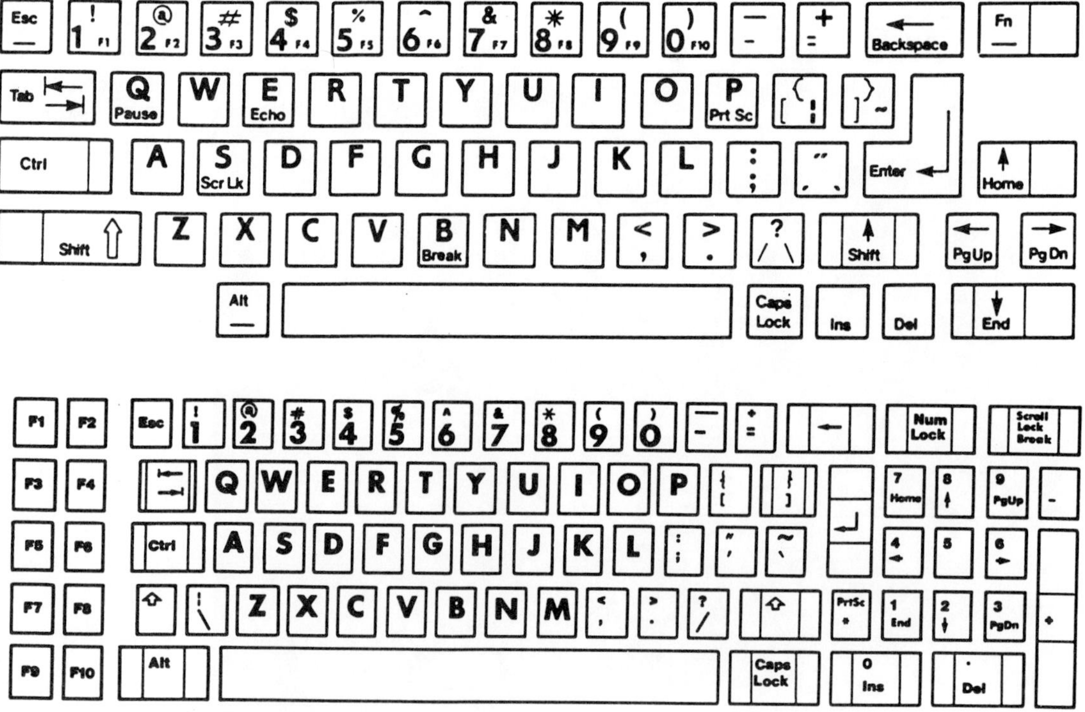

Table 7–1 lists some important keys and their functions for both the IBM PC and PCjr. These keys save time when you are programming or running a program. Familiarize yourself with the keys before beginning to work on the computer.

DEFINITIONS

It is not necessary to know everything that goes on inside the computer to use it. It is necessary, however, to be familiar with some computer terminology. Table 7–2 defines some commonly used computer terms with which you should become familiar if you have not yet read Part I of this text. Other terms will be introduced as they are needed. The glossary in the back of the book provides a quick reference for many of the terms used throughout this section.

LEARNING CHECK

1. ________ ________ are programs that are already written for the user.
2. The computer itself, the monitor, the disk drive, and the computer chips are called ________.
3. A ________ is a series of step-by-step instructions that tells the computer what to do.
4. The mechanical input device that rotates the disk and reads what is on it is the ________ ________.
5. To reset the system instead of turning the computer off and on, the keys that must be depressed are the ________, ________, and ________ keys.

ANSWERS:

1. Software packages. 2. hardware. 3. program. 4. disk drive. 5. Alt, Ctrl, Del.

Table 7–1 HELPFUL KEYSTROKES

KEY	FUNCTION
Home (Fn-Home)	Moves cursor to upper left corner of screen.
Ctrl-Home (Ctrl-Fn-Home)	Clears the screen and moves the cursor to upper left corner of the screen. (Typing CLS also clears the screen.)
Esc	Erases the current display line in BASIC mode.
Ctrl-Break (Fn-Break)	Interrupts program execution and returns control to keyboard.
Ctrl-Num Lock (Fn-Pause)	Causes the computer to pause, temporarily stopping program execution or printing, until another key is pressed.
Alt-Ctrl-Del	Causes the system to reset, the same as turning the computer off and back on.

Notes:

- Hyphens between keys indicate that the keys should be pressed at the same time.
- The first set of commands names the keys used for the IBM PC; the second set (shown in parentheses) shows the keys for the PCjr. If only one set is listed, there is no difference between the PC and the PCjr.

Table 7–2 COMMON COMPUTER TERMS DEFINED

TERM	DEFINITION
BASIC	Beginners' All-Purpose Symbolic Instruction Code, one of many computer languages. BASIC consists of special words the computer understands. Just as there are different languages, however, there are different versions of BASIC. Two versions of BASIC are offered with the IBM PC: cassette and disk BASIC. Advanced BASIC, a type of disk BASIC, is the version that will be covered in this text.
bit	The smallest piece of data the computer can use.
byte	A unit of storage, typically eight bits.
disk drive	The mechanical input device that rotates the disk during data transmission.
floppy disk	A flexible disk with a magnetic coating on which data can be stored and from which it can be retrieved.
hard copy	Any output listed on paper.
hardware	The computer itself, the monitor, the disk drive, and the computer chips inside.
K	A unit of storage. One K of memory is equal to 1,024 bytes. (The larger the memory, the greater the amount of information that can be stored.)
peripherals	The devices that expand what you can do with your computer (for example, monitors, printers, disk drives).
program	A series of step-by-step instructions written in a programming language that tells the computer exactly what to do.
RAM	Random-access memory, the memory used to store programs. The contents of RAM can be read or changed at any time.
ROM	Read-only memory, a permanent part of storage. Whatever is stored in ROM remains there even after the power to the computer has been turned off. ROM cannot be changed or added to.
soft copy	Any output listed on the monitor.
software	The programs or sets of instructions that tell the computer what to do. These include the programs typed on the keyboard or loaded into the computer from floppy disks, as well as the operating system software stored permanently within the computer.

GETTING STARTED ON THE COMPUTER

The method used to load a software program into your IBM PC varies depending on the package. Before doing anything, read the instructions included with the package.

Many times the program disk simply needs to be inserted. To do this, remove the disk from its envelope and slide it into the disk drive, right side up with the label toward you. (Use Disk Drive A if there are two disk drives.) Turn the latch on the disk drive to the vertical position. Now turn on the monitor and the computer. Wait until the disk drive stops making a whirring noise before pressing any keys. Then proceed as the program instructions specify.

Another common method used to run packaged software requires some type of operating system software to be located first. In this case, follow the instructions that came with your software package.

FORMATTING A DISK

Format (or initialize)
To prepare a disk so that programs can be saved on it.

Before a blank disk can be used, you must **format,** or **initialize,** it. Formatting prepares the disk so programs can be saved on it for later use. Used disks may be reformatted so that their old contents are removed and new programs can be stored on them. Keep in mind that all your files will be destroyed permanently when a used disk is reformatted.

You will need a disk operating system (DOS) disk for the IBM PC and a blank or old disk. The following steps are used to format a disk:

1. Insert the DOS disk in Disk Drive A (the drive on the left), close the door, and turn on the computer. (For the PCjr or any system with one disk drive, just insert the disk in the drive.) When the system prompt *A>* appears, type the following command:

```
FORMAT B:/S    (for a two-drive system)
   or
FORMAT A:/S    (for a one-drive system)
```

and press the RETURN, or ENTER, key. On the IBM PC, the RETURN key <↵> is located to the left of the numeric keypad. On the IBM PCjr, the RETURN key <Enter ↵> is located on the right side of the keyboard (see Figure 7–1 for the location of both keys). The B tells the computer that the blank disk is in Drive B. The A tells the computer that only one drive is being used. The /S, which is optional, copies three operating system files to the disk. One of the files reads the commands when they are entered and decides what function they should perform.

2. When the following message appears:

```
Insert new diskette for drive B: (A for one drive)
and strike any key when ready
```

insert the blank diskette in Disk Drive B (or remove the DOS disk and insert the blank disk in Drive A) and close the door. Then press any key. You should see the following message:

```
Formatting. . .Format complete
System transferred
```

along with some information about the byte space available. Never remove a disk while the red light on the drive is still on.

3. You will then be asked if you need to format another disk. Type a Y if you do and an N if you are finished.

Now you can format a disk by following these steps:

1. Place the DOS disk in disk drive A, close the door, and turn on the computer.

2. Type: FORMAT B:/S (or FORMAT A:/S for one drive).
3. Press the ENTER key, and follow the instructions that are given on the screen.

DISK OPERATING SYSTEM COMMANDS

Operating system (OS)
A program that controls the operation of the computer.

Disk operating system (DOS)
A portion of the operating system which resides on disk and manages disk operations and input/output to peripheral devices not controlled by the OS in ROM.

The **operating system (OS)** is a program that controls the operation of the computer. A portion of the OS permanently resides in the read-only memory (ROM) of the IBM PC and PCjr. This portion contains many of the primary operating functions of the computer. When the computer is first turned on, it is this part of the OS that performs the initial start-up procedures.

The remaining portion of the OS, the **disk operating system (DOS),** resides on disk and must be loaded into the computer. DOS's primary concern is the managing of disk operations, and input and output to other peripheral devices not controlled by the portion of the OS resident in ROM. For example, DOS controls the reading of a file from disk and the writing of a file back out to disk.

The two basic types of DOS commands are internal and external. Internal commands are those DOS commands that are part of the DOS program in memory. Once they have been entered, they are executed immediately. Examples of internal commands include DIR, COPY, and CLS. External commands are DOS commands that reside on disk as separate programs. When an external command is entered, DOS must first load the corresponding program into memory and then execute it. Examples of external commands include DISKCOPY, FORMAT, and BASICA.

DISKCOPY

You should make copies of all your important disks in case the originals are damaged or lost. Keep these backup disks in a place where they will not be damaged by heat, moisture, or other harmful substances.

To copy the contents of one disk to another, type the following command:

```
DISKCOPY source drive: target drive:
```

You must specify the letter of the source drive (drive containing the disk to be copied) and the letter of the target drive (drive containing the disk to be copied to). If you have only one disk drive, specify only one drive. The program will tell you when to switch disks during the copying process.

For example, to copy the contents of the disk in Drive A onto the disk in Drive B, the command should be as follows:

```
DISKCOPY A:B:
```

For the IBM PCjr or a system with only one disk drive, the following command should be used:

```
DISKCOPY A:
```

After copying, the following message will appear:

```
Copy another (Y/N)?_______
```

Type Y to continue copying on the same drives indicated, or type N if you are finished.

When the copying process is completed, type the following command, which checks to see if the disks are identical:

```
DISKCOMP source drive: target drive:
```

The disk in the first drive specified will be compared to the disk in the second drive. Again, for a one-drive system, only specify one drive (you will have to switch disks). If there are any errors, a message will indicate the location of the error. Check your user's manual if an error occurs.

DIRECTORY

A list of the names of all files stored on a disk can be obtained by using the DIRECTORY command. Just type

```
DIR
```

and press the RETURN key. The names of all files stored on the disk will be displayed on the screen along with the type of file, size of the file in bytes, and the date and time that the file was created.

RENAME

The name of a file stored on a disk can be changed while in the system mode. Type

```
RENAME drive: old filename new filename
```

Because BASIC files (shown in the directory as .BAS) may not be the only files on the disk, the type of file must also be specified. For example, a BASIC program called GRADES loaded in Disk Drive A could be renamed to SCORES by typing the following:

```
RENAME A: GRADES.BAS SCORES.BAS
```

If the filename is not spelled the correct way or if the type of file is not specified when needed, the message FILE NOT FOUND will be displayed. Check the directory for the correct spelling and file type; then retype the command.

ERASE

A file can be erased from a disk by typing

```
ERASE file name
```

or

```
DEL file name
```

and pressing the RETURN key. DEL stands for DELETE. Again, you must specify the type of file. After this command has been executed, the file is permanently erased. So make sure the file you are erasing is the correct one. For example, to erase a BASIC program named GRADES, just type

```
ERASE GRADES.BAS
```

or

```
DEL GRADES.BAS
```

and then press the RETURN key.

BASIC COMMANDS

BASIC commands, similar to DOS commands, instruct the OS to perform certain tasks on BASIC programs.

The IBM PC has two versions of BASIC: cassette and disk. Cassette BASIC is built into the computer. Disk BASIC, which is more advanced, must be loaded into the computer. Advanced BASIC, one type of disk BASIC, is the type discussed throughout this book.

Before you can write or run programs in Advanced BASIC, you must load a formatted DOS disk and then get into the BASIC mode. First, insert a formatted disk in Disk Drive A and turn on the computer or reset the system, if it is already on, by pressing the <Ctrl>, <Alt>, and <Del> keys at the same time. With the IBM PCjr, the BASIC cartridge must also be inserted in the cartridge slot. When the DOS prompt *A>* appears, type the following:

```
BASICA
```

and press the RETURN key. The BASIC prompt, *Ok,* should appear on the screen. At the bottom of the PC screen, the ten function keys are listed with the functions they perform. Only five keys are shown on the PCjr screen. To see all ten, change the screen width to eighty columns. Refer to the "Screen Width" section, which appears later in this chapter, to change the IBM PCjr screen width. The function keys can be used instead of typing commands. Consult the IBM PC user's manual for further instructions. Now you are ready to write, save, load, and run programs in Advanced BASIC.

FILES

In BASIC, the command used to list the names of all programs stored on a disk is different from the command used when in DOS. (Remember, the

DOS prompt is *A>*, while the BASIC prompt is *Ok.*) To get a list of program names, type

```
FILES
```

and press the RETURN key. Notice that the extension .BAS has been added to some of the BASIC program names. This extension is added automatically when the programs are saved. When specifying program names with certain BASIC commands, you may need to include the .BAS extension, or the system will not access the file.

SAVE

Once a BASIC program has been entered into the computer, it can be stored on disk by typing the following:

```
SAVE ''drive: program name''
```

and pressing the RETURN key. If the disk containing the program is not in Disk Drive A, you must specify the letter of the disk drive. The program name may be from one to eight characters long. It may include an extension of one to three characters. A period (.) must separate the program name from the extension. Extensions can be used when you have more than one version of the same program. For example, the program TAXES may have two versions: TAXES.84 and TAXES.85. The extension .BAS will be added if the name is eight characters long or less and has no extension.

The filename and extension may include the alphabetic characters A through Z, the digits 0 through 9, and the following special characters: |, @, #, $, %, &, (,), ', and -. No spaces are allowed in a program name. Each program should have a unique name that identifies it. As more programs are stored on a disk, it will become increasingly important that they have descriptive names.

When the light on the disk drive goes off and the BASIC prompt, *Ok,* appears, the program should have been saved. To verify that it has been saved, types FILES and press the RETURN key. A list of all stored programs will appear. If the name of the program just saved is listed, it has been stored on the disk.

LOAD

To get a BASIC program that is stored on disk back into the computer's main memory, simply type

```
LOAD ''drive: program name''
```

and press the RETURN key. The drive letter must be specified if the disk is not in Drive A. The program must be spelled exactly as it is listed in the directory. Use the FILES command to check on spellings of program names. The light on the disk drive will be on while the computer searches the disk for the program. If the program is on the disk, the light will go off when it has been loaded, and the BASIC prompt will appear on the screen. The program has been transferred to the computer's main memory. You may then list, change, or run the program.

RUN

To execute a BASIC program currently in the computer's memory, simply type

```
RUN
```

and then press the RETURN key.

YOUR TURN

1. Insert a formatted disk in Disk Drive A and turn on the computer. Type NEW and the following program lines exactly as shown, including line numbers. Use your birth date in place of MONTH, DAY in Line 40.

```
10  PRINT ''A DAY ON WHICH''
20  PRINT ''MANY GREAT PEOPLE WERE BORN''
30  PRINT ''IS:''
40  PRINT ''MONTH, DAY''
99  END
```

2. Check the program for typing errors. If there is an error, simply retype that line.
3. Now execute the program by typing RUN and pressing the RETURN key.
4. Save the program under the name BIRTHDAY. Type SAVE "BIRTHDAY" or SAVE "A: BIRTHDAY" and press the RETURN key.

NAME

When in BASIC, program names can be changed in a similar fashion as they are when in DOS. Type

```
NAME ''drive: old filename'' AS ''new filename''
```

and press the RETURN key. If the disk is in Drive A, the drive letter need not be specified. The old filename must exactly match the name listed in the directory, and there cannot be an existing program with the same name as the new filename. You must include the .BAS after the filenames. For example, to change the name of a BASIC program named AUTO, loaded on Disk Drive B, to FORD, type the following:

```
NAME ''B:AUTO.BAS'' AS ''FORD.BAS''
```

and press the RETURN key.

KILL

A file can be deleted from a disk when in BASIC by typing

```
KILL ''drive: filename''
```

and pressing the RETURN key. Again, you must include the .BAS when indicating which file to delete. For example, to erase a BASIC file named FORD from the disk loaded in Drive A, type

```
KILL ''A: FORD.BAS''
```

and press the RETURN key. Check to see if the file has successfully been deleted by typing the FILES command.

SCREEN WIDTH

When the IBM PC is in DOS mode (shown by the *A>* prompt), the screen width is set for eighty columns; the PCjr screen is set for forty columns when in DOS mode. However, both models allow for screen widths of either forty or eighty columns. Type the following command to change the screen width from eighty columns to forty columns:

```
MODE BW40
```

Similarly, type the following command to change the screen width from forty to eighty columns:

```
MODE BW80
```

When working in BASIC (shown by the *Ok* prompt), the commands are different:

```
WIDTH 40
```

changes the screen to forty columns while

```
WIDTH 80
```

changes the screen to eighty columns.

LEARNING CHECK

1. Disks should be inserted into the disk drive with the label ________ you.
2. Preparing a blank disk so that programs can be stored on it is referred to as ________ the disk.
3. The ________ controls the operation of the computer.
4. The BASIC command that stores a program on disk is ________.
5. The BASIC command that executes a program in main memory is ________.

ANSWERS:

1. toward. 2. formatting (or initializing). 3. operating system. 4. SAVE. 5. RUN.

GUIDE TO THE WEST FAMILY OF INSTRUCTIONAL SOFTWARE

The guides in the following four chapters accompany the West Publishing Company Instructional Diskettes, which include a word processor (WestWord™) an electronic spreadsheet (WestCalc™), a data manager (WestFile™), and a graphics package (WestGraph™). These programs are designed to be self-explanatory. By using the step-by-step instructions at the bottom of each screen, the user will be guided through the various operations within a particular program.

The purpose of the guides included in each of the next four chapters is to familiarize the user with both the computer and the format of the programs in order to optimize the time the user spends in the computer lab. This version of the instructional software is designed to be used with an IBM PC and 128K of internal memory or a PCjr.

Documentation Design

The information within these guides can serve as an interactive walk-through and manual for programs on the four diskettes. Each of these programs (WestWord™, WestCalc™, WestFile™, and WestGraph™) is explained in the guide at the end of the appropriate chapter. Each guide gives a brief overview of its respective program, which explains the various functions of that program (with exhibits of the associated screens) and includes hands-on activities for the user, indicated in the left margin of the text by this special figure:

YOUR TURN

Throughout the guides, items displayed on the screen are shown in capital letters to help the user associate what is seen on the screen with what is written in the documentation. User input to the program is shown by capital letters. Before beginning the program sections, it may be useful to review the IBM PC and PCjr keyboards shown in Figure 7–1 earlier in the chapter.

The Keyboard and Diskettes

Throughout the documentation, the term *RETURN key* refers to the < ↵ > key, known as the ENTER or RETURN key on the IBM PC and PCjr keyboards. This key, located on the right side of the keyboards, is used to signal the end of user input throughout the programs on the instructional diskettes. User responses that require only one key to be pressed do not require the use of the RETURN key. User responses that require more than one key to be pressed, however, must be followed by pressing the RETURN key.

The backspace key, located next to the < = / + > key on the upper right of the keyboard, is represented by <←>. If you discover a mistake prior to pressing the RETURN key, the backspace key can be used to erase the incorrect characters.

The left arrow <←>, right arrow <→>, up arrow < ↑ >, and down arrow < ↓ > keys are used to move the cursor in the word processor and the spreadsheet. These keys are located on the numeric key pad of the PC and on the lower right side of the PCjr keyboard.

The <Esc> key can be used throughout the programs to abort an operation from several of the user input locations. This key is located on the left side of the keyboard near the number 1 key.

The less than (<) and greater than (>) signs are used in the instructions at the bottom of the screens to signify the required user input. The following instruction, for example, indicates that a Y should be entered to allow a record to be deleted, or an N should be entered in order to prevent a record from being deleted:

```
1.  (A) ENTER <Y> IF IT IS OK TO
        DELETE THE DISPLAYED RECORD
    (B) ENTER <N> IF IT IS NOT OK TO
        DELETE THE RECORD
```

The program diskette should be left in the drive at all times. When you are finished using the diskette, the proper time to remove it is when the MAIN MENU for a particular program is displayed on the screen.

Program Instructions

Each program (WestFile™, WestWord™, WestGraph™, and WestCalc™) contains special help screens. Each screen will assist the user in using a particular program. After you select a program, the question WOULD YOU LIKE INSTRUCTIONS? (Y/N) appears on the screen. To gain access to the help screens, simply press Y. Press N to go to the program's MAIN MENU.

Operating Instructions

The following operating instructions should be used when self-booting diskettes (explained in the next section) have not been made.

1. Insert the DOS 2.XX diskette into Drive A.
2. Turn on the monitor and computer.
3. Press the RETURN key in response to the prompt:

```
Current date is Tue 1-01-1980
Enter new date:__
```

4. Press the RETURN key in response to the prompt:

```
Current time is 0:02:32.74
Enter new time:__
```

5. The following should appear on the screen:

```
The IBM Personal Computer DOS
Version 2.XX ©Copyright IBM Corp 1981, 1982, 1983

A>
```

6. Remove the DOS diskette and insert the appropriate diskette into drive A. At the prompt *A>*, type:

```
WESTFILE (if using the data manager WestFile)

WESTWORD (if using the word processor WestWord)

WESTCALC (if using the spreadsheet WestCalc)

WESTGRAF (if using the graphics package WestGraph)
```

and then press the RETURN key.

Creating Self-Booting Diskettes

1. Insert the DOS 2.XX diskette into Drive A.
2. Turn on the monitor and computer.
3. Press the RETURN key in response to the prompt:

```
Current date is Tue 1-01-1980
Enter new date:__
```

4. Press the RETURN key in response to the prompt:

```
Current time is 0:01:33.09
Enter new time:__
```

5. The following should appear on the screen:

```
The IBM Personal Computer DOS
Version 2.XX ©Copyright IBM Corp 1981, 1982, 1983

A>_
```

6. Type:

```
FORMAT B:/S (for a two-drive system)
FORMAT A:/S (for a one-drive system)
```

and then press the RETURN key.
7. After the prompt:

```
Insert new diskette for Drive B (or Drive A)
and strike any key when ready
```

insert a new diskette into Drive B (or Drive A) and press any key.
8. The following should appear on the screen:

```
Formatting. . .
```

9. When the following appears:

```
Formatting. . .Format Complete
System transferred

  XXXXXX bytes total disk space
   XXXXX bytes used by system
  XXXXXX bytes available on disk

Format another (Y/N)?_
```

type: N
10. Remove the DOS 2.XX diskette from Drive A.
11. Insert the diskette labeled WestFile into Drive A.
12. Type:

```
COPY *.* B:
```

and then press the RETURN key.
13. A list of files will appear on the screen. When the *A>* appears, the copying of the WestFile diskette is complete.
14. To create self-booting diskettes for WestWord, WestCalc, and WestGraph, insert the DOS 2.XX diskette back into Drive A and repeat steps 6 through 13 for each diskette. In step 11, insert the appropriate diskette instead of the diskette labeled WestFile.

To use the diskettes from now on, simply insert the appropriate diskette into Drive A, and turn on the monitor and computer.

SUMMARY POINTS

- Software packages are programs that are already written for the user.
- Some examples of packaged software are word processors, spreadsheets, data managers, and graphics packages.
- The IBM PCjr keyboard has sixty-two keys, while the IBM PC has eighty-three keys, including ten function keys and a numeric keypad.
- Both the IBM PC and PCjr can accommodate screen widths of either forty columns or eighty columns.
- *Hardware* refers to the physical components of the computer system, whereas *software* consists of the instructions that make the computer work.
- Disks are used to store programs. The disk drive rotates the disk during data transmission.
- Disks must be formatted before programs can be stored on them. Formatting a used disk erases the old contents stored on it.
- The operating system (OS) is a program that controls the operation of the computer.
- Disk operating system (DOS) commands can make copies of files, list the files stored on a disk, erase files, or rename files.
- The DISKCOPY command can be used to make duplicate copies of disks.
- The DOS command used to list all the files on a disk is DIR. The command used when in the BASIC mode is FILES.
- While in the BASIC mode, programs in main memory can be stored on disk by using the SAVE command.
- While in the BASIC mode, programs stored on disk can be loaded into the computer's main memory by using the LOAD command.
- The RUN command executes programs currently in the computer's main memory when in the BASIC mode.
- The RENAME command is used to change the name of a file when in DOS mode, while NAME is used when in the BASIC mode.
- A file can be deleted from a disk by using the ERASE command when in DOS mode and the KILL command when in the BASIC mode.

REVIEW QUESTIONS

1. Give some examples of the types of packaged software that can be purchased.

2. Explain the difference between computer hardware and software.

3. What tasks are performed by the disk operating system?

4. What is hard copy? What is soft copy? Give an example of when each might be useful.

5. Which commands covered in this chapter can be used only when in the DOS mode? In the BASIC mode?

6. List some peripherals you might use with your computer system.

7. List the steps necessary to format a disk.

8. What steps are used to store a program on a disk?
9. How can a program stored on disk be loaded into main memory? List the necessary steps.
10. What is one way to reset the IBM PC without turning it off and then back on?

EXERCISES

Follow these steps to practice using some DOS commands and BASIC commands.

1. Insert a DOS formatted disk (and a BASIC cartridge for the PCjr), wait for the *A>* prompt, then access BASIC by typing BASICA.
2. Type NEW and press the RETURN key. (NEW clears the computer's memory. It is discussed in Chapter 12.)
3. Type this program:

```
10  PRINT ''THE DOS COMMANDS COVERED IN THIS CHAPTER ARE''
20  PRINT ''DISKCOPY, DIR, ERASE, AND RENAME''
30  PRINT ''THE BASIC COMMANDS COVERED ARE''
40  PRINT ''FILES, SAVE, LOAD, RUN, NAME, AND KILL''
99  END
```

4. Use the SAVE command to store this program on disk under the name TEST.
5. Type FILES and press ENTER. Is TEST listed in the disk directory? What extension, if any, has been added?
6. Load TEST back into the computer's memory.
7. Run the program TEST.
8. Change the program name TEST to SAMPLE.
9. Delete the program SAMPLE.
10. Type FILES and press the RETURN key. Neither SAMPLE nor TEST should be listed in the disk directory.

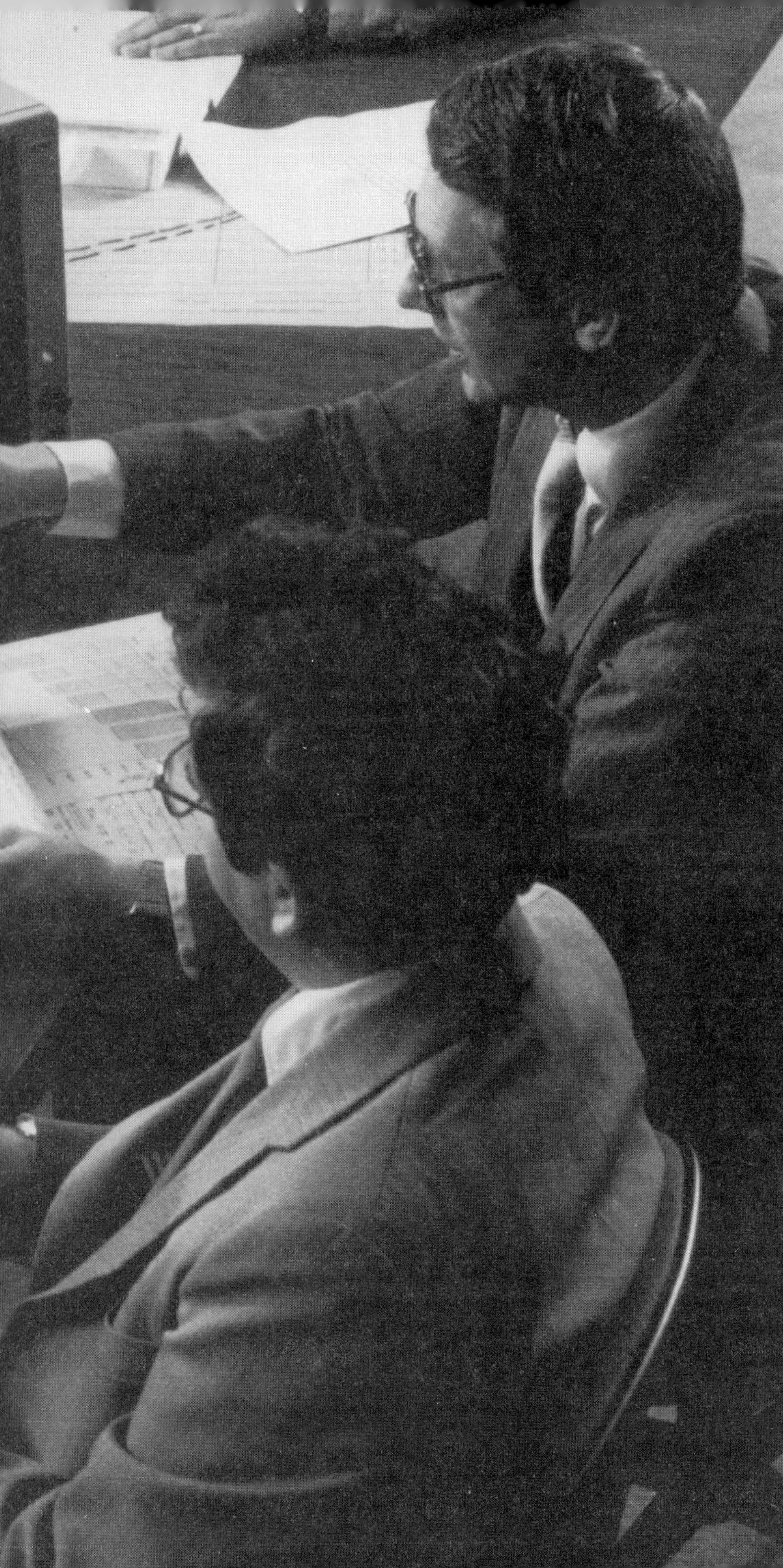

CHAPTER 8

DATA MANAGER

Chapter Outline

INTRODUCTION

Computer software can be used in a variety of ways to assist us in our everyday duties and tasks. Data managers, like word-processors (see Chapter 10) and spreadsheet packages (see Chapter 11), are designed to speed and simplify an otherwise tedious manual process—in this case, recording and filing information. Data managers are often used in place of conventional wheel card index files or manila file folders and file cabinets. For this reason, they are often referred to as file handlers, file cabinets, or file managers.

File handlers
Data management software packages designed to access only one data file at a time.

Data base packages
Data management software packages that consolidate data files into an integrated whole, allowing access to more than one data file at a time.

This chapter will discuss some of the common uses of data managers, as well as explore the differences between **file handlers** and **data base packages.** Common features of file handlers and the hardware requirements for using a data manager will also be presented. The chapter also describes some of the things to look for when choosing a data manager and lists some of the popular data managers and their features available for the IBM PC and the IBM PCjr computers. The chapter concludes with user documentation for the data manager called WestFile™.

DEFINITIONS

Everyone is familiar with file cabinets and their uses. File cabinets and data manager software packages are used for nearly identical purposes. Data managers allow you to computerize traditional filing systems that use wheel card index files or manila folders and file cabinets. There are two types of data managers: file handlers and data base packages. The differences between them will be discussed shortly. Before discussing what a data manager is, however, it might be helpful to review the key terms relating to computerized data management in Table 8–1.

Data managers (data management packages), like word processors and spreadsheets, are software packages that computerize a normal, everyday

Table 8–1 KEY DATA MANAGEMENT TERMS

TERM	DEFINITION
Data base	A grouping of independent data files into an integrated whole that can be accessed through one central point. A data base is designed to meet the information needs of a wide variety of users within an organization.
Field	A meaningful item of data, such as an employee number.
File	A grouping of related data records, such as an employee file.
Menu driven program	A program designed to prompt the user for choices by presenting a menu from which to choose (much like selecting dinner from a restaurant menu).
Record	A collection of related data fields that relate to a single unit, such as an employee record.
Sort	To arrange data elements into some order to facilitate processing or printing.
Update	To alter a data field within a record to reflect accurate information, such as changing an employee's address after he or she has moved.

task—that of recording and filing information. Data is recorded using a computer terminal and keyboard, and it is stored on the computer's secondary storage devices (see Chapter 2), where it can be accessed.

Most data managers are menu driven and contain a number of standard features, including the following:

- The ability to add or delete information within a file.
- The ability to search a file for information based on some criteria.
- The ability to update, or modify, information within a file.
- The ability to sort information into some order.
- The ability to print reports or mailing labels.

However, the overall capabilities of the two types of data managers (file handlers and data base packages) differ. These differences are discussed in the following sections.

File Handlers

File handlers and data base packages differ primarily in the way in which the data is organized and, hence, how it can be accessed. One way to view the difference between the two types of data managers is by reviewing their development through time.

File handlers, which were developed first, were designed to duplicate the traditional manual methods of filing. Before the use of computers for filing, sections or departments in a business generally kept records that pertained only to their particular area of interest. The payroll department, for example, kept an employee's name, number, address, salary, and number of deductions so it could write paychecks. The personnel department, in contrast, kept its own information on employees, including name, number, salary, job title, address, employment history, and spouse's name. The information was kept independently in a file for each department's own use.

With the advent of computers and computerized record keeping, the procedures and methods of recording and filing data were simply converted from paper, file folders, and file cabinets to computer software and storage devices. Each department had computer access to maintain its own independent files. For example, the personnel department would have access to the employee file, whereas the payroll department would have access to the payroll file.

File handlers, therefore, are designed to access only one data file at a time. The information that is stored on the computer's secondary storage devices is organized in such a way that only records within a single file can be accessed at a given time. There is only one, two-way path that data can travel between the data files and the file handler software (see Figure 8–1).

Because of the way data is organized by a file handler, duplication of data between files can result in a situation where many files containing similar information must be maintained, particularly as in a large corporation. This is not to say, however, that file handlers are not useful in certain

Figure 8–1 A FILE HANDLER'S DATA ORGANIZATION

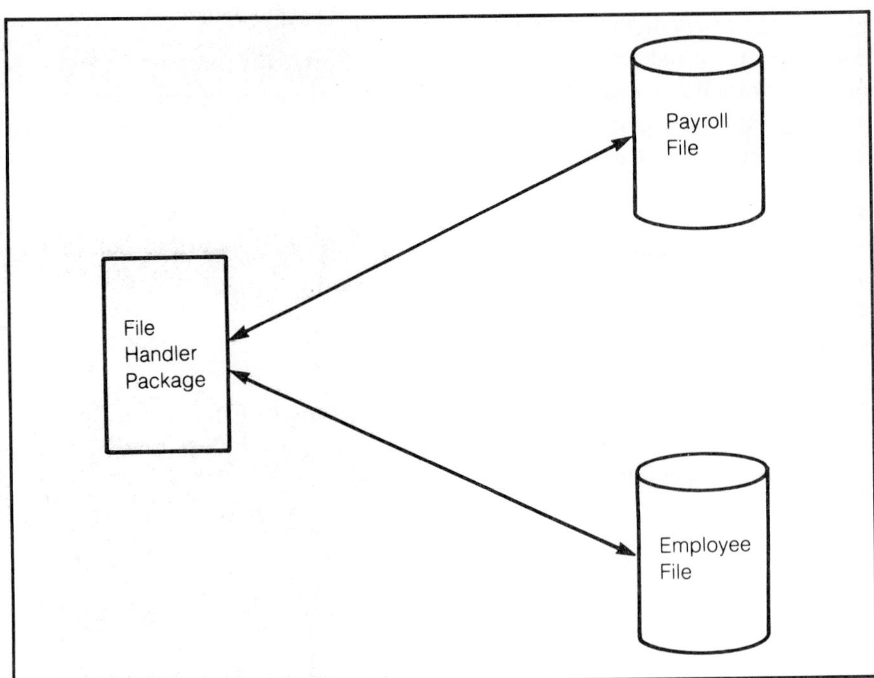

situations. A small business, for example, can benefit greatly from the use of a file handler package that helps organize and properly maintain the business's inventory.

Data Base Packages

The file-handling software had some drawbacks for companies with enormous amounts of data and limited computer resources. Because of the duplication of data and the difficulty in keeping one piece of information—such as an employee address—accurate across several files, large companies began to develop data bases.

Data bases are designed to consolidate various independent files into one integrated whole giving all users access to the information they need. The information that is stored in the data base is organized so that data in more than one file can be accessed. There are a number of two-way paths that data can travel between data files and the data base package (see Figure 8–2).

A piece of data thus needs to be located in only one place, making it easier to maintain. You can still search for, update, add, or delete data as you would with a file handler. What differs is the way in which the data is organized and stored.

A data base, therefore, can be likened to a large, centrally located room containing file cabinet after file cabinet of information. Because it is kept in a central location and all personnel can have access to the information they require for their work, information is easy to access, can be updated in one location, and is not duplicated (see Figure 8–3a).

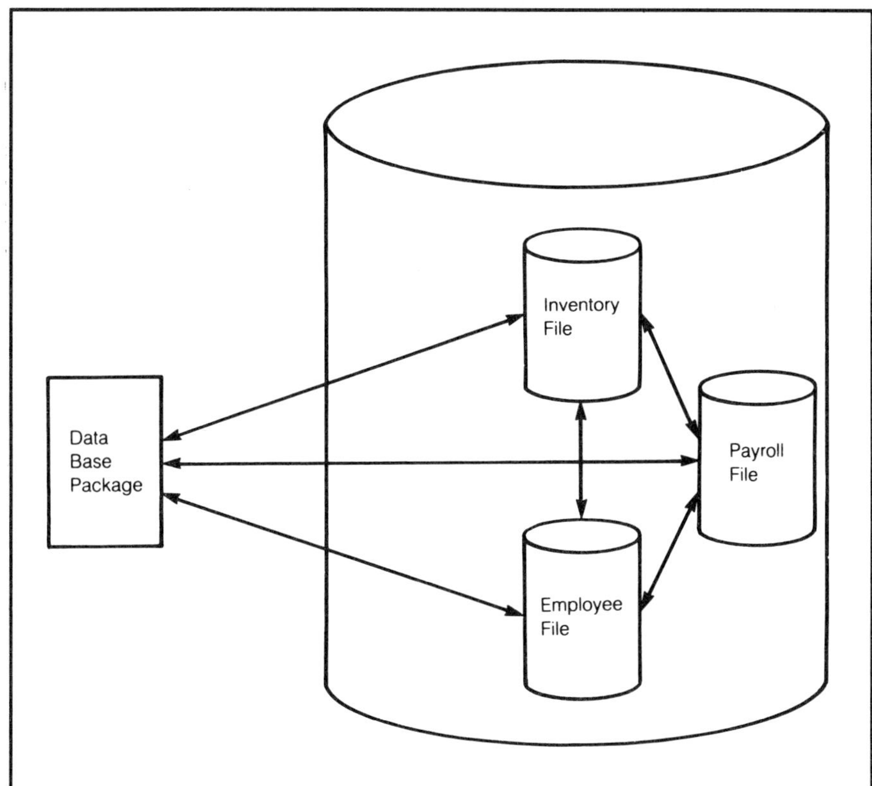

Figure 8–2 A DATA BASE'S DATA DATA ORGANIZATION

A file handler, in contrast, can be likened to a single file cabinet kept in a particular department where only the department's employees have access to the data. Another department's employees would find it difficult to get access to the data, so data would be duplicated across departments within the organization (see Figure 8–3b).

Since microcomputers were introduced, a large number of both file handler and data base packages have been written for them. File handler packages have been popular with small businesses and home users, whereas data base packages have been popular with medium to large companies. Because file handlers have been popular with home computer users and small businesses, the discussions throughout the remainder of the chapter will concentrate on file handlers and their features. A detailed discussion of data base concepts and applications is beyond the scope of this text.

USES OF A DATA MANAGER

Data managers have a number of uses in the home, in business, and for specialized purposes. Some of the uses in each of these categories are explored here. Later in the chapter, some of the popular data management packages are listed, using the same categories.

Figure 8–3 A DATA BASE VERSUS FILE HANDLERS

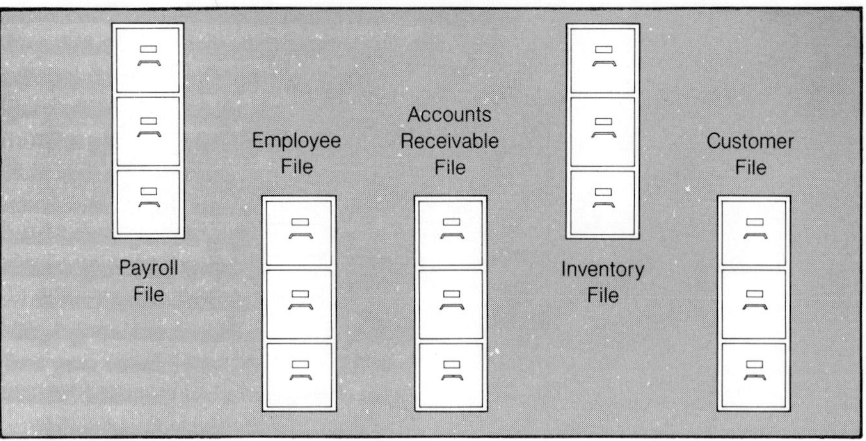

Company A's Data Base System—Information Accessible by All Departments

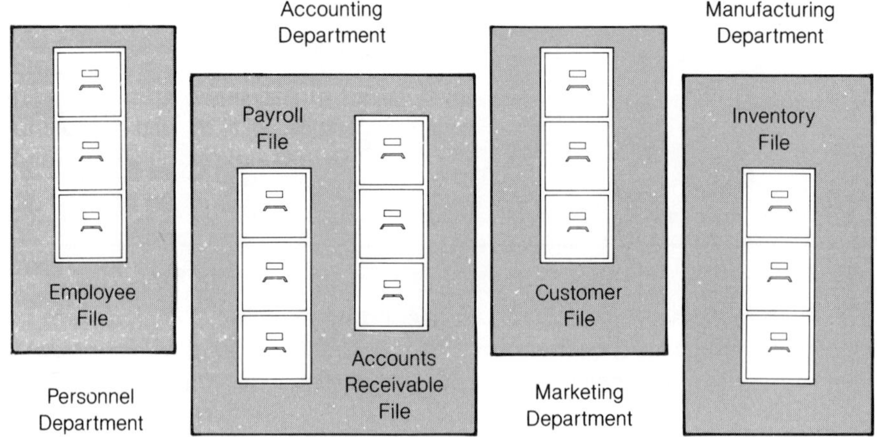

Company B's File-handling System—Information Accessible by Only Certain Departments

Home Uses

Data managers, and file handlers in particular, have proved to be very popular software packages for use in the home. Data managers can be used for such things as creating a computerized Christmas card list, making a computerized recipe index card file, and balancing a checkbook. The data manager can be used for just about any type of record keeping and filing that you may do in your home.

Computerizing record-keeping and filing duties around the home means records can be kept in a central location and in a compact form. Rather than having numerous books and files that must be maintained manually, you can enter the information into the computer and store it on compact floppy diskettes (see Chapter 2).

Aside from their usefulness as an alternative method of record keeping, data managers offer other benefits in the home. The ability to generate reports for the preparation of taxes, for example, can be very helpful. You could use a data manager to keep a record of financial transactions throughout the year. You could place a field labeled "Tax Deductible" in the data record to indicate whether a transaction was tax related. Once this was done, the data manager could be used at tax time to pick out the tax-related transactions and print a report of them (see Figure 8–4).

Other possible uses of data managers in the home include personal property inventory record keeping, listing important documents and their locations, keeping a computerized address book and telephone listing, creating a mailing list, keeping an appointment calendar, and keeping track of works within a personal library. File handlers offer a means of computerizing a manual record-keeping task—that of keeping organized, readily accessible records.

Business Uses

File handlers have been particularly popular with small businesses that can benefit from the conversion of manual record-keeping processes to computerized record keeping. Converting manual filing systems to computerized filing systems has possibly been the single greatest use of data managers. Any aspect of a business that uses some form of file system—such as a wheel card index file or file cabinet—could potentially be computerized using a data manager.

Business applications that are easily adapted to use with a data manager include the maintaining of employee records, inventory control, and listings

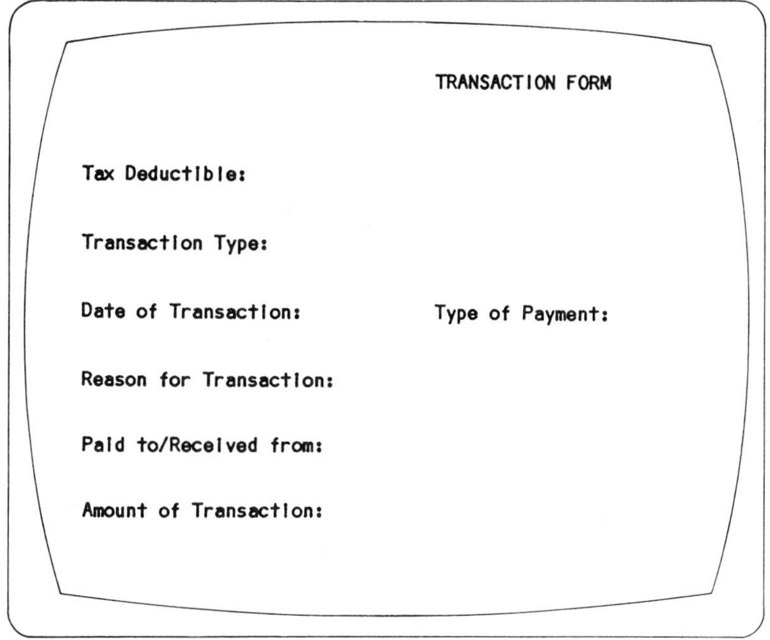
TRANSACTION FORM

Tax Deductible:

Transaction Type:

Date of Transaction: Type of Payment:

Reason for Transaction:

Paid to/Received from:

Amount of Transaction:

Figure 8–4 SAMPLE TRANSACTION FORM FOR TAX PURPOSES

of suppliers and customers. A small sporting goods retail store, for example, can computerize its inventory to improve sales and overall business through more efficient and timely record keeping (see Figure 8–5). Managers of the store can use the data manager to inform them when goods are reaching a reorder point: by recording daily sales using the data manager, the managers can see when the stock level of a particular item is low. By doing so, the store can have ample supply of an item on hand when customers come to purchase it.

If a data manager also has mathematical capabilities, it can be used for such things as determining dollar sales of an item for a certain period. This is one method managers can use to track sales of an item. The mathematical capabilities of the data manager also can be used for inventory control. Rather than hand count items in the store, the data manager can subtotal and total inventory on hand for tax reporting at the end of the year, saving a great deal of time. The data manager can be used for these applications if the required data is included within the record.

Perhaps the greatest benefit to computerized record keeping in business is the amount of time that potentially can be saved. In the case of a small retail store, the managers' time can be a very valuable commodity.

Specialized Uses

Most of the discussion to this point has considered data managers in a general manner. It has been stated that they can be used for just about any record-keeping purpose in the home and in business. However, some data managers are designed for use in special or unique situations. One such specialized use of data managers is in the area of mass mailing.

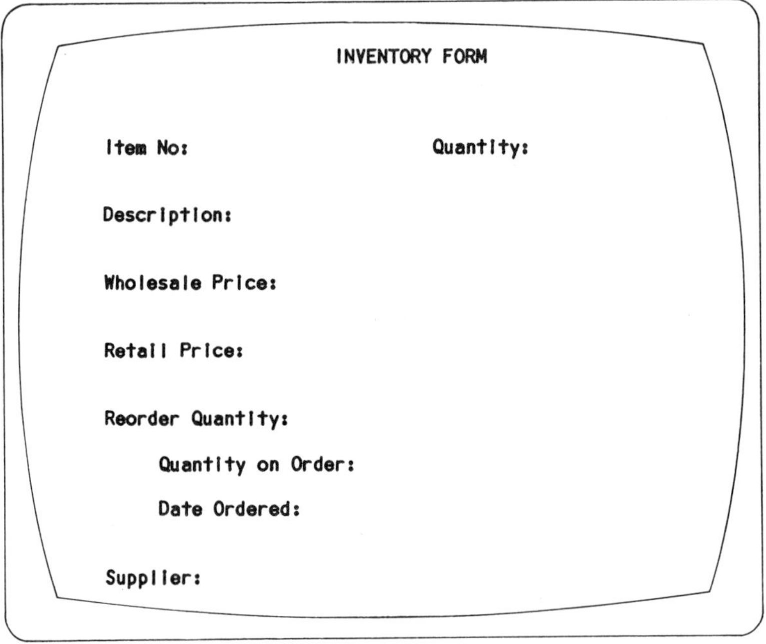
INVENTORY FORM

Item No: Quantity:

Description:

Wholesale Price:

Retail Price:

Reorder Quantity:

Quantity on Order:

Date Ordered:

Supplier:

Figure 8–5 SAMPLE INVENTORY FORM FOR A SMALL RETAIL SPORTING GOODS STORE

Creating mailing lists is a popular application. Mailing list data managers provide the user with the ability to store, update, sort, and print data that can be used for creating mailing lists or mailing labels. In some cases, the mailing list capability is built into the package; in others, it can be added to the base package for an additional cost; and in still other cases, the entire data manager is designed for the purpose of creating and maintaining mailing lists.

Not only can data managers be used to create mailing lists; they also can be used along with word processors to generate form letters to send to the individuals or organizations found on the mailing lists. Data man-

LEARNING CHECK

1. Data manager software packages are designed to speed up and simplify the ________ and ________ of information.

2. A ________ is *not* another name for a data manager.

a. file cabinet

b. file filer

c. file handler

d. file manager

3. A ________ is a meaningful item of data, such as an employee number.

4. File handlers can access ________ data file(s) at one time.

a. one

b. two

c. three

d. multiple

5. ________ are designed to consolidate various independent files into one integrated whole.

a. file handlers

b. data bases

c. records

d. cabinets

6. ________ often result in duplicate information.

a. file handlers

b. data bases

c. records

d. cabinets

ANSWERS: **1.** recording, filing. **2.** b. **3.** field. **4.** a. **5.** b **6.** a.

agers, therefore, can be used in conjunction with word processors to create form letters for mass-mailing purposes.

FEATURES OF DATA MANAGERS

Many of the popular data managers offer what can be considered a standard group of features. In most packages, these features can be selected through choices displayed in menus on the screen. For the most part, the standard file handlers are menu driven and prompt you to select features from a main menu and submenus (see Figure 8–6). Figure 8–6 is only an example of a menu and does not contain standard features. These standard features include adding records; deleting records; searching for records, updating records, or both; sorting the data file, and printing. Additional features contained in some data managers include making mathematical calculations, creating screen displays, and displaying help screens containing available menu choices and explanations to guide the inexperienced user through the use of the package.

Add/Delete

Adding and deleting records are features essential to data management. Once a file has been created, data is entered to the file using the add feature. This feature allows you to place records of information into the data file. The delete, or remove, feature serves just the opposite function; by choosing the delete feature, you can erase a record of information from the data file.

Search/Update

The search feature of data managers allows you to search an existing data file for a record or records based on certain criteria. If, for example, you wanted to find all tennis rackets within your sports equipment inventory with a price of over $25, you would use the search feature. The update feature, in contrast, allows you to change the value of a data field once you have located it. If the price of the tennis rackets had changed from $25 to $27.50, for example, you would use the update feature to make the change within your inventory file. In many data managers the search and update features are used in conjunction with each other to locate a record and then change it.

Sort

The sort feature in data managers can be very valuable. The data in the file is generally stored in the order in which it is entered, and the sort feature provides the user with a way to alter that order of storage. For example, the data file containing the names and addresses for a mailing list can be sorted, or arranged according to last names, prior to printing the list. This

DATA MANAGER III

1. Add a Record

2. Delete a Record

3. Search for a Record

4. Update a Record

5. Print

6. Exit the Program

Please Enter the Number of the Choice: 1

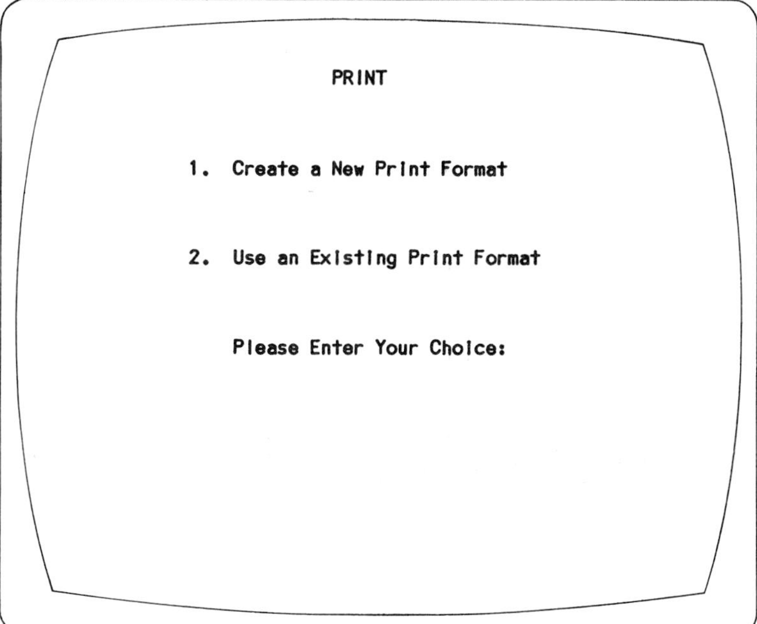

Figure 8–6 SAMPLE MAIN MENU AND SUBMENU

allows the list to be printed in alphabetical order. If you were using a data manager to help balance your checkbook, the entries you had made into the data file could be sorted according to either date or check number prior to balancing the checkbook.

Print

The print feature of data managers is also very valuable. Some packages, however, have limited printing capabilities. If you intend to do a great deal of printing or creating reports, you should investigate the printing capabilities of the package before purchasing it. Some software publishers offer an independent report-generating package or package add-on to use with the data files that have been created. Again, these packages have different capabilities and limitations, which should be investigated before one is purchased. If all you wish to do is print mailing lists and mailing labels, most data managers have adequate print capabilities to meet your needs.

Additional Features

A number of data managers have the capability to make mathematical calculations on the data contained within the files. These calculations include subtotaling or totaling a particular field within the data records and can include calculating statistics such as means or averages. File handlers, for the most part, offer limited mathematical capabilities, whereas data base packages typically offer more complex computations.

A special feature in many data managers allows you to design the screen on which the data will be displayed. By designing the screen display format, you indicate to the data manager the fields that will be contained within a record of the data file. Data managers that do not allow you to create a display format generally require you to enter data through a text entry mode similar to the manner in which text is entered using a word processor. Figure 8–7 illustrates a possible screen display format for a file that contains product supplier information.

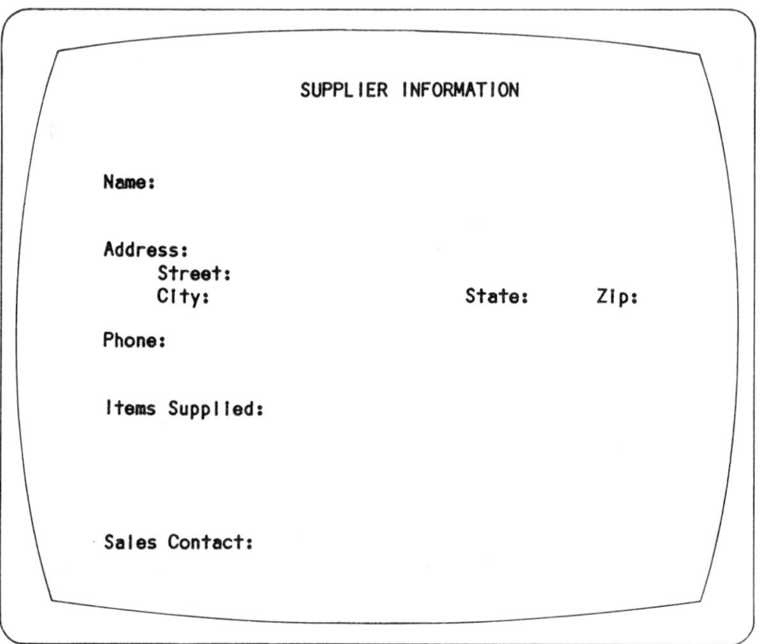

Figure 8–7 SAMPLE SUPPLIER INFORMATION FORM

Data managers that offer you the ability to design your own screen display format also provide a way to modify the existing display format. The design can be altered either before or after data has been entered into the file. Making a change in the screen display before data is added to the file is simple. Fields within the record can be changed, added, or deleted without affecting any data. Making a change to a screen display after data has been entered into the file, however, is more difficult. Although you can still change, add, or delete fields within the data record, you must be careful. Once the screen display and data file have been changed, it can be very difficult (if not impossible) to restore the original screen and data. To be safe, therefore, make a backup copy of the original before changing the screen display after data has been entered into the file.

Another feature used in some data managers is the display of help screens upon request from the user. If you are confused about your available choices at a certain point within the program, you can request a display of the available options and possibly even a brief explanation of what each option will do. This feature is especially valuable for inexperienced users of the package. Once they have gained experience, however, the need for the help screens decreases. Since the screens are displayed only on request, experienced users are not slowed by the additional display of menu screens and explanations of available choices.

CHOOSING A DATA MANAGER

There are a number of considerations involved in choosing a data manager. The way in which the package is to be used is the primary consideration. Additional considerations include the following:

- Storage capacities.
- Available features.
- Package flexibility.

By determining how you want to use the package, you establish a set of criteria by which to judge the available packages.

The storage capacity of the package is a vital consideration. Many software publishers specify either how many characters can be stored using the package or how many average-sized records can be stored. If the publisher uses the record as a means of determining how much data can be stored in a file, it normally provides some means of calculating the number of average-sized records that can be stored. If the number of characters is used, you will have to determine the average number of characters a record will contain to determine approximately how many records can be stored in a file. The storage capacity is very important, because if you have 1,000 records to store and the package is only capable of functioning with 800 records, the package will be of very little value to you. Thus, determine your storage capacity requirements prior to shopping for a data manager.

The features offered by a data manager are also important. If you know that it will be necessary to do a considerable amount of mathematical calculations when using the data manager, you must consider only those packages capable of providing the necessary calculations. If you require the creation of detailed reports, you must evaluate only those packages that provide the necessary printing capabilities. If you will require a great deal of sorting, it is essential that you consider only those packages that offer sorting as an available feature.

The flexibility of a particular data manager also should be considered. If you intend to use your data manager to create data files for use with your word processor, you should consider only those packages that can create compatible data files. Consult with the data manager manual or the software salesperson to determine if the data managers you are considering will create compatible data files.

All these things must be taken into consideration when choosing a data manager. The important thing to remember is to be sure to choose a package that meets your particular needs. If you have any questions regarding features included in the packages and their overall capabilities, the software salesperson and software magazines and journals are potential sources of answers.

HARDWARE REQUIREMENTS

Hardware requirements for data managers, much like hardware requirements for other software packages, vary from package to package, depending largely on the capabilities of the particular package. Evaluate each package according to the hardware required for its use. The hardware requirements for the given package should then be considered in relation to either your current computer system or the system you would like to purchase. The following are some of the things to consider in relation to hardware requirements:

- Internal memory size requirements.
- Secondary storage requirements, including disk drive requirements.
- Printer requirements.
- Monitor requirements.

All software packages require a certain amount of internal storage (see Chapter 2). If the package you are considering does not specify a particular internal storage requirement but is designed to run on your computer or the one you are considering purchasing, you can assume it will run on the amount of internal storage provided with the computer when it comes from the factory. If the package states that it requires a certain amount of memory and you are uncertain whether your own computer has enough, consult the software salesperson or an independent knowledgeable person. The amount of internal storage required for data managers generally ranges from 48K to 256K of RAM. The size of the internal storage will limit the amount of information you can store in a file using your data manager. This limit is normally specified by the software publisher according to either the total number of characters or the number of records based on the record size. Software publishers provide some means of determining the storage capacity so that you can determine if enough room is available for your particular application.

As you learned in Chapter 2, secondary storage for microcomputers is normally in the form of floppy diskettes. Before purchasing your software, determine the secondary storage requirements, if any, of the package you are considering. Most data managers are designed to run with floppy diskettes because of the speed at which the data on the disk can be loaded to internal storage.

Along with internal storage requirements, data managers designed to run on a floppy disk system will also state the number of disk drives required by the package. Some packages will run with only one disk drive, but most require at least two, and some will handle up to eight. The more disk drives used, the larger the amount of data accessible to the data manager without having to switch floppy disks in and out of the disk drives. Hard disk drives are an alternative to the floppy disk system normally used with the standard microcomputer system. A hard disk drive increases both the amount of storage available to the data manager and the speed at which data is retrieved from disk and saved to disk.

The choice of a printer can be important, depending on how you intend to use your package. If you intend to use your data manager in conjunction with a word processor for form letter creation and printing, a letter quality printer will be required. A data manager used for inventory control, in contrast, may only require a dot matrix printer, which is less expensive than a letter quality printer. Your choice of printer should be based on the intended use of your software packages or your computer system in general.

LEARNING CHECK

1. The ________ feature is used to enter data once the file has been created.

2. Most data managers are menu driven. (True or false?)

3. List four features that a data manager typically includes.

4. Home versions of data manager packages are usually ________ (more/less) sophisticated than business versions.

5. ________ are not a consideration in relation to hardware requirements.

a. Internal memory size requirements

b. Printer requirements

c. Monitor requirements

d. Package feature requirements

6. Some data manager software packages are capable of running on a single disk drive. (True or false?)

ANSWERS:

1. add. **2.** true. **3.** add/delete, search/update, sort and print. **4.** less. **5.** d. **6.** false.

The choice of a monitor, like the choice of a printer, also depends on the application for which you intend to use your data manager. If you are going to use your package for mailing list applications, a monochrome monitor of average quality may be sufficient. If, however, you intend to integrate your data files from your data manager with a graphics software package, you may need a color monitor with graphics capability. The same is true for your choice of printer; if you intend to use your data manager for graphic purposes; you may need a color printer with graphics capability. Assess your needs to determine what printer and monitor you will require.

An additional item that should be considered is the eighty-column display option available for some computer systems. Some data managers may require an eighty-column display, whereas others may list it as an option. An eighty-column display can increase the amount of text that is displayed on the monitor screen. Again, review the package documentation and investigate the hardware requirements before making a final choice of a data manager.

POPULAR DATA MANAGMENT PACKAGES

In the following listing of some of the popular file handlers available for the IBM PC and PCjr family of computers, the packages will be grouped under the headings "Home Versions," "Business Versions," and "Specialized Versions." The manner in which the packages have been categorized is based primarily on their level of sophistication and their ability to meet the needs of the users in each of the three categories.

The listing of packages that follows does not endorse any of them but is simply a list of some of the more popular data managers and their features. To make a choice based on your needs, you must evaluate the packages according to your intended use. This listing serves only as a beginning in the process of evaluating data managers.

Home Versions

The home version packages are usually less sophisticated in their features and provide for the storage of fewer total records than packages in either of the two other categories. Home versions are also more suitable to the novice computer user. The following data managers typify those available for the home market:

- ***PFS: File***

  Available from: Software Publishing Corp.
  1901 Landings Dr.
  Mountain View, CA 94043
  Price range: $125–$150
  Features: See Table 8–2
  Available for: IBM PC, IBM PCjr

- ***Data Handler***

  Available from: Miller Microcomputer Services
  61 Lakeshore Road
  Natick, MA 01760

Table 8–2 HOME VERSION PACKAGES AND THEIR FEATURES

Package \ Feature	Menu driven	Add/delete/search/update	Sort	Print	Mathematical calculations	Create screen formats	Help screens
PFS: File	x	x	x	x		x	
Data Handler	x	x	x	x	x		
PC-File III	x			x	x	x	
UltraFile	x	x	x	x	x	x	
Personal Data Base II	x	x	x	x		x	

Price range: $50–$75
Features: See Table 8–2
Available for: IBM PC, IBM PCjr

- ***PC-File III***

Available from: Jim Button
P.O. Box 5786
Bellevue, WA 98006
Price range: $25–$50
Features: See Table 8–2
Available for: IBM PC

- ***UltraFile***

Available from: Arrays Inc./Continental Software
11223 S. Hindry Ave.
Los Angeles, CA 90045
Price range: $175–$200
Features: See Table 8–2
Available for: IBM PC

- ***Personal Data Base II***

Available from: SuperSoft Inc.
P.O. Box 1628
Champaign, IL 61820
Price range: $125–$150
Features: See Table 8–2
Available for: IBM PC, IBM PCjr

Business Versions

Business version data manager packages have been rated as such because of a greater overall sophistication than the home packages and because of their higher price. Business version packages are also somewhat more difficult to learn to use, and in some cases they provide greater storage capacities. The following are some popular business versions:

- ***VersaForm***

  Available from: Applied Software Technology
  170 Knowles Drive
  Los Gatos, CA 95030
  Price range: $375–$400
  Features: See Table 8–3
  Available for: IBM PC, IBM PCjr

- ***Dbase III***

  Available from: Ashton-Tate
  10150 W. Jefferson Blvd.
  Cover City,CA 90230
  Price range: $650–$700
  Features: See Table 8–3
  Available for: IBM PC

Condor Series 20

Available from: Condor Computer Corporation
2051 S. State St.
Ann Arbor, MI 48104
Price range: $625–$650
Features: See Table 8–3
Available for: IBM PC, IBM PCjr

Specialized Versions

The specialized data manager packages have been placed in this category because they are designed for a particular data-management application.

Table 8–3 BUSINESS VERSION PACKAGES AND THEIR FEATURES

PACKAGE / FEATURE	Menu driven	Add/delete/search/update	Sort	Print	Mathematical calculations	Create screen formats	Help Screens
VersaForm		x	x	x	x	x	
Dbase III	x	x	x	x	x	x	x
Condor Series 20	x	x	x	x	x	x	x

Although First Class Mail can be adapted for general data-management applications, its design reflects its primary purpose—creating and maintaining mailing lists. Sapana-Cardfile-Index-I, in contrast, is designed to record and file information relating to magazines and books. Addressor is a data manager that stores addresses and also serves as a date reminder. The user can request a display of addresses and associated dates that are close to the requested dates.

- ***First Class Mail***

  Available from: Continental Software
  11223 S. Hindry Ave.
  Los Angeles, CA 90045
  Price range: \$100–\$125
  Available for: IBM PC, IBM PCjr

- ***Sapana-Cardfile***

  Available from: Sapana Micro Software
  1305 S. Rouse
  Pittsburg, KS 66762
  Price range: \$25–\$50
  Available for: IBM PC, IBM PCjr

- ***Addressor***

  Available from: Info Soft Computers
  2699 Clayton Road
  Concord, CA 94519
  Price range: \$50 – \$75
  Available for: IBM PC, IBM PCjr

GUIDE TO WESTFILE™

WestFile data manager, which is included on the diskette labeled WestFile, is a file handler. Packages such as WestFile have become popular in business because they allow the user to store data in a convenient and easily accessed location. For example, a rock concert promoter who wants to store the addresses, capacities, and names of various stadiums around the country could use a program such as WestFile. By using a data manager, the promoter can store this information, retrieve it, sort it, update it, or delete it as desired.

The WestFile program can be accessed by first booting DOS 2.XX and then inserting the disk into the disk drive and typing WESTFILE, if it is not a self-booting diskette, or by inserting the self-booting disk into the disk drive and turning on the monitor and computer. After you boot WestFile, the program asks, WOULD YOU LIKE INSTRUCTIONS? (Y/N). Press Y (yes) for instructions and N (no) to go to the WestFile MAIN MENU shown in Figure 8–8. This menu contains both operational and nonoperational functions. The nonoperational functions are the utility functions, which are accessed by Selection 7 (see Figure 8–9). Although they are nonoperational on this diskette, they have been included to familiarize you with the way they would function in a typical data management package. The data manager menu offers six operational functions, which are selected by pressing the numbers 1, 2, 3, 4, 5, and 6 (see Figure 8–8).

Selecting a File

The first function listed in the WestFile MAIN MENU, SELECT A FILE, allows you to create your own data file or to open one of the existing data files. To select functions 2, 3, or 4 in the data manager MAIN MENU, a file must first be selected. To choose the SELECT A FILE option, press 1 when the MAIN MENU is presented (refer again to Figure 8–8).

Selecting an Existing File. After you choose the SELECT A FILE option, a new screen is displayed. This screen shows the existing data files and asks for a file name to be entered. To open an existing file, enter one of the file names listed under the heading EXISTING FILES. The file name that is entered must exactly match the file name shown on the screen, or a new file is accidentally created. (If this should happen, simply press the <Esc> key, and you will return to the data manager menu.) The software package then opens the data file.

YOUR TURN

As a hands-on activity, the SELECT A FILE function can be used to select the STADIUMS file. The following steps serve as a guide:

1. Press 1 when the WestFile MAIN MENU is presented.
2. The program then shows the SELECT screen and waits for a file name

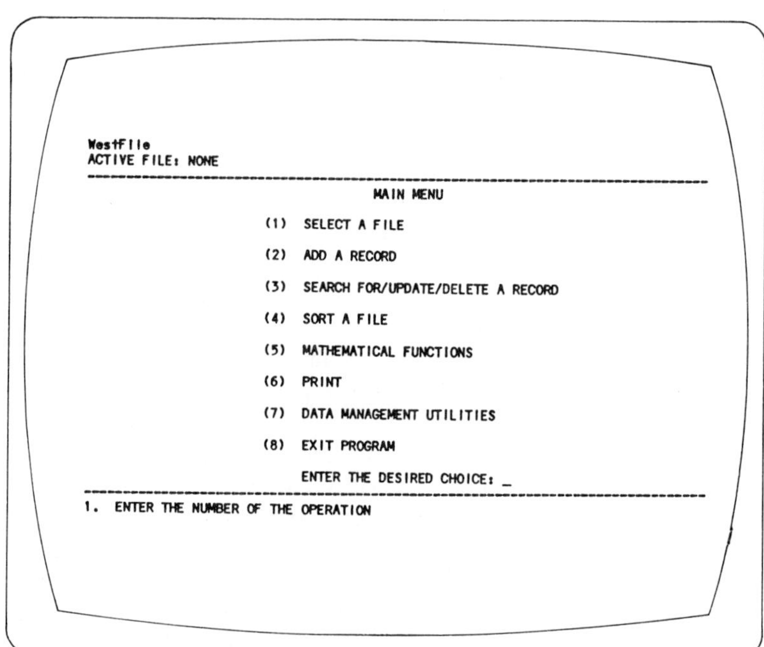

WestFile
ACTIVE FILE: NONE
MAIN MENU
(1) SELECT A FILE
(2) ADD A RECORD
(3) SEARCH FOR/UPDATE/DELETE A RECORD
(4) SORT A FILE
(5) MATHEMATICAL FUNCTIONS
(6) PRINT
(7) DATA MANAGEMENT UTILITIES
(8) EXIT PROGRAM
ENTER THE DESIRED CHOICE: _
1. ENTER THE NUMBER OF THE OPERATION

Figure 8–8 WESTFILE MAIN MENU

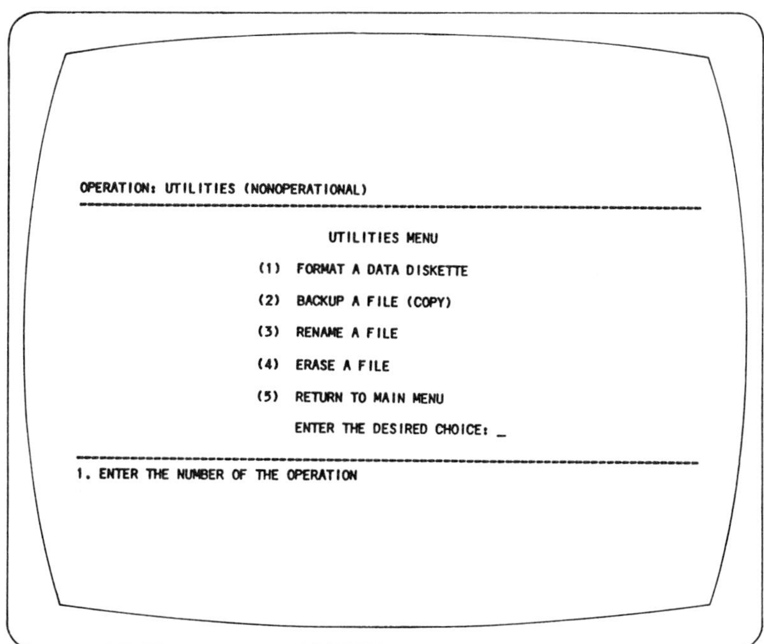

OPERATION: UTILITIES (NONOPERATIONAL)
UTILITIES MENU
(1) FORMAT A DATA DISKETTE
(2) BACKUP A FILE (COPY)
(3) RENAME A FILE
(4) ERASE A FILE
(5) RETURN TO MAIN MENU
ENTER THE DESIRED CHOICE: _
1. ENTER THE NUMBER OF THE OPERATION

Figure 8–9 UTILITIES MENU

to be entered. Enter STADIUMS (see Figure 8–10), and press the RETURN key.

3. The program then returns to the WestFile MAIN MENU and displays the ACTIVE FILE above the dashed line.

Defining a New File. The SELECT A FILE function also allows new files to be created. This version of the data manager program is limited because it allows two files to be added. If you wish to create more than two data files, one of the old files must be erased first. To erase an old data file, answer yes (press Y) in response to the question that asks you if a particular file should be erased.

To define a new file, enter Selection 1 from the data manager menu. The program then displays the SELECT screen and waits for a file/name to be entered. Enter a file name from one to eight characters long, and press the RETURN key. (The file name may consist of any letters from *A* to *Z* and the numbers 1 to 9.) Next, the program displays the DEFINE screen and asks for the name of field #1. Enter a field name from one to ten characters in length, and press the RETURN key. Next, the cursor moves to the right of LENGTH and waits for the length of Field #1 to be entered. (The length is the number of characters you allow for each data item in each field and cannot be greater than sixty.) Enter the length (a number between 1 and 60), and press the RETURN key. The program then asks for the name of field #2 and its length. Enter another field name and its length. The program asks for the data field names and their lengths until twelve data fields have been entered, or until only the RETURN key is pressed when the program asks for a field name. The program then asks, DEFINITIONS OK? (Y/N). Press

Figure 8–10 SELECTING THE STADIUMS FILE

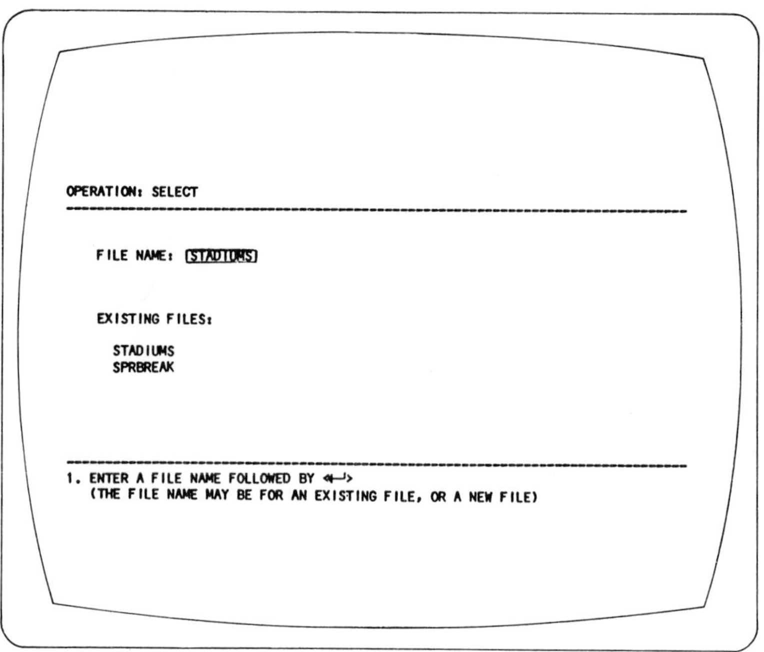

OPERATION: SELECT
FILE NAME: STADIUMS
EXISTING FILES:
STADIUMS
SPRBREAK
1. ENTER A FILE NAME FOLLOWED BY <↵>
(THE FILE NAME MAY BE FOR AN EXISTING FILE, OR A NEW FILE)

Y if the definitions are correctly typed. If the definitions are not correctly typed, press N. If N is entered, the field names and lengths can be changed by using the TAB key to position to a field name or length and editing it. After Y is entered, the program accepts the data record definition and returns to the data manager menu.

To further explain, consider how the STADIUMS file included on your diskette was created; however, there is no need for you to use the DEFINE screen, since the STADIUMS file is provided on your diskette. When the STADIUMS file was created, Selection 1 was entered when the data manager menu was presented. Next, the program waited for a file name to be entered. STADIUMS was entered, and the RETURN key was pressed. The program then displayed the DEFINE screen. The names and lengths of the fields used in the STADIUMS file have been defined as follows:

Field Number	Field Name	Length/(Number of Characters)
1	STAD. NAME	25
2	CAPACITY	7
3	ADDRESS	25
4	CITY	20
5	STATE	2
6	ZIP	10

STAD. NAME was entered for FIELD #1 NAME, and the RETURN key was pressed. Next, the program waited for the LENGTH to be entered. The number 25 was entered, and the RETURN key was pressed (see Figure 8–11). The program then asked for the name of field #2. CAPACITY was

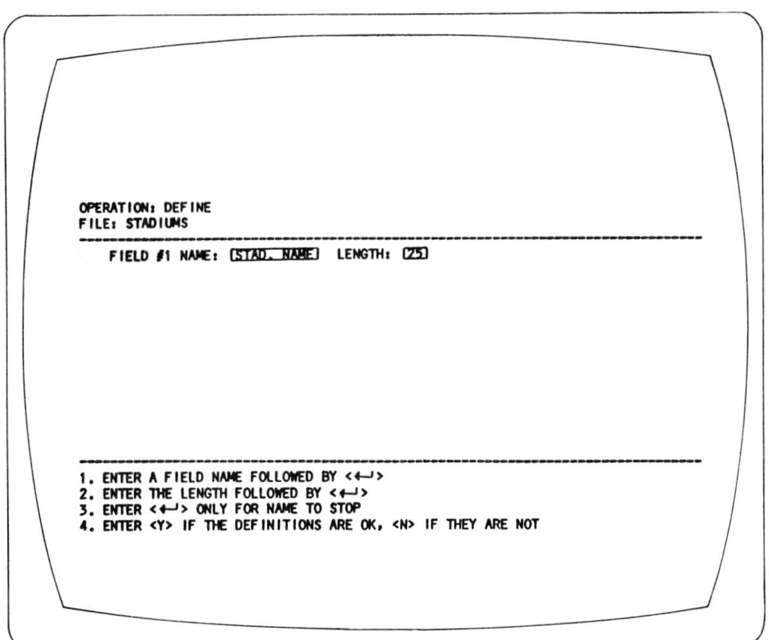

OPERATION: DEFINE
FILE: STADIUMS
FIELD #1 NAME: STAD. NAME LENGTH: 25
1. ENTER A FIELD NAME FOLLOWED BY <←┘>
2. ENTER THE LENGTH FOLLOWED BY <←┘>
3. ENTER <←┘> ONLY FOR NAME TO STOP
4. ENTER <Y> IF THE DEFINITIONS ARE OK, <N> IF THEY ARE NOT

Figure 8–11 DEFINING THE FIRST FIELD NAME OF THE STADIUMS FILE

entered, and the RETURN key was pressed. Next, the program moved the cursor to the length of field #2. The number 7 was entered and the RETURN key was pressed. The program then asked for the names and lengths of fields 3, 4, 5, and 6. ADDRESS and 25 were entered for the name and length of field #3. CITY and 20 were entered for the name and the length of field #4. STATE and 2 were entered for the name and the length of field #5. ZIP and 10 were entered for the name and the length of field #6. (Each entry was followed by pressing the RETURN key.) Next, the program asked for #7 NAME. The RETURN key was pressed to stop. The program asked, DEFINITIONS OK? (Y/N) (see Figure 8–12). Y was entered to signify that the definitions were correctly typed. The program then accepted the STADIUMS file record definition and returned to the data manager menu. After this, ten records were added to the STADIUMS file using Selection 2 from the WestFile MAIN MENU. These records and their data item values are shown in Figure 8–13.

Searching for a Record

The SEARCH FOR/UPDATE/DELETE A RECORD function is capable of searching through a file for a specific value of a data item. The program uses two types of searches: a full value and a numeric search. A full value search tries to find an exact match for an item. For example, if the search were for the value ATLANTA, the program would find only the value ATLANTA, not a value such as A TLANTA. A numeric search tries to find a number either greater than, less than, or equal to the number specified. The greater than, less than, or equal sign is placed before the specified numeric value. The program then finds the values according to the indicated

Figure 8–12 DEFINING THE FIELDS OF THE STADIUMS FILE

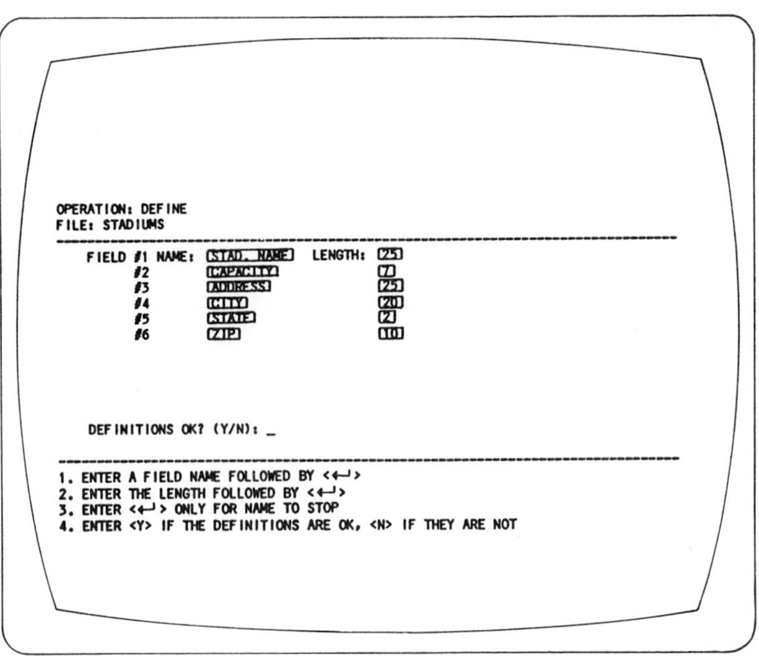
OPERATION: DEFINE
FILE: STADIUMS
FIELD #1 NAME: STAD. NAME LENGTH: 25
#2 CAPACITY 7
#3 ADDRESS 25
#4 CITY 20
#5 STATE 2
#6 ZIP 10
DEFINITIONS OK? (Y/N): _
1. ENTER A FIELD NAME FOLLOWED BY <↵>
2. ENTER THE LENGTH FOLLOWED BY <↵>
3. ENTER <↵> ONLY FOR NAME TO STOP
4. ENTER <Y> IF THE DEFINITIONS ARE OK, <N> IF THEY ARE NOT

operator (>, <, =,). For example, if the greater than operator and 20000 are entered for the field CAPACITY in the STADIUMS example, the program looks for all values greater than 20000 within the CAPACITY field.

To enter the SEARCH function, press 3 when the data manager menu is presented. After selecting the SEARCH FOR/UPDATE/DELETE A RECORD option, the SEARCH screen appears. To begin the search for a value, the program asks for a field name to be entered. (The field names are listed at the top of the screen under the dotted line.) Enter one of the field names, and press the RETURN key. After you select the field name, the cursor is placed next to it. This indicates that the value to be located needs to be entered. Enter the operator and the value to search for (for a numeric search) or just a value (for a full value search), and press the RETURN key. The program then asks, OK TO BEGIN SEARCH? (Y/N). Simply press Y or N for yes or no. If you press Y, the program automatically searches through the file for the value. If the data item value can be found, the program displays it (and all other values in the same record) on the screen. If the data item value cannot be found, the program displays the message NO MATCHING RECORDS FOUND. For example, if the search were on the field name STATE for a value of OH (for Ohio), no record could be found containing that value in the STADIUMS file; the program would display the message NO MATCHING RECORDS FOUND. Next, the program asks, DO ANOTHER SEARCH? (Y/N). Enter N to return to the WestFile MAIN MENU, or enter Y to do another search.

Figure 8–13 CONTENTS OF THE STADIUMS FILE

```
STAD. NAME: ARROWHEAD STADIUM
CAPACITY  : 78067
ADDRESS   :
CITY      : KANSAS CITY
STATE     : MO
ZIP       : 64129

STAD. NAME: THE SUPERDOME
CAPACITY  : 80982
ADDRESS   : 944 ST. CHARLES AVE.
CITY      : NEW ORLEANS
STATE     : LA
ZIP       : 70130

STAD. NAME: THE ORANGE BOWL
CAPACITY  : 75459
ADDRESS   : 1400 NW 4TH ST.
CITY      : MIAMI
STATE     : FL
ZIP       : 33101

STAD. NAME: SHEA STADIUM
CAPACITY  : 60372
ADDRESS   : 126TH ST. AND ROOSEVELT
CITY      : FLUSHING
STATE     : NY
ZIP       : 11368

STAD. NAME: ANAHEIM STADIUM
CAPACITY  : 69000
ADDRESS   : 2000 S STATE COLLEGE BLVD
CITY      : ANAHEIM
STATE     : CA
ZIP       : 92803

STAD. NAME: THE OMNI
CAPACITY  : 15785
ADDRESS   : 100 TECHWOOD DR. NW
CITY      : ATLANTA
STATE     : GA
ZIP       : 30303

STAD. NAME: THE SPECTRUM
CAPACITY  : 18482
ADDRESS   : BROAD AND PATTERSON STS.
CITY      : PHILADELPHIA
STATE     : PA
ZIP       : 19148

STAD. NAME: PONTIAC SILVERDOME
CAPACITY  : 80638
ADDRESS   : 1200 FEATHERSTONE RD.
CITY      : PONTIAC
STATE     : MI
ZIP       : 48057

STAD. NAME: MADISON SQUARE GARDEN
CAPACITY  : 19591
ADDRESS   : 4 PENNSYLVANIA PLAZA
CITY      : NEW YORK
STATE     : NY
ZIP       : 10001

STAD. NAME: THE KINGDOME
CAPACITY  : 64752
ADDRESS   : 201 S. KING
CITY      : SEATTLE
STATE     : WA
ZIP       : 98101
```

YOUR TURN

To illustrate this concept, the following hands-on activity will show you how to search the STAD. NAME field of the STADIUMS file for the value SHEA STADIUM:

1. When the WestFile MAIN MENU is presented, press 3.
2. The program asks for the field name. Since the value SHEA STADIUM belongs in the field called STAD. NAME, enter STAD. NAME (see Figure 8–14), and press the RETURN key.
3. The program waits for the value of the data item to be entered.
4. Since SHEA STADIUM is not a numeric value, a full value search must be done. Enter SHEA STADIUM without including a numeric search operator (see Figure 8–15), and press the RETURN key.

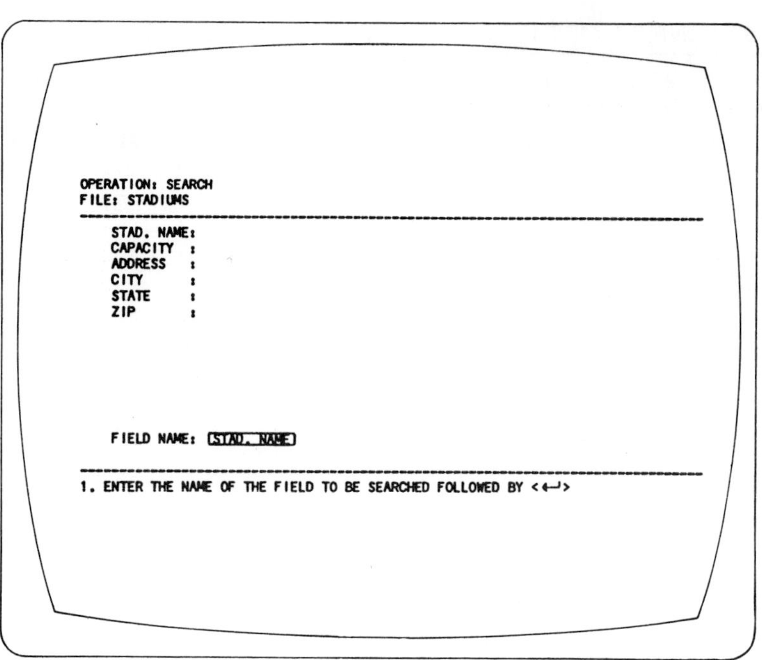

Figure 8–14 ENTERING THE FIELD NAME TO SEARCH ON

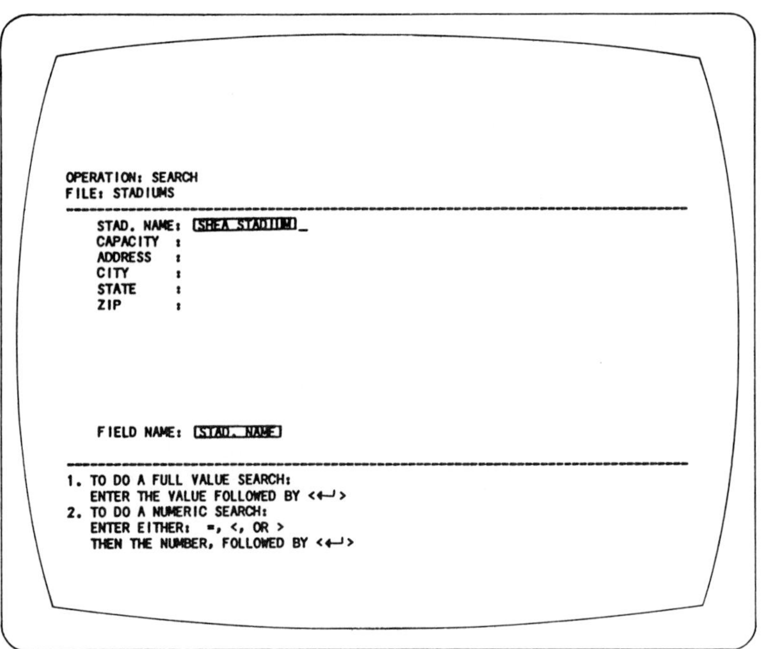

Figure 8–15 ENTERING THE VALUE TO SEARCH FOR

5. The program asks, OK TO BEGIN SEARCH? (Y/N). Enter Y (for yes) if everything is correctly typed or N (for no) if anything has been mistyped, and return to Step 2.
6. When SHEA STADIUM is correctly typed, press Y. The program then searches for SHEA STADIUM.

7. Since SHEA STADIUM is in the file, the program displays all the information related to SHEA STADIUM on the screen.

Continuing the Search

While searching for a specific value, it is sometimes desirable to locate one or more records with the same value. For example, two stadiums may be located in the same state. It is possible to locate these two records with only one search, since WestFile is capable of looking for more than one record with the same value.

To locate these records, choose Selection 3 from the WestFile MAIN MENU. Next, indicate the field name and the value to be searched for (refer to the previous section, "Searching for a Record"). The program asks, OK TO BEGIN SEARCH? (Y/N). Enter Y (for yes); the program finds the first record containing that value and displays it on the screen. The program then asks if it should CONTINUE, STOP, UPDATE, OR DELETE (C/S/U/D). Since you would like to continue searching for records with the same value, press C for CONTINUE. The program continues until it finds the next record with the identical data item value. The program displays the record and again asks if it should CONTINUE, STOP, UPDATE, OR DELETE (C/S/U/D). This continues until a response other than C is entered or until the data item value cannot be found in the remaining records of the file. If there are no remaining records, the message NO MORE MATCHING RECORDS is displayed. The program then asks, DO ANOTHER SEARCH? (Y/N). If Y is entered, you can begin the search process again. If N is entered, the program leaves the SEARCH function and returns to the MAIN MENU.

YOUR TURN

As a hands-on activity, the CONTINUE function can be used to search for the two stadiums located in New York (NY). The following steps serve as a guide:

1. Follow the guidelines for the search using STATE as the field name and NY as the value to be searched for (refer to the previous section, "Searching for a Record").
2. The program finds the first stadium located in NY and displays it on the screen.
3. The question CONTINUE, STOP, UPDATE, OR DELETE (C/S/U/D) is displayed. Press C for CONTINUE to search for the next stadium in NY (see Figure 8–16).
4. The program locates the next record containing NY within the field named STATE and displays it (see Figure 8–17).
5. The program asks if it should CONTINUE, STOP, UPDATE, OR DELETE (C/S/U/D). To continue looking for stadiums in NY, enter a C for CONTINUE.

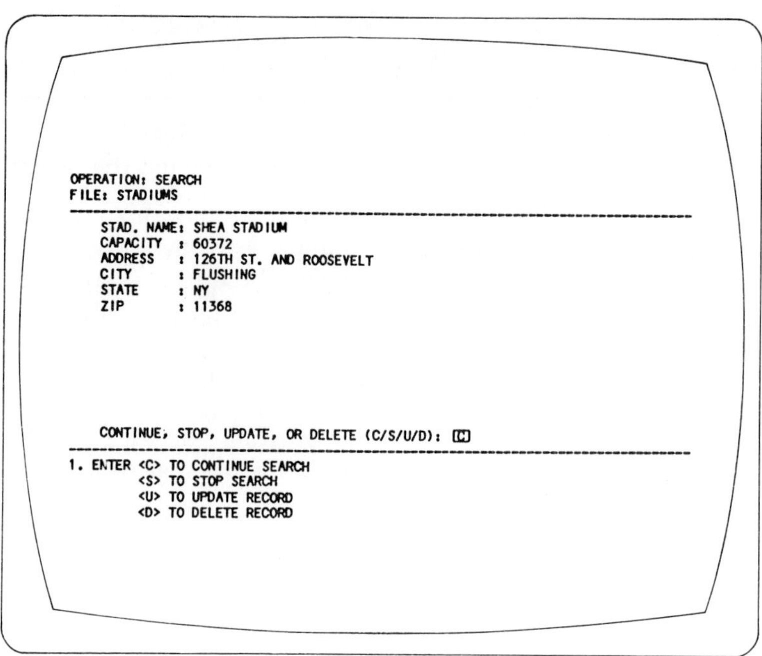

OPERATION: SEARCH
FILE: STADIUMS
STAD. NAME: SHEA STADIUM
CAPACITY : 60372
ADDRESS : 126TH ST. AND ROOSEVELT
CITY : FLUSHING
STATE : NY
ZIP : 11368
CONTINUE, STOP, UPDATE, OR DELETE (C/S/U/D): C
1. ENTER <C> TO CONTINUE SEARCH
<S> TO STOP SEARCH
<U> TO UPDATE RECORD
<D> TO DELETE RECORD

Figure 8–16 CONTINUING THE SEARCH

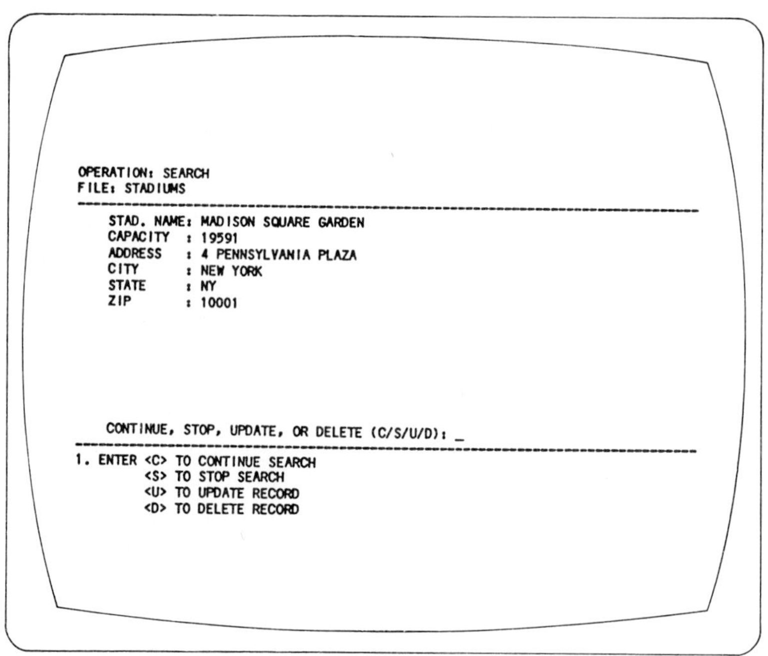

OPERATION: SEARCH
FILE: STADIUMS
STAD. NAME: MADISON SQUARE GARDEN
CAPACITY : 19591
ADDRESS : 4 PENNSYLVANIA PLAZA
CITY : NEW YORK
STATE : NY
ZIP : 10001
CONTINUE, STOP, UPDATE, OR DELETE (C/S/U/D): _
1. ENTER <C> TO CONTINUE SEARCH
<S> TO STOP SEARCH
<U> TO UPDATE RECORD
<D> TO DELETE RECORD

Figure 8–17 PROGRAM DISPLAYS THE NEXT RECORD IN NY

6. Since there are no more stadiums in NY, the program displays the message NO MORE MATCHING RECORDS and asks, DO ANOTHER SEARCH? (Y/N).

7. Enter N, and the program returns to the MAIN MENU.

Deleting a Record

The data manager program is also capable of erasing a record from a data file. If a record does not belong in the file, it can be erased. Choosing the DELETE option when the question CONTINUE, STOP, UPDATE, OR DELETE (C/S/U/D) is displayed allows you to erase a record from the data file. However, remember that once a record has been deleted, it cannot be accessed again.

To use the DELETE function, choose Selection 3 from the WestFile MAIN MENU. Next, search for the record by entering a field name and a data item value in that field (refer to the "Searching for a Record" section). After the record has been found, the program asks if it should CONTINUE, STOP, UPDATE, OR DELETE (C/S/U/D). Press D for DELETE. The program then asks, OK TO DELETE RECORD? (Y/N). Press Y to delete the record, and the program then deletes the record. If you do not wish to delete the record, press N. After you enter either N or Y, the program asks, DO ANOTHER SEARCH? (Y/N). Press Y to do another search, and press N to return to the MAIN MENU.

YOUR TURN

As a hands-on activity, the DELETE function can be used to delete the record containing information about SHEA STADIUM. The following steps serve as a guide:

1. Search the STADIUMS file on the field name STAD. NAME for the value SHEA STADIUM (refer to the "Searching for a Record" section).
2. After finding the record, the program asks if it should CONTINUE, STOP, UPDATE, OR DELETE (C/S/U/D). Enter D for DELETE (see Figure 8–18).
3. The program then asks, OK TO DELETE RECORD? (Y/N). Press Y to delete the record. We will replace it later with the ADD function.
4. The program then deletes the record and asks, DO ANOTHER SEARCH? (Y/N). Press N, and the program returns to the MAIN MENU.

Notice that the program asks for a second confirmation of any action that will permanently change the file. This feature is designed to make it difficult for you to accidentally spoil or destroy your data.

Adding a Record

The data manager program also allows records to be added to an existing data file. The ADD function is somewhat limited in this version because the program allows only ten records to be in any one data file at a time. To use the ADD option, enter the number 2 when the WestFile MAIN MENU is displayed. The program then displays the name of the first field and places the cursor next to it. The program waits for the data item value of the first field name to be entered. After the value has been entered and the

Figure 8–18 DELETING A RECORD

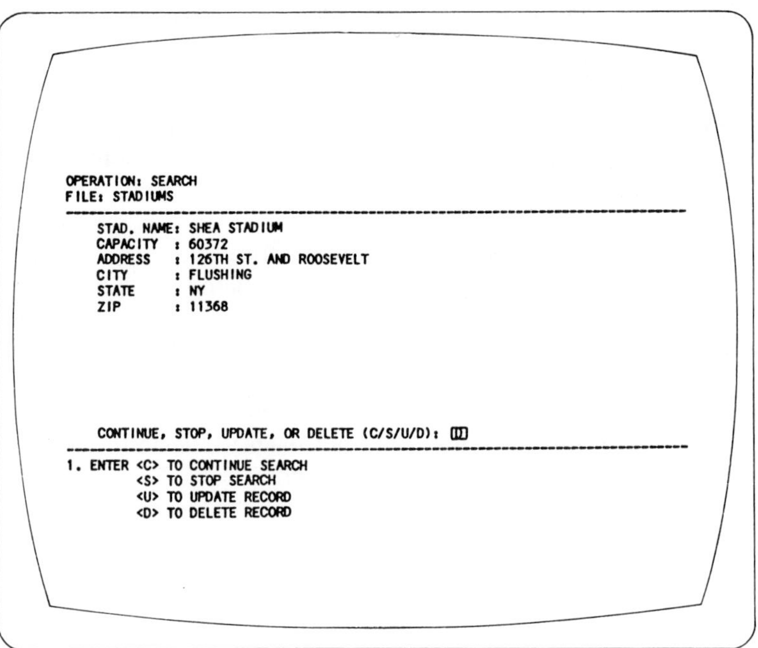

OPERATION: SEARCH
FILE: STADIUMS
STAD. NAME: SHEA STADIUM
CAPACITY : 60372
ADDRESS : 126TH ST. AND ROOSEVELT
CITY : FLUSHING
STATE : NY
ZIP : 11368
CONTINUE, STOP, UPDATE, OR DELETE (C/S/U/D):
1. ENTER <C> TO CONTINUE SEARCH
<S> TO STOP SEARCH
<U> TO UPDATE RECORD
<D> TO DELETE RECORD

RETURN key pressed, the program goes to each consecutive field and waits for a value to be entered and the RETURN key to be pressed. When all the data item values have been entered, the program asks, DATA ENTRIES OK? (Y/N). Enter Y if all the entries are correctly typed, and enter N if any entries have a mistake. If an N is entered, the entries can be changed by using the TAB key to position to the entry you desire to edit. After a Y is entered, the program adds the record as it was typed. Next, the program asks, ADD ANOTHER RECORD? (Y/N). Press Y if another record needs to be added, and press N if there are no more records to be added. The program returns to the MAIN MENU when N is pressed.

As a hands-on activity, the ADD function can be used to add the record containing the information about SHEA STADIUM. The following steps serve as a guide:

1. Enter the number 2 when the WestFile MAIN MENU is displayed.
2. The program waits for a value STAD. NAME to be entered. Enter SHEA STADIUM (see Figure 8–19) and press the RETURN key.
3. The program then asks for the value of CAPACITY. Enter 60372, and press the RETURN key.
4. The cursor is moved next to ADDRESS and waits for the value to be entered. Enter 126TH ST. AND ROOSEVELT, and press the RETURN key.
5. The program asks for the city, for the state, and then for the zip. Enter FLUSHING and press RETURN, NY and press RETURN, and 11368 and press RETURN (see Figure 8–20).

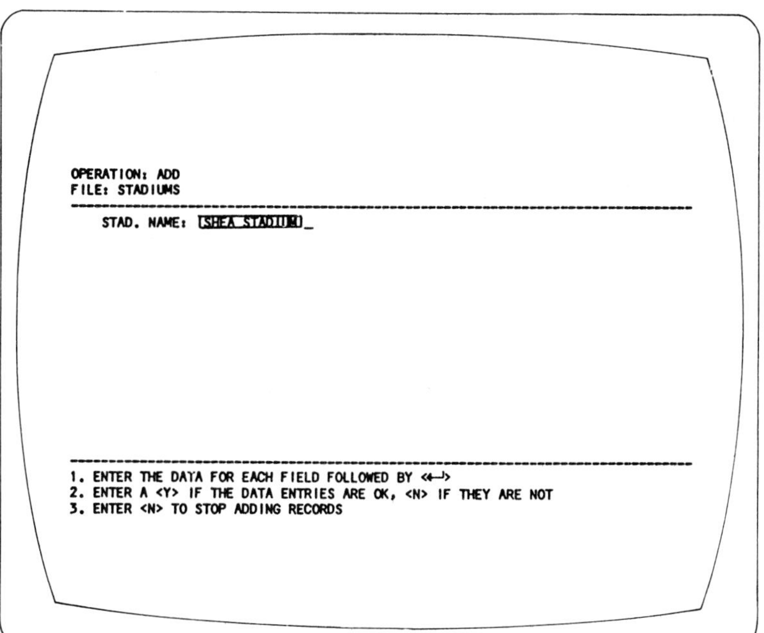

OPERATION: ADD
FILE: STADIUMS
STAD. NAME: SHEA STADIUM _
1. ENTER THE DATA FOR EACH FIELD FOLLOWED BY <↵>
2. ENTER A <Y> IF THE DATA ENTRIES ARE OK, <N> IF THEY ARE NOT
3. ENTER <N> TO STOP ADDING RECORDS

Figure 8–19 ENTERING A VALUE FOR STAD. NAME

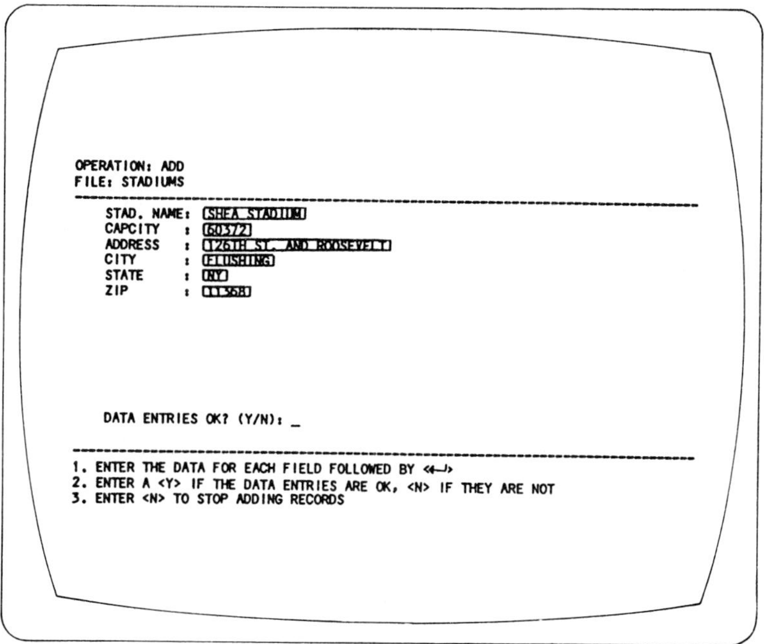

OPERATION: ADD
FILE: STADIUMS
STAD. NAME: SHEA STADIUM
CAPCITY : 60372
ADDRESS : 126TH ST. AND ROOSEVELT
CITY : FLUSHING
STATE : NY
ZIP : 11368
DATA ENTRIES OK? (Y/N): _
1. ENTER THE DATA FOR EACH FIELD FOLLOWED BY <↵>
2. ENTER A <Y> IF THE DATA ENTRIES ARE OK, <N> IF THEY ARE NOT
3. ENTER <N> TO STOP ADDING RECORDS

Figure 8–20 ADDING A RECORD

6. The program then asks, DATA ENTRIES OK? (Y/N). Enter a Y, and the record is added to the STADIUMS file. Enter N to edit the entries.
7. The program asks, ADD ANOTHER RECORD? (Y/N). Enter an N, and the MAIN MENU is returned to the screen.

Updating a Record

The data manager program is capable of updating a record; any data item value within a record can be changed. To update a data item value, enter Selection 3 when the WestFile MAIN MENU is displayed. First, a search is performed to find the record to be updated (refer to the "Searching for a Record" section). After the record is found, the program displays it on the screen and asks if it should CONTINUE, STOP, UPDATE, OR DELETE (C/S/U/D). Press U for UPDATE, and the program waits for a field name to be entered. Enter the field name of the value to be changed (the field names appear between the dotted lines and to the left of the data record), and press the RETURN key. The program moves the cursor to the value next to the field name indicated. Simply edit the information as it should be, and press RETURN. The program asks for another field name to be entered. If any of the other values in the record are not correct, enter another field name, press the RETURN key, edit the value, and press the RETURN key again. The program continues the updating process until only the RETURN key is pressed when the program asks for a field name. The program then asks, OK TO UPDATE RECORD? (Y/N). Enter Y, and the program updates the record with the given values. Enter N and the record will not be changed. Next, the program asks, DO ANOTHER SEARCH? (Y/N). Enter N, and the program returns to the MAIN MENU.

YOUR TURN

As a hands-on activity, the UPDATE function can be used to update the ARROWHEAD STADIUM record in the STADIUMS file. In this record, two data item values are incorrect. First, the address has not been entered. Second, the zip was incorrectly typed. The following steps serve as a guide to help you update the ARROWHEAD STADIUM record:

1. Enter the number 3 when the WestFile MAIN MENU is shown on the screen; then do a search on STAD. NAME for ARROWHEAD STADIUM.
2. When the record containing ARROWHEAD STADIUM has been found, the program places it on the screen and asks if it should CONTINUE, STOP, UPDATE, OR DELETE (C/S/U/D). Press U for UPDATE (see Figure 8–21).
3. Next, the program asks for the field name of the incorrect data. Enter ADDRESS, and press the RETURN key (see Figure 8–22).
4. The program places the cursor next to ADDRESS and waits for the correct address to be entered. Enter ARROWHEAD DRIVE, and press the RETURN key (see Figure 8–23).
5. The program again asks for a field name. Enter ZIP, and press the RETURN key so that the zip code can be changed.
6. The cursor appears next to ZIP. Enter the new zip code, 64108, and press the RETURN key (see Figure 8–24).
7. The program then asks for a field name to be entered. Press the RETURN key to stop.

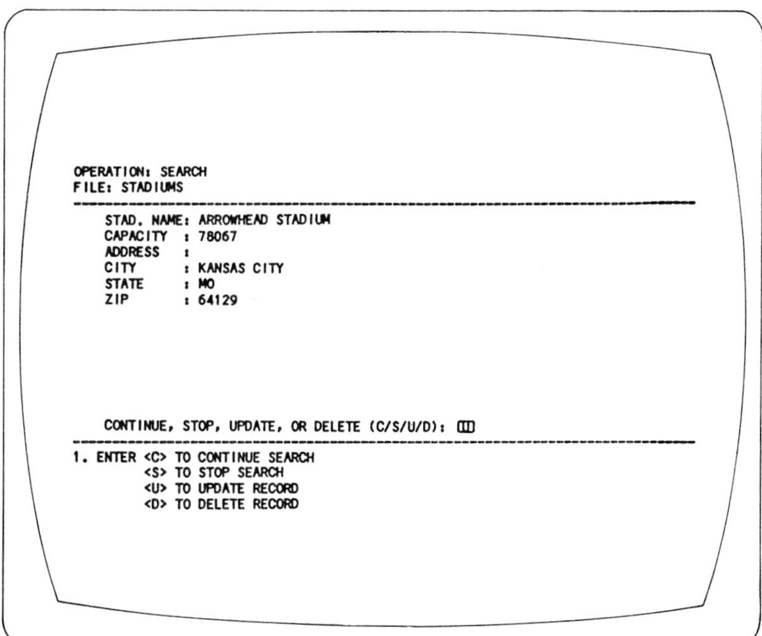

OPERATION: SEARCH
FILE: STADIUMS
STAD. NAME: ARROWHEAD STADIUM
CAPACITY : 78067
ADDRESS :
CITY : KANSAS CITY
STATE : MO
ZIP : 64129
CONTINUE, STOP, UPDATE, OR DELETE (C/S/U/D): U
1. ENTER <C> TO CONTINUE SEARCH
<S> TO STOP SEARCH
<U> TO UPDATE RECORD
<D> TO DELETE RECORD

Figure 8–21 UPDATING A RECORD

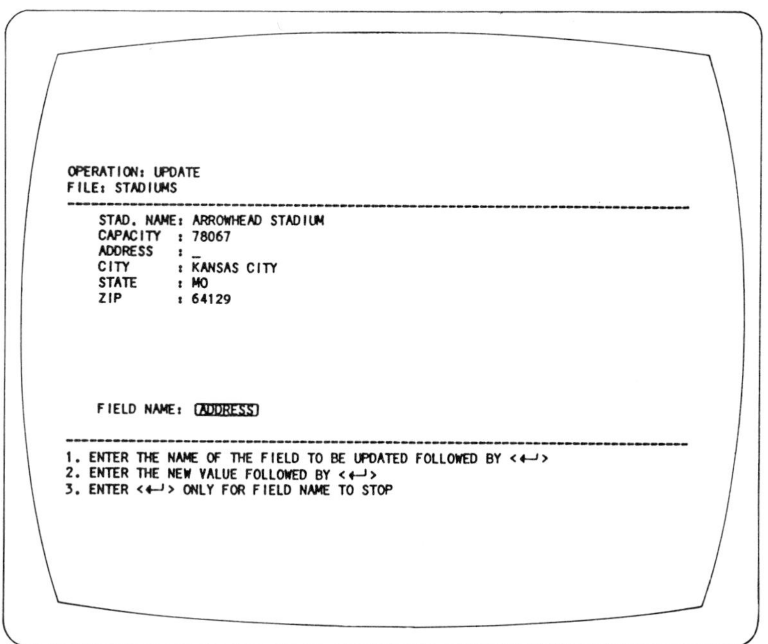

OPERATION: UPDATE
FILE: STADIUMS
STAD. NAME: ARROWHEAD STADIUM
CAPACITY : 78067
ADDRESS : _
CITY : KANSAS CITY
STATE : MO
ZIP : 64129
FIELD NAME: ADDRESS
1. ENTER THE NAME OF THE FIELD TO BE UPDATED FOLLOWED BY <↵>
2. ENTER THE NEW VALUE FOLLOWED BY <↵>
3. ENTER <↵> ONLY FOR FIELD NAME TO STOP

Figure 8–22 ENTERING THE FIELD NAME OF THE FIELD TO BE UPDATED

8. Next, the program asks, OK TO UPDATE RECORD? (Y/N). Press Y, and the program updates the record with the new information. Press N and the original record is not changed.
9. The program then asks, DO ANOTHER SEARCH? (Y/N). Enter N, and the program returns to the MAIN MENU.

Figure 8–23 UPDATING THE ADDRESS FIELD OF THE STADIUMS FILE

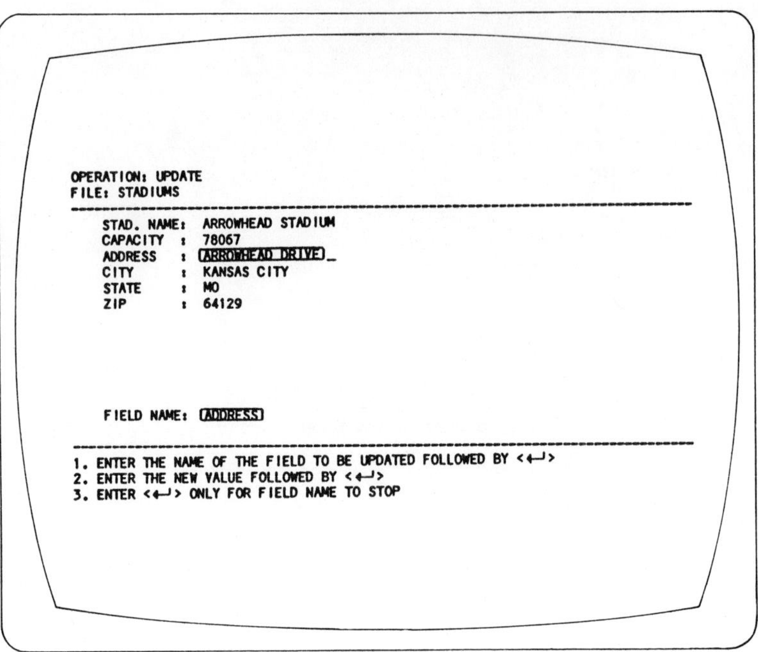

Figure 8–24 ENTERING THE FIELD NAME OF THE VALUE TO BE UPDATED

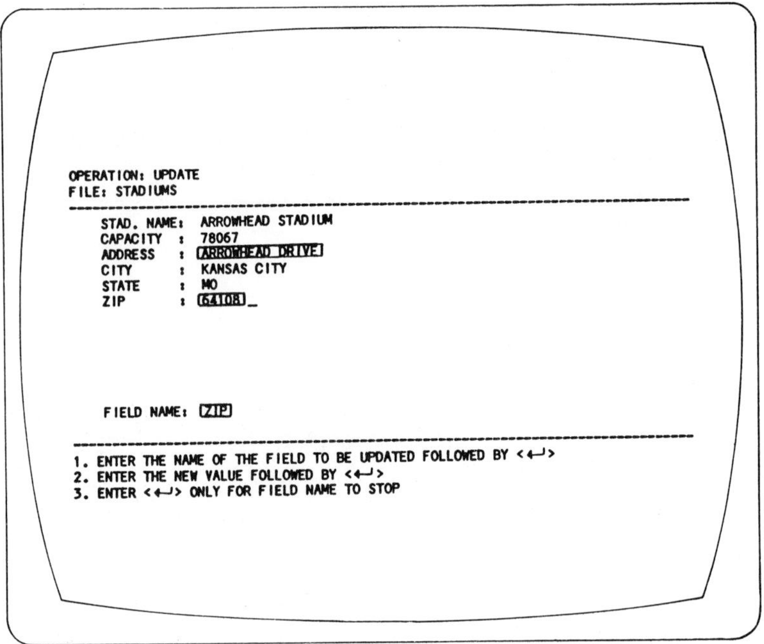

Sorting a File

The WestFile data manager also allows the records in a data file to be sorted, or rearranged into either an ascending (forward) or descending (backward) order. There are two types of sorts: a numeric sort and a nonnumeric (string)

sort. A numeric sort sorts numeric values of differing lengths. This means that numbers of smaller lengths have leading zeros added to them before sorting. For example, if you do an ascending numeric sort of the numbers 5 and 25, the number 5 is placed ahead of 25. A nonnumeric sort sorts characters and numbers; it compares the first character or characters of a string. For example, the numbers 5 and 25, if sorted as a string in ascending order, would result in 25 being placed ahead of the 5 (because 2 is less than 5). Therefore, if you desire a sort that considers just numeric values (such as CAPACITY in the STADIUMS example), you must enter Y to the question NUMERIC SORT? (Y/N).

To sort the records in a selected file, choose Selection 4 when the WestFile MAIN MENU is displayed. The program displays all the field names of the file and waits for a field name to be entered. Enter a field name, and press the RETURN key. The program asks, NUMERIC SORT? (Y/N). Enter Y to do a numeric sort or an N to do a nonnumeric sort. Next, the program asks, ASCENDING OR DESCENDING ORDER? (A/D). Press A for ASCENDING or D for DESCENDING. The program then sorts the records. The PRINT function must be used to display or print the records in the sorted order.

YOUR TURN

As a hands-on activity, the SORT function can be used to sort the records in the STADIUMS file based on the field name CAPACITY. Use the following as a guideline:

1. Press the number 4 when the WestFile MAIN MENU is displayed.
2. The program displays the SORT screen and waits for a field name to be entered. Enter CAPACITY (see Figure 8–25), and press the RETURN key.
3. The program asks, NUMERIC SORT? (Y/N). Enter Y to do a numeric sort.
4. Next, the program asks ASCENDING OR DESCENDING ORDER? (A/D). Press A for ASCENDING.
5. The program then sorts the records in numeric ascending order.

Mathematical Functions

The WestFile program can also perform some mathematical calculations on data fields within a file. The mathematical or statistical calculations contained in the program include: a total or sum function, an average function, a maximum value function, and a minimum value function.

The mathematical functions in the WestFile program are accessed by pressing 5 when the WestFile MAIN MENU is displayed. After selecting MATHEMATICAL FUNCTIONS from the menu, the program displays the MATHEMATICAL CALCULATIONS screen and waits for a field name to be entered. The available field names are displayed under the dotted line near the top of the screen. Once a correct field name is entered, the program

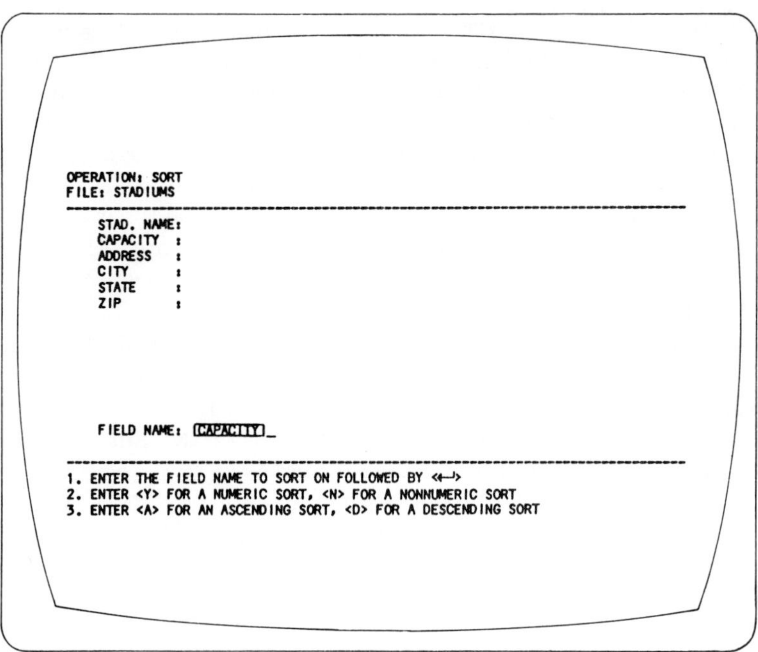

OPERATION: SORT
FILE: STADIUMS
STAD. NAME:
CAPACITY :
ADDRESS :
CITY :
STATE :
ZIP :
FIELD NAME: CAPACITY_
1. ENTER THE FIELD NAME TO SORT ON FOLLOWED BY <↵>
2. ENTER <Y> FOR A NUMERIC SORT, <N> FOR A NONNUMERIC SORT
3. ENTER <A> FOR AN ASCENDING SORT, <D> FOR A DESCENDING SORT

Figure 8–25 ENTERING THE FIELD NAME TO SORT ON

calculates the four statistics and displays them on the screen. After displaying the statistics, the program also asks if you would like to print the statistics. If you would like the statistics printed, press Y (for yes) when the program displays the question PRINT STATISTICS? (Y/N), or N (for no) if you do not want the statistics printed.

An important note should be made about the mathematical functions contained in the program, however. Only fields that contain numeric data can be used for the calculation of the values listed above. If none of the values in the field name selected are numeric data, the following error message will be displayed:

```
FIELD NAME CHOSEN DOES NOT
    CONTAIN NUMERIC DATA
```

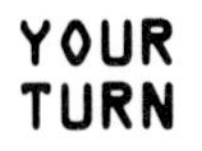

The following hands-on activity demonstrates how the mathematical functions can be used.

1. Press 5 when the WestFile MAIN MENU is displayed.
2. When the MATHEMATICAL CALCULATIONS screen is displayed, enter the field name CAPACITY (see Figure 8–26) and then press RETURN.
3. The program then displays the total, average, maximum value, and minimum value for the CAPACITY data field (see Figure 8–27). Press N (for no) in response to the question PRINT STATISTICS? (Y/N), and the program will return to the MAIN MENU.

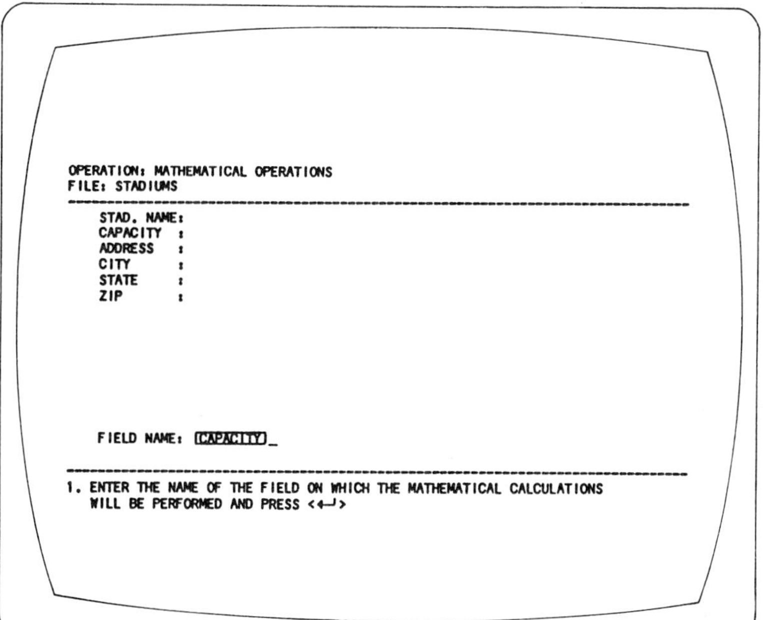

Figure 8–26 ENTERING THE FIELD NAME FOR MATHEMATICAL CALCULATIONS

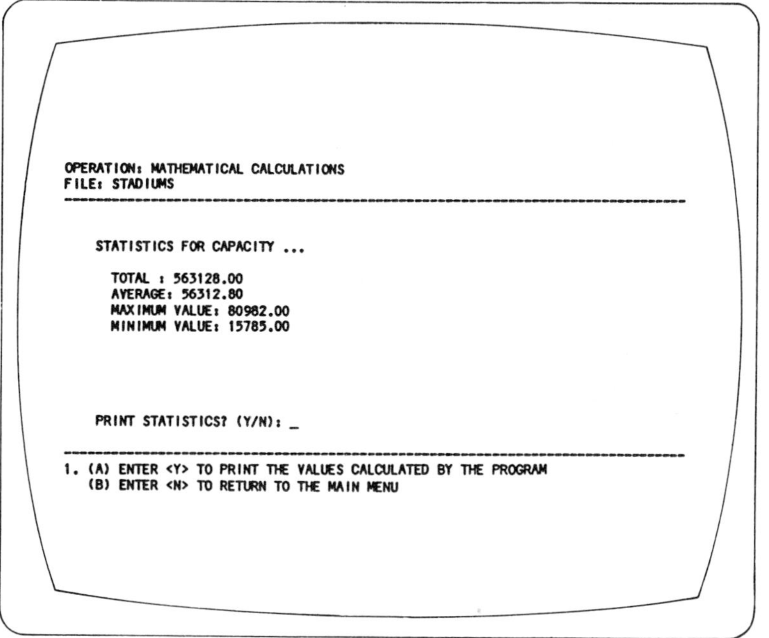

OPERATION: MATHEMATICAL CALCULATIONS
FILE: STADIUMS
STATISTICS FOR CAPACITY ...
TOTAL : 563128.00
AVERAGE: 56312.80
MAXIMUM VALUE: 80982.00
MINIMUM VALUE: 15785.00
PRINT STATISTICS? (Y/N): _
1. (A) ENTER <Y> TO PRINT THE VALUES CALCULATED BY THE PROGRAM
(B) ENTER <N> TO RETURN TO THE MAIN MENU

Figure 8–27 DISPLAYING THE CAPACITY STATISTICAL VALUES

Printing a File

In order to print the contents of a data file, choose Selection 6 from the WestFile MAIN MENU. The program will then display the PRINT MENU which includes the options: (1) SELECT FILE FOR PRINTING, (2) SELECT FILE FOR DISPLAY, and (3) PRINTER DEFAULTS, and (4) RETURN TO MAIN

MENU. Selection 1 of the PRINT MENU allows you to select the file you wish to print. After the number 1 is pressed, the program will display the names of the data files that are available for printing. Enter the name of the file you wish to print, and press the RETURN key.

The program will then ask you to ready your printer by turning it on, if it is not already on, and to make sure that it is on-line, (connected to the computer), and loaded with paper. Once the printer is turned on, on-line, and loaded with paper, you can press the RETURN key to begin printing. When printing is complete, the program will return to the PRINT MENU.

Selection 2 on the PRINT MENU allows the user to select a data file for display to the monitor screen. If a hard copy of the data file is not needed but you would like to look at the contents of the file, use option 2 on the PRINT MENU.

Selection 3 on the PRINT MENU displays to the user the printer defaults used for printing. In order to display these printer defaults, press 3 when the PRINT MENU is displayed.

YOUR TURN

As a hands-on activity, the PRINT function can be used to print the data contained in the STADIUMS file. The following steps can be used as a guide:

1. Press 6 when the WestFile MAIN MENU is displayed.
2. Press 1 when the PRINT MENU is displayed (see Figure 8–28).
3. The program then displays the SELECT FILE FOR PRINTING screen and waits for a file name to be entered. When the printer is ready to print, enter STADIUMS (see Figure 8–29) and press the RETURN key.

Figure 8–28 THE PRINT MENU

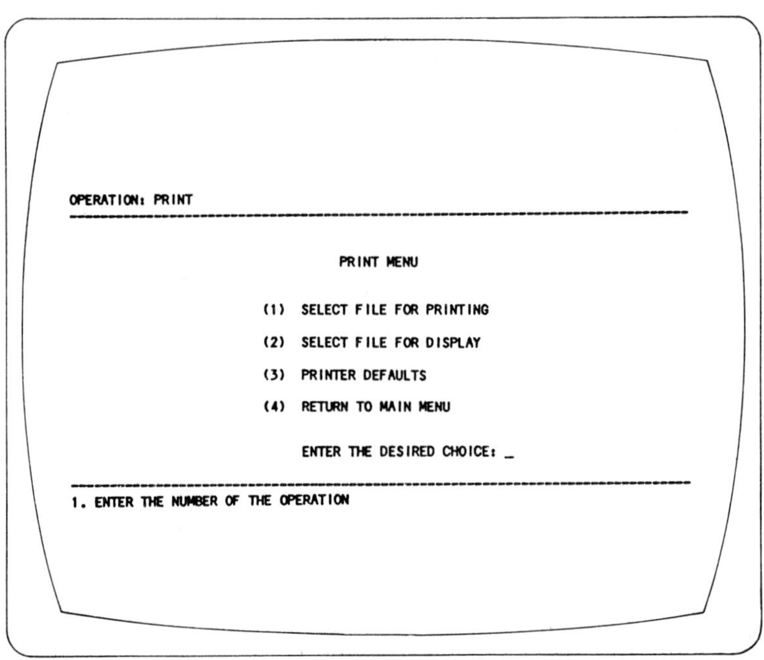

OPERATION: PRINT
PRINT MENU
(1) SELECT FILE FOR PRINTING
(2) SELECT FILE FOR DISPLAY
(3) PRINTER DEFAULTS
(4) RETURN TO MAIN MENU
ENTER THE DESIRED CHOICE: _
1. ENTER THE NUMBER OF THE OPERATION

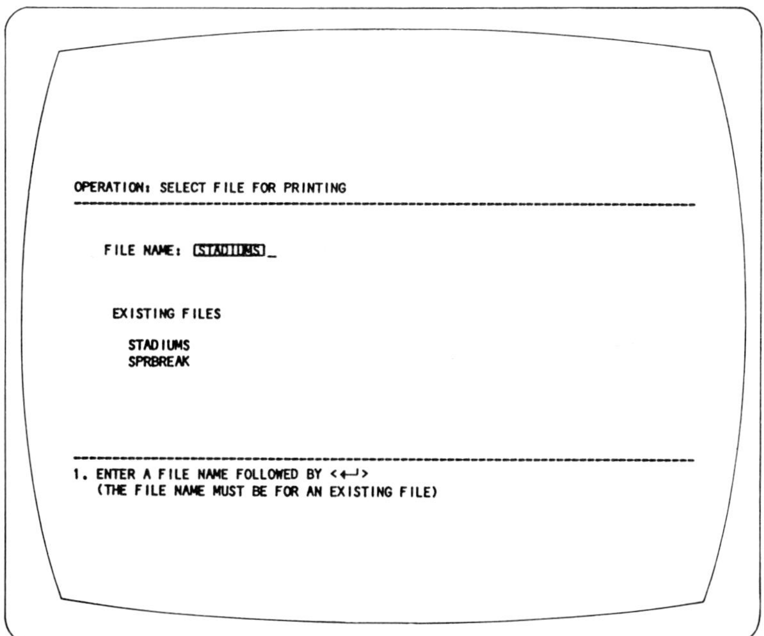

OPERATION: SELECT FILE FOR PRINTING
FILE NAME: STADIUMS_
EXISTING FILES
STADIUMS
SPRBREAK
1. ENTER A FILE NAME FOLLOWED BY <↵>
(THE FILE NAME MUST BE FOR AN EXISTING FILE)

Figure 8–29 SELECTING A DATA FILE FOR PRINTING

4. The program then prints the contents of the STADIUMS file and returns to the PRINT MENU. Enter the number 4 to return to the MAIN MENU.

Defining the ADDRESS Data File

Since there was not a hands-on activity included in the "Defining a New File" section, a hands-on activity for defining a new data file entitled ADDRESS follows. The ADDRESS file is designed to store the addresses and phone numbers of friends and acquaintances.

As a hands-on activity, the following steps serve as a guide to creating the ADDRESS data file.

1. Press 1 for SELECT A FILE when the WestFile MAIN MENU is displayed.
2. The SELECT screen is displayed and the program waits for a file name to be entered. Enter ADDRESS (see Figure 8–30) and press RETURN.
3. The program then displays the DEFINE screen and waits for the first field name to be entered. When the cursor is positioned next to FIELD #1 NAME:, enter LAST NAME and press RETURN. The cursor then positions next to the word LENGTH. Enter 25 and press RETURN. Continue

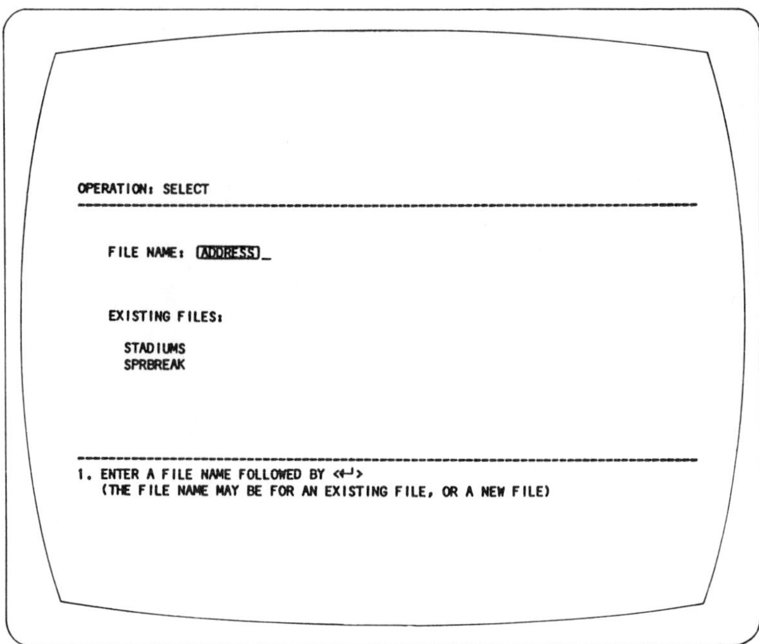
OPERATION: SELECT
FILE NAME: ADDRESS_
EXISTING FILES:
STADIUMS
SPRBREAK
1. ENTER A FILE NAME FOLLOWED BY <↵>
(THE FILE NAME MAY BE FOR AN EXISTING FILE, OR A NEW FILE)

Figure 8–30 ENTERING ADDRESS AS A NEW FILE NAME

entering the field names and lengths by typing FIRST NAME and RETURN, 20 and RETURN, ADDRESS and RETURN, 25 and RETURN, CITY and RETURN, 20 and RETURN, STATE and RETURN, 2 and RETURN, ZIP and RETURN,10 and RETURN, PHONE and RETURN, and 13 and RETURN. Press the RETURN key only when the cursor is positioned next to #8 (see Figure 8–31).

4. The program then asks, DEFINITIONS OK? (Y/N). Enter Y (for yes) if the definitions are typed correctly, N (for no) if they are not (see Figure 8–32).If you type N, the TAB key can be used to position the cursor to the entry that should be changed.

5. Once Y is entered for the question DEFINITIONS OK? (Y/N), the program will return to the MAIN MENU.

WestFile Messages

1. ENTER <A> OR <D> ONLY

   A number or character other than A or D has been entered.

2. ENTER <C>, <S>, <U>, OR <D> ONLY

   A number or character other than C, S, U, or D has been entered.

3. ENTER <Y> OR <N> ONLY

   A number or character other than Y or N has been entered.

4. FIELD NAME CHOSEN DOES NOT
   CONTAIN NUMERIC DATA

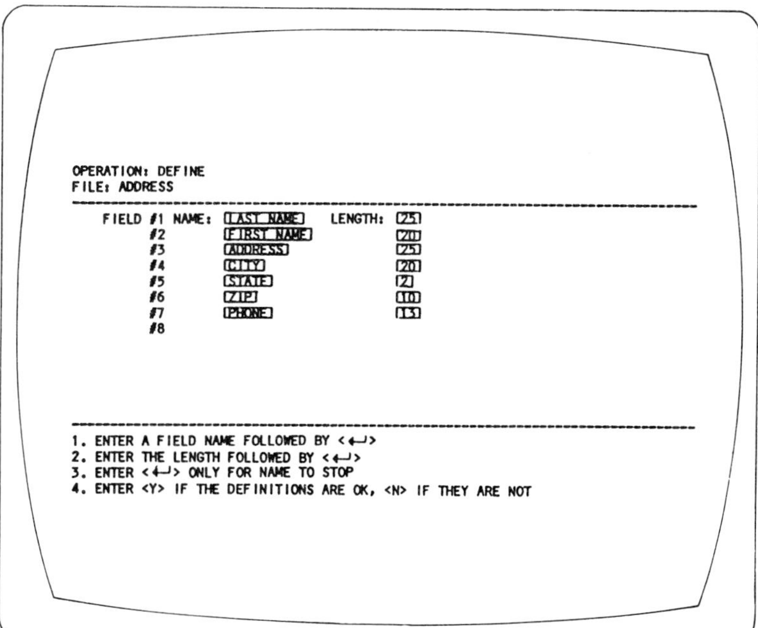

OPERATION: DEFINE
FILE: ADDRESS
FIELD #1 NAME: LAST NAME LENGTH: 25
#2 FIRST NAME 20
#3 ADDRESS 25
#4 CITY 20
#5 STATE 2
#6 ZIP 10
#7 PHONE 13
#8
1. ENTER A FIELD NAME FOLLOWED BY <↵>
2. ENTER THE LENGTH FOLLOWED BY <↵>
3. ENTER <↵> ONLY FOR NAME TO STOP
4. ENTER <Y> IF THE DEFINITIONS ARE OK, <N> IF THEY ARE NOT

Figure 8–31 DEFINING THE FIELD NAMES AND LENGTHS OF THE ADDRESS FILE

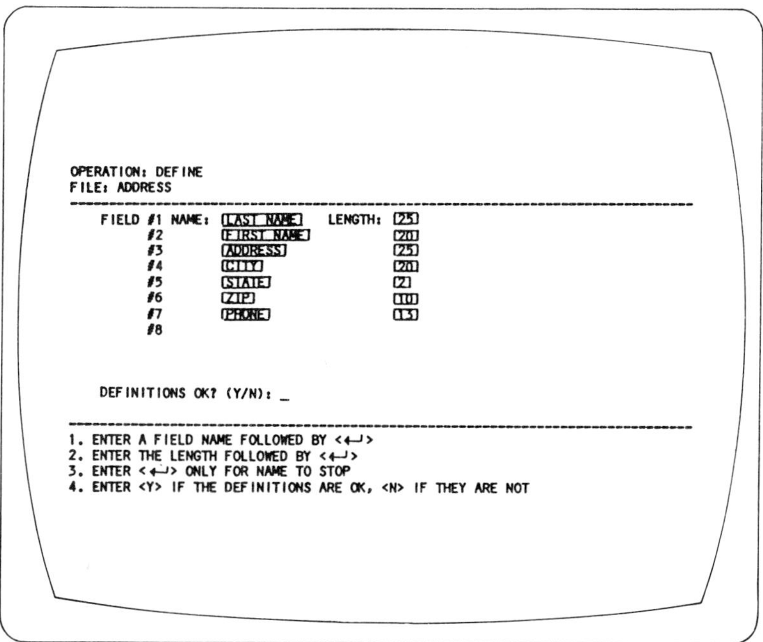

OPERATION: DEFINE
FILE: ADDRESS
FIELD #1 NAME: LAST NAME LENGTH: 25
#2 FIRST NAME 20
#3 ADDRESS 25
#4 CITY 20
#5 STATE 2
#6 ZIP 10
#7 PHONE 13
#8
DEFINITIONS OK? (Y/N): _
1. ENTER A FIELD NAME FOLLOWED BY <↵>
2. ENTER THE LENGTH FOLLOWED BY <↵>
3. ENTER <↵> ONLY FOR NAME TO STOP
4. ENTER <Y> IF THE DEFINITIONS ARE OK, <N> IF THEY ARE NOT

Figure 8–32 THE PROGRAM ASKS, DEFINITIONS OK? (Y/N)

The field name chosen for mathematical calculations did not contain numeric information and therefore the calculations cannot be completed.

5. `FILE NAME DOES NOT EXIST`

   The file name selected for printing or display does not exist.

```
6.  INCORRECT DATA FIELD LENGTH
   THE DATA FIELD LENGTH MUST FALL
        IN THE RANGE 1 - 60
```

The length of the data field can only be from one to sixty characters. Therefore, a number from 1 to 60 must be entered.

```
7.         INVALID FIELD NAME
THE NAME MUST MATCH ONE LISTED ABOVE
```

A field name that does not exist in the selected file has been entered.

```
8.          INVALID FILE NAME
FILE NAMES CAN CONTAIN THE CHARACTERS:
          A - Z AND 1 - 9
```

A file name that contains characters other than the letters *A* to *Z* or the numbers 1 to 9 has been entered.

```
9.  INVALID MENU SELECTION PLEASE
    ENTER CHOICE AGAIN USING 1 - 5.
```

A number or character other than 1, 2, 3, 4, or 5 has been entered. (These numbers represent menu selections.)

```
10.  INVALID MENU SELECTION PLEASE
     ENTER CHOICE AGAIN USING 1 - 8.
```

A number or character other than 1, 2, 3, 4, 5, 6, 7 or 8 has been entered. (These numbers represent menu selections.)

```
11.  INVALID SEARCH CRITERIA
```

The search criteria specified must be preceded by either <, >, or = or must be for a full value search.

```
12. NO MATCHING RECORDS FOUND
```

The program cannot find the indicated record. Either the data item value has been mistyped, or the record does not currently exist.

```
13. NO MORE MATCHING RECORDS FOUND
```

The program cannot find any more of the indicated records. There are no more records containing the specified data item value.

```
14.  ONLY TWO FILES CAN BE CREATED USING
     THIS VERSION OF THE DATA MANAGER
```

Only two extra files can be created. To create another file, an old file must first be erased.

```
15. PRESS SPACE BAR TO CONTINUE
```

To continue execution of the program, press the space bar.

```
16.  THE MAXIMUM OF TEN RECORDS
 HAS ALREADY BEEN ADDED TO THIS FILE
```

The program only allows ten records to be in any file. Ten records have already been added; therefore, another record cannot be added.

```
17. YOU MUST SELECT A FILE BEFORE CHOOSING
     THIS OPERATION. USE MAIN MENU CHOICE
           (1) TO SELECT A FILE
```

To select numbers 2 through 4 from the main menu, a file must be selected. Selection 1 from the main menu selects a file.

18. YOU MUST ENTER AT LEAST ONE FIELD
    NAME AND LENGTH PAIR

Once on the DEFINE screen, you must enter at least one FIELD NAME value and one LENGTH or abort the operation by pressing the <Esc> key.

Contents of Spring Break File

```
HOTEL      : BEST WESTERN
ADDRESS    : 5727 N. FEDERAL HIGHWAY
CITY       : FORT LAUDERDALE
STATE      : FL
ZIP        : 33308
COST/ROOM  : 62.00
ADDITIONAL : 10.00

HOTEL      : BEACH PLAZA HOTEL
ADDRESS    : 625 N. ATLANTIC BLVD.
CITY       : FORT LAUDERDALE
STATE      : FL
ZIP        : 33304
COST/ROOM  : 88.00
ADDITIONAL : 8.00

HOTEL      : PARK LANE MOTOR LODGE
ADDRESS    : 2949 N. FEDERAL HIGHWAY
CITY       : FORT LAUDERDALE
STATE      : FL
ZIP        : 33306
COST/ROOM  : 45.00
ADDITIONAL : 6.00

HOTEL      : FORT LAUDERDALE MOTEL
ADDRESS    : 501 SE 17TH STREET
CITY       : FORT LAUDERDALE
STATE      : FL
ZIP        : 33316
COST/ROOM  : 70.00
ADDITIONAL : 10.00

HOTEL      : HOLIDAY INN-NORTH
ADDRESS    : 4116 N. OCEAN DRIVE
CITY       : FORT LAUDERDALE
STATE      : FL
ZIP        : 33308
COST/ROOM  : 100.00
ADDITIONAL : 10.00
```

```
HOTEL      : BEST WESTERN CONTINENTAL
ADDRESS    : 1885 S. VIRGINIA ST.
CITY       : RENO
STATE      : NV
ZIP        : 89502
COST/ROOM  : 40.00
ADDITIONAL : 6.00

HOTEL      : HOLIDAY INN-DOWNTOWN
ADDRESS    : 1000 E. 6TH ST.
CITY       : RENO
STATE      : NV
ZIP        : 89512
COST/ROOM  : 54.00
ADDITIONAL : 4.00

HOTEL      : RENO HILTON
ADDRESS    : 255 N. SIERRA STREET
CITY       : RENO
STATE      : NV
ZIP        : 89501
COST/ROOM  : 54.00
ADDITIONAL : 10.00

HOTEL      : MGM GRAND HOTEL-RENO
ADDRESS    : 2500 E. 2ND STREET
CITY       : RENO
STATE      : NV
ZIP        : 89595
COST/ROOM  : 65.00
ADDITIONAL : 8.00

HOTEL      : SANDS HOTEL
ADDRESS    : 345 N. ARLINGTON AVE.
CITY       : RENO
STATE      : NV
ZIP        : 89501
COST/ROOM  : 85.00
ADDITIONAL : 6.00
```

Summary of WestFile Functions

Function Name	*Description*
`ADD`	Permits a record to be added to an existing or new data file.
`SEARCH`	Looks for a record based on the desired field name and a particular data value.
`UPDATE`	Changes the data value of one or more fields within a data record.
`DELETE`	Erases an existing data record from a data file.
`SORT`	Arranges the records of a data file in either an ascending or descending order based on the selected field.
`MATHEMATICAL FUNCTIONS`	Calculates the total, average, maximum value, and minimum value for the chosen data field within a data file.
`PRINT`	Prints the contents of the chosen data file.

SUMMARY POINTS

- Data managers (data management packages) can be used for the same purposes as a manual filing system: to record and file information.
- There are two types of data managers: file handlers and data base packages.
- File handlers were developed first to replace manual filing systems, whereas data base packages were developed after file handlers to organize independent files into an integrated whole.
- Data managers can be used in the home for such tasks as creating a computerized Christmas card list or a computerized recipe index card file, for helping you balance your checkbook, and for keeping a personal appointment calendar.
- In business, data managers can be used for keeping employee and inventory control records and to catalog lists of customers and suppliers, to mention just a few uses.
- Data managers provide businesses with the ability to save time and maintain a more efficient record-keeping process.
- Specialized uses of data managers exist in such areas as mass mailing and in conjunction with word processors to create form letters.
- Features considered to be standard in all data managers include adding records, deleting records, searching for records, updating records, sorting the data file, and printing information from records. Additional features might include making mathematical calculations, formatting screen displays, and displaying help screens.
- When considering hardware requirements for data managers, the following items must be evaluated: internal memory size requirements, sec-

ondary storage requirements (including disk drive requirements), printer requirements, and monitor requirements.

- The purpose for which the data manager is going to be used is the prime consideration in evaluating a package.
- Once the package use has been defined, areas that should be considered for meeting the needs of the intended use are storage capacities, available features, and package flexibility.
- Reviewing a list of potential data managers should be only the first step in evaluating packages for your use. Each package must be reviewed carefully, and its ability to meet your specific needs must be considered.

REVIEW QUESTIONS

1. What is a data manager, and how is it used?

2. Give a short explanation of the difference between a file handler and a data base package.

3. Other than the uses presented in the chapter, name two possible uses for data managers in each of the following categories: home uses and business uses.

4. Describe each of the standard features contained within data managers.

5. What do you think is the advantage of being able to create your own screen display formats for use with a data manager?

6. What is the most important question that must be resolved before you shop for a data manager? Why is it the most important question?

7. Why is storage capacity an important consideration when selecting a data manager for your use?

8. If you were to consider purchasing a data manager for use at home, for what types of things would you want to use it?

9. What areas of hardware requirements should be considered prior to purchasing a data manager?

10. Briefly explain why the choice of a printer can be very important if it is going to be used with a data manager.

WestFile™ Exercises

1. Use the SPRBREAK file included on your diskette to do the following exercises:

a. Select the SPRBREAK file presented on your diskette.

b. Delete the record containing the information about Fort Lauderdale Motel.

c. Add the following record to your SPRBREAK file:

```
HOTEL:        OCEAN MANOR RESORT HOTEL
ADDRESS:      4040 GALT OCEAN DRIVE
CITY:         FORT LAUDERDALE
STATE:        FL
ZIP:          33308
COST/ROOM:    125.00
ADDITIONAL:   10.00
```

d. Update the record containing information about the Reno Hilton. Insert Box 1291 for the address.

e. Search for all the Fort Lauderdale hotels. What are their names?

f. Using a numeric sort, sort all the records by cost in descending order. Which hotel costs the least? Which costs the most?

2. Create your own data file called EMPLOYEE. Use the following fields and lengths:

Field Name	Length
NAME	25
BIRTH	8
SEX	1
TITLE	15
HIRE DATE	8
WAGE	6
DEPT	3

a. Use the following information to create the records for the EMPLOYEE file:

Name	Birth	Sex	Title	Hire Date	Wage	Dept
Tami Thomas	01–15–56	F	Clerk	06–01–74	7.50	004
Jerry Johnson	03–08–60	M	Bagger	04–07–80	6.75	002
Nancy Neumeyer	04–09–60	F	Assistant Mgr.	10–10–79	10.50	001
Karl Klineschmidt	10–05–40	M	Supervisor	01–01–60	10.25	006
Evelyn Evans	10–18–39	F	Clerk	03–16–64	8.25	004
Bonnie Beechum	07–09–29	F	Secretary	11–10–56	8.75	001
Don Deft	05–28–29	M	Janitor	12–15–60	8.50	007

b. Jerry Johnson no longer works for the company; delete his record.

c. Bonnie Beechum has received a pay raise; her salary is now $9.25 per hour. Update her record.

d. Paul Hindle has been hired today. He will work in Department 002 as a bagger, and his pay rate will be $4.75 per hour. Hindle was born on December 12, 1964. Add his record to the file.

e. Search for all wages greater than $8.00. Whose salaries are they?

f. Using an alphanumeric search, sort all the records by department. How many work in Department 001? In 002? In 004? In 006? In 007?

CHAPTER 9

GRAPHICS AND OTHER SOFTWARE PACKAGES

Chapter Outline

INTRODUCTION

As you are discovering, software packages can turn your home microcomputer into an extremely useful tool. This chapter discusses even further the seemingly endless number of possible uses for your computer, beginning with computer graphics. Computer graphics packages can be useful in designing objects and drawing plans or simply can be fun to use, allowing you to be creative and imaginative. Other categories of software packages presented in this chapter are home business and finance programs, home and personal interest programs, recreational programs, and educational programs. The uses and features of these packages are described, and lists of several popular packages on the market today for your IBM computer also are included. Table 9–1 provides a quick reference to terms you may encounter when reading about graphics software, some of which have been covered in Section I.

Table 9–1 GRAPHICS TERMS

TERM	DEFINITION
Analytical graphics	Charts and graphs used for financial analysis and other types of numeric comparison.
Graphics set	The complete set of graphics images available in a software package.
Graphics tablet	A small tablet that is sensitive to pressure. When you press on the surface of the tablet, the position of that pressure is transmitted to the computer, and the corresponding location on the display screen is illuminated. Most graphics tablets permit only two-dimensional drawings.
Light pen	A stylus connected to the computer by a wire. It tells the computer the *x,y* coordinates of the spot where the pen is pointing (*x* being the horizontal axis and *y* being the vertical axis). It is most often used to create graphics and to point to menu options.
Mouse	A small hand-controlled device that rolls on a flat surface. Its movement controls the cursor's position on the display screen, allowing you to draw graphic images and select from menu options.
Pixel	The smallest graphic point addressable by a computer. Pixels are turned on or off to form the characters and graphic images on a computer screen.
Plotter	A computer-controlled graphics output device that moves pens or paper to specified *x,y* coordinates to make a hard copy of graphics images.
Resolution	The number of pixels on the display screen. This determines the clarity of the image; the more pixels on a screen, the higher the resolution, or quality, of the image.
Simulation	Computer graphics created to model an actual process in appearance and usually in performance, such as the flying of an airplane.
Touch screen	A video screen or plastic overlay that allows you to draw, write, and make menu selections from the screen with the touch of a finger or stylus.

GRAPHICS PACKAGES

Graphics software packages are designed to allow the user to display images on a computer monitor and to print the images with a printer. A wide variety of images can be produced—ranging from a simple bar graph to complicated designs done by an engineer—in a wide selection of colors.

Using a graphics package can be as simple as selecting shapes from a menu of options or as complex as controlling the individual dots (**pixels**) on the display screen. Turning the pixels on and off forms the images on the screen. A display screen contains a certain number of pixels; some have as few as 1,920, whereas others have 128,000 or more. By controlling which pixels are on and off, the user can create images as detailed as the computer will allow. The greater the number of pixels in the screen, the higher the quality, or **resolution,** of the image. The higher the resolution, the clearer or sharper the images will be when displayed.

pixel
Individual dots on the display screen that can be turned on or off.

resolution
The number of pixels on a display screen. The greater the number of pixels, the higher the resolution.

Uses of Graphics Packages

Three basic types of graphics packages are available: analytical business graphics packages, design graphics packages, and creative drawing and painting packages.

Analytical Business Applications. Business graphics packages help the user develop charts and **analytical graphs** for financial analysis. These programs transform numeric statistics into multicolored charts and graphs. They can be useful for analyzing markets, forecasting sales, comparing stock trends, and planning business and home finance. Business graphics packages produce different types of graphs, such as line, bar, stacked bar, and scatter graphs, as well as pie charts (see Figures 9–1 and 9–2). In many cases it is possible to merge graphs. For example, a line graph showing net income could be overlaid with a bar graph showing net sales.

analytical graphics
Charts and graphics used for financial analysis and other types of numeric comparison.

Design Applications. Design graphics packages are useful for drawing plans that an architect, engineer, or interior designer would create. These programs eliminate the need for drafting tools such as T squares and french curves and allow the user to produce designs much faster than when working with pencil and paper. Many design packages include **simulation** capabilities, which can be used to create a model of an object on the display screen and to replicate the object's actual use, as well as animation capabilities, which let you move your image around the screen. Changes in a design can easily be made on the screen, and variations can be printed and saved on a disk. To do this, only the original design must be created from scratch. After the original design has been saved, you can make changes and save the new version under a new name.

simulation
Creating a model of an object on the display screen, making it easy to change the design without building an actual model.

Creative Drawing and Painting Applications. Computer art is different from traditional art. Many problems a traditional artist might have can be avoided by the computer artist. For instance, the "paint" will not drip or run, colors will not fade or dominate one another, and pastel colors can easily cover dark or bright colors. Computer art has a crude, machinelike

Figure 9–1 PIE CHART AND LINE GRAPH

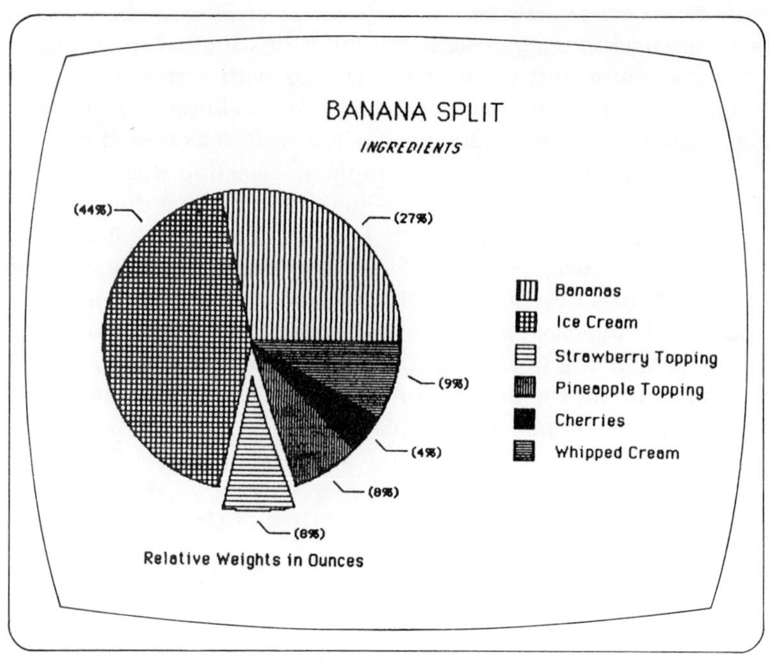

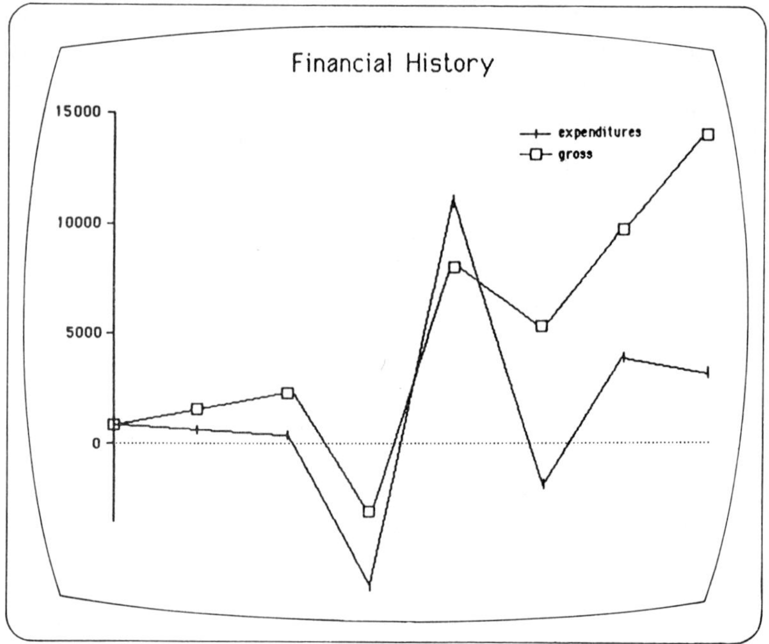

appearance; the texture and line of the medium make it distinctive. However, advanced equipment is now capable of "air brushing" and blending fine tones to diminish the computerized look.

With computer art there is no need to perform color tests using markers or acetate overlays, and the time spent waiting for paint to dry is eliminated.

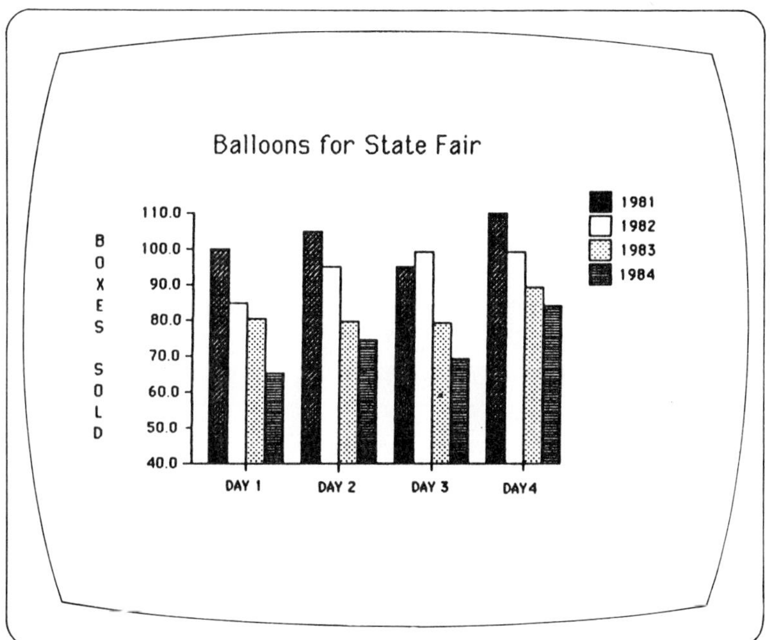

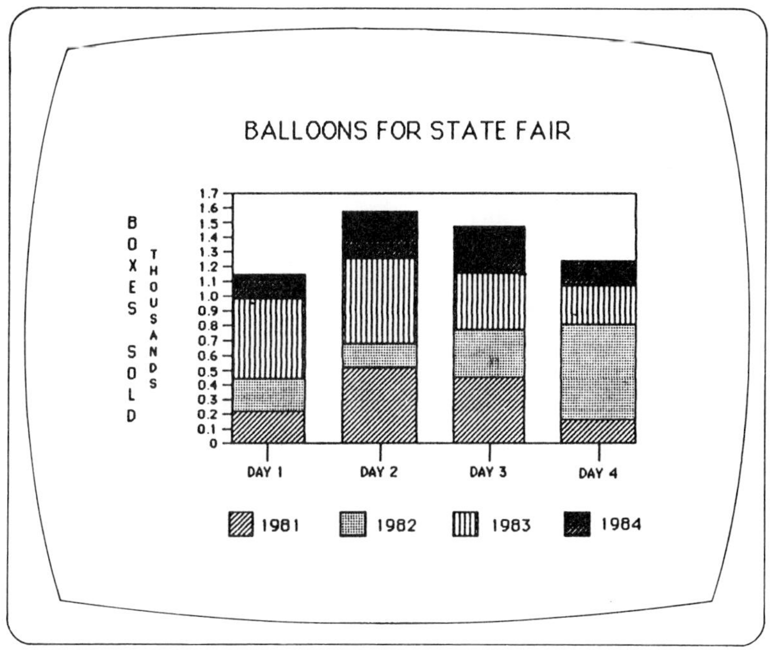

Figure 9–2 BAR GRAPH, STACKED BAR GRAPH, AND SCATTER GRAPH

These programs make color changes instantly, which gives you more time to try different color combinations. You can save a picture, reload it, and make changes until you are satisfied with the result. Examples of computer art are shown in Figure 9–3.

Figure 9–2
continued

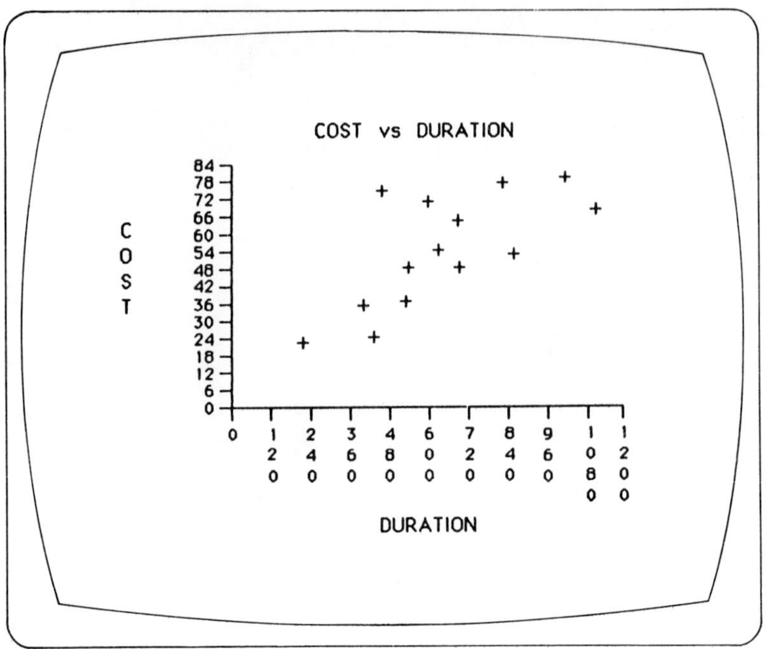

Features of Graphics Packages

Some of the common features available in graphics software summarized here may not be found in all types of packages. For example, business graphics packages probably will not have animation or automatic dimensioning, because these features are not needed to develop graphs and charts.

Two and Three-Dimensional Display. Some graphics packages offer only a two-dimensional display, which is adequate for many applications, such as graphs and simple drawings. However, for more realistic images and more impressive results (Figure 9–4), three-dimensional capabilities may be necessary. Three-dimensional representations are very helpful in designing objects such as the one shown in Figure 9–5.

Save. The save feature stores on a disk what you have created on the screen. By saving the screen display, it can be used with other programs. You also can use the save feature to create two or more similar displays. The original display can be changed (after it has been saved) and then saved under a new name, eliminating the need to re-create a new display from scratch.

High Resolution. A graphics package with high-resolution capability creates clearer and sharper images than would be displayed in the normal display mode. High-resolution graphics packages must be used on video monitors capable of displaying high-resolution graphics.

Figure 9–3 COMPUTER ART

Color. If a computer system has a color monitor and the capability to display color, the graphics package can make images much more appealing. Several packages offer a rotate function, which can change the entire color scheme of an image once it has been created. Producing many different color combinations instantly can be extremely enjoyable and useful to the artist.

Figure 9–4 THREE-DIMENSIONAL GRAPHICS PRESENTATION

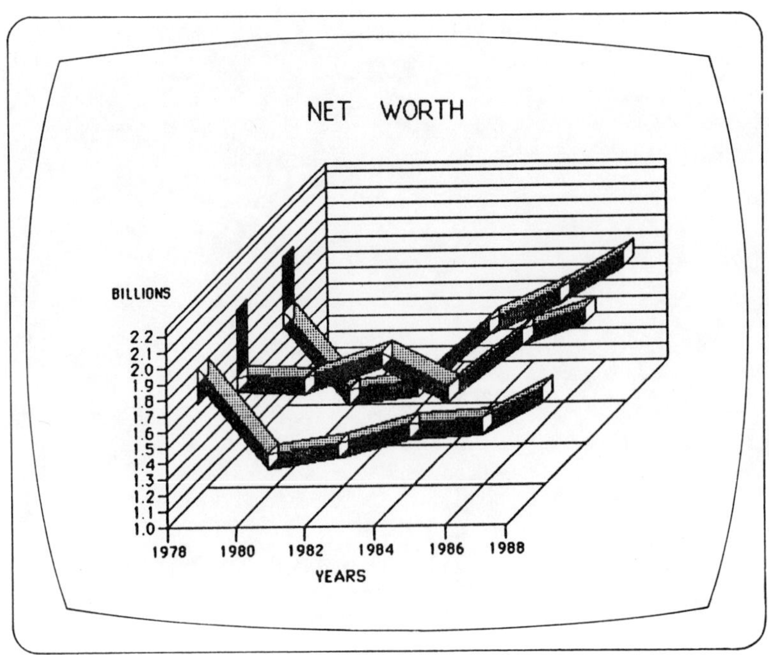

Figure 9–5 THREE-DIMENSIONAL DESIGN GRAPHICS

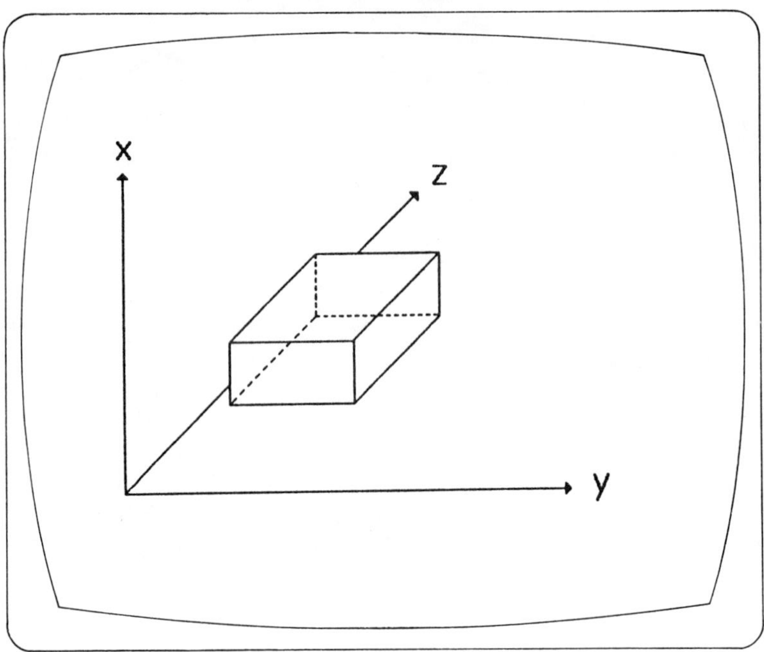

Animation. Animation of images involves moving objects about the screen. The images can be moved horizontally, vertically, or diagonally, or they can be rotated about a point. Software packages with this feature are useful in video game development and in designing and engineering objects with moving parts.

Zoom. The zoom feature allows you to enlarge or shrink a specific portion of the display screen. The magnified mode makes it easier to create detail or examine text or figures that are not legible when the image is displayed in its original size. When an image is reduced, it is possible to see an entire display that is too large to fit on the screen at one time.

Pan. The pan feature moves the display horizontally or vertically across the screen. Panning lets you select the center of the area on which you wish to zoom in.

Automatic Dimensioning. Automatic dimensioning is useful for applications in which specific measurements are required, such as creating architectural drawings. This feature automatically measures the distance between two points and will draw the dimension line if you want it to. You can also specify the number of decimal places to be used in a dimension label (the measurement for a particular dimension line), as well as the size and location of the dimension label.

Automatic Drawing. Many software packages have standard geometric shapes stored in a special file called a **graphics set.** Using a joystick, **mouse, touch screen, light pen,** or **graphics tablet,** and sometimes the keyboard, you can tell the computer to draw an image from the software's graphics set, place it where you want it, and designate its size.

graphics set
The complete set of graphics images available in a software package.

mouse
A small hand-controlled device that rolls on a flat surface and is connected to the computer by a wire. It tells the computer which point on the screen to activate.

touch screen
A video screen or plastic overlay that allows a stylus or the touch of a finger to tell the computer which point on the screen to activate.

light pen
A stylus connected to the computer by a wire. It tells the computer which point on the screen to activate.

graphics tablet
A tablet sensitive to pressure; when a point is pressed, the coordinating point is illuminated on the display screen.

Choosing a Graphics Package

The first step in choosing a graphics software package is deciding what its uses will be. Do you want to analyze numeric data using graphs and charts? Do you want to design objects? Would you like to create art? For example, if you desire more effective communication by using visual images so that your viewer can immediately grasp the relationships of your numbers, you need a package that will create graphs. Charts and graphs are easier to understand than lists of numbers, and graphs sometimes make it easier to spot trends and relationships.

When you examine graphics packages, make sure you have the hardware required to use the program. If you do not, you may have to purchase it. Graphics software packages, although they may be designed to run on IBM computers, may have different hardware requirements. Check the amount of memory required to run the program. If it is more memory than your computer has, the package will not be of use to you. Also, see what type of input device is required. If the package requires a graphics tablet or light pen and you only have a keyboard, you will have to decide whether to buy the device or not. Other important considerations are the number of disk drives, type of printer, and type of monitor or display screen necessary to run the graphics package.

Graphics software packages are available in many price ranges. In most cases, the more expensive the package, the better the program. When there is a limit on price, the number of features included will also be limited. You will have to decide which features are essential and which features you can do without; then look for a package that meets those needs and is within your price range.

The program should offer the variety of graphs and colors you require. You may also want to superimpose graphs on one another or combine groups of data on one graph. For example, the bar graph in Figure 9–6 shows the number of boxes of balloons sold during the first four days of a state fair over a period of four years.

When purchasing a package for design purposes, useful features are zoom, pan, automatic dimensioning, save, automatic drawing, and possibly three-dimensional display with animation and rotation capabilities. (Rotation capabilities allow an object to be turned in any direction on the display screen.) All packages do not have every feature. Three-dimensional displays and animation capabilities usually cost more, so you must decide if these features are necessary and worth the added cost. Rotation and three-dimensional displays allow the image to be viewed from all directions. The save feature enables you to store the original design on disk so that you can alter the image and experiment with new designs. The automatic drawing feature produces straight lines and perfect arcs, circles, and ovals instantly.

To create art or draw pictures, many useful features are the same as those for design packages. Other important features to check are high-resolution capabilities and the variety of colors and brush or line sizes available. The method used to control cursor position is also important in art applications. Light pens, mouses, touch screens, and graphics tablets used with the keyboard usually make it easier to move the cursor than using the keyboard alone.

A final feature that may be useful, especially for animated games, is collision detection. This feature automatically checks to see if two objects

Figure 9–6 BAR GRAPH COMPARING RANGES OF DATA

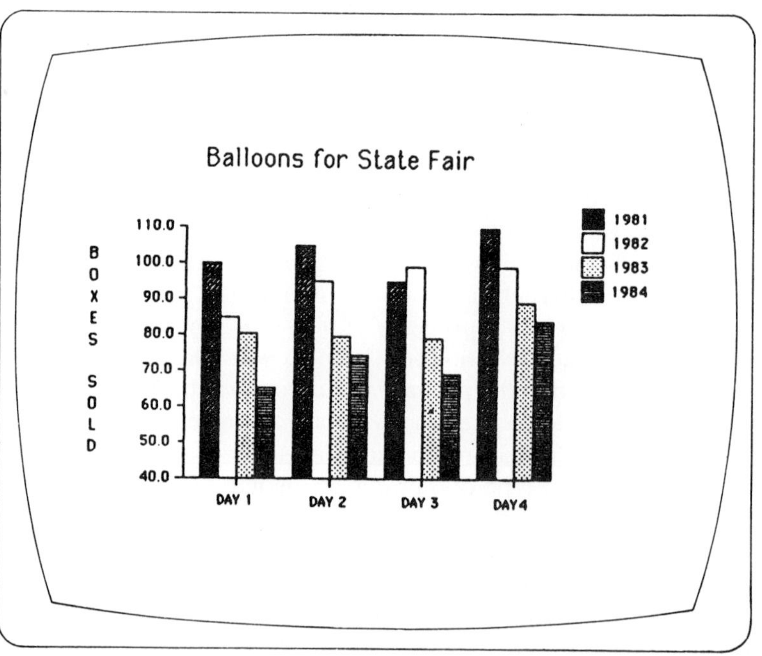

Table 9–2 COMPUTER GRAPHICS SOFTWARE PACKAGES AND THEIR FEATURES

PACKAGE \ FEATURE	CONTROLS	ANIMATED GRAPHICS	SAVE DISPLAY	CREATE THREE-DIMENSIONAL GRAPHICS	NUMBER OF KINDS OF CHARTS	COLORS	REQUIREMENTS	TYPE
BUSINESS GRAPHICS SYSTEM	Keyboard	No	Yes	Yes	8	8, with a color monitor	128K of RAM, two disk drives color graphics board	Business graphics
LENIPEN/PC	Keyboard, light pen, mouse, graphics tablet, joystick	Yes	Yes	Yes	N/A	16	64K of RAM one disk drive, color graphics board	Art and design
PC CRAYON	Keyboard	Yes	Yes	Yes	N/A	Draws in 4 paints in 10	64K of RAM one disk drive, color graphics board	Art
VIDEOGRAM	Keyboard	No	Yes	Yes	N/A	16	128K of RAM, one disk drive, plantronics color plus graphics board	Art and design

are being plotted on the same point, such as a missile and its target. When a collision is detected, you may want to create an explosion. This feature eliminates the constant need to compare the missile to its target to see if they are at the same point.

Software graphics packages often combine the three types of packages discussed. For example, one program may be used both for designing objects and creating works of art.

Popular Graphics Packages

The following is a list of some of the popular packages that are now available for the IBM PC and PCjr.

- ***Business Graphics System***

  Available from: Peachtree Software, Inc.
  3445 Peachtree Rd. NE
  Atlanta, GA 30326
  Price range: $275–$300
  Features: See Table 9–2
  Available for: IBM PC

- ***Lenipen/PC***

Available from:	Duncan-Atwell Computerized Technologies 1200 Salem Ave. Hillside, NJ 07205
Price range:	\$475–\$500
Features:	See Table 9–2
Available for:	IBM PC, Lenipen/jr is available for the PCjr.

- ***PC Crayon***

Available from:	PC Software 9120 Grammercy Dr. #416 San Diego, CA 92123
Price range:	\$50 – \$75
Features:	See Table 9 – 2
Available for:	IBM PC and PCjr

- ***Videogram***

Available from:	Softel, Inc. P. O. Box 365 Stoddard, NH 03464
Price range:	\$100–\$125
Features:	See Table 9–2
Available for:	IBM PC

LEARNING CHECK

1. The individual dots on the display screen, which can be turned on and off, are called ________.
2. The greater the number of pixels in the display screen, the higher the ________ of the image.
3. How can design graphics be used for simulation?
4. Describe what the zoom feature is designed to do.
5. A ________ feature automatically checks to see if two objects are plotted on the same point.

ANSWERS:

1. pixels. **2.** resolution. **3.** An object can be designed and tested on a computer screen without actually being built. **4.** magnify or reduce a portion of the display. **5.** collision detection.

BUSINESS AND FINANCE PACKAGES

If you understand the uses and features of business and finance software packages and are familiar with some other considerations, you can choose a package that will best fit your needs. This section explains these factors and briefly describes a few specific business and finance packages you can buy.

Uses of Business and Finance Packages

Business and finance software packages help you keep track of your assets, bills, monthly payments, income, and taxes. These packages can keep a running total of all accounts and help you determine your net worth at any time. There are basically two types of business and finance software packages. Some are designed to fit a specific business's needs, and others are general in nature and can be tailored by the user to fit a particular home business or personal financial situation.

Specific business packages are available for many different applications, including apartment, property, and real estate management; home building and contracting businesses; farm management; restaurant management; and many more. These packages have predefined accounts (accounts already set up), such as maintenance expense, utilities expense, wage expense, and accounts receivable, and they are tailored to fit a certain type of business. Although accounts are already set up, some packages still allow changes to be made.

General business or finance packages can be set up by users to fit their needs. These packages have many applications, such as checkbook balancing, organization of stocks and investments, and financial management.

Both specific and general business or finance packages provide a systematic method of keeping track of expenditures. When the time comes to report taxes, you do not have to sort through receipts to find deductible expenses. These packages can show you where and when your money was spent, as well as how much was spent. You can then plan to increase or decrease spending. Tax planning and tax preparation packages are available for both business and home finance. Tax planners help determine tax options, so you pay the government no more than its share of your income. Tax preparers help prepare tax forms, provide accurate numbers, and save the expense of paying a professional to do your tax returns.

The advantages of investing in a business or finance software package are having your finances organized and being able to understand them. By periodically spending a small amount of time entering new data into your computer, you will not have the chores of recording receipts in ledger books, manually balancing checkbooks, or manually reconciling bank statements. The right software package can handle these tasks for you. Business and finance software packages are powerful tools that can bring organization into your business or home finances and, at the same time, help you interpret your financial status.

Features of Business and Finance Packages

Business and finance software packages have features that make them easy to operate. Some important features you may find useful are discussed here.

Data Entry. The method of entering data is an important feature to consider. A good package will require that a transaction be entered only once. The greater the number of times you enter a transaction, the greater the chance of error. Also, reentering transactions is time consuming. Some programs require that the transaction be entered once to register it and again when it is time to reconcile the account. When possible, avoid programs like this. However, if cost is a consideration, you may have to give up the convenience of entering data only once.

The format of data entry (the way in which data is requested on the screen) can make the transition to computerizing your finances simple. Most people enter their checkbook transactions in a check register. If this same format appears on the screen, it is easy to understand. Since one transaction appears on one line, the check register format allows multiple transactions to appear on the screen. Some packages, though, display only one transaction per screen, which makes searching for a certain transaction a slower process.

The amount of information about each transaction you can enter is also important. You probably want to enter the date, payee, amount, whether or not the check has cleared the bank, whether the amount is tax deductible, and under what expense account the transactions fall. Make sure the package has enough fields (spaces for individual data items relating to each transaction) to allow you to enter all the information you need about each transaction.

Printing. The ability to print checks and reports is a feature you may want. For this you will need a printer and blank checks you can order from your software supplier. Some packages also offer a variety of formatted reports that can be used to produce income statements and balance sheets.

Budgeting. The ability to set budget amounts for expense categories means that the program will store the amounts you set as the limits to be spent in each expense category. The program should be capable of producing a report to notify you if you are over or under your budgeted amount, and if so, by how much.

Graphics. Many business and finance software packages also feature graphics. They produce graphs that are easy to understand, allowing you to see trends in spending and income or assets in relation to liabilities. Some programs display only line or bar graphs, whereas others offer a choice of line, bar, or pie graphs. Some packages offer color, which makes the graphs more interesting. Not all packages allow the graphics to be printed. If the software does enable you to print the graphic images, you must have a printer or **plotter** capable of printing them.

plotter
A computer controlled graphics output device that moves pens or paper to specified x,y coordinates to make a hard copy of graphics images.

Choosing a Business and Finance Package

When it comes time to choose the software for your business or home finances, you will want to evaluate each package partly on the basis of the features just discussed. However, one of the most important aspects of any software package is ease of use. If a program is not easy to understand and use, it probably will not be used. Therefore, before you purchase a package, read the documentation. Is it easy to understand? Does it clearly explain how to get started and continue using the program? Test the program before purchasing it to determine whether you are comfortable using it.

The following are some other ways to help determine if a package will be easy to use:

- Make sure each transaction has to be entered only once.
- Look at the capacity of the program. How many checking or savings accounts can the program handle? If you have six checking or savings accounts but the program only allows for four, it will not be useful to you.
- Determine how many budget or expense categories you will need, allowing for a few extra. Does the package have enough space for them? If the program has predefined categories, can they be changed if necessary?
- Is the package flexible? That is, will it do everything you would like it to do? Is it easy to use? For instance, some programs search for transactions by date or payee, but not by amount or tax status. Furthermore, some packages will not graph your information.
- Before purchasing a tax preparation package, go through your previous tax forms and determine what forms you may need in coming years. Make sure that the package you have chosen includes all needed forms. Above all, make sure that the software company offers yearly updates to its programs.
- As with any type of software package, check the hardware requirements. Does your computer have enough memory to run the program? Do you have enough disk drives? Will your printer work with the program and print what you need?

You must weigh the importance of all these features versus the cost of the package and then decide which package best fits your needs. After purchasing a package, take time to learn how to use the program and how to set it up. You should be able to enjoy the advantages of an accurate and organized financial system.

Popular Business and Finance Packages

The following is a list of some of the popular packages that are now available for the IBM PC and PCjr.

General Business and Finance Packages.

- ***Dollars and $ense***

Available from:	Monogram 8295 S. LaCienega Blvd. Inglewood, CA 90301
Price range:	$175 – $200
Features:	See Table 9–3
Available for:	IBM PC and PCjr with 128K of RAM and one disk drive

- ***Money Maestro***

Available from:	InnoSYS, Inc. 2150 Shattuck Ave., Suite 901 Berkeley, CA 94704
Price range:	$125–$150
Features:	See Table 9–3
Available for:	IBM PC and PCjr with 64K of RAM and one disk drive

Table 9–3 GENERAL BUSINESS AND FINANCE SOFTWARE PACKAGES AND THEIR FEATURES

PACKAGE \ FEATURE	NUMBER OF EXPENSE AND BUDGET CATEGORIES	NUMBER OF TRANSACTIONS PER MONTH	NUMBER OF CHECKING ACCOUNTS	NUMBER OF TRANSACTIONS ON SCREEN	FLEXIBLE BUDGET CATEGORIES	GRAPHICS	BANK RECONCILIATION	CHECK PRINTING	AMORTIZATION AND APPRECIATION
DOLLARS AND $ENSE	120	Unlimited	12	20	Yes	Yes	Yes	Yes	Yes
MONEY MAESTRO	210	Unlimited	1	3	Yes	No	Yes	Yes	No
PC/PERSONAL FINANCE PROGRAM	45	400	1	18	Yes	Yes	Yes	Yes	No
PC/PROFESSIONAL FINANCE PROGRAM	45	400	26	18	Yes	Yes	Yes	Yes	No
THE SMART CHECKBOOK II	200	300	Unlimited	12	Yes	No	Yes	Yes	No

- ***PC/Personal Finance Program***

  Available from: Best Programs
  5134 Leesburg Pike
  Alexandria, VA 22305
  Price range: $75–$100
  Features: See Table 9–3
  Available for: IBM PC with 128K of RAM

- ***PC/Professional Finance Program***

  Available from: Best Programs
  5134 Leesburg Pike
  Alexandria, VA 22305
  Price range: $75–$100
  Features: See Table 9–3
  Available for: IBM PC with 128K of RAM

- ***The Smart Checkbook II***

  Available from: Softquest, Inc.
  P. O. Box 3456
  McLean, VA 22103
  Price range: $125–$175
  Features: See Table 9–3
  Available for: IBM PC and PCjr with 64K of RAM and one disk drive

Table 9–4 TAX PREPARATION SOFTWARE PACKAGES AND THEIR FEATURES

PACKAGE \ FEATURE	NUMBER OF SCHEDULES AND FORMS	ON-SCREEN CALCULATIONS	YEAR-TO-YEAR TRANSFER	FORM-TO-FORM TRANSFER	ABILITY TO PRINT IRS FORMS
PC/TAXCUT	19	Yes	Yes	Yes	Yes
THE TAX ADVANTAGE	10	Yes	No	No	No
TAX MANAGER	25	Yes	No	Yes	Yes
TAX PREPARER	22	Yes	Yes	Yes	Yes

Tax Preparation Packages.

- ***PC/Taxcut***

  Available from: Best Programs
  5134 Leesburg Pike
  Alexandria, VA 22305
  Price range: \$225–\$250
  Features: See Table 9–4
  Available for: IBM PC with 128K of RAM and two disk drives

- ***The Tax Advantage***

  Available from: Arrays, Inc./Continental Software
  11223 S. Hindry Ave.
  Los Angeles, CA 90045
  Price range: \$50 – \$75
  Features: See Table 9 – 4
  Available for: IBM PC with 128K and one disk drive

- ***Tax Manager***

  Available from: Micro Lab
  2699 Skokie Valley Rd.
  Highland Park, IL 60035
  Price range: \$250 – \$275
  Features: See Table 9 – 4
  Available for: IBM PC with 64K of RAM and two disk drives

- ***Tax Preparer***

  Available from: HowardSoft
  8008 Girard Ave., Suite 310
  LaJolla, CA 92037
  Price range: \$275–\$300
  Features: See Table 9–4
  Available for: IBM PC with 64K of RAM and one disk drive

HOME AND PERSONAL INTEREST PACKAGES

A wide variety of software is available for use with hobbies, in-home management, and other personal interests. This category includes such programs as loan analyzers, IRA organizers, menu and meal planners, nutrition analyzers, horoscope analyzers, and schedule organizers.

Choosing a Home and Personal Interest Package

In choosing a software package, the first thing you must decide is what you would like it to do. Then decide how much money you can spend before examining the packages available. Since there are many different programs for home and personal interests, the features vary somewhat with each package. Several popular packages are described below and this information should give you an idea of what these packages can do.

There is, however, one general feature that is important for any type of package: quality of documentation. The package should have clear, straightforward documentation. Read through the documentation, and actually run the program in the store before purchasing it. If the program is hard to understand and use, you may not want it. Also, check that your computer has the hardware components required and enough memory to run the program.

Popular Home and Personal Interest Packages

The following is a brief sample of home and personal interest software now available for the IBM PC and PCjr.

- ***Catman***

  Available from: Zephyr Services
  306 S. Homewood Ave.
  Pittsburgh, PA 15208

  Price range: \$20–\$45

  Features: Catman generates catalogs of books, tapes, and records. Catman can store up to 3,500 items by category or title. Users can use Catman to prepare catalog listings and to perform sorts.

  Available for: IBM PC and PCjr with 64K of RAM and one disk drive

- ***Diet Analyzer***

  Available from: Natural Software Limited
  7 Lake St., #7E
  White Plains, NY 10603

  Price range: \$50–\$75

  Features: Diet Analyzer is designed to aid the users with menu planning. The program keeps a record of foods consumed, exercise, and body weight. Users enter the amounts and types of foods consumed in English, using common measuring units. The program then analyzes the user's food consumption for up to twenty-four nutrients. Foods, meals, days, or any selected period can be used for the analysis. Diet Analyzer has a dictionary of USDA foods. Users can add their favorite foods to the dictionary.

  Available for: IBM PC and PCjr with 128K and one disk drive

- ***Family Medical Advisor***

Available from: Navic Software
P. O. Box 14727
North Palm Beach, FL 33408
Price range: \$25–\$50
Features: Family Medical Advisor diagnoses common ailments, diseases, and childhood illnesses by analyzing symptoms and determining the most probable medical condition. This program asks a series of yes or no questions to which the user responds. The program then analyzes the answers against a data base of 200 illnesses and 10,000 combinations of symptoms. Disorders with similar symptoms are also listed in descending order of probability. Family Medical Advisor also defines any medical term it uses.
Available for: IBM PC with 64K of RAM and one disk drive and PCjr with 64K of RAM and cartridge BASIC

- ***InShape***

Available from: Power Up
P. O. Box 306
125 Main St.
Half Moon Bay, CA 94019
Price range: \$75–\$100
Features: InShape is a health package that monitors the user's aerobic exercise performance, weight, and diet. This program evaluates the user's progress based upon aerobic values. The program then reports if the user is working hard enough. InShape breaks down the user's food intake into fats, carbohydrates, and proteins. The program also has a graphing function which shows the impact on the user's body weight.
Available for: IBM PC with 128K and one disk drive

- ***Micro Cookbook***

Available from: Virtual Combinatics
P. O. Box 755
Rockport, MA 01966
Price range: \$25–\$50
Features: Micro Cookbook contains recipes for 150 international dishes. Micro Cookbook also manages, stores, searches for, and retrieves recipes, and will add or delete recipes according to the user's needs. Micro Cookbook produces a shopping list of ingredients for a recipe and shows recipes for ingredients that have already been purchased.
Available for: IBM PC and PCjr with 64K of RAM and one disk drive

- ***Personal Calendar***

Available from:	Peachtree Software, Inc. 3445 Peachtree Rd. NE Atlanta, GA 30326
Price range:	\$175–\$200
Features:	Personal Calendar manages time for individuals, groups, or facilities. This program uses reminders and priority and flexible-time analysis. The program schedules meetings in the first available time slot and then schedules recurring activities. The time interval of the appointment is determined by the user.
Available for:	IBM PC with 128K and one disk drive

LEARNING CHECK

1. Name the two types of business and finance software packages.

2. Most business and finance software packages do not include a graphics feature, because graphics are seldom used. (True or false?)

3. When selecting any type of software package, it is important to read the ________ explaining how to use it.

4. The number of times a transaction must be entered with a business or finance software package is an important feature to consider. (True or false?)

5. It is not important to check the hardware requirements when selecting a business or finance software package. (True or false?)

ANSWERS:

1. those designed to fit specific business needs and general packages that can be tailored to a user's needs. **2.** false. **3.** documentation. **4.** true. **5.** false.

RECREATIONAL PACKAGES

There are hundreds of recreational software packages on the market today. How do you begin to select ones that you will enjoy? This section describes some of the games available and suggests which features to look for when purchasing them.

Types of Recreational Packages

So many games are now available that it would be impossible to describe them all here. Recreational games can be found for almost any interest, including sports, puzzles, strategy, adventure, board games, war games, and arcade games. Many packages combine two or more types of games into one. Because they seem to be the most popular, board, arcade, and adventure games are the main types discussed here.

When playing board games on the computer, your opponent is the computer. Having the computer as an opponent has advantages. The computer is always ready and able to play, and it does not have good and bad days. The computer can almost always match the user's skill level, which is important when trying to improve at a game. Board game software often offers advice about good moves to make. You can also watch the computer play itself and learn new strategies in this way.

Arcade games are wonderful for developing hand-eye coordination, and they are now much more advanced than the earliest games, such as Pong. Tactical planning and the ability to make correct decisions on the spur of the moment are skills needed for many games. Games that require intense thinking tend to hold the player's interest longer.

Adventure games vary with regard to the degree of player involvement. Some adventure games exercise hand-eye coordination more than imagination, whereas others are so mind boggling that user support groups have been formed to exchange clues. Some adventures are so involved that they may take months to solve, and others may take only hours.

Features of Recreational Packages

Common features to look for in recreational packages include the level of challenge, the quality of the package's graphics, the amount of fun involved with using the package, and the method of input required by the package.

Challenge. The most important feature of recreational games software seems to be the ability to continually challenge the user. The only way a game can maintain interest is by challenging the user as his or her skill level improves. A program that offers only one level of skill will not be interesting for long; once it has been mastered, it will no longer be fun. Most games offer a choice of several skill levels from beginner to expert. Each level should be challenging initially, forcing the user to try new techniques and master new skills. The best games will challenge not only reflexes and coordination, but also the user's ability to think.

Some board games even offer an infinite level of play. At the lowest levels, the computer responds almost instantly. At the highest levels, it may take minutes or even hours to respond. At the infinite level, the computer considers all possible moves, which sometimes takes hours or, in some instances, days. A force-move feature tells the computer to make the best move it has found so far, rather than wait to finish its complete search. The force-move feature can be used at any level.

Graphics. Graphics play an important part in successful computer games, especially in arcade and adventure games. Graphics must have a realistic appearance (at least realistic enough so that the objects are recognizable). Fast action is also important; the graphics must be able to keep a fast pace to challenge the player's reflexes. The program also should offer several different screens (game set-ups) on which to play.

Fun. A game should be fun, of course. Games with interesting stories or intriguing characters will keep the user fascinated and maybe prevent discouragement during play at a difficult level.

Input Method. There are several ways to let the computer know your decisions or moves. The most common are by using the keyboard or a joystick; some programs allow both. For board games, the keyboard is easy to use. For example, in a game of chess, you would just type E2–E4 to move a piece from Square E2 to Square E4. This might be tiresome, at least until the notation is mastered. Simpler methods are to use the keyboard arrows or joysticks. Joysticks and game paddles are the easiest to use for fast-action games or games in which precise movements are needed. For instance, keyboard arrows allow only horizontal and vertical movement, which makes traveling in curves or diagonals difficult. Joysticks work much better for these moves.

Listed here are some desirable features of typical board games.

Advice. Most board games offer opportunities to ask the computer for advice. The computer will usually show a suggested move or two; however, some games give a series of best moves for each side. The user can either accept or reject the computer's advice.

Switch Sides. Some programs allow the user to switch sides with the computer when the user is in a tough situation or a predicament he or she is unable to handle. This allows the user to see how the computer would handle the situation.

Change Move. In many games, the computer will let you take back your move once or several times. This lets you correct an input mistake, as well as to try various moves to see what will happen.

List Moves. This feature permits you to see a list of all moves made in the game thus far. A few games will even show an instant replay. Many games can be saved on tape or disk to be continued at a later date.

Two Players. This feature allows two players to play each other, giving both the opportunity to ask the computer for advice.

Choosing a Recreational Package

When it comes time to choose a recreational package for your home computer, you will have to decide what type of game you are interested in (arcade, board, adventure, strategy, or sports simulation). Look at the number of levels of play available and the number of game screens in the package, which should indicate whether or not the game will provide continuing interest. Whenever possible, test the package before you buy it. Another consideration is the type of input device the package requires (joystick, keyboard, or game paddles).

Popular Recreational Packages

The following is a list of some of the popular packages now available for the IBM PC and PCjr.

Board Games.

- ***Backgammon***

Available from: C & C Software
54 Sonoma Ave.
Goleta, CA 93117
Price range: $25–$50
Features: Backgammon provides interactive play between player and computer; it allows the game to be saved and then returned to at any time. It gives advice, keeps score, and never cheats
Available for: IBM PC with 128K of RAM and a color graphics adaptor

- ***Bluebush Chess***

Available from: Bluebush
P. O. Box 3585
Santa Clara, CA 95055
Price range: $50–$75
Features: Bluebush Chess has eight skill levels to which the user can switch at any time. It gives advice, allows the board to be set up in any arrangement, and provides lists of both possible and previous moves. The program also allows the user to switch sides with the computer and to take back unwanted moves. Bluebush Chess checks all moves for legality and can select the best move for the user.
Available for: IBM PC and PCjr with 64K of RAM and one disk drive

- ***Chess-Champ***

Available from: Zephyr Services
306 S. Homewood Ave.
Pittsburgh, PA 15208
Price range: $25–$50
Features: Chess-Champ offers the full range of chess moves and gives advice on the best move to make; it allows the user to rearrange the board at any time, to set up a new game or a chess problem, and to switch sides with the computer. Chess-Champ has twenty-four levels of play.
Available for: IBM PC and PCjr with 64K of RAM and one disk drive

- ***Cross Clues*** (a combination of Scrabble and Hangman)

Available from: Science Research Associates
155 N. Wacker Dr.
Chicago, IL 60606
Price range: $25–$50
Features: Cross Clues allows the user to play against the computer or a friend. Cross Clues has an automatic timer and score keeper and is played by using the cursor control keys.
Available for: IBM PC and PCjr with 64K of RAM and one disk drive

- ***Desdemona*** (a version of Othello)

  Available from: Zephyr Services
  306 S. Homewood Ave.
  Pittsburgh, PA 15208

  Price range: $20–$45

  Features: Desdemona allows the user to play against the computer or a friend. Desdemona has automatic scoring and sound effects.

  Available for: IBM PC and PCjr with 64K of RAM and one disk drive

- ***Tiao Chi*** (a version of Chinese checkers)

  Available from: Microclassics
  315 W. Grand Ave.
  El Segundo, CA 90245

  Price range: $25–$50

  Features: Tiao Chi has three skill levels, color graphics, and sound effects. Tiao Chi allows up to six players (including the computer).

  Available for: IBM PC with 64K of RAM and one disk drive

Arcade Games.

- ***Astro Dodge***

  Available from: Digital Marketing Corp.
  2363 Boulevard Circle
  Walnut Creek, CA 94595

  Price range: $25–$50

  Features: See Table 9–5

  Available for: IBM PC and PCjr with 64K of RAM, one disk drive, and a color graphics board

- ***Crossfire***

  Available from: Sierra On-Line, Inc.
  Sierra On-Line Building
  Coarsegold, CA 93614

  Price range: $25–$50

  Features: See Table 9–5

  Available for: IBM PC and PCjr with 64K of RAM, one disk drive, and a color graphics board

- ***Dig Dug***

  Available from: Atari
  1272 Borregas Ave.
  Sunnyvale, CA 94086

  Price range: $25–$50

  Features: See Table 9–5

  Available for: IBM PC and PCjr with 64K of RAM and a color graphics adaptor

Table 9–5 *ARCADE GAMES AND THEIR FEATURES*

PACKAGE \ FEATURE	INPUT DEVICE (J = JOYSTICK; K = KEYBOARD)	NUMBER OF LEVELS	NUMBER OF SCREENS
ASTRO DODGE	K	1	1
CROSSFIRE	K/J	99	1
DIG DUG	K/J	2	8
FROGGER	K/J	99	1
JUMPMAN	J	5	30
SEA DRAGON	K/J	2	24
SERPENTINE	K/J	99	20

- ***Frogger***

  Available from: Sierra On-Line, Inc.
  Sierra On-Line Building
  Coarsegold, CA 93614
  Price range: $25–$50
  Features: See Table 9–5
  Available for: IBM PC and PCjr with 64K, one disk drive, and a color graphics board

- ***Jumpman***

  Available from: Epyx-Automated Simulations, Inc.
  1043 Kiel Court
  Sunnyvale, CA 94086
  Price range: $25 – $50
  Features: See Table 9–5
  Available for: IBM PC with 64K of RAM

- ***Sea Dragon***

  Available from: Adventure International
  P. O. Box 3435
  Longwood, FL 32750
  Price range: $25–$50
  Features: See Table 9–5
  Available for: IBM PC with 128K, one disk drive, and a color graphics board

- ***Serpentine***

  Available from: Broderbund
  1938 Fourth St.
  San Rafael, CA 94901
  Price range: $25–$50
  Features: See Table 9–5
  Available for: IBM PC with 64K of RAM and a color graphics adaptor

Adventure Games.

- ***Asylum***

Available from:	Software Resources Group 1095 Airport Rd. Minden, NV 89423
Price range:	\$25–\$50
Features:	See Table 9–6
Available for:	IBM PC and PCjr with 64K of RAM and one disk drive

- ***Cyborg***

Available from:	Sentient Software, Inc. P. O. Box 4929 Aspen, CO 81612
Price range:	\$25–\$50
Features:	See Table 9–6
Available for:	IBM PC and PCjr with 64K of RAM and one disk drive

- ***Starcross***

Available from:	Infocom, Inc. 55 Wheeler St. Cambridge, MA 02138
Price range:	\$25–\$50
Features:	See Table 9–6
Available for:	IBM PC and PCjr with 48K of RAM

- ***Ulysses and the Golden Fleece***

Available from:	Sierra On-Line, Inc. Sierra On-Line Building Coarsegold, CA 93614
Price range:	\$25–\$50
Features:	See Table 9–6
Available for:	IBM PC with 48K of RAM, one disk drive, and a color graphics board

- ***The Witness***

Available from:	Infocom, Inc. 55 Wheeler St. Cambridge, MA 02138
Price range:	\$25–\$50
Features:	See Table 9–6
Available for:	IBM PC and PCjr with 48K of RAM

- ***Zork I, II, III***

Available from:	Infocom, Inc. 55 Wheeler St. Cambridge, MA 02138
Price range:	\$25–\$50 each
Features:	See Table 9–6
Available for:	IBM PC and PCjr with 48K of RAM and one disk drive

Table 9–6 ADVENTURE GAMES AND THEIR FEATURES

PACKAGE \ FEATURE	NUMBER OF PLAYERS	TYPE OF GAME (T = TEXT; G = GRAPHICS)	GAME CAN BE SAVED
ASYLUM	1	G	Yes
CYBORG	1	T	Yes
STARCROSS	1	T	Yes
ULYSSES AND THE GOLDEN FLEECE	1	T/G	Yes
THE WITNESS	1	T	Yes
ZORK I, II, III	1	T	Yes

EDUCATIONAL PACKAGES

Educational software is becoming popular as a teaching aid in classrooms. Computer-aided instruction, as mentioned in Chapter 5, helps students learn new concepts or drills them on certain subjects. At the same time, students learn more about the computer itself.

Educational software packages are also becoming popular to help students practice their skills at home. With good software, learning on the computer can be exciting for both adults and children.

Uses of Educational Packages

Educational software packages are available for many applications and for students of all ages. Although this section concentrates on programs available for students from preschool through high school, there are many packages that adults find helpful, such as programs that teach speed reading, typing, programming in BASIC, foreign languages, and playing musical instruments.

There are three basic types of educational programs. Tutorial programs actually present and explain the material and then test on it, concentrating on building knowledge and understanding. Drill programs drill and test the user on a subject that has already been learned; they do not explain the material. Testing programs only test the student on the material, giving practice in test situations.

Most educational software packages are designed to cover specific areas of study, such as geometry, history, or spelling. However, these packages may not follow the same sequence of lessons being taught in school. Some software follows right along with the student's lessons, but the student must provide the questions and answers. Eazylearn described in Table 9–7 is an example. Students learn from making up their own questions and answers.

Features of Educational Packages

When selecting educational software packages, consider the following important features.

Table 9–7 EDUCATIONAL SOFTWARE PACKAGES AND THEIR FEATURES

PACKAGE \ FEATURE	TYPE	AUDIENCE	EXPLANATION OF ANSWERS	DOCUMENTATION	COLOR REQUIRED	SCORING
ABsCENES I	letter and word recognition	children	No	User's manual	No	No
APTITUDE/ACHIEVEMENT TEST PREPARATION	simulation of the SAT exam	college bound high school students	Yes	On-screen documentation	No	Yes
EAZYLEARN	creation of essay, fill in the blank, and word/phrase recognition tests	business teachers	Yes	User's manual	No	No
FRENCH I	vocabulary and verb conjugation drills	beginning French students	Yes	User's manual	No	Yes
KEYS TO RESPONSIBLE DRIVING	simulation and explanation of safe driving principles	beginning to experienced driver	Yes	User's manual and driving and car care manual	Yes	Yes
MATH BLASTER!	basic arithmetic skills	grades 1 to 6 and remedial or learning disabled	Yes	User's manual	No	No
THE MUSIC TEACHER SERIES: THE NOTABLE PHANTOM	read music and play keyboard	Ages 5 to 10	Yes	User's manual	Yes	Yes
SAT ENGLISH	develops vocabulary, reasoning, and interpretive skills	college bound high school students	Yes	Practice and study aids	No	Yes
SAT MATH	practice in arithmetic skills covered by the SAT exam	college bound high school students	Yes	Study aids	No	Yes
SPANISH I	vocabulary and verb conjugation drills	beginning Spanish students	Yes	User's manual	No	Yes
SPEED READER II	speed reading tutorial	8th grade and up	N/A	User's manual	No	Yes
STATES AND TRAITS	recognition, placement, and geography of the states in the U.S.	ages 9 to adult	Yes	User's manual	Yes	Yes
TYPING INSTRUCTOR	typing tutorial	beginning typists	N/A	User's manual	No	Yes
WORD ATTACK!	word definition	ages 8 to adult	yes	User's manual	No	No

Age Level. The software package should match the age level of the person for whom it is intended. A program that is too difficult will only create frustration and confusion, and one that offers no challenge or progresses too slowly will not be effective.

Presentation of Material. Good educational programs have clear and complete instructions appearing on the screen both at the beginning of the program and throughout its execution. The younger the user, the more often instructions and reminders need to appear in the program. Children can quickly forget how to select different options or stop the program.

Instructions should be simple enough for young students to understand and complete enough so students can run the program on their own after an introduction and trial run with a parent's help. Older students (high school level) should be able to operate a program from a well-written instruction manual.

Help Screens. The program should allow the student to ask for help and receive it by providing a list of keys to press and their functions. This is important to children when they are struggling with an answer or when they forget how to make the program do what they want it to do.

Graphics. The best educational packages make learning enjoyable. In fact, good educational software for children often uses a game format. When evaluating software packages for children, pay close attention to the graphics. Make sure that captivating graphics and colors will draw the child's attention to the educationally important aspects of the display. The graphics should motivate rather than distract. Preschoolers need simplicity and color. Be wary of software that seems too busy or sophisticated, as preschoolers can easily become confused with too much detail.

A game structure or colorful graphics displays are not as important for older students, because they realize that the purpose is to learn. Speed is important, especially in programs designed to drill and test, such as the SAT educational software packages. In packages designed to test, slow graphics displays will only distract the student and slow down the learning process.

Reward. Students need to see the results of their accomplishments, such as a score or rating level. For children, scores are not as important as rewards for correct answers. Rewards such as musical tunes or special graphics displays give children a feeling of success and accomplishment. However, the rewards should not be excessively long or distract students from the purpose of the program.

Also, pay attention to the manner in which the program responds to incorrect answers. Good educational software programs should give a hint to, or demonstration of, the correct answer rather than a loud nasty noise or no response at all. The program should teach children new information rather than make them feel "wrong" when they answer incorrectly.

Choosing an Educational Package

Your computer can only be transformed into an educational tool if it is used with high-quality educational software. The hard part is choosing the best software to fit your needs out of the thousands of educational packages on the market today. As you evaluate a program, look at what it is designed to teach, as well as how it teaches and reinforces a particular skill.

First, determine the area or areas that the user of the package wants to develop or strengthen, along with the areas in which the user could benefit most from computer-aided instruction. Next, determine which is needed: a tutorial program, a drill program, or a testing program. Note that the student may also gain practice in test taking from the drill type of program.

For an educational package to be useful, it must be designed for the user's age level. Test the program before buying it to be sure that the person for whom it is intended will be able to understand and use it easily. Make sure instructions are clear and complete. Also, read the instruction manual and any other documentation to make sure the instructions take the user step by step through the program.

Once you have chosen a package, be sure you have the necessary hardware needed to implement it. For instance, if the program places a heavy importance on color, the package may not be of great value to you unless you have a color monitor or plan to buy one.

Popular Educational Packages

Listed below are a number of educational packages for the IBM PC and PCjr. These packages can be used for such things as learning a foreign language, improving your reading speed, and learning to type.

- ***ABsCenes I***

  Available from: CompuTeach
  353 W. Lancaster Ave.
  Wayne, PA 19087
  Price range: $25–$50
  Features: See Table 9–7
  Available for: IBM PC with 128K of RAM and one disk drive

- ***Aptitude/Achievement Test Preparation***

  Available from: Microphys Programs
  1737 W. Second St.
  Brooklyn, NY 11223
  Price range: $200–$225
  Features: See Table 9–7
  Available for: IMB PC and PCjr with 64K of RAM and one disk drive

- ***Eazylearn***

  Available from: Miracle Computing
  313 Clayton Ct.
  Lawrence, KS 66044
  Price range: $250–$275
  Features: See Table 9–7
  Available for: IBM PC with 128K of RAM and two disk drives

- ***Keys to Responsible Driving***

Available from:	CBS Software 1 Fawcett Pl. Greenwich, CT 06836
Price range:	\$75–\$100
Features:	See Table 9–7
Available for:	IBM PC with 128K of RAM, one disk drive, and a color garphics board and IBM PCjr with 128K of RAM and cartridge BASIC

- ***The Music Teacher Series: The Notable Phantom***

Available from:	DesignWare, Inc. 185 Berry St. San Francisco, CA 94107
Price range:	\$50–\$75
Features:	See Table 9–7
Available for:	IBM PC and PCjr with 64K of RAM, one disk drive, and a color graphics board

- ***SAT Math and SAT English***

Available from:	Micro Lab 2699 Skokie Valley Rd. Highland Park, IL 60035
Price range:	\$25–\$50
Features:	See Table 9–7
Available for:	IBM PC with 128K of RAM and one disk drive

- ***Spanish I and French I***

Available from:	Acorn Software Products 353 W. Lancaster Ave. Wayne, PA 19087
Price range:	\$25–\$50 each
Features:	See Table 9–7
Available for:	IBM PC with 128K of RAM and one disk drive and IBM PCjr with 128K of RAM and cartridge BASIC

- ***States and Traits***

Available from:	DesignWare, Inc. 185 Berry St. San Francisco, CA 94107
Price range:	\$25–\$50
Features:	See Table 9–7
Available for:	IBM PC and PCjr with 64K of RAM, one disk drive, and a color graphics board

- ***Speed Reader II***

Available from:	Davidson and Associates 6069 Groveoak Pl. #12 Rancho Palos Verdes, CA 90274

Price range: $50–$75
Features: See Table 9–7
Available for: IBM PC and PCjr with 64K of RAM and one disk drive

- ***Typing Instructor***

Available from: Individual Software
24 Spinnaker Pl.
Redwood City, CA 94065
Price range: $50–$75
Features: See Table 9–7
Available for: IBM PC and PCjr with 64K of RAM

- ***Word Attack! and Math Blaster!***

Available from: Davidson and Associates
6069 Groveoak Pl. #12
Rancho Palos Verdes, CA 90274
Price range: $50–$75 each
Features: See Table 9–7
Available for: IBM PC with 64K of RAM and one disk drive and IBM PCjr with cartridge BASIC

TELECOMMUNICATIONS

Definitions

Data communications is the electronic transmission of data from one location to another. Telecommunications requires the use of data communications facilities, such as the telephone system, to allow the user to access information from across town or across the country. Data communications has allowed the development of computer networks—the linking together of computers, allowing them to share information and hardware.

There are two types of networking systems: remote and local area networks (LANs). Remote networks rely on telecommunications systems; commercial data bases such as CompuServe and The Source are examples. CompuServe is the largest general information service available. A CompuServe customer can choose from a large number of available services, such as games or the ability to check on stock prices. The Source offers information on everything from astrology to bonds, as well as an advice column. Commercial data bases are often used by people doing in-depth research. Electronic bulletin boards are another type of remote network. These are run by other microcomputer users and can be accessed using a telecommunications system. Electronic bulletin boards are used by anyone who wants any kind of general information, from software evaluations to a copy of a public domain program.

Local-area networks operate within a well-defined and generally self-enclosed area such as an office building. They can be formed by hooking up one microcomputer to talk to other microcomputers, usually with a cable. These networks are used by a variety of small and large companies who have realized the benefits associated with linking their computers to share information and hardware.

Commercial Data Bases. **Commercial data bases,** also called *information services* or *information utilities,* charge their customers for using their service. Passwords are often used to insure that only paying customers can access the information from the data base. Information services charge either by connect time or by charging a flat rate in the form of a general fee. **Connect time** refers to the actual time a customer is using the data base; if a customer does not use the data base one month, that customer will not be charged. If a general fee is charged, however, a set monthly fee will be charged no matter how much or how little the data base is used. The customer is charged for having the data base available instead of being charged for the actual use of it.

commercial data base
A data base set up by a specific company for the purpose of allowing other companies and individuals to access information in the data base for a fee; also called information services or information utilities.

connect time
The amount of time a customer is hooked up to and is using the commercial data base.

Another cost that must be considered is the telephone cost. A long-distance telephone call often is required to access a data base. Not only will the information service bill the customer, but the telephone company will have to be paid, too. After all, its services are being used, just as if a personal long-distance call were being made. Some telephone companies also charge an extra fee (separate from the long-distance charges) for customers who use modems.

Telecommunicating with a commercial data base can obviously be very expensive. It is important to weigh the importance of the information that will be received with the cost of receiving that information before establishing the network.

Electronic Bulletin Boards. Electronic bulletin boards are operated by computer enthusiasts and can be accessed at no cost. Of course, a bulletin board will not contain as much information as a commercial data base, but a well-constructed one could provide a user with all the information needed on a particular topic.

Bulletin boards are usually set up for the users of a particular type of computer system, for example, the owners of IBM computers. Information is selected from a main menu, just as it is from an information service. The main menu lists all the available topics. A particular category is selected by entering the specified code, and that information is then accessed.

Bulletin boards are also used for writing messages to and from different operators. This option is helpful for finding buyers and sellers for hardware, locating user groups in different communities, and getting evaluations of new software packages.

Although passwords are not required to access most bulletin boards, it may be necessary to contact the operator before downloading or uploading (copying) one of the many public domain programs to or from the bulletin board. The operator may give you a password or terminal program that will allow the program to be copied. Bulletin boards are perpetuated by users who contribute programs they have written to the library of programs on the bulletin board. This allows a great deal of new software to be available at any time. Many bulletin boards may be accessed by a variety of computers. For a listing of general bulletin boards, contact Novation, Inc.; 20409 Prairie St.; Chatsworth, CA 91311; (213) 996–5060.

Local-Area Networks. Local-area networks allow computers in the same area (usually within a few thousand feet, since they are directly connected by a cable hookup) to talk to each other. Teachers use them to leave homework on their students' terminals and to monitor their progress by checking in occasionally. In the office, LANs are used to send electronic mail and to check on the progress of projects that involve more than one person.

Hardware Requirements

Before any type of telecommunicating can be accomplished, the proper hardware must be set up. In addition to a computer and the appropriate software, two extra pieces of hardware are needed for telecommunications: a telephone and a modem. The telephone physically links the systems together. A modem translates the data into a type of information that the telephone lines can transmit, and another modem then translates the information back to computer-readable form once it is received on the other end. Figure 9–7 illustrates the function of a modem.

Modems are either half-duplex or full-duplex. A half-duplex modem can transmit and receive data, but not at the same time. A full-duplex modem can send and receive data at the same time. Modems typically transmit data at one of two speeds: 300 or 1,200 baud. A 1200-baud modem is much faster and much more expensive than a 300-baud modem. When using a modem to access an information service, skimming through the material will be much faster with a 1,200-baud modem than with a 300-baud modem.

Choosing a Communications Software Package

Microcomputers cannot do anything unless they are told to, and telecommunicating is no different. A software program must be used to tell the computer how the information is to be manipulated, transmitted, and received. A good communications package can do all that, as well as set up the computer to handle various forms of data, change transmission speeds,

Figure 9–7 TELECOMMUNICATIONS DATA TRANSMISSION

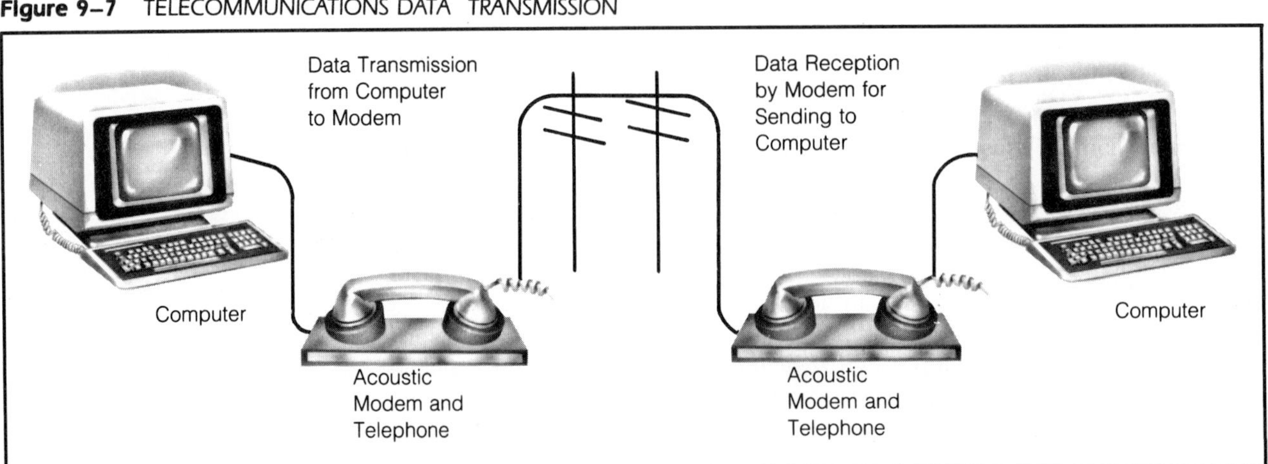

store telephone numbers, and automatically reconnect each time the user needs to communicate. Not all packages provide every function, and you may not need them all. The software you choose should perform all the functions that you need and that your modem is able to perform. Remember, the more the software package does, the more it costs.

Features of Communications Packages. The most simple communications software package should be able to transmit data in the American Standard Code for Information Interchange (ASCII) form. Most information utilities send their data in ASCII form, and personal computers can store their data in ASCII form. Check with your dealer to be sure the software you purchase transfers data in the form you need.

Another feature to look for is the ability to transfer data to and from a disk drive. The software package should be able to save the information on the disk. It also should provide a screen display of the data coming in or going out.

The software should also be responsible for controlling the operation of the modem. If, for example, the modem has an autodial feature, the software should activate it. If the modem can transfer data at different speeds, the software should be able to make the changes when necessary. If the modem can operate in either full- or half-duplex modes, the software should make those changes, too.

Some less essential but very convenient features follow. Keep in mind that the more the software does, the more it is going to cost. Therefore, buy a package that performs only the functions you will need.

The ability to transfer data that is not in ASCII form can save the user much unnecessary work. Files written from word processors (often in binary form) and files written in programming languages will not have to be converted if this feature is available.

The transmission of data can be affected by noise on the telephone line, atmospheric conditions, and other interference. An error-checking feature in the software package can check for transmission accuracy and find many of the errors that occur when data is transferred over the telephone lines. Two common types of error-checking abilities are parity checking and checksumming. Consult your dealer to determine which type of error checking is most important for your particular applications.

The automatic buffer save is another convenient feature. When data is transferred, it is first put into a temporary storage area called the **buffer.** If the buffer that is sending the information is larger than the receiving computer's buffer, some information can be lost in overflow. When the receiving computer's buffer is full, the automatic buffer save utility automatically issues a stop character to the transmitter and saves the full buffer. It then continues to receive data. This proves invaluable if you work with large files, since data can be easily lost if the receiving buffer size is different from the sending buffer size.

buffer
A temporary storage area used to compensate for a difference in the rate of the flow of data, or time occurrence of events when transmitting data from one device to another.

Some programs store log-on routines, the series of steps needed to open the communications line between two computers. Some users may find it convenient to have a feature that allows the editing of files while still in the communications program without having to download to a word-processing program.

The best way to find out if a program fits all your needs is to try it out. If it performs the functions you need, if you are comfortable using it, and if it is within your budget, it is the software package you need.

Popular Communications Packages

Some of the more popular communications software packages for the IBM PC and PCjr are listed here.

- ***The Apple-IBM Connection***

  Available from: Alpha Software
  12 New England Executive Park
  Burlington, MA 01803
  Price range: $175–$200
  Features: See Table 9–8
  Available for: IBM PC with 128K of RAM and a RS-232C serial port and PCjr with 48K of RAM, an internal modem, and a modem cable

- ***Data Capture/PC***

  Available from: Southeastern Software
  7743 Briarwood Dr.
  New Orleans, LA 70128
  Price range: $25–$50
  Features: See Table 9–8
  Available for: IBM PC with 64K of RAM, one disk drive, BASIC, and a RS-232C serial port

- ***ERA 2***

  Available from: MicroCom, Inc.
  1400A Providence Hwy.
  Norwood, MA 02062
  Price range: $475–$500
  Features: See Table 9–8
  Available for: IBM PC with 64K of RAM and a RS-232C seial port and PCjr with 64K of RAM, an internal modem, and a modem cable

- ***Intelliterm***

  Available from: MicroCorp
  913 Walnut St.
  P. O. Box Q
  Philadelphia, PA 19107
  Price range: $150–$175
  Features: See Table 9–8
  Available for: IBM PC with 320K of RAM, two disk drives, and a RS-232C serial port and PCjr with 320K of RAM, an internal modem, and a modem cable

Table 9–8 COMPARISON OF COMMUNICATIONS SOFTWARE PACKAGES

PACKAGE \ FEATURE	ASYNCH	VARIFIED DATA TRANSFER	BAUD RATE	MODEMS SUPPORTED	FILE TYPE
THE APPLE-IBM CONNECTION	Yes	Yes	110 to 9600	Hayes Micromodem with Apple Super Serial Card, California Computer System 7710A Serial Card, or Mountain Multifunction Serial Card	ASCII
DATA CAPTURE/PC	Yes	No	300	Most popular modems	ASCII
ERA 2	Yes	Yes	300 or 1200	modem board included	text
INTELLITERM	Yes	Yes	110 to 9600	Any	MS-DOS PL-DOS
LOGON	Yes	Yes	300 or 1200	Hayes Micromodem	ASCII, text, binary
PC/INTERCOMM	Yes	Yes	up to 9600	any	binary, ASCII
TELECOMMUNICATIONS	Yes	Yes	300 to 9600	Any RS-232 modem, Hayes Smartmodem, or Smartmodem 1200	ASCII

- ***Logon***

Available from: Ferox Microsystems, Inc.
1701 N. Fort Myer Dr., Suite 611
Arlington, VA 22209
Price range: \$150–\$175
Features: See Table 9–8
Available for: IMB PC with 128K of RAM and a RS-232C serial port

- ***PC/InterComm***

Available from: Mark of the Unicorn
222 Third St.
Cambridge, MA 02142
Price range: \$100–\$125
Features: See Table 9–8
Available for: IBM PC with 64K of RAM, one disk drive, and a RS-232C serial port

- ***Telecommunications***

Available from: Peachtree Software, Inc.
3445 Peachtree Rd. NE
Atlanta, GA 30326
Price range: \$150–\$175
Features: See Table 9–8
Available for: IBM PC with 64K of RAM, two disk drives and a RS-232C serial port

LEARNING CHECK

1. Arcade games are especially useful for developing ______.
2. The challenge of game software often depends on the level of ______ involved.
3. Name the two most common ways to let the computer know what move you are making when playing a computer game.
4. What are the three basic types of educational programs?
5. Educational software should have clear instructions appearing only at the beginning of the program. (True or false?)
6. Most information utilities send their data in ______ form.
7. Information is usually selected from a ______ when a commercial data base or electronic bulletin board is accessed.

ANSWERS:

1. hand-eye coordination. **2.** skill. **3.** keyboard and joystick. **4.** tutorial, drill, and testing. **5.** false. **6.** ASCII. **7.** menu.

GUIDE TO WESTGRAPH™

A graphics package is a computer program that lets you display data in a pictorial fashion. Graphics packages have become popular in business because they allow users to view summarized data in picture instead of numeric form. By viewing pictures, the user can understand the data faster and easier than by looking at numbers. For example, a rock concert promoter might want to view net income figures from various concert sites in a pie chart or bar or line graph. By using the graphics package, the promoter can see all the net income figures at once and determine which concert site contributes the most profit.

To access WestGraph, insert the diskette labeled WestGraph into the disk drive and turn on the power to the system unit and the monitor. The program then displays the WestGraph MAIN MENU (see Figure 9–8).

Creating a Data File

The first function listed in the WestGraph MAIN MENU, CREATE A DATA FILE, allows you to create a new data file. This data file contains a title, labels, and numeric data that can be used to create a pie chart, line graph, or bar graph. To select the CREATE A DATA FILE option, press 1 when the WestGraph MAIN MENU is displayed (refer to Figure 9 – 8).

After you select the CREATE A DATA FILE option, the GRAPH CREATION screen is displayed. This screen shows the existing data files (graph files) and asks for a GRAPH NAME to be entered. To define a new data file, enter a graph name from one to eight characters long, and press the RETURN key. (The graph name may consist of any character from *A* to *Z* and any number from 1 to 9.)

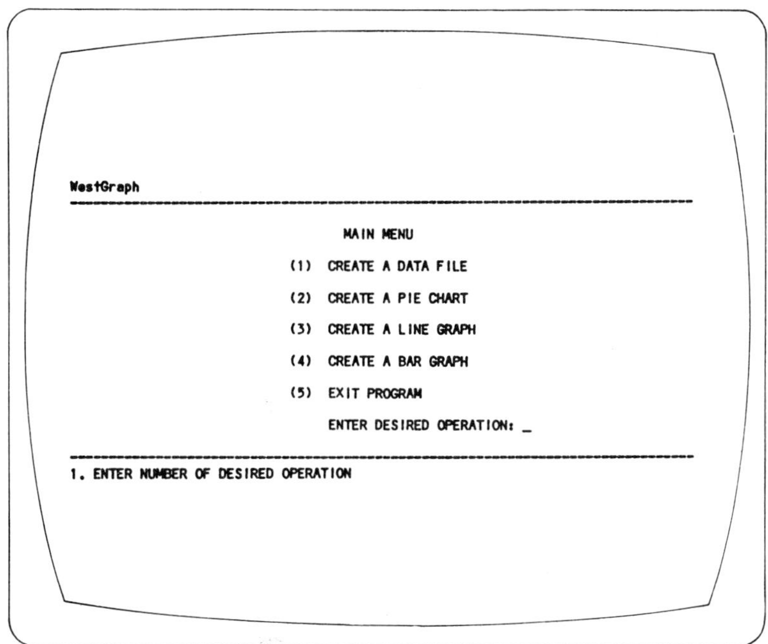

WestGraph
MAIN MENU
(1) CREATE A DATA FILE
(2) CREATE A PIE CHART
(3) CREATE A LINE GRAPH
(4) CREATE A BAR GRAPH
(5) EXIT PROGRAM
ENTER DESIRED OPERATION: _
1. ENTER NUMBER OF DESIRED OPERATION

Figure 9–8 GRAPHICS MENU

Next, the program asks for a TITLE to the graph. Enter a title from one to thirty characters long and press the RETURN key. The program then waits for the DESCRIPTION (label) of the first data item. Enter a description from one to five characters long, and press the RETURN key. Next, the program waits for the NUMERIC DATA of the first data item to be entered. Enter a numeric value from one to eight numbers in length, and press the RETURN key. (*Note:* Negative numbers cannot be used.) The program then waits for the DESCRIPTION and the NUMERIC DATA of the second data item. Enter the description, press the RETURN key, enter the numeric value, and press the RETURN key again. The program continues asking for descriptions (and their numeric values) until ten of each have been entered or until only the RETURN key is pressed for the DESCRIPTION. The program then asks, ARE ENTRIES OK? (Y/N). Enter Y if the descriptions and their numeric values have been correctly typed, and enter N if the descriptions or numeric values are incorrect. If N is entered, all the descriptions and their numeric values must be retyped. After Y is entered, the program returns to the graphics menu.

As an example, consider the STADIUMS file that is included on your diskette. The following discussion will explain how the STADIUMS file was created; however, there is no need to create the file, since it is already provided on your diskette.

The description names and numeric values of the STADIUMS graph file follow. (*Note:* The numeric values were taken from the spreadsheet analysis of net income.)

Description	Numeric Value
ARROW	450500
SUPER	457375
ORANG	383625
SHEA	320611.1
ANAHE	413500
OMNI	110199.4
SPECT	132786.8
PONTI	532386.2
MADIS	132279.1
KINGD	229250

When the STADIUMS graph file was created, Selection 1 was entered when the graphics menu was displayed. Next, the program waited for a GRAPH NAME to be entered (see Figure 9–9). STADIUMS was entered, and the RETURN key was pressed. The program then displayed the TITLE GRAPH screen and waited for the TITLE of the graph to be entered (see Figure 9–10). NET INCOME was entered, and the RETURN key was pressed. Next, the program displayed the DATA ENTRY screen and waited for the DESCRIPTION of Data Item 1 (see Figure 9–11). ARROW (for ARROWHEAD STADIUM) was entered, and the RETURN key was pressed. Next, the program waited for the NUMERIC DATA of Data Item 1 to be entered. The number 450500 was entered, and the RETURN key was pressed. The program then asked for the DESCRIPTION of Data Item 2. SUPER (for SUPERDOME) was entered, and the RETURN key was pressed. Next, the program waited for the NUMERIC DATA of Data Item 2 to be entered. After 457375 was entered, the RETURN key was pressed.

Figure 9–9 CREATING A NEW DATA GRAPH FILE

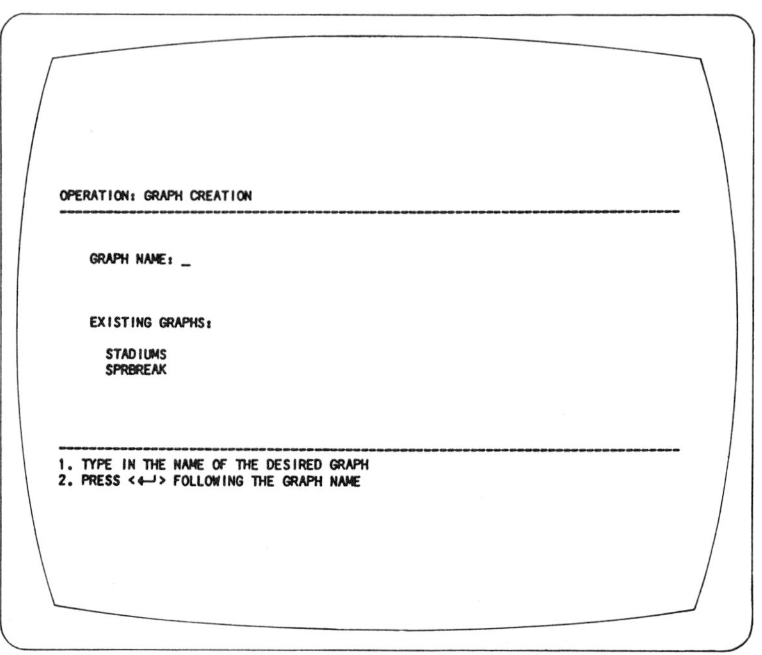

OPERATION: GRAPH CREATION
GRAPH NAME: _
EXISTING GRAPHS:
STADIUMS
SPRBREAK
1. TYPE IN THE NAME OF THE DESIRED GRAPH
2. PRESS <↵> FOLLOWING THE GRAPH NAME

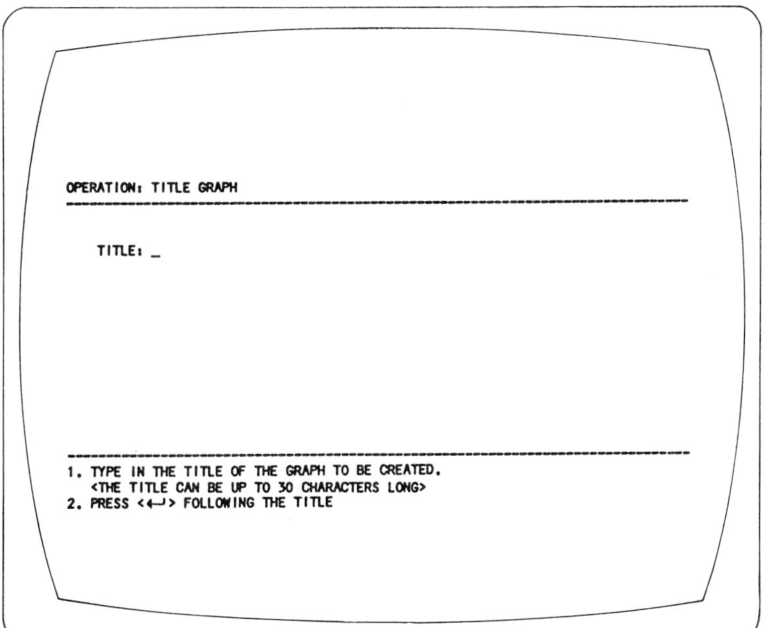

OPERATION: TITLE GRAPH
TITLE: _
1. TYPE IN THE TITLE OF THE GRAPH TO BE CREATED.
<THE TITLE CAN BE UP TO 30 CHARACTERS LONG>
2. PRESS <↵> FOLLOWING THE TITLE

Figure 9–10 ENTERING THE TITLE OF THE STADIUMS GRAPH DATA FILE

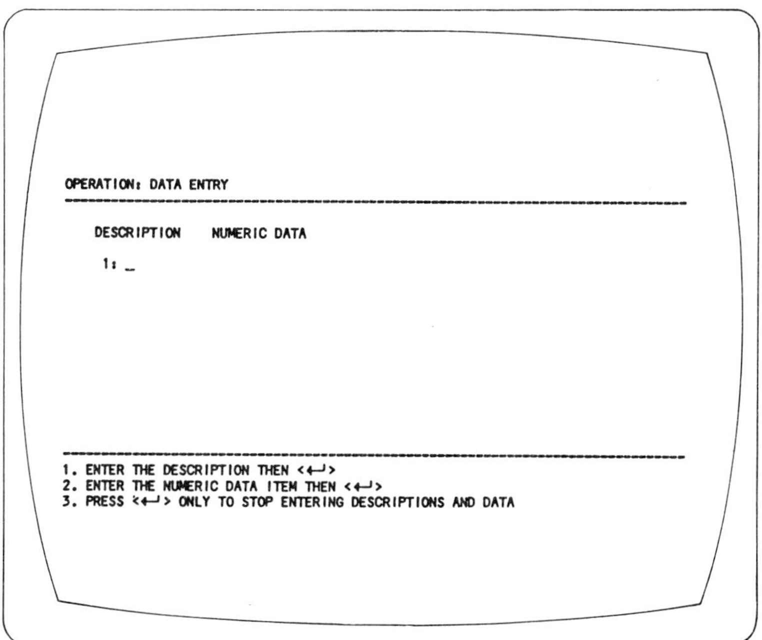

Figure 9–11 DATA ENTRY SCREEN

The program then waited for the remaining eight descriptions and numeric values to be entered. ORANG (for THE ORANGE BOWL) and 383625 were entered for Data Item 3. SHEA (for SHEA STADIUM) and 320611.1 were entered for Data Item 4. ANAHE (for ANAHEIM STADIUM) and 413500 were entered for Data Item 5. OMNI (for THE OMNI) and 110199.4 were entered for Data Item 6. SPECT (for THE SPECTRUM) and 132786.8 were entered for Data Item 7. PONTI (for PONTIAC SILVERDOME) and 532386.2 were entered for Data Item 8. MADIS (for MADISON SQUARE GARDEN) and 132279.1 were entered for Data Item 9. KINGD (for THE KINGDOME) and 229250 were entered for Data Item 10. The RETURN key was pressed after each entry. The program then asked, ARE ENTRIES OK? (Y/N) (see Figure 9–12). Y was entered, and the program created the STADIUMS graph file using the data given to it. The program then returned to the WestGraph MAIN MENU.

Creating a Pie Chart

To CREATE A PIE CHART, enter Selection 2 from the WestGraph MAIN MENU. The program then asks for a GRAPH NAME to be entered. Enter one of the graph names listed under the heading EXISTING GRAPHS, and press the RETURN key. The program then creates a pie chart using the numeric data in the file. First, the pie itself is created. Next, the title of the graph is displayed at the top center of the screen. Each of the numeric values in the file are then assigned a percentage of the pie based on the total of all the numeric values in the file. The descriptions and their percentages are displayed either next to or within each slice (division) of the pie. After viewing the pie, press the space bar to return to the WestGraph MAIN MENU.

YOUR TURN

As a hands-on activity, the CREATE A PIE CHART function can be used to create a pie chart of the STADIUMS graph. The following steps serve as a guide:

1. Enter the number 2 when the WestGraph MAIN MENU is displayed.
2. The program then asks for the GRAPH NAME (see Figure 9–13).
3. Enter STADIUMS, and press the RETURN key. (Note that STADIUMS is listed under EXISTING GRAPHS.)
4. The program then displays the pie chart as indicated in the preceding paragraph (see Figure 9–14).
5. Press the space bar to return to the WestGraph MAIN MENU.

Bar and Line Graph Labels

Graph labels are used to help the user understand the numeric values on the y-axis of the bar and line graphs. There are four different labels used in the program: THOUSANDS, MILLIONS, 1/THOUSANDS, and 1/MILLIONTHS. The label THOUSANDS, for example, indicates to the user that all numeric values listed on the y-axis should be multiplied by 1,000. For example, if the label THOUSANDS appears along with the number 345, the

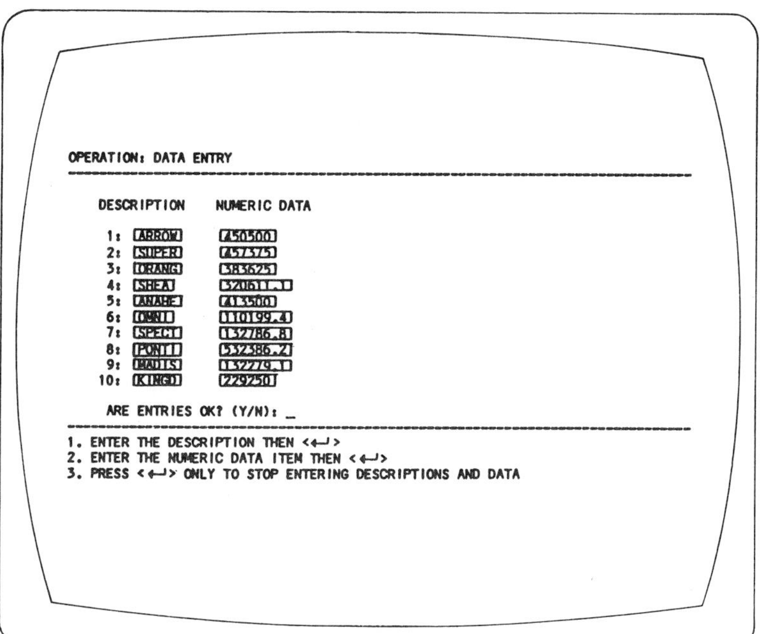

Figure 9–12 ENTERING THE DATA FOR THE STADIUMS FILE

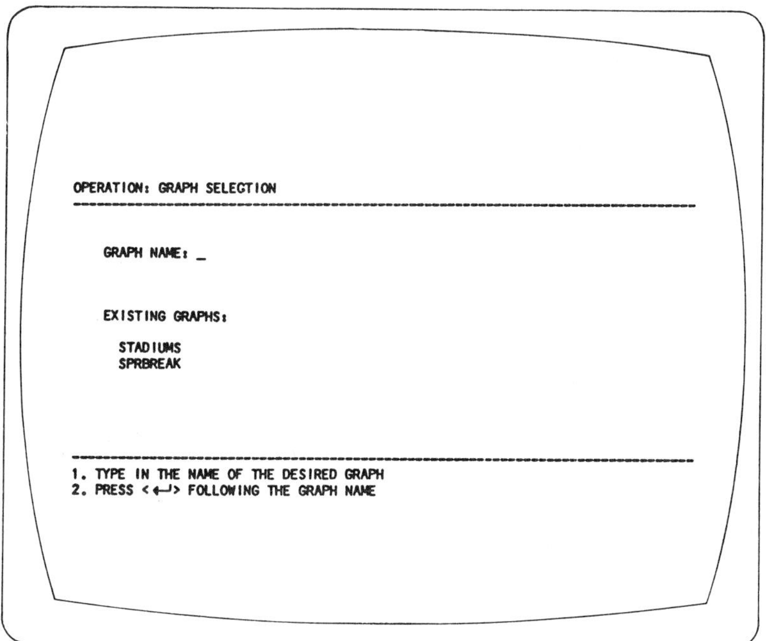

Figure 9–13 GRAPH SELECTION SCREEN

number would be interpreted as 345,000. When the label MILLIONS is used, all numeric values should be multiplied by 1,000,000. Therefore, the number 67.5 would be interpreted as 67,500,000. The label 1/THOUSANDS indicates that any numeric value should be multiplied by 1/1,000. For example, the number .54 can be interpreted as .54/1,000 or 0.00054. In the same manner,

Figure 9–14 PIE CHART

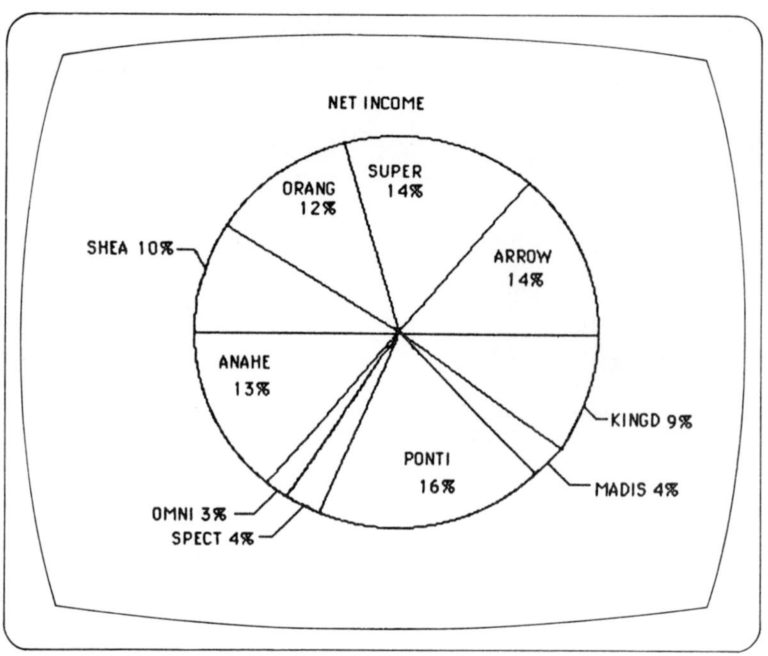

when the label 1/MILLIONTHS is used, all numeric values are multiplied by 1/1,000,000. As an example, the numeric value 2.2 would be interpreted as 2.2/1,000,000 or 0.0000022.

Creating a Line Graph

To CREATE A LINE GRAPH, enter Selection 3 from the WestGraph MAIN MENU. The program then asks for a GRAPH NAME to be entered. Enter one of the graph names listed under the heading EXISTING GRAPHS, and press the RETURN key. The program then creates a line graph using the numeric data in the graph file. First, the program places a vertical line (the y-axis) and its line divisions on the left side of the screen. The program also places a label at the top of the y-axis (refer to the previous section, "Bar and Line Graph Labels"). Second, the program displays the title of the graph at the top center of the screen. Next, the program displays a horizontal line (the x-axis), its line divisions, and the descriptions at the bottom of the screen. Last, the line graph is displayed to the right of the y-axis and above the x-axis. The actual line graph has square points to represent each numeric value and its description. To return to the WestGraph MAIN MENU, press the space bar.

As a hands-on activity, the CREATE A LINE GRAPH function can be used to create a line graph of the STADIUMS graph file. The following steps serve as a guide:

1. Enter the number 3 when the WestGraph MAIN MENU is displayed.

2. The program then waits for the GRAPH NAME to be entered (refer to Figure 9–13). Enter STADIUMS, and press the RETURN key.
3. Next, the program creates the line graph as indicated in the preceding paragraph (see Figure 9–15).
4. After viewing the line graph, press the space bar to return to the WestGraph MAIN MENU.

Creating a Bar Graph

To CREATE A BAR GRAPH, enter Selection 4 when the WestGraph MAIN MENU is displayed. The program then asks for a GRAPH NAME to be entered. Enter one of the graph names listed under the heading EXISTING GRAPHS, and press the RETURN key. The program then creates a bar graph using the numeric data in the graph file. First, the program places a vertical line (the y-axis) and its line divisions on the left side of the screen. The program also places a label at the top of the y-axis (refer to the section "Bar and Line Graph Labels"). Second, the program displays the title of the graph at the top center of the screen. Next, the program displays a horizontal line (the x-axis), its line divisions, and the descriptions at the bottom of the screen. Finally, the bar graph is displayed to the right of the y-axis and above the x-axis. Each bar represents a numeric value and its description. The height of each bar is determined by the numeric value; the greater the numeric value, the higher the bar. After viewing the bar graph, press the space bar to return to the WestGraph MAIN MENU.

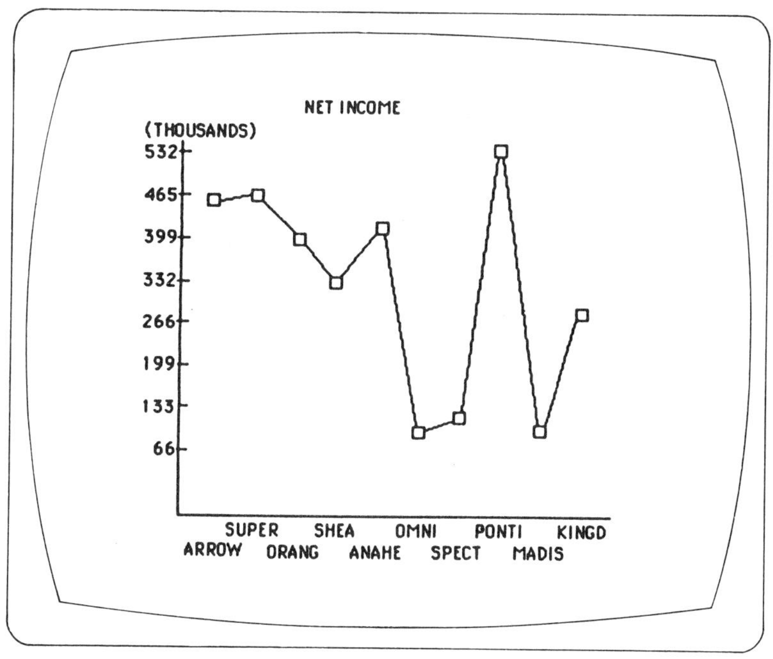

Figure 9–15 LINE GRAPH

YOUR TURN

As a hands-on activity, the CREATE A BAR GRAPH function can be used to create a bar graph of the STADIUMS graph file. The following steps serve as a guide:

1. Enter the number 4 when the WestGraph MAIN MENU is displayed.
2. The program then waits for the GRAPH NAME to be entered (refer to Figure 9–13). Enter STADIUMS, and press the RETURN key.
3. Next, the program creates the bar graph using the numeric data in the file as indicated in the preceding paragraph (see Figure 9–16).
4. After viewing the graph, press the space bar to return to the WestGraph MAIN MENU.

Printing a Graph

To print an existing graph, choose Selection 5 from the WestGraph MAIN MENU. The program then displays the PRINT MENU which includes the options: (1) SELECT GRAPH FOR PRINTING and (2) PRINTER DEFAULTS. Selection 1 of the PRINT MENU allows you to select a graph for printing. After the number 1 is pressed, the program will display the names of the existing graphs and wait for one of these graph names to be entered. Enter the name of the graph you wish to print and press the RETURN key.

The program will then ask you to ready your printer by turning it on, if it is not already on, and to make sure that it is on-line, and that the printer is loaded with paper. Once the printer is ready, you can press the RETURN key to begin printing. When printing is complete the program will return to the PRINT MENU.

Figure 9–16 BAR GRAPH

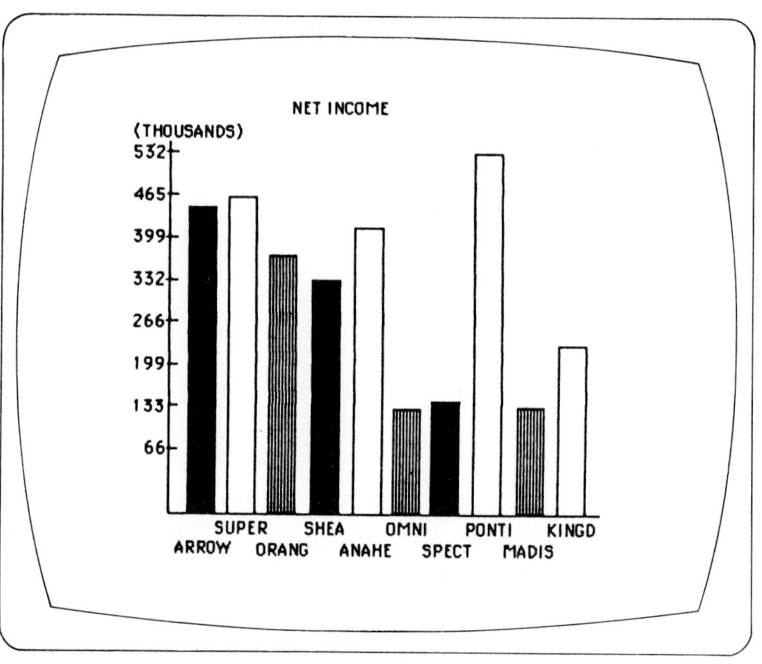

Selection 2 on the graphics PRINT MENU displays the printer defaults used for printing the graphs. In order to display these printer defaults press 2 when the PRINT MENU is displayed.

YOUR TURN

As a hands-on activity, the PRINT function can be used to print the STADIUMS graph. The following steps serve as a guide:

1. Press 5 when the WestGraph MAIN MENU is displayed.
2. Press 1 when the PRINT MENU is displayed (see Figure 9–17).
3. The program then displays the SELECT GRAPH FOR PRINTING screen and waits for a GRAPH NAME to be entered. Enter STADIUMS (see Figure 9–18) and press the RETURN key.
4. Once an existing graph name has been entered, the program will ask you to ready your printer. When the printer is ready to print, press the RETURN key.
5. The program will then print the STADIUMS graph and then return to the graphics PRINT MENU. Enter the number 3 to return to the WestGraph MAIN MENU.

Creating the ENROLL Data File

Since there was not a hands-on activity provided in the "Creating a Data File" portion of the chapter, this section provides a hands-on activity for

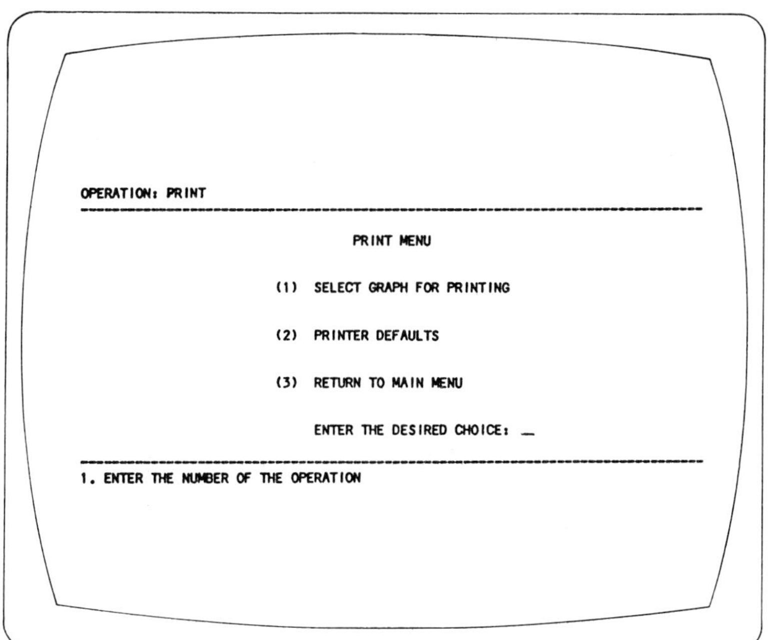

OPERATION: PRINT
PRINT MENU
(1) SELECT GRAPH FOR PRINTING
(2) PRINTER DEFAULTS
(3) RETURN TO MAIN MENU
ENTER THE DESIRED CHOICE: _
1. ENTER THE NUMBER OF THE OPERATION

Figure 9–17 THE GRAPH PRINT MENU

creating a new graph data file entitled ENROLL. The ENROLL data file contains the student enrollment at a university for the years 1955 through 1985.

YOUR TURN

As a hands-on activity, the following steps serve as a guide to creating the ENROLL graph data file.

1. Enter 1 when the WestGraph MAIN MENU is displayed.
2. The GRAPH CREATION screen is then displayed. Enter the name ENROLL (see Figure 9–19).
3. Once the graph name has been entered the program waits for a TITLE to be entered. Type STUDENT ENROLLMENT (see Figure 9–20) and press RETURN.
4. The third and final screen in the CREATE A DATA FILE function is the DATA ENTRY screen. When the cursor is sitting next to 1:, under the word DESCRIPTION, enter the description 1955 and press RETURN (see Figure 9–21). Next, the cursor is positioned under NUMERIC DATA. Enter 6459 and press RETURN. To complete entering data for the ENROLL file, enter 1960 and press RETURN, 7237 and press RETURN, 1965 and press RETURN, 9300 and press RETURN, 1970 and RETURN, 11490 and RETURN, 1975 and RETURN, 14690 and RETURN, 1980 and RETURN, 16330 and RETURN, 1985 and RETURN, 15680 and press RETURN.
5. In order to stop entering DESCRIPTIONs and NUMERIC DATA, press the RETURN key only for description 8. The program then asks, ARE

Figure 9–18 SELECTING A GRAPH FOR PRINTING

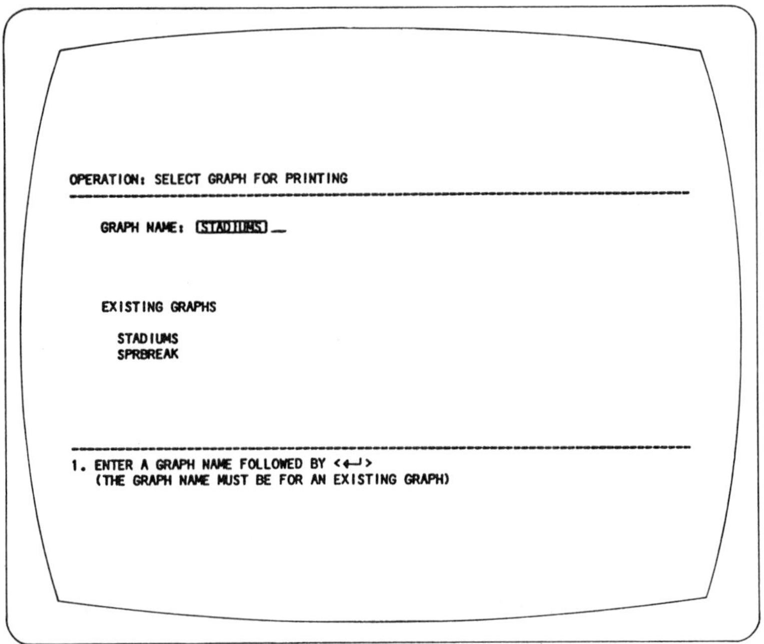

OPERATION: SELECT GRAPH FOR PRINTING
GRAPH NAME: [STADIUMS] _
EXISTING GRAPHS
STADIUMS
SPRBREAK
1. ENTER A GRAPH NAME FOLLOWED BY <↵>
(THE GRAPH NAME MUST BE FOR AN EXISTING GRAPH)

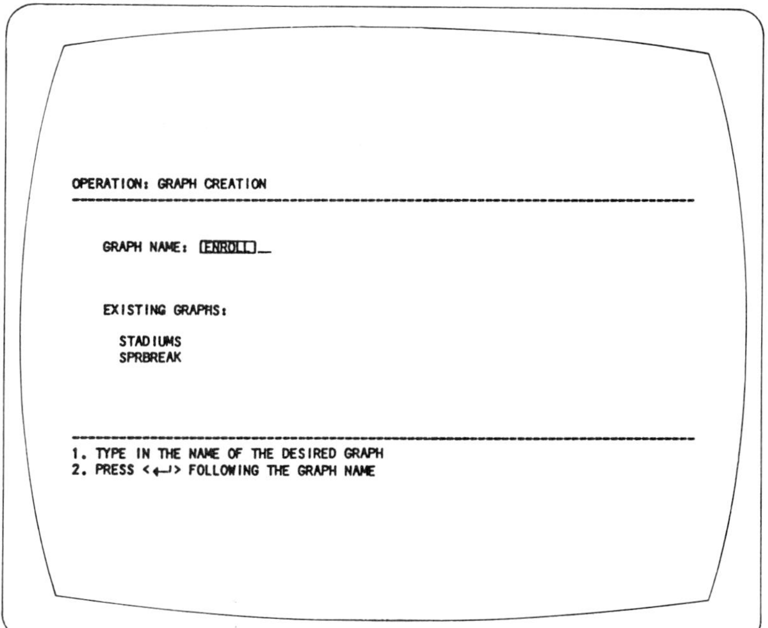
OPERATION: GRAPH CREATION
GRAPH NAME: ENROLL_
EXISTING GRAPHS:
STADIUMS
SPRBREAK
1. TYPE IN THE NAME OF THE DESIRED GRAPH
2. PRESS <↵> FOLLOWING THE GRAPH NAME

Figure 9–19 CREATING THE ENROLL GRAPH DATA FILE

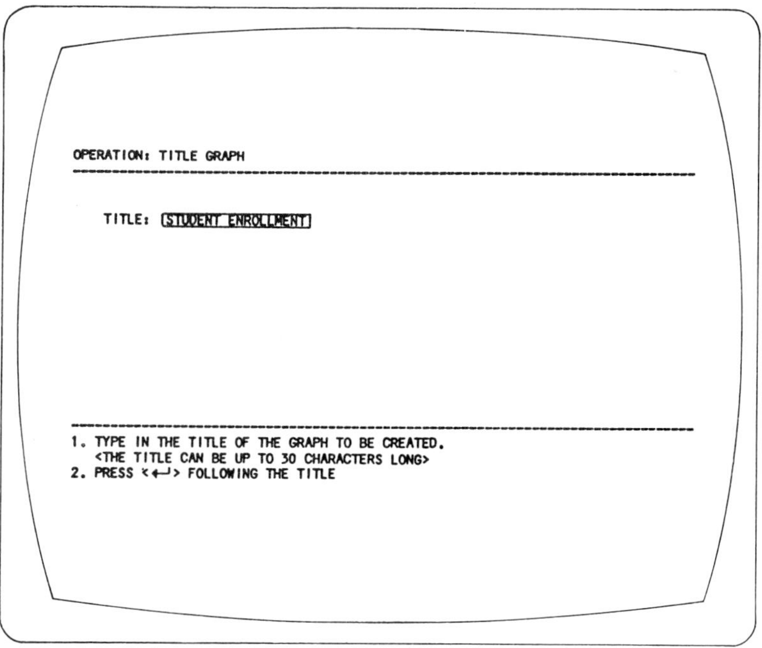
OPERATION: TITLE GRAPH
TITLE: STUDENT ENROLLMENT
1. TYPE IN THE TITLE OF THE GRAPH TO BE CREATED.
<THE TITLE CAN BE UP TO 30 CHARACTERS LONG>
2. PRESS <↵> FOLLOWING THE TITLE

Figure 9–20 ENTERING THE TITLE OF THE ENROLL GRAPH DATA FILE

ENTRIES OK? (Y/N) (see Figure 9–22). Press Y (for yes) if the entries are correct. Enter N (for no) if they are not and return to step 4 above.

6. Once the DESCRIPTIONs and NUMERIC DATA entries have been entered correctly, the program returns to the WestGraph MAIN MENU

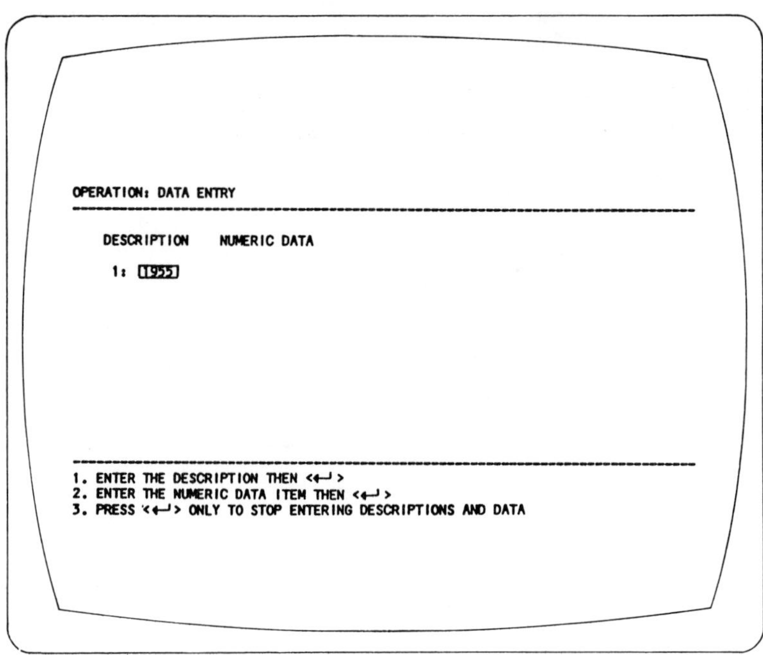

Figure 9–21 ENTERING THE FIRST DESCRIPTION OF THE ENROLL GRAPH DATA FILE

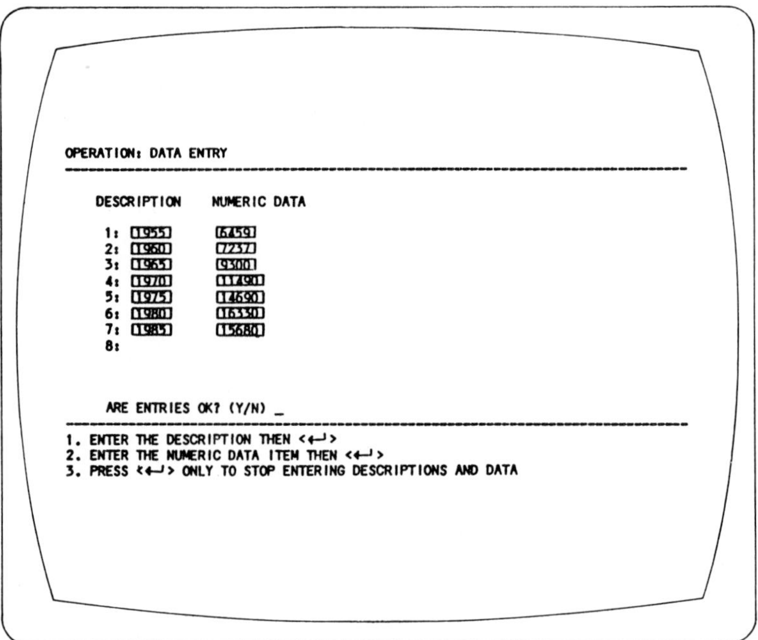

Figure 9–22 ENTERING THE DATA FOR THE ENROLL FILE

where you can enter numbers 2, 3, or 4 to create a graph of the ENROLL data file.

1. DATA FILE ERROR
NUMERIC DATA FOR GRAPH TOTALS ZERO

The numeric data entered into the graph data file totals 0.

2. ENTER <Y> OR <N> ONLY

A number or character other than Y or N has been entered.

3. INVALID GRAPH NAME
GRAPH NAMES CAN CONTAIN THE CHARACTERS:
A – Z AND 1 – 9

A graph name that contains characters other than the letters *A* to *Z* or the numbers 1 to 9 has been entered.

4. INVALID GRAPH NAME
NAME ALREADY IN USE

SPRBREAK and STADIUMS have already been used as a graph name and cannot be used again.

5. INVALID GRAPH NAME
THE GRAPH CHOSEN DOES NOT EXIST

The graph name that has been entered does not match an existing graph name.

6. INVALID MENU SELECTION. PLEASE ENTER
CHOICE AGAIN USING THE NUMBERS 1 – 5.

A number or character other than 1, 2, 3, 4, or 5 has been entered. (These numbers represent menu selections.)

7. NO DATA IN DATA FILE

The RETURN key was pressed before any description or numeric data was entered.

8. ONLY ONE GRAPH CAN BE CREATED USING THIS
VERSION OF THE GRAPHICS PACKAGE

Only one extra graph data file can be created. To create another graph data file, the old graph data file must first be erased.

9. PRESS SPACE BAR TO CONTINUE

To continue execution of the program, press the space bar.

Contents of Spring Break File

TITLE: COST OF SPRING BREAK VACATION

DESCRIPTION	NUMERIC DATA
BW–FL (Best Western–Fort Lauderdale)	667.5
BP–FL (Beach Plaza–Fort Lauderdale)	797.5
PL–FL (Park Lane–Fort Lauderdale)	582.5

```
FL-FL (Fort Lauderdale-Fort Lauderdale)          707.5
HI-FL (Holiday Inn-Fort Lauderdale)              857.5
BWC-R (Best Western Continental-Reno)            557.5
HID-R (Holiday Inn Downtown-Reno)                627.5
HIL-R (Hilton-Reno)                              627.5
MGM-R (MGM Grand-Reno)                           682.5
SAN-R (Sands Hotel-Reno)                         782.5
```

Summary of WestGraph Functions

Function	Description
Pie Chart	Creates a circular chart that is divided into slices based on one unit's portion of the total.
Line Graph	Creates a graph that connects data values by a line in the X and Y plane.
Bar Graph	Creates a graph that displays data values as vertical or horizontal bars in the X/Y plane.

SUMMARY POINTS

- Graphics software packages allow the user to display images on a computer monitor and print these images on paper.
- There are three basic types of graphics packages: analytical business graphics, design graphics, and creative drawing and painting graphics packages.
- Business and finance software packages are available for specific types of businesses or almost any type of home business or financing.
- Home and personal interest packages are available in many different areas of interests.
- The wide variety of available recreational packages includes board, arcade, adventure, strategy, and sports games.
- An important feature of recreational packages is the number of levels of play and the challenge the program can present to the user.
- Educational software is available to teach age levels from preschoolers to adults.
- An important consideration for educational software is that it correspond to the age level of the student.
- Clear and complete documentation is a very important aspect of any software package.
- Instructions on how to run an educational program should be described not only in the printed documentation, but also on the screen. Instructions and menus should be both simple to understand and complete enough so that students can run the program on their own after an introduction and trial run.

REVIEW QUESTIONS

1. What is the purpose of graphics software packages?
2. What is the save feature, and why is it important in graphics packages?
3. Name two important features of any software package.
4. What are the two main types of home business and finance packages?
5. Name three types of software packages that fall under the general category of home and personal interest software.
6. Name three types of computer games.
7. List four important features of recreational software.
8. To whom can educational software be useful?
9. What is one of the most important features to look at when choosing an educational package? Why?
10. Describe the differences among commercial data bases, electronic bulletin boards, and local-area networks.

WESTGRAPH EXERCISES

1. SPRING BREAK Exercises (the data file SPRBREAK is included on your diskette)

a. Select the CREATE A PIE CHART option from the graphics menu, and create a pie chart using the SPRBREAK data file. Which hotel has the largest slice of the pie? Which has the smallest?

b. Select the CREATE A LINE GRAPH option from the graphics menu, and create a line graph using the SPRBREAK data file. Which hotel costs the most? Which costs the least?

c. Select the CREATE A BAR GRAPH option from the graphics menu, and create a bar graph using the SPRBREAK data file. Which hotel costs the most? Which costs the least?

2. Student Tuition Exercises

a. Select the CREATE A DATA FILE option from the graphics main menu.

b. Enter a new graph name, TUITION.

c. Enter a TITLE called STATE UNIVERSITY TUITION.

d. Enter the DESCRIPTION and NUMERIC DATA for the following records:

Description	Numeric Data
1950	200
1955	350
1960	500
1965	775
1970	1001
1975	1309
1980	1578
1985	2000
1990	2324
2000	3100

(*Note:* The numeric data for 1990 and 2000 represent an estimated tuition.)

e. Select the CREATE A PIE CHART option from the graphics menu, and create a pie chart using the TUITION data file.

f. Select the CREATE A LINE GRAPH option from the graphics menu, and create a line graph using the TUITION data file.

g. Select the CREATE A BAR GRAPH option from the graphics menu, and create a bar graph using the TUITION data file.

CHAPTER 10

WORD PROCESSOR

Chapter Outline

INTRODUCTION

Human beings are constantly in search of more efficient and effective methods to accomplish their tasks. The written word has been no exception in this search. The evolution of the writing instrument has taken us from rocks and twigs straight through to what many thought to be the ultimate writing instrument—the typewriter. But the evolution did not stop there; the computer revolution has brought the word processor.

To gain a little perspective, think of the difference between writing with a pen and pad and writing with a typewriter; this approximates the difference between using a typewriter and using a word processor. In terms of speed, power, and capabilities, the word processor is to the pen and pad as the Ferrari is to the Model T.

One of the biggest advantages of word processing is that the words typed are not immediately committed to paper, but rather are displayed on a video screen, where they can be easily manipulated electronically. Word processors have made it simple to insert or delete text and to move text from one place to another without having to retype or spend hours cutting and pasting. Gone are the days of overflowing wastepaper baskets and irritating correction paper or fluid. A word processor allows the writer to be completely satisfied with what has been written before one word gets committed to paper.

This chapter will introduce you to word processing—what it is, what its uses are, and how to get started. In addition, descriptions of some of the popular word-processing packages will be given.

DEFINITIONS

Most of you probably have heard of word processors, word processing, and word-processing systems. However, for the benefit of those who have not or those who may still be a bit unsure about their definitions, this section will sort them out.

Word processor
A program or set of programs designed to allow you to enter, manipulate, format, print, store, and retrieve text.

A **word processor** is a program (software) or set of programs designed to allow you to enter, manipulate, format, print, store, and retrieve text (each of these processes is discussed in detail later in this chapter). The logic and overall design of the program or programs determine the capabilities and ease of use of a particular word processor.

Word processing
The act of composing and manipulating text.

Word processing refers to the actual act of composing and manipulating text. The words are composed and rearranged in your mind; the word processor and the hardware simply allow you to conveniently display, store, and recall what you have done.

Word-processing system
The hardware that allows you to operate a word processor.

Dedicated systems
Computers equipped to handle only one function, such as word processing.

A **word-processing system** is the hardware and software that is put together to allow you to operate a word processor. There are two general types of word-processing systems: (1) **dedicated systems,** which are basically microcomputers equipped to handle only word processing; and (2) multipurpose microcomputers, which are equipped to handle a wide variety of processing tasks, including word processing. In the early days of word processing, the serious user's only real choice was a dedicated system. However, with the development of faster and more sophisticated microcomputers came the development of microcomputer-compatible word processors. Word-processing systems were no longer only dedicated machines. Today most, if not all, multipurpose microcomputers on the market have a word processor available for them. Many of these word processors are approaching the dedicated systems in sophistication and ease of use.

Although a word processor is actually a program or programs, many people refer to the combination of both software and hardware as a word processor, especially when referring to dedicated systems. However, this book will use the definitions previously presented. Table 10–1 provides a quick reference to other terms frequently encountered when reading about word processors.

This chapter will focus in general on word processors that run on multipurpose microcomputer systems, and specifically on the IBM PC and IBM PCjr, rather than on dedicated word-processing systems. Much of the general description of word processors, however, can be applied to dedicated systems as well.

A word processor has two primary functions: text editing and print formatting. The following sections give a general description of each of these functions, and a more detailed look at some of the common features of each function can be found in the section entitled "Features of Word Processors."

Text Editing

The **text-editing** function of a word processor, the function that probably comes to most people's minds first when thinking about word processing, allows the user to enter and edit text. The most fundamental aspect of this function is the word processor's ability to accept and store internally the text that is typed in at the keyboard. Without this ability, all the other functions and procedures would be useless.

Text editing
The function of a word processor that allows the user to enter and edit text.

Text editing also includes the ability of the word processor to insert and delete characters, words, lines, paragraphs, and larger blocks of text. The insert and delete modes are probably two of the most often used text-editing features of any word processor. The text-editing function of most, if not all, word processors also allows blocks of text to be moved and copied. These features facilitate the rearranging and retyping of documents, and their ease of use is an important consideration in choosing a word processor. Many other text-editing features are also available to help manipulate text. These include word wrap, search and find, search and replace, cursor controls, and scrolling. These and other features will be discussed later in this chapter.

Line versus Screen Editors. There are two basic forms of text editors: **line editors,** which work on only one line at a time, and **screen editors,** which work on an entire screen at a time. Word processors that use line editors are generally inexpensive, but limited in their features. Their major limitation is their lack of screen-formatting capabilities; they cannot duplicate on the screen the formatting features that are implemented. For example,

Line editor
The type of editor that allows the user to edit only one line at a time.

Screen editor
The type of editor that allows the user to edit an entire screen at a time.

Table 10–1 FREQUENTLY ENCOUNTERED WORD-PROCESSING TERMS

TERM	DEFINITION
Automatic pagination	A feature that enables a word processor to automatically number the pages of the printed copy.
Block	A group of characters, such as a sentence or paragraph.
Block movement	A feature that allows the user to define a block of text and then perform a specific operation on the entire block. Common block operations include block move, block copy, block save, and block delete.
Boldface	Heavy type, for example, **this is boldface.**
Character	A letter, number, or symbol.
Character enhancement	Underlining, boldfacing, subscripting, and superscripting.
Control character	A coded character that does not print but is part of the command sequence in a word processor.
Cursor	The marker on the display screen indicating where the next character can be displayed.
Default setting	A value used by the word processor when not instructed to use any other.
Deletion	A feature in which a character, word, sentence, or larger block of text may be removed from the existing text.
Document-oriented word processor	A word processor that operates on a text file as one long document.
Editing	The act of changing or amending text.
Format	The layout of a page; for example, the number of lines, margin settings, and so on.
Global	An instruction that will be carried out throughout an entire document, for example, global search and replace.
Header	A piece of text that is stored separately from the text and printed at the top of each page.
Incremental spacing	A method in which the printer inserts spaces between words and letters to produce justified margins; also called *microspacing.*
Insertion	A feature in which a character, word, sentence, or larger block of text is added to the existing text.
Justification	A feature for making lines of text even at the margins.
Line editor	The type of editor that allows the user to edit only one line at a time.
Memory-only word processor	A word processor that cannot exchange text between internal memory and disk during the editing process.
Menu	A list of commands or prompts on the display screen.
Page-oriented word processor	A word processor that operates on a text file as a series of pages.
Print formatting	The function of a word processor that communicates with the printer to tell it how to print the text on paper.

Table continued on next page

Print preview	A feature that allows the user to view a general representation on the screen of how the document will look when printed.
Screen editor	The type of editor that allows the user to edit an entire screen at a time.
Screen formatting	A function of a word processor that controls how the text will appear on the screen.
Scrolling	Moving a line of text onto or off of the screen.
Search and find	A routine that searches for, and places the cursor at, a specified string of characters.
Search and replace	A routine that searches for a specified character string and replaces it with the specified replacement string.
Status line	A message line above or below the text area on a display screen that gives format and system information.
Subscript	A character that prints below the usual text baseline.
Superscript	A character that prints above the usual text baseline.
Text buffer	An area set aside in memory to temporarily hold text.
Text editing	The function of a word processor that enables the user to enter and edit text.
Text file	A file that contains text, as opposed to a program.
Virtual representation	An approach to screen formatting that allows the user to see on the screen exactly how the printed output will look.
Word wrap	The feature in which a word is automatically moved to the beginning of the next line if it goes past the right margin.

the screen will show the words that were typed, but it will not show the proper margins, spacings, indentations, page breaks, and so on.

A screen editor, in contrast, allows you to see on the screen how the text will be formatted when printed. A common way to tell the word processor how you want the text to look when printed is to embed control characters in the text that appears on the screen. For example, if you wanted to center the title *Chapter 1,* it might appear on the left side of the screen as ^CChapter 1^C. Some programs, instead of using control characters to represent the various formatting features selected, let the user actually see the text indented, centered, double spaced, and so on. Some word processors are now offering virtual representation, more commonly referred to as a "what you see is what you get" approach to screen formatting. This means that when a particular formatting feature is implemented (for example, a **character enhancement** such as underlining, boldfacing, subscripting, or superscripting), the text on the screen actually appears underlined, boldfaced, subscripted, or superscripted instead of being surrounded by control characters. However, many screen editors are still unable to show character enhancement.

Character enhancement *Underlining, boldfacing, subscripting, and superscripting.*

Most word processors that use a screen editor and support eighty columns of text (eighty characters per line) give at least a fair representation of how the text will look when printed. However, some word processors only display forty or fewer characters per line on the screen, even though they have the ability to print more than forty characters per line on paper. This can make formatting of the text difficult if the final copy is to be more than forty characters per line, because you will not be able to see how it looks before it is printed.

Print preview
A feature that allows the user to view a general representation on the screen of how the document will look when printed.

Some word processors attempt to get around the screen-formatting problem by offering a **print preview** feature. This feature allows you to view a representation on the screen of how the document will look when printed. Although you generally will not be able to see the whole document or even a whole page on the screen at one time, you can move through the document in sections to see spacings, where pages will end, how paragraphs will appear, and so on, before the document is printed. If a word processor does not have a screen editor that offers or comes near a "what you see is what you get" feature or a print preview feature, the only way to accurately tell how your document will look is to print a copy and then make any necessary modifications to the format.

Modes. The text-editing portion of some word processors has all the text-editing features available in one mode; that is, you can write and then edit immediately without switching to an edit mode. Others have separate modes for writing and editing, requiring the user to switch back and forth between modes. A program that uses specific modes to accomplish different tasks can be very flexible while using only a relatively few commands. However, a single-mode word processor permits more convenient and faster editing, because you do not have to switch modes, and any command can be used at any point within the program.

Memory-only word processors
Word processors that cannot exchange text between internal memory and disk during the editing process.

Text Files. To save and edit text requires you to create a text file on a disk. There are several methods in which a word processor might treat a text file. Many of the early programs, referred to as **memory-only word processors,** limited the size of a text file to only what could fit into internal memory at one time. They could not swap text between internal memory and disk, so longer documents had to be broken up and worked on as separate files.

Page-oriented word processors
Word processors that operate on a text file as a series of pages.

Most programs on the market today, however, either treat a text document as a series of pages or as one long document. Those that treat the text document as a series of pages are referred to as **page-oriented word processors.** Using them, you can create and display only one page at a time. A series of commands must be used to swap pages in memory to and from disk. A page-oriented word processor can make it difficult to edit paragraphs that start on one page and end on another. Other operations, such as moving or copying blocks of text from one page to another, can also be more involved. However, because the amount of text stored in memory at any one time is relatively small, page-oriented word processors may operate faster than those that treat text as one long document.

Document-oriented word processors
Word processors that operate on a text file as one long document.

Document-oriented word processors—those that treat a text file as one long document—can make editing a document easier, because pages do not need to be worked on separately. The bottom portion of one page and the top portion of another page can appear on the screen at the same time. This type of word processor can be slower than page-oriented word processors, because larger blocks of text are stored in memory at any one time, slowing down processing time.

There are also several ways in which a word processor might format the text that is stored on disk. Typically, the text will be stored either in binary or ASCII format. Ideally, the text should be stored so it can be read by other programs and by your computer's disk operating system. For example, if the files were stored in ASCII format, they would be readable by your computer's DOS, and you could use your word processor as a BASIC program editor to write and edit programs. Many word processors that store text in a binary format supply a utility program that will convert a binary file to ASCII format.

Print Formatting

The **print-formatting** function involves a variety of features that communicate with the printer to tell it how to print the text on paper. Some of the more common print-formatting features include the ability to set margins and tab stops; single or double space text; reformat paragraphs after editing; mark page breaks; position header and footer notes and page numbers; and perform character enhancements such as underlining, boldfacing, superscripts and subscripts. The section entitled "Features of Word Processors" will take a closer look at these and other print-formatting features.

Print formatting
The function of a word processor that communicates with the printer to tell it how to print the text on paper.

The number and type of print-formatting features available differ from word processor to word processor. When considering these features, make sure your printer can handle the ones you need. You probably will not need the more sophisticated features if you are using the word processor at home to type memos to yourself, recipes, or informal correspondence. However, if your word-processing needs include typing manuscripts, papers for formal presentation, business reports, or formal correspondence, you will need a word processor with some of the more sophisticated print-formatting features. The closer you can get to the "what you see is what you get" approach to screen formatting, the easier your job will be.

USES OF WORD PROCESSORS

There are three general categories of uses for word processors: home, business, and specialized uses. The following is a brief overview of each of these categories.

Home Uses

One of the most likely uses the average person will have for a personal computer at home is word processing. To determine if you are one of these people, ask yourself a few questions: Do you use a typewriter often to write letters, correspondence, papers, or reports? Do you despise rewriting or even refuse to rewrite your text because it seems to be too much work? If you have answered yes to at least one of these questions, you probably will benefit from owning and using a word processor at home.

Most home word processors cost less than $150, and many fall in the $50-to-$100 range. It is generally said that you get what you pay for, but in the case of the home user, what you pay for in a lower-priced word processor may be all you need. Do not be fooled into buying a Cadillac when all you really need is a Chevy. This will be covered in more detail in the section on choosing a word processor.

A home word processor will generally let you write letters, memos, short papers, and similar documents relatively easily, but the print-formatting capabilities may be limited. For many users this is not a problem. The trend, however, appears to be toward offering more powerful word processors at lower costs, so it may be well worth your time and effort to shop around.

Some word processors that bill themselves as home word processors go a step further and include additional capabilities such as mail-merge programs, which allow you to insert names and addresses into a form letter, and spelling checkers to help find spelling errors. These capabilities extend the usefulness of a home word processor, and many small businesses find them a good bargain. These word processors tend to be at the high end of the price scale for home programs.

Business Uses

The possible uses for a word processor in a business setting are more obvious, since the amount of paperwork generated is staggering in many businesses. One of these uses is merging names and addresses into a form letter; others include report generation, formal correspondence, and memos. Word processing makes typing and editing these documents relatively simple. Because the documents can be edited and arranged in final form before they ever get put on paper, the business saves a tremendous amount of time and money in both labor and supply costs. Business-oriented word processors fall in the $150-to-$500 range and vary markedly in their features. Most allow for powerful manipulation of text- and print-formatting procedures, although they are not always easy to use.

Lately there has been an emphasis on user friendliness and the human engineering factors in designing programs. However, in some word processors, user friendliness can mean a tradeoff in power. This is not necessarily true, however, and hopefully this attitude will continue until even the most powerful word processors become user friendly.

Many business word-processing programs offer additional help in the form of a spelling checker, on-line dictionary, on-line thesaurus, or other aids (usually at an additional cost, although a few offer them as part of the word-processing package). For the serious writer or secretary, these tools can be invaluable.

Specialized Uses

The final category is the specialized word processor, which is designed for specific applications. For example, some word processors allow you to work in foreign languages, and others allow special symbols used in scientific formulas. Remember, though, that to print any special characters, your printer must have the capability.

To sum up, whether you use a home, business, or specialized word processor, many of the mechanical functions associated with writing and editing can be eliminated. Inserting and deleting text, as well as myriad other operations, are as easy as striking a few keys. These operations are definitely easier on some word processors than on others. In general, however, you will find that word processing lets you concentrate more on organizing your thoughts clearly and precisely than on the mechanics of writing.

LEARNING CHECK

1. A ______ is a program (software) or set of programs designed to allow you to enter, manipulate, format, print, store, and retrieve text.
   a. word processor
   b. word processing
   c. word-processing system
   d. dedicated system
2. The two primary functions of a word processor are ______ and ______.
3. Line editors cannot duplicate on the screen the formatting features that are implemented. (True or false?)
4. ______ can make editing a document easier, because pages do not need to be worked on separately, but can also slow down processing time, because larger blocks of text are stored in memory.
   a. Memory-only word processors
   b. Page-oriented word processors
   c. Document-oriented word processors
   d. The print preview feature
5. The ______ function tells the printer how to print the text on paper.

ANSWERS: 1. a. 2. text editing, print formatting. 3. true. 4. c. 5. print-formatting.

FEATURES OF WORD PROCESSORS

A word processor is essentially a collection of routines or features, each performing a particular function. The previous section described three general categories of word processors: home, business, and specialized. Each of these supports a number of common basic features as well as some convenient special-purpose features.

In general, you will want the combination of keys used to implement a feature to be logical and easy to remember. For example, striking the control key and the C key is a logical choice of keys to center a word. The following general description of the features should help you understand what they are, as well as help you determine the importance of each feature to you. Be aware, though, that there is no standardization between feature names and the functions they perform. This book attempted to select commonly used names that are indicative of their functions; however, different word processors may refer to the same functions differently.

There also may be differences among the different word processors in how similarly named features operate. Remember, both having the particular features you want and being able to easily use and remember these features are important. This is especially important for the most-used functions, since you do not want to have to memorize a complex series of keystrokes or be constantly referring to a manual to perform them. The features discussed in this section will be divided into the following categories: writing and editing features, screen-formatting features, print-formatting features, and additional features.

Writing and Editing Features

The writing and editing features facilitate the rapid and easy typing and editing of text. They remove many of the mechanics, such as cutting, pasting, and retyping, typically associated with manually writing or revising a document.

Cursor
The marker on the display screen indicating where the next character can be displayed.

Cursor-positioning Features. The **cursor** is a marker (usually a line or box) on the screen that indicates where the next character can be displayed. Use the cursor-positioning features to position the cursor on the screen. These features can considerably speed up the typing and editing of a document, since they allow you to jump the cursor a set distance, such as a word or page at a time, instead of moving it only a character or line at a time.

On the IBM PC and IBM PCjr, the cursor is moved a character or line at at time by the use of the four arrow keys. Their combined use with other keys, such as the control key, allows for movement in large jumps. The IBM PC and PCjr also have four special keys labeled, <Home>, <End>, <PgUp>, and <PgDn>, which are normally used to move the cursor over larger distances.

Some of the more common cursor-positioning features include the following:

- Home: Jumps the cursor to the upper left corner of the screen in a page-oriented process.
- Top of page: Jumps the cursor to the first character at the beginning of the current screen display.
- End of page: Jumps the cursor to the last character at the end of the current screen display.
- Tab: Jumps the cursor a preset number of spaces to the right from the left margin.

- Page up: Displays the portion of the document that is directly above that portion of the document currently on the display screen. If fifteen lines of a document are displayed at once, the preceding fifteen lines will be displayed.
- Page down: Displays the portion of the document that is immediately below that portion of the document currently on the display screen. If fifteen lines of a document are displayed at once, the next fifteen lines will be displayed.
- Next word: Jumps the cursor to the beginning of the next word.
- Previous word: Jumps the cursor to the beginning of the previous word.
- Next page: Displays the next page on the screen, jumping the cursor to the first character on the page.
- Previous page: Displays the previous page on the screen, jumping the cursor to the first character on the page.
- Goto: Jumps the cursor to a specified location, such as another page.

Word Wrap. If you have ever used a typewriter, you know that when you reach the end of a line you have to press the RETURN key to get to the beginning of the next line. Most word processors have a feature called **word wrap,** or word wraparound, which lets you keep typing when you reach the end of a line without having to press the RETURN key. If a word extends past the margin, the whole word is automatically moved to the beginning of the next line. If you want to end a line and start a new one before you reach the margin (for instance, the last line of a paragraph), you simply press the RETURN key.

Word wrap
The feature in which a word is automatically moved to the beginning of the next line if it goes past the right margin.

Scrolling. If your document is long, you will not be able to view it on the screen all at once. **Scrolling** is the process of moving a line or lines of text onto or off of the screen. When you move the cursor up or down past the lines on a full screen, the new line or lines move onto the screen, and the line or lines at the opposite edge of the screen moves off. Vertical scrolling from the top to the bottom or from the bottom to the top of the screen is the norm; however, horizontal scrolling is available with some word processors. Some computers that only allow a forty-column display will scroll the screen horizontally when you reach the fortieth column. The characters on the left side of the screen will scroll off, and blank spaces will be scrolled onto the right side of the screen, allowing you to continue typing on the same line until you reach the margin. With a forty-column word/processor you cannot use the whole width of the page at once, but formatting an eighty-column document for printing is easier with horizontal scrolling.

Scrolling
Moving a line or lines of text onto or off of the screen.

Insertion and Replacement. A word processor should allow for the **insertion** of characters, words, sentences, or larger blocks of text into the existing text. There are several ways in which this can be done. One of these is to **overstrike** a character—that is, to type directly over an existing character, replacing it with a new character. This makes editing of errors such as spelling mistakes or typographical errors quick and simple. Another method is to insert new text in the middle of existing text by opening up space for it while the existing text automatically adjusts to allow room for

Insertion
A word-processing feature in which a character, word, sentence, or larger block of text is added to the existing text.

Overstrike
To type directly over an existing character, replacing it with a new character.

the inserted text. Some word processors automatically reformat the whole paragraph; others require you to run a separate reformatter program, whereas some require you to reformat manually.

Deletion
A word-processing feature in which a character, word, sentence, or larger block of text may be removed from the existing text.

Deletion. A word processor allows for the **deletion** of a character, word, sentence, or larger block of text from the existing text. The backspace key may operate as a "destructive" backspace, erasing any characters that the cursor moves over.

To delete a block of text of any length, many programs allow you to use the cursor to mark the beginning and end of the text to be deleted. Many also highlight the selected text so that you can be sure of what you are about to delete. Most word processors automatically adjust the remaining text to fill the gap left by the deleted text.

Block movements
A feature that allows the user to define a block of text and then perform a specific operation on the entire block. Common block operations include block move, block copy, block save, and block delete.

Block Movements. Manipulating a document a character at a time is extremely slow when working with large blocks of text. To help speed operations, most word processors allow you to use **block movements,** which define a block of text to work with by using the cursor to mark its beginning and end. The entire block of text can then be manipulated at once. The following are some of the more common block operations:

- Block move: Moves the specified block of text to a new location, destroying the original
- Block copy: Copies the specified block of text to a new location, leaving the original intact.
- Block save: Saves the specified block of text on disk in a separate file for later use in the same or another document.
- Block delete: Deletes the specified block of text.

Search and find
A routine that searches for, and places the cursor at, a specific string of characters.

Search and replace
A routine that searches for a specified character string and replaces it with the specified replacement string.

Global search and replace
A search and replace operation that will be carried out throughout the entire document without user intervention.

Searching. If you have ever written a large document and discovered that you misspelled a key term throughout, you know how difficult and time-consuming it can be to find and change each occurrence of the word or string of characters. Most word processors have alleviated this problem by incorporating various search routines. The most basic is the **search and find** routine. You tell the program the specific character string to search for, and it will find and position the cursor at the first occurrence of the specified string. Usually you will have the option of continuing the search to find each successive occurrence of the specified string.

Another type of search routine is the **search and replace** routine, in which the word processor searches for each occurrence of a specified string and replaces it with a specified replacement string. There are usually two options for this search routine. In the first option, the cursor moves to the first occurrence of the string to be replaced, and the user is asked if that particular occurrence of the string should be replaced. The user responds accordingly here and at each successive occurrence of the string. The second option is what is known as **global search and replace.** The word processor searches for all occurrences of a specified string and replaces them with the specified replacement string without user intervention.

Another search option overlooks the case of a letter and finds a word whether it starts with an uppercase or lowercase letter. Some search features also allow you to use a wild card symbol to search for strings that contain a specified group of characters. For example, if the wild card character is a dollar sign, *run$* will help you find all the words that began with *run,* such as *running, runners,* and so on.

Undo. If you are a person who likes to "leap before you look," the undo feature found in some word processors will be a blessing. It allows you to undo the action just taken, leaving the text in the form in which it appeared prior to the action. For example, if you just deleted a whole page when you only meant to delete a word, the undo feature lets you recall the page back into main memory and onto the screen. However, your word processor must be able to set up a **text buffer** to use this feature. The text buffer is an area set aside in memory by the word processor to temporarily hold the text. The amount of text that can be stored in the text buffer varies and is usually replaced each time a new operation is performed.

Text buffer
An area set aside in memory to temporarily hold text.

Save and Re-enter. When typing in a large amount of text, it is a good idea to periodically save the text on a disk. This avoids losing everything you have typed if a power outage or voltage irregularity occurs, or if you make a fatal mistake that destroys the contents of memory while operating the computer. Most word processors allow you to save your text stored in the computer's RAM on a disk by simply striking a key or combination of keys; you then automatically re-enter the program at the same point and continue typing or editing. A few word processors, however, assume you are finished with a document when you save it and remove the document from memory. In this case, you have to load the document back into memory and find the place where you stopped in order to continue work.

Screen-formatting Features

The **screen-formatting** features control how the text will appear on the screen and include status displays that give on-screen information concerning the document. The following are some of the more common screen-formatting features.

Screen formatting
A function of a word processor that controls how the text will appear on the screen.

Status Displays. A number of word processors have a **status line,** a message line above or below the text area on the display screen that gives format and system information. The status line is either constantly displayed or displayed on request. Some of the more common items in the status line are the following:

Status line
A message line above or below the text area on a display screen that gives format and system information.

- Current line number of cursor.
- Current column number of cursor.
- Current page number on screen.
- Current available memory space.
- Number of words the document contains.

Tab Settings. The basic tab feature of most word processors works the same way as the tab key on a typewriter. Some word processors offer additional tab capabilities, such as the ability to line up columns of numbers along their decimal points or to center columns of words on the tab setting.

Displayed Page Breaks. Page-oriented word processors have only one page in memory at a time. With the help of a status line indicating the current line number of the page, however, you can easily see where to break the current page and start a new page when writing. When editing, you can also easily tell when additions or deletions change the length of the text on the page, so you can make the appropriate adjustments.

With document-oriented word processors, pages are not noticeably swapped between the disk and memory, so some kind of marker is needed in the text to indicate on the screen where one page will end and another will begin when printing. This can help avoid unnatural breaks, such as putting the last word from a list on one page at the top of the next page.

Print-formatting Features

The print-formatting features communicate with the printer and tell it how to print the document on paper. Some of the more common print-formatting features are described in the following paragraphs.

Margin Settings. Some word processors let you set margins for all four sides of the paper, whereas others do not. For user-changeable margins, many word processors provide **default settings,** or values the word processor will use when the user does not instruct it to use any others. The default settings are typically for the normal 8½ × 11–inch business letter. Some allow you to change the default settings to coincide with your most frequently produced document so that you will not have to change them every time you run the word processor.

Default settings
Values used by the word processor when not instructed to use any other.

Some word processors also provide **justification.** This feature makes lines of text even at the margin, such as those found in textbooks, as opposed to the ragged appearance found in letters. Justification of left, right, or both margins is possible, depending on the word processor.

Justification
A feature for making lines of text even at the margins.

The right margin can be justified in two ways. In one, the printer inserts additional spaces between words as needed until the line lengths match. This method can cause the output to look odd, however, since some of the spaces between words can become quite large. The second method avoids this by using **incremental spacing,** or microspacing. In this method the printer inserts small spaces not only between words, but also between letters, to help avoid unnaturally large spaces between words. Your printer must be capable of incremental spacing to take advantage of this feature.

Incremental spacing
A method in which the printer inserts spaces between words and letters to produce justified margins; also called microspacing.

Line Spacing. All word processors allow single spacing of a document, and many also allow you to switch to double or triple spacing. The line spacing is usually reflected only in the printed output, and the screen displays only single spacing.

Centering. To center text using a typewriter, you must count the number of characters in the text to be centered, divide this by 2, and then backspace from the center line of the document. Most word processors allow you to automatically center a word by simply pressing one or two keys.

Automatic Page Numbering. Automatic page numbering enables the word processor to automatically number the pages of the printed copy. Some word processors will not give you a choice of where the page number is printed, whereas others will let you choose its location. Other options include omitting the number on the first page and the ability to choose the page number with which to start numbering.

Headers and Footers. A **header** is a piece of text that is printed at the top of a page, such as a chapter title. A **footer** is a piece of text that is printed at the bottom of a page. Both are stored separately from the text. Many word processors require you to define a header or footer just once and then automatically print it at the top or bottom of each page.

Header
A piece of text that is stored separately from the text and printed at the top of each page.

Footer
A piece of text that is stored separately from the text and printed at the bottom of each page.

Character Enhancements. The most common character enhancements include underlining, boldfacing, subscripting, and superscripting. Both the

LEARNING CHECK

1. The combination of keys used to implement any word processor feature should be ________ and ________.
2. The ________ feature allows the user to define a certain amount of text, which then can be manipulated at one time.
   a. cursor-positioning
   b. block movements
   c. scrolling
   d. searching
3. ________ are values the word processor will use when you do not instruct it to use any others.
   a. Status displays
   b. Tab settings
   c. Character enhancements
   d. Default settings
4. An important aspect in the ease and use of a word processor is the amount and quality of the ________ or ________ that are available.
5. To be able to undo an action just taken—to recover the text in the form it appeared prior to the action—your computer must have a(n) ________.

ANSWERS:
1. logical, easy to remember. **2.** b. **3.** d. **4.** documentation, operational aids. **5.** text buffer.

word processor and the printer must be capable of a particular character enhancement before it can be used.

Additional Features

An important factor in the ease of using a word processor is the amount and quality of the available documentation or operational aids. Operational aids to look for include help menus within the word processor that are easy to access and truly helpful. Other valuable aids include quick-reference cards; tutorials that walk you through the actual operation of the word processor; and thorough, well-written, and readable manuals.

Among the other available features are disk-handling routines that permit the performance of such operations as formatting, cataloging, and copying disks without requiring the user to quit the word processor and reboot the disk operating system. Some word processors also have the ability to use enhancement programs, such as spelling and grammar checkers and on-line dictionaries.

HARDWARE REQUIREMENTS

There are certain minimum hardware requirements to be met before a word-processing system will be functional on the IBM PC, but again there is a wide range of possibilities, depending on your needs and finances. The basic hardware for the IBM PC system includes the following:

- An IBM PC computer.
- One disk drive (some word processors may require two).
- A monitor and a monochrome or color/graphics card.
- A printer and printer interface card.

The IBM PC comes with 256K of RAM. This should be sufficient to run most of the word processors currently available for the IBM PC. You will need at least one disk drive to operate a word processor. In most cases, two disk drives make operation much easier, and two are required with some word processors. Next, you will need a monitor on which to view the text you have typed. Although color monitors will work, they are not well suited for word processing; their text resolution is generally very poor. A high-resolution monochrome monitor is the best choice.

You will also need a printer, as a word processor without a printer would not make much sense. There are many printers to choose from, so where should you start your search? First, determine what will be the uses of your word processor. If you will simply be producing short letters to friends, memos, or informal correspondence, a dot matrix printer should do. However, if you intend to use your word processor for business or formal documents, you probably will need a letter quality printer. Many articles on choosing a printer are published in the wide variety of computer journals on the market, so do a little research before you wade into the sea of printers. Along with the printer, you will need a parallel or serial interface card (depending on the type of printer) to instruct it. Parallel printers, which are typically much faster than serial printers, are connected to most home systems.

In addition to these basic hardware items, you may wish to add some additional items now or later. One of these is a spooler, a hardware device that acts as a buffer between the computer and the printer (many printers come equipped with at least a small buffer built in). Since a computer can send out characters much faster than the printer can print them, the computer is slowed down and has to wait for the printer to catch up so that no characters will be lost. The spooler can accept and hold these characters at a rate equal to what the computer can send; the spooler then passes the characters on to the printer at a rate that it can receive. In this way, the computer is free to keep working while the printer is printing.

People who work with large volumes of text could benefit from using a hard disk. A hard disk has a much greater storage capacity, eliminating the need to change data disks; it also enables a much faster transfer of data between the disk and internal memory. Finally, the addition of the CP/M operating system will allow you to run a number of CP/M-based word processors, enabling you to choose from a greater selection of software.

CHOOSING A WORD PROCESSOR

Once you have all the necessary hardware, the next step is to choose your word processor. This can be difficult, given the number of word processors currently on the market and the constant influx of new entries. Furthermore, if you buy a word processor and discover later that it really does not fit your needs, you could be stuck with it, because a computer software warranty does not cover "fitness for purpose." It is your responsibility to make sure the package you buy will perform the functions you need. You may have some legal recourse if you relied on the dealer's expertise to suggest a software package, such as a word processor; properly informed him or her of your needs; and then discovered that the program does not meet them. However, this is a tricky legal area involving many factors. Therefore, how should you choose a word-processing package that will meet your needs? This section will set forth some guidelines to help you.

The first step in choosing a word processor is to analyze your needs. Consider the type of writing for which you will be using the word processor. Will you be doing considerable rewriting, requiring you to insert, delete, and move or copy portions of your text? If so, pay close attention to how easily and efficiently those operations can be performed. Do your needs include formal applications that require specific print-formatting techniques, or will you be using the word processor primarily for informal or personal applications? Consider this carefully, because there is a wide range of differences in the print-formatting capabilities among word processors.

Once you have a solid understanding of what you require or want out of a word processor, the next step is to decide how much you want to spend. That $500 word processor may do everything except make coffee for you, but you may not be able to afford it or, more importantly, even need it.

People choosing a word processor often overbuy or underbuy. Many users initially feel more secure buying a more expensive model, because they feel that without a doubt it will have everything they need. However, many who purchase a higher-priced word processor use only one-third to two-thirds of the program's capabilities, and a good midpriced program would have met their needs. On the other extreme are those who buy a low-priced word processor only to discover upon using it that it does not meet their needs or that their needs soon expand beyond its capabilities. There are good and bad word processors at both the high and low price ranges, and what is good or bad may depend on your needs. Do not make the mistake of letting price be your only guide.

After carefully considering your needs and budget constraints, the next step is to research what is available to meet them. This might include reading reviews in the computer journals at the library, asking friends or users groups for opinions on the word processors they use, or talking with the salesperson at the local computer store. These are good ways to get a general feeling for a word-processing package; remember, though, that because many of these people probably own or are trying to sell the word processors in question, their comments may be biased. Between the reviews and comments gathered and your own constraints, however, you should be able to narrow the field to a select few. At this point you will want to go to your local dealer and ask for a hands-on demonstration. Make either a written or mental checklist of the type of functions you will be using most often, and run the word processor through its paces. Make sure the text-editing and print-formatting features meet your needs and that their implementation is logical and easy to understand.

LEARNING CHECK

1. Most sophisticated word processors require only 48K of RAM. (True or false?)

2. A ________ monitor is the best choice for word processing.

3. Having greater storage capacity, a ________ eliminates the need to change data disks and facilitates a much faster transfer of data between the disk and internal memory.

4. Which one of the following is not a step in the process of selecting a word processor?

a. analyzing your needs

b. determining budget constraints

c. researching available word processors

d. having the salesperson walk you through the word processor

5. Good documentation includes ________, ________, and ________.

ANSWERS:
1. false. **2.** high-resolution monochrome. **3.** hard disk. **4.** d. **5.** help menus, quick-reference cards, thorough and easy-to-read manuals.

Good documentation is important. The best way to determine its quality is to *not* let the salesperson show you the word processor at work. Instead, pick up the manuals yourself, and see how long it takes you to start using the basic features of the word processor. If you cannot begin with relative ease in the store, imagine the frustration you will have at home after buying the package. Look for help menus, quick-reference cards, and thorough and easy-to-read manuals. Tutorials, step-by-step teaching aids that walk you through a word processor, are an excellent teaching aid for the first-time computer user.

Probably more than one word processor will contain all the features you need, so hands-on testing is a particularly important way to obtain a feel for the "personality" of a word processor. Remember, you are the one who will have to use it, so make sure you are satisfied and can live with the program you select.

POPULAR WORD-PROCESSING PACKAGES

This section lists some of the popular word processors available for the IBM microcomputer. The packages are grouped into home versions, business versions, and specialized versions. The programs presented do not reflect an endorsement of the product. They were selected to represent the wide variety of word processors available for the IBM PC. Refer to the previous section for some tips on selecting a word processor to fit your needs.

Home Versions

The home versions of word processors are generally less sophisticated in their features and thus more limited in their uses. They tend, however, to be cheaper and easier to use than word processors in the other two categories. The following word processors typify those available for the home market:

- ***Easy Writer***

  Available from: IBM Corp.
P.O. Box 1328
Boca Raton, FL 33432
  Price range: $150–$200
  Features: See Table 10–2
  Available for: IBM PC

- ***Select Write***

  Available from: Select Information Systems
919 Sir Francis Drake Blvd.
Kentfield, CA 94904
  Price range: $50–$100
  Features: See Table 10–2
  Available for: IBM PC

Table 10–2 HOME VERSIONS OF WORD PROCESSORS

PROGRAM \ FEATURES	Minimum memory requirement	Wordwrap	Horizontal scrolling	Cursor to beginning of current line	Cursor to end of current line	Cursor to top of screen	Cursor to bottom of screen	Cursor to next screen	Cursor to marker	Copy block	Move block	Insert block	Delete block	Save block	Justification	Underlining	Boldface	Overstrike	Automatic footnotes	Decimal tabs	Undo command	Search and replace	Split screens/windows	Automatic reformatting	User-definable defaults	Display page length/width	Display help menu/screens	Display foreign language symbols
EASY WRITER	64K	x		x	x	x		x		x	x	x				x	x	x			x	x			x		x	
SELECT WRITE	128K	x		x	x	x	x	x	x	x	x	x	x	x	x	x	x	x		x	x	x		x	x	x	x	
TEXTRA	128K	x		x	x	x	x	x	x	x	x	x				x	x				x	x		x	x	x	x	
VOLKSWRITER	128K	x	x	x	x	x	x	x		x	x	x	x	x	x		x	x	x		x	x		x		x	x	
THE WRITER	64K	x	x	x	x	x	x	x							x	x	x	x	x			x	x		x	x	x	

- ***Textra***

  Available from: Ann Arbor Software
407 N. Main
Ann Arbor, MI 48104
Price range: $50–$100
Features: See Table 10–2
Available for: IBM PC

- ***Volkswriter***

  Available from: Lifetree Software Inc.
411 Pacific Street
Monterey, CA 93940
Price range: $200–$250
Features: See Table 10–2
Available for: IBM PC

- ***The Writer***

  Available from: Hayden Software Co.
600 Suffolk Street
Lowell, MA 01853
Price range: $50–$100
Features: See Table 10–2
Available for: IBM PC

Business Versions

The business versions of word processors are usually more sophisticated in the features they offer, allowing greater flexibility in their uses. Because of their greater sophistication, however, they also tend to be more difficult to learn and more expensive than home versions. The following word processors typify those available for the business market:

- ***Leading Edge Word Processing***

Available from:	Leading Edge Products Inc. Headquarters and Retail Division 225 Turnpike St. Canton, MA 02021
Price range:	$300–$350
Features:	See Table 10–3
Available for:	IBM PC

- ***MultiMate***

Available from:	MultiMate International 52 Oakland Avenue, North East Hartford, CT 06108
Price range:	$450–$500
Features:	See Table 10–3
Available for:	IBM PC

- ***Word***

Available from:	Microsoft Corp. 10700 Northrup Box 97200 Bellevue, WA 98004
Price range:	$350–$400
Features:	See Table 10–3
Available for:	IBM PC

- ***Wordstar***

Available from:	MicroPro International 33 San Pablo Ave. San Rafael, CA 94903
Price range:	$450–$500
Features:	See Table 10–3
Available for:	IBM PC with CP/M operating system

Specialized Versions

Although word-processing packages in the specialized versions category can be used for general-purpose writing, they actually have been designed for a specific task. For example, some word processors allow you to write in a foreign language. One of these, the Select Bilingual, allows you to write in both Spanish and English:

Table 10–3 BUSINESS VERSIONS OF WORD PROCESSORS

PROGRAMS \ FEATURES	Minimum memory requirement	Wordwrap	Horizontal scrolling	Cursor to beginning of current line	Cursor to end of current line	Cursor to top of screen	Cursor to bottom of screen	Cursor to next screen	Cursor to marker	Copy block	Move block	Insert block	Delete block	Save block	Justification	Underlining	Boldface	Overstrike	Automatic footnotes	Decimal tabs	Undo command	Search and replace	Split screens/windows	Automatic reformatting	User-definable defaults	Display page length/width	Display help menu/screens	Display foreign language symbols
LEADING EDGE WORD PROCESSING	256K	x	x	x	x	x	x	x	x	x	x	x	x	x	x		x	x	x	x	x	x	x	x		x	x	
MULTIMATE	256K	x	x	x	x	x	x	x		x	x	x	x	x	x	x	x	x		x	x	x		x	x	x	x	
WORD	128K	x	x	x	x	x	x	x	x	x	x	x	x	x	x	x	x	x	x	x	x	x	x	x	x	x	x	
WORDSTAR	64K	x	x	x	x	x	x	x	x	x	x	x	x	x	x	x	x	x	x	x		x	x		x	x	x	

- ***Select Bilingual***

  Available from: Select Information Systems
  919 Sir Francis Drake Blvd.
  Kentfield, CA 94902
  Price range: $350–$400
  Features: See Table 10–4
  Available for: IBM PC

GUIDE TO WESTWORD™

Word processors are computer programs that let the user edit and print documents. They are popular in business, because they allow the user to type, save, and edit documents easily. For example, a rock concert promoter might want to type a letter to send to various stadiums around the country. By using a word processor, the promoter can use the same document and yet obtain an individualized letter to send to each stadium by simply changing the stadium name and address.

The WestWord program is on the disk labeled WestWord and can be accessed by first booting DOS 2.XX and then inserting the disk into the disk drive and typing WESTWORD, if it is not a self-booting diskette, or by inserting the self-booting disk into the disk drive and turning on the monitor and computer. The program then displays the WestWord MAIN MENU (see Figure 10–1). This menu contains both operational and nonoperational

Table 10–4 SPECIALIZED VERSIONS OF WORD PROCESSORS

FEATURES / PROGRAM	Minimum memory requirement	Wordwrap	Horizontal scrolling	Cursor to beginning of current line	Cursor to end of current line	Cursor to top of screen	Cursor to bottom of screen	Cursor to next screen	Cursor to marker	Copy block	Move block	Insert block	Delete block	Save block	Justification	Underlining	Boldface	Overstrike	Automatic footnotes	Decimal tabs	Undo command	Search and replace	Split screens/windows	Automatic reformatting	User-definable defaults	Display page length/width	Display help menu/screens	Display foreign language symbols
SELECT BILINGUAL	128K	x	x	x	x	x	x	x	x	x	x	x	x	x	x	x	x	x		x	x	x		x	x	x	x	x

functions. The nonoperational function (accessed by selection number 4) is the menu shown in Figure 10–2. Although the DISK UTILITIES function, is nonoperational in this program, the menu (Disk Utilities Menu) and associated function screens are included to familiarize you with the utility functions used in a typical word processor package.

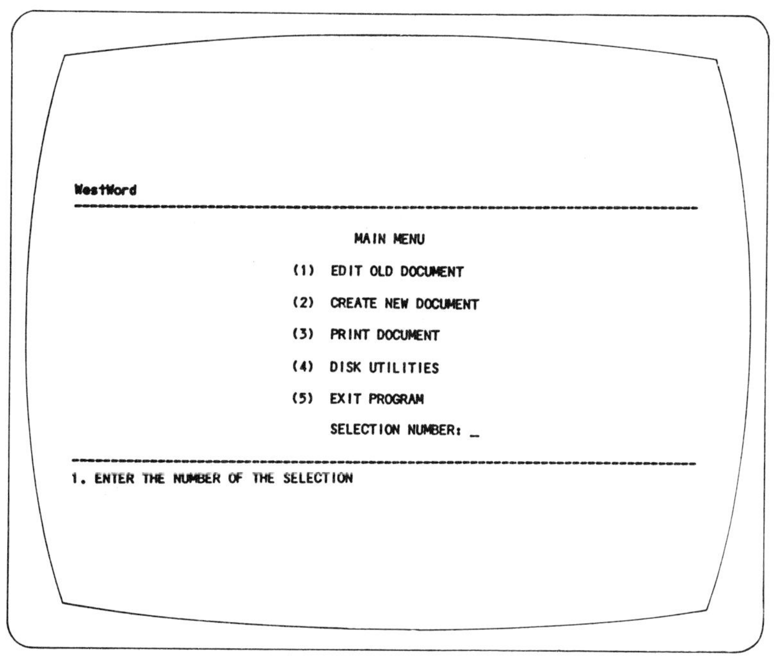

Figure 10–1
WESTWORD WORD PROCESSOR MENU

Figure 10–2
DISK UTILITIES MENU

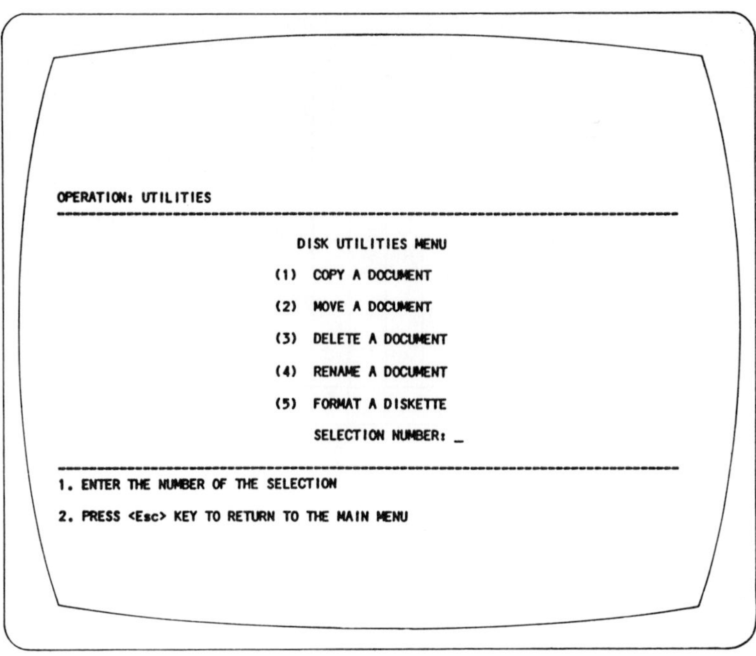

OPERATION: UTILITIES
DISK UTILITIES MENU
(1) COPY A DOCUMENT
(2) MOVE A DOCUMENT
(3) DELETE A DOCUMENT
(4) RENAME A DOCUMENT
(5) FORMAT A DISKETTE
SELECTION NUMBER: _
1. ENTER THE NUMBER OF THE SELECTION
2. PRESS <Esc> KEY TO RETURN TO THE MAIN MENU

Editing an Old Document

The first function of the word processor, EDIT OLD DOCUMENT, allows an existing document to be edited (changed). To choose this option, press 1 when the WestWord MAIN MENU is shown (refer to Figure 10–1).

After you have chosen the EDIT OLD DOCUMENT option from the WestWord MAIN MENU, the edit screen is displayed. The program places the cursor next to DOCUMENT TO EDIT and then waits for a document name to be entered. Enter one of the document names listed under the heading EXISTING DOCUMENTS, and press the RETURN key.

Next, the program displays a new screen showing the first fifteen lines of the requested document. This screen contains many helpful features. First, at the top of the screen is a line showing the name of the document. This line also shows the position of the cursor by giving the line and column numbers where the cursor is presently located. At the beginning, the cursor is located in Line 1 and in Column 1. Next, at the bottom of the screen is a list of the various commands available for use while editing the document. Finally, the first fifteen lines of the document are shown between the dashed lines. (Throughout the documentation, this area between the dashed lines will be referred to as the text window.)

YOUR TURN

As a hands-on activity, you can now actually select the STADIUMS document by using the EDIT OLD DOCUMENT command. The following steps serve as a guide:

1. Press 1 when the word processor menu is shown (see Figure 10–1).
2. The program then waits for you to enter any document name listed

under EXISTING DOCUMENTS. Enter STADIUMS (see Figure 10–3), and press the RETURN key.

3. The first fifteen lines of the STADIUMS document are then displayed in the text window (see Figure 10–4).

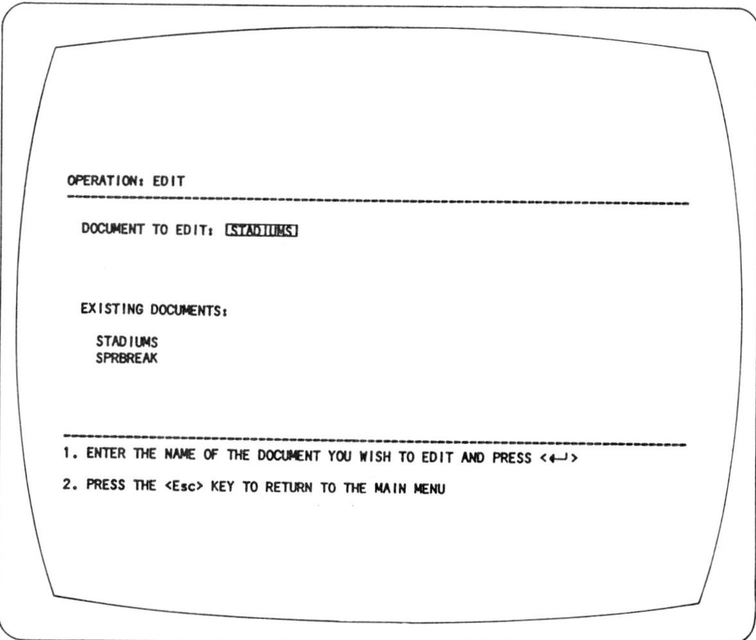

Figure 10–3
SELECTING THE STADIUMS DOCUMENT

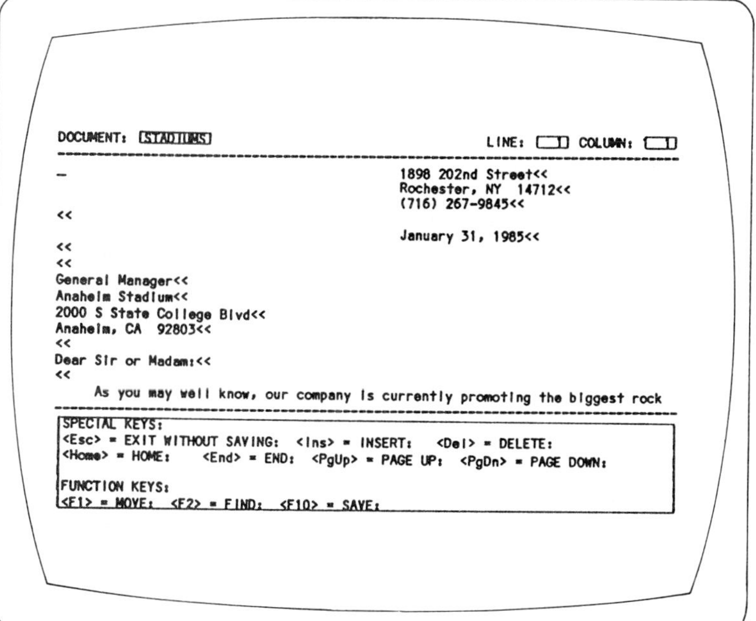

DOCUMENT: STADIUMS
LINE: COLUMN:
1898 202nd Street<<
Rochester, NY 14712<<
(716) 267-9845<<
January 31, 1985<<
General Manager<<
Anaheim Stadium<<
2000 S State College Blvd<<
Anaheim, CA 92803<<
Dear Sir or Madam:<<
As you may well know, our company is currently promoting the biggest rock
SPECIAL KEYS:
<Esc> = EXIT WITHOUT SAVING: <Ins> = INSERT: <Del> = DELETE:
<Home> = HOME: <End> = END: <PgUp> = PAGE UP: <PgDn> = PAGE DOWN:
FUNCTION KEYS:
<F1> = MOVE: <F2> = FIND: <F10> = SAVE:

Figure 10–4
EDIT SCREEN DISPLAYING THE STADIUMS DOCUMENT

The left, right, up, and down arrow keys are used to move the cursor to the desired location within the text window. In order to move the cursor within the document, the <Num Lock> key must be toggled off. If the <Num Lock> key is toggled on, numbers are output to the screen. To change the toggle state of the <Num Lock> key, simply press the key once.

One important note should be made. The cursor can only be positioned in a column which contains a character or a carriage return. For example, the cursor cannot be positioned at Line 12, Column 79 if Line 12 contains a carriage return (represented by the << symbol). The cursor cannot be positioned in any column (other than column 1) in Line 12 because no characters were entered in those positions. The cursor, therefore, can only be positioned to locations where a character or a carriage return has been typed.

YOUR TURN

Use the arrow keys to move the cursor in the STADIUMS document, which should already be on your screen from the previous hands-on activity. The following serves as a guide.

1. The cursor should presently be located at the top left corner of the text window. If it is not, return the cursor to the top left corner by pressing the key labelled <PgUp>. (*Note:* on the PCjr, you must press the <Fn> key prior to pressing the <PgUp> key.) Move the cursor to the *'1'* in *1898* by using the right arrow key.
2. Now move the cursor down to the line containing *'General Manager'* (line 8) by using the down arrow key.
3. Now move the cursor to the *'M'* in *Manager* (Column 9) by using the left arrow key.
4. Now move the cursor up two lines by using the up arrow key.This positions the cursor at the carriage return in Line 6, Column 1.

Other commands that are available to edit your document are listed at the bottom of the screen and are discussed in detail in the following sections.

HOME. The HOME command places the cursor at the top left corner of the text window (Line 1, Column 1). To use the HOME command on the IBM PC, press the special key marked <Home> (located on the numeric keypad). On the PCjr, just press the <Fn> (function) key, and then press the arrow key labelled <Home>. The cursor is then placed at the top left corner of the text window.

YOUR TURN

Use the HOME command to place the cursor in the first position of the text window. (*Note:* The STADIUMS document should still be displayed from the previous activity, and the cursor should still be located in Line 6, Column 1.) The following steps serve as a guide:

1. If you are using an IBM PC, press the <Home> key located on the

numeric keypad. If you are using a PCjr, just press the <Fn> key and then the arrow key labelled <Home>.
2. The cursor is then placed at the top left corner of the text window (which is a blank at Line 1, Column 1).

END. The END command, positions the cursor one column beyond the last character of the text window. If a document fills the text window, the END command places the cursor at the lower right corner of the text window. However, if the text window is not full, the END command will place the cursor one position beyond where the last character was typed. For example, if the last character to be typed is a blank at Line 5, Column 32, the END command places the cursor at Line 5, Column 33. To use the END command on the IBM PC, press the special key marked <End> (located on the numeric keypad). For the PCjr, just press the <Fn> key, and then press the arrow key labelled <End>. The cursor is then placed at the last typed character of the text window.

YOUR TURN

As a hands-on activity, the END command can be used to place the cursor at the end of the text window. The STADIUMS document should still be displayed in the text window, and the cursor should still be in the upper left corner. The following steps serve as a guide:

1. If you are using an IBM PC, press the <End> key. For the PCjr, press the <Fn> key, and then press the arrow key labelled <End>.
2. The cursor is then placed at the blank character in Line 15, Column 80.

PAGE DOWN. The PAGE DOWN command places the cursor at the top of the next fifteen lines of the document page. If the cursor is not located at the lower right corner of the text window, the PAGE DOWN command will function as an END command. If the cursor is in the word position, the next fifteen lines of the document will be brought into the text window, and the cursor will be moved to the home position. To use this command on the IBM PC, press the <PgDn> key (located on the numeric keypad). For the PCjr, just press the <Fn> key, and then press the arrow key labelled <PgDn>.

YOUR TURN

Use the PAGE DOWN command to move the cursor. The STADIUMS document should still be displayed in the text window. The following steps serve as a guide:

1. If you are using an IBM PC, press the <PgDn> key. If you are using a

PCjr, press the <Fn> key and then press the arrow key labelled <PgDn>.
2. The cursor will jump to Line 15, Column 80.
3. Press the <PgDn> key.
4. The current fifteen lines in the text window will scroll off the top of the screen, being replaced by the next fifteen lines of the STADIUMS document.

PAGE UP. The PAGE UP command, places the cursor at the bottom of the preceding fifteen lines of the document page. If the cursor is not located at the top left corner of the text window, the PAGE UP command will function as the HOME command. If the cursor is in the home position, the preceding fifteen lines of the document will be brought into the text window, and the cursor will be moved to the end position. To use this command on the IBM PC, press the <PgUp> key (located on the numeric keypad). For the PCjr, just press the <Fn> key, and then press the arrow key labelled <PgUp>.

YOUR TURN

As a hands-on activity, use the PAGE UP command to move the cursor. The STADIUMS document should still be displayed in the text window (after you have executed the PAGE DOWN command). The following steps serve as a guide:

1. If you are using an IBM PC, press the <PgUp> key. If you are using a PCjr, press the <Fn> key, and then press the arrow key labelled <PgUp>.
2. The cursor will jump to Line 1, Column 1.
3. Press the <PgUp> key.
4. The current fifteen lines in the text window will scroll off the bottom of the screen being replaced by the previous fifteen lines of the STADIUMS document.

DELETE. To delete text, move the cursor to the first character that you want deleted. Next, press the <Del> key (located at the bottom of the numeric keypad on the IBM PC and at the bottom right of the keyboard on the PCjr). Move the cursor to the last character you want deleted. (*Note:* As you move the cursor, the text is shown in reverse video, so that the background surrounding the character(s) is lit up rather than the character itself.) Press the <Del> key. The text is then deleted.

YOUR TURN

As a hands-on activity, delete text from the STADIUMS document (this document should still be displayed in the text window from the previous hands-on activity). *Anaheim Stadium* can be deleted from the STADIUMS

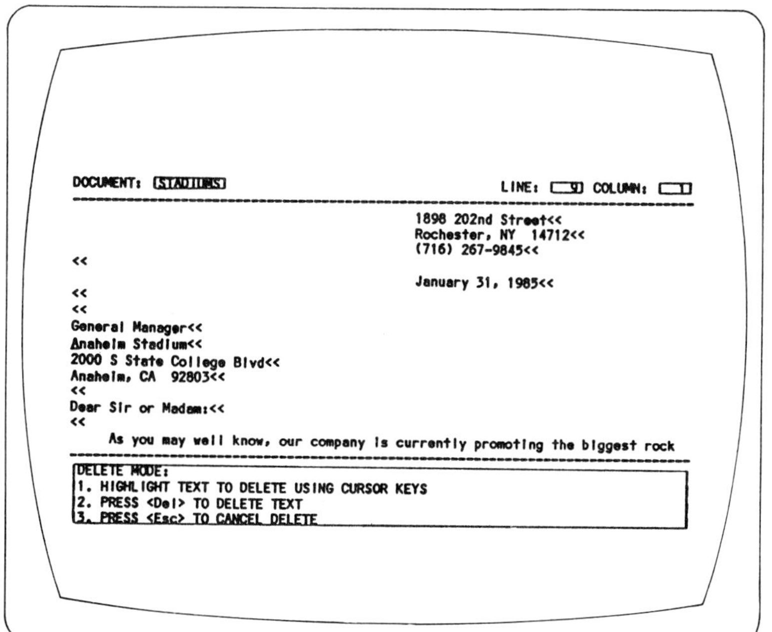
DOCUMENT: STADIUMS
LINE: 9 COLUMN: 1
1898 202nd Street<<
Rochester, NY 14712<<
(716) 267-9845<<
<<
January 31, 1985<<
<<
<<
General Manager<<
Anaheim Stadium<<
2000 S State College Blvd<<
Anaheim, CA 92803<<
<<
Dear Sir or Madam:<<
<<
As you may well know, our company is currently promoting the biggest rock
DELETE MODE:
1. HIGHLIGHT TEXT TO DELETE USING CURSOR KEYS
2. PRESS <Del> TO DELETE TEXT
3. PRESS <Esc> TO CANCEL DELETE

Figure 10–5
DELETE COMMAND

document by using the DELETE command (the <Del> key). The following steps serve as a guide:

1. Move the cursor to the first *A* in *Anaheim* (Line 9, Column 1). Execute the DELETE command by pressing <Del> key (see Figure 10–5).
2. Move the cursor one column past the *m* in *Stadium* (Line 9, Column 16). You will notice that all the text in Line 9 is shown in reverse video. By positioning to Line 9, Column 16, the carriage return at the end of the line will also be deleted. This will cause Line 10 to be moved up to Line 9, where the text is being deleted. Terminate the DELETE command by pressing the <Del> key.
3. The text *Anaheim Stadium* is now deleted.

INSERT. To insert text, move the cursor to the position where you wish to insert the text. Next, press the <Ins> key (located at the bottom of the numeric keypad on the IBM PC and at the bottom right of the keyboard on the PCjr). After pressing the <ins> key, the screen is cleared from the indicated position to the bottom of the text window. Type the text to be inserted, and press the <Ins> key to stop inserting text.

As a hands-on activity, insert the text that was previously deleted back into the STADIUMS document by using the INSERT command (the <Ins> key). The following steps serve as a guide:

YOUR
TURN

1. The cursor should be positioned at Line 9, Column 1 (on the 2 in *2000 S. State College Blvd.*). Execute the INSERT command by pressing the <Ins> key (see Figure 10–6).
2. The text window should be filled with spaces from Line 9 to the bottom. Type in the following text:

Anaheim Stadium

and press the RETURN key.
3. Terminate the INSERT command by pressing the <Ins> key. The text is then inserted.

MOVE. The MOVE command, can be used to delete text from one position and then place it in another position. To use this command, position the cursor at the first character that you wish to move. Next, on the IBM PC, press the function key <F1> (located on the far left side of the keyboard). For the PCjr, press the <Fn> key, and then press the numeric key 1 (located on the top row of the keyboard). (You will notice that this key has a green F1 written on it.) Each numeric key, 1 through 0, is labelled in green with its corresponding function key number. Next, move the cursor to the last character that you wish to move. For the IBM PC, press the function key <F1>. For the PCjr, press the <Fn> key and then the numeric key labelled <F1>. Next, position the cursor to where you would like the text moved. Again press the <F1> on the IBM PC or <Fn> and <F1> keys on the IBM PCjr, and the text is then deleted and inserted at the specified position.

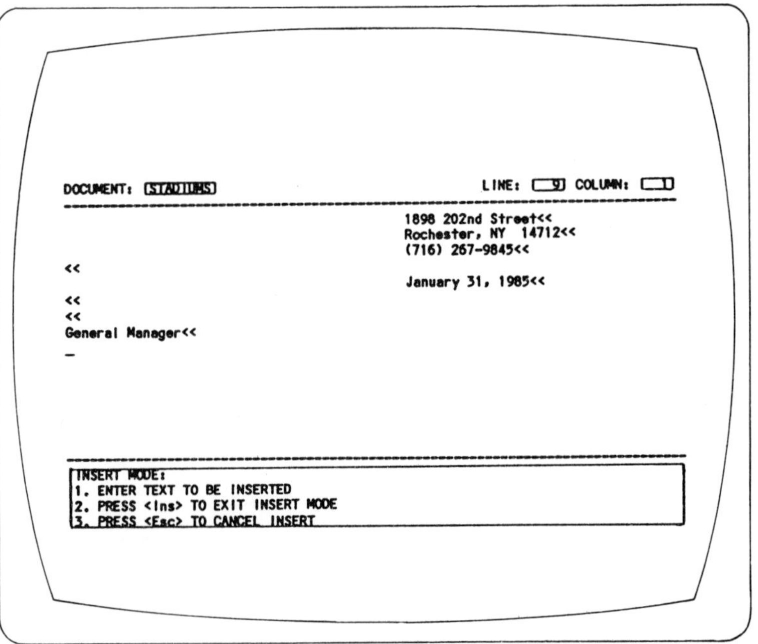

Figure 10–6
INSERT COMMAND

YOUR TURN

Text can be moved within the STADIUMS document by using the MOVE command. For example, the line *General Manager,* can be moved to the line before *2000 S. State College Blvd.* The following steps serve as a guide:

1. Position the cursor at the *G* in *General* (Line 8, Column 1). If you are using the IBM PC, begin the MOVE command by pressing the <F1> key. For the PCjr, press the <Fn> key and then the <F1> key.
2. Position the cursor one column past the << in *Manager* << (Line 8, Column 17); see Figure 10–7. Execute the MOVE command again.
3. Position the cursor at the *2* in *2000* (Line 10, Column 1). Press <F1> if you are using an IBM PC, or <Fn> and then <F1> for the PCjr, and the text is deleted from its previous position and moved to the new position (see Figure 10–8).

SEARCH. The SEARCH command is used to locate a specified character string (the search string) within a document and gives you the option to replace that string individually or globally with another specified character string (the replacement string). To use this command on the IBM PC, press the function key <F2>. For the PCjr, press the <Fn> key and then press the numeric key labelled <F2> (the 2 key). The search will begin at the current cursor location. To search the entire document, the cursor must be positioned at the beginning before pressing the <F2> key.

After you press the <F2> key, the program will display the prompt SEARCH AND REPLACE? (Y/N). Press N to search only or Y to search and replace.

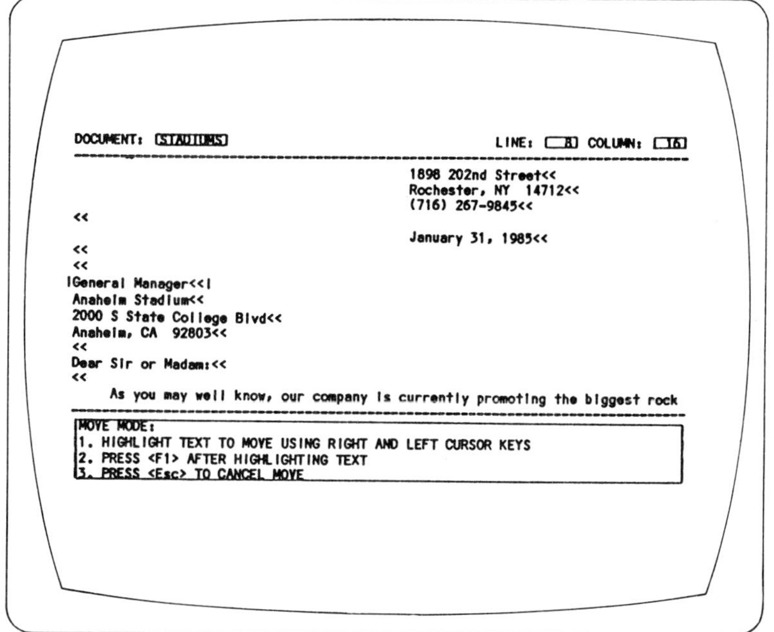
DOCUMENT: STADIUMS
LINE: 8 COLUMN: 16
1898 202nd Street<<
Rochester, NY 14712<<
(716) 267-9845<<
<<
January 31, 1985<<
<<
<<
General Manager<<
Anaheim Stadium<<
2000 S State College Blvd<<
Anaheim, CA 92803<<
<<
Dear Sir or Madam:<<
<<
As you may well know, our company is currently promoting the biggest rock
MOVE MODE:
1. HIGHLIGHT TEXT TO MOVE USING RIGHT AND LEFT CURSOR KEYS
2. PRESS <F1> AFTER HIGHLIGHTING TEXT
3. PRESS <Esc> TO CANCEL MOVE

Figure 10–7
POSITIONING THE CURSOR FOR THE MOVE COMMAND

Figure 10–8
MOVING TEXT USING THE MOVE COMMAND

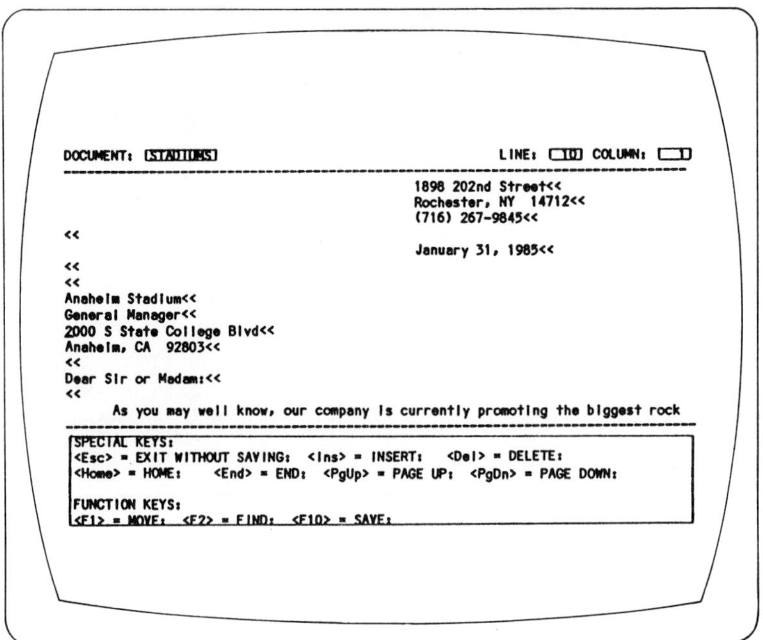

DOCUMENT: STADIUMS
LINE: 10 COLUMN: 1
1898 202nd Street<<
Rochester, NY 14712<<
(716) 267-9845<<
<<
January 31, 1985<<
<<
<<
Anaheim Stadium<<
General Manager<<
2000 S State College Blvd<<
Anaheim, CA 92803<<
<<
Dear Sir or Madam:<<
<<
As you may well know, our company is currently promoting the biggest rock
SPECIAL KEYS:
<Esc> = EXIT WITHOUT SAVING: <Ins> = INSERT: <Del> = DELETE:
<Home> = HOME: <End> = END: <PgUp> = PAGE UP: <PgDn> = PAGE DOWN:
FUNCTION KEYS:
<F1> = MOVE: <F2> = FIND: <F10> = SAVE:

If you press N, the program will prompt you to enter the search string. The search does not discriminate between upper- and lower-case characters, and thus all occurrences of the search string, no matter what combination of upper- and lower-case characters, will be found. Enter the search string, and press the RETURN key. The program then finds the first occurrence of the search string and places the cursor at the beginning of the string. The program then asks, CONTINUE SEARCH? (Y/N). Enter Y to continue looking for the search string, or enter N to stop the search. If the program cannot find the specified search string, the message NO MATCH FOUND will appear, and you must press the space bar to continue.

YOUR TURN

Use the SEARCH command to find the first two occurrences of the word *information* in the STADIUMS document. The following steps serve as a guide:

1. Press <PgUp> to position the cursor at the beginning of the text. Press the <F2> key on the IBM PC or the <Fn> key and then the <F2> key on the PCjr. The program then prompts you with SEARCH AND REPLACE? (Y/N) (see Figure 10–9). Enter N to do a search only.
2. The program then asks you to enter the string to search for. Enter the word *information* (see Figure 10–10), and press the RETURN key. The program then finds the first occurrence of the word *information.*
3. Next, the program asks if you want to CONTINUE SEARCH? (Y/N). Press Y, and the program will search for the next occurrence of *information* and places the cursor next to it (see Figure 10–11).

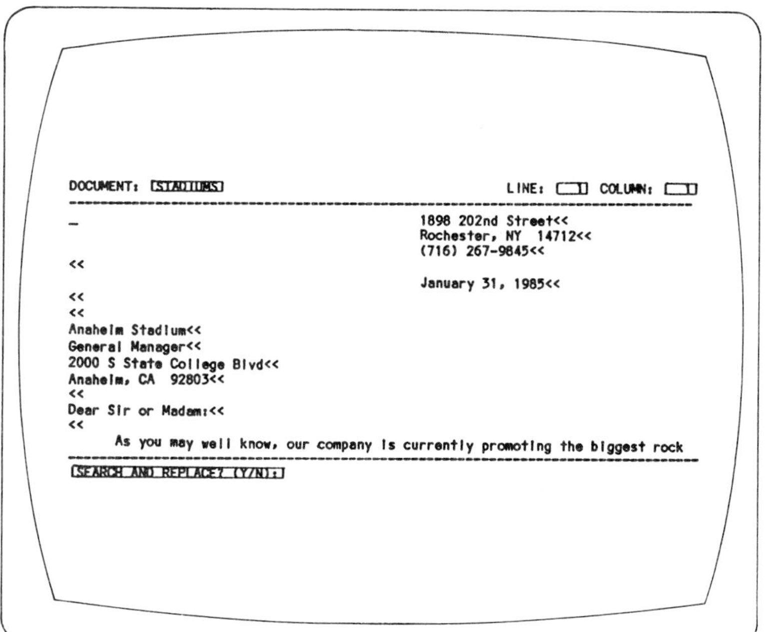

DOCUMENT: STADIUMS
LINE: 1 COLUMN: 1
1898 202nd Street<<
Rochester, NY 14712<<
(716) 267-9845<<
January 31, 1985<<
Anaheim Stadium<<
General Manager<<
2000 S State College Blvd<<
Anaheim, CA 92803<<
Dear Sir or Madam:<<
As you may well know, our company is currently promoting the biggest rock
SEARCH AND REPLACE? (Y/N):

Figure 10–9
SEARCH ONLY OPTION

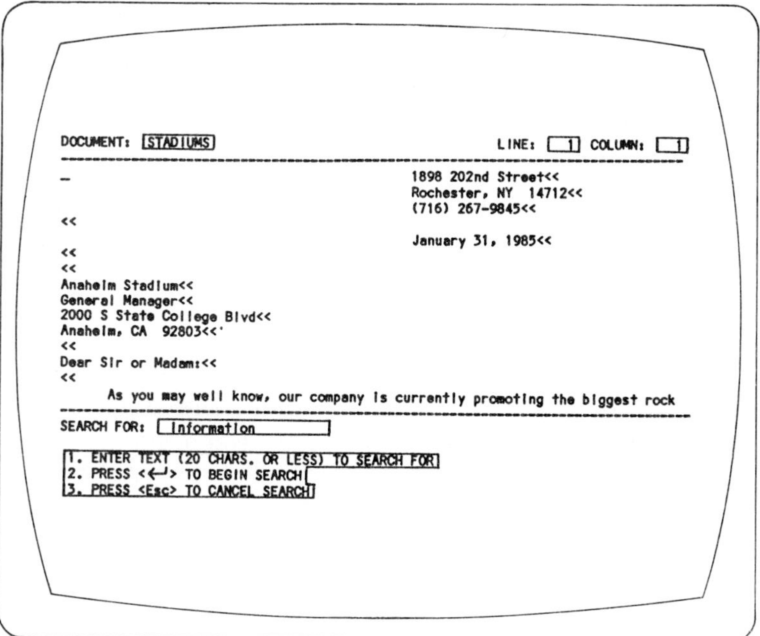

DOCUMENT: STADIUMS
LINE: 1 COLUMN: 1
1898 202nd Street<<
Rochester, NY 14712<<
(716) 267-9845<<
January 31, 1985<<
Anaheim Stadium<<
General Manager<<
2000 S State College Blvd<<
Anaheim, CA 92803<<
Dear Sir or Madam:<<
As you may well know, our company is currently promoting the biggest rock
SEARCH FOR: information
1. ENTER TEXT (20 CHARS. OR LESS) TO SEARCH FOR
2. PRESS <↵> TO BEGIN SEARCH
3. PRESS <Esc> TO CANCEL SEARCH

Figure 10–10
ENTERING THE SEARCH STRING

4. The program then asks, CONTINUE SEARCH? (Y/N). Press N, and the program allows you to continue editing the STADIUMS document.

If you pressed Y in response to the SEARCH AND REPLACE? (Y/N) prompt, the program will prompt you to enter the search string. Enter the string

Figure 10–11
FINDING THE SECOND OCCURRENCE OF THE WORD INFORMATION

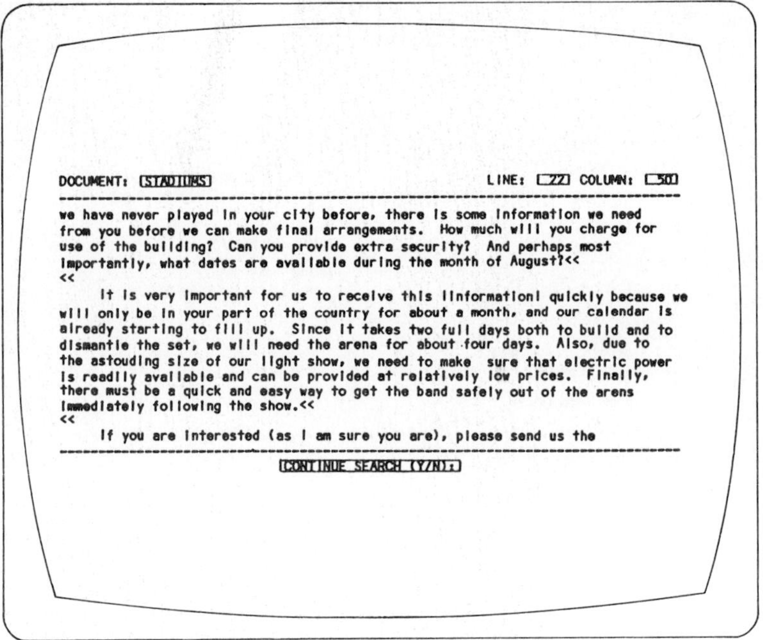

and press RETURN. Next the program prompts you to enter a replacement string. Enter the string and press RETURN. Following this the program displays the prompt GLOBAL SEARCH AND REPLACE? (Y/N). If you answer N and the search string is found, the program displays the prompt REPLACE? (Y/N). If you enter Y in response to the REPLACE? (Y/N) prompt, the search string is replaced with the replacement string. Immediately following this or if you answered N to the REPLACE? (Y/N) prompt, the program displays the prompt CONTINUE SEARCH? (Y/N). Enter Y to continue looking for the search string or N to stop the search.

YOUR TURN

Use the SEARCH command to replace the first occurrence of the word *information* in the STADIUMS document with the word *data*. The following steps serve as a guide:

1. Press <PgUp> to position the cursor at the beginning of the text. Press the <F2> key on the IBM PC or the <Fn> key on the PCjr. The program then prompts you with SEARCH AND REPLACE? (Y/N). Enter Y to do a search and replace.
2. The program then asks you to enter the string to search for. Enter the word *information* and press the RETURN key.
3. Next, the program asks you to enter the replacement string. Enter the word *data* (see Figure 10–12) and press the RETURN key.
4. The program then displays the prompt GLOBAL SEARCH AND REPLACE? (Y/N) (see Figure 10–13). Enter N and press the RETURN key.

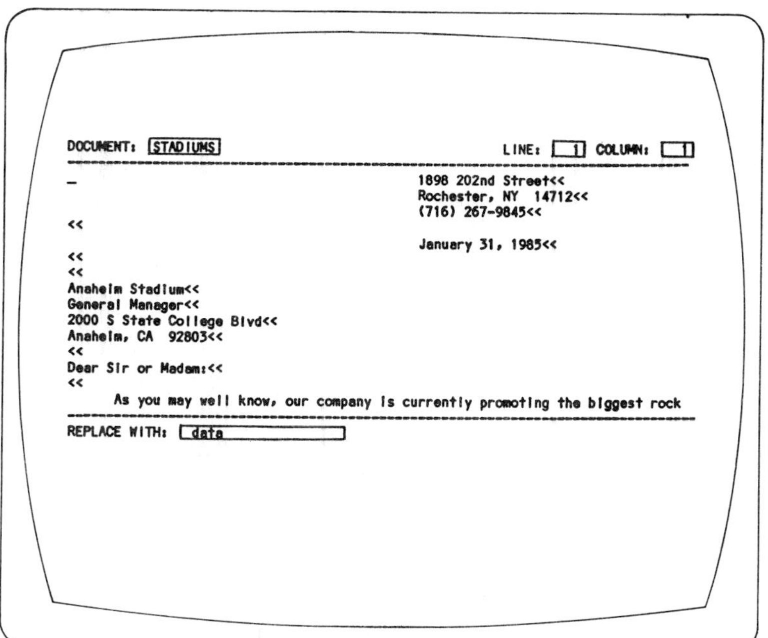
DOCUMENT: STADIUMS
LINE: 1 COLUMN: 1
1898 202nd Street<<
Rochester, NY 14712<<
(716) 267-9845<<
<<
January 31, 1985<<
<<
<<
Anaheim Stadium<<
General Manager<<
2000 S State College Blvd<<
Anaheim, CA 92803<<
<<
Dear Sir or Madam:<<
<<
As you may well know, our company is currently promoting the biggest rock
REPLACE WITH: data

Figure 10–12
ENTERING THE REPLACEMENT STRING

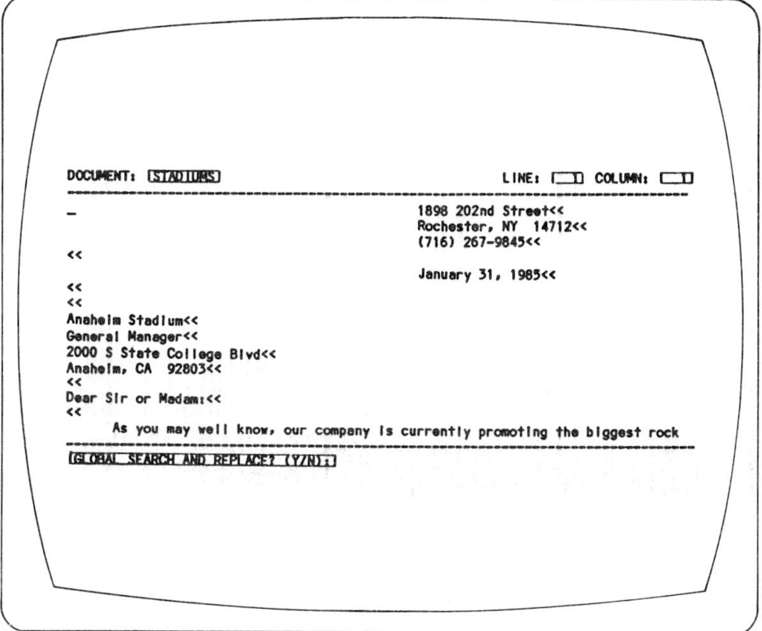
DOCUMENT: STADIUMS
LINE: 1 COLUMN: 1
1898 202nd Street<<
Rochester, NY 14712<<
(716) 267-9845<<
<<
January 31, 1985<<
<<
<<
Anaheim Stadium<<
General Manager<<
2000 S State College Blvd<<
Anaheim, CA 92803<<
<<
Dear Sir or Madam:<<
<<
As you may well know, our company is currently promoting the biggest rock
GLOBAL SEARCH AND REPLACE? (Y/N):

Figure 10–13
GLOBAL SEARCH AND REPLACE PROMPT

5. The program then finds the first occurrence of the word *information* and displays the prompt REPLACE? (Y/N) (see Figure 10–14). Enter Y to replace this occurrence of the word *information* with the word *data.*

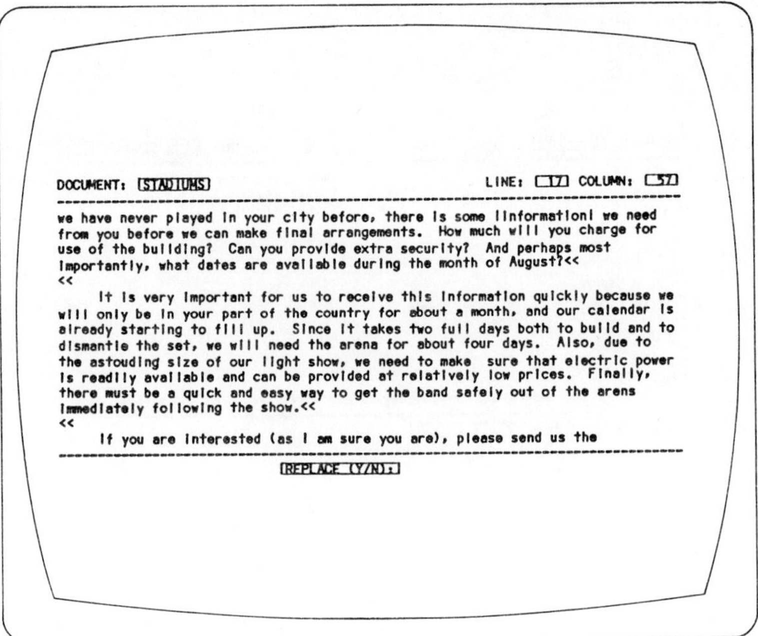

DOCUMENT: STADIUMS
LINE: 17 COLUMN: 57
we have never played in your city before, there is some |information| we need
from you before we can make final arrangements. How much will you charge for
use of the building? Can you provide extra security? And perhaps most
importantly, what dates are available during the month of August?<<
<<
It is very important for us to receive this information quickly because we
will only be in your part of the country for about a month, and our calendar is
already starting to fill up. Since it takes two full days both to build and to
dismantle the set, we will need the arena for about four days. Also, due to
the astouding size of our light show, we need to make sure that electric power
is readily available and can be provided at relatively low prices. Finally,
there must be a quick and easy way to get the band safely out of the arens
immediately following the show.<<
<<
If you are interested (as I am sure you are), please send us the
REPLACE (Y/N):

Figure 10–14
REPLACE OPTION

6. The program then asks, if you want to CONTINUE SEARCH? (Y/N). Press N, and the program allows you to continue editing the STADIUMS document.

If you entered Y to the prompt GLOBAL SEARCH AND REPLACE? (Y/N), all the occurrences of the search string will be replaced with the specified replacement string.

YOUR TURN

Use the SEARCH command to replace all the occurrences of the word *information* in the STADIUMS document with the word *data*. The following steps serve as a guide:

1. Press the <PgUp> key to position the cursor at the beginning of the text. Press the <F2> key on the IBM PC or the <Fn> key and <F2> key on the IBM PCjr. The program then prompts you with SEARCH AND REPLACE? (Y/N). Enter Y to do a search and replace.
2. The program then asks you to enter the string to search for. Enter the word *information* and press the RETURN key.
3. Next, the program asks you to enter the replacement string. Enter the word *data* and press the RETURN key.
4. The program then displays the prompt GLOBAL SEARCH AND REPLACE? (Y/N). Enter Y and press the RETURN key. All the occurrences of the word *information* are now replaced with the word *data*.

5. Now, repeat Steps 1 through 4 using the word *data* as the search string and the word *information* as the replacement string.

SAVE. There are two ways in which you can exit the editor portion of the word processor. The first one, pressing the <Esc> key, does not allow you to save a document so that you can come back and work on it later. The second option is to execute the SAVE command, the function key, <F10>, which allows you to save a document.

To save a document on the IBM PC, press the <F10> key. For the PCjr, just press the <Fn> key and then the numeric key labelled <F10>. The document is then saved, and the program returns to the word processor menu.

This word processor is limited, because it allows only two documents to be added. If you wish to create more than two documents, one of the old documents must be erased first. To erase the old document, press Y (for yes) when the program displays the message asking if you want to erase a particular file. If you press N (for no), the file in question is not erased. To save a document, press the <F10> key. The document is then saved, and the program returns to the WestWord MAIN MENU.

YOUR TURN

The changes that have been made to the STADIUMS document do not have to be saved. Use the <Esc> key to exit the editor portion of WestWord. The following steps serve as a guide:

1. Press the <Esc> key.
2. The program then asks, ESCAPE WITHOUT SAVING? (Y/N). Press Y (for yes) and you are returned to the MAIN MENU.

Creating a New Document

The WestWord program also allows new files to be created. This version of WestWord is limited, because it allows only two files to be added. Therefore, if you wish to save another document, one of the old ones must first be erased. Erasing the document is done by answering yes (pressing Y) when the program displays the message asking if you want to erase a particular file. Answering yes will only erase the document you previously created. It will not erase the STADIUMS or SPRBREAK documents. This version is also limited, because the document cannot be longer than three pages.

To create your own document, press 2 when the WestWord MAIN MENU is shown. The program then shows the CREATE screen and places the cursor next to DOCUMENT TO CREATE. To create your own document, enter a name from one to eight characters in length, and press the RETURN key. (The file name may consist of any letter from *A* through *Z* and any number from 1 through 9.) The program then creates the file and allows

Figure 10–15
TYPING THE STADIUMS DOCUMENT

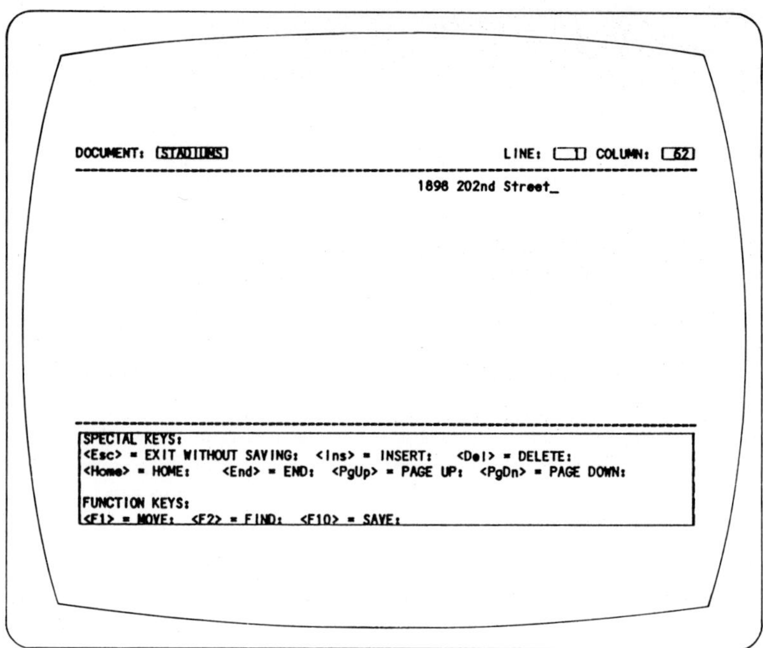

you to begin typing a new document. Refer to the Section "Editing an Old Document" to see the commands available.

An example is how the STADIUMS document was created. Since this document is already on your diskette, there is no need for you to create it. First, 2 was entered when the word processor menu was displayed. Next, the program displayed the CREATE screen and waited for the DOCUMENT TO CREATE. STADIUMS was entered, and the RETURN key was pressed. The program then created the file. Next, the first line of the STADIUMS document was typed (see Figure 10–15), and then the entire STADIUMS document (see Figure 10–16).

Printing a File

In order to print the contents of a document file, choose Selection 3 from the WestWord MAIN MENU. The program will then display the Print Menu which includes the options: (1) SELECT DOCUMENT and (2) CHANGE PRINTER DEFAULTS. Selection 1 of the PRINT MENU allows you to select the file you wish to print. After the number 1 is pressed, the program will display the names of the document files that are available for printing. Enter the name of the file you wish to print and press the RETURN key.

The program will then ask you to ready your printer by turning it on, if it is not already on, and to make sure that it is on-line (connected to your computer). Once the printer is turned on and on-line, you can then press the RETURN key to begin printing. When printing is complete, the program will return to the print menu.

Selection 2 on the print menu displays to the user the printer defaults used for printing and also the printers that can be used by the program

```
                                     1898 202nd St.<<
                                     Rochester, NY 14712<<
                                     (716) 267-9845<<
<<
                                     January 31, 1985<<
<<
<<
General Manager<<
Anaheim Stadium<<
2000 S. State College Blvd.<<
Anaheim, CA 92803<<
<<
Dear Sir or Madam:<<
<<
     As you may well know, our company is currently promoting the biggest rock
concert tour in history, and we would like to bring it to your arena! Because
we have never played in your city before, there is some information we need
from you before we can make final arrangements. How much will you charge for
use of the building? Can you provide extra security? And perhaps most
importantly, what dates are available during the month of August?<<
<<
     It is very important for us to receive this information quickly because we
will only be in your part of the country for about a month, and our calendar is
already starting to fill up. Since it takes two full days both to build and to
dismantle the set, we will need the arena for about four days. Also, due to
the astounding size of our light show, we need to make sure that electric power
is readily available and can be provided at relatively low prices. Finally,
there must be a quick and easy way to get the band safely out of the arena
immediately following the show.<<
<<
     If you are interested (as I am sure you are), please send us the
information as soon as possible. All of us, especially the band, hope
something can be worked out. We very much look forward to hearing from you.<<
<<
                                     Sincerely yours,<<
<<
<<
<<
                                     Stevie Star<<
                                     (The Stardusters)<<
```

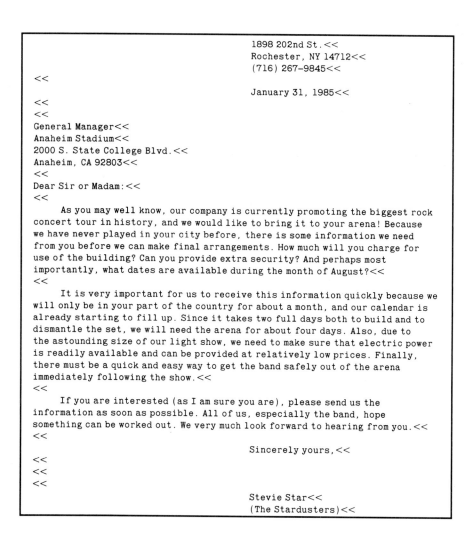

Figure 10–16
CONTENTS OF THE STADIUMS DOCUMENT

for printing. In order to display these printer defaults, press 2 when the PRINT MENU is displayed.

The PRINT function can be used to print the document STADIUMS. The following steps can be used as a guideline:

1. Choose Selection 3 from the MAIN MENU.
2. Choose Selection 1 from the PRINT MENU (see Figure 10–17).
3. Enter STADIUMS as the file to print (see Figure 10–18), and press the RETURN key.
4. The prompt READY YOUR PRINTER, THEN PRESS RETURN will be displayed. Make sure your printer is turned on and connected to your computer, and then press RETURN. Your document will now print.

Figure 10–17
PRINT MENU

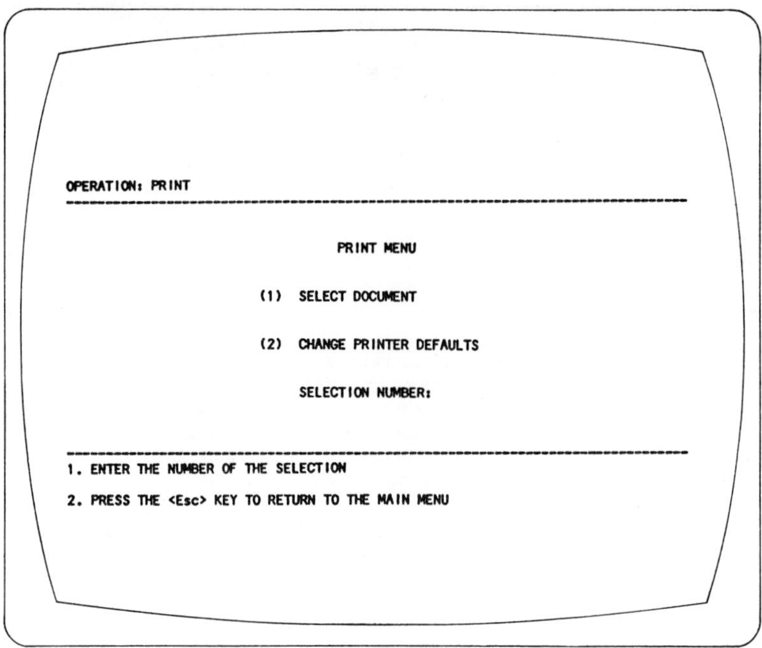

OPERATION: PRINT
PRINT MENU
(1) SELECT DOCUMENT
(2) CHANGE PRINTER DEFAULTS
SELECTION NUMBER:
1. ENTER THE NUMBER OF THE SELECTION
2. PRESS THE <Esc> KEY TO RETURN TO THE MAIN MENU

WestWord Messages

1. BUFFER FULL
   NO MORE TEXT CAN BE ADDED
   TO THE DELETE BUFFER

   You have tried to delete more text than the buffer will hold. The buffer will allow only five lines to be deleted.

2. BUFFER FULL
   NO MORE TEXT CAN BE ADDED
   TO THE MOVE BUFFER

   You have tried to move more text than the buffer will hold. The buffer will allow only five lines to be moved.

3. CONTINUE SEARCH? (Y/N)

   After the FIND operation has found a matching string in the document, it asks you if you would like to continue searching for the same string. Answering N (No) terminates the search, while a Y (Yes) answer causes the search to continue.

4. ENTER <Y> OR <N> ONLY

   A number or character other than Y or N has been entered.

5. ESCAPE WITHOUT SAVING? (Y/N)

   Answering Y (Yes) to this question allows you to leave the editor without saving what you have entered. Answering N (No) to this question returns you to the editor at the position the <Esc> key was pressed.

6. FILE NOT FOUND

   The file name that was entered does not currently exist.

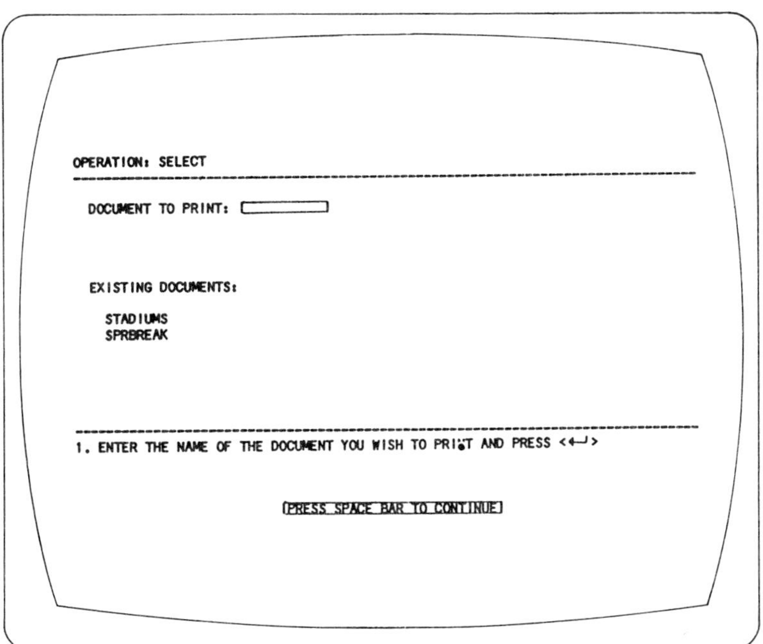

OPERATION: SELECT
DOCUMENT TO PRINT:
EXISTING DOCUMENTS:
STADIUMS
SPRBREAK
1. ENTER THE NAME OF THE DOCUMENT YOU WISH TO PRINT AND PRESS <←┘>
PRESS SPACE BAR TO CONTINUE

Figure 10–18
SELECTING THE DOCUMENT TO PRINT

```
7.     BUFFER FULL
   NO MORE TEXT CAN BE ADDED
      TO THE INSERT BUFFER
```

The buffer that is used for inserting text is full. The buffer will allow only five lines to be inserted.

```
8. INVALID MENU SELECTION. PLEASE
   ENTER CHOICE AGAIN USING 1-2.
```

A number or character other than 1 or 2 has been entered (these numbers represent menu selections.)

```
9. INVALID MENU SELECTION. PLEASE
   ENTER CHOICE AGAIN USING 1-5.
```

A number or character other than 1, 2, 3, 4, or 5 has been entered (these numbers represent menu selections.)

```
10. NO MATCH FOUND
```

The string that has been entered for a FIND does not have a match in the document that is currently being edited.

```
11. ONLY ONE DOCUMENT CAN BE CREATED USING
      THIS VERSION OF THE WORD PROCESSOR
```

Only one extra document can be created. To create another document, the old document must first be erased.

```
12. ONLY THE CHARACTERS A..Z AND 1..9 CAN
        BE USED IN A DOCUMENT NAME
```

A document name that contains characters others than A..Z or 1..9 has been entered.

13. PRESS SPACE BAR TO CONTINUE

To continue execution of the program press the space bar.

14. THE FILE NAME ENTERED IS
ALREADY IN USE

Documents with the names STADIUMS and SPRBREAK have already been created and cannot be used again.

Contents of the Spring Break Document

```
                                                802 Sixth St.
                                                Marion, NC 28752
                                                (704) 555-8179

                                                January 7, 1985

Manager
Park Lane Motor Lodge
625 N. Atlantic Blvd.
Fort Lauderdale, FL 33304

Dear Sir or Madam:

Would you send information on the cost of your rooms per night and the number
of vacancies you have available from March 9 through March 16? If we should
decide to make a reservation, what will you accept as a deposit, and how soon
will this deposit need to be sent? Please provide information on your refund
policy, the maximum number of occupants allowed per room, the facilities
available, and the services provided for your guests.

Since this is our first time in Fort Lauderdale, a detailed description of how
to get to your motel would be greatly appreciated. Are you located near the
ocean (within a five-minute walking distance), or will there be a need to have
a car? If there is public transportation, when is it available, and where is
the closest pick-up/drop-off point in relation to your motel?

Please provide brochures from the entertainment areas surrounding your motel, or
provide the name of an organization that we can contact for brochures.

                                                Sincerely yours,


                                                Russ Stevens
```

Summary of WestWord Commands

Special Key	Function Name	Description
<Home>	HOME	Positions the cursor at the top left corner of the text window.
<End>	END	Positions the cursor one column past the last character of the text window or to the lower right corner of the text window if the document fills the text window.
<PgDn>	PAGE DOWN	Positions the cursor at the end of the current screen, to the next screen if you are at the end of the current screen, or to the next page if you are at the end of the current page.

Special Key	Function Name	Description
<PgUp>	PAGE UP	Positions the cursor at the beginning of the current screen, to the previous screen, if you are at the beginning of the current screen or to the previous page if you are at the beginning of the current page.
<Del>	DELETE	Deletes a character or block of characters up to five lines in length from the current cursor position.
<Ins>	INSERT	Inserts up to five lines of characters into document from the current cursor position.
<F1>	MOVE	Deletes the specified text from the current cursor position and then inserts it at the specified cursor location.
<F2>	FIND	Locates a specified character string within a document and provides the option of replacing the search string individually or globally with a specified replacement string.
<F10>	SAVE	Saves a document to disk.

SUMMARY POINTS

- A word processor is a program or set of programs designed to allow you to enter, manipulate, format, print, store, and retrieve text.
- Word processing is the act of composing and manipulating text.
- A word-processing system is the hardware that allows you to operate a word processor. There are two general types: (1) dedicated systems, which only handle word processing, and (2) multipurpose microcomputers, which handle a variety of processing tasks, including word processing.
- The two primary functions of a word processor are text editing (which involves entering and manipulating text) and print formatting (which involves communicating to the printer how to format the printed copy).
- A word processor with a line editor works on only one line at a time, whereas a word processor with a screen editor works on a screen at a time.
- Memory-only word processors cannot swap text between disk and internal memory and are limited to working on only what can be stored in memory at one time. Page-oriented word processors treat a text file as a series of pages, swapping the pages between memory and disk. Document-oriented word processors treat a text file as one long document.
- Word processors are available for home, business, and specialized uses.
- Common writing and editing features of a word processor include cursor positioning, word wrap, scrolling, insertion and replacement, deletion, block movements, searching, undo, and save and re-enter.
- Common screen-formatting features include status displays, tab settings, and displayed page breaks.
- Common print-formatting features include margin settings, justified margins, line spacing, centering, automatic pagination, headers and footers, and character enhancements.

- The basic hardware needed for an IBM PC system to run a word processor includes the following:
  —An IBM PC computer.
  —One disk drive (some word processors may require two).
  —A monitor and a monochrome or color/graphics card.
  —A printer and printer interface card.
- The following steps are recommended when selecting a word processor:
  —Analyze your needs.
  —Determine budget constraints.
  —Research available word processors.
  —Narrow the selection to a few, based on your research and constraints.
  —Perform hands-on testing.

REVIEW QUESTIONS

1. Define the terms *word processor*, *word processing*, and *word-processing system*.

2. What are the two primary functions of a word processor? Briefly define each.

3. What is the difference between a line editor and a screen editor?

4. Describe the uses a person might have for a word processor in the home. What uses might a business have?

5. What is a cursor, and how might controlling its movements help the user write and edit? What are some common cursor-positioning features?

6. Define *word wrap*.

7. Name and discuss three different types of searches.

8. Discuss the basic equipment (hardware) that is needed for the IBM PC to run a word processor.

9. What are some things to consider when choosing a word processor?

10. Analyze your own writing needs. Would you benefit by using a word processor?

WESTWORD EXERCISES

1. Use the SPRING BREAK file, included on your diskette, to complete the following exercises.

a. Using the EDIT OLD DOCUMENT option, enter the SPRBREAK document into the word processor.

b. Move the cursor to the end of the first paragraph of the document.

c. Delete the following text (which begins at Line 22, Column 1):

```
Since this is our first time in Fort Lauderdale, a de-
tailed description of how to get to your motel would
be greatly appreciated.
```

(*Note*: Make sure you delete the two spaces following this text.)

d. Place the cursor at Line 20, Column 12, and insert the following text:

```
a map to locate your establishment,
```

(*Note*: Make sure you include a space following this text.)

e. Move the *and* in Line 15, Column 64, to Line 16, Column 33 following the word *available.* Make sure you also move the space following the *and.*

f. Move the following text (found in Line 15, Column 31) to the space presently held by the *f* in from (found in Line 16, Column 34):

```
the cost of your rooms per night
```

2. Create a new document called CLETTER using the CREATE NEW DOCUMENT option. Type the following letter into the CLETTER document:

```
                                                        309 Parsons Ave.
                                                        Twinsburg, OH 41517
                                                        (215) 384-3498

                                                        March 25, 1985

Service Manager
Chemco Corp.
456 Chemco Ave.
Cleveland, OH 41319

Dear Sir or Madam:

In the March 24 issue of the Cleveland Plain Dealer, you advertised for a
chemical engineer. I wish to apply for the position.

I am well qualified for this position. In May, I will graduate from Akron
University. My degree is in space technology.

Please send me the necessary details to apply for this position. I look
forward to hearing from you. If you have any questions, please phone (215)
384-3498.

                                                        Sincerely yours,


                                                        Edward C. Yale
```

a. Delete the following text starting with the period from the previous sentence (located at the end of the second paragraph):

```
My degree is in space technology.
```

b. Insert the following text with the cursor located on carriage return following *University.*: Type a blank (press the spacebar) before typing the word *with.*

```
with a bachelor's degree in chemical engineering.
```

c. Move the following text to the space after *(216) 425-8583.:*

```
I look forward to hearing from you.
```

(*Note*: Make sure you include the two spaces before the text.)

d. If you look at the text on your screen, you will notice that there are eight spaces between the words *look* and *forward.* These are the spaces that were at the end of the line following the word *look* before you moved the text. The MOVE routine moves everything that is highlighted, including the spaces, so to close up the line, place the cursor at Line 22, Column 53 and press the <Del> key. Highlight all the spaces up to the *f* but not including the *f,* and then press the <Del> key.

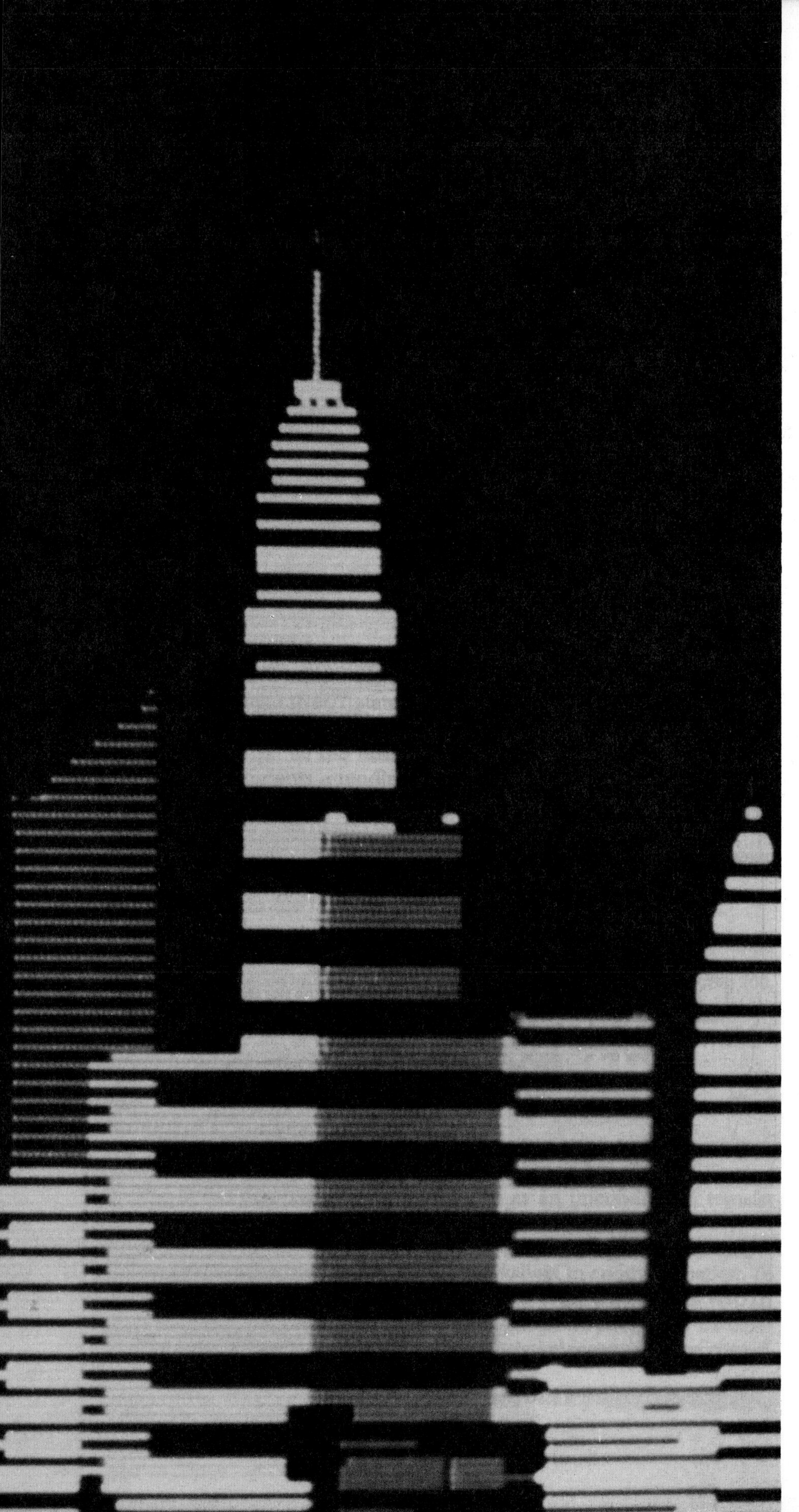

CHAPTER 11

THE SPREADSHEET

Chapter Outline

INTRODUCTION

Spreadsheet
A ledger or table used in a business environment for financial calculations and for the recording of transactions.

Like most computer programs, a **spreadsheet** is designed to take care of a simple, commonly encountered manual task. Also like many computer programs, it has a fancy name that tells very little about what it does. A spreadsheet program is simply a calculator that uses a computer's memory capability to solve a mathematically oriented problem.

A pencil, a piece of paper, and a calculator are common tools normally used to solve these mathematical problems. With a spreadsheet program, the computer can modify your calculations at the speed of electricity. This capability proves more and more useful the larger your formulas and calculations become. For example, imagine doing your tax returns and realizing after finishing that you forgot to include your new car as an expense. All your calculations following that part of the form would be wrong! If you were using a spreadsheet program, however, you would simply have to insert the forgotten number, and the program would recalculate all the following totals for you. This is only one example of what a spreadsheet can do. With the ability to recalculate, as well as store, print, merge, and sort numeric information, a spreadsheet becomes the ultimate replacement for pencil, paper, and calculator.

This chapter will look at the features that make this software so popular. It will also review some of the more popular spreadsheet programs and give you some suggestions on what to look for when purchasing a spreadsheet program.

DEFINITIONS

Unlike the terms *word processor* and *file manager,* the term *spreadsheet* does not give any real insight into what the program actually does. A definition of some of the common terms associated with this type of program will clarify this matter. Table 11–1 provides a quick reference to terms often encountered when reading about spreadsheets.

Electronic spreadsheet
A spreadsheet that uses computer storage and computational capabilities.

Spreadsheet program
A set of computer instructions that generates and operates an electronic spreadsheet.

Spreadsheet analysis
A mental process of evaluating information contained within an electronic spreadsheet; also called what-if analysis.

Model
A numeric representation of a real-world situation.

A spreadsheet, in the traditional sense, is actually a ledger sheet like the one shown in Figure 11–1. It is primarily used in the business environment by accountants and managers for financial calculations and the recording of transactions. An **electronic spreadsheet,** in contrast, is a table of columns and rows used to store and manipulate any kind of numeric information. This table (or matrix) is displayed on a computer's display screen, and its contents are stored in the computer's memory.

A **spreadsheet program** is a set of computer instructions that generates and operates an electronic spreadsheet. **Spreadsheet analysis** (or what-if analysis) is the mental process of evaluating information contained within an electronic spreadsheet. It often involves the comparing of different results generated by the spreadsheet. A **model,** or modeling, in terms of a spreadsheet, is a numeric representation of a real-world situation. For example, a home budget is a numeric representation of the expenses involved in maintaining a household and therefore can be considered a model.

In this chapter, the term *spreadsheet* will always mean "electronic spreadsheet." Also, all applications of a spreadsheet cited in this chapter can be considered numeric models of real-world situations.

TERM	DEFINITION
Cell	A storage location within a spreadsheet used to store a single piece of information relevant to the spreadsheet.
Coordinate	The location of a cell within a spreadsheet; a combination of the column letter and row number that intersect at a specific cell.
Formula	A mathematical equation used in a spreadsheet.
Label	Information used for describing some aspect of a spreadsheet. A label can be made up of alphabetic or numeric information, but no arithmetic may be performed on a label.
Value	A single piece of numeric information used in the calculations of a spreadsheet.
Window	The portion of a worksheet that can be seen on the computer display screen.

Table 11–1 TERMS ASSOCIATED WITH ELECTRONIC SPREADSHEETS

Figure 11–1 LEDGER SHEET

HOME BUDGET	
Expenses:	
Rent	235 00
Food	100 00
Gas	97 00
Electric	75 00
Phone	25 00
Car	100 00
TOTAL EXPENSES	632 00

How a Spreadsheet Works

After loading a spreadsheet program into your computer, the first thing you are likely to see is something similar to Figure 11–2. The numbers on the left side of the screen represent the rows of the table, and the letters at the top represent the columns. Even though you can see only 16 rows and 4 columns, there are in fact (on most spreadsheets) 254 rows and 64 columns. It is as though you are looking through a **window** at a much larger sheet, but you just cannot see all of it at once. The arrow keys on your keyboard are commonly used to move the cursor around so that any part of the sheet can be seen. The spreadsheet is used by entering labels, values, or formulas into the cells of the spreadsheet.

Cells are storage locations named according to their location on the spreadsheet. The name (or **coordinate**) of a cell is made up of a letter

Window
The portion of a worksheet that can be seen on the computer display screen.

Cells
Storage locations within a spreadsheet.

Coordinate
The location of a cell within a spreadsheet.

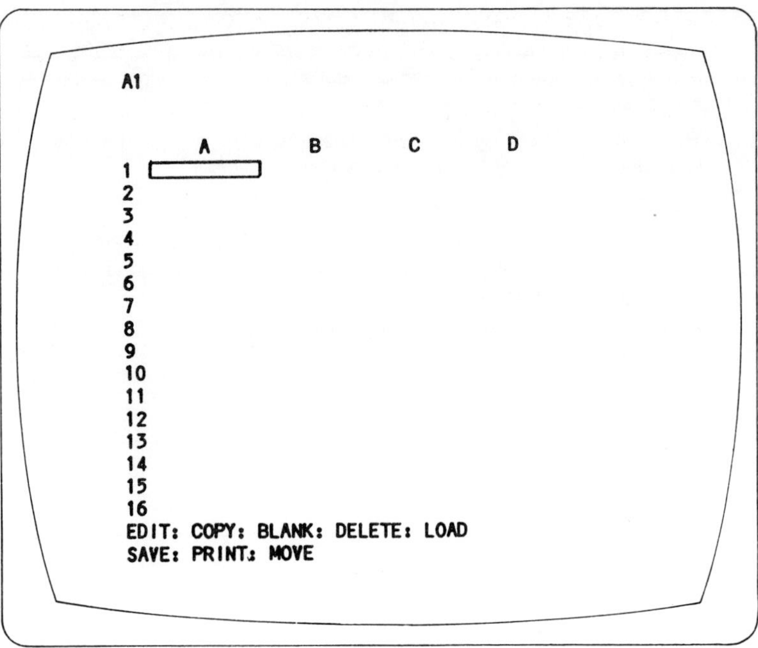

Figure 11–2
A CLEAN SPREADSHEET AT INITIAL LOADING

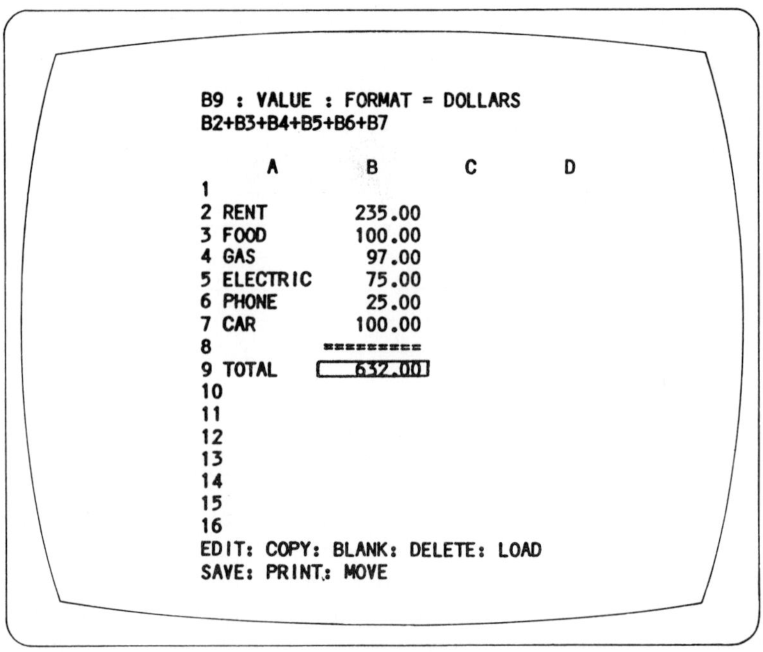

Figure 11–3
HOME BUDGET

representing the column that the cell is in and a number representing the row that the cell is in. For example, A1, B10, and C16 can all be seen in the window in Figure 11–2. Information is entered to the spreadsheet via the keyboard and is placed in the cell on which the cursor is currently located. In Figure 11–3, for example, information entered would be placed in Cell B9.

A cell can hold three types of information: **labels, values,** and **formulas.** Figure 11–3 shows a home budget with labels in Column A and their corresponding values in Column B. At coordinate B9, a formula is used to sum the preceding values in Column B.

Labels
Information used for describing some aspect of a spreadsheet.

Values
Single pieces of numeric information used in the calculations of a spreadsheet.

Formulas
Mathematical equations used in a spreadsheet.

The area at the top of the display screen is the status area, so named because it contains all the information that is important to the cell that the cursor is on. In Figure 11–3, the top left corner of the status area displays the current location of the cursor (in this case, B9). The next line of the status area shows what was typed into B9. Notice that what was typed into the cell and what is displayed in the window are not the same; the spreadsheet interpreted the formula and displayed the results on the sheet. It is the use of formulas that gives a spreadsheet its power and flexibility. The use of formulas will be discussed shortly.

One other area is common to most spreadsheets: the command area. This area displays all the commands that are available to the user at any given time. Figure 11–3 shows a command area at the bottom of the screen. These commands are additional features of the spreadsheet that will be explained in greater detail later in this chapter.

Formulas and How to Use Them

A formula is simply a mathematical equation that the user assigns to a cell in the spreadsheet. The big advantage of using a spreadsheet is that you can use other cell locations (instead of just numbers) in the mathematical expression. As shown in Figure 11–3, the total of the budget was made by adding the contents of the preceding cells. This is useful, because if you wanted to know how much the total would be if rent were only $175.00, all you would have to change would be the value in the rent cell (Figure 11–4 shows the effect of changing the rent value).

Any equation using addition, subtraction, multiplication, division, or exponentiation can be used for the value of a cell. In addition, most spreadsheet programs offer predefined functions as well. Common functions are sum, minimum, maximum, and average. These functions are simply shortcuts that are used instead of the operators + − / *. For example, the addition of the cells in Figure 11–4 could have been done with the statement *Sum B1 through B8.* The minimum and maximum functions will give the smallest and largest numbers in a specified range (Cells B11 and B12), respectively, and the average function will return the average of a specified range (Cell B13).

Other Standard Commands

To make the spreadsheet easier to read, formatting options are available that will rearrange the data on the sheet. For example, numeric data (such as values and formulas) can be displayed as integers, percentages, dollar values, or full floating-point numbers. Label entries can be right justified, left justified, or centered in a column. It is common practice for value entries

Figure 11–4
BUDGET ANALYSIS USING PREDEFINED FUNCTIONS

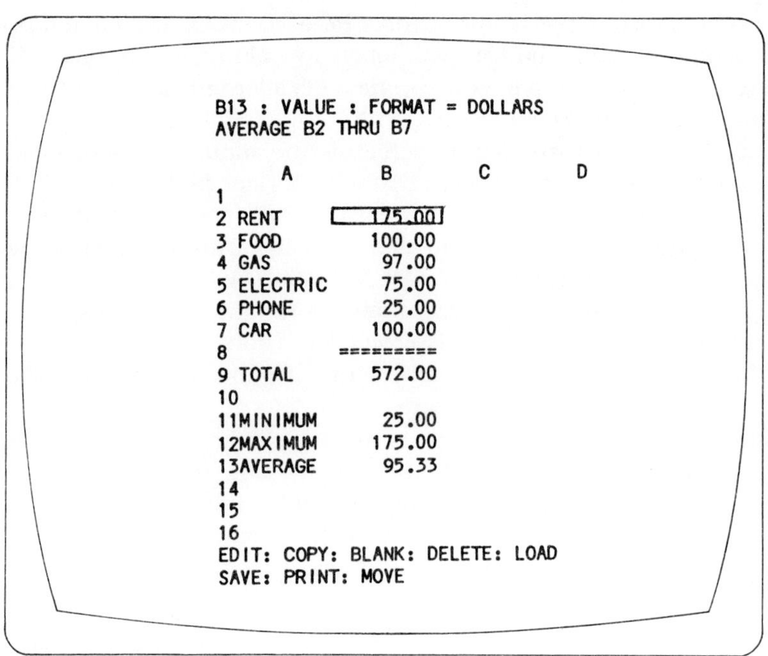

to be displayed as right justified. Once the final spreadsheet has been made, it can be stored for future use on a disk or printed as a report.

USES OF A SPREADSHEET

A spreadsheet automates a commonly encountered manual task. However, unlike other programs, a spreadsheet can also be used as a tool for decision making.

Business Uses

In most business situations there are many different ways to achieve the same goal. For example, a manager of a department must combine labor, materials, and equipment to produce a sellable good. The question is, what is the best combination of labor, materials, and equipment that will produce the desired quantity of sellable goods within the time allotted? To answer this question, the manager must construct a model of the job in which all inputs (labor, material, and equipment) and outputs (sellable goods) are identified. Then, through a process of trial and error, the manager calculates the different combinations until the best one is found. It is easy to see that this process can become very long and cumbersome when many options are available to the manager. Nevertheless, the manager must evaluate all possible alternatives to find an optimal solution.

By using a spreadsheet instead of a pencil and calculator, the manager can concentrate on the decision at hand instead of the calculations required to find each result. This type of what-if analysis capability has caused spreadsheet programs to become popular; as managers learned how to use a spreadsheet program, they began to find many new applications to which the program could be adapted.

Within the business environment, sales and industry data are put on a spreadsheet to identify trends and external factors influencing the company's profitability. In fact, any bits of information that can be manipulated mathematically are stored on a spreadsheet to be combined with other information and evaluated at a later date. Analysis that once was considered too trivial or extensive to justify the time and cost involved in evaluation has suddenly become acceptable.

Home Uses

With the passing of time, new and different ways of applying spreadsheets outside the business environment began to emerge; these range from recording church donations to keeping track of weekly bowling scores. The spreadsheet user must think in a new way. Although it is true that a calculator is fine for balancing your checkbook, have you ever wondered what percentage of your income goes to food, housing, or entertainment? Or how much of your monthly pay goes to interest charges for the use of a credit card? Is there a cheaper way to borrow the money? Have you ever been halfway through a grading period in school and pondered what kind of scores you would need to receive on your remaining tests to achieve a certain grade point average? Or how that grading period would affect your cumulative average? These are a few examples of home and personal uses

LEARNING CHECK

1. Spreadsheets store data in a ________ and ________ format.

2. A ________ is the name of a cell and represents that cell's location in the spreadsheet.

3. The ________ area of the spreadsheet displays the current location of the cursor.

4. The ________ area of the spreadsheet displays all commands available to the user.

5. A formula is a mathematical equation that the user assigns to a cell in the spreadsheet. (True or false?)

6. Business uses of a spreadsheet include all of the following except ______.

a. modeling real-world situations

b. storing data in a data base

c. what-if analysis

d. profitability analysis

ANSWERS: **1.** column, row. **2.** coordinate. **3.** status. **4.** command. **5.** true. **6.** b.

for a spreadsheet. Although it is not recommended that you buy a $300 spreadsheet package without a particular application in mind, the uses of a spreadsheet seem to grow as the user becomes more familiar with all its capabilities.

In addition to the previous examples, spreadsheet analysis has also been applied in the fields of science and engineering. In the course of research and development, people in these fields are required to make extensive use of the trial-and-error method of evaluation. By using a spreadsheet program, these people can calculate different alternatives rapidly and then save each of their results as documentation of their progress.

SPECIAL FEATURES OF SPREADSHEET PROGRAMS

Because of its wide acceptance in the business world and its flexibility in adapting to many applications, spreadsheet programs are currently the Number 1 best-selling programs for microcomputers. There are more than two hundred different brands of spreadsheet programs for sale today. Many of these programs have special features that make them easier to operate. Others have special features designed to help the user solve a certain type of problem, and still others try to increase the overall flexibility and speed of the spreadsheet.

User-Friendly Software

User friendliness is a term that is used ambiguously in the microcomputer industry. Although it brings visions of your personal computer laying quietly at your feet in front of a toasty fire, *user friendly* generally translates into "easy to use." But even the translation can be misleading, because what is easy for a seasoned programmer may very well not be easy for the first-time computer user.

The important aspects of user friendliness of a spreadsheet program involve (1) the amount of time it takes to learn how to operate a spreadsheet program and (2) the user's ability to remember how the program works after the training is completed. Both are closely related to how easy the program is to use.

The primary foundation for learning how to operate a spreadsheet (or any other program) is the user's manual. If it is not clear and well-organized, learning and operating a spreadsheet program can be extremely frustrating. Another aid to the user of a spreadsheet program is the use of a command area to display all the commands the spreadsheet offers. Although this function was listed as a common characteristic of spreadsheets at the beginning of the chapter, not all spreadsheet programs offer this assistance. A few spreadsheet programs take this concept one step further by storing in the computer's memory a summary description of each command, which can be referred to by the user as a quick reminder instead of having to dig through the user's manual.

Speed and Flexibility

Nearly all spreadsheet programs written today try to be user friendly, but most try to differentiate themselves from the rest of the market by supplying the user with extra commands that increase the flexibility and speed with which the spreadsheet operates. The following sections briefly describe some of these commands.

Variable Column Width. Labels are very important to the operation of a spreadsheet. Being able to rapidly manipulate numbers can prove useful only if you know what the numbers stand for. The ability to set the width of a column containing labels to a length that will fit a good description of the numbers with which they are associated is a functional, as well as cosmetic, enhancement to the display of a spreadsheet.

Automatic Spillover. In cases where variable column width is not possible, some spreadsheet programs allow the entry of an extralong label that "spills over" into the next cell. This function is handy when making a title at the top or bottom of the spreadsheet.

Insertions and Deletions. Some spreadsheets have functions that let the user insert or delete rows or columns as needed. The program automatically adds or deletes any values within a formula in which the row or column is embedded.

Graphics. Many spreadsheet programs offer a function to generate standard horizontal bar graphs using the asterisk character to represent the bar. A few spreadsheets offer additional graphs, such as a pie chart and a line graph.

Templates. A template, when referring to spreadsheet programs, is a predefined set of formulas used over and over. For example, a church donation spreadsheet and a weekly bowling average tally would be good applications for templates. The formulas could be saved on a diskette, and each week the new figures could be entered to obtain the result. All spreadsheet programs with the ability to save files have this capability, but some take it one step further by supplying ready-to-use templates for specific purposes like real estate management and investment tracking.

Locking Cells. To prevent the user or someone else from altering or destroying formulas in a template, the cells containing these formulas can be "locked" so that no one (without a password) can change them. This locking is done by using a special command supplied by the spreadsheet program that tells the spreadsheet not to let any new information be put into that cell.

Hiding Cells. The ability to hide cells lets the designer of a template make certain cells invisible to the screen so that the person entering the data cannot see the results.

Naming Cells. When working through a large spreadsheet, it is easy to forget the coordinates of a cell needed in a formula. To avoid the user's having to scroll all the way back to a cell just to look at its coordinates, some spreadsheet programs let the user give the cells useful names that act the same as the original coordinates. For example, in calculating an income statement, you could have a formula in a cell that said "income − expense," and you could call that cell PROFIT.

Windows. Yes, a spreadsheet even does windows, but not the kind you are thinking of. Because a spreadsheet is so big (254 rows by 64 columns) and the computer screen is so small (25 lines with 80 characters per line), it is hard to tell what is going on in all the cells you cannot see. The window feature lets you split the screen into two, three, or four miniscreens, or windows, that can look at any part of the spreadsheet independently of the others.

Titles. A title feature works in a manner similar to the window function, except it is used to stop labels from being scrolled off the screen. For example, suppose you have a budget for the next twelve months on a spreadsheet with a column for each month and a row for each of your expenditures. The labels for those expenditures are in Column 1. If you tried to scroll over to the "April" column, the labels for your expenditures would disappear off the left side of the screen. The titles feature lets you lock the labels in place so that all other cells work normally, but the labels do not move.

Replication. Replication (or copying) is one of the most used commands on a spreadsheet. It allows the user to copy any cell or group of cells to another part of the spreadsheet. With this feature, the user does not need to waste time entering redundant data.

Manual Recalculation. When the contents of a cell in a formula are changed, the result of that formula will change accordingly. This is known as *recalculation.* Most spreadsheet programs are designed to automatically update the formula result when a cell within that formula is changed. This is a useful feature, but it has its drawbacks. For example, if the user is working with a very large formula, the spreadsheet could take from five seconds to well over a minute to recalculate it. During this time, the user must sit and wait for the computer to finish before entering any more information. Furthermore, if the user wants to change two or more cells before checking the result, the spreadsheet is wasting time. To overcome this problem, some spreadsheets can be set so that they only recalculate a result when they are asked (hence, the term *manual recalculation*).

Sorting. To produce a more meaningful display, some spreadsheet programs will sort information within the spreadsheet. This sorting can be done alphabetically with labels or numerically with constant values and formula values.

HARDWARE REQUIREMENTS

Many spreadsheet programs are written to run on a variety of computers, each with different hardware requirements. This section will discuss the hardware needed to run spreadsheets on the IBM PC family of microcomputers.

Memory

With a spreadsheet program, the internal random-access memory (RAM) in your computer is used for two distinct purposes. Part of the RAM is used to store the actual spreadsheet program, and the remaining RAM is used to store the information you enter into the cells of the spreadsheet. Therefore, if you have extra memory in your computer, you will be able to construct larger spreadsheet models. All spreadsheet programs list on their packaging the minimum amount of RAM that the computer must have. This number is often just higher than the actual size of the program, so if you have more memory than is required, it probably will not go to waste.

Monitor Display

The monitor on the IBM PC can display twenty-five lines with eighty characters per line. A circuit board available exclusively for use with spreadsheet programs will increase the monitor display to 132 columns. This board increases the size of the spreadsheet window to 16 rows by 12 columns. Unless you plan to do a good deal of work on a spreadsheet, though, the standard monitor display should be adequate.

CHOOSING A SPREADSHEET PROGRAM

The most important factor to consider when purchasing a spreadsheet (or any other program) is its application. For example, if the spreadsheet program you purchase is to be used primarily for home and personal applications, special functions and business graphics will be of little use to you. However, if you are planning to use a spreadsheet program to supply other people with information or for a specific business application, some of the advanced features could be useful. A second factor to consider is how easy the spreadsheet program is to use. Again, the presence of sophisticated commands is useless unless you know how they work and when to use them.

The prices and abilities of spreadsheet programs on the market today vary widely, as does the relationship between price and performance. The prices for spreadsheets range from under $30 to $700, with the majority of programs falling between $150 and $300. Spreadsheet programs designed specifically for home and personal use are nearly nonexistent, as you can tell from the price range.

In general, the same procedure used in buying a word-processing program should be followed in choosing a spreadsheet program. Weed out the programs that obviously do not serve your purpose, and then test-drive each of the remaining programs to find the one with which you are most comfortable.

LEARNING CHECK

1. Commands that increase the flexibility and speed with which the spreadsheet operates include all of the following except ________.

   a. graphics

   b. replication

   c. cell finding

   d. sorting

2. RAM is needed to store the spreadsheet program only. (True or false?)

3. What is a template?

4. What is the most important factor when choosing a spreadsheet?

5. Which of the following is not a user's aid of spreadsheet operation?

   a. formulas

   b. command area

   c. user's manual

   d. command summary descriptions

ANSWERS:

1. c. **2.** false. **3.** a predefined set of formulas used over and over. **4.** the application for which the spreadsheet will be used. **5.** a.

POPULAR SPREADSHEET PROGRAMS

This portion of the chapter will list spreadsheet programs available for the IBM PC family of microcomputers. Specific information pertaining to each of the programs listed can be obtained by writing to the addresses provided. The programs selected do not reflect an endorsement of the product. This list is not an attempt to cover the entire market of IBM-compatible spreadsheets, but rather a brief sample of the available programs.

Home Versions

Because spreadsheet programs are designed for versatility, their differentiation into home and business versions is vague. The main criteria used for the selection of these home versions were price and special features. The following programs represent the lower end of the price range into which spreadsheet programs fall. Table 11–2 compares features offered by each of these programs.

Table 11–2 COMPARISON OF SPREADSHEETS AND FEATURES

PROGRAM \ FEATURE	VARIABLE COLUMN WIDTH	AUTOMATIC SPILLOVER	INSERT AND DELETE	STANDARD GRAPHICS	TEMPLATE ABILITY	LOCKING CELLS	HIDING CELLS	NAMING CELLS	NUMBER OF WINDOWS	TITLES	REPLICATION	MANUAL RECALCULATION	SORTING	COMMAND AREA	HELP SCREENS
EASYCALC	X	X	X		X				1		X				X
NOVACALC	X								1						X
THE THINKER			X						1		X				X
LOTUS 1–2–3	X	X	X	X	X	X		X	2	X	X	X	X	X	X
MULTIPLAN	X	X	X	X	X	X	X	X	8	X	X	X	X	X	X
PEACHCALC	X		X		X	X			2	X	X	X			X
PERFECTCALC	X	X	X		X	X		X	2		X	X	X	X	X
SUPERCALC3	X	X	X	X	X	X	X	X	2	X	X	X	X		X
VISICALC IV	X	X	X	X	X	X	X		2	X	X	X		X	X

Some of the following spreadsheet packages require a special card (known as the CP/M card) to be installed into the IBM computer before they will work. This card is essentially a second computer that enables the IBM computer to run programs written for other computers.

- ***EasyCalc***

  Available from: Norell Data Systems Corp.
  3400 Wilshire Blvd.
  Los Angeles, CA 90010
  Price range: $75–$100
  Features: See Table 11–2
  Available for: 64K IBM PC (128K recommended), PCjr, one drive

- ***NovaCalc***

  Available from: Hourglass Systems
  P.O. Box 312
  Glen Ellyn, IL 60137
  Price range: $25–$50
  Features: See Table 11–2
  Available for: IBM PC, two drives

- ***The Thinker***

  Available from: TexaSoft
  1028 N. Madison Ave.
  Dallas, TX 75208
  Price range: $25–$50
  Features: See Table 11–2
  Available for: 64K IBM PC (128K recommended), 80 column screen, and one drive

Business Versions

The following business spreadsheet programs reflect the average price range into which most spreadsheet programs fall:

- ***Lotus 1-2-3***

  Available from: Lotus Development Co.
  161 First Street
  Cambridge, MA 02142
  Price range: $450–$500
  Features: See Table 11–2
  Available for: 192K IBM PC, 2 drives, color graphics boards

- ***Multiplan***

  Available from: Microsoft Corp.
  10700 Northup Way
  Bellevue, WA 98004
  Price range: $250–$300
  Features: See Table 11–2
  Available for: 64K IBM PC, PCjr

- ***PeachCalc***

  Available from: Peachtree Software Inc.
  3445 Peachtree Rd., NE, 8th Floor
  Atlanta, GA 30326
  Price Range $350–$400
  Features: See Table 11–2
  Available for: 64K IBM PC

- ***PerfectCalc***

  Available from: Perfect Software
  1400 Shattuck Ave.
  Berkeley, CA 94710
  Pricc range: $200 $250
  Features: See Table 11–2
  Available for: 128K IBM PC

- ***SuperCalc 3***

  Available from: Sorcim/IUS Micro Software
  2195 Fortune Dr.
  San Jose, CA 95131
  Price range: $300–$350
  Features: See Table 11–2
  Available for: 128K IBM PC

- ***VisiCalc IV***

  Available from: VisiCorp
  2895 Zanker Rd.
  San Jose, CA 95134
  Price range: $200–$250
  Features: See Table 11–2
  Available for: 128K IBM PC, color graphics converter

New Enhancements

Two new enhancements recently have been made available for spreadsheet programs. The first is the concept of integrated software, where files created with a spreadsheet program can be saved on a diskette and then reloaded back into a word processor to be reformatted with the special editing features of the word processor. This sharing of files also allows all or part of a spreadsheet to be inserted into an existing report or letter that was created with the word processor.

The second enhancement is special input devices for the IBM PC and other personal computers. These devices—the mouse, light pen, and voice recognizer (see Chapter 2)—are substitutes for the computer keyboard that make entering data to a spreadsheet much easier.

With the passing of time, applications for spreadsheet programs will continue to grow. Also, the power and ease of use of the microcomputer itself will increase. The effect on the uses of information caused by these advances is analogous to the effect on the uses of communication caused by the introduction of the telephone and television. The information age is upon us and is growing fast.

GUIDE TO WESTCALC™

Spreadsheets are computer programs that let you keep track of numeric information that can be organized in a column-and-row format. Spreadsheet programs have become very popular in business, because they allow the user to ask what-if questions by changing different variables within the spreadsheet. For example, a rock concert promoter might be asked to prepare a net income forecast for an upcoming concert tour. By using an electronic spreadsheet to prepare an income statement for each of the concert sites, the promoter can forecast the net income from each concert. Once the income forecast for a rock concert has been entered, variables within the statement (such as ticket price) can be changed to determine what effect the change will have on net income.

The WestCalc spreadsheet can be accessed by loading the diskette labeled WestCalc into the disk drive and turning on the system unit and monitor. When the system prompt, *A>*, is displayed on the monitor, type WestCalc and press RETURN.

Common Spreadsheet Terms

The following are common terms used in the WestCalc spreadsheet:

- **Worksheet:** The portion of the spreadsheet that holds the data and the information. The worksheet is a matrix (table) of twenty columns and fifteen rows that displays the data (see Figure 11–5). Columns I through T (the remaining fifteen columns) are loaded into the worksheet but cannot be seen until the cursor is moved toward these columns. The same is true for rows eleven through fifteen.
- **Cell:** A single location within the worksheet. A cell can hold a label, value, or formula. Each cell displays from two characters or numbers up to thirty

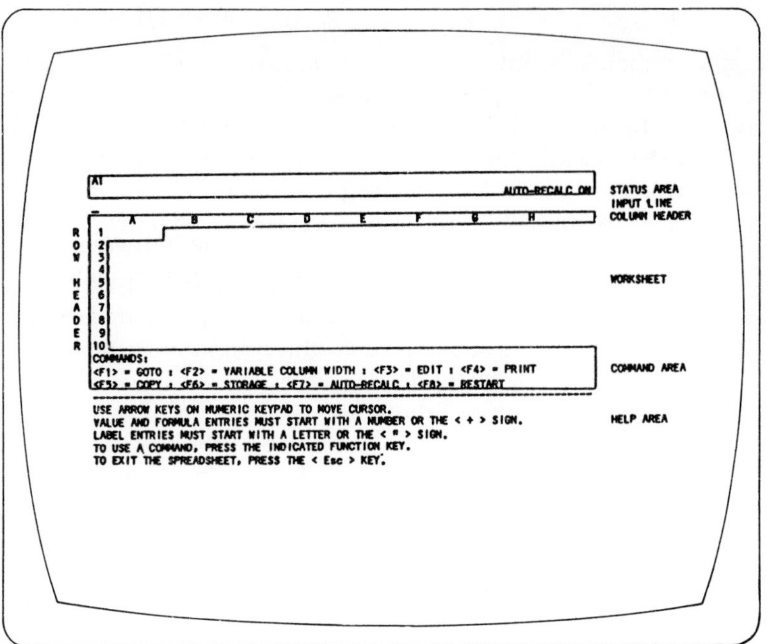

Figure 11–5
LAYOUT OF THE SPREADSHEET

characters or numbers depending on the format selected for the cell. The WestCalc spreadsheet has three hundred cells (fifteen rows by twenty columns).

- **Cursor:** A pointer to the cell that you are currently working on. It appears as a block that occupies one cell within the worksheet. The cursor can be moved to any cell within the worksheet by using the arrow keys located on the numeric keypad of the IBM PC or on the right side of the keyboard for the IBM PCjr.
- **Coordinate:** The location of a cell within the worksheet. The columns of the worksheet are named from A to T. The rows are named from 1 to 15. A cell located in Column D and in Row 6 is identified by the coordinate D6.
- **Label:** An entry to the worksheet that acts as an identifier. Usually, label entries are letters or symbols that describe some portion of the worksheet (TOTAL, for example).
- **Formula:** A mathematical expression. A spreadsheet formula can contain both constants and coordinates. For example, both 100 + 60 (using constants) and D6*(100 + 60) − E4 (using coordinates and constants) are valid. The operators are + (addition), − (subtraction), * (multiplication), / (division), and ^ (exponentiation).
- **Value:** An entry made into a cell that is assigned a number. A value can be either a formula (B7 + D1) or a constant (the number 30).

Description of the Spreadsheet

A spreadsheet is composed of different areas (refer to Figure 11–5). The first area is the *status area,* which tells you the location of the cursor within the worksheet, the type of entry in a coordinate, the cursor movement, and the format of a value. It also shows you what was actually entered into the cell. The second area of the spreadsheet is the *input line.* When you type a valid character, that character is displayed on the input line. The *column header* is the third area of the spreadsheet. Column headers indicate the various column positions, which range from A to T. The *row header* is the next area of the spreadsheet. The row headers indicate the various row positions, which range from 1 to 15. The *worksheet* is the fifth area of the spreadsheet. This area holds the data relating to the numeric analysis of the spreadsheet in a table. The *command area* makes up the next part of the spreadsheet. Eight FUNCTION commands are listed in this area; these will be discussed in the following sections. The last area of the spreadsheet, the *help area,* lists information to help you use the spreadsheet.

Helpful Hints

The WestCalc spreadsheet program uses the arrow keys to move the cursor within the worksheet. The arrow keys are situated on the right side of the keyboard. Refer to Figure 11–6 for the layouts of the IBM PC and PCjr keyboards.

The following hints will help you move the cursor within the WestCalc worksheet. For the IBM PC, the <NumLock> key, located at the top right side of the keyboard, must be off. If the <NumLock> key is on, the numbers on the keys will be activated rather than the arrow keys. For the IBM PCjr, the arrow keys are located to the right of the RETURN key.

When inputting labels, values, or formulas, the RETURN key is used to terminate the entry. This key is on the right side of the keyboard. The arrow keys may also be used to input labels, values, and formulas. To exit the WestCalc spreadsheet, press the ESCAPE (<Esc>) key located in the upper left corner of the keyboard.

To activate one of the spreadsheet's eight FUNCTION commands, you must press the FUNCTION key that designates that command. For example, to use the RESTART command, press the <F8> key. The FUNCTION keys are located on the extreme left side of the keyboard on the IBM PC and on the top row of the PCjr. See the command area in Figure 11–5 for the FUNCTION commands available.

To backspace on the input line, press the backspace key. On the IBM PC, the backspace key is located to the left of the <NumLock> key. On the IBM PCjr, it is located on the left of the <Fn> key.

Value entries (for example, 3.50 and 1000) must start with a number, or the plus sign (+), whereas label entries (for example, RENT and TAXES) must begin with a letter. Label entries such as ********* and = = = = = = must begin with double quotation marks ("). Refer to Figure 11–6 for the location of the double quotation marks and plus sign keys. Remember to press the shift key when you want double quotation marks or the plus sign.

Formula entries (for example, 100 + 60, B5 + D7), and A10 + (100*1.5^2) − 2/H4 must begin with the plus sign (+). The plus sign is needed to tell the program that a formula (and not a label) is being entered. The plus sign

Figure 11–6 KEYBOARD LAYOUT OF IBM PC (TOP) AND PCjr (BOTTOM)

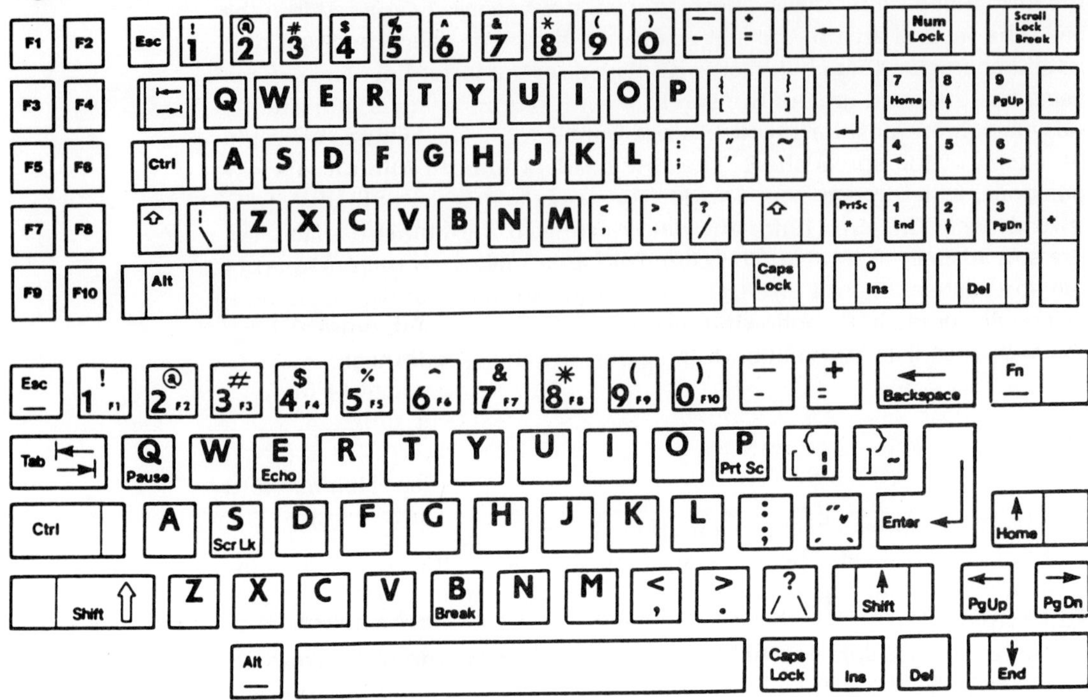

key is located on the right side of the keyboard. Make sure there are no spaces in the formulas because the program does not accept spaces.

If you enter a value that is too big to fit into a worksheet cell, such as 9999999997776521, the message *TOO BIG* is printed in the cell instead of the numeric value. Even though you get the *TOO BIG* message, the value that was entered is still in memory and is used on the computations.

When the message ERROR appears in a cell, there is a computational error in your formula or the numeric range of the computer has been exceeded. For instance, division by 0 or unmatching parentheses both display ERROR. Should this happen, clear the cell by executing the BLANK A CELL command, and then start over. Remember to type the plus sign before reentering the formula.

The following sections will introduce you to the FUNCTION commands used in the spreadsheet program. In the remainder of the text, a key such as <F3> represents a function key. The function keys for the IBM PC are located on the left side of the keyboard. For the IBM PCjr, the <Fn> key and the appropriate number key, such as <F1>, must be pressed at the same time. To help you understand the commands, the STADIUMS NET INCOME example provided with your diskette will be used.

FUNCTION Commands

STORAGE. The STORAGE command is a general command used to access the LOAD WORKSHEET, SAVE WORKSHEET, and LOAD EXAMPLE WORK-

SHEET commands. To access the specific storage commands, press the <F6> function key (for the PCjr, press the <Fn> and <F6> keys at the same time); this will access the STORAGE submenu. The specific storage commands are discussed in the following three sections.

LOAD EXAMPLE WORKSHEET. The LOAD EXAMPLE WORKSHEET command is used to copy one of the two examples provided with the WestCalc spreadsheet program into the worksheet. The first example, STADIUMS NET INCOME, shows the net income associated with a concert at SHEA STADIUM. The second example, SPRING BREAK VACATION, contains spring break vacation options.

To execute the LOAD EXAMPLE WORKSHEET command, press <F6> to access the STORAGE submenu (see Figure 11–7) and then press <F3>. Next, the program waits for 1 or 2 to be pressed. If 1 is pressed, the STADIUMS NET INCOME example is copied into the spreadsheet program. If 2 is pressed, the SPRING BREAK VACATION example is copied. To abort the LOAD EXAMPLE WORKSHEET command, press the <Esc> key. Aborting does not change the worksheet on which you are currently working.

YOUR TURN

Use the LOAD EXAMPLE WORKSHEET command to copy the STADIUMS NET INCOME example into the worksheet. The following steps serve as a guide:

1. Press the <F6> key, and then press the <F3> key. After doing this, the screen appears as shown in Figure 11–8.

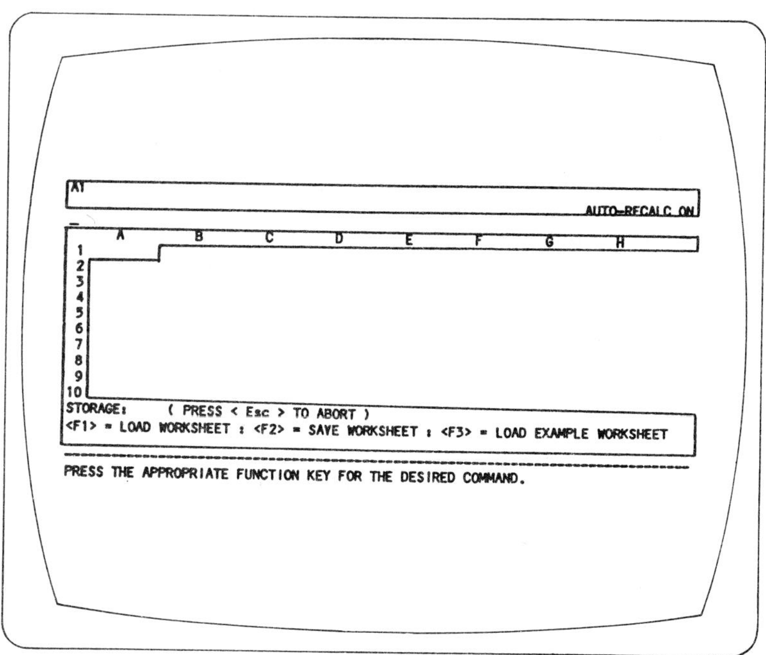

Figure 11–7
STORAGE SUBMENU

Figure 11–8
LOAD EXAMPLE WORKSHEET COMMAND

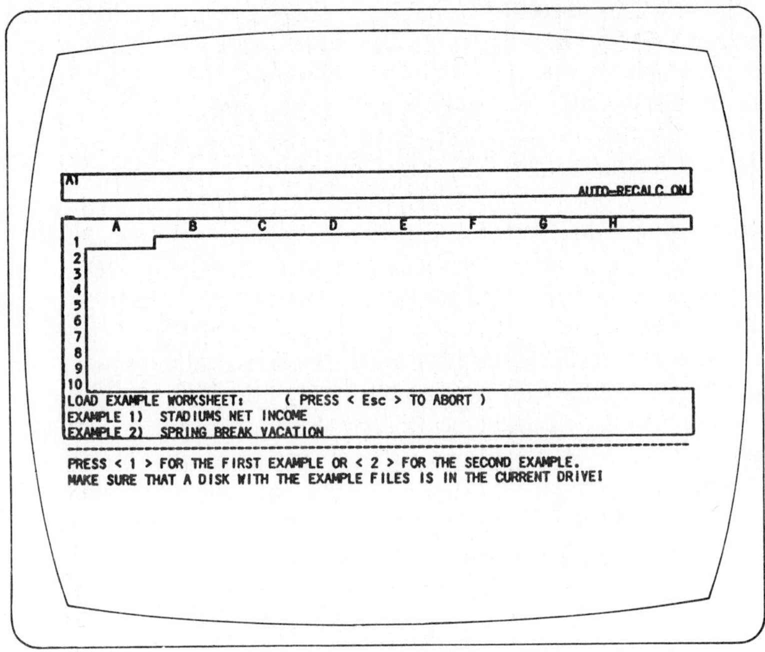

2. Press 1, and the STADIUMS NET INCOME example is loaded into the worksheet (see Figure 11–9).

SAVE WORKSHEET. The SAVE WORKSHEET command allows for a maximum of two worksheets to be saved. Once a worksheet has been saved, you can load it and work on it later. If, for any reason, you exit the WestCalc spreadsheet program, the worksheet currently displayed on the monitor is lost unless the SAVE WORKSHEET command is executed.

To execute the SAVE WORKSHEET command, press the <F6> function key to access the STORAGE submenu; then press <F2>. The program then asks, ARE YOU SURE THAT YOU WANT TO SAVE YOUR WORK AT THIS TIME? (Y/N) If you press N (for no), the worksheet is not saved and the normal command and help area messages are returned to the screen. If you press Y (for yes), the program displays the number of worksheets saved and the instruction ENTER NAME OF WORKSHEET TO BE SAVED. The name may contain a maximum of eight characters, and the valid characters include the letters A through Z and the numbers 1 through 9.

If you have saved fewer than two worksheets, entering the worksheet name and pressing the RETURN key will save the worksheet displayed on the screen. If you have already saved two worksheets, the program will ask if one of the worksheets should be erased. If you press Y (for yes), the indicated worksheet will be erased and the worksheet displayed on the screen will be saved. If you press N (for no), the program will ask if the second worksheet should be erased. If you press Y (for yes), the second worksheet will be erased and the worksheet displayed on the monitor will be saved. If you press N (for no) or <Esc>, neither worksheet will be erased.

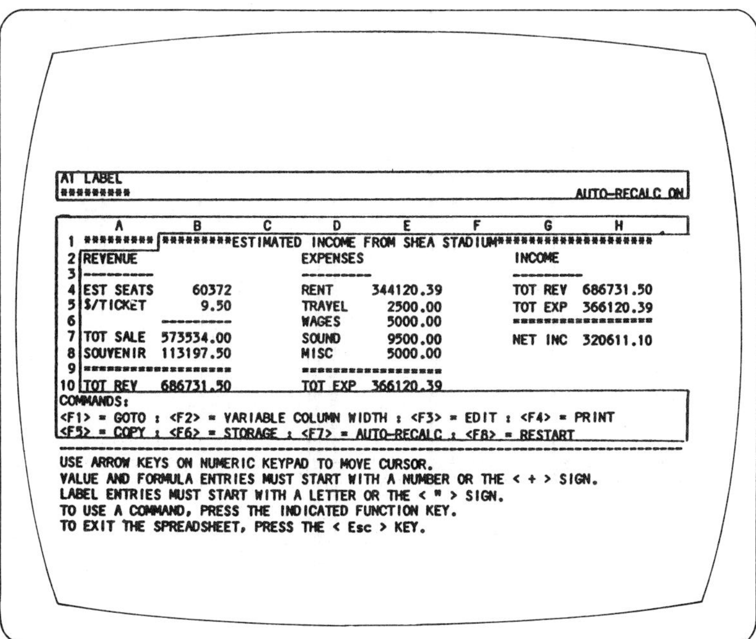

Figure 11–9
STADIUMS NET INCOME EXAMPLE SCREEN

The command and help areas will then be cleared and new messages displayed.

An important point to remember is when you try to save a worksheet and there are already two worksheets saved, you will have to erase one of the two in storage. Be careful not to erase a worksheet you need. Once a worksheet is erased, there is no way to access it again.

YOUR TURN

As a hands-on activity, use the SAVE WORKSHEET command with the STADIUMS NET INCOME example. The following steps serve as a guide:

1. Execute the SAVE WORKSHEET command by pressing <F6> to access the STORAGE submenu (see Figure 11–7) and then press <F2> When this is done, the command and help areas are cleared and new messages appear (see Figure 11–10).
2. The program asks, ARE YOU SURE THAT YOU WANT TO SAVE YOUR WORK AT THIS TIME? (Y/N). Press Y (for yes), and the command and help areas appear as in Figure 11–11. Enter the name STADIUMS and press the RETURN key. Now you have saved a worksheet entitled STADIUMS.

LOAD WORKSHEET. The LOAD WORKSHEET command loads a previously saved worksheet into the spreadsheet program and erases the worksheet currently in use. To activate this command, press the <F6> key to enter

Figure 11–10
SCREEN 1 OF THE SAVE WORKSHEET COMMAND

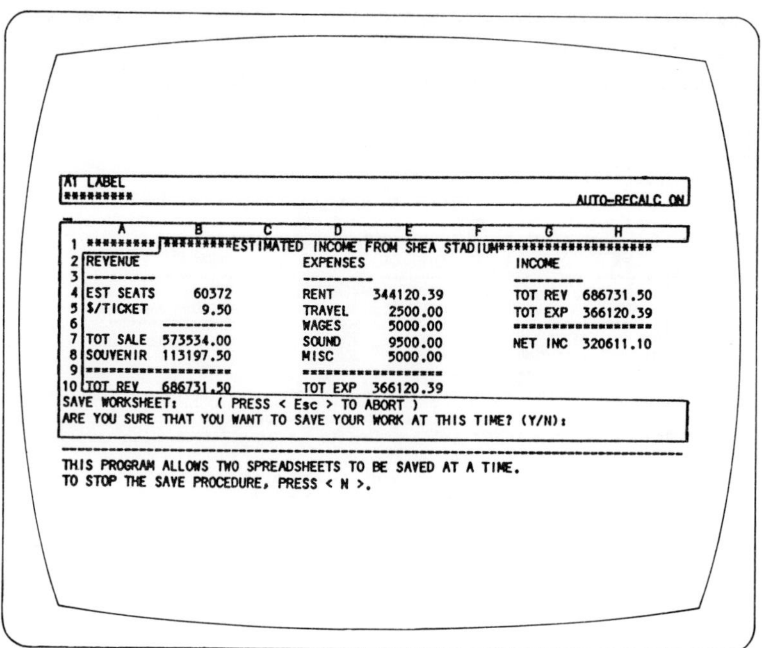

Figure 11–11
SCREEN 2 OF SAVE WORKSHEET COMMAND

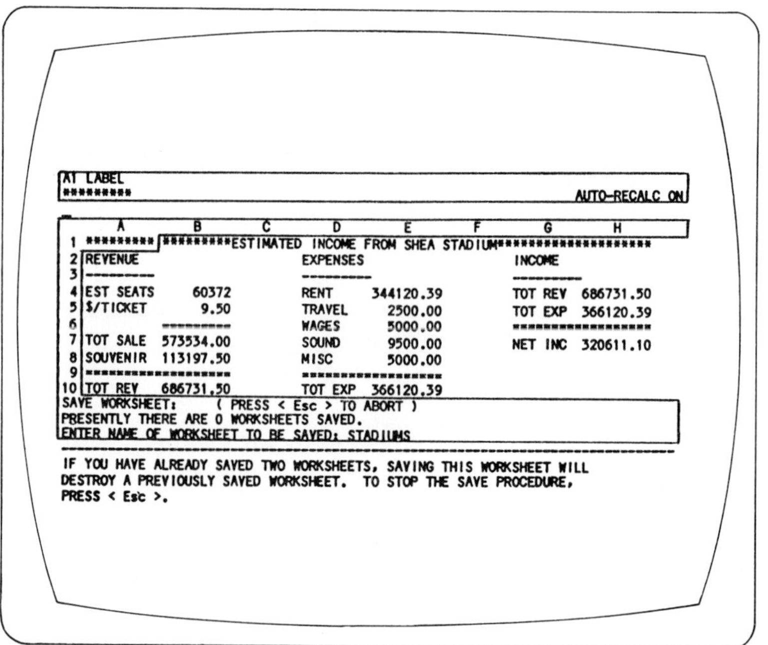

the STORAGE submenu and then press <F1>. To load a worksheet, press 1 or 2 and the program loads the indicated worksheet. (If there is no previously saved worksheet, the program loads a blank worksheet.) If you do not want to load a worksheet, press <Esc>. This will not change the worksheet currently in the spreadsheet program.

YOUR TURN

Use the LOAD WORKSHEET command to load the STADIUMS worksheet (which was previously saved) into the spreadsheet program. The following steps serve as a guide:

1. Execute the LOAD WORKSHEET command by pressing the <F6> to access the STORAGE submenu and then pressing <F1>.
2. You are then prompted to select a worksheet (see Figure 11–12). Press 1, and the worksheet is loaded.

RESTART. To start a new worksheet, you must execute the RESTART command (<F8>) by pressing the <F8> key. When this command is executed, the program asks, ARE YOU SURE YOU WANT TO START OVER AT THIS TIME? (Y/N). If you are certain that you want to start over, press Y (for yes). If you do not want to start over, press N (for no). If you press N, the worksheet is not changed. If you press Y, however, the worksheet is cleared, and all label, value, and formula entries currently in the worksheet are destroyed.

Use the RESTART command to restart the STADIUMS NET INCOME worksheet saved in the previous section. (This worksheet should still be displayed on the screen.) The following steps serve as a guide:

1. Execute the RESTART command (press <F8>).
2. You are then asked, ARE YOU SURE YOU WANT TO START OVER AT

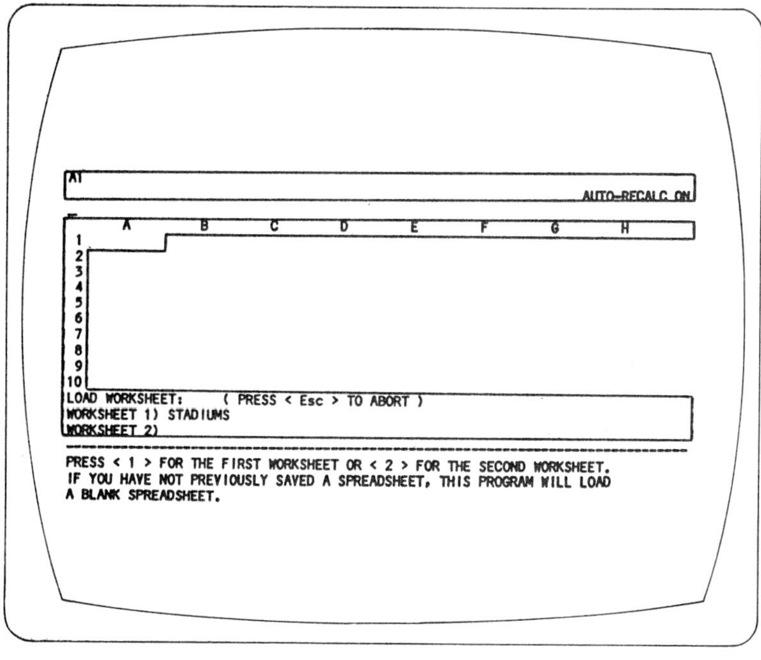

Figure 11–12
LOAD WORKSHEET COMMAND

THIS TIME? (Y/N) (see Figure 11–13). Press Y; the STADIUMS NET INCOME worksheet is removed from the screen, and a blank worksheet appears.

GOTO. The GOTO command is used to move the cursor directly from one cell to another without using the arrow keys. To execute this command, press the <F1> function key. When executed, the program asks you to enter the coordinate of the cell you would like to go to. Enter the coordinate in column and row format and press the RETURN key. To cancel the GOTO command, press <Esc>.

For instance, if the cursor were located at coordinate A1 and you wanted to move the cursor to coordinate T15, first execute the GOTO command by pressing <F1>. The program would then prompt you to enter the coordinate of the cell you wanted to go to. In this case, you would enter T15 and press the RETURN key. The cursor would then be positioned at coordinate T15.

Use the GOTO command to go to a coordinate in the STADIUMS NET INCOME example worksheet. The following steps serve as a guide:

1. The STADIUMS NET INCOME worksheet should already be loaded. Execute the GOTO command by pressing the <F1> function key. When

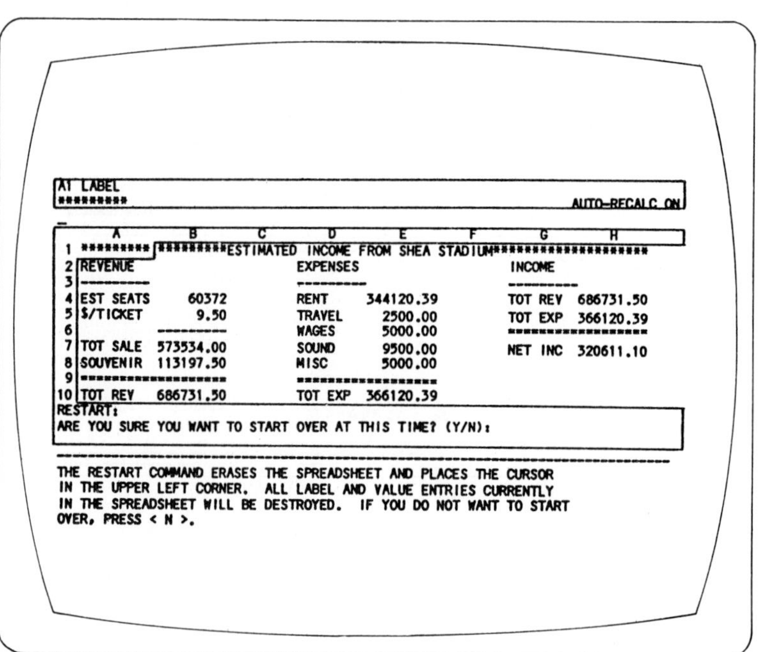

Figure 11–13
RESTART COMMAND

this is done, the command and help areas are cleared, and new messages appear (see Figure 11–14).

2. The program instructs, ENTER THE COORDINATE OF THE CELL YOU WOULD LIKE TO GOTO. Enter D10 and press the RETURN key. The cursor is now located at coordinate D10.

VARIABLE COLUMN WIDTH. The VARIABLE COLUMN WIDTH command allows the column width to be changed. For example, if you have a title that is twenty characters long, you can change the width of the column so the entire title will be displayed on the screen. This command is executed by pressing the <F2> function key. A column width may be as small as three or as large as thirty characters. To abort this command, press the <Esc> key.

YOUR TURN

Use the VARIABLE COLUMN WIDTH command to vary the width of a column in the STADIUMS NET INCOME example. The following steps serve as a guide:

1. The STADIUMS NET INCOME worksheet should be loaded from the previous hands-on activity. Position the cursor at coordinate A1, and execute the VARIABLE COLUMN WIDTH command by pressing <F2>. When this is done, the command and help areas are cleared, and new messages appear (see Figure 11–15).

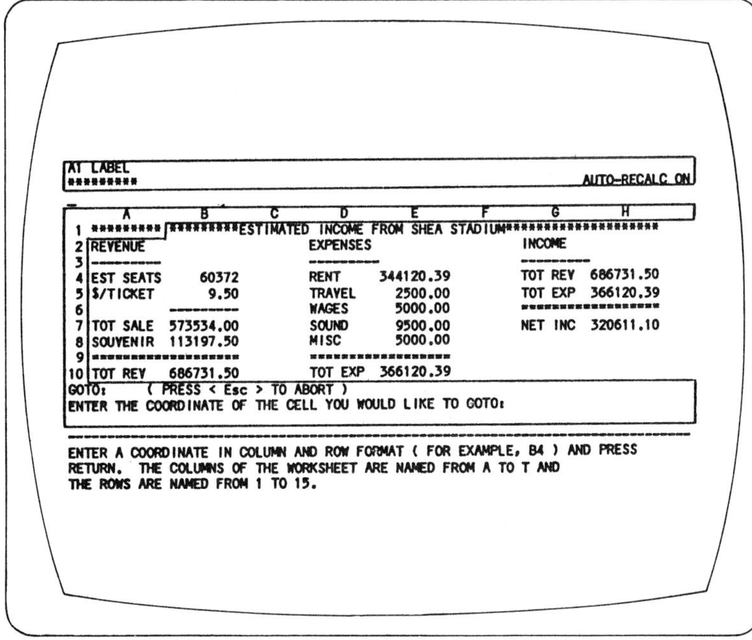

Figure 11–14
GOTO COMMAND

Figure 11–15
VARIABLE COLUMN WIDTH COMMAND

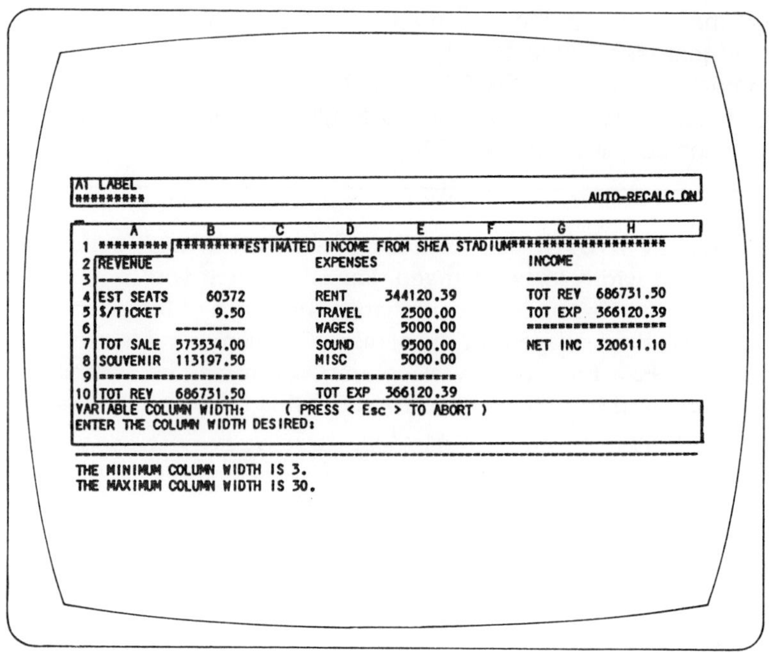

2. The program then instructs, ENTER THE COLUMN WIDTH DESIRED. Enter 3 and notice what happens to the worksheet. Execute the command again and enter 30. Now, go back and change the column width to 9.

EDIT. The EDIT command is a general command used to access the FORMAT A CELL, BLANK A CELL, INSERT ROW/COLUMN, and DELETE ROW/COLUMN commands. To access the edit commands, first press the <F3> function key (for the PCjr, press the <Fn> and <F3> keys at the same time), which accesses the EDIT submenu. The specific edit commands are discussed in the following four sections.

FORMAT A CELL. The FORMAT A CELL command, is used to display the numeric data in three forms: integer, floating point, and dollar. The integer form specifies that the numeric data does not contain decimal places. The floating-point form specifies that the numeric data contains as many decimal places as you desire. The dollar form specifies that the numeric data contains two decimal places. To use the FORMAT A CELL command, first press <F3> to access the EDIT submenu (see Figure 11–16). Then press <F1>. If you do not execute this command, the format automatically defaults to the dollar form.

As a hands-on activity, use the FORMAT A CELL command in the STADIUMS NET INCOME example. The following steps serve as a guide:

1. The STADIUMS NET INCOME example should already be loaded into

A1
AUTO-RECALC ON
A B C D E F G H
1
2
3
4
5
6
7
8
9
10
EDIT: (PRESS < Esc > TO ABORT)
<F1> = FORMAT A CELL : <F2> = BLANK A CELL
<F3> = DELETE ROW/COLUMN : <F4> = INSERT ROW/COLUMN
PRESS THE APPROPRIATE FUNCTION KEY FOR THE DESIRED COMMAND.

Figure 11–16
EDIT SUBMENU

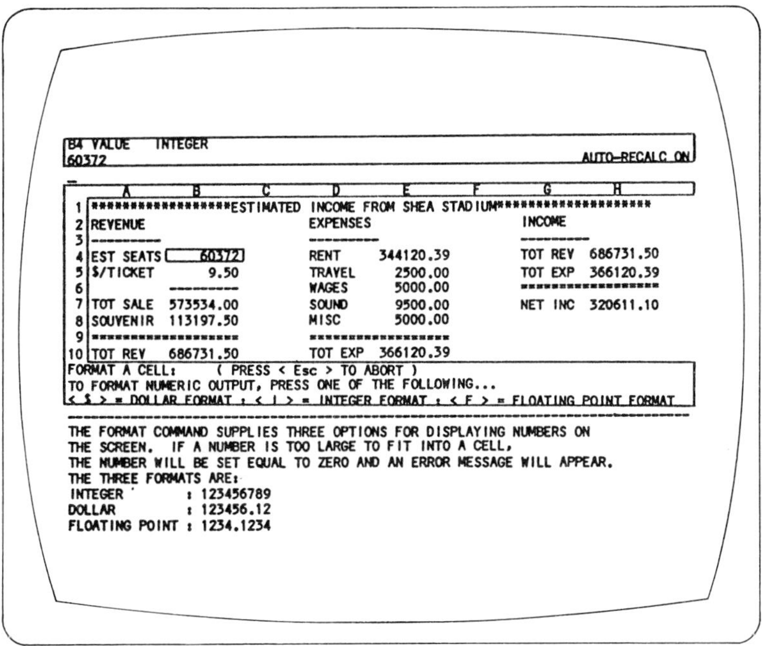

B4 VALUE INTEGER
60372
AUTO-RECALC ON
A B C D E F G H
1 ******************ESTIMATED INCOME FROM SHEA STADIUM******************
2 REVENUE EXPENSES INCOME
4 EST SEATS 60372 RENT 344120.39 TOT REV 686731.50
5 $/TICKET 9.50 TRAVEL 2500.00 TOT EXP 366120.39
6 WAGES 5000.00
7 TOT SALE 573534.00 SOUND 9500.00 NET INC 320611.10
8 SOUVENIR 113197.50 MISC 5000.00
10 TOT REV 686731.50 TOT EXP 366120.39
FORMAT A CELL: (PRESS < Esc > TO ABORT)
TO FORMAT NUMERIC OUTPUT, PRESS ONE OF THE FOLLOWING...
< $ > = DOLLAR FORMAT : < I > = INTEGER FORMAT : < F > = FLOATING POINT FORMAT
THE FORMAT COMMAND SUPPLIES THREE OPTIONS FOR DISPLAYING NUMBERS ON
THE SCREEN. IF A NUMBER IS TOO LARGE TO FIT INTO A CELL,
THE NUMBER WILL BE SET EQUAL TO ZERO AND AN ERROR MESSAGE WILL APPEAR.
THE THREE FORMATS ARE:
INTEGER : 123456789
DOLLAR : 123456.12
FLOATING POINT : 1234.1234

Figure 11–17
FORMAT A CELL COMMAND

the spreadsheet from the previous hands-on-activity. Move the cursor over to the coordinate B4 by using the arrow keys.

2. Execute the FORMAT A CELL command by pressing <F3> to access the EDIT submenu, and then pressing <F1> (see Figure 11–17). Now select FLOATING POINT by pressing <F>. The status area now reads B4

VALUE FLOATING POINT, and the coordinate B4 contains 60372.0 instead of 60372.

BLANK A CELL. The BLANK A CELL command is used to clear an individual cell. To execute the BLANK A CELL command, first press <F3> to access the EDIT submenu. Then press <F2>. When you execute this command, the cell containing the cursor is cleared; that is, the contents of that cell are erased.

Once the cell location has been cleared, you may enter a value, label, or formula. You may also elect to enter nothing in that particular cell location and move the cursor to another cell location.

YOUR TURN

Use the BLANK A CELL command to erase the label RENT from the coordinate D4. The following steps serve as a guide:

1. The STADIUMS NET INCOME example should still be loaded from the previous hands-on activity.
2. Move the cursor to the coordinate D4. Execute the BLANK A CELL command (press <F3> to access the EDIT submenu, and then press <F2>), and you will notice that the label RENT is erased (see Figure 11–18).
3. Go back to the coordinate D4, and reenter the label RENT.

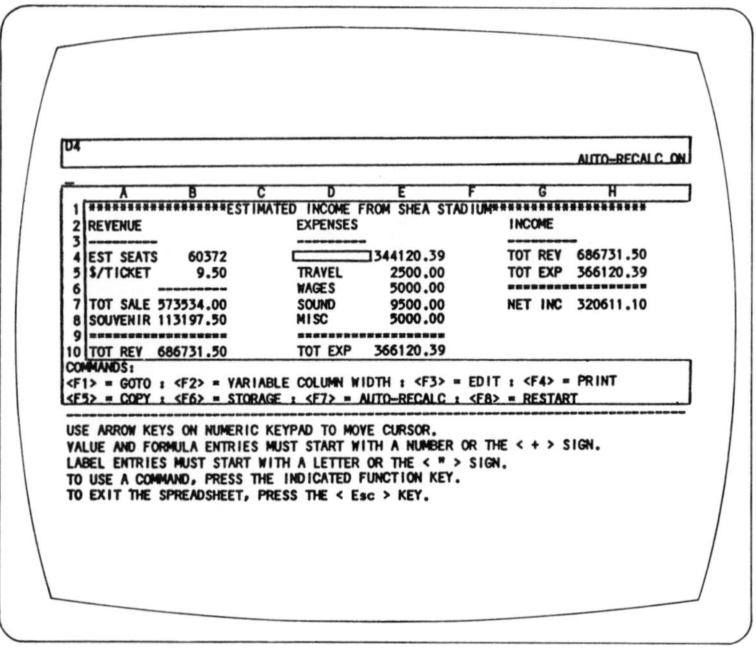

Figure 11–18
BLANK A CELL COMMAND

INSERT ROW/COLUMN. The INSERT ROW/COLUMN command is used to insert a blank row or column into the worksheet. To execute this command, press <F3> to access the EDIT submenu, and then press <F4>. The program will prompt you to enter an R for ROW INSERTION, or C for COLUMN INSERTION. After you have made your selection, the program will insert a blank row or column for the length of the worksheet.

If a ROW INSERTION is executed, all of the rows below the cursor will shift down one row to make room for the new row. Also, the last row of the worksheet will be moved off the screen entirely. If the last row contains data, the program will not perform the insertion. Instead, an error message is displayed and the insertion is aborted (see Figure 11–19).

If a COLUMN INSERTION is executed, all of the columns to the right of the cursor will be shifted to the right to make room for the new column. If there is data entered in the last column, an error message is displayed and the insertion is aborted (see Figure 11–20).

YOUR TURN

As a hands-on activity, use the INSERT ROW/COLUMN command in the STADIUMS NET INCOME example. The following steps serve as a guide:

1. The STADIUMS NET INCOME example should be loaded. Move the cursor to coordinate C1. Execute the INSERT ROW/COLUMN command by pressing <F3> to access the EDIT submenu, and then press <F4> (see Figure 11–21).

2. The program prompts, ENTER R FOR ROW INSERTION, OR C FOR COLUMN INSERTION. Enter a C for COLUMN INSERTION. Note how the

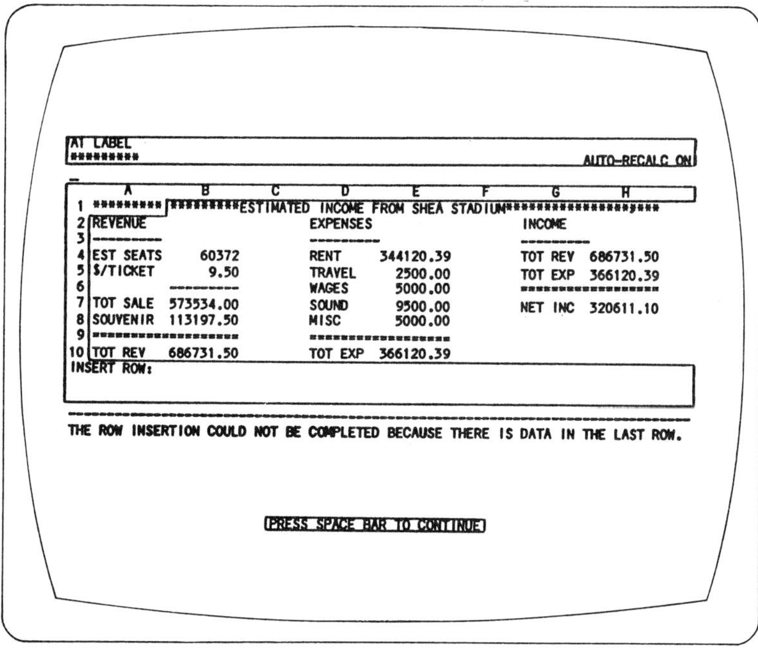

Figure 11–19
ROW INSERTION ERROR

Figure 11–20
COLUMN INSERTION ERROR

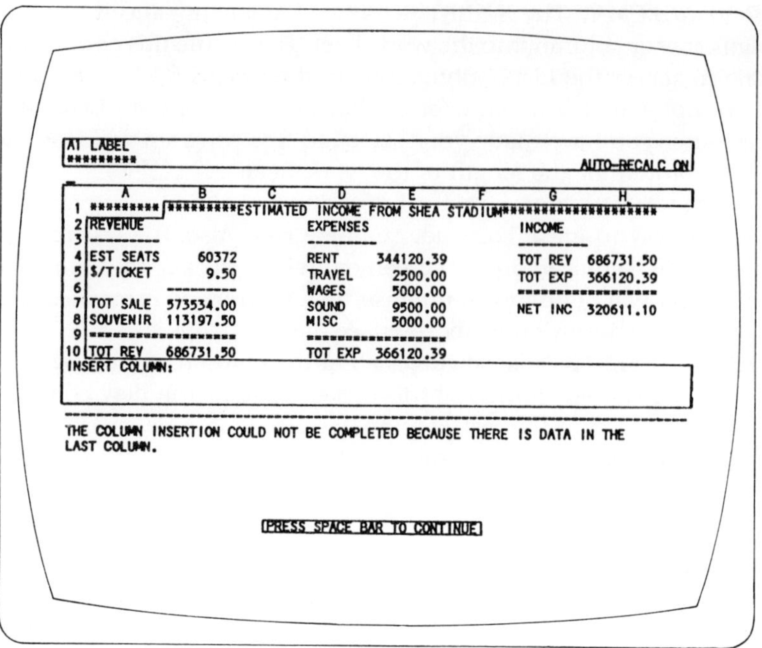

Figure 11–21
INSERT ROW/COLUMN COMMAND

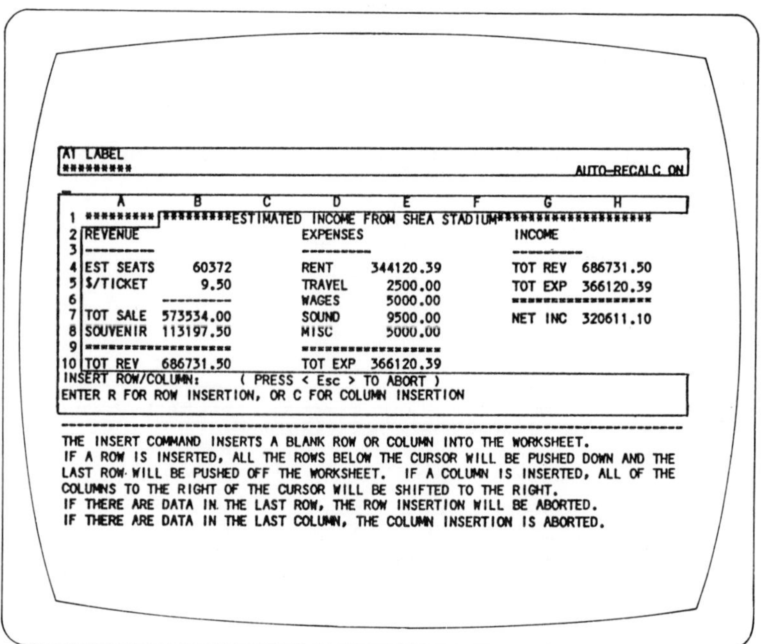

columns to the right of the cursor have shifted right one column. At this point you type in formulas, labels, or numeric entries.

3. Execute the LOAD EXAMPLE WORKSHEET command, and select the STADIUMS NET INCOME example. Now execute the INSERT ROW/ COLUMN command, and do a row insertion. Note how the rows below the cursor have shifted down one row. At this point you may enter formulas, labels, or numeric entries.

4. Load the STADIUMS NET INCOME example for the next hands-on activity.

DELETE ROW/COLUMN. The DELETE ROW/COLUMN command will delete, or remove, a row or column from the worksheet. To use the DELETE ROW/COLUMN command, press <F3> to access the EDIT submenu. Then press <F3> again, and the program will prompt, ENTER R FOR ROW DELETION, OR C FOR COLUMN DELETION. After you have made your selection (R or C), the program will delete the row or column where the cursor is positioned for the length of the worksheet. If you execute the DELETE ROW/COLUMN command by mistake, press the <Esc> key to abort the operation.

YOUR TURN

As a hands-on activity, use the DELETE ROW/COLUMN command in the STADIUMS NET INCOME example. The following steps serve as a guide:

1. With the STADIUMS NET INCOME example already loaded, move the cursor to coordinate A1.

2. Execute the DELETE command by pressing <F3> to access the EDIT submenu. Then press <F3> again (see Figure 11–22).

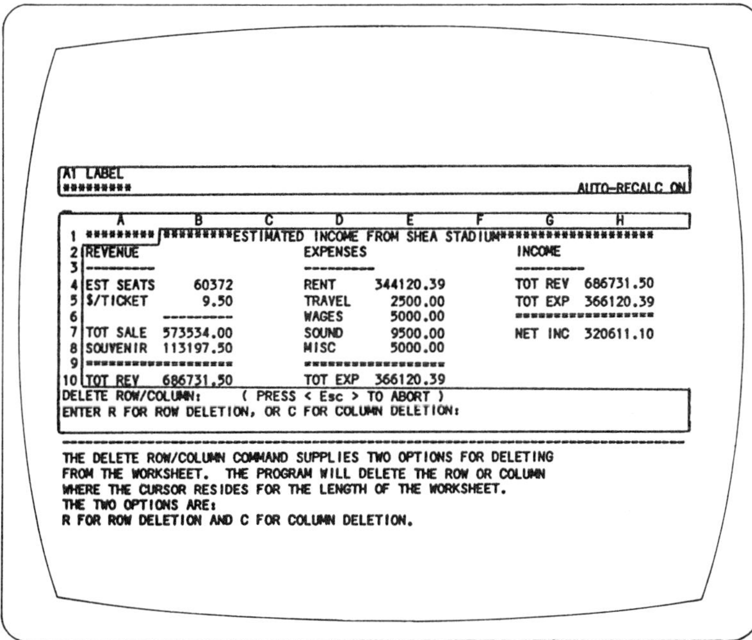

Figure 11–22
DELETE ROW/COLUMN COMMAND

3. The program prompts, ENTER R FOR ROW DELETION, OR C FOR COLUMN DELETION. Enter an R, and notice that the row has been deleted. Execute the DELETE command again, and enter a C. Now, the entire column has been deleted.
4. Do not save this worksheet! Instead, load the STADIUMS NET INCOME example again (see the LOAD EXAMPLE WORKSHEET command).

PRINT. The PRINT command prints all or any part of the worksheet currently in memory. This command is executed by pressing the <F4> key. The program asks you to enter the first cell location where printing should begin. To print the entire worksheet enter A1.

After entering the first cell location where printing should begin, the program prompts you to enter the location of the last cell to be printed. Enter the cell location where printing should stop. To print the entire worksheet, enter T15.

After the last cell is entered, the program displays the printer defaults. Printer defaults represent the conditions under which the spreadsheet or a portion of the spreadsheet will be printed.

The program then tells you to ready the printer. This is the last message from the spreadsheet program before it begins to send information to the printer. Make sure that the power to the printer is on, that the printer is on-line (connected to the computer), and that you have enough paper installed in the printer. Once you are satisfied that these conditions are met, the RETURN key should be pressed.

YOUR TURN

As a hands-on activity, the PRINT command can be used so that you can print the STADIUMS NET INCOME worksheet. The following steps serve as a guide:

1. Press <F4>. The screen then looks like the one shown in Figure 11–23.
2. Next, the instruction ENTER FIRST CELL LOCATION TO BE PRINTED appears. Enter A1 and press RETURN.
3. The program then prompts, ENTER LAST CELL LOCATION TO BE PRINTED (see Figure 11–24). Enter H7, and press the RETURN key.
4. The program then displays the ENTER PRINTER DEFAULTS (see Figure 11–25).
5. Next, the program prompts, READY PRINTER (see Figure 11–26). Make sure that the printer is on, that the printer is on-line, and that you have enough paper installed in the printer. Next, press the RETURN key to begin printing.
6. Once printing is complete, the program will return to the worksheet currently being worked on.

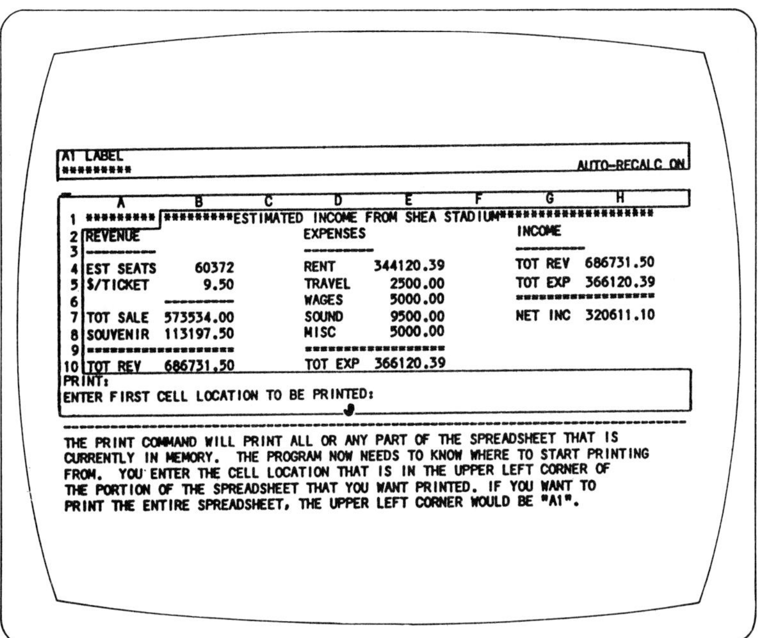

Figure 11–23
SCREEN 1 OF PRINT COMMAND

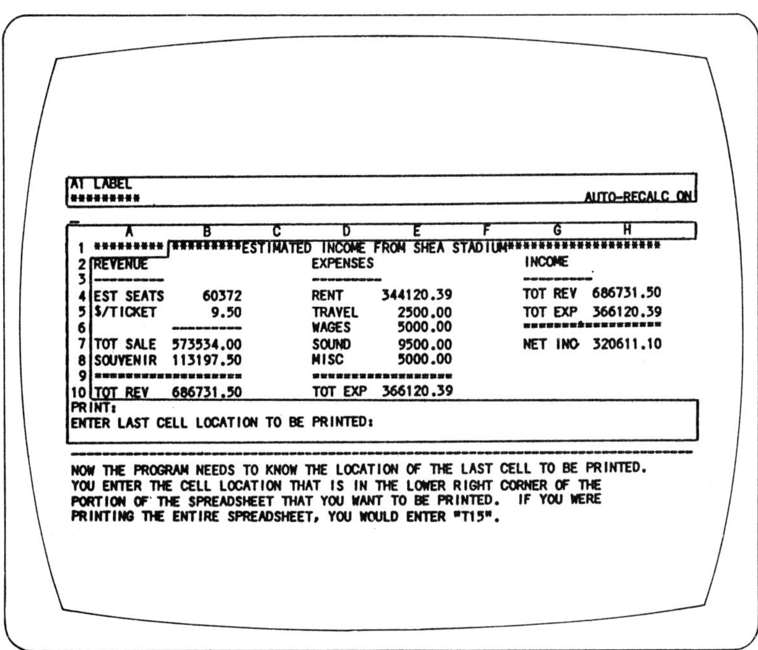

Figure 11–24
SCREEN 2 OF PRINT COMMAND

COPY. The COPY command will copy a single cell, a row of cells, or a column of cells from one location in the worksheet to another location. To execute the COPY command, press the <F5> key.

The program will prompt, ENTER THE CELL LOCATION(S) TO BE COPIED. You then enter the coordinates of the first and last cells to be copied,

Figure 11–25
SCREEN 3 OF PRINT COMMAND

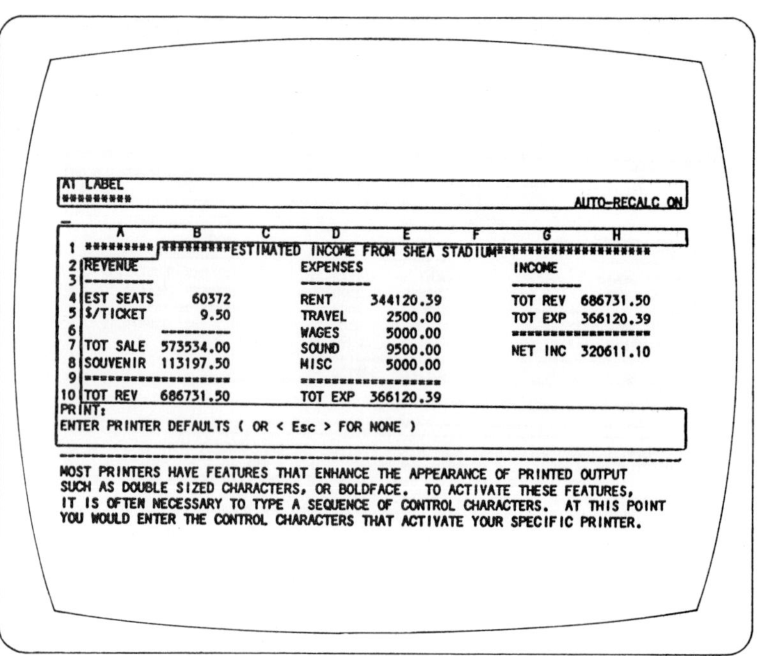

Figure 11–26
SCREEN 4 OF PRINT COMMAND

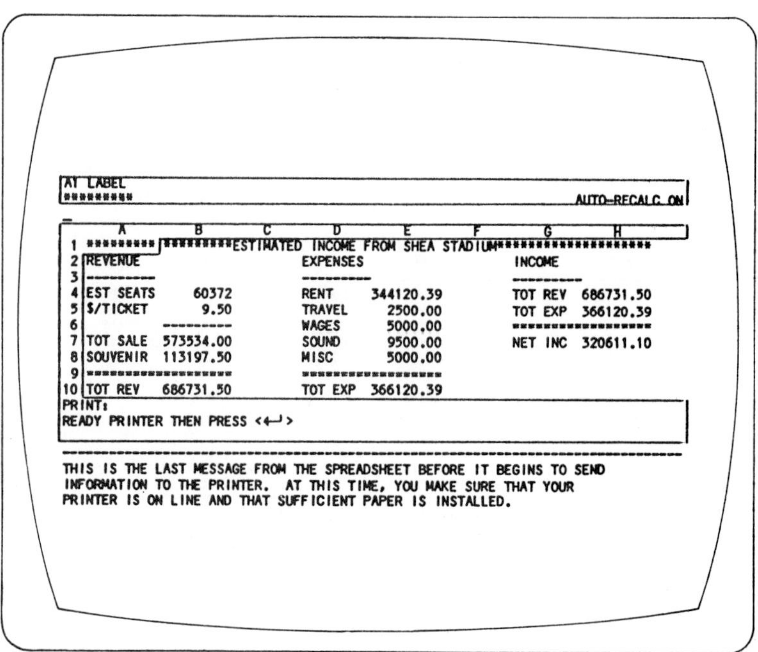

separated by a hyphen. For example, to copy cells D1 through D9, type D1-D9 and press the RETURN key.

The program responds by prompting, ENTER THE CELL LOCATION(S) WHERE DATA IS TO BE COPIED TO. You would then enter the coordinates of the first and last cells to receive the copy, separated by a hyphen. For example, type F1-F9, and press the RETURN key. The program will copy the cells to the new location.

If you want to copy a single cell, enter the cell coordinate to be copied and press the RETURN key. Then enter the cell coordinate that will receive the copy and press the RETURN key.

If the number of cells copied does not equal the number of cells to receive the copy, the computer alerts you to the situation. If you try to copy, for example, cells A1-A4 (four cells) to D1-D3 (three cells), the program will ask, DO YOU WANT TO CONTINUE COPY? (Y/N). If you respond with Y (for yes), the program will copy as many cells as room allows. In this case, cells A1-A3 will be copied to cells D1-D3. If you answer N (for no), the copy will be aborted.

YOUR TURN

As a hands-on activity, use the COPY command with the STADIUMS NET INCOME example. The following steps serve as a guide:

1. The STADIUMS NET INCOME example should be loaded from the previous hands-on activity. Move the cursor to coordinate G2. Execute the COPY command by pressing <F5>.
2. The program will prompt, ENTER THE CELL LOCATION(S) TO BE COPIED. Enter G2-G7, and press the RETURN key (see Figure 11–27). The program prompts with ENTER CELL LOCATION(S) WHERE DATA IS TO BE COPIED TO. Enter J8-J13, and press the RETURN key (see Figure 11–28). Note the result.

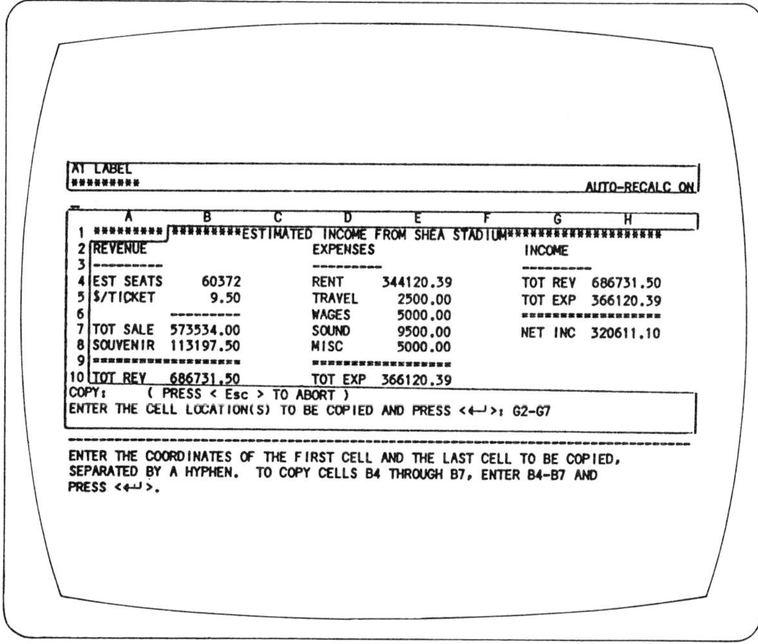

Figure 11–27
SCREEN 1 OF COPY COMMAND

Figure 11–28
SCREEN 2 OF COPY COMMAND

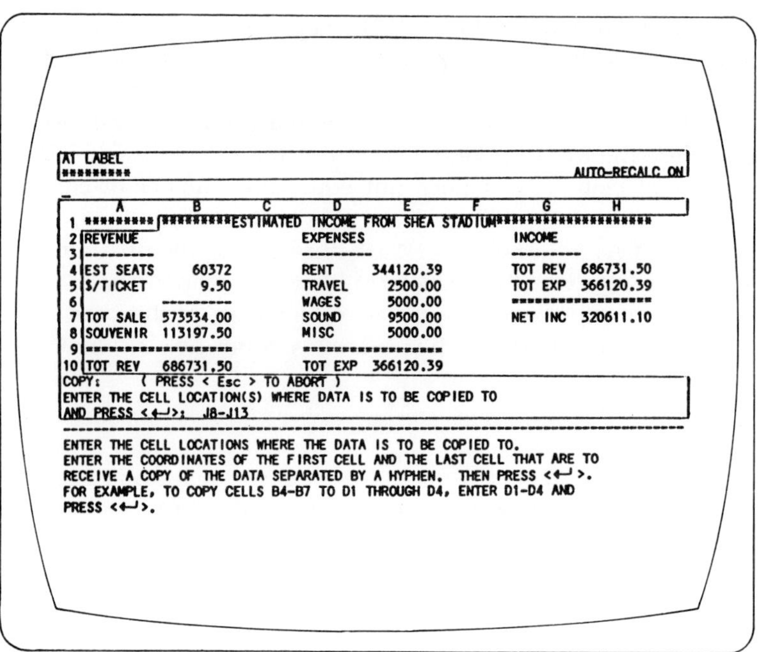

Figure 11–29
ERROR IN COPY SCREEN

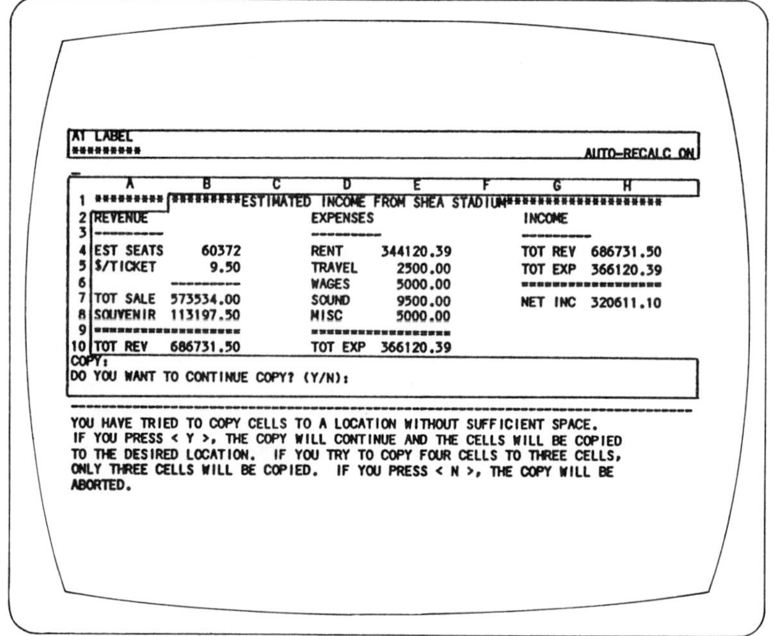

3. Delete cells J8-J13. Copy cells G2-G7 to cells J1-J3. The program will ask, DO YOU WANT TO CONTINUE COPY? (Y/N) (see Figure 11–29). Enter Y (for yes), and note the result.
4. Delete cells J1-J3.

AUTO-RECALC. The AUTO-RECALC command automatically recalculates all the cells that contain formulas every time a numeric entry is made into the worksheet.

When you first enter the WestCalc spreadsheet program, the STATUS area will display AUTO-RECALC ON. This indicates that the AUTO-RECALC command is on. When the status area displays AUTO-RECALC OFF, the AUTO-RECALC command is off. To switch, or toggle, between the ON and OFF states, press <F7>.

The purpose of the AUTO-RECALC command is to shorten the time it takes the program to accept the data you are entering. If you are building a new spreadsheet model, you may not need to constantly update the cells.

As a hands-on activity, use the AUTO-RECALC command with the STADIUMS NET INCOME example. The following steps serve as a guide:

1. With the STADIUMS NET INCOME example loaded, move the cursor to coordinate B4. Execute the AUTO-RECALC command by pressing <F7>.
2. The STATUS AREA now says OFF. Change the integer value 60372, to the integer value 50000. Note that the program does not recalculate (see Figure 11–30).
3. Execute the AUTO-RECALC command again, and notice that the program recalculates and displays the new values. Also, the STATUS AREA says ON (see Figure 11–31).
4. Change cell B4 back to its original integer value of 60372.

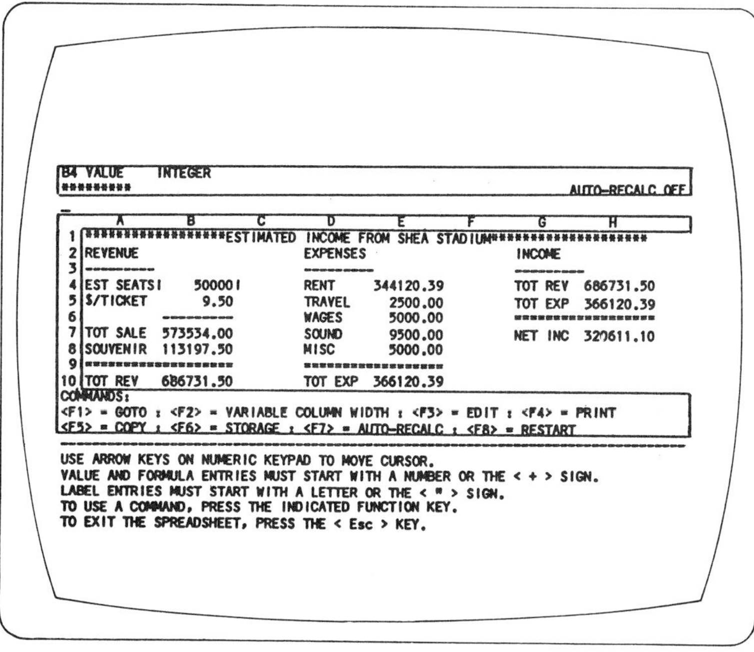

Figure 11–30
SCREEN 1 OF AUTO-RECALC EXAMPLE

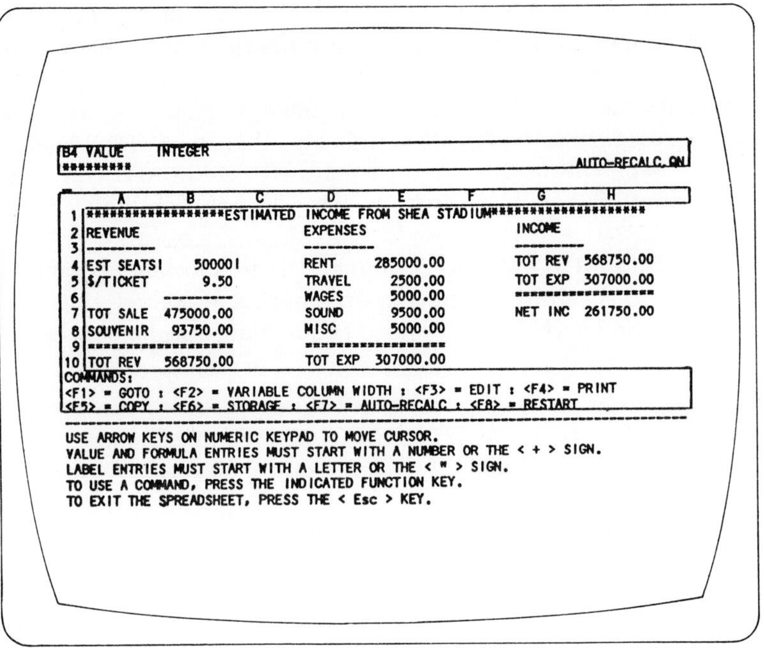

Figure 11–31
SCREEN 2 OF AUTO-RECALC EXAMPLE

Creating the GPA Worksheet

The following activity provides a step-by-step explanation for creating a new worksheet. The worksheet contains the data necessary to compute a student's grade-point average (GPA) at a local university.

YOUR TURN

As a hands-on activity, the following steps serve as a guide to creating the GPA worksheet.

1. At the coordinate C1, enter the label COURSE. At D1, enter the label HOURS with four spaces before the H. At E1, enter the label GRADE with four spaces before the G. At F1, enter the label POINTS with three spaces before the P. And at G1, enter the label GPA with six spaces before the G (see Figure 11–32).

2. At C4, enter the label MIS 200. For the coordinates C5-C8, enter the following labels:

Coordinate	Label
C5	ACCT 221
C6	CALCULUS
C7	PHYS ED
C8	ENGLISH

3. At D4, execute the FORMAT A CELL command by pressing <F3> to access the EDIT submenu. Then press <F1>. Next, press the letter I to

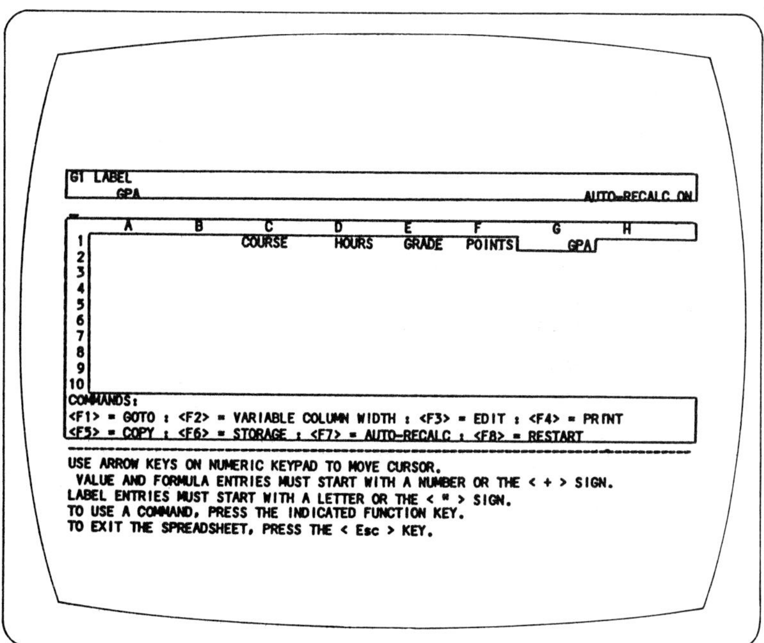

Figure 11–32
ENTERING LABELS INTO GPA WORKSHEET

format the cell for an integer value (see Figure 11–33). Then enter the value 3. For the coordinates D5-D8, format the cell as integer values, and then enter the values as shown below:

Coordinate	Format	Value
D5	INTEGER	3
D6	INTEGER	4
D7	INTEGER	1
D8	INTEGER	3

4. At E4, format the cell for floating point, and enter the value 4.0. For the coordinates E5-E8, format the cell as floating point values and enter the values.

Coordinate	Format	Value
E5	FLT. PT.	3.0
E6	FLT. PT.	3.5
E7	FLT. PT.	4.0
E8	FLT. PT.	3.0

5. At F4, enter the points earned. First, format the cell for floating point. Second, press the plus sign key (+) to enter a formula. Enter the formula D4*E4 to calculate total points for MIS200. Notice that the formula is displayed in the status area and the answer is displayed in Cell F4. For the coordinates F5-F8 enter the following:

Coordinate	Format	Formula
F5	FLT. PT.	D5*E5 (total points for ACCT 221)
F6	FLT. PT.	D6*E6 (total points for CALCULUS)
F7	FLT. PT.	D7*E7 (total points for PHYS ED)
F8	FLT. PT.	D8*E8 (total points for ENGLISH)

Figure 11–33
FORMATTING A CELL

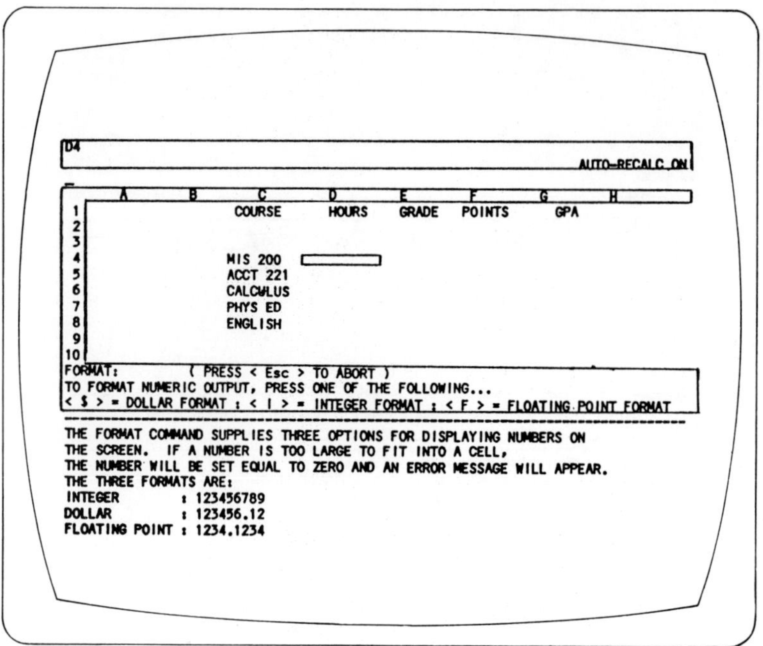
D4
AUTO-RECALC ON
A B C D E F G H
1 COURSE HOURS GRADE POINTS GPA
2
3
4 MIS 200
5 ACCT 221
6 CALCWLUS
7 PHYS ED
8 ENGLISH
9
10
FORMAT: (PRESS < Esc > TO ABORT)
TO FORMAT NUMERIC OUTPUT, PRESS ONE OF THE FOLLOWING...
< $ > = DOLLAR FORMAT : < I > = INTEGER FORMAT : < F > = FLOATING POINT FORMAT
THE FORMAT COMMAND SUPPLIES THREE OPTIONS FOR DISPLAYING NUMBERS ON
THE SCREEN. IF A NUMBER IS TOO LARGE TO FIT INTO A CELL,
THE NUMBER WILL BE SET EQUAL TO ZERO AND AN ERROR MESSAGE WILL APPEAR.
THE THREE FORMATS ARE:
INTEGER : 123456789
DOLLAR : 123456.12
FLOATING POINT : 1234.1234

6. At C2, enter the label --------. Remember to press the double quotation mark key (") first. Enter the same label for the coordinates D2, E2, F2, and G2.
7. At the coordinates D9 and F9, enter the label = = = = = = = = = .
8. At D10, format the cell for an integer value. Then enter the formula D4 + D5 + D6 + D7 + D8. Remember, a formula must begin with the plus sign (+). (See Figure 11–34).
9. At F10, format the cell for a floating point value and enter the formula F4 + F5 + F6 + F7 + F8.
10. At G10, format the cell for a dollar value and enter the formula F10/D10. This displays the student's grade point average (see Figure 11–35).

WestCalc Messages

```
1. CURRENTLY THAT CHARACTER IS NOT ALLOWED
   IN A VALUE ENTRY. YOUR OPTIONS ARE. . .
   NUMBERS 0 THRU 9
   CELLS A1 THRU T15
   CHARACTERS + - . (
```

Numbers other than 0 through 9 have been entered, cell locations other than A1 through T15 have been entered or characters other than + − . (have been entered in a value entry.

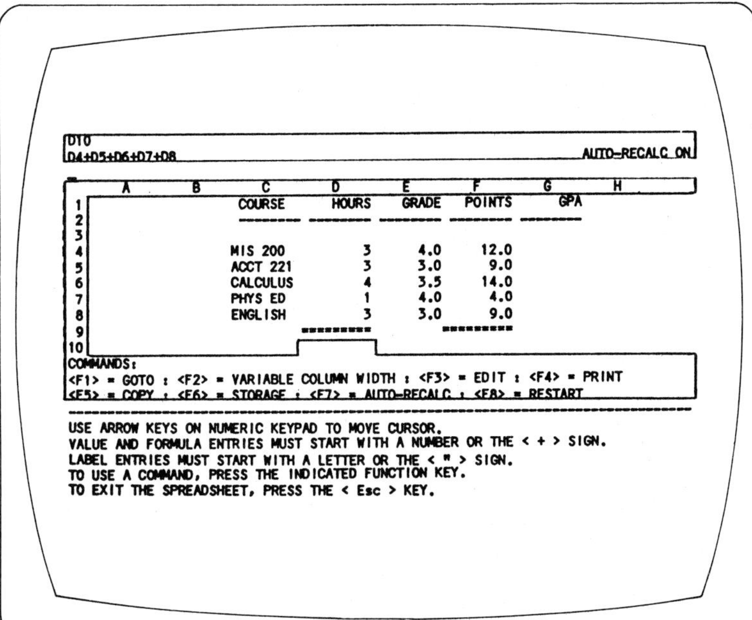

Figure 11–34
ENTERING A FORMULA INTO GPA WORKSHEET

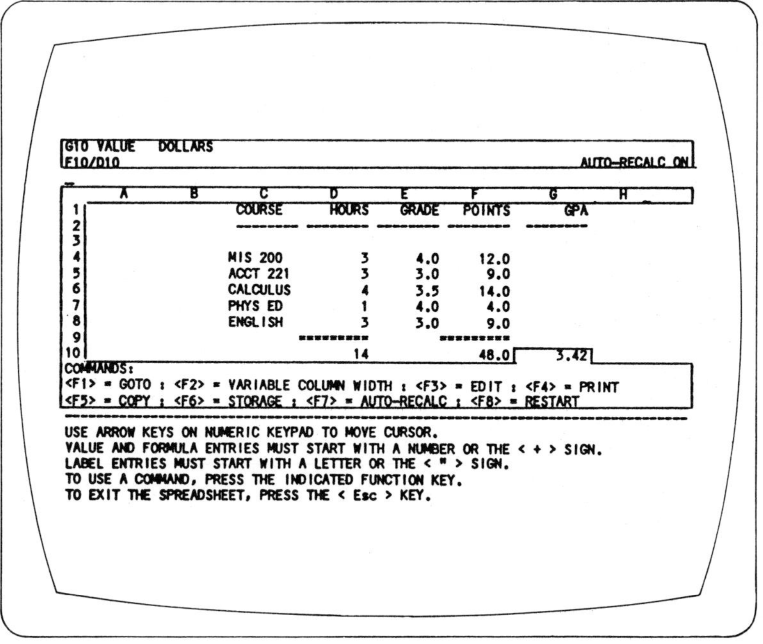

Figure 11–35
ENTERING A FORMULA INTO CELL G10

2. CURRENTLY THAT CHARACTER IS NOT ALLOWED
   IN A VALUE ENTRY. YOUR OPTIONS ARE. . .
   NUMBERS 0 THRU 9
   CHARACTERS + – * / .)

   You have tried to use a character that cannot be used for a value entry. You may enter the numbers 0 through 9 and the following characters: + – * / .).

3. EACH CELL CAN HOLD ONLY 30 CHARACTERS
IF YOU NEED TO ENTER MORE THAN 30, YOU
MUST DIVIDE THE ENTRY BETWEEN 2 CELLS

A label, value, or formula entry that has more than thirty characters has been entered.

4. ERROR

You have tried to perform an incorrect computation, such as dividing by 0 or you have exceeded the numeric range of the computer.

5. PRESS SPACE BAR TO CONTINUE

To continue execution of the program, press the space bar.

6. SORRY, THE KEY YOU HAVE PRESSED
IS NOT USED AT THIS TIME

A number or character that is not used by the program has been entered. Remember, formulas must be preceded by the plus sign. Labels must be preceded by double quotation marks or a letter.

7. THE CHARACTER YOU TYPED IS NOT PRINTABLE
AND MAY NOT BE USED IN A LABEL

Labels must consist of printable characters. The available characters follow:

SPACE ! " # $ % & ' ( ) * + COMMA – /
The numbers 0 through 9
: ; < = > ? @

Contents of the Spring Break Vacation Example

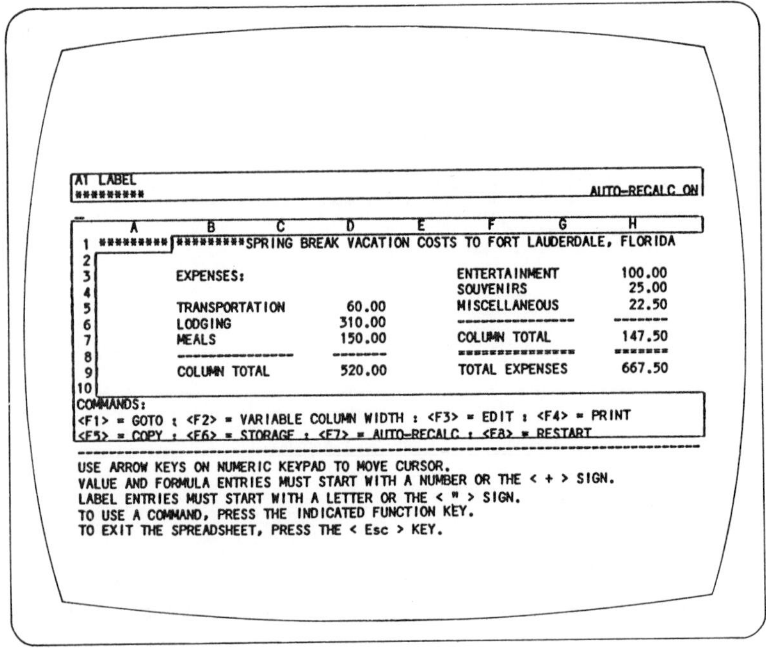

The capital letters from *A* to *Z*
[\ ] ^_ `
The lowercase letters from *a* to *z*

8. *TOO BIG*

You have tried to enter a value that is too large for the cell at this time. The number allowed depends on the format (whether dollar, integer, or floating point).

9. YOU ARE NOW IN ''VALUE ENTRY'' MODE
THE CHARACTERS THAT YOU MAY ENTER ARE. . .
NUMBERS 0 THRU 9, CELLS A1 THRU T15
CHARACTERS + – * / . ( )

You have tried to enter an inappropriate value (such as the arrow key) while in the value entry mode. You may enter the numbers from 0 through 9, cell locations A1 through T15, and the characters + – * / . ( ).

Summary of WestCalc Commands

Command	Function Name	Description
<F3> <F2>	Blank A Cell	Erases the contents of the cell containing the cursor.
<F6> <F3>	Load Example Worksheet	Loads one of the two worksheets provided with the WestCalc spreadsheet program.
<F3> <F1>	Format A Cell	Displays the numeric data in one of three different forms: integer, floating point, or dollar, depending on the input after the format command has been executed.
<F4>	Print	Displays the contents of all or part of a worksheet on paper.
<F8>	Restart	Erases the worksheet currently in the spreadsheet program and then replaces it with a blank worksheet.
<F6> <F2>	Save Worksheet	Saves the worksheet currently in the WestCalc spreadsheet program to disk.
<F6> <F1>	Load Worksheet	Loads a worksheet (that was previously saved) into the WestCalc spreadsheet program.
<F1>	GOTO	Moves the cursor directly from one cell to another.
<F2>	Varible Column Width	Allows the column width to be changed. Width may range from 3 to 30.
<F3> <F3>	Delete Row/Column	Deletes a row or column from the WestCalc spreadsheet.
<F3> <F4>	Insert Row/Column	Inserts a blank row or column into the WestCalc spreadsheet.

continued on next page

Command	Function Name	Description
<F5>	Copy	Copies a single cell, a row of cells, or a column of cells from one place to another within the worksheet.
<F7>	Auto-Recalc	Automatically recalculates all of the cells that contain formulas every time a numeric entry is made into the worksheet.

SUMMARY POINTS

- A spreadsheet program simulates the operations of a calculator and stores the results in the computer's memory.
- An electronic spreadsheet is displayed as a table of columns and rows.
- The three items that can be entered into an electronic spreadsheet are labels, values, and formulas.
- There are two areas common to most spreadsheet programs: the command area and the status area.
- A formula is a mathematical expression that is assigned to a cell in the spreadsheet.
- A predefined function is used in a formula instead of the operators + − / *.
- The spreadsheet program was initially intended for use by managers for modeling and what-if analysis.
- Many spreadsheet programs supply the user with special commands that enhance the performance of the spreadsheet.
- No special hardware is required for the IBM PC or PCjr to run a spreadsheet program, but special options are available.
- When purchasing a spreadsheet program, the intended purpose of the spreadsheet should be the most important deciding factor.

REVIEW QUESTIONS

1. In the traditional sense, what is a spreadsheet, and for what is it used?
2. What does the term *coordinate* mean when referring to a spreadsheet?
3. What are the dimensions (columns and rows) of an average spreadsheet?
4. What information is displayed in the status area of an electronic spreadsheet?
5. Formulas contained within a spreadsheet can include coordinates as well as numbers. (True or false?)
6. Describe what is meant by *what-if analysis.*
7. In terms of a spreadsheet, what is a model, and how is it used?
8. All spreadsheet programs have a command area, where all commands available to the user are displayed. (True or false?)
9. What is meant by the term *user friendly,* and why is it important?
10. In terms of a spreadsheet, what is a template, and for what is it used?

WESTCALC EXERCISES

1. Use the SPRING BREAK VACATION example included on the WestCalc diskette to complete the following exercises.

   a. Using the LOAD EXAMPLE WORKSHEET command, load the SPRING BREAK VACATION example into the worksheet.

   b. Using the BLANK A CELL command, erase the contents of the coordinate B7.

   c. Place the label FOOD in the coordinate B7.

   d. Change the formula of the coordinate in H5 to be 20 percent of the cost of the entertainment (in Cell H3).

   e. Change the format of Cell D5 to integer.

   f. Using the SAVE WORKSHEET command, save the worksheet currently in the spreadsheet program.

   g. Using the RESTART command, place a blank worksheet into the spreadsheet program.

   h. Using the LOAD WORKSHEET command, place the previously saved worksheet into the spreadsheet program.

2. Create a new spreadsheet file by first clearing the worksheet with the RESTART command.

   a. Enter the following labels:

Label Name	Coordinate Location
TUITION	A1
RM/VOARD	A2
SPEC FEES	A3
BOOKS	A4
PARKING	A5
=========	A6
TOTAL	A7

   b. Correct the label at the coordinate A2 to read RM/BOARD.

   c. Enter the following values:

Format	Coordinate	Value/Label
DOLLAR	B1	950
DOLLAR	B2	1200
DOLLAR	B3	150
DOLLAR	B4	179.50
DOLLAR	B5	15.00
------	B6	=========

   d. At B7, create a formula to sum the values entered in Part c. The answer should be displayed at B7.

   e. Change the value at B2 (in Part c) to 1125.

f. Create the following labels and values:

Coordinate	Label	Coordinate	Format	Value
D1	PIZZA	E1	DOLLAR	100
D2	MUNCHIES	E2	DOLLAR	60
D3	LAUNDRY	E3	DOLLAR	48
D4	PHONE	E4	DOLLAR	200
D5	MOVIES	E5	DOLLAR	32
D6	=========			
D7	GRAND TOTAL			

g. At E7, create a formula to sum the values from Part f and the value from Part d.

h. Change your pizza expenditure in Part f from 100 to 200.

i. Save this worksheet.

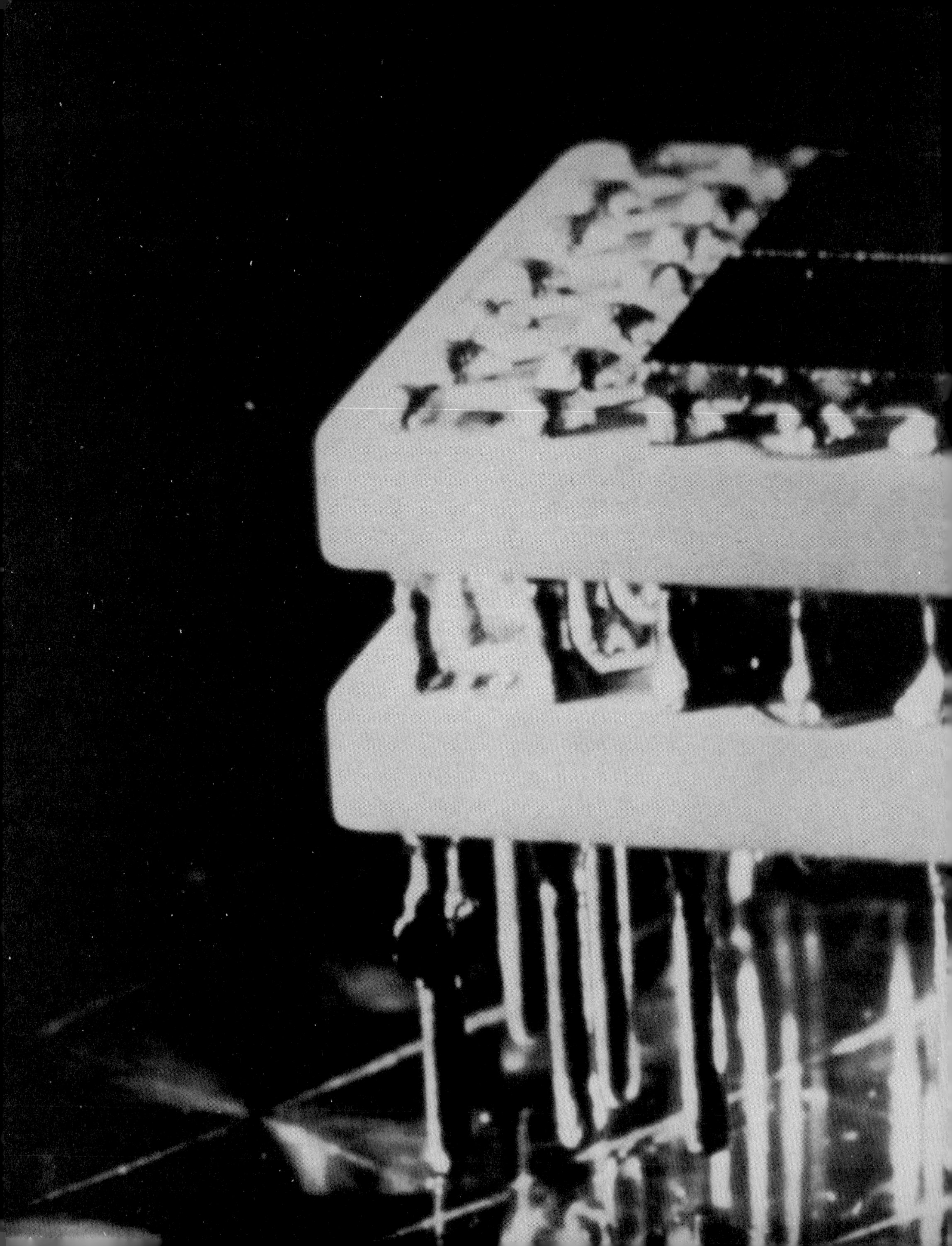

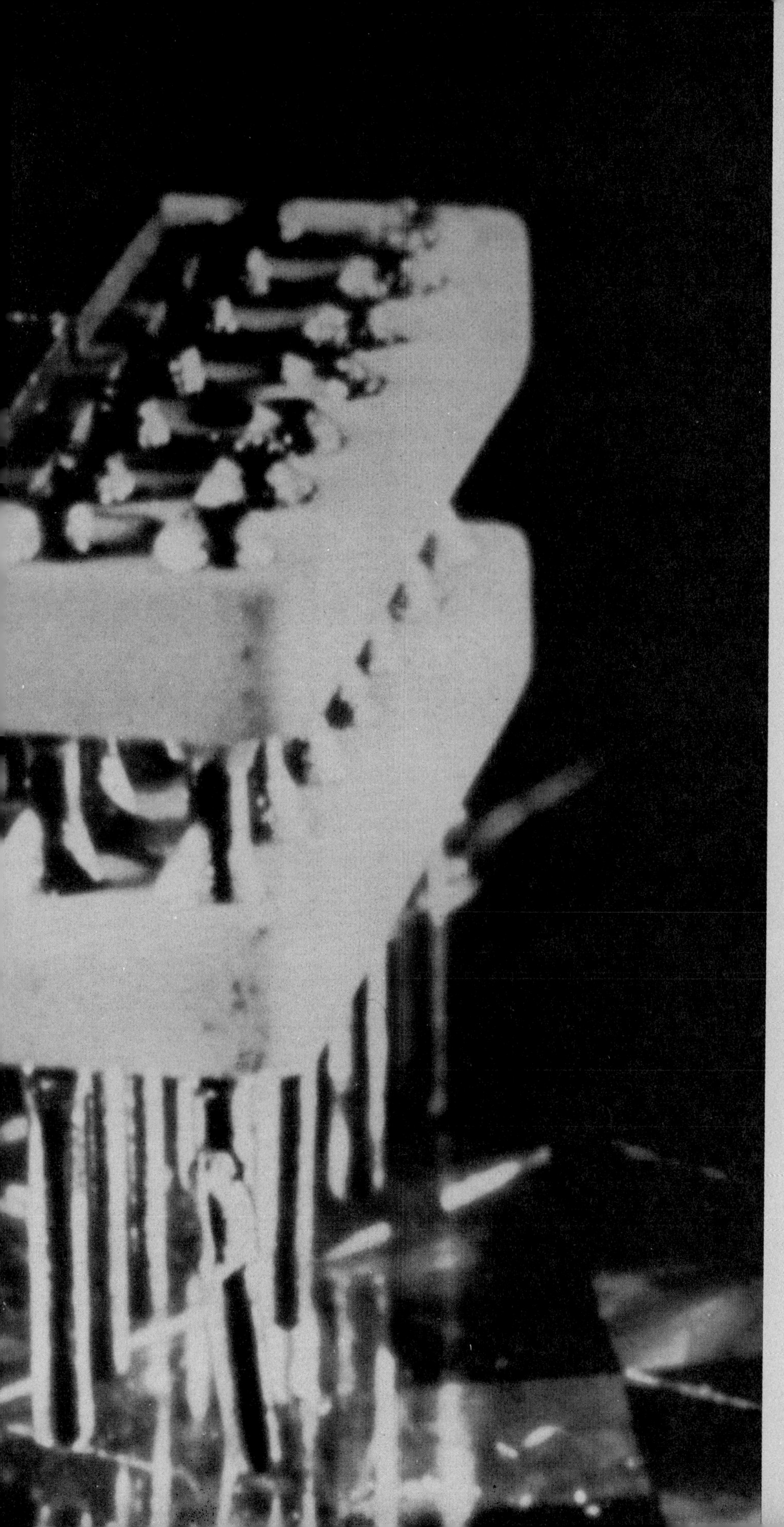

PART III

BASIC PROGRAMMING

カキクケコサシスセソタチツテ

ノハヒフヘホマミムメモヤユヨ

ワンャュョッ/：＊ー，．゛゜

IJKLMNOPQRSTUVWXYZ0123456789

コサシスセソタチツテトナニヌネノハヒフヘホマミムメモヤユヨ

ッ/：＊ー，．゛゜X

KLMNOPQRSTUVWXYZ0123456789 アイウエオカキクケコサ

ハヒフヘホマミムメモヤユヨラリルレロワンャュョッ/：＊ー，．゛゜X

PQRSTUVWXYZ0123456789 アイウエオカキクケコサシスセソタチツテトナニヌネノハヒフヘホマミムメモヤ

゜X

KLMNOPQRSTUVWXYZ0123456789 アイウエオカキクケコサシ

ハヒフヘホマミムメモヤユヨラリルレロワンャュョッ/：＊ー，．゛゜X

IJKLMNOPQRSTUVWXYZ0123456789

コサシスセソタチツテトナニヌネノハヒフヘホマミムメモヤユヨ

ッ/：＊ー，．゛゜X

EFGHIJKLMNOPQR

XYZ0123456789

カキクケコサシスセソタチツテ

ノハヒフヘホマミムメモヤユヨ

CHAPTER 12

BASIC COMMANDS AND VARIABLE TYPES

Chapter Outline

INTRODUCTION

Languages used for communication between humans and computers are called programming languages. All instructions given to a computer must follow the syntactic (grammatical) rules of whatever programming language is being used. One significant difference exists between programming languages and languages such as English or German. The rules for programming languages are precise; there are no exceptions to them. An error in writing an instruction will change the meaning of a program and cause the computer to perform the wrong action.

This section of the book concentrates on IBM BASIC. BASIC is a high-level but relatively simple language. It is similar to English and therefore is a good language for beginners.

Chapter 12 will cover five BASIC commands: NEW, RUN, SAVE, LOAD, and LIST. All these commands permit the programmer to manipulate entire programs and perform tasks involving memory management.

GETTING STARTED IN BASIC

It is easy to start writing BASIC programs on the IBM Personal Computer. To use BASIC, you need to start the DOS (disk operating system). To do so, insert the IBM DOS diskette in Disk Drive A (the disk drive on the left side of the machine). After responding to the DATE and TIME prompts, the prompt sign A will appear.[1]

Type

```
BASIC
```

The screen will now look like this:

```
The IBM Personal Computer Basic
Version D2.10 Copyright IBM Corp. 1981, 1982, 1983
61327 Bytes free
Ok
```

[1]**Note on the IBM PCjr.:** The IBM PCjr has only one disk drive. If this is the computer you are using, insert the IBM DOS diskette into the drive. Then insert the BASIC cartridge into either of the cartridge slots. Next, move the power switch on the back of the main unit to the ON position. The computer will immediately prompt you for a new date and a new time. Press the ENTER key once for each request. IBM Corp. copyright information will appear along with the prompt sign A.

Type

```
BASIC
```

The screen will now look like this:

```
The IBM PC jr Basic
Version J1.00
Copyright IBM Corp. 1981, 1982, 1983
59694 Bytes free
Ok
```

The word "Ok" that appears on the screen means that the computer is ready to be used. Note that the computer defaults to a screen width of forty characters.

Now type

```
WIDTH 80
```

and press the ENTER key to obtain a screen width of eighty characters.

Notice the word "Ok" on the screen. It is the BASIC prompt. It tells you the computer is ready to accept BASIC commands and statements.

BASIC COMMANDS

BASIC commands are similar to operating system commands. They instruct the operating system to perform specified tasks on BASIC programs. Five regularly used BASIC commands are NEW, RUN, SAVE, LOAD, and LIST.

NEW

The NEW command tells the computer that the programmer is ready to enter a new program. It does so by instructing the computer to erase anything in main memory, thereby making room for the new program. The syntax is

NEW (return)

For example:

```
NEW
```

If you want to store the program currently in main memory for future use, you must save it before entering the NEW command. Otherwise the NEW command will erase the old program from main memory to make room for the new program.

RUN

When a program is entered, it is stored in the computer's main memory. To see if the program works, use the RUN command. This command will cause the computer to **execute** the program currently in main memory; that is, the computer will carry out the instructions in the program.

Execution
The computer's carrying out of the instructions in a program.

There are three forms of the RUN command. The first form simply executes the program currently in memory from start to finish (unless an error is encountered). The syntax is

RUN (return)

For example:

```
10 PRINT " THIS IS A TEST"
RUN
 THIS IS A TEST
```

The second form also executes the program currently in main memory. However, it begins at the position specified—the line number you indicate. (Line numbers must accompany every program. They will be discussed in the next chapter.) The syntax is

RUN line number

For example:

```
10 PRINT " THIS IS "
20 PRINT "A TEST"
30 PRINT " ON RUN"
40 PRINT "COMMANDS"
RUN 30
 ON RUN
COMMANDS
```

The third form gets a file from the diskette, puts it into main memory, and runs it. This form will delete anything currently in main memory. The syntax is

RUN "filename" (return)

For example:

```
RUN "PAYROLL"
```

This command gets the program PAYROLL from the diskette, places it (loads it) into main memory, and executes it.

Notice that quotation marks have been placed around the filename. The quotation mark on the right side of the filename is optional. Thus the file PAYROLL could also be executed by this statement:

```
RUN "PAYROLL
```

SAVE

Once a program has been entered into main memory, you can save it on a diskette by using the SAVE command. This command will copy the program from main memory, which is temporary, to a diskette for long-term storage. Once the program is copied to a diskette, the programmer can perform various other tasks that access the computer's main memory without worrying about erasing or changing the program. The syntax is

SAVE "filename" (return)

For example:

```
SAVE "PAYROLL"
```

This command will save the program in main memory as PAYROLL. The filename must be eight or fewer characters. If a filename already on the diskette is the same as the filename just used, it will be written over. That is, the earlier program will be lost.

LOAD

A program that has been saved is stored on a diskette. When it is needed, it can be retrieved from the diskette and placed into the computer's main memory. The procedure for doing so is called loading a program, and it is carried out by the BASIC command LOAD. When the program you request is retrieved from the diskette and placed into main memory, anything currently in main memory is erased.

There are two basic forms of the LOAD command. The first form simply loads the specified program from the diskette into main memory. The syntax is

LOAD "filename" (return)

For example:

```
LOAD "PAYROLL"
```

The second form loads the specified program from the diskette to the computer's main memory and runs it. The syntax is

LOAD "filename",R

For example:

```
LOAD "PAYROLL",R
```

This command loads the program PAYROLL and executes it.

LIST

It is often necessary to view part or all of a program being worked on. The LIST command will display the complete program or part of the program that is currently in main memory to either the screen or the printer. There are two basic forms of the LIST command, one for the entire program and the other for only part of the program.

To view the entire program in main memory, use the following syntax:

LIST (return)

When the LIST command is used to display a program on the monitor screen, the program will **scroll;** that is, the display image will move vertically in such a way that the next line of the program will appear at the

Scrolling
The vertical movement of lines on the display screen in such a way that the next line appears at the bottom of what is already on the screen.

bottom of what is already on the screen. Thus the entire program will not be viewable at one time. To view a section before it disappears at the top of the screen, press the <Ctrl> and <NumLock> keys at the same time. To continue with the listing, press any key other than the SHIFT, the <Break>, or the <Ins> key. To stop the LIST command from either displaying the program on the screen or printing it with the printer, press the <Ctrl> and <Break> keys at the same time.[2]

For example:

```
LIST
```

This command will list on the screen the program that is in main memory.

For example:

```
LIST,"LPT1:"
```

"LPT1" stands for line printer. Now the complete program in main memory will be printed as a hard copy.

To view a portion of the program, use the following syntax:

LIST Line1 – Line2

The lines between Line 1 and Line 2 will then be displayed. This form of the LIST command has several options. If only Line 1 is given with the hyphen following it, that line and all higher numbered lines will be listed.

LEARNING CHECK

1. When is the NEW command used?
2. What is the syntax of the instruction to execute a program that has been saved on a diskette?
3. The LOAD command erases anything currently in the computer's main memory. (True or false?)
4. What is the command to list a program through Line 990 on the printer?

1. When the programmer is ready to enter a new program. **2.** RUN "filename". **3.** true. **4.** LIST – 990, "LPT1:".

[2]**Note on the PCjr.:** On the PCjr, the keys used to stop a scrolling program are different from those on the PC. To temporarily view a section of a program or a portion of a run before it disappears at the top of the screen, press the FN key and then the PAUSE key. To continue the listing, press the space bar or any other valid key. To permanently stop the listing or the run, press the FN key and then the BREAK key.

COMMAND	EXPLANATION
LIST	List the entire program on the screen.
LIST, "LPT1:"	List the entire program on the printer.
LIST 10	List Line 10 on the screen.
LIST 10-20	List Lines 10 through 20 on the screen.
LIST 10-20, "LPT1:"	List Lines 10 through 20 on the printer.
LIST 100-	List the program from Line 100 to the end of the program.
LIST -200	List the program from the beginning through Line 200.

Table 12–1 LIST COMMANDS

If only Line 2 is given with the hyphen preceding it, all lines from the beginning of the program through Line 2 will be listed. These three ways of listing parts of a program require the use of a hyphen in the line range. If only Line 1 is given and no hyphen follows it, only that line will be printed. (See Table 12–1 for the forms of the LIST command.)

VARIABLES

Values that change during the execution of a program are **variables.** There are two types of variables: numeric and string. **Numeric variables** are variables used to represent numbers. **String variables** are variables used to represent one or more characters.

Variables
Values that change during the execution of a program.

Numeric variables
Variables used to represent numbers.

String variables
Variables used to represent one or more characters.

Variables are represented by variable names (see Table 12–2). IBM BASIC variable names can be any length. However, only the first forty characters are relevant to the computer. Letters, numbers, and a decimal point are the characters allowed in a variable name. The variable name must match the type of data it represents, either string or numeric. Each name must start with a letter. For string variables, each name must end with a dollar sign ($). Numeric variable names may also end with special symbols (see sample names in Table 12–2).

Certain words, called reserved words, have special meaning in the BASIC language (see Table 12–3 for a complete list of these words). The reserved words cannot be used as variable names. However, they can be contained within variable names. This statement is invalid because the variable name KEY is a reserved word:

```
10 KEY = 5
```

STRING VARIABLE NAMES	NUMERIC VARIABLE NAMES
NAMES$	PAY!
ADDRESS$	HOURS!
EMPLOYEE.NUMBER1$	MONEY#
	EMPLOYEE.NUMBER

Table 12–2 SAMPLE VARIABLE NAMES

Table 12–3 RESERVED WORDS

CALL	INPUT#	OPEN	SCREEN
CLEAR	INPUTS	OR	SIN
CLOSE	INSTR	OUT	SOUND
COLOR	KEY	PEEK	SPACE$
DATA	KILL	PLAY	SQR
DELETE	LEFT$	POINT	STEP
DIM	LEN	POKE	STOP
DRAW	LET	PRINT	STR$
ERROR	LINE	PRINT#	STRINGS
EXP	LIST	PUT	SWAP
FIELD	LLIST	READ	TAB
FILES	LOAD	REM	TAN
FOR	LOCATE	RESTORE	THEN
GET	NAME	RESUME	TIMES
GOSUB	NEW	RETURN	TO
GOTO	NEXT	RIGHT$	USING
IF	NOT	RUN	WAIT
INPUT	OFF	SAVE	WHILE
	ON		WIDTH
			WRITE
			WRITE#

This statement is valid because KEY is only part of the variable name:

```
10 EMPLOYEE.KEY = 5
```

A variable name can be assigned a variable that is the result of a computation, or it can be assigned a constant value. To assign a value to a variable name, use the LET command (which will be discussed in detail in Chapter 13).

- Examples of assigning a constant:

```
10 LET EMPLOYEE.NUMBER = 99
20 LET LAST.NAME$ = "SMITH"
```

- Examples of assigning the result of a computation:

```
10 LET PAY = 4.25 * 40
20 LET A = A + PAY
```

Numeric Variables

As indicated earlier, numeric variables represent numbers. Their variable names can be any length (with only the first forty characters being recognized by the computer). They can also be a combination of letters, numbers, and decimal points; and they must begin with a letter.

Numeric variables can be declared as one of three types: integer, single-precision, or double-precision. The declaration is made by adding a symbol to the end of the variable name. (See Table 12–4 for a list of these symbols.) If the variable type is not explicitly declared, then it will default to single-precision. (More details on these types of numeric variables will be provided later in the chapter.)

Although computations done with integer and single-precision variables are not as accurate as those done with double-precision variables, there are two reasons for using them. First, double-precision variables take up more storage room. This is an important point because space is a consideration in most programs. Second, it takes more time to do arithmetic computations with double-precision numbers. A program with repeated calculations will run faster with integer variables. Table 12–5 provides examples of all three types of numeric variables.

Integer Variables. Integers are whole numbers: 1, 2, 3, and so on. **Integer variables** are variables used to represent whole numbers between −32768 and +32768. They do not have a decimal point. The last character of an integer variable name must be the percent symbol (%). For example:

Integer variables
Variables used to represent whole numbers between −32768 and +32768 and having no decimal point.

AREA% (an integer variable name)

Single-Precision Variables. Variables used to represent numbers with a decimal point and seven or fewer digits are **single-precision variables.** An example of a single-precision number is 9.38. For a variable name to be declared single-precision, the last character of the name should be an exclamation point (!). Since the default on an undeclared variable type is single-precision, the last symbol of the variable does not have to be the exclamation point, although it is recommended. For example:

Single-precision variables
Variables used to represent numbers with a decimal point and seven or fewer digits.

AREA! (a numeric single-precision variable name)

Table 12–4 DECLARATION SYMBOLS

SYMBOL	VARIABLE TYPE
$	String
!	Single-precision
#	Double-precision numeric
%	Integer

Table 12–5 EXAMPLES OF NUMERIC VARIABLES

VARIABLE NAME	VARIABLE	TYPE OF VARIABLE
LENGTH!	12.89	Single-precision
TOTAL%	31	Integer
LIMIT#	39.0567784	Double-precision

Double-precision variables *Variables used to represent numbers with a decimal point and eight or more digits.*

Double-Precision Variables. Variables used to represent numbers with a decimal point and eight or more digits are **double-precision variables.** An example of a double-precision number is 34.9836981. The last character of the double-precision variable name must be the number sign (#). For example:

AREA# (a numeric double-precision variable name)

String Variables

As indicated earlier, a **string variable** contains one or more characters. These characters can be words, sentences, or descriptive phrases composed of numeric, alphabetic, or other special characters. The character string can be as long as desired, and it must always be enclosed in quotation marks.

A string variable name can be any length, but if it exceeds forty characters the computer will see only the first forty. The first character must be a letter, and the last character must be a dollar sign ($). Table 12–6 gives some examples of string variables.

LEARNING CHECK

1. What is wrong with the statement 20 LET NAME = "MICHAEL"?
2. What is wrong with the following program segment?

```
10 LET $NAME = "MICHAEL"
20 LET NEW = "NEW EMPLOYEE"
```

3. If no variable type is declared for numeric variables, double-precision is assumed. (True or false?)
4. ________ variables are numbers with a decimal point and eight or more digits.
5. Which of the following is not a valid variable name? H23, A!B, G1$, X%, NAME.A1$

ANSWERS:

1. The statement needs a dollar sign ($) at the end of the variable name to represent a string variable. **2.** The dollar sign ($) should be the last character of the variable name, and NEW is a reserved word. **3.** false; single-precision is assumed. **4.** Double-precision. **5.** A!B.

Table 12–6 EXAMPLES OF STRING VARIABLES

STRING VARIABLE NAME	CHARACTER STRING
EMPLOYEE.NAME$	"MICHAEL MEEK"
EMPLOYEE.ADDRESS$	"1234 SOMEPLACE AVE."
STORE$	"THE 123/ABC STORE"

SUMMARY POINTS

- The BASIC command NEW clears the computer's main memory in preparation for a new program.
- The command RUN causes the computer to execute a program.
- The command SAVE transfers a program from main memory to diskette. The command LOAD places a saved program into main memory.
- The command LIST is used to display on the screen or to print a hard copy of all or part of a program that is in main memory.
- Variables are values that may change during program execution.
- Variable names must start with a letter; they may be a combination of letters, numbers, and decimal points.
- Only the first forty characters of a variable name are recognized by the computer.
- Numeric variables may be of the following types: integer, single-precision, or double-precision. They are declared by the use of a special symbol as the last character of the variable name.
- String variables contain characters and are enclosed in quotation marks. The last character of the variable name must be the dollar sign ($).

REVIEW QUESTIONS

1. Name the five regularly used BASIC commands.
2. When is the NEW command used? What does it do?
3. Give examples of the three different ways the LIST command can be used.
4. What are the three types of numeric variables discussed in the chapter?
5. Which numeric variable names in the following list are invalid? Why?

a. TOTAL!
b. AMOUNT#
c. NUM1$
d. ADD
e. X%
f. ADD.TOGETHER

6. What type of variable are each of these variable names?

a. AMOUNT
b. NUM1%
c. B
d. N$
e. PERCENTAGE#
f. MONEY!

7. Give an appropriate variable name for each of the following:

a. "1220 Frazer Ave."
b. 14.80
c. 9185.70698
d. 14
e. −170

8. Give one reason for using an integer or single-precision numeric variable rather than a double-precision numeric variable.
9. Between what values can an integer variable range?
10. How does the computer determine if a variable represents an integer, a single-precision number, a double-precision number, or a character string?

CHAPTER 13

BEGINNING PROGRAMMING

Chapter Outline

INTRODUCTION

In Chapter 12 you learned about commands that are used to manipulate BASIC programs. This chapter introduces you to some BASIC statements that are used within the BASIC program and that are executed when the program is run. The chapter also discusses common syntax and logic errors and how to correct them.

LINE NUMBERS

Direct mode
The communication mode in which commands are executed as soon as they are entered.

There are two possible ways to communicate with the computer: direct mode and indirect mode. In **direct mode,** you are telling the computer to execute your command immediately after you enter it. This type of communication is accomplished by *not* preceding the statement with a line number. The command itself is not saved after it is executed. Direct mode is useful for debugging and for quick computations that do not require a complete program. If you type

```
PRINT 20 + 2
```

and then press ENTER ↵, the result will be

```
22
```

Indirect mode
The communication mode in which program statements are stored in main memory and not executed until the RUN command is given.

In **indirect mode,** you are telling the computer that the statements you are entering are part of a program and should be stored in main memory and not executed until the RUN command is given. In this mode, every line must begin with a line number. The line is then stored in main memory as part of the program.

Type

```
10 PRINT 20 + 2
20 PRINT 20 + 3
```

Then execute the program.

```
RUN
 22
 23
```

Line numbers
Numbers at the beginnings of lines that are used to show the order in which program lines are stored in main memory.

The **line numbers** are used to show the order in which the program lines are stored in main memory. They also are used as reference points for branching and editing (discussed later in the chapter). Figure 13–1 gives an example of a program using line numbers.

Line numbers can be from one to five digits long and must range between 0 and 65529.

Figure 13–1 LINE NUMBERS

```
10 REM   THIS IS AN EXAMPLE
20 REM   OF LINE NUMBERS
30 LET MESSAGE$ = "YOU NEED LINE NUMBERS"
40 PRINT MESSAGE$
99 END
RUN
YOU NEED LINE NUMBERS
```

Usefulness of Line Numbers

Line numbers tell the computer the order in which to execute the program statements. In the following example, since 15 comes before 20, the computer will process Line 15 first. Type

```
10 LET NUMBER = 10
20 PRINT NUMBER
15 LET NUMBER = NUMBER + 1
```

and then execute the program.

```
RUN
 11
```

Line numbers allow you to edit a specific line rather than the whole program.

Incrementing Line Numbers

Although lines can be numbered in any way desired (1, 2, 3,; 10, 20, 30; 100, 200, 300; and so on), it is best to use a numbering system that leaves some open line numbers in case a statement needs to be inserted later. If, for example:

```
60 LET NUMBER = 10
70 PRINT NUMBER,NUMBER2
```

had been entered and a line had been omitted, you could enter it out of sequence as

```
60 LET NUMBER = 10
70 PRINT NUMBER,NUMBER2
65 LET NUMBER2 = 11
```

and the computer would rearrange the lines in the correct order. To verify, just type LIST. Now the program should be in the following sequence:

```
60 LET NUMBER = 10
65 LET NUMBER2 = 11
70 PRINT NUMBER,NUMBER2
```

EDITING AND DEBUGGING

Syntax
The rules of computer "grammar" that must be followed in writing program instructions.

Syntax errors
Errors caused by the incorrect use of the rules of a programming language.

Logic errors
Errors caused by incorrect solutions to programming problems.

Programmers make and must correct two general types of errors: syntax errors and logic errors. Each error requires the programmer to change (edit) the program to make it correct. **Syntax** is the rules of computer "grammar" that must be followed in writing program instructions. **Syntax errors** are errors caused by the incorrect use of the rules of a programming language. They are often produced by inaccurate typing. **Logic errors** are errors caused by incorrect solutions to programming problems. Examples are missing or misplaced statements.

Editing Syntax Errors

Sooner or later you will make a syntax error. If you are typing a line and discover that you've typed something incorrectly, you can correct the error. Use the keyboard diagrams in Figures 13–2 and 13–3 to help you locate the various keys discussed in this section. Use the cursor left key [4 ←] to move the cursor to the position where the mistake occurred, and type the correct letter on top of the wrong one. Then, using the cursor right key [6 →], move the cursor back to the end of the line and continue typing the line. If the incorrect letter is the last character you typed, just use the backspace key to delete it, and then type the correct character.

If you notice an error after you press the enter key [↵], use the cursor up key [8 ↑] to get the cursor onto the correct line. Then use the cursor

Figure 13–2 THE IBM PC KEYBOARD

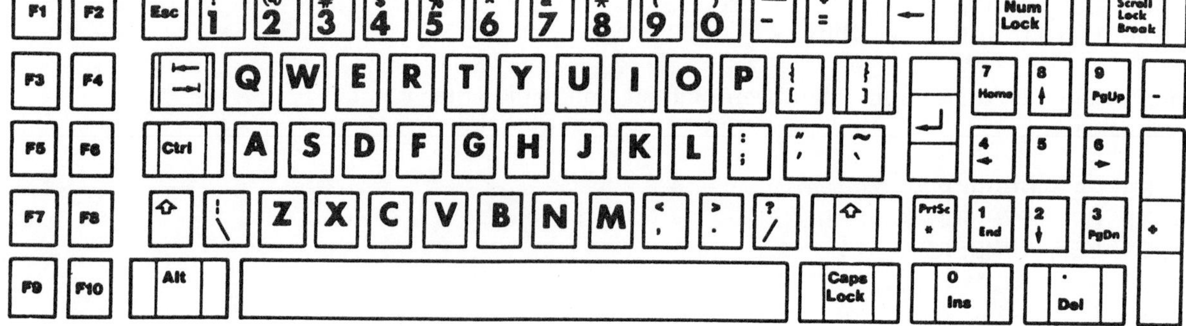

Figure 13–3 *THE IBM PCjr KEYBOARD*

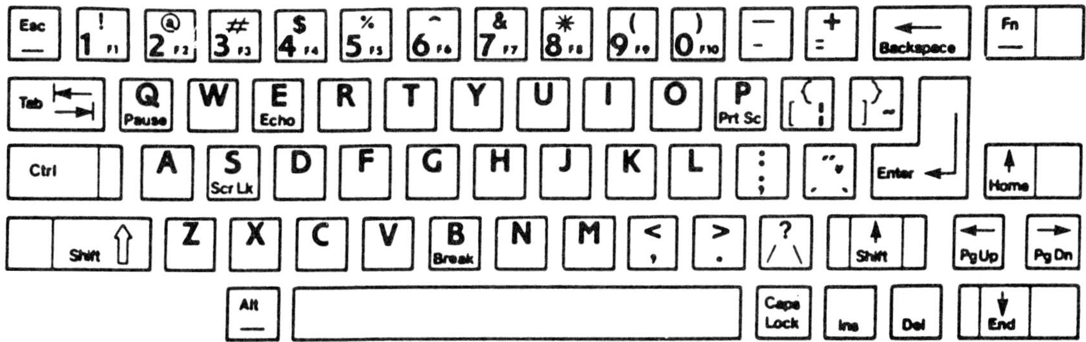

right or cursor left key to move the cursor to the position where the mistake occurred, and type the correct letters on top of the wrong ones. When the correction is made, press the enter key.

If you notice that you have put an extra character in the line you are typing or have typed, you can erase (delete) it using the <Del> key. Use the cursor movement keys to move the cursor to the character you want to erase. Press the <Del> key, and the character will be deleted. Then use the cursor right or <End> key to move the cursor back to the end of the line, and continue typing or press ENTER. For example, if you have typed

```
DEELETE_
```

use the cursor left key to move the cursor under the extra E:

```
DEELETE
```

Press the <Del> key, and the extra E will be deleted:

```
DELETE
```

Press the END key and continue:

```
DELETE_
```

If you have omitted a character in a line, move the cursor to the position where you want to put the new character. Press the <Ins> key and type the character you want to insert. The character you type will be inserted at the cursor, and the characters following it will be pushed to the right. When you have finished adding characters, press the cursor right or <End> key to move the cursor to the end of the line, and continue typing or press ENTER. For example:

`LIS 10_` (you forgot the T in LIST)

Press the cursor left key until the cursor is under the space:

```
LIS_10
```

Press the <Ins> key and type the letter T:

```
LIST_10
```

Press the <End> key and then press ENTER.

Debugging Logic Errors

Debugging
The task of finding and correcting program errors.

If a program runs but yields incorrect output, it contains logic errors, or bugs. A logic error may be the result of an incorrect arithmetic formula or a similar problem. The task of finding and correcting the program error is known as **debugging.** A common method of debugging is to look through the program one statement at a time, thinking about what the computer would do in the execution of each statement.

Many logic errors are caused by processing steps that are missing, incorrect, or unnecessary. To insert a missing step, type the line number of where the step should be positioned and the line itself. To change or replace an incorrect program line, type the line number of the incorrect line and the correct statement. For example:

```
10 PRINT "HELLO DAISY"
20 PRINT "GOODBYE DAISY"
```

If you want to change Line 10, type

```
10 PRINT "GOOD DAY DAISY"
```

If you list the program now, it will appear as follows:

```
10 PRINT "GOOD DAY DAISY"
20 PRINT "GOODBYE DAISY"
```

If your program contains an unnecessary processing step, you need to delete it. This is done by typing the line number alone. For example:

```
10 PRINT "GOOD DAY DAISY"
20 PRINT "GOODNIGHT DAISY"
30 PRINT "HOW ARE YOU?"
```

If you wish to delete Line 20, type

```
20 (ENTER)
```

Now type LIST, and Line 20 will have disappeared:

```
10 PRINT "GOOD DAY DAISY"
30 PRINT "HOW ARE YOU?"
```

LEARNING CHECK

1. Line numbers are of no importance to the computer but are helpful in debugging. (True or false?)
2. What is wrong with the following program segment?

```
10 LET W$ = G$
LET X% = 1298
30 LET A$ = "STEVE BARTH"
```

3. Two types of errors are ________ and ________.
4. A syntax error is usually a typing mistake and will be caught by the computer. (True or false?)
5. Debugging is the term given to the process of correcting syntax errors. (True or false?)

ANSWERS:

1. false. 2. A line number is needed for the second line. 3. syntax, logic. 4. true. 5. false.

REM STATEMENT

REM is short for "remark." The format for the REM statement is

Line# REM comment

Following is an example of a REM statement:

```
10 REM THIS PROGRAM DEMONSTRATES THE REM STATEMENT
```

REM is a nonexecutable statement; that is, it does not cause any program action. The computer simply skips to the next executable line. Since the REM statement is not executable, it can be placed anywhere in a program without affecting the program's process.

REM statements are used to explain what the program is about and are therefore helpful at the beginning of the program. They should explain the general purpose of the program, list the variable names to be used, and indicate what each variable represents. They should also be inserted every so often throughout the program as a reminder of what a particular section of the program is doing at a particular point.

LET STATEMENT

The LET statement is used to assign values to variables. The syntax is

LET variable = expression

The expression is the value that the variable will hold. Figure 13–4 is a program using the LET statement. Look at Line 20 in the figure. Upon execution of Line 20, the number 9 is stored in the memory location defined as NUMBER1. The variable name NUMBER1 will now represent the number 9 until that variable name is redefined.

The variable in a LET statement can be numeric or string. The expression can be a constant (an expression that has a value that does not change), an arithmetic formula, other variables, or a character string. Table 13–1 gives examples of valid LET statements.

Until otherwise defined, all variables are equal to 0 when the computer is turned on and after the execution of the NEW command. The variables to the left of the equals sign signify a storage location in main memory. On the right side of the equals sign is the value that is stored in that location. It must match the type of variable name. The word LET is optional; that is, the equals sign is sufficient when an expression is assigned to a variable. Table 13–2 gives examples of invalid LET statements.

THE HIERARCHY OF OPERATIONS

Often mathematics is used in programs. Do not worry if you are not a mathematics wizard; the computer will do all the calculations. All you need to do is type in the correct formulas and understand the order in which the computer will perform the calculations. Table 13–3 explains some of the arithmetic symbols the computer uses.

Hierarchy of operations
The order in which mathematical calculations are performed by the computer.

The computer performs mathematical calculations in a particular order, called the **hierarchy of operations.** (This hierarchy is shown in Table 13–4.) For example, in the following equation, the final value of A will be 4:

A = 3 ^ 2 − 6 + (8 − 5) / 3

Let us look at how the computer arrived at this answer. Table 13–4 shows that any operation within parentheses will be performed first, so 8 − 5 = 3 is the first operation. Now the equation is 3 ^ 2 − 6 + 3 / 3.

Figure 13–4 LET STATEMENT

```
10 REM  THIS PROGRAM ADDS TWO NUMBERS
20 LET NUMBER1 = 9
30 LET NUMBER2 = 4
40 LET ANSWER = NUMBER1 + NUMBER2
50 LET MESSAGE$ = "THE ANSWER IS "
60 PRINT MESSAGE$;ANSWER
99 END
```

Table 13–1 SOME VALID LET STATEMENTS

STATEMENT	EXPLANATION
10 LET X = 4	The variable X is assigned the number 4.
10 X = 4	Same as above (the word LET is optional).
30 K$ = "HELLO"	The variable K$ is assigned the character string HELLO.
100 LET T = A + B	The values of A and B are added together and placed in T.
200 LET C = C + 1	The current value of C is increased by 1.
300 B = X	The value of X is entered into the location defined as B.
450 LET A$ = B$	The value in the string variable name B$ is copied into location A$.

Table 13–2 SOME INVALID LET STATEMENTS

STATEMENT	EXPLANATION
10 LET 8 + B = X	Only a variable name can be on the left side of the equals sign.
20 B$ = DON	A string must be enclosed in quotes.
40 LET T$ = A	A numeric value cannot be assigned to a string variable.
60 X = "PAUL"	A string cannot be assigned a numeric variable.

Table 13–3 ARITHMETIC SYMBOLS

ARITHMETIC SYMBOL	MEANING
+	Addition, as in 3 + 2 = 5
–	Subtraction, as in 3 – 1 = 2
*	Multiplication, as in 3 * 2 = 6
/	Division, as in 6 / 3 = 2
^	Exponentiation, as in 2 ^ 3 = 8 (2 raised to the third power)

Table 13–4 HIERARCHY OF OPERATIONS

PRIORITY	OPERATION
First	Any operation within parentheses
Second	Exponentiation
Third	Multiplication or division
Fourth	Addition or subtraction

The next priority is exponentiation. Thus, 3 ^ 2 = 9 is performed, creating the equation 9 – 6 + 3 / 3. Multiplication or division is next, so the division will be performed: 3 / 3 = 1, leaving an equation of 9 – 6 + 1.

When the final equation is simplified to A = 9 – 6 + 1, all the operations are at the same level (addition and subtraction have last priority). When this is the case, the computer works from left to right. Thus, 9 – 6 = 3 and 3 + 1 = 4, so 4 is the final answer. Two consecutive operators must be separated by parentheses, as shown in Figure 13–5.

Figure 13–5 SEPARATING CONSECUTIVE OPERATORS

SEPARATING CONSECUTIVE OPERATORS
X * (−Y)
14 / (+121)
NUM * (−12.25)

LEARNING CHECK

1. The REM statement is a ________ statement.
2. Write a LET statement to assign the value 212 to a single-precision variable.
3. The * is the ________ symbol for BASIC.
4. The ________ is the exponential sign for IBM BASIC.
5. The particular order in which a computer does mathematical calculations is called the ________.
6. 4 * (2 + 3) + 2 ^ 2 − 1 = ________.

ANSWERS:

1. nonexecutable. **2.** LET N = 212 or LET N! = 212. **3.** multiplication. **4.** ^. **5.** hierarchy of operations. **6.** 23.

PRINT STATEMENT

The PRINT statement is used to display data and to arrange the output of the display. It displays whatever is to the right of it. The general format for this statement is

Line# PRINT expression

The expression can be numbers, variables, or strings. (Any string constants in the expression must be enclosed in quotation marks.) For example, Line 60 in Figure 13–4 will display the value of the variables, not the variable names themselves. The following is the result of the PRINT statement in Line 60:

```
THE ANSWER IS 13
```

The PRINT statement is also used to display such strings as headings or messages. Lines 50 and 60 in Figure 13–4 could have been written as follows:

```
60 PRINT "THE ANSWER IS ";ANSWER
```

In this way the program could have been shortened by the elimination of Line 50 and still would have resulted in the same output. The inclusion of spaces in the quotes can vary the output display. For example:

```
50 PRINT "THE        ANSWER        IS        ";ANSWER
```

will result in output that looks like this:

```
THE        ANSWER        IS        13
```

Another use of the PRINT statement is to print values of arithmetic expressions. Figure 13–6 shows a program and its output using a PRINT statement in this fashion.

Print Zones

The BASIC language considers the print or display area to be divided into vertical zones called **print zones.** IBM BASIC divides the display area into five print zones, each consisting of fourteen spaces. Table 13–5 shows the zone columns, with a total of 80 spaces horizontally per line. If the output to be printed is longer than fourteen columns, it will continue into the next print zone.

Print zones
Vertical zones into which the print or display area is divided.

```
10 LET TWO = 2
20 LET THREE = 3
30 PRINT TWO + THREE
99 END
RUN
 5
```

Figure 13–6 PRINT STATEMENT EXAMPLE

Table 13–5 COLUMNS OF PRINT ZONES

ZONE	COLUMNS
1	1–14
2	15–28
3	29–42
4	43–56
5	57–80

Use of Commas

A comma tells the computer to skip over to the next print zone before printing the contents to the right of the comma (see Figure 13–7). If two commas are used, two print zones are skipped, and printing will start in Zone 3. Figure 13–8 illustrates this technique.

A comma at the end of a PRINT statement causes the output of the next PRINT statement to be printed in the next zone, not on the next line. In other words, there is no line feed after the computer executes a PRINT statement that ends with a comma (see Figure 13–9).

Use of Semicolons

A semicolon causes the output to be printed immediately after the last value. (However, printed numbers are always followed by a space, and positive numbers are preceded by a space.) Figure 13–10 shows the use of the semicolon in a program. Figure 13–11 shows a sample program that uses both commas and semicolons.

A semicolon at the end of a PRINT statement will cause the next PRINT statement to continue on the same line without skipping a space. Figure 13–12 gives an example. Notice that no space was left between IS and JOE. To overcome this problem, it is necessary to enclose a space either after the S in IS or before the J in JOE. For example, look at Figure 13–13.

This use of commas and semicolons may seem confusing at first, but all that is required is a little practice and a good deal of patience. Practice using commas and semicolons to help you understand print zones and

Figure 13–7 USING THE COMMA

```
10 PRINT "ONE","TWO"
RUN
ONE             TWO
```

Figure 13–8 ZONE 3

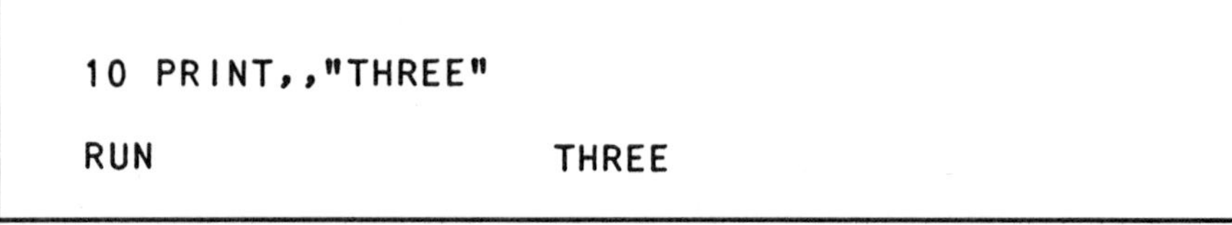

```
10 PRINT,,"THREE"

RUN                           THREE
```

Figure 13–9 PRINT STATEMENT ENDING WITH A COMMA

```
10 PRINT "ONE","TWO",
20 PRINT "THREE"

RUN
ONE             TWO             THREE
```

```
10 PRINT 1;2;3;4
RUN
 1  2  3  4
```

Figure 13–10 PROGRAM WITH SEMICOLONS

```
10 PRINT 1,2;3,4;5
RUN
 1              2  3            4  5
```

Figure 13–11 COMMAS AND SEMICOLONS

```
10 PRINT "MY NAME IS";
20 PRINT "JOE"
RUN
MY NAME ISJOE
```

Figure 13–12 PRINT STATEMENT ENDING WITH A SEMICOLON

```
10 PRINT "MY NAME IS ";
20 PRINT "JOE"
RUN
MY NAME IS JOE
```

Figure 13–13 SPACING WITH A SEMICOLON

the formatting of output displays. Your output displays will be greatly enhanced if you know how to use commas and semicolons correctly.

TAB

The TAB function is similar to the TAB key on a typewriter. It is used with the PRINT statement. The TAB function will move the cursor only to the right of its present position. If the current print position is already beyond the space specified in the TAB function, the print will occur at the specified position in the next line. The TAB function prints blank spaces, erasing anything it passes over on the screen.

The number of columns at which the tab is to be set must be in the range of 1 to 80 and be enclosed in parentheses to the right of the word TAB. Figure 13–14 gives an example in which the computer is told to move to the fifth column to the right before it starts to print. Figure 13–15 shows how more than one TAB function can be used in one statement. The second

Figure 13–14 TAB FUNCTION

```
10 PRINT TAB(5) "START"
RUN
    START
```

Figure 13–15 MULTIPLE TAB FUNCTIONS

```
10 PERSON$ = "DON"
20 NUMBER = 3
30 PRINT TAB(15) PERSON$ TAB(20) NUMBER
99 END
RUN
              DON  3
```

TAB function will not move the output an additional twenty columns. Instead it will move the output only to the column specified (in this example to Column 20).

SPC

The SPC (space) function is used in the same general way as the TAB function (see Figure 13–16). The difference between the SPC and TAB functions can be seen when more than one function is used in a single statement. Recall that when two TAB functions are in a line, the second TAB moves over to the column indicated. The second SPC function will move over an additional number of spaces from the last output. Figure 13–17 illustrates the difference between the two functions.

When TAB is used, the output is printed in Columns 5 and 10. With the SPC function, however, the output is printed in Columns 5 and 15, because the SPC function spaces over ten columns from the last output (A) before executing the second PRINT statement (B). The number of positions at which SPC is to be set must be in the range 1 through 80 and must be enclosed in parentheses to the right of the SPC function.

END STATEMENT

The END statement does exactly what it says; it indicates the end of the program. It is usually the last line of the program, in which case it has the highest line number. Many programmers give the END statement a line number of all 9s to make it easy to distinguish from the rest of the program. The format for the END statement is as follows:

Line# END

```
10 PRINT SPC(25) "START"
RUN
                         START
```

Figure 13–16 SPC FUNCTION

```
10 PRINT TAB(5) "A" TAB(10) "B"
RUN
     A    B

10 PRINT SPC(5) "A" SPC(10) "B"
RUN
     A          B
```

Figure 13–17 DIFFERENCE BETWEEN SPC AND TAB FUNCTIONS

Here is an example of the END statement:

```
999 END
```

The END statement at the end of a program is optional but recommended. BASIC always returns to command level after an END is executed.

LEARNING CHECK

1. The statement 10 PRINT "STEVE" SPC(20) "BETH" will print BETH in columns ________.
2. What is the difference between the TAB and SPC functions?
3. The END statement must be the last line of a program. (True or false?)
4. The END statement is given a value of ________ by many programmers.

ANSWERS: **1.** 26–29. **2.** TAB causes the output to start in a specified column; SPC causes the output to start after a specified number of spaces. **3.** false. **4.** all 9s.

SUMMARY POINTS

- Every BASIC statement in the indirect mode requires a line number. The computer will execute the statements in order, according to the number given to each line.
- Although you can number your lines in any sequence, it is best to leave some open line numbers in case you need to insert additional lines in your program.

- Syntax errors are grammatical errors in the program (usually typing errors).
- Logic errors are errors in the actual statements given to the computer. They cause incorrect output.
- REM is a nonexecutable statement used to explain the program.
- The LET statement is one way to enter data into programs; the word LET is optional.
- The PRINT statement is used to display data, to arrange the output of the display, and to skip lines.
- The comma, used in conjunction with the PRINT statement, tells the computer to skip to the next print zone before printing.
- The semicolon used in a PRINT statement causes output to be printed in the next column instead of the next print zone.
- The TAB function is used with the PRINT statement and is followed by the expression to be printed.
- The SPC function spaces over from the last output; the TAB function moves the output to a specified column regardless of what has been printed.
- The END statement indicates the end of a program.

REVIEW QUESTIONS

1. Explain the difference between syntax errors and logic errors.
2. Explain how to delete a line in a BASIC program.
3. Why is a REM statement referred to as a nonexecutable statement? Why are REM statements so important?
4. Write the following LET statements:

a. Assign the character string MARVIN K. MOONEY to an appropriate string variable.
b. Increase the value of the integer variable LC% by 2.
c. Assign the value of ADDRESS$ to STREET$.

5. Write BASIC statements to do the following:

a. Assign GEORGE HOSSLER to the string variable EMPLOYEE$.
b. Assign 379-50-5288 to the string variable SSNO$.
c. Assign 9.50 to the numeric variable PAY.
d. Print these values so that EMPLOYEES$ starts in Column 1, SSNO$ in Column 15, and PAY in Column 30. Do this by using commas in the PRINT statement.
e. Print these values so that EMPLOYEE$ starts in Column 10, SSNO$ in Column 25, and PAY in Column 40. Use the TAB function.

6. List the hierarchy of operations in IBM BASIC.
7. Find the correct value of X for each of the following statements:

a. `20  X = 2 ^ 2 + 1 * 3`
b. `30  X = (8 + 4) * 6 - 1`
c. `80  X = 8 + 9 / 3 ^ 2`

8. Write the following BASIC statements:

a. Add 4 to 2 and multiply the result by 6. Assign this value to the variable COST.
b. Divide 12 by 4 and subtract 8 from the result. Assign this value to RESULT.
c. Raise 4 to the second power and divide the result by 2. Assign this value to NUM.

9. Write the necessary BASIC statements to print your name on the display screen, starting at Column 10.
10. What is the difference between the TAB function and the SPC function?

SAMPLE PROGRAM

1. This program produces a calendar of events. It illustrates the use of PRINT statements for formatting output and the use of string variables for printing headings. Try formatting your own output for practice.

```
10  REM  * * * A CALENDAR OF EVENTS * * *
20  REM  * * * A PRACTICE IN FORMATTING * * *
30  REM
40  LET MONTH1$ = "JUNE"
50  LET BIRTHDAY$ = "BIRTHDAYS"
60  LET SPECIAL$ = "SPECIAL DAYS"
70  LET DAY1$ = "1 - BOB"
80  LET DAY2$ = "8 - ANNIVERSARY"
90  LET DAY3$ = "16 - FATHER'S DAY"
100 LET DAY4$ = "23 - GRANDMA'S"
110 LET MONTH2$ = "JULY"
120 LET DAY5$ = "16 - MOM"
130 LET DAY6$ = "29 - UNCLE VITO"
140 PRINT
150 PRINT,MONTH1$
160 PRINT,"-----"
170 PRINT,BIRTHDAY$
180 PRINT
190 PRINT DAY1$,DAY4$
200 PRINT
210 PRINT,SPECIAL$
220 PRINT
230 PRINT DAY2$,DAY3$
240 PRINT : PRINT
250 PRINT,MONTH2$
260 PRINT,"----"
270 PRINT,BIRTHDAY$
280 PRINT
290 PRINT DAY5$,DAY6$
300 END
999 END
```

```
RUN
                 JUNE
                 -----
                 BIRTHDAYS

1 - BOB          23 - GRANDMA'S

                 SPECIAL DAYS

8 - ANNIVERSARY                16 - FATHER'S DAY

                 JULY
                 ----
                 BIRTHDAYS

16 - MOM         29 - UNCLE VITO
```

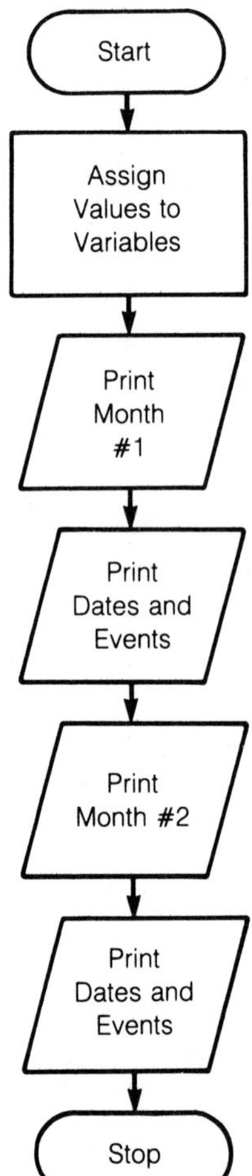

Pseudocode
Assign all headings, names, and dates to variables
Print each month followed by dates and events

PROGRAMMING EXERCISES

1. Write a short program that assigns your name to a string variable, and have the computer print that string variable.

2. Extend the program in Exercise 1 to print your age beside your name. Your output should be as follows:

```
XXXXXXXXXXXXX IS XX YEARS OLD
```

3. Write the same program as in Exercise 2, but now have the computer calculate your age in days (365 × your age) and list your age in days next to your age in years. Use REM statements to document your program properly. The output should be formatted as follows:

```
NAME                 YEARS   DAYS

XXXXXXXXXXXXXX       XX      XXXXX
```

4. Write a properly documented program that calculates the Centigrade temperature equivalents of −25, 6, and 80 degrees Fahrenheit; the formula for the temperature conversion is $C = 5/9 \times (F - 32)$. Use the SPC function to format your output in the following manner:

```
CENTIGRADE         FAHRENHEIT

XXX.XXXXXXX          XXX
XXX.XXXXXXX          XXX
XXX.XXXXXXX          XXX
```

5. Write a properly documented program that uses integer variables and calculates the square footage of a 25 × 32–foot room (square feet = length × width). Your output should be formatted this way:

```
THE LENGTH IS 32
THE WIDTH IS 25
THE SQUARE FOOTAGE = 800
```

CHAPTER 14

INPUTTING DATA AND SIMPLE CONTROL STATEMENTS

Chapter Outline

INTRODUCTION

In Chapter 13, the LET statement was used to enter data to programs. The LET statement is fine for small programs or for programs in which the data does not change. However, if a program is more involved and there is a great deal of data to enter, or if the data changes every time the program is run, a more efficient way to enter data is needed.

This chapter will expand your programming capabilities by introducing the INPUT, READ/DATA, and RESTORE statements as alternatives to the LET statement for entering data to programs. It will also discuss the use of the GOTO, IF/THEN/ELSE, and ON/GOTO statements in programs.

INPUT STATEMENT

The INPUT statement is commonly used to enter data to programs at the keyboard. The INPUT statement is used when a question-and-answer environment is required. The general format for this statement follows:

Line# INPUT "prompt";variable1,variable2, . . .

Prompt *A statement that tells the user of a program that data should be entered.*

A **prompt** is a statement that tells the user of a program that data should be entered. It also should tell the user what type of data to enter. Suppose, for instance, that you want to write a program that will calculate the gas mileage for your family's car. You also want everyone who drives the car to be able to enter the data, although none of the family members knows anything about computer programming. This would be an ideal situation in which to use an INPUT statement, because the data is different each time the program is run and the only thing the person entering the data needs to know is how far the car has been driven and how much gas has been used. The computer will ask for the information when it needs it. Figure 14–1 shows the gas mileage program.

When the computer reaches an INPUT statement, it prints the prompt and stops. This is the cue for the user to enter data. For example in Figure 14–1, when the user types RUN and presses the ENTER key, the computer executes the program. When it gets to the first INPUT statement, it prints the message ENTER THE DISTANCE TRAVELED?. Once the user has entered the data (105.0 in the example) and pressed the ENTER key, the program will continue. For the program in Figure 14–1, it will execute Line 30 in the same way as Line 20. Once this data has been entered (4.8), the computer will make the calculations and print the following results:

```
RUN
ENTER THE DISTANCE TRAVELED ? 105.0

ENTER THE GAS USED ? 4.8

DISTANCE         GAS USED         MILEAGE

 105              4.8              21.875
```

```
10 REM  COMPUTE GAS MILEAGE
20 REM
30 INPUT "ENTER THE DISTANCE TRAVELED ";DISTANCE
40 PRINT
50 INPUT "ENTER THE GAS USED ";GAS
60 LET MILES = DISTANCE / GAS
70 PRINT
80 PRINT "DISTANCE","GAS USED","MILEAGE"
90 PRINT
100 PRINT DISTANCE,GAS,MILES
999 END

RUN
ENTER THE DISTANCE TRAVELED ? 105.0

ENTER THE GAS USED ? 4.8

DISTANCE          GAS USED          MILEAGE

 105               4.8               21.875
```

Figure 14–1 GAS MILEAGE PROGRAM

If it is necessary to enter different data, simply run the program again to enter the new data. Try it yourself.

One INPUT statement can contain more than one variable. When the INPUT statement has two or more variables, the user must enter data for each variable specified. If enough data is not entered, the program will not continue.

An INPUT statement can be used to enter string data as well as numeric data—for example:

```
10 INPUT "ENTER NAME AND AGE ";A$,B
```

In this case, the information required is the user's name and age. Be sure to enter the data in the order it was requested. If a string is entered where a numeric variable is requested, the computer will print an error message.

The INPUT statement can be used without a prompt if one is not desired or if PRINT statements are used to tell the user what data is desired. In this instance, the computer will print a question mark when it is ready for data to be entered. Figure 14–2 shows the INPUT statement used with PRINT statements instead of prompts. This program segment will work exactly the same as Lines 20 through 30 in Figure 14–1.

READ/DATA STATEMENTS

The READ and DATA statements go hand in hand; one cannot be used without the other. Like the LET and INPUT statements, the READ/DATA statements are used to enter data. However, data is not entered in response

Figure 14–2 INPUT STATEMENT WITH NO PROMPT

```
10 PRINT "ENTER THE DISTANCE TRAVELED "
20 INPUT DISTANCE
30 PRINT
40 PRINT "ENTER THE GAS USED "
50 INPUT GAS

RUN
ENTER THE DISTANCE TRAVELED
? 105.0

ENTER THE GAS USED
? 4.8
```

to a prompt; instead it is listed in a group of input lines. READ/DATA statements are best used when a large amount of data must be entered. The general format is as follows:

Line# READ variable1, variable2, . . .
Line# DATA value1, value2, . . .

The DATA statement values may be numeric or string. However, no expressions (such as A + B or 13 + 7) are allowed in the list. The numeric constant may be in any format. String constants in DATA statements do not need to be surrounded by quotation marks, unless the string contains commas, colons, or significant leading or trailing blanks.

When the computer sees a READ statement, it stops and looks for data. Once it has the required data, it continues executing the program. An example is shown in Figure 14–3. In Line 10, the READ statement tells the computer to look for a DATA statement and to get two numeric data values. The computer finds the first DATA statement in Line 40 and reads the first two pieces of data. Notice that each data value is separated by a comma; 50 is assigned to NUMBER1, and 100 is assigned to NUMBER2. The computer then will continue and the output will be printed.

As with the INPUT statement, the data for READ/DATA statements can be numeric or string, as long as it matches the variables. Some examples of possible READ/DATA statements are given in the program segments shown in Figure 14–4. All these examples will produce the same results. The READ statements will cause the data values to be taken from the DATA statements. The DATA statements can come before or after the READ statements.

A single READ statement can access one or more DATA statements, or several READ statements can access one DATA statement. If the number of variables specified is fewer than the number of values in the DATA statement(s), subsequent READ statements will begin reading data at the first unread value. The READ statement accesses the DATA statement in line number order. If there are no subsequent READ statements, the extra data is ignored. If the number of variables in the list in the READ statement exceeds the number of values in the DATA statement, an error message will

```
10 READ NUMBER1,NUMBER2
20 LET TOTAL = NUMBER1 + NUMBER2
30 PRINT TOTAL
40 DATA 50,100
99 END

RUN
 150
```

Figure 14–3 READ/DATA EXAMPLE

```
10 READ PERSON$,AGE,FRIEND$
60 DATA "JOE",69,"DALE"

10 READ PERSON$
20 READ AGE
30 READ FRIEND$
40 DATA "JOE",69,"DALE"
```

Figure 14–4 READ/DATA STATEMENTS IN USE

```
10 READ NUMBER1,NUMBER2
50 DATA 12,20,30,40
          :
80 RESTORE
90 READ NUMBER3,NUMBER4
```

Figure 14–5 RESTORE STATEMENT

appear. The first READ statement encountered will take as many values of data as required from the top of the list. The next data item will then advance to the top of the list, and so on.

RESTORE STATEMENT

The RESTORE statement can be used with the READ/DATA statements when the same set of data is needed more than once in a given program. It enables the programmer to avoid entering redundant data. After a RESTORE statement is executed, the next READ statement accesses the first item in the first DATA statement, as shown in Figure 14–5.

The RESTORE statement tells the computer to go back to the first piece of data in the original data list. In Figure 14–5, the variables NUMBER3 and NUMBER4 will be given the values of 12 and 20, respectively—the same values as those stored in variables NUMBER1 and NUMBER2. Now that you know how to enter data to programs, you can learn how to manipulate the data once it has been entered. Although the techniques may be difficult at first, with practice they will become easier to understand and use.

LEARNING CHECK

1. Three statements used for entering data are the ________, ________, and ________ statements.
2. ________ statements are best used when data is frequently changing.
3. The PRINT statement can be used to enter data. (True or false?)
4. The ________ statement can be used instead of a prompt in the INPUT statement.
5. The INPUT statement must include a prompt. (True or false?)
6. One READ statement may access several DATA statements. (True or false?)
7. What values will be stored in variables Y and Z in the following program segment?

```
10 READ W,X
20 READ Y
30 RESTORE
40 READ Z
50 DATA 21,32,12,34,15,32,66
```

ANSWERS:

1. INPUT, READ/DATA, RESTORE. **2.** INPUT. **3.** false. **4.** PRINT. **5.** false. **6.** true. **7.** Y = 12, Z = 21.

GOTO STATEMENT

The GOTO statement tells the computer to execute the line indicated after the word GOTO. For example, if the computer came across the sequence of statements shown in Figure 14–6, it would execute Line 30; then, after reading Line 40, it would skip over Lines 50 and 60 and execute Line 70. The GOTO statement, which always transfers control to a specified line, is known as an **unconditional transfer statement.**

Unconditional transfer statement *A statement that always transfers control to another part of the program.*

If the line number specified by the GOTO statement is of an executable statement, that statement and those following are executed. If it is a non-executable statement, such as REM or DATA, the program will continue at the first executable statement encountered after the specified line number.

The GOTO statement is very useful in programs containing the INPUT statement. Using the process known as **looping** (executing part of a program as many times as needed), the GOTO statement eliminates the need to run the program each time more data is needed. In the mileage program in Figure 14–1, for example, after the data had been entered and the program run, the program had to be run again in order for the user to enter new data.

Looping *Executing part of a program as many times as needed.*

Figure 14–6 GOTO STATEMENT

```
30 LET NUMBER = NUMBER + 1
40 GOTO 70
50 PRINT "SUBTOTAL = ";NUMBER + NUMBER2
60 PRINT "CONTINUING"
70 INPUT NUMBER2
```

The program in Figure 14–7 illustrates the use of the GOTO statement and looping to simplify the program in Figure 14–6. Line 70 automatically transfers the program back to Line 20 to allow new data to be entered; thus the program forms a loop going from Line 70 to Line 20. Notice that this program will never end on its own. To stop the program, press the BREAK key while depressing the CONTROL key. Methods for avoiding these **infinite loops** (loops that never stop executing) will be discussed later.

Infinite loop
A loop that never stops executing.

IF/THEN/ELSE STATEMENT

The IF/THEN/ELSE statement is a **conditional transfer statement:** If a specified condition is true, the computer will transfer control to the line or statement following the THEN clause. If the condition is not true, the computer will follow a path specified by the ELSE and will perform a different task. What the computer does depends on whether or not the condition is true.

Conditional transfer statement
A statement that transfers program control only if a specified condition is true.

There are two basic formats for the IF/THEN statement:

Line# IF condition THEN Line# ELSE statement

or

Line# IF condition THEN statement ELSE statement

Figure 14–7 LOOPING WITH A GOTO STATEMENT

```
10 REM   COMPUTE GAS MILEAGE
15 REM
20 INPUT "ENTER THE DISTANCE TRAVELED ";DISTANCE
25 PRINT
30 INPUT "ENTER THE GAS USED ";GAS
40 LET MILES = DISTANCE / GAS
45 PRINT
50 PRINT "DISTANCE      GAS USED      MILEAGE"
55 PRINT
60 PRINT "  ";DISTANCE;"  ";GAS;"  ";MILES
70 GOTO 20
99 END
```

(The ELSE portion of these statements is optional.) In the first format, if the condition is true, the computer will skip to whatever line number is indicated after the THEN. (This is similar to the procedure for the GOTO statement.) If the condition is false, the computer will perform the task indicated after the ELSE. If the ELSE condition is omitted, the next statement in the program will be executed.

In Figure 14–8, which illustrates this idea, NUMBER1 = 2 is the condition. If NUMBER1 does indeed equal 2, control of the program is sent to Line 140, and the program prints NUMBER1 IS EQUAL TO 2 and stops. If the condition is not true—say NUMBER1 = 6—control goes to Line 120, which tells the computer to print a message saying that NUMBER1 is not equal to 2. Then control of the program is sent to Line 999, which is executed, and the program stops.

In the second format, instead of branching to a line number, a statement can be specified in the THEN clause. In the program in Figure 14–8, for example, Line 100 could have been written as follows:

```
100 IF NUMBER1 = 2 THEN PRINT "NUMBER1 IS EQUAL TO 2" ELSE 120
```

In this case, the PRINT statement would perform the same function as the line number.

Relational symbols
Symbols used to compare one expression with another.

The condition in an IF/THEN/ELSE statement can involve numeric or string variables. Mathematical **relational symbols** (symbols used to compare one expression with another) can also be used within the condition statement (see Table 14–1). Figure 14–9 gives examples of valid IF/THEN/ ELSE statements. Notice the different conditions that are possible and the statements that can be used.

AND/OR Clauses

The IF/THEN/ELSE statement can be expanded by adding the AND and OR clauses to it. The program in Figure 14–10 gives examples of both clauses. As is easily seen by going through this program line by line, the IF/AND/ THEN statement in Line 50 requires that both conditions be true before control is transferred to Line 90. With the IF/OR/THEN statement in Line 60, in contrast, only one of the conditions must be true. If either NUMBER1 = 1 or NUMBER2 = 2 (or both), the computer will skip to Line 130 and continue from there. If neither statement is true, the computer will continue on Line 70. Remember that if the appropriate conditions are not met for

Figure 14–8 IF/THEN/ELSE EXAMPLE

```
100 IF NUMBER1 = 2 THEN 140 ELSE 120
120 PRINT "NUMBER1 IS NOT EQUAL TO 2"
130 GOTO 999
140 PRINT "NUMBER1 IS EQUAL TO 2"
999 END
```

Table 14–1 RELATIONAL SYMBOLS

RELATIONAL SYMBOL	MEANING
<	Less than
>	Greater than
<=	Less than or equal to
>=	Greater than or equal to
=	Equal to
<>	Not equal to

```
40 IF A = 6 THEN 60              10 IF X = Y THEN PRINT "X = Y"
70 IF A >= 10 THEN 90            30 IF C > 2 * D THEN LET A = A + 1
30 IF A <= 4 + B THEN 65         80 IF C$ <> "CONTINUE" THEN END
60 IF A = B + C THEN 10          40 IF X = 5 THEN LET Y = X + 1
90 IF G$ = "YES" THEN 80         60 IF N$ = "M" THEN PRINT "MONDAY"
50 IF X = Y / Z THEN 85          55 IF A = 5 * A ^ B THEN PRINT X$
```

Figure 14–9 VALID IF/THEN/ELSE STATEMENTS

the corresponding IF/THEN/ELSE statements, control of the program will always pass to the next line in sequence.

Dummy Values

In Figure 14–7, the mileage program is in an infinite loop. By adding an IF/THEN/ELSE statement, control can be transferred to Line 99 to end the program, as shown in Figure 14–11. The prompt in Line 30 tells the user what values to enter to terminate the program. The 0 is called a **dummy value.** It is not data needed for the program; instead, it is used strictly to indicate to the computer that the end of the input data has been reached. When the dummy values are read into the program and the computer executes the IF statement, it will test for that condition and will know when to send control to another part of the program (usually the end). Make sure that the dummy values used are never actual data values, or a logic error may occur.

Dummy value
A value used to indicate that the end of the input data has been reached.

The program in Figure 14–11 also could have been written using READ/DATA statements, with dummy values at the end of the DATA statement to indicate the actual end of usable data (see Figure 14–12). Notice that in Line 30 the last two data items are 0s, but Line 50 tests the value of only one variable, DISTANCE, to determine if it is 0. You may wonder why that last 0 is not just left off. Recall that the discussion about READ/DATA statements indicated that an appropriate value must be entered for each variable

Figure 14–10 AND AND OR CLAUSES

```
10 PRINT
20 PRINT "ENTER THE NUMBER 1, 2, 3 "
30 PRINT "IN ANY ORDER"
40 INPUT NUMBER1,NUMBER2,NUMBER3
50 IF NUMBER1 = 1 AND NUMBER2 = 2 THEN 90
60 IF NUMBER1 = 1 OR NUMBER2 = 2 THEN 130
70 IF NUMBER1 <> NUMBER2 + NUMBER3 THEN 170
80 GOTO 200
90 PRINT
100 PRINT "BOTH CONDITIONS ARE MET"
110 PRINT "NUMBER1 = 1 AND NUMBER2 = 2"
120 GOTO 70
130 PRINT
140 PRINT "ONE OF THE CONDITIONS IS MET"
150 PRINT "EITHER NUMBER1 = 1 OR NUMBER2 = 2"
160 GOTO 70
170 PRINT
180 PRINT "NUMBER1 <> NUMBER2 + NUMBER3"
190 GOTO 220
200 PRINT
210 PRINT "NUMBER1 = NUMBER2 + NUMBER3"
999 END


RUN

ENTER THE NUMBER 1, 2, 3
IN ANY ORDER
? 1,2,3

BOTH CONDITIONS ARE MET
NUMBER1 = 1 AND NUMBER2 = 2

NUMBER1 <> NUMBER2 + NUMBER3
```

in the READ statement or an error message will result. In this case, if the last 0 had been left off, an OUT OF DATA error message would have appeared (the very condition we were trying to avoid) and program execution would have terminated.

Counter
A numeric variable that is increased or decreased each time a loop is executed, thereby controlling how many times the loop will be executed.

Terminal value
The value that, when reached by the loop variable, will stop loop repetition.

Counters

Dummy values are one way of ending a loop. Another way is to use a **counter,** a numeric variable that is increased or decreased, usually by 1, each time the loop is executed, thereby controlling how many times the loop is executed. When the number set for the counter variable in an IF/THEN/ELSE statement (the **terminal value**—the value that, when reached

```
10 REM    COMPUTE GAS MILEAGE
20 REM
30 PRINT "ENTER 0 TO QUIT"
40 INPUT "ENTER THE DISTANCE TRAVELED ";DISTANCE
50 IF DISTANCE = 0 THEN 999
60 PRINT
70 INPUT "ENTER THE GAS USED ";GAS
80 LET MILES = DISTANCE / GAS
90 PRINT
100 PRINT "DISTANCE","GAS USED","MILEAGE"
110 PRINT
120 PRINT DISTANCE,GAS,MILES
130 PRINT
140 GOTO 30
999 END


RUN
ENTER 0 TO QUIT
ENTER THE DISTANCE TRAVELED ? 375

ENTER THE GAS USED ? 18.5

DISTANCE      GAS USED      MILEAGE

 375           18.5          20.27027

ENTER 0 TO QUIT
ENTER THE DISTANCE TRAVELED ? 0
```

Figure 14–11 MILEAGE PROGRAM WITH DUMMY VALUE

by the loop variable, will stop loop repetition) is reached, the THEN clause will be executed and control can be sent out of the loop.

Figure 14–13 illustrates the use of a counter. In Line 30 the terminal value is set at 7. Line 50 is the counter. Each time the loop is executed, COUNTER is increased by 1. The counter does not have to be set to 0, since all variables are automatically set to 0 after the NEW command is used to clear memory. After the seventh time the loop is executed, COUNTER will equal 7. Line 30 tells the computer go to Line 999 if COUNTER = 7, and the program then will end. Be sure the statement that increases the counter and the IF/THEN/ELSE statement that tests the condition are both within the loop. If they are not, the program will never end, and a logic error will result.

ON/GOTO STATEMENT

The ON/GOTO statement is an extension of the GOTO statement. It transfers control to other statements in the program on the basis of the value of a mathematical expression. Any of several transfers may occur, depending

Figure 14–12 READ/DATA WITH DUMMY VALUE

```
10 REM   COMPUTE GAS MILEAGE
20 REM
30 DATA 600,60,40,20,0,0
40 READ DISTANCE,GAS
50 IF DISTANCE = 0 THEN 999
60 PRINT
70 LET MILES = DISTANCE / GAS
80 PRINT
90 PRINT "DISTANCE","GAS USED","MILEAGE"
100 PRINT
110 PRINT DISTANCE,GAS,MILES
120 PRINT
130 GOTO 40
999 END
RUN

DISTANCE         GAS USED        MILEAGE

 600              60              10


DISTANCE         GAS USED        MILEAGE

 40               20              2
```

Multiple conditional transfer statement
A statement that transfers program control to other statements on the basis of the value of a mathematical expression.

on the value computed. Therefore, the ON/GOTO statement is a **multiple conditional transfer statement.** The format is as follows:

Line# ON expression GOTO Line#, Line#, Line#, ...

Here is an example:

```
40 ON X GOTO 100, 200, 300
```

If X is equal to 1, control goes to the first line number after the word GOTO (Line 100 in this case). If X is equal to 2, control transfers to the second line number (Line 200). If X is equal to 3, control transfers to Line 300. The ON/GOTO statement recognizes only integer values. If X had been computed and was not a whole number (say 2.16), the numeric expression would have been rounded (leaving X = 2). If the expression value (X in this example) is 0 or is greater than the number of items in the list, IBM BASIC continues with the next executable statement.

Figure 14–14 shows how to use the ON/GOTO statement in a program. If the expression NUMBER / 2 in Line 40 is equal to 1 or is rounded to 1,

Figure 14–13 COUNTER PROGRAM

```
10 REM *** PROGRAM TO SEE IF A NUMBER IS ***
20 REM *** DIVISIBLE BY 3                ***
25 REM
30 IF COUNTER = 7 THEN 999
40 READ NUMBER
50 LET COUNTER = COUNTER + 1
60 REM *** INT IS FOR INTEGER, WHICH IS JUST THE ***
70 REM *** WHOLE NUMBER AND NOT THE DECIMAL PART ***
80 REM *** EXAMPLE INT(4.25) = 4                 ***
90 IF NUMBER / 3 = INT(NUMBER/3) THEN 110
100 GOTO 30
110 PRINT NUMBER;" IS DIVISIBLE BY 3"
120 GOTO 30
130 DATA 11,9,22,15,14,18,21
999 END

RUN
 9  IS DIVISIBLE BY 3
 15  IS DIVISIBLE BY 3
 18  IS DIVISIBLE BY 3
 21  IS DIVISIBLE BY 3
```

Figure 14–14 ON/GOTO PROGRAM

```
10 PRINT "ENTER A NUMBER FROM 1 TO 10"
20 INPUT NUMBER
30 IF NUMBER / 2 > 4 THEN 500
40 ON NUMBER / 2 GOTO 100,200,300,400
100 PRINT "THE NUMBER WAS 1 OR 2"
110 GOTO 999
200 PRINT "THE NUMBER WAS 3 OR 4"
210 GOTO 999
300 PRINT "THE NUMBER WAS 5 OR 6"
310 GOTO 999
400 PRINT "THE NUMBER WAS 7 OR 8"
410 GOTO 999
500 PRINT "THE NUMBER WAS 9 OR 10"
999 END

RUN
ENTER A NUMBER FROM 1 TO 10
? 3
THE NUMBER WAS 3 OR 4
```

control will be transferred to Line 100. If NUMBER / 2 is equal to 2 or is rounded to 2, control will be transferred to Line 200, and so on. Line 30 is inserted to prevent an error message if NUMBER / 2 exceeds the values in the ON/GOTO statement (that is, if NUMBER / 2 is greater than 4).

The ON/GOTO statement may seem difficult at first. However, with practice in writing short programs using this statement, you will find it much easier to understand.

LEARNING CHECK

1. Is the GOTO statement a conditional or an unconditional transfer statement?

2. Is the IF/THEN/ELSE statement a conditional or an unconditional transfer statement?

3. If A = 72 in the following program, what line will be executed after Line 10?

```
10 IF A > 72 THEN 70
20 IF B = 61 THEN A = 12
70 PRINT "FINISHED"
99 END
```

4. A ________ value is used to mark the end of a data file.

5. ________ and ________ are methods for exiting a loop.

ANSWERS:

1. unconditional. 2. conditional. 3. Line 20. 4. dummy. 5. Dummy values, counters.

SUMMARY POINTS

- The INPUT, READ/DATA, and RESTORE statements are all used for entering data to programs.
- The INPUT statement is used when a question-and-answer environment is needed.
- A prompt included in an INPUT statement should tell the person entering the data exactly what information is required. If more than one variable is specified in the INPUT statement, the specified number of values must be entered or the program will not continue.
- The READ/DATA statements must be used together and are best suited for use with large amounts of data.
- The DATA statements can come before or after the READ statement, and as many READ and DATA statements as are needed can be used in a program.
- The RESTORE statement is used in conjunction with the READ/DATA statements. When inserted, the RESTORE statement tells the computer to go back to the beginning of its list of data items and start over. By using this statement, a programmer can avoid entering redundant data.
- The GOTO statement tells the computer to execute the line following the word GOTO. It is an unconditional transfer statement, since control is sent without regard to any conditions.
- The IF/THEN/ELSE statement is a conditional transfer statement. Depending on a specified condition, the computer will take one of two different paths.

- The condition in an IF/THEN/ELSE statement can involve numeric or string variables. Mathematical relational symbols also can be used within the condition.
- The AND and OR clauses can expand the flexibility of the IF/THEN/ELSE statement.
- When the IF/AND/THEN statement is used, both conditions specified must be true for the THEN clause to be executed.
- When the IF/OR/THEN statement is used, one or both of the statements must be true for the THEN clause to be executed.
- A dummy value indicates when the last data item has been reached. It is used in conjunction with the IF/THEN/ELSE statement to exit a loop.
- Counters are numeric variables that increase or decrease, usually by 1, each time a loop is executed. When the specified number (terminal value) is reached, the computer will exit the loop, transferring control to the line specified in the IF/THEN/ELSE statement.
- The ON/GOTO statement is a multiple conditional transfer statement; when the computer executes this statement, it can follow two or more paths.

REVIEW QUESTIONS

1. Explain how the INPUT statement works.

2. Write two BASIC statements that will ask the user to enter two values. The first one should be the name of a school, and the second should be the number of students attending that school. Assign these values to appropriate variables.

3. When are the READ and DATA statements useful?

4. Write READ and DATA statements to assign the odd numbers between 8 and 26 to the correct number of numeric variables.

5. What does the RESTORE statement do?

6. Study this program segment:

```
10 READ A,B,D,E,F
20 RESTORE
30 READ B,C
40 RESTORE
50 READ F
60 DATA 20,40,27,1,8,13,17,26
```

After these statements are executed, what will be the values of A, B, C, D, E, and F?

7. Why is the GOTO statement referred to as an unconditional transfer statement?

8. Write an IF/THEN/ELSE statement that will print the value of X only if X is greater than 0.

9. Write an IF/THEN/ELSE statement that will print the value of WIDTH only if WIDTH is greater than LENGTH and greater than 44.

10. How are dummy values used in controlling loop execution?

SAMPLE PROGRAMS

1. This program uses the LET, INPUT, and READ/DATA statements. The program is documented with REM statements to help you understand what it is telling the computer to do, and when.

```
10 REM *** PROGRAM WITH THREE DATA ***
20 REM *** ENTRY METHODS           ***
30 REM *** READ/DATA               ***
40 READ TITLE$
50 DATA "STOSH"
60 REM *** INPUT ***
70 PRINT "INPUT ONE NUMBER AND DEPRESS"
80 PRINT "RETURN"
90 INPUT FIRST
100 PRINT
110 INPUT "ENTER A NUMBER FROM 1 TO 9 ";NUMBER
120 IF NUMBER < 1 THEN 100
130 IF NUMBER > 9 THEN 100
140 REM *** LET ***
150 LET TOTAL = FIRST * NUMBER
160 PRINT
170 PRINT "NAME","INPUTS","FIRST * NUMBER"
180 PRINT
190 PRINT TITLE$,FIRST;" & ";NUMBER,TOTAL
999 END
```

```
RUN
INPUT ONE NUMBER AND DEPRESS
RETURN
? 45

ENTER A NUMBER FROM 1 TO 9 ? 3

NAME           INPUTS         FIRST * NUMBER

STOSH           45  &  3       135
```

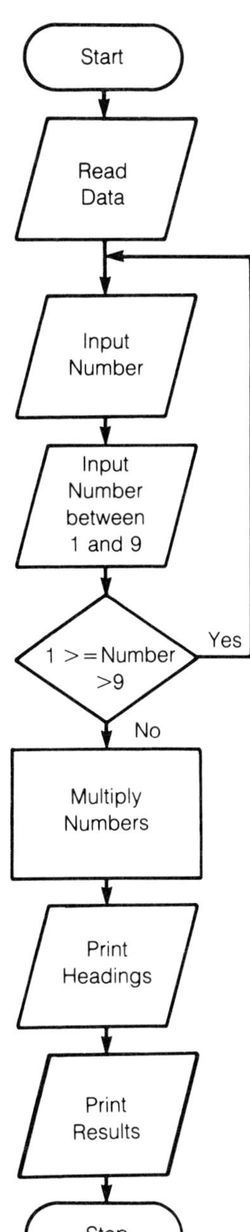

Pseudocode
Read name from data list
Input first number
Input second number between 1 and 9
Multiply first and second numbers
Print headings
Print results

2. This program uses LET and READ/DATA statements. A loop is formed using the GOTO statement in Line 140. The dummy value END is used to signify the end of the data records, and the loop is exited via the IF/THEN/ ELSE conditional transfer command in Line 95.

```
10 REM *** BASEBALL PROGRAM                                ***
20 REM *** AVE = BATTING AVERAGE                           ***
30 REM *** BATS = AT BATS, HIT = HITS                      ***
40 REM *** SINGLES = SINGLES, DOUBLES = DOUBLES ***
50 REM *** TRIPLES = TRIPLES, HOME = HOME RUNS   ***
60 PRINT
70 PRINT "NAME","BAT AV","EXTRA"
80 PRINT ,,"HITS"
85 PRINT
90 READ PERSON$,BATS,HIT,SINGLES,DOUBLES,TRIPLES,HOME
95 IF PERSON$ = "END" THEN 999
100 LET AVE = HIT / BATS
110 LET TOTAL = DOUBLES + TRIPLES + HOME
120 PRINT
130 PRINT PERSON$,AVE,TOTAL
140 GOTO 90
150 DATA JOHN,20,8,2,4,2,0,TOM,30,18,6,0,2,2
160 DATA DAN,50,25,14,6,2,3,LEE,20,6,2,1,2,1
170 DATA END,0,0,0,0,0,0
999 END
```

```
RUN

NAME              BAT AV            EXTRA
                                    HITS


JOHN               .4                6

TOM                .6                4

DAN                .5                11

LEE                .3                4
```

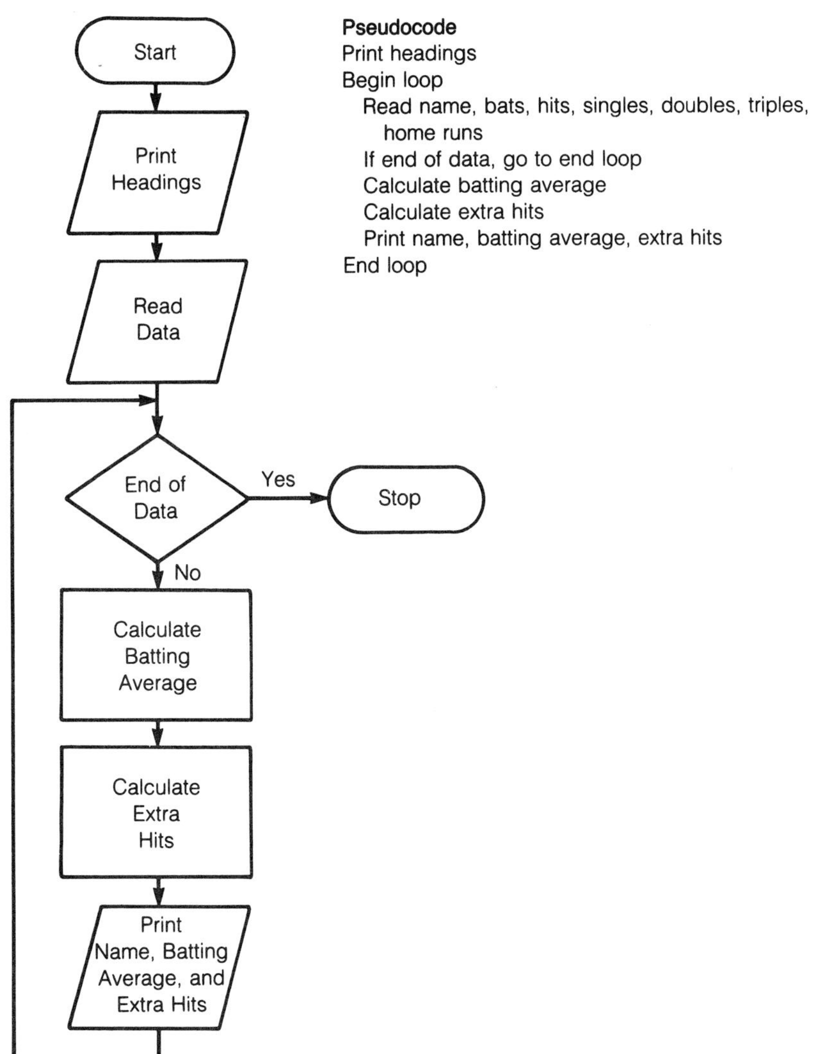

Pseudocode

Print headings
Begin loop
  Read name, bats, hits, singles, doubles, triples,
    home runs
  If end of data, go to end loop
  Calculate batting average
  Calculate extra hits
  Print name, batting average, extra hits
End loop

PROGRAMMING EXERCISES

1. Write a properly documented program that uses a question-and-answer environment to enter data. The program should print the total of any two numbers when they are added, subtracted, multiplied, and divided. The output should be as follows:

```
ENTER ANY TWO NUMBERS
(SEPARATE THE NUMBERS WITH A COMMA) XXX,XXX

XXX + XXX = XXXX

XXX - XXX = XXXX

XXX * XXX = XXXX

XXX / XXX = XXXX
```

2. Write a program to help students with their math (simple addition). Use READ/DATA statements to enter your data and the INPUT command for the students to enter their answers. You will need to use a GOTO command to form a loop and a dummy value to escape and end the program. The program should test the students on adding 1 + 1, 2 + 2, 3 + 3, 4 + 4, and 5 + 5. The prompts and output should be in the following format:

```
1 + 1 =
WHAT IS THE ANSWER

? 2

HOORAY, YOU GOT IT RIGHT!

2 + 2 =

WHAT IS THE ANSWER

?5

OOPS! THAT'S WRONG, TRY AGAIN.

WHAT IS THE ANSWER
?
      .
      .
      .
```

3. Write a program using an INPUT statement, a loop, and a counter to calculate your total gas bill for last year. Assume that you receive bills monthly, so you will be entering twelve bills, which should be totaled. The output should be similar to this:

```
THIS PROGRAM WILL CALCULATE YOUR
GAS BILL FOR ONE YEAR

ENTER ONE MONTH'S GAS BILL  $ XXX

ENTER ONE MONTH'S GAS BILL  $ XXX
              .
              .
              .
YOUR GAS BILL FOR LAST YEAR WAS  $ XXXX
```

4. Write a program that explains and demonstrates the use of the RESTORE command. The program should use four data items in one DATA statement, as well as two READ statements. First, add the first two data items; then READ the same DATA statement again, and total all four data items. Your output should be formatted as follows:

```
THE FIRST TWO DATA ITEMS  =  XXXX

ALL FOUR DATA ITEMS  =  XXXXX
```

5. Write a program using the IF/THEN/ELSE statement to determine a semi-annual insurance premium. The base premium for persons under the age of twenty-five is $160. Those who are twenty-five years of age or older have a base premium of $120. For a person who has had one or more accidents, the premium is the base premium plus $60. Otherwise, the base premium is the premium charged. At the end of the program, print the data along with the final premium.

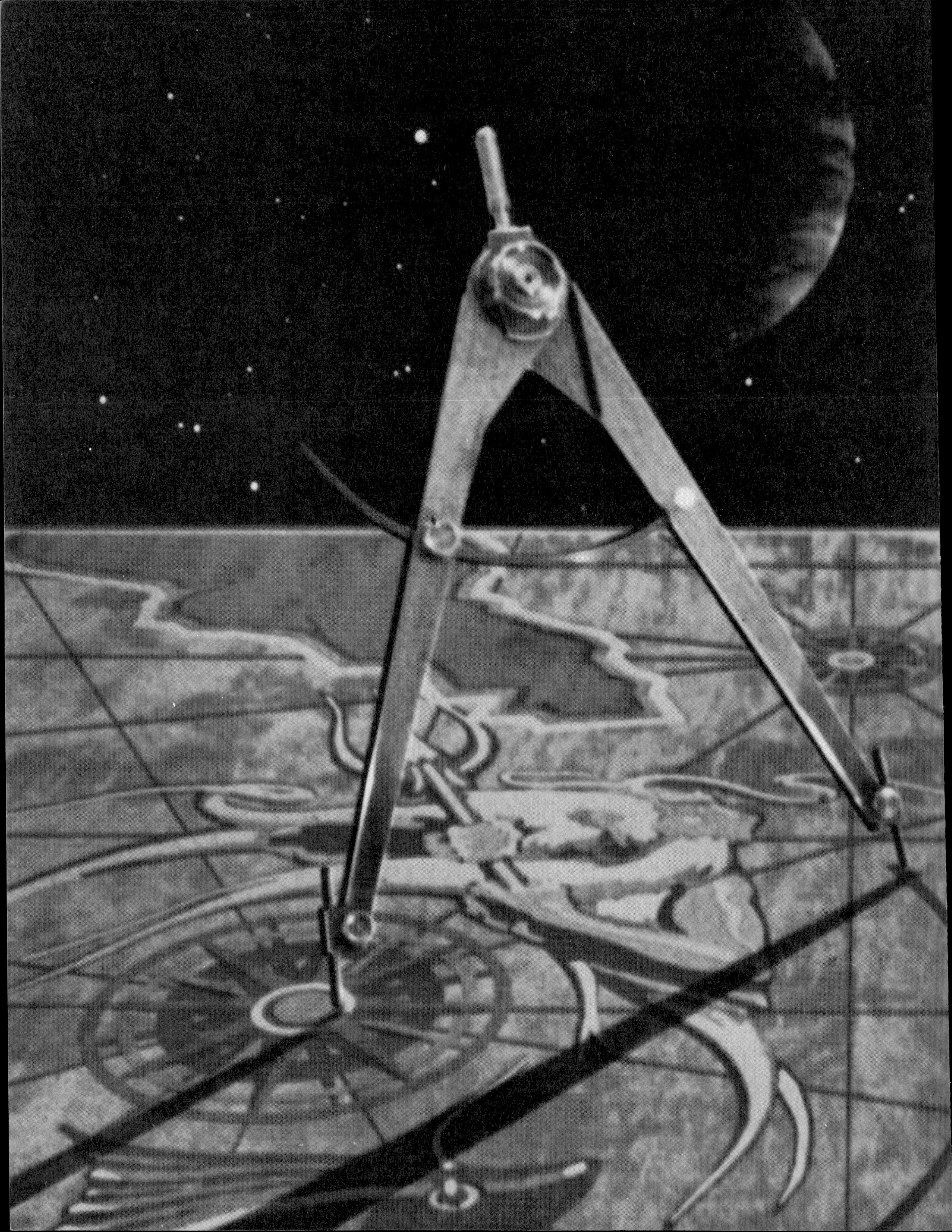

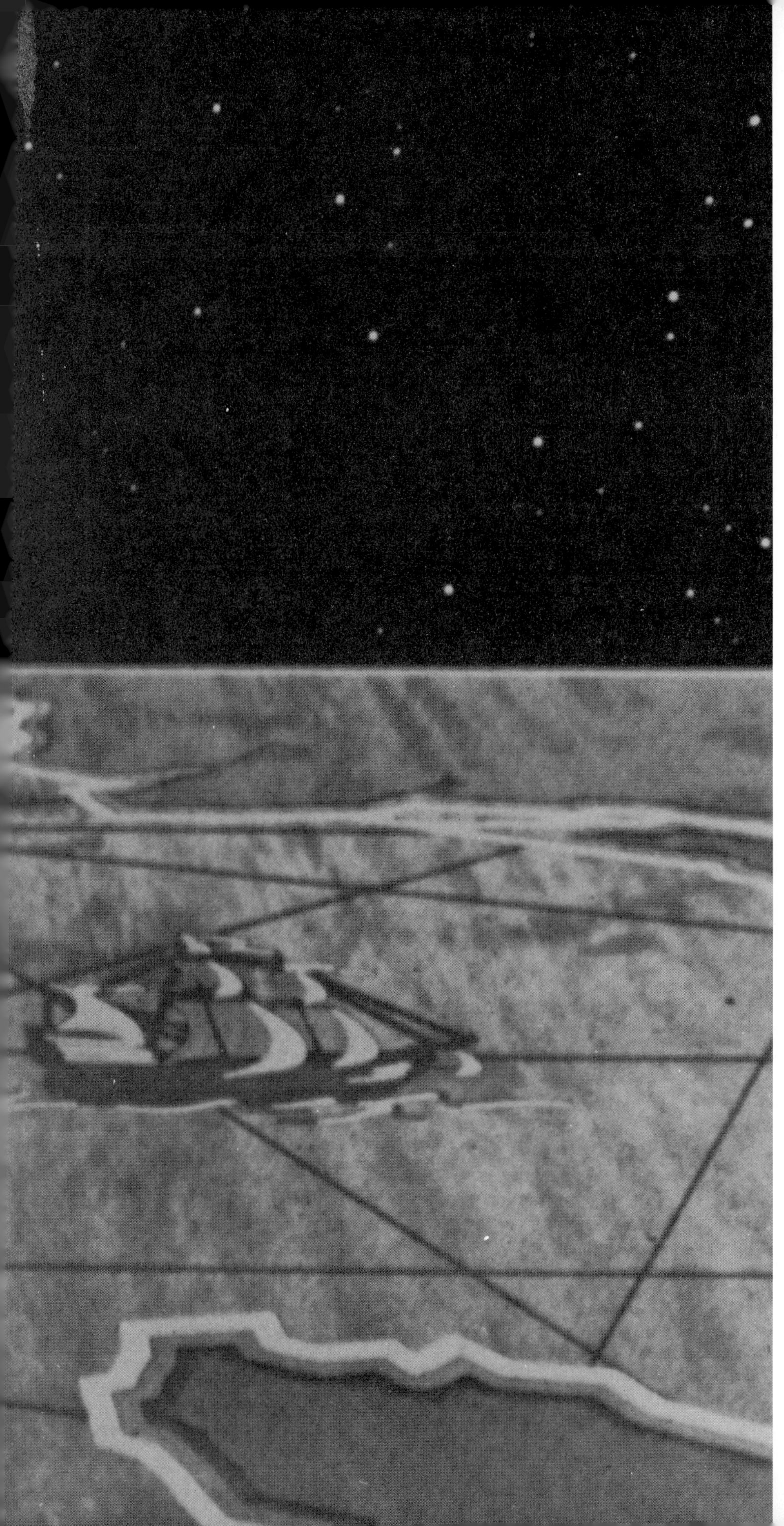

CHAPTER 15

LOOPING AND USING SUBROUTINES

Chapter Outline

INTRODUCTION

Now that the primary BASIC commands have been discussed, it is time to deal with a few of the more advanced commands. This chapter will begin by introducing two looping techniques: the FOR/NEXT loop and the WHILE/WEND loop. It will also introduce subroutines so you will be able to break down large, complex programs into manageable parts. Finally, the chapter will cover commands used with subroutines: GOSUB, RETURN, STOP, and ON/GOSUB.

FOR/NEXT STATEMENTS

The FOR and NEXT statements, a useful combination of commands, allow programmers to specify how many times a loop will be executed. The general formats for the FOR and NEXT statements follow:

```
Line# FOR lv = initial value TO terminal value STEP value
        .
        .  } loop body
        .
Line# NEXT lv
```

In the general format, lv stands for loop variable. The loop body is executed for each value of the lv from the initial value through the terminal one. Initial and terminal values can be constants, variables, or expressions.

The FOR and NEXT statements are always used together. Figure 15–1 shows how they work. The FOR J = 1 clause in Line 10 tells the computer to start counting the times the loop is executed at 1. Therefore, the first

Figure 15–1 FOR/NEXT PROGRAM

```
10 FOR J = 1 TO 12 STEP 1
20      PRINT J
30 NEXT J
99 END

RUN
 1
 2
 3
 4
 5
 6
 7
 8
 9
 10
 11
 12
```

time the computer sees Line 10, it will assign a value of 1 to J. The TO 12 clause tells the computer to stop executing the loop when J exceeds 12 (J > 12). The ending expression (12, in this case) is the **terminal value**— the value at which loop execution will be stopped. The final clause in Line 10, STEP 1, tells the computer how much to add or subtract from the loop variable each time the loop is executed. In the example in Figure 15–1, the loop will be executed twelve times. If the STEP value were 6, as in Figure 15–2, the loop would be executed only two times; 6 would be added to the loop variable with each execution of the loop, and the terminal value of 12 would be surpassed in only two loop executions.

Terminal value
The value at which loop execution will be stopped.

For clarity it is recommended that you indent when using FOR/NEXT loops. This will make it easier to distinguish the beginning and end of each loop. Figures 15–1 and 15–2 show properly indented programs.

There are two ways of controlling the number of times a FOR/NEXT loop is executed. One is to vary the difference between the loop variable and the terminal value. For example, FOR J = 1 TO 10 will be executed ten times, whereas FOR J = 1 TO 5 will be executed only five times. The other way to control the number of times a loop is executed is to increase or decrease the STEP value. If the STEP value is omitted, the computer assumes a STEP value of +1. Line 20 in Figure 15–2 displays the value of J during each execution of the loop. The NEXT statement in Line 30 signifies the end of the loop. At this point, control is sent back to Line 10. When J reaches a value greater than 12, control will go to Line 99, which, in this case, ends the program.

The program in Figure 15–3 uses the GOTO statement in conjunction with a counter to perform and exit a loop. Line 40 increments the counter. When N reaches a value greater than 5, the program will go to Line 99 and end. Figure 15–4 shows how the same results can be obtained using FOR/NEXT statements. Both programs do exactly the same thing, but FOR and NEXT statements are more efficient.

Suppose the Indian who sold Manhattan Island for $24 in 1626 had put that money in a bank to earn 6 percent interest compounded annually every year since. How much money would his descendants have today? The program in Figure 15–5 uses a FOR/NEXT loop to determine the answer. PRICE is set to 24 rather than 0 because the Indian started out with $24. The loop will run 359 times (1985 − 1626). The answer is as follows:

```
RUN
 3.092587E+10
```

```
10 FOR J = 1 TO 12 STEP 6
20     PRINT J
30 NEXT J
99 END

RUN
 1
 7
```

Figure 15–2 FOR/NEXT PROGRAM WITH STEP VALUE OF 6

Figure 15–3 LOOP FORMED BY GOTO COMMAND

```
10 LET N = 1
20 IF N > 5 THEN 99
30     PRINT N;TAB(10);N ^ 2;TAB(20);N ^ 3
40 LET N = N + 1
50 GOTO 20
99 END

RUN
 1         1         1
 2         4         8
 3         9         27
 4         16        64
 5         25        125
```

Figure 15–4 FOR/NEXT LOOP

```
10 FOR N = 1 TO 5
20     PRINT N;TAB(10);N ^ 2;TAB(20);N ^ 3
30 NEXT N
99 END

RUN
 1         1         1
 2         4         8
 3         9         27
 4         16        64
 5         25        125
```

Figure 15–5 INDIAN INTEREST PROGRAM

```
10 LET PRICE = 24
20 FOR YEAR = 1626 TO 1985
30     LET PRICE = PRICE + PRICE * 0.06
40 NEXT YEAR
50 PRINT PRICE
99 END
```

This answer is the same as $30,925,870,000, or a little over $30 billion—not a bad price.

Increment
To increase a value.

Decrement
To decrease a value.

Increments

A programmer may want to **increment** or **decrement** (increase or decrease) the loop variable by something other than 1s. This change can be incorporated in the FOR statement. For instance, to increase J by 2 instead of 1, the STEP value can be changed to 2, as illustrated here:

```
10 FOR J = 1 TO 5 STEP 2
```

It is also possible to step backward using negative STEP values, as shown in Figure 15–6. Be sure Line 10 reads J = 10 TO 1, not J = 1 TO 10, when stepping backward. Otherwise, a logic error will result. For a positive STEP value, the initial value must be smaller than the terminal value; for a negative STEP value, the initial value must be larger than the value. Remember, any valid constant, numeric expression, or arithmetic formula can be used as an expression. Figure 15–7 gives some examples of valid FOR/NEXT statements.

Nested Loops

Sometimes more than one loop is needed to accomplish a task. When one or more loops are contained within another loop, they are called **nested loops.** One loop must be totally within another to be properly nested.

Nested loop
A loop that is contained within another loop.

Figure 15–8 illustrates a nested loop. In this example, every time the inner loop executes five times, the outer loop is incremented (increased) by 1. When this program is run, the loop values are displayed as in Figure 15–9. The first column of numbers represents the outer loop (I), and the second column represents the inner loop (J). In Line 10, I is set to 1. Then control goes to Line 20, and J is set to 1. The first NEXT statement encountered is NEXT J. Control is returned to Line 20, J is increased to 2, and so on. Once the inner loop exceeds 5, the statement NEXT I is encountered. This statement sends control to Line 10 and increases the outer loop by 1, to 2. The process then starts all over again and continues until I exceeds 3 and control passes to the statement following Line 50.

Figure 15–10 and 15–11 contain examples of valid and invalid nested loops. The computer will give the error message NEXT without FOR if the loops are intertwined.

Another example of valid nested loops appears in Figure 15–12. When A

```
10 FOR J = 10 TO 1 STEP -2
20     PRINT J
30 NEXT J
99 END

RUN
 10
 8
 6
 4
 2
```

Figure 15–6 NEGATIVE STEP VALUES

Figure 15–7 VALID FOR/NEXT STATEMENTS

```
FOR X = (10 - B) TO (35 + G) STEP 5
     .
     .
     .
NEXT X

FOR T = P TO 10 STEP 2
     .
     .
     .
NEXT T

FOR I = A TO 3 STEP -1
     .
     .
     .
NEXT I
```

Figure 15–8 NESTED LOOP

```
10 FOR I = 1 TO 3
20     FOR J = 1 TO 5
30         PRINT I,J
40     NEXT J
50 NEXT I
99 END
```

is initialized to 1, B runs its loop until its terminal value is greater than 2. Thus, after one cycle of the B loop, the output is as follows:

```
RUN
1 X 1 = 1                    2 X 1 = 2
```

When the terminal value of B is exceeded, the outer loop, A, increments by 1 giving a new loop value of 2, and the process begins again. Notice that the loops in Figures 15–10, 15–11, and 15–12 have been correctly indented.

WHILE/WEND STATEMENTS

The WHILE and WEND statements in IBM BASIC allow programming in a more structured form. Although the programmer may be tempted to use the GOTO statement, the WHILE and WEND statements should be incor-

LEARNING CHECK

1. Initial and final values in the FOR loop variable can be ________, ________, or ________.

2. Which of the following is a valid FOR statement?

   a. `10 FOR X = 12 TO 6 STEP -5`

   b. `10 FOR J = 1 TO 427 STEP 43`

   c. `10 FOR I = 7 TO 8`

   d. all of the above

3. When the terminal value is surpassed in a FOR/NEXT loop, the loop will begin to execute. (True or false?)

4. If no STEP value is indicated, the computer will assume it to be ________.

5. Is the following program segment valid or invalid?

```
10 FOR I = 1 TO 3 STEP 1
20     FOR J = 5 TO 1 STEP -1
30         PRINT I,J
40     NEXT I
50 NEXT J
```

ANSWERS:

1. constants, variables, expressions. 2. d. 3. false. 4. +1. 5. invalid (has intertwined loops).

Figure 15–9 LOOP VALUES

```
10 FOR I = 1 TO 3
20     FOR J = 1 TO 5
30         PRINT I,J
40     NEXT J
50 NEXT I
99 END
RUN
 1            1
 1            2
 1            3
 1            4
 1            5
 2            1
 2            2
 2            3
 2            4
 2            5
 3            1
 3            2
 3            3
 3            4
 3            5
```

Figure 15–10 VALID NESTING

```
10 FOR A = 1 TO 10

20    FOR B = 1 TO 10

30       FOR C = 1 TO 10

40          PRINT A,B,C

50       NEXT C

60    NEXT B

70 NEXT A

99 END
```

Figure 15–11 INVALID NESTING

```
10 FOR A = 1 TO 10

20    FOR B = 1 TO 10

30       PRINT A,B

40    NEXT A

50 NEXT B

99 END
```

Figure 15–12 VALID NESTED LOOP WITH OUTPUT

```
10 FOR A = 1 TO 3
20    FOR B = 1 TO 2
30       PRINT B;" X ";A;" = ";B * A,
40    NEXT B
50    PRINT
60 NEXT A
99 END

RUN
 1  X  1  =  1                   2  X  1  =  2
 1  X  2  =  2                   2  X  2  =  4
 1  X  3  =  3                   2  X  3  =  6
```

porated instead, because the flow of the program will be more easily followed when they are used. The general format for the WHILE/WEND statements follows:

```
Line# WHILE expression
        .
        .  } loop body
        .
Line# WEND
```

In the general format, the WHILE statement is the beginning of the loop. The expression may also be a simple variable. (The reason for this will be discussed later.) The WEND statement is the end of the loop. All statements between the two are repeated each time the loop is executed.

Like the FOR and NEXT statements, the WHILE and WEND statements are always used together. Figure 15–13 shows how they work. The LET statement in Line 10 simply initializes the variable A to a specific value. It need not be there if A has previously attained a value. The WHILE/WEND loop is then entered at Line 20. If the expression is evaluated as true, the loop is executed. In this short program, the expression does evaluate as true, so the loop body is entered. The loop will continue to execute until A is no longer less than 3. The loop body prints A and then adds 1 to A. The addition of 1 to A is vital to the execution of the WHILE/WEND statement. If 1 is not added to A, the expression will remain true, and the program will be stuck in an infinite loop.

The WEND statement is reached on Line 99. The computer rechecks the expression, and if it is true, the statements in the loop body are executed again. A false evaluation will cause the first statement following the WEND statement to be executed. The loop in this example will execute three times and will exit when A equals 3.

As mentioned before, a variable may replace the expression in the WHILE statement. An example is given in Figure 15–14. The loop will execute until the variable equals 0. Each time through the loop, 1 is subtracted from B before the WEND statement causes the variable to be evaluated again. This

```
10 LET A = 0
20 WHILE A < 3
30     PRINT A
40     A = A + 1
50 WEND
99 END

RUN
 0
 1
 2
```

Figure 15–13 WHILE/WEND PROGRAM WITH EXPRESSION

Figure 15–14 WHILE/WEND PROGRAM WITH VARIABLE

```
10 LET B = 3
20 WHILE B
30      PRINT B
40      B = B - 1
50 WEND
99 END

RUN
 3
 2
 1
```

LEARNING CHECK

1. WHILE/WEND loops are used to eliminate the need for which of the following?

   a. FOR/NEXT loops

   b. GOTO statements

   c. IF/THEN statements

   d. none of the above

2. Which of the following is a valid WHILE statement?

   a. `10 WHILE X < 6 DO`

   b. `10 WHILE X = 6 THEN`

   c. `10 WHILE X = 1 TO 4`

   d. `10 WHILE X`

3. A WHILE/WEND loop always executes at least once. (True or false?)

4. A constant can be used instead of the expression in the WHILE statement. (True or false?)

5. Is the following program segment valid or invalid?

```
10 LET Y = 0
20 LET X = 10
30 WHILE X
40      WHILE Y = 0
50           PRINT Y,X
60           IF X = 6 THEN Y = 1
70      WEND
80      X = X - 2
90 WEND
```

ANSWERS: **1.** b. **2.** d. **3.** false. **4.** false. **5.** valid.

loop executes three times and then exits to the first line following the WEND statement (if there is such a line).

Like FOR/NEXT loops, WHILE/WEND loops can be nested to any level. Indentation should be used as described earlier. Be sure to check that each WHILE has a WEND and each WEND has a WHILE. An unmatched WHILE statement results in a WHILE without WEND error statement, and an unmatched WEND statement results in a WEND without WHILE error statement.

SUBROUTINES

A subroutine is a part of a program that can be executed any number of times in a given program. Rather than rewrite a sequence of instructions over and over, a programmer can place it in a subroutine and type it in only once. The commands necessary for executing a subroutine, GOSUB and RETURN, are always used together.

GOSUB Statement

The general format of the GOSUB statement follows:

```
Line#  GOSUB Line#
```

For example, when the computer sees 50 GOSUB 600, it will go to Line 600 and proceed to execute a subroutine. The line number after the word GOSUB always indicates the first line of the subroutine. Once the computer is at Line 600, it executes the subroutine until it reads the RETURN command. At this time control goes to the statement directly under the GOSUB statement.

For example, Line 20 in Figure 15–15 will send control to Line 500, skipping everything in between. The program then will execute sequentially from Line 500 until it reaches Line 520, where the RETURN command will tell the computer to go back to where it left off before. Since Line 20 has already been read, the computer will continue at Line 30.

RETURN Command

The RETURN command, which is used to return the control of the program to the statement immediately following the GOSUB statement, is always put at the end of the subroutine. No line number is needed after RETURN because if there is more than one GOSUB statement, the computer automatically remembers which GOSUB was the last one executed and returns control there.

For clarity, subroutines are usually located at the end of a program to distinguish them from the main program. However, it is acceptable to place them anywhere within the program. Figure 15–16 illustrates the structure typically used for incorporating a subroutine.

Figure 15–15 GOSUB/RETURN EXAMPLE

```
10 REM *** GOSUB EXAMPLE ***
20 GOSUB 500
30 PRINT X
40 GOTO 999
      .
      .
      .
500 LET X = 25
510 LET Y = 40
520 RETURN
999 END
```

Figure 15–16 SUBROUTINE PROGRAM

```
10 REM *** MAIN PROGRAM ***
      .
      .
      .
50 REM *** GOSUB SENDS CONTROL TO SUBROUTINE ***
60 GOSUB 200
70 PRINT X
      .
      .
      .
190 STOP
200 REM *** SUBROUTINE ***
210 LET X = 3 * A
220 REM *** RETURN SENDS CONTROL BACK TO 70 ***
230 RETURN
999 END
```

STOP Command

The STOP command causes the program to terminate execution without closing files. One of the main reasons this command is used is to prevent any unnecessary execution of statements after a program has reached its logical conclusion. When a subroutine is used, a STOP statement usually is placed immediately before it so the subroutine is not executed at this point. The STOP in Line 190 of Figure 15–16, for example, prevents the subroutine from being executed after the program reaches its logical conclusion.

The STOP instruction can come anywhere in the program and can be used as many times as needed (unlike the END statement, which can be used only once). When the STOP command is used in a program, the message "Break In nnnnn" will appear on the screen; "nnnnn" is the line where the STOP occurred. BASIC always returns to command level after it executes a STOP. Execution can be resumed by issuance of the CONT command.

ON/GOSUB Statement

Just as ON is used with the GOTO statement, it can also be used with the GOSUB command. The following is the general format of the ON/GOSUB statement:

Line# ON expression GOSUB Line#[,Line#,Line#] . . .

Consider the example in Figure 15–17. If X = 1, the computer will go to the subroutine starting at the first line number listed, in this case Line 100. If X = 2, the computer will execute the subroutine starting at Line 200. If X = 3, the subroutine starting at Line 300 will be executed. In each case, when one of the subroutines is finished, control will come back to Line 60.

The expression in an ON/GOSUB statement is always evaluated to an integer. If the expression is a real number (for example, 3.5), the computer will round to the nearest integer (in this case, the integer 4). The expression must evaluate to a nonnegative integer in the range 0 to 255 or the error message "ILLEGAL FUNCTION CALL" will result. If the expression evaluates to 0 or to a positive integer greater than the number of items in the list, the program ignores the statement and continues with the statement following the ON/GOSUB statement.

LEARNING CHECK

1. The commands necessary for executing a subroutine are ________ and ________.

2. What does the line number after the word GOSUB in the GOSUB statement indicate?

3. To where does the RETURN command send control?

4. The ________ command is used to prevent unnecessary execution of statements.

5. What line number will be executed following Line 20 in this program segment?

```
10 LET X = 4
20 ON X GOSUB 200,300,400,500,600
30 PRINT X
      .
      .
      .
99 END
```

ANSWERS:

1. GOSUB, RETURN. 2. the first line of the subroutine. 3. to the statement immediately following the GOSUB statement. 4. STOP. 5. 500.

Figure 15–17 ON/GOSUB PROGRAM

```
40 LET X = A / B
50 ON X GOSUB 100,200,300
60 PRINT Y
```

SUMMARY POINTS

- The initial and terminal values in the FOR statement can be constants, variables, or expressions.
- The FOR and NEXT statements, which are always used together, are valuable commands for forming loops.
- The STEP value in a FOR statement tells the computer how much to add or subtract to the value of the loop variable each time the loop is executed. It is possible to STEP backward.
- The terminal value is the ending expression in the FOR statement. When the terminal value is surpassed, the computer will exit the loop.
- Indentation should be used when implementing FOR/NEXT or WHILE/WEND loops to make it easier to distinguish the beginning and end of each loop.
- When one or more loops are entirely contained within another loop, they are called nested loops.
- A WHILE/WEND loop will be exited when the expression in the WHILE statement evaluates to false or the variable in the WHILE statement acquires a value of 0.
- The body of the WHILE/WEND loop must contain a statement that will eventually change the result of the WHILE statement expression evaluation.
- Subroutines are used to avoid having to type the same instructions over and over. GOSUB and RETURN statements are necessary for implementing subroutines.
- The RETURN command sends control of the program back to the line immediately following the GOSUB statement.
- Subroutines are usually located at the end of the program to distinguish them from the main program.
- The STOP command causes the program to terminate execution without closing files.
- The STOP command is usually placed immediately before the subroutine to insure that the subroutine will not be executed when it is not needed.

REVIEW QUESTIONS

1. How many times will each of these loops be executed? What will be printed?

```
10 LET I = 10
20 LET J = 20
30 WHILE I - 3 > 1
```

```
40     PRINT I
50     WHILE J
60        PRINT J
70        J = J - 10
80     WEND
90     I = I - 3
100 WEND
999 END
```

2. How many times will this loop be executed? What will be the final value of I?

```
10 FOR I = 1 TO 12 STEP 3
20    PRINT I
30 NEXT I
99 END
```

3. What will be the output of the following program segment?

```
10 FOR X = 5 TO 15 STEP 2
20    LET Y = X + 1
30    PRINT X,Y
40 NEXT X
99 END
```

4. What will be printed by this program segment?

```
10 FOR SUM = 10 TO 2 STEP -2
20    PRINT SUM
30 NEXT SUM
99 END
```

5. What is a nested loop?
6. What will be printed by this program segment?

```
10 FOR I = 1 TO 6 STEP 2
20    FOR J = 6 TO 6 STEP 1
30       PRINT I,J
40    NEXT J
50 NEXT I
99 END
```

7. Write a statement that will cause a subroutine starting at Line 250 to be executed.
8. What happens when a RETURN statement is encountered in a subroutine?
9. Write an ON/GOSUB statement that will cause a transfer to Line 250 if X = 1, to Line 280 if X = 2, and to Line 500 if X = 3.
10. Explain how the ON/GOSUB statement works.

SAMPLE PROGRAMS

1. This program, which illustrates the use of FOR/NEXT loops, provides both the yearly total and the monthly average of each type of expense (gas, electric, grocery and phone).

```
10  REM   * * * PROGRAM FOR YEARLY ACCUMULATION * * *
20  REM   * * * OF BILLS, AND MONTHLY AVERAGE   * * *
30  PRINT
40  PRINT "THIS PROGRAM WILL TOTAL YOUR"
50  PRINT "MONTHLY BILLS AND GIVE YOU"
60  PRINT "AN AVERAGE."
70  PRINT : PRINT
80  REM   * * * GAS BILL CALCULATION * * *
90  PRINT "ENTER EACH MONTH'S GAS BILL"
100 FOR I = 1 TO 12
110    INPUT GAS
120    LET TOT.GAS = TOT.GAS + GAS
130 NEXT I
140 LET AVE.GAS = TOT.GAS / 12
150 PRINT
160 REM  * * * ELECTRIC BILL CALCULATION * * *
170 PRINT "ENTER EACH MONTH'S ELECTRIC BILL"
180 FOR I = 1 TO 12
190    INPUT ELECT
200    LET TOT.ELECT = TOT.ELECT + ELECT
210 NEXT I
220 LET AVE.ELECT = TOT.ELECT / 12
230 PRINT
240 REM  * * * GROCERY BILL CALCULATION * * *
250 PRINT "ENTER EACH MONTH'S GROCERY BILL"
260 FOR I = 1 TO 12
270    INPUT GROC
280    LET TOT.GROC = TOT.GROC + GROC
290 NEXT I
300 LET AVE.GROC = TOT.GROC / 12
310 PRINT
320 REM  * * * PHONE BILL CALCULATION * * *
330 PRINT "ENTER EACH MONTH'S PHONE BILL"
340 FOR I = 1 TO 12
350    INPUT PHONE
360    LET TOT.PHONE = TOT.PHONE + PHONE
370 NEXT I
380 LET AVE.PHONE = TOT.PHONE / 12
390 PRINT : PRINT
400 REM  * * * PRINT HEADINGS AND TOTALS * * *
410 PRINT "BILL","YEARLY","MONTHLY"
420 PRINT ,"TOTAL","AVERAGE"
430 PRINT
440 PRINT "GAS",TOT.GAS,AVE.GAS
450 PRINT
460 PRINT "ELECTRIC",TOT.ELECT,AVE.ELECT
470 PRINT
```

```
480 PRINT "GROCERY",TOT.GROC,AVE.GROC
490 PRINT
500 PRINT "PHONE",TOT.PHONE,AVE.PHONE
999 END
```

(Program continued)

```
RUN

THIS PROGRAM WILL TOTAL YOUR
MONTHLY BILLS AND GIVE YOU
AN AVERAGE.


ENTER EACH MONTH'S GAS BILL
? 12
? 24
? 12
? 24
? 36
? 12
? 12
? 12
? 12
? 12
? 24
? 12

ENTER EACH MONTH'S ELECTRIC BILL
? 13
? 11
? 24
? 10
? 14
? 20
? 28
? 28
? 20
? 12
? 12
? 24

ENTER EACH MONTH'S GROCERY BILL
? 144
? 100
? 188
? 96
? 108
? 120
? 120
? 152
? 96
? 1424
? 108
? 144
```

(Program continued)

```
ENTER EACH MONTH'S PHONE BILL
? 12
? 24
? 48
? 96
? 36
? 36
? 12
? 12
? 12
? 12
? 24
? 12

BILL           YEARLY        MONTHLY
               TOTAL         AVERAGE

GAS             204           17

ELECTRIC        216           18

GROCERY         1500          125

PHONE           336           28
```

Pseudocode

Print message telling program purpose
Print message to input gas bills
Begin loop to input 12 values
    Input gas bill
    Accumulate totals
End loop
Calculate average monthly gas bill
Print message to enter electric bills
Begin loop to input 12 values
    Input electric bill
    Accumulate total
End loop
Calculate average monthly electric bill
Print message to enter grocery bills
Begin loop to input 12 values
    Input grocery bill
    Accumulate total
End loop
Calculate average monthly grocery bill
Print message to enter phone bill
Begin loop to enter 12 values
    Input phone bill
    Accumulate total
End Loop
Calculate average
Print headings
Print totals and averages

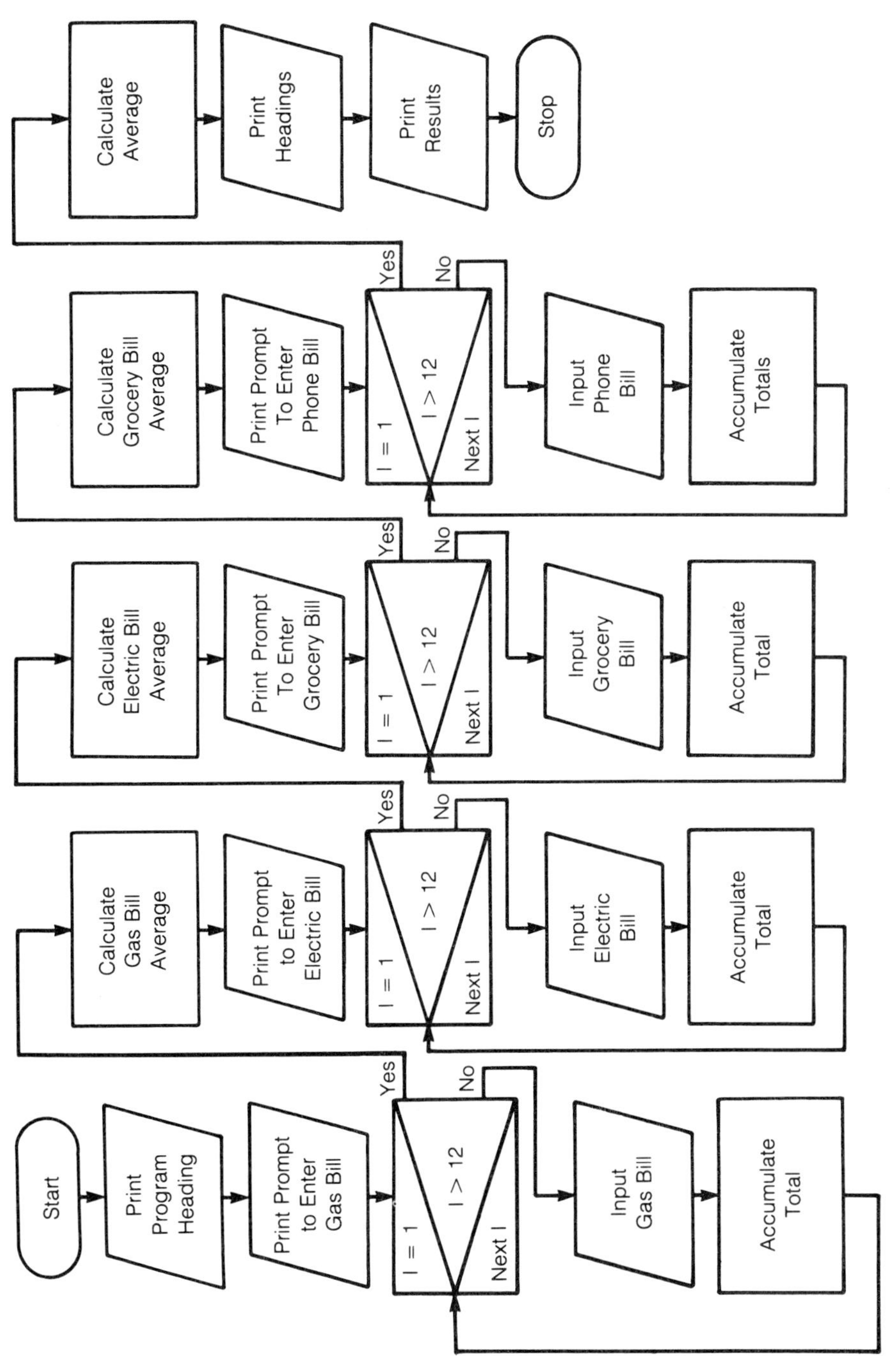

2. The following program uses a subroutine to calculate a bowler's average and what is needed to raise the average by one pin next week. Notice the use of the TAB command for formatting the bowling pin display.

```
10   REM    * * * FINDING YOUR BOWLING AVERAGE * * *
20   REM    * * * AND WHAT YOU NEED TO DO NEXT * * *
30   REM    * * * WEEK TO IMPROVE YOUR AVERAGE * * *
40   REM
50   PRINT
60   PRINT "ENTER YOUR GAMES BOWLED AND TOTAL PINS"
70   INPUT GAMES,PINS
80   REM    * * * CONTROL IS SENT TO LINE 700 * * *
90   GOSUB 320
100  PRINT
110  PRINT "GAMES    AVERAGE    SCORE TO RAISE"
120  PRINT "                   AVERAGE ONE PIN"
130  PRINT "                  (TOTAL SERIES SCORE)"
140  PRINT
150  PRINT "  ";GAMES;"       ";AVE;"          ";TARGET.SERIES
160  PRINT : PRINT
170  PRINT TAB(13);"O"; TAB(17);"O"; TAB(21);"O"; TAB(25);"O"
180  PRINT TAB(15);"O"; TAB(19);"O"; TAB(23);"O"
190  PRINT TAB(17);"O"; TAB(21);"O"
200  PRINT TAB(19);"O"
210  PRINT
220  PRINT TAB(14);"A QUICK TIP"
230  PRINT
240  PRINT "IF YOU CONSISTENTLY HIT TO THE LEFT"
250  PRINT "OF THE HEADPIN, MOVE YOUR FEET A FEW"
260  PRINT "BOARDS LEFT, AND THROW OVER THE SAME"
270  PRINT "SPOT AS BEFORE.  IF YOU CONSISTENTLY"
280  PRINT "GO TO THE RIGHT OF THE HEADPIN, MOVE"
290  PRINT "RIGHT A FEW BOARDS AND THROW OVER"
300  PRINT "THE SAME SPOT"
310  GOTO 410
320  REM   * * * SUBROUTINE * * *
330  REM   * * * INT TRUNCATES THE DIGITS FOLLOWING THE DECIMAL * * *
340  LET AVE =INT(PINS / GAMES)
350  REM   * * * COMPUTING WHAT IS NEEDED NEXT WEEK * * *
360  REM   * * * INT STANDS FOR INTEGER * * *
370  LET TARGET.AVE = INT(AVE + 1)
380  LET TARGET.TOT.PINS = TARGET.AVE * (GAMES + 3)
390  LET TARGET.SERIES = TARGET.TOT.PINS - PINS
400  RETURN
999  END
```

```
RUN

ENTER YOUR GAMES BOWLED AND TOTAL PINS
? 3,450
```

(Program continued)

```
GAMES     AVERAGE     SCORE TO RAISE
                     AVERAGE ONE PIN
                    (TOTAL SERIES SCORE)

  3          150              456


            0   0   0   0
              0   0   0
                0   0
                  0

            A QUICK TIP

IF YOU CONSISTENTLY HIT TO THE LEFT
OF THE HEADPIN, MOVE YOUR FEET A FEW
BOARDS LEFT, AND THROW OVER THE SAME
SPOT AS BEFORE.  IF YOU CONSISTENTLY
GO TO THE RIGHT OF THE HEADPIN, MOVE
RIGHT A FEW BOARDS AND THROW OVER
THE SAME SPOT
```

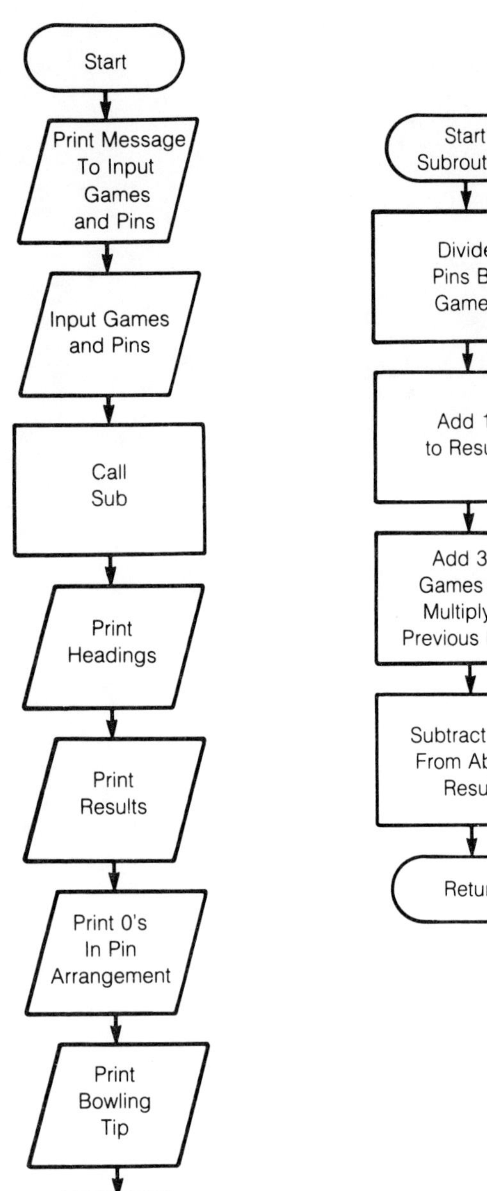

Start Subroutine
Divide Pins By Games
Add 1 to Result
Add 3 to Games and Multiply by Previous Result
Subtract Pins From Above Result
Return

Pseudocode
Print message to enter number of games bowled and total pins
Input data
Call subroutine to find average and needed score
Print headings
Print number of games and results
Print zeros to form the pin arrangement
Print tip

Subroutine
Divide pins by games to get average
Add 1 to average to get score
Add 3 to games, multiply with score to get points
Subtract pins from points

3. This program allows the user to input the number of days jogged every day for four weeks. The average miles jogged per week and per day are printed. The program uses a WHILE loop nested inside a FOR loop to allow the user to input the number of miles jogged each day.

```
10   REM  * * * THIS PROGRAM KEEPS TRACK OF THE NUMBER * * *
20   REM  * * * OF MILES A PERSON JOGS EVERY DAY FOR 4 * * *
30   REM  * * * WEEKS.  THE AVERAGE MILES JOGGED PER   * * *
40   REM  * * * WEEK AND PER DAY ARE THEN PRINTED.     * * *
50   FOR WEEK = 1 TO 4
60      LET DAY = 1
70      WHILE DAY <= 7
80         PRINT "HOW MANY MILES WERE RUN ON WEEK";WEEK;"DAY";DAY
90         INPUT MILES
100        LET TOT.MILES = MILES + TOT.MILES
110        LET DAY = DAY + 1
120     WEND
130  NEXT WEEK
140  LET AVE.DAY = TOT.MILES / 28
150  LET AVE.WEEK = TOT.MILES / 4
160  PRINT "THE AVERAGE MILES JOGGED PER DAY WERE:";AVE.DAY
170  PRINT "THE AVERAGE MILES JOGGED PER WEEK WERE:";AVE.WEEK
999  END
```

```
RUN
HOW MANY MILES WERE RUN ON WEEK 1 DAY 1
? 1
HOW MANY MILES WERE RUN ON WEEK 1 DAY 2
? 3
HOW MANY MILES WERE RUN ON WEEK 1 DAY 3
? 4
HOW MANY MILES WERE RUN ON WEEK 1 DAY 4
? 5
HOW MANY MILES WERE RUN ON WEEK 1 DAY 5
? 2
HOW MANY MILES WERE RUN ON WEEK 1 DAY 6
? 6
HOW MANY MILES WERE RUN ON WEEK 1 DAY 7
? 2
HOW MANY MILES WERE RUN ON WEEK 2 DAY 1
? 6
HOW MANY MILES WERE RUN ON WEEK 2 DAY 2
? 5
HOW MANY MILES WERE RUN ON WEEK 2 DAY 3
? 7
HOW MANY MILES WERE RUN ON WEEK 2 DAY 4
? 3
HOW MANY MILES WERE RUN ON WEEK 2 DAY 5
? 3
HOW MANY MILES WERE RUN ON WEEK 2 DAY 6
? 3
HOW MANY MILES WERE RUN ON WEEK 2 DAY 7
? 5
```

(Program continued)

```
HOW MANY MILES WERE RUN ON WEEK 3 DAY 1
? 6
HOW MANY MILES WERE RUN ON WEEK 3 DAY 2
? 2
HOW MANY MILES WERE RUN ON WEEK 3 DAY 3
? 7
HOW MANY MILES WERE RUN ON WEEK 3 DAY 4
? 7
HOW MANY MILES WERE RUN ON WEEK 3 DAY 5
? 6
HOW MANY MILES WERE RUN ON WEEK 3 DAY 6
? 6
HOW MANY MILES WERE RUN ON WEEK 3 DAY 7
? 7
HOW MANY MILES WERE RUN ON WEEK 4 DAY 1
? 5
HOW MANY MILES WERE RUN ON WEEK 4 DAY 2
? 8
HOW MANY MILES WERE RUN ON WEEK 4 DAY 3
? 3
HOW MANY MILES WERE RUN ON WEEK 4 DAY 4
? 4
HOW MANY MILES WERE RUN ON WEEK 4 DAY 5
? 4
HOW MANY MILES WERE RUN ON WEEK 4 DAY 6
? 4
HOW MANY MILES WERE RUN ON WEEK 4 DAY 7
? 5
THE AVERAGE MILES JOGGED PER DAY WERE: 4.607143
THE AVERAGE MILES JOGGED PER WEEK WERE: 32.25
```

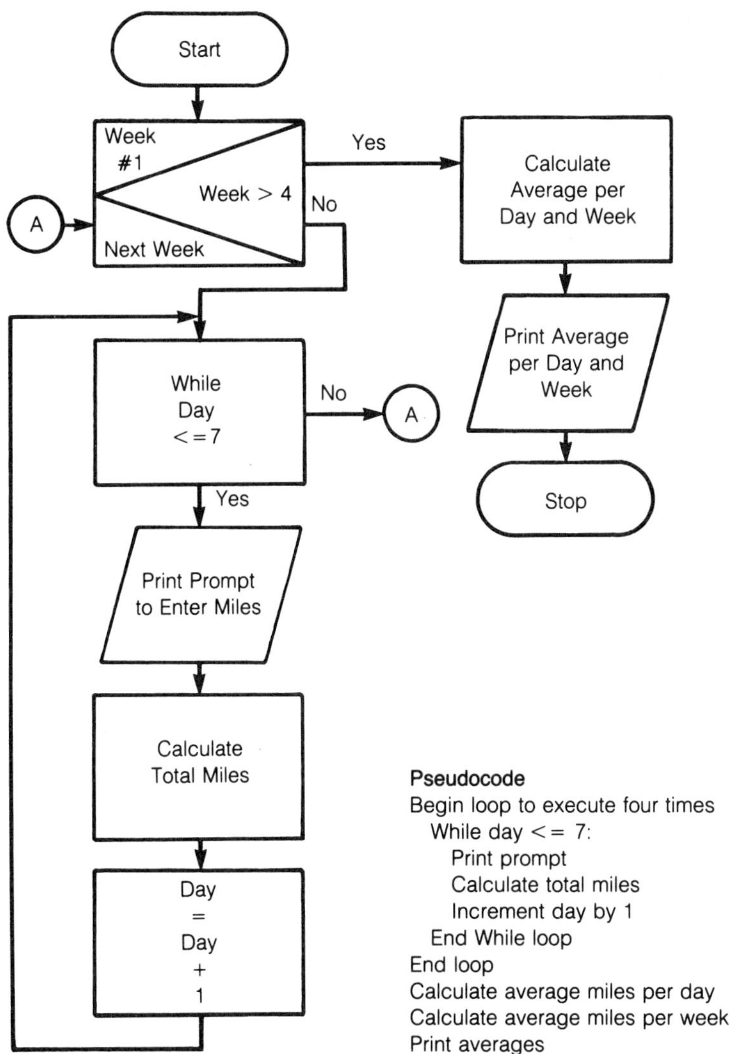

Pseudocode

```
Begin loop to execute four times
   While day <= 7:
      Print prompt
      Calculate total miles
      Increment day by 1
   End While loop
End loop
Calculate average miles per day
Calculate average miles per week
Print averages
```

PROGRAMMING EXERCISES

1. Write a program to calculate pay, including time-and-a-half for overtime (any hours over 40). Use the GOSUB statement and the following data:

Don earns $10.00 per hour and worked 43 hours.
Joe earns $7.50 per hour and worked 37 hours.
Steve earns $4.50 per hour and worked 48 hours.
Beth earns $8.50 per hour and worked 25 hours.

Your output should be formatted as follows:

```
NAME     HOURS    PAY
XXXXX    XX       XXXXX
XXXXX    XX       XXXXX
```

2. Write a program using the ON/GOSUB statement to display one of the following messages, depending on which is requested by the person entering the data:

FEBRUARY 22, PRESIDENTS' DAY
MAY 28, MEMORIAL DAY
JUNE 6, D-DAY

Your output should be formatted in the following manner:

THIS PROGRAM TELLS THE SIGNIFICANCE
OF 3 HOLIDAYS

ENTER 1 FOR FEBRUARY 22,
ENTER 2 FOR MAY 28,
OR ENTER 3 FOR JUNE 6.

MAY 28, MEMORIAL DAY

3. Write a program using FOR/NEXT loops to calculate a bowler's average score for a series of nine games of bowling. Use the INPUT command to enter the data. Your prompts and output should be as follows:

```
WHAT WAS THE SCORE OF GAME 1?  XXX
WHAT WAS THE SCORE OF GAME 2?  XXX
         .
         .
         .
WHAT WAS THE SCORE OF GAME 9?  XXX
YOUR 9 GAME AVERAGE IS XXX
```

Refer to the sample programs in this chapter for assistance in writing the program.

4. Steve Hoffman has a carpet cleaning business. Use a WHILE loop in a program for him to determine how much to bill each of an unknown number of customers. Hoffman charges

- 13 cents per square foot for normal carpets.
- 2 cents more per square foot for extra-dirty carpets.
- 5 cents more per square foot for deodorizing the carpet.
- 3 cents more per square foot if the carpet is to be treated with carpet shield protector.

Allow Hoffman to enter the length and width of each room in inches, and have the program compute the number of square feet. Assume the rooms are rectangular. Use prompts to determine if there is another customer, if the carpet is extra-dirty, if it is in need of deodorant, or if it should be treated with carpet shield protector. Print the amount of each bill and Hoffman's gross income to the monitor.

TY

CHAPTER 16

ARRAYS

Chapter Outline

INTRODUCTION

Array
An ordered set of data items, such as a table.

An **array** is a systematic way of naming large numbers of variables; it is an ordered set of data items, such as a table. When two or more data items need to be entered, instead of giving each one a separate variable name, the programmer can give one variable name to the entire collection of related data items. This becomes increasingly important when larger quantities of data items are needed in a program.

A single array can be used to store numeric or string values. However, all the values in a given array must be of the same type. Thus, if an array is given a string variable name, a numeric data item cannot be entered to it; only string variables are allowed. Each array must be given a unique name (array name), and each data item (array element) must be given a specific location within that array.

SUBSCRIPTED VARIABLES

Subscripted variables
Variable names that include a subscript in parentheses.

Subscript
A value used to indicate the position of a data item in an array.

The variables described in earlier chapters represented a single location in main memory. For example, B might represent the storage location of a numeric value, say 500. An array, in contrast, is used to store a whole series of values in a number of locations. This group of values is stored under a single array name.

Since a single array can contain numerous data items, a system for labeling each of the data items is necessary. The system uses **subscripted variables,** which consist of a valid variable name followed by a **subscript** in parentheses—for example:

A(1)   B(3)   C(K)   D(K + N)

The letter in front of the parentheses is the name of the array. The subscript tells which storage location in the array holds the data item desired; it indicates the position of the data item in the array. If the subscript is a variable—for example, C(K)—the computer will find the current value of K. It then will use this value to determine the position of the element in the array. Likewise, if the subscript is an arithmetic expression—for example, D(K + N)—the computer will evaluate the expression using the current values of the variables. It will truncate the result to the nearest integer and use this final answer to determine the position of the data element within the array.

In IBM BASIC, a subscript must be a 0 or a positive integer from 1 through 255. The first position in an array has a subscript of 0. However, IBM BASIC allows the user to change the minimum value for array subscripts by using the OPTION BASE statement. The general format is shown here:

Line#   OPTION BASE n

The n in the general format must be a 1 or 0. As mentioned, the default base is 0. If the default base is not desired, the statement

```
OPTION BASE 1
```

can be placed before the definition of or reference to any arrays to change the lowest value of an array subscript to 1. Although this statement is not vital to any programming practice, it is convenient when a FOR/NEXT loop variable designates the subscripts. FOR/NEXT loops with a range of 1 to 10 are less likely to cause confusion than are such loops with a range of 0 to 9.

Suppose that in a program, C = 1, D = 2, and E = 3. The following then would be true for Table 16–1:

- A(0) refers to the first position in Array A, which has a value of 10.
- A(C) refers to A(1)—the second position in Array A, or 20.
- A(C + D) refers to A(1 + 2), or A(3)—the fourth position, or 40.

To print the contents of storage location A(4)—in this case, 50—a number of commands could be used, including the following:

```
PRINT A(C + E)
```

or

```
PRINT A(4)
```

Using a numeric variable as the array name defines that array as one containing numeric data (see Table 16–2). Arrays also can be defined to hold string data if a string variable is used as the array name. By using subscripted variables, we can gain access to any of the names in the array. In Table 16–2, F$(0) refers to DON, or the first position in the string array F$. SUE is represented by F$(1), STACY by F$(2), and PAUL by F$(3).

The same rules that apply to naming simple variables also apply to naming arrays. Since the subscript uniquely identifies a variable as an array variable, it is possible to use the same name for both a subscripted and an unsubscripted variable. For example, the variables A and A(X) can be used in the same program. However, to avoid confusion it is best to use different variable names whenever possible.

DIM STATEMENT

When an array is used in a program, the computer automatically sets aside eleven storage locations (0 through 10) for the elements in the array. If the array contains more than eleven data elements, the computer will recognize the first eleven but will print an error message, since no space has been

Table 16–1 ARRAY EXAMPLE

ARRAY A	SUBSCRIPT
10	0
20	1
30	2
40	3
50	4

Table 16–2 STRING AND NUMERIC ARRAY EXAMPLES

ARRAY F$	ARRAY X
Don	25
Sue	135
Stacy	6
Paul	98

set aside for the additional data. Remember, the computer must be told everything it is to do. If only eleven storage spaces have been set aside, twelve data items cannot be entered. Additional space can be set aside in an array by the use of the DIM (dimension) statement. Its general format is as follows:

Line# DIM variable (limit)

The variable is the name of the array, and the limit is the largest subscript the array can have. For instance, the following statement shows how the computer can be told to save space for twenty-six items (locations 0 through 25):

```
10 DIM K(25)
```

This statement will set aside twenty-six storage locations in main memory. If fewer than the twenty-six data items are inserted, there is no problem, but Array K can contain no more than twenty-six pieces of data.

More than one array can be used in a single program. The dimensions for multiple arrays can be set on a single line—for example:

```
10 DIM A(10),B(20),C(100)
```

A, B, and C are the array names. Array A can contain up to 11 elements, Array B up to 21 elements, and Array C up to 101 elements. Remember, arrays can store fewer than the maximum number of data items but never more than this limit.

It is good programming practice always to use the DIM statement, even if the array contains eleven or fewer elements. This statement will help document the array usage. It is also a good idea to put the DIM statements at the very beginning of the program to insure that they are executed before the array is encountered.

ONE-DIMENSIONAL ARRAYS

One-dimensional array
An array that has only one column.

A **one-dimensional array** is an array with only one column, as in Table 16–3. This array has five data elements (15, 20, 27, 8, and 16) in one column. Array X is stored in main memory, as represented in Table 16–4. If the computer is told to do this:

```
10 PRINT X(2)
```

the number in the third position, 27, will be displayed.

LEARNING CHECK

1. A(n) ________ is a systematic way of naming large numbers of variables.
2. One array can be used to store more than one type of variable (string, integer, or real). (True or false?)
3. ________ are used with variables to identify a particular storage location within an array.
4. The statement 10 PRINT A(12) tells the computer to display the value stored in position ________ of Array ________.
5. If a DIM statement is not used for an array, ________ storage locations are automatically set aside for the data elements.
6. Write a DIM statement to set aside twenty-eight storage locations for a string array.

ANSWERS: 1. array. 2. false. 3. Subscripts. 4. 13, A. 5. eleven. 6. 10 DIM F$(27).

Entering Data

The next step is to determine how to fill the array with data. The discussion will focus on two different ways of accomplishing this: using READ/DATA statements and using the INPUT statement. The READ/DATA method should be used when the data needed rarely changes; the INPUT method is best suited for programs that require changing data to be entered. In the examples, data will not be stored in the first location—that is, the location with a 0 subscript.

Table 16–3 ONE-DIMENSIONAL ARRAY

ARRAY X
15
20
27
8
16

Table 16–4 STORAGE OF ARRAY X

		ARRAY A			
Rows	0	50	35	4	8
	1	200	63	100	17
	2	19	102	5	181
	3	41	11	230	118
		0	1	2	3
		Columns			

READ/DATA Entry. One method of entering data to an array is by using of the READ and DATA commands. Remember, READ and DATA statements are always used together. A FOR/NEXT loop can be incorporated into the program to read the data. As an example, the program in Figure 16–1 reads ten numbers to Array D. The first time through the loop (Lines 20 through 40), the loop variable X equals 1. When Line 30 is executed, the computer reads the first number (10) from the data list and stores it in location D(1). The second time through the loop, X equals 2. The next number in the data list (20) is read into D(2). The processing continues until all ten numbers have been read and stored.

The READ/DATA method is useful as long as the data needed for the array is constant. To use the program again for a new set of data, however, the data lines would have to be rewritten, or another method of data entry, such as the INPUT statement, would have to be used.

INPUT Data Entry. When the computer executes an INPUT statement, it stops and waits for a piece of data. Thus, it can be used to enter data to an array, as shown in Figure 16–2. The program works the same way as in the previous example. Now, however, different data can be entered, as required by the program, without any program lines having to be rewritten.

Displaying Data

The next step is to learn how to display the data stored in the array. Again, a FOR/NEXT loop can be used, as shown in Figure 16–3. Once a value has been entered to an array, it does not have to be read again in order to be used. In the example in Figure 16–3, all that is needed to display the contents of the array is to put a PRINT statement inside the loop.

Figure 16–4 combines the statements from Figures 16–2 and 16–3. Notice the prompts and the display of data stored in Array K.

Computations

Figure 16–5 illustrates a program that might be used in a small business. The total sales for the day are calculated using three different arrays. Arrays COST and NUM are used to enter data. Array SALES is used to hold the information obtained from multiplying Arrays COST and NUM together so

Figure 16–1 READ/DATA STATEMENTS AND ARRAYS

```
10 DIM (10)
20 FOR X = 1 TO 10
30     READ D(X)
40 NEXT X
50 DATA 10,20,30,40,50
60 DATA 60,70,80,90,100
99 END
```

```
10 OPTION BASE 1
20 DIM K(10)
30 PRINT "INPUT 10 NUMBERS INTO ARRAY K"
40 FOR T = 1 TO 10
50     INPUT K(T)
60 NEXT T
```

Figure 16–2 INPUT DATA-ENTRY PROGRAM

```
60 FOR N = 1 TO 10
70     PRINT K(N)
80 NEXT N
99 END
```

Figure 16–3 PRINTING AN ARRAY

that the sales for each individual item can be calculated. An explanation of the commands appears in Table 16–5. If this program were to be used every day with changing data, the INPUT statement could be used instead of the READ/DATA statement.

LEARNING CHECK

1. A ________ array contains only one column.

2. What values are held in positions J(2) and J(3) in Array J?

```
Array J
    25
    13
     3
    89
    55
```

3. Write a PRINT statement that will display the value 89 from Array J in Question 2.

4. Write a program to enter five names in Array F$. Place the names Pam, Tom, Jill, Tim, and Bob in positions 1 through 5, respectively.

ANSWERS: **1.** one-dimensional. **2.** 3, 89. **3.** 10 PRINT J(3).
4. 10 DIM F$(5).
20 FOR I = 1 TO 5.
30 READ F$(I).
40 NEXT I.
50 DATA "PAM", "TOM", "JILL", "TIM", "BOB".

Figure 16–4 ENTERING AND DISPLAYING DATA WITH ARRAYS

```
10 OPTION BASE 1
20 DIM K(10)
30 PRINT "INPUT 10 NUMBERS INTO ARRAY K"
40 FOR T = 1 TO 10
50     INPUT K(T)
60 NEXT T
70 FOR N = 1 TO 10
80     PRINT K(N)
90 NEXT N
999 END

RUN
INPUT 10 NUMBERS INTO ARRAY K
? 106.6
? 9.8
? 100.8
? 95.5
? 78.4
? 45.5
? 55.0
? 70.80
? 7.45
? 0.05
 106.6
 9.8
 100.8
 95.5
 78.4
 45.5
 55
 70.8
 7.45
 .05
```

TWO-DIMENSIONAL ARRAYS

Two-dimensional array
An array with both rows and columns.

As indicated earlier, one-dimensional arrrays are arrays that have only one column. **Two-dimensional arrays,** in contrast, have both rows and columns. Figure 16–6 graphically shows a two-dimensional array.

To find a specific data item in a one-dimensional array, only the row has to be specified (since there is only one column with which to work). In a two-dimensional array, however, both the row and the column must be specified. In Figure 16–6, for example, the number 181 is stored in lo-

Figure 16–5 TOTAL SALES PROGRAM

```
10 REM *** SALES PROGRAM ***
20 OPTION BASE 1
30 DIM COST(10),NUM(10),SALES(10)
40 PRINT "COST","SOLD","SALES"
50 PRINT
60 REM *** ENTER COST DATA INTO ARRAY COST ***
70 FOR I = 1 TO 10
80    READ COST(I)
90 NEXT I
100 REM *** ENTER NUMBER OF EACH ITEM IN ARRAY NUM ***
110 FOR I = 1 TO 10
120    READ NUM(I)
130 NEXT I
140 REM *** COMPUTE ARRAY SALES FOR ITEM SALES ***
150 FOR I = 1 TO 10
160    LET SALES(I) = COST(I) * NUM(I)
170    PRINT COST(I),NUM(I),SALES(I)
180 NEXT I
190 REM *** CALCULATE TOTAL SALES ***
200 FOR I = 1 TO 10
210    LET TOT.SALES = TOT.SALES + SALES(I)
220 NEXT I
230 REM *** END OF CALCULATIONS ***
240 PRINT
250 PRINT "THE TOTAL SALES ARE $ ";TOT.SALES
260 DATA .99,1.39,.59,.19,2.49,1.00
270 DATA 1.98,.43,.39,9.49,10,3,17
280 DATA 15,12,23,40,4,63,37
999 END
```

```
RUN
COST          SOLD          SALES

 .99           10            9.899999
 1.39          3             4.17
 .59           17            10.03
 .19           15            2.85
 2.49          12            29.88
 1             23            23
 1.98          40            79.2
 .43           4             1.72
 .39           63            24.57
 9.49          37            351.13

THE TOTAL SALES ARE $  536.45
```

Table 16–5 EXPLANATION OF FIGURE 16–5

LINE NUMBER	WHAT IS OCCURRING
20	Minimum value for array subscripts is set to 1.
30	Dimensions arrays to reserve storage space.
40	Prints headings for output.
60–90	Reads cost items from the data list to Array COST by using a FOR/NEXT loop. When the loop variable is set to 1, the first item in the data list is assigned to COST(1). As the loop continues to 2, a second piece of data is read and assigned to COST(2), and so on until the looping is completed. Control then passes to the next line.
100–130	Loop for entering number of each item to Array NUM. NUM(1) will be 10, NUM(2) will be 3, and so on.
140–180	Loop that takes the information in Arrays COST and NUM, multiplies them together, and stores the results in Array SALES.
190–220	The total sales of each item are stored in Array SALES. Adding the contents of Array SALES will then give the total sales for all the items combined.
260–280	Data list; remember to separate each item by a comma.

Figure 16–6 GRAPHIC REPRESENTATION OF A TWO-DIMENSIONAL ARRAY

MEMORY LOCATION	VARIABLE REPRESENTING MEMORY LOCATION
15	X(0)
20	X(1)
27	X(2)
8	X(3)
16	X(4)

cation A(2,3). If only the row is specified—location A(2), for instance—the computer will not know which data item in Row 2 is desired (19, 102, 5, or 181).

The row is always designated before the column. For example, the number 11 is stored in A(3,1), the number 4 in A(0,2), and so on. Remember, subscripts can be any legal expression.

Since both rows and columns must be specified, two subscripts must be used to set the dimensions of a two-dimensional array. The dimension for Array T, with twenty-one rows and eleven columns, can be set with the following DIM command:

```
10 DIM T(20,10)
```

Entering and Displaying Data

The same basic method is followed to enter and display data for two-dimensional arrays as was followed for one-dimensional arrays. The difference is that subscripts now must be used for both rows and columns. FOR/NEXT loops are used to store and retrieve data.

Figure 16–7 shows a program segment that enters data to a two-dimensional array. The data in Lines 60 through 80 will be read to a two-dimensional array called HEIGHT, filling a table row by row. Notice that there are two FOR/NEXT loops. The outer loop (I = 1 TO 3) controls the number of rows, and the inner loop (J = 1 TO 3) controls the number of columns. Row 1 is filled first, then Row 2, and then Row 3. When the outer loop is executed once, the inner loop is executed three times. Thus, the first three data items read are stored in HEIGHT(1,1) HEIGHT(1,2), and HEIGHT(1,3). After this sequence, the outer loop is incremented to 2. The inner loop then runs its course again, and the second row is filled: HEIGHT(2,1), HEIGHT(2,2), and HEIGHT(2,3). The outer loop is incremented again, and the next row is stored in HEIGHT(3,1), HEIGHT(3,2) and HEIGHT(3,3).

Displaying data contained in a two-dimensional array is very similar to entering the data. Figure 16–8 shows how it can be done. Nested loops are used again in displaying the data once it has been entered to an array. Notice the comma at the end of Line 110. It tells the computer to print the entire row on one line. Line 130 is present to provide a line feed so the next row will be displayed on the next line.

Computations

The program in Figure 16–9 is designed to help a teacher organize students' grades. The data being entered is as follows:

STUDENT	QUIZ 1	QUIZ 2	QUIZ 3
Bob	80	80	85
Jim	95	75	83
Kathy	73	90	84

The previous sections showed how to enter and display the data. Suppose the teacher wants to average all the quiz grades or average an individual student's quiz grades. This can be done by manipulating the array by row, by column, or in its entirety.

```
10 FOR I = 1 TO 3
20     FOR J = 1 TO 3
30         READ HEIGHT(I,J)
40     NEXT J
50 NEXT I
60 DATA 80,80,85
70 DATA 95,75,83
80 DATA 73,90,84
99 END
```

Figure 16–7 ENTERING DATA TO A TWO-DIMENSIONAL ARRAY

Figure 16–8 DISPLAYING DATA FROM A TWO-DIMENSIONAL ARRAY

```
90  FOR I = 1 TO 3
100     FOR J = 1 TO 3
110         PRINT HEIGHT(I,J),
120     NEXT J
130     PRINT
140 NEXT I
999 END
```

Figure 16–9 COMPUTING WITH ARRAYS

```
10 OPTION BASE 1
20 FOR I = 1 TO 3
30     FOR J = 1 TO 3
40         READ QUIZ(I,J)
50     NEXT J
60 NEXT I
70 DATA 80,80,85
80 DATA 95,75,83
90 DATA 73,90,84
100 FOR I = 1 TO 3
110     FOR J = 1 TO 3
120         PRINT QUIZ(I,J),
130     NEXT J
140     PRINT
150 NEXT I
999 END

RUN
 80             80             85
 95             75             83
 73             90             84
```

To find the average of Bob's grades, add all his quiz grades together. The following statements show how this can be done:

```
10 FOR J = 1 TO 3
20     LET BOB = BOB + QUIZ(1,J)
30 NEXT J
```

Remember, the first subscript refers to the row. The subscript 1 in QUIZ(1,J) restricts all computations to Row 1 of the array (the row that contains only Bob's scores). The column will increment each time the loop is executed, thereby allowing all the columns in Row 1 to be processed.

The first time through the loop the computer will take the value from storage location QUIZ(1,1), or 80, since J is set to 1 initially. The next time through the loop, the data item from location QUIZ(1,2), or 80, will be taken and added to the value of BOB. The third and final time through the loop, Bob's final quiz grade will be read from location QUIZ(1,3), or 85. This number will be added to the total, the result being BOB = 245. To get the average, add another line outside the loop to divide the total by 3:

```
40 LET BOB.AVE = BOB / 3
```

Adding columns is very similar to adding rows. When a row is added, the row subscript is kept constant to insure that the particular row will be the only one added. When columns are being added, the column subscript must be held constant so that each row in that particular column can be added. To find the average of Quiz 1, for example, restrict the calculations to the elements in Column 1 while I varies from 1 to 3. This can be accomplished as shown here:

```
50 FOR I = 1 TO 3
60     LET QUIZ.ONE = QUIZ.ONE + QUIZ(I,1)
70 NEXT I
```

To find the class average for all three quizzes, divide QUIZ.ONE by 3 after the looping has been completed:

```
80 LET AVE.ONE = QUIZ.ONE / 3
```

Thus, rows or columns can be added by keeping one of the subscripts constant and using a FOR/NEXT loop to add the row or column until each value has been read and computed.

Suppose the teacher wants to know the average of all the quiz grades for the entire class. Each item in each row and column must be added together. This addition involves the use of nested FOR/NEXT loops, as shown in Figure 16–10. The outer loop controls the rows, and the inner loop controls the columns. The totals will be accumulated in the variable TOTAL. Again, for an average, divide TOTAL by 9 after the looping is finished. Figure 16–11 shows the entire program and its output. Notice that REM statements are included throughout the program for clarification.

```
10 FOR I = 1 TO 3
20     FOR J = 1 TO 3
30         LET TOTAL = TOTAL + QUIZ(I,J)
40     NEXT J
50 NEXT I
```

Figure 16–10 TOTALING AN ENTIRE ARRAY

Figure 16–11 TOTALING AN ARRAY PROGRAM AND OUTPUT

```
10 REM *** STUDENTS' QUIZ GRADES ***
20 REM *** DEMONSTRATION OF ARRAY MANIPULATION ***
30 REM
40 OPTION BASE 1
50 DIM QUIZ(3,3)
60 REM *** READ DATA INTO ARRAY ***
70 FOR I = 1 TO 3
80    FOR J = 1 TO 3
90       READ QUIZ (I,J)
100    NEXT J
110 NEXT I
120 DATA 80,80,85
130 DATA 95,75,83
140 DATA 73,90,84
150 DATA "BOB","JIM","SUE"
160 PRINT "STUDENT   QUIZ 1      QUIZ 2      QUIZ 3"
170 REM *** PRINT NAME AND SCORES FROM ARRAY ***
180 REM *** PRINT NAME AND SCORES FROM ARRAY ***
190 FOR I = 1 TO 3
200    READ N$
210    PRINT N$;"   ";
220    FOR J = 1 TO 3
230       PRINT "      ";QUIZ(I,J);"    ";
240    NEXT J
250    PRINT
260 NEXT I
270 PRINT
280 REM *** CALCULATE BOB'S AVERAGE ***
290 FOR J = 1 TO 3
300    BOB = BOB + QUIZ(1,J)
310 NEXT J
320 LET BOB.AVE = BOB / 3
330 PRINT
340 PRINT "BOB'S AVERAGE IS ";BOB.AVE
350 PRINT
360 REM *** CALCULATE AVERAGE SCORE OF QUIZ 1 ***
370 FOR I = 1 TO 3
380    LET QUIZ.ONE = QUIZ.ONE + QUIZ(I,1)
390 NEXT I
400 LET AVE.ONE = QUIZ.ONE / 3
410 PRINT "QUIZ 1 AVERAGE IS ";AVE.ONE
420 PRINT
430 REM *** CALCULATE AVERAGE OF ENTIRE ARRAY (ALL QUIZZES ) ***
440 FOR I = 1 TO 3
```

Figure 16–11 continued

```
450     FOR J = 1 TO 3
460         LET TOTAL = TOTAL + QUIZ(I,J)
470     NEXT J
480 NEXT I
490 LET TOTAL.AVE = TOTAL / 9
500 PRINT "QUIZZES AVERAGE ";TOTAL.AVE
999 END


RUN
STUDENT    QUIZ 1         QUIZ 2         QUIZ 3
BOB          80             80             85
JIM          95             75             83
SUE          73             90             84


BOB'S AVERAGE IS  81.66666

QUIZ 1 AVERAGE IS  82.66666

QUIZZES AVERAGE  82.77778
```

MANIPULATING ARRAYS

In addition to manipulations with rows and columns, entirely separate arrays can be manipulated. One such operation is **merging** (combining two arrays). Another is **searching** (locating a particular value).

Merging
Combining two arrays into one, usually in a particular order.

Searching
Locating a particular value; often used in the attempt to find a given value in an array.

Merging

It is possible to merge two separate arrays into one array. That is, Array A and Array B can be manipulated to create a new Array C. If A and B each contain five data items, to have Array C contain the elements in the order A1, B1, A2, B2, A3, B3, and so on, the program segment in Figure 16–12 can be used. Line 20 of the figure sets up a loop that will be executed five times. The first time through the loop, Line 30 will have the values

LET C(1) = A(1)

Line 40 adds 1 to C(I), so the first time through the loop

C(2) = B(1)

Figure 16–12 MERGING ARRAYS

```
10 LET X = 1
20 FOR I = 1 TO 10 STEP 2
30     LET C(I) = A(X)
40     LET C(I+1) = B(X)
50     LET X = X + 1
60 NEXT I
```

After these two lines have been executed, Array C will have values for positions C(1) and C(2). Those values will have come from position 1 of Array A and position 1 of Array B, respectively. The next time through, the loop will be incremented and new values will be placed in positions C(3) and C(4), and so on.

Searching

A particular array can be searched to find a certain value or to count how many times that value is in the array. In Figure 16–13, an array containing one hundred items is searched to see how many times a score of 70 or better is listed. Line 110 checks to see if a score is less than 70. If it is, the line checks the next value in the array. If the score is 70 or greater, the value of NUMBER is incremented by 1.

Suppose a program is needed to determine if a score of 55 exists in the array. The program segment in Figure 16–14 could be used in this instance. Line 110 searches to determine if the number 55 exists. If it does not, the line checks the next data position in the array. If there is a number 55 in the array, Line 120 will display it.

Arrays can be merged, searched, and manipulated in many other ways. These are just a few simple examples to get you started. Refer to your user's manual for further instructions, and do not forget to experiment.

Figure 16–13 SEARCHING AN ARRAY

```
100 FOR I = 1 TO 100
110     IF SCORE(I) < 70 THEN 130
120     LET NUMBER = NUMBER + 1
130 NEXT I
```

Figure 16–14 SEARCHING FOR A SCORE

```
100 FOR I = 1 TO 100
110     IF SCORE(I) <> 55 THEN 130
120     PRINT SCORE(I)
130 NEXT I
```

LEARNING CHECK

1. What value is represented in location A(2,3) in Figure 16–6?
2. Given the statement 10 DIM T(20,10), how many elements could this array contain?
3. Each item in each row and column of two arrays can be added together and stored in a single array. (True or false?)
4. ________ is the combining of two separate arrays into a third separate array.
5. The attempt to find a particular value in an array is called ________.

ANSWERS: 1. 181. 2. 231. 3. true. 4. Merging. 5. searching.

SUMMARY POINTS

- An array is a method of storing a large number of variables under one name.
- An array can be used to store integer, real, or string values. Once an array has been defined as either a numeric or a string array, however, it can include only that specified type of data.
- Subscripts are used to label each data item in an array. A valid subscripted variable consists of a variable name followed by a subscript in parentheses.
- If the subscript is an expression, the computer will determine the current value of the expression and use its numeric equivalent for operations.
- The minimum value for array subscripts can be changed using an OPTION BASE statement.
- If fewer than the specified number of data items are entered into an array, there is no problem. If the programmer tries to enter more than the dimensioned limits, however, an error message will result.
- It is good programming practice to dimension an array, even if the array contains eleven or fewer data items.
- A one-dimensional array contains only one column.
- Arrays can be filled in two ways: using the READ/DATA statement and using the INPUT statement. FOR/NEXT loops are used to insure that all the data items are entered.
- Two-dimensional arrays have both rows and columns.
- Two subscripts must be used for two-dimensional arrays. The row is always designated before the column.
- When data items are read to an array, they fill it row by row.
- It is possible to manipulate arrays by rows or columns. This is done by restricting the row numbers or column numbers desired so that only the specific information contained in those rows or columns will be included.
- When nested loops are used to manipulate arrays, the outer loop controls the rows and the inner loop controls the columns.
- Before two arrays are merged to create a third array, the third array must be dimensioned.
- Arrays can be searched for particular values. An IF/THEN/ELSE statement can be used to determine if the desired value has been located.

REVIEW QUESTIONS

1. What is an array?

2. Look at this array in storage. Then answer the questions that follow it.

ARRAY AMOUNT	SUBSCRIPT
	0
8.2	1
8.2	2
7.5	3
	4
	5

a. What value is stored in AMOUNT(1 + 1)?
b. What value is stored in AMOUNT(4 − 1)?
c. Write a statement that stores 104.75 in AMOUNT(5).

3. Write the following DIM statements:

a. An integer array that can contain up to twenty-six values.
b. A real array that can contain up to eighty values.
c. A string array that can contain up to thirty-nine values.

4. Assume that no OPTION BASE statement was used. How many elements can an array hold if it has not been dimensioned? What if the OPTION BASE statement was used?

5. What is the difference between a one-dimensional and a two-dimensional array?

6. Use this program segment to answer the following questions:

```
10 DIM VALUE(14)
20 FOR X = 1 TO 7
30    LET VALUE(X) = X + 2
40    PRINT VALUE(X)
50 NEXT X
99 END
```

a. What will be the first number printed?
b. What is the maximum number of data items this array can hold?
c. How many positions in Array VALUE will be filled by this program?
d. What will the value of VALUE(6) be after this program is executed?

7. Write a DIM statement for an integer array that will contain eighteen rows and nine columns.

8. Write statements to assign a value to each of the following positions in the array dimensioned in Question 7:

a. Assign the value 14 to Row 10, Column 2.
b. Assign the value 102 to Row 3, Column 8.
c. Assign the value 29 to Row 6, Column 1.

9. What is the maximum number of elements each of the following arrays can hold?

a. `DIM Z(4,8)`
b. `DIM STUDENTS(11,40)`
c. `DIM NUM%(2,12)`

10. What happens when two arrays are merged?

SAMPLE PROGRAMS

1. This program fills a one-dimensional array with twenty numbers using the READ/DATA method. The numbers represent the winning numbers of a lottery game. Notice that an INPUT statement is used to enter each player's guess and an IF/THEN/ELSE statement is used to determine if the number guessed is in the array.

```
10 REM * * * LOTTERY GAME * * *
20 REM * * * DON'T FORGET TO DIMENSION ARRAYS * * *
30 OPTION BASE 1
40 DIM L(20)
50 PRINT
60 FOR I = 1 TO 20
70     READ L(I)
80 NEXT I
90 PRINT "ENTER YOUR TICKET NUMBER, (1 - 1000)"
100 INPUT N
110 FOR I = 1 TO 20
120     IF L(I) = N THEN WIN = 1
130 NEXT I
140 IF WIN = 1 THEN PRINT "YOU WIN!!!!" ELSE PRINT "YOU LOSE!"
150 DATA 3,872,991,32,543,219,4,701,843,47
160 DATA 952,106,88,672,714,152,98,76,542,31
170 END

RUN

ENTER YOUR TICKET NUMBER, (1 - 1000)
? 254
YOU LOSE!

RUN

ENTER YOUR TICKET NUMBER, (1 - 1000)
? 672
YOU WIN!!!!
```

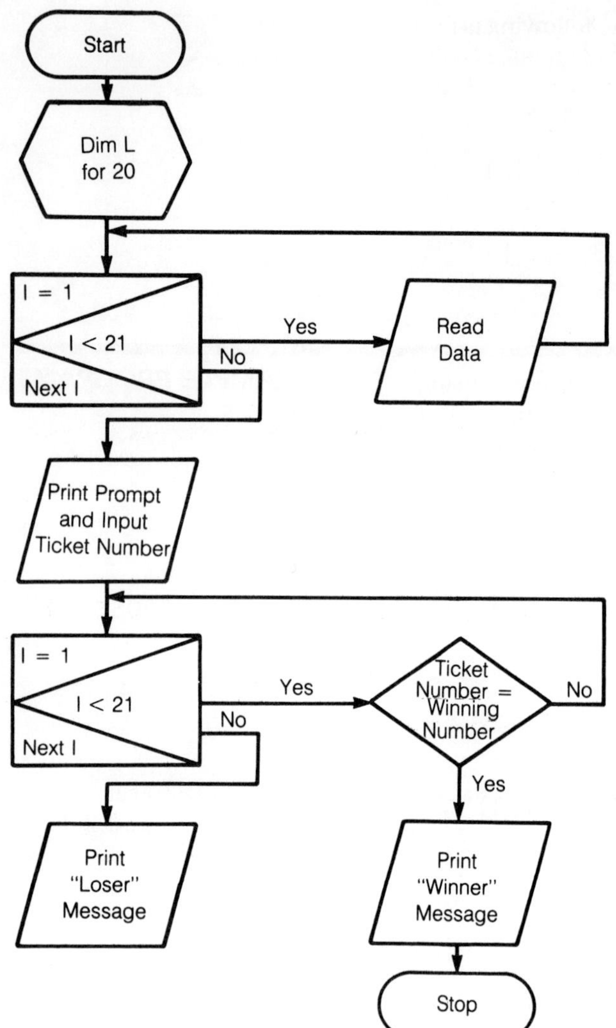

Pseudocode

Dimension an array to hold twenty values
Begin loop to execute twenty times
  Read one number into array
End loop
Print prompt and input ticket number
Begin loop to execute twenty times
  If ticket number equals winning number, go to end loop
End loop
If value does not equal winning value, print loser message
If value equals winning value, print winner message

2. This program contains four arrays that calculate the payroll for The Brassy Niblick Golf Company. Notice that only three of the arrays have been dimensioned in Line 40. Also notice that the data is read and printed within the same FOR/NEXT loop.

```
10   REM   * * * MORE CALCULATIONS WITH ONE * * *
20   REM   * * * DIMENSIONAL ARRAYS           * * *
30   OPTION BASE 1
40   DIM PERSON$(10),HOURS(10),RATE(10)
50   PRINT
60   PRINT TAB(5);"THE BRASSY NIBLICK GOLF COMPANY"
70   PRINT
80   PRINT TAB(16);"PAYROLL"
90   PRINT : PRINT
100   PRINT "NAME";TAB(10);"HOURS";TAB(20);"RATE";TAB(29);"GROSS PAY"
110   PRINT
120 FOR I = 1 TO 10
130    READ PERSON$(I),HOURS(I),RATE(I)
140    LET GROSS(I) = HOURS(I) * RATE(I)
150    LET TOT.EXP = TOT.EXP + GROSS(I)
160    PRINT PERSON$(I);TAB(10);HOURS(I);TAB(20);RATE(I);TAB(29);GROSS(I)
170 NEXT I
180 PRINT : PRINT
190 PRINT "TOTAL PAID OUT.............";TOT.EXP
200 DATA  ARNIE,40,10.00,JACK,40,12.00
210 DATA  DON,35,7.50,RALPH,18,9.00
220 DATA  HERB,15,7.00,ED,38,8.00,JUDY
230 DATA  20,7.50,PAUL,37,9.00,STAN,16
240 DATA  4.50,BERT,40,9.75
999 END
```

```
RUN

    THE BRASSY NIBLICK GOLF COMPANY

               PAYROLL


NAME     HOURS     RATE     GROSS PAY

ARNIE     40        10       400
JACK      40        12       480
DON       35        7.5      262.5
RALPH     18        9        162
HERB      15        7        105
ED        38        8        304
JUDY      20        7.5      150
PAUL      37        9        333
STAN      16        4.5      72
BERT      40        9.75     390


TOTAL PAID OUT............. 2658.5
```

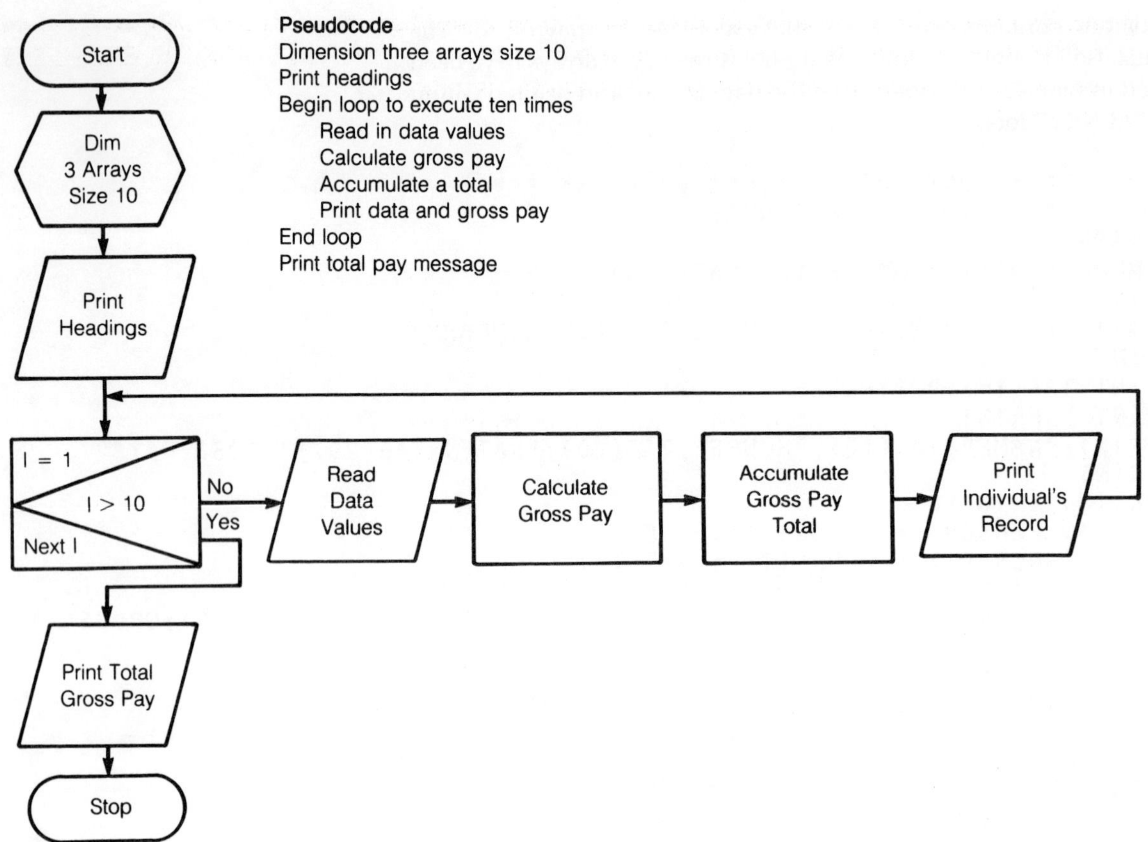

Pseudocode

```
Dimension three arrays size 10
Print headings
Begin loop to execute ten times
    Read in data values
    Calculate gross pay
    Accumulate a total
    Print data and gross pay
End loop
Print total pay message
```

PROGRAMMING EXERCISES

1. Write a program that will enter the following five names to one array and each of the annual incomes to another array. Then display the data in the following format:

```
NAME                INCOME

JOE SWARTZ          $10000
STEVE ZOLLOS        $90000
MARY DOUGH          $55000
ANDY TJOLAKIS       $15000
PAULA JOHN          $25000
```

2. Using the program from Exercise 1, add the data items in the income array and display the following message under the list of names and income:

```
TOTAL INCOMES = $195000
```

3. Write a program to read the following gymnastic scores to a two-dimensional array with three rows and four columns. You will need a separate array for the names. Your output should be in the following format:

```
          GYMNASTIC EVENT AND SCORE

NAME      1      2      3      4

OLGA      9      7.5    8      7
CATHY     9      9.5    8      7.5
NADIA     8      8.5    9      9.5
```

4. Total Cathy's score from the array in Exercise 3 and display the following message under your previous output display (assume that the location of Cathy's name in the list is not known):

CATHY'S OVERALL SCORE = 34

5. Write a program that reads the names of ten colleges and the number of wins each had in football games. Print this information in table form; then print the name of the school with the most wins and the name of the school with the least wins.

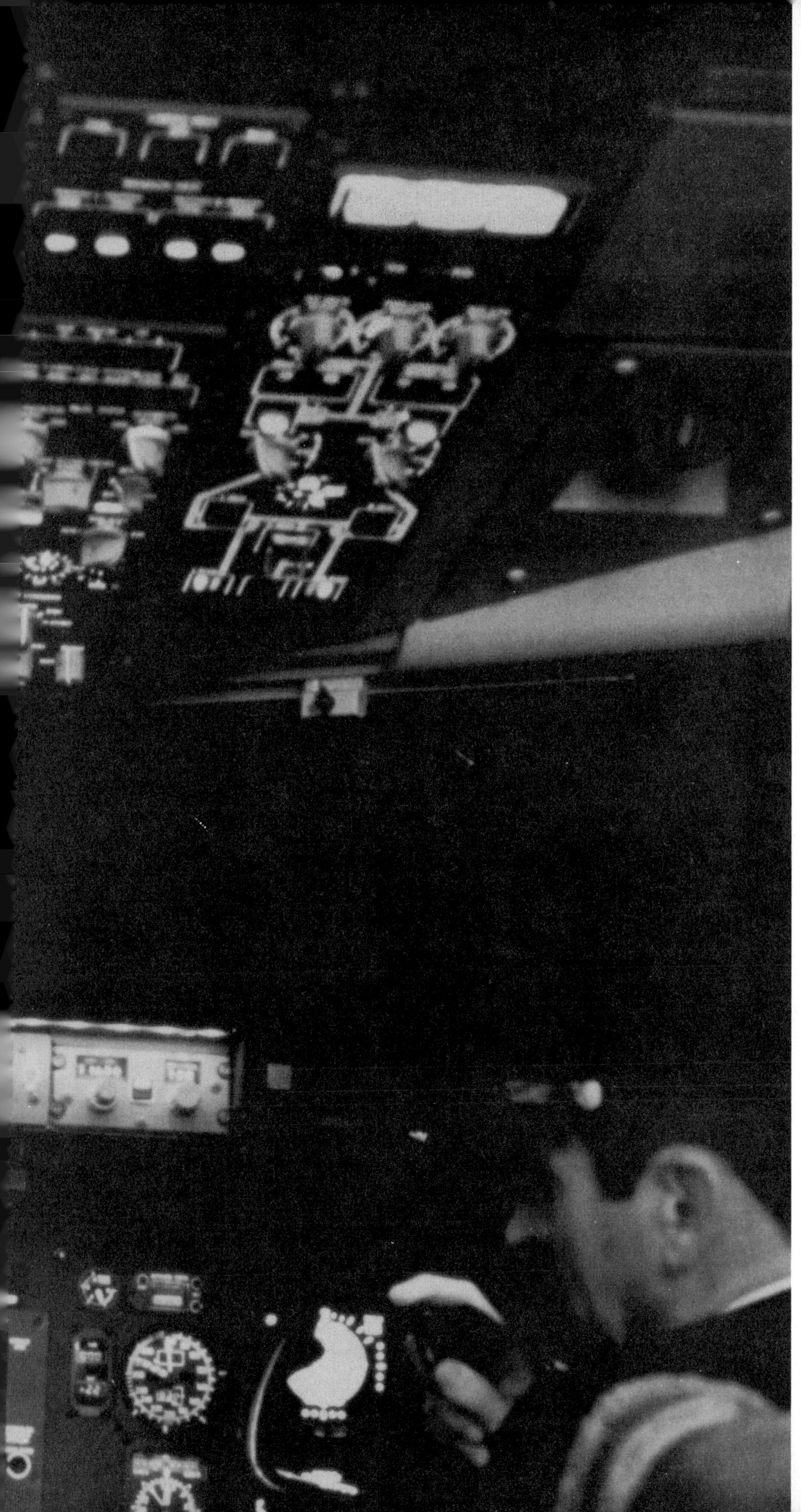

CHAPTER 17

GRAPHICS AND SOUND

Chapter Outline

INTRODUCTION

Programming a computer for graphics and sound is enjoyable. Graphics can be used to enhance programs, making otherwise dull material interesting and readable. Sounds produced by the computer can be used to attract attention to specific prompts or displays. They can also be grouped into musical notes and even entire songs.

DISPLAY MODES

The IBM PC screen operates in three display modes: Text, medium-resolution graphics, and high-resolution graphics. Until now, only the text mode has been used in this section. Although some simple graphics programs can be written in this mode, most graphics programming is done in the medium- and high-resolution graphics modes. In order to use these modes, you must equip your IBM PC with a special circuit board called a color/graphics interface. If this device has not been installed in your computer, then you can use only the text mode.

The SCREEN command switches the format of the screen from one display mode to another. Its format is as follows:

Line# SCREEN mode-number

The mode-number must be an integer between 0 and 2. For example, the command SCREEN 0 will activate the text mode, SCREEN 1 will activate the medium-resolution graphics mode, and SCREEN 2 will activate the high-resolution graphics mode. The screen is automatically set to the text mode when it is turned on.

Preparing the Screen for Graphics

In order to produce graphics displays that are clear and easy to read, you should first clear the screen of any existing characters through the use of the CLS (CLEAR SCREEN) command. Then you should remove the key-word messages at the bottom of the screen by using the statement KEY OFF. For example, the statements shown here will clear the screen and turn off the key-word messages:

```
10 CLS
20 KEY OFF
```

Text Mode Graphics

While the screen is in text mode, it displays twenty-five rows, each containing eighty characters (columns). This means that there are 25 × 80, or 2,000, possible character positions on the screen. From the top of the screen to the bottom, the rows are numbered 1 through 25. The columns, from left to right, are numbered 1 through 80. For example, in Figure 17–1, the char-

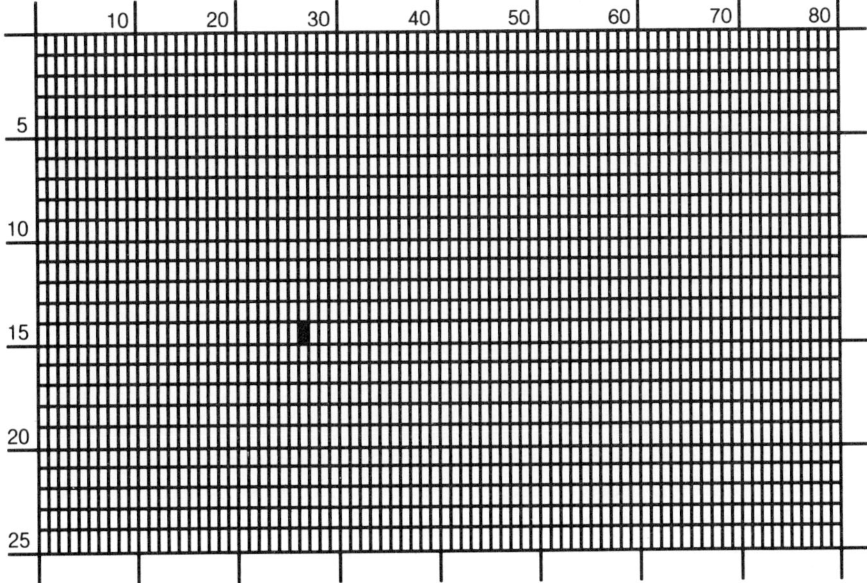

Figure 17–1 TEXT MODE GRAPHICS SCREEN

acter position at Row 15 and Column 27 is colored in. Notice that each of the character positions has the shape of a rectangle.

All the programs thus far have caused their output to be printed sequentially (character after character, line after line, starting at the position at which the cursor is currently located). But the concept of text mode graphics requires that characters be printable at any of the 2,000 character positions, regardless of what position the cursor left off at. To do this, we can use the LOCATE command.

LOCATE. The LOCATE command allows us to place the cursor at a specified character position. Printing occurs where the cursor is located. Thus, by placing a PRINT statement right after a LOCATE command, it is possible to print a character anywhere on the text screen, disregarding the previous position of the cursor. The format of the LOCATE command is as follows:

Line# LOCATE row, column

Figure 17–2 contains a program that puts the computer into the text mode and prints the word HELLO at character position 10,20. Line 20 uses the CLS command to clear the screen and place the cursor in the top-left corner at character position 1,1. Line 30 removes the key-word messages at the bottom of the screen. Line 40 tells the computer to activate the text mode. Line 50 places the cursor at Row 10 and Column 20. Line 60 prints the word HELLO at that position.

ASCII Character Set. Until now, we have been able to print only those characters that can be found on a traditional typewriter keyboard—letters, numbers, and punctuation marks, for example. The IBM PC, however, allows many different types of characters to be printed on the screen, including a set of graphics characters. (Not all printers will print the graphics char-

Figure 17–2 THE LOCATE COMMAND

```
10 REM *** PROGRAM TEXT-GRAPHICS ***
20 CLS
30 KEY OFF
40 SCREEN 0
50 LOCATE 10,20
60 PRINT "HELLO"
99 END
```

acters. If you need to print them, make sure you buy a printer that has the capability of doing so.) Each printable character has a corresponding numeric code. The numeric codes are part of the Extended ASCII code for the IBM PC. In fact, these codes can be used to represent any character or action that can be generated by the keyboard. Figure 17–3 lists all possible Extended ASCII codes (0 through 255) and their corresponding keyboard representations.

It is possible during program execution to code any of the characters or functions on the keyboard by using the CHR$ command. For example, instead of using the statement PRINT "A" to print the character A at the current cursor position, it is possible to use the command PRINT CHR$(65). It is also possible to move the cursor one character position to the right with the command PRINT CHR$(28). Figure 17–4 produces a bar chart using the graphics commands while in the text mode.

In most cases, the screen is already in text mode and setting the screen mode to 0 is not necessary. However, when the medium- and high-resolution graphics modes are used, setting of the screen mode will be necessary. These modes are discussed in the next section.

Figure 17–3 EXTENDED ASCII CODES AND CORRESPONDING KEYBOARD REPRESENTATION

ASCII VALUE	CHARACTER	ASCII VALUE	CHARACTER	ASCII VALUE	CHARACTER	ASCII VALUE	CHARACTER	ASCII VALUE	CHARACTER
000	(null)	051	3	102	f	153	Ö	204	╠
001	☺	052	4	103	g	154	Ü	205	═
002	☻	053	5	104	h	155	¢	206	╬
003	♥	054	6	105	i	156	£	207	╧
004	♦	055	7	106	j	157	¥	208	╨
005	♣	056	8	107	k	158	Pts	209	╤
006	♠	057	9	108	l	159	ƒ	210	╥
007	(beep)	058	:	109	m	160	á	211	╙
008	(backspace)	059	;	110	n	161	í	212	╘
009	(tab)	060	<	111	o	162	ó	213	╒
010	(line feed)	061	=	112	p	163	ú	214	╓

continued on next page

ASCII VALUE	CHARACTER	ASCII VALUE	CHARACTER	ASCII VALUE	CHARACTER	ASCII VALUE	CHARACTER	ASCII VALUE	CHARACTER
011	(home)	062	>	113	q	164	ñ	215	╫
012	(form feed)	063	?	114	r	165	Ñ	216	╪
013	(carriage return)	064	@	115	s	166	ª	217	┘
014	♫	065	A	116	t	167	º	218	┌
015	☼	066	B	117	u	168	¿	219	█
016	►	067	C	118	v	169	⌐	220	▄
017	◄	068	D	119	w	170	¬	221	▌
018	↕	069	E	120	x	171	½	222	▐
019	‼	070	F	121	y	172	¼	223	▀
020	¶	071	G	122	z	173	¡	224	α
021	§	072	H	123	{	174	«	225	β
022	▬	073	I	124	¦	175	»	226	Γ
023	↨	074	J	125	}	176	░	227	π
024	↑	075	K	126	~	177	▒	228	Σ
025	↓	076	L	127	⌂	178	▓	229	σ
026	→	077	M	128	Ç	179	│	230	µ
027	←	078	N	129	ü	180	┤	231	τ
028	(cursor right)	079	O	130	é	181	╡	232	Φ
029	(cursor left)	080	P	131	â	182	╢	233	Θ
030	(cursor up)	081	Q	132	ä	183	╖	234	Ω
031	(cursor down)	082	R	133	à	184	╕	235	δ
032	(space)	083	S	134	å	185	╣	236	∞
033	!	084	T	135	ç	186	║	237	Ø
034	"	085	U	136	ê	187	╗	238	ε
035	#	086	V	137	ë	188	╝	239	∩
036	$	087	W	138	è	189	╜	240	≡
037	%	088	X	139	ï	190	╛	241	±
038	&	089	Y	140	î	191	┐	242	≥
039	'	090	Z	141	ì	192	└	243	≤
040	(	091	[	142	Ä	193	┴	244	⌠
041	)	092	\	143	Å	194	┬	245	⌡
042	*	093	]	144	É	195	├	246	÷
043	+	094	^	145	æ	196	─	247	≈
044	,	095	_	146	Æ	197	┼	248	°
045	-	096	`	147	ô	198	╞	249	•
046	.	097	a	148	ö	199	╟	250	·
047	/	098	b	149	ò	200	╚	251	√
048	0	099	c	150	û	201	╔	252	^{n}
049	1	100	d	151	ù	202	╩	253	^{2}
050	2	101	e	152	ÿ	203	╦	254	■
								255	(blank 'FF')

Figure 17–4 BAR CHART PROGRAM

```
10 CLS
20 SCREEN 0
30 FOR ROW = 5 TO 20
40      LOCATE ROW,20
50      PRINT CHR$(222)
60 NEXT ROW
70 FOR COL = 21 TO 60
80      LOCATE 20,COL
90      PRINT CHR$(95)
100 NEXT COL
110 FOR ROW = 10 TO 20
120     LOCATE ROW,30
130     PRINT CHR$(177)
140 NEXT ROW
150 FOR ROW = 7 TO 20
160     LOCATE ROW,40
170     PRINT CHR$(177)
180 NEXT ROW
190 FOR ROW = 17 TO 20
200     LOCATE ROW,50
210     PRINT CHR$(177)
220 NEXT ROW
230 LOCATE 5,15
240 PRINT "RAIN"
250 LOCATE 22,38
260 PRINT "MONTH"
```

LEARNING CHECK

1. Three display modes of the IBM PC are the ________, ________, and ________.

2. The ________ command switches the screen from one display mode to another.

3. The text mode screen is divided into ________ rows and ________ columns, producing a total of ________ possible character positions.

4. The ________ command is used to place the cursor at a specified character position on the text mode screen.

5. A statement that uses Extended ASCII code to perform the same function as the HOME command is ________ (see Figure 17–3 for Extended ASCII Codes).

ANSWERS:
1. text, medium-resolution graphics, high-resolution graphics. **2.** SCREEN. **3.** 25, 80, 2,000. **4.** LOCATE. **5.** PRINT CHR$(11).

Medium-Resolution Graphics

If your IBM PC is equipped with a color/graphics interface, you can design more detailed graphics that include a variety of colors. The medium-res-

Table 17–1 COLORS USED IN MEDIUM-RESOLUTION GRAPHICS

BACKGROUND COLORS			
COLOR	NUMBER	COLOR	NUMBER
Black	0	Gray	8
Blue	1	Light blue	9
Green	2	Light green	10
Cyan	3	Light cyan	11
Red	4	Light red	12
Magenta	5	Light magenta	13
Brown	6	Yellow	14
White	7	Bright white	15

FOREGROUND COLORS			
PALETTE 0		PALETTE 1	
COLOR	NUMBER	COLOR	NUMBER
Green	1	Cyan	1
Red	2	Magenta	2
Brown	3	White	3

olution graphics mode divides the screen into 320 image points across and 200 down. That means there is a total of 64,000 (320 × 200) image points.

Each image point is referred to as a **picture element,** or **pixel.** A pixel is specified by a pair of coordinates consisting of a column number, 0 through 319, and a row number, 0 through 199. Unlike in the text mode, the column number must be specified before the row number. Also, in the medium- and high-resolution graphics modes, the columns and rows begin with the number 0, whereas in the text mode they began with 1.

Pixel
(picture element) One of the many image points that make up a graphics display.

Color Graphics. Of the three display modes for the IBM PC, the medium-resolution graphics mode is the only one that allows for color graphics. In order to use the available colors in your display, you must first turn on the color switch with the statement SCREEN 1,0. The number 1 activates the medium-resolution graphics mode, and the number 0 activates the color capabilities. (You turn the color off with the statement SCREEN 1,1.)

Once the color has been turned on, you must choose a background color, which will be the color of all the 64,000 pixels before any individual pixels are lit up. Table 17–1 lists the 16 possible background colors, numbered 0 through 15. After choosing a background color, you must pick a set of foreground colors. These colors will be used to light up the individual pixels that you specify. Therefore, a **foreground pixel** is any pixel that is not the same color as the background pixels.

Foreground pixel
Any pixel that is not the same color as the background pixels.

The colors used with foreground pixels can be chosen from one of two groups of colors, or palettes, shown in Table 17–1. When you use Palette 0, your choice of foreground colors is limited to green, red, and brown. The three colors offered by Palette 1 are cyan, magenta, and white.

The COLOR statement is used to set the background color and to select one of the two palettes. For example, the statement 10 COLOR 1,0 will set the background color as blue and select the colors provided in Palette 0.

PSET and PRESET. The PSET statement is used to turn on (color in) a specific pixel. Its format is as follows:

Line# PSET (column,row),color-number

To see how the PSET statement is used, look at the following program segment:

```
10 CLS
20 KEY OFF
30 SCREEN 1,0
40 COLOR 7,0
50 PSET (100,100),2
99 END
```

Line 30 switches the display mode to medium-resolution graphics. It also turns on the color switch. Line 40 selects white as the background color. It also selects the foreground colors offered by Palette 0. Line 50 causes the color of the pixel at Column 100 and Row 100 to be changed to red.

The PRESET statement is used to turn off a specific pixel. Actually, it causes the color of the pixel to be returned to the background color. Its format is as follows:

Line# PRESET (column,row)

LINE. In the design of graphics displays, it is often necessary to draw lines and rectangles. It is possible to draw a line using the PSET statement within a FOR/NEXT loop. Figure 17–5 is an example of a program that connects four lines to form a rectangle.

Notice that the GOTO statement in Line 260 forms an infinite loop. This loop keeps the graphics display on the screen. To terminate program execution, hold down the <Ctrl> key and then press the <Break> key. If you are using the IBM PCjr, press the <Fn> (function) key and then press the <Break> key (the B key).

Drawing in this manner is effective but not efficient. If you execute the program shown in Figure 17–5, you will notice that the lines are produced rather slowly. For this reason, the IBM PC and PCjr versions of BASIC offer the use of the LINE statement. Its format is as follows:

Line# LINE(X_1,Y_1) – (X_2,Y_2),color number

This statement is used to draw a line that connects the pixel at character position X_1,Y_1 to the pixel at X_2,Y_2. Specifying the color of the line is optional. If the color number is not specified, the line will be drawn in Color 3 of the active palette. Using the LINE statement decreases the complexity of drawing lines and greatly increases the speed at which they are drawn. Fig-

```
10 REM *** PROGRAM RECTANGLE ***
20 REM *** X = COLUMN COORDINATE ***
30 REM *** Y = ROW COORDINATE ***
40 REM
50 REM *** PREPARE MEDIUM-RESOLUTION
           GRAPHICS SCREEN ***
60 CLS
70 KEY OFF
80 SCREEN 1,0
90 COLOR 7,0
100 REM *** DRAW TOP SIDE OF RECTANGLE ***
110 FOR X = 100 TO 200
120     PSET(X,75),2
130 NEXT X
140 REM *** DRAW RIGHT SIDE OF RECTANGLE ***
150 FOR Y = 75 TO 125
160     PSET(X,Y),2
170 NEXT Y
180 REM *** DRAW BOTTOM SIDE OF RECTANGLE ***
190 FOR X = X TO 100 STEP -1
200     PSET(X,Y),2
210 NEXT X
220 REM *** DRAW LEFT SIDE OF RECTANGLE ***
230 FOR Y = Y TO 75 STEP -1
240     PSET(X,Y),2
250 NEXT Y
260 GOTO 260
999 END
```

Figure 17–5 RECTANGLE PROGRAM USING THE PSET STATEMENT

ure 17–6 shows this by modifying the rectangle program of Figure 17–5. It uses the LINE statement instead of the PSET statement inside a FOR/NEXT loop.

There is even an easier way to draw a rectangle, however. In fact, the LINE statement has an extended format just for drawing rectangles. But before looking into exactly how to use it, let's examine the rectangle diagrammed in Figure 17–7. This rectangle has Corner A opposite Corner C and Corner B opposite Corner D. Each of the sides meet to form a corner at a right (45°) angle. One LINE statement can be used to draw this rectangle by specifying the coordinates of opposite corners, such as A and C. Following the color number should be the letter B, which tells the computer to box in the two corners. It is also possible to color in the box by using the letters BF (box filled) instead of the letter B (box). For example, the statement

```
110 LINE (100,75)-(200,125),2,B
```

will draw the same rectangle that is produced by the four LINE statements in Figure 17–6. That is, it will draw a 100 × 50 rectangle (see Figure 17–8). Its top-left corner will be at pixel 100,75, and its bottom-right corner will be at pixel 200,125.

Using this form of the LINE statement greatly decreases the complexity of designing graphics displays. For example, the program shown in Fig-

Figure 17–6 RECTANGLE PROGRAM USING THE LINE STATEMENT

```
10 REM *** PROGRAM RECTANGLE ***
20 REM *** X = COLUMN COORDINATE ***
30 REM *** Y = ROW COORDINATE ***
40 REM
50 REM *** PREPARE MEDIUM-RESOLUTION GRAPHICS SCREEN ***
60 CLS
70 KEY OFF
80 SCREEN 1,0
90 COLOR 7,0
100 REM *** DRAW TOP SIDE OF RECTANGLE ***
110 LINE (100,75)-(200,75),2
120 REM *** DRAW RIGHT SIDE OF RECTANGLE ***
130 LINE (200,75)-(200,125),2
140 REM *** DRAW BOTTOM SIDE OF RECTANGLE ***
150 LINE (200,125)-(100,125),2
160 REM *** DRAW LEFT SIDE OF RECTANGLE ***
170 LINE (100,125)-(100,75),2
180 GOTO 180
999 END
```

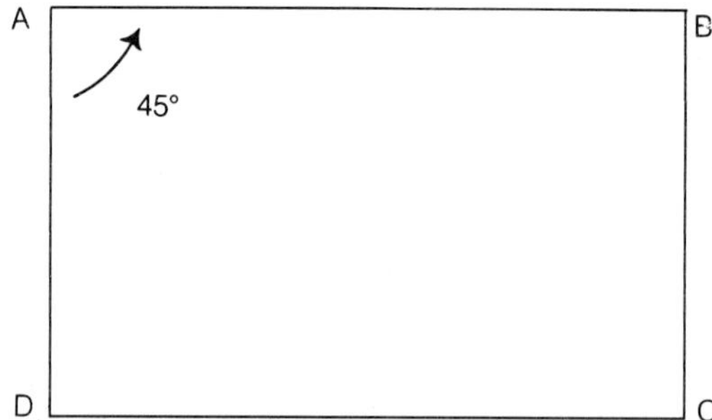

Figure 17–7 DRAWING A RECTANGLE

ure 17–9 will draw the same 100 × 50 rectangle produced by the program in Figures 17–5 and 17–6 with only a fraction of the statements.

Graphics and Text

Many graphics displays require character string messages to clarify or explain their purpose. For this reason, it is possible to include text with graphics displays. The PRINT and PRINT USING statements will perform exactly as they would in the text mode. However, the cursor is hidden while in the graphics modes.

A suggested method for printing text within graphics displays is to start by moving the cursor to the desired character position. This can be done with the LOCATE statement. A common mistake of beginning programmers is to specify the coordinates for the LOCATE statement in the form column,

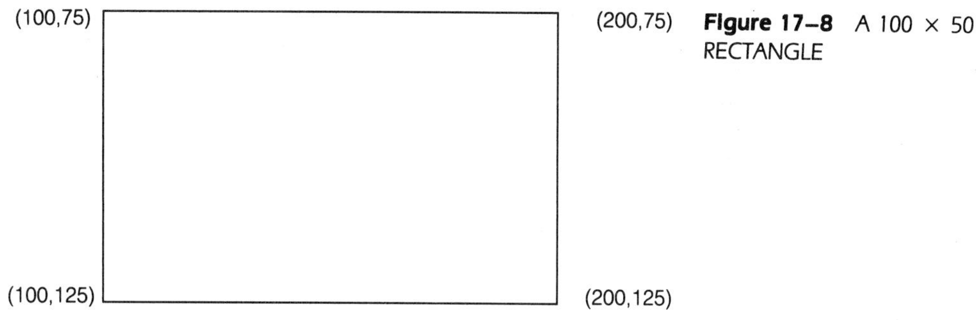

Figure 17–8 A 100 × 50 RECTANGLE

```
10 REM *** PROGRAM RECTANGLE ***
20 REM *** X = COLUMN COORDINATE ***
30 REM *** Y = ROW COORDINATE ***
40 REM
50 REM *** PREPARE MEDIUM-RESOLUTION GRAPHICS SCREEN ***
60 CLS
70 KEY OFF
80 SCREEN 1,0
90 COLOR 7,0
100 REM *** DRAW RECTANGLE ***
110 LINE (100,75)-(200,125),2,B
180 GOTO 180
999 END
```

Figure 17–9 RECTANGLE PROGRAM USING THE LINE STATEMENT AND BOX PARAMETER

row. The coordinates must be specified in the form row, column, even while in graphics modes. Points to remember

1. All characters are displayed in a box eight pixels wide by eight pixels high.
2. In both medium- and high-resolution graphics modes, only characters with ASCII codes less than 128 can be used. See Figure 17–3 for details.
3. In the medium-resolution graphics mode, text can be printed only within the first forty columns and will be displayed in Color 3 of the active palette.

Since the size of each character is 8 × 8, it is possible to erase an entire character string by drawing a rectangle on top of it. The color of the rectangle should be the same as the background that surrounds the text. For example, consider the string JANUARY printed at character position 1,1. Assume that the background color black (0) surrounds the string. The string contains seven characters, so the width of the rectangle in pixels should be 56 (7 × 8). Also, because each character is eight pixels high, the dimensions of the rectangle should be 56 × 8. Therefore, to erase the given text string, the following statement is used:

```
40 LINE (0,0)-(55,7),0,BF
```

LEARNING CHECK

1. The screen of the medium-resolution graphics mode is divided into ________ columns and ________ rows.
2. Each character position is called a ________ and is specified by a pair of ________.
3. A ________ is any pixel that is not the same color as the background pixels.
4. The ________ statement is used to illuminate a specified pixel.
5. A statement that will draw a line connecting two pixels is a ________ statement.

ANSWERS: 1. 320,200. 2. pixel, coordinates. 3. foreground pixel. 4. PSET. 5. LINE.

High-Resolution Graphics

The high-resolution graphics mode divides the screen into 640 columns and 200 rows. Each of the 128,000 (640 × 200) pixels can be controlled by any of the statements presented in the previous section. Although the high-resolution mode allows for sharper, more detailed graphics displays, each pixel can be only one of two colors: white (1) or black (0).

The high-resolution graphics mode is activated by the statement SCREEN 2. Therefore, for a high-resolution graphics display, the first three lines of the program should be

```
10 CLS
20 KEY OFF
30 SCREEN 2
```

Although there are only two colors available in the high-resolution mode, it is possible to create different shades of white by turning on different combinations of pixels. For example, consider the rectangular portion of the graphics screen shown in Figure 17–10. It is possible to color the rectangle pure white by lighting up all the pixels in the rectangle with the statement

```
10 LINE (X1,Y1)-(X2,Y2),1,BF
```

But if the rectangle is to be filled in with a darker shade of white, the LINE statement could be used within a FOR/NEXT loop to color in every column of pixels. The following program segment will fill in the rectangle shown in Figure 17–10:

```
40 FOR X1 = X1 TO X2 STEP 2
50       LINE (X1,Y1)-(X1,Y2),1
60 NEXT X1
```

Figure 17–10 CREATING DIFFERENT SHADES OF WHITE

If the STEP value in Line 40 is increased to 3, the program segment will light up every third column, thereby creating a darker shade of white.

The program shown in Figure 17–11 divides the high-resolution screen into six 213 × 100 rectangles. Each is shaded differently. (Study the algorithms used to shade each rectangle.) Below the program in Figure 17–11 is a sketch of the graphics display produced. (To see the actual display, you may wish to type in the program and run it yourself.)

The program in Figure 17–12 draws a three-dimensional hallway by shading different portions of the screen differently. When you run the program, notice that the ceiling and floor are pure colors, whereas the walls are a shaded white. Lines 70 through 120 show this process.

CIRCLE. If you are programming in BASICA, you can include circles in your graphics displays by using the CIRCLE command. This statement can be used in both the medium- and high-resolution graphics modes. But because of the limited resolution of the medium-resolution mode, the circles produced are not smooth and often are unclear. For this reason, only high-resolution examples of the CIRCLE statement are provided here. The format of this statement is as follows:

Line# CIRCLE (column,row),radius,color

The column and row positions specify the coordinates of the center of the circle, and the radius specifies the distance from the center to any coordinate on the curve of the circle. For example, the statement

```
40 CIRCLE (100,75),40,1
```

will draw a circle with a radius of forty pixels at Column 100 and Row 75.

The program shown in Figure 17–13 will produce a circle (ball) that rolls slowly across the screen. The FOR/NEXT statements increase the X-coordinate for the center of the circle, which creates the horizontal rolling effect.

Figure 17–11 PROGRAM TO SHADE

```
10 REM *** PROGRAM SHADES ***
20 REM *** THIS PROGRAM DIVIDES THE SCREEN INTO SIX RECTANGLES
30 CLS
40 KEY OFF
50 SCREEN 2
60 REM *** BEGIN DRAWING IN TOP LEFT CORNER AT 0,0
70 REM *** COLOR RECTANGLE I
80 LINE (0,0)-(212,99),1,BF
90 REM *** COLOR RECTANGLE II HORIZONTAL LIGHT GRAY
100 FOR Y = 0 TO 99 STEP 2
110     LINE (213,Y)-425,Y),1
120 NEXT Y
130 REM *** COLOR RETANGLE III VERTICAL LIGHT GRAY
140 FOR X = 426 TO 639 STEP 2
150    LINE (X,0)-(X,99),1
160 NEXT X
170 REM *** COLOR RECTANGLE IV VERTICAL DARK GRAY
180 FOR X = 0 TO 212 STEP 3
190     LINE (X,100)-(X,199),1
200 NEXT X
210 REM *** COLOR RECTANGLE V HORIZONTAL DARK GRAY
220 FOR Y = 100 TO 199 STEP 3
230     LINE (213,Y)-(425,Y),1
240 NEXT Y
250 GOTO 250
999 END
```

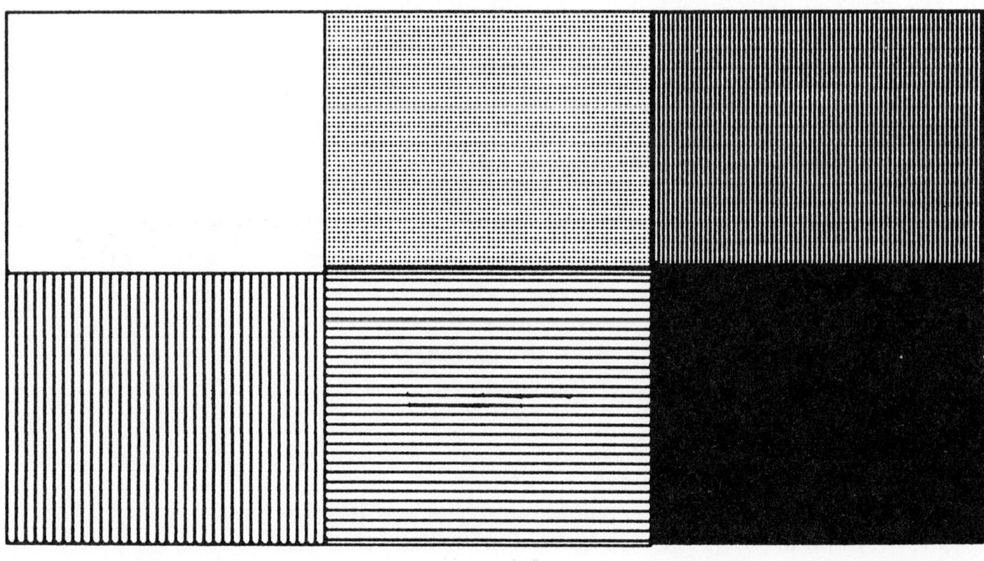

```
10 CLS
20 KEY OFF
30 SCREEN 2
40 LET Y1 = 0
50 LET Y2 = 199
60 LET X2 = 639
70 FOR X1 = 0 TO 290 STEP 4
80      LINE (X1,Y1)-(X2,Y2),1,B
90      LET Y1 = Y1 + 1
100     LET X2 = X2 - 4
110     LET Y2 = Y2 - 1
120 NEXT X1
130 LOCATE 11,39
140 PRINT "EXIT"
150 LOCATE 13,43
160 PRINT "."
999 GOTO 999
```

Figure 17–12 PROGRAM TO DRAW HALLWAY

```
10 REM *** PROGRAM ROLLING BALL ***
20 CLS
30 KEY OFF
40 SCREEN 2
45 REM *** DRAW THE GROUND LINE ***
47 LINE (0,199)-(639,199),1
50 FOR X = 63 TO 574
60     CIRCLE (X+1,170),64,1
65     CIRCLE (X,170),64,0
70 NEXT X
80 GOTO 80
99 END
```

Figure 17–13 PROGRAM FOR THE ROLLING BALL

LEARNING CHECK

1. The high-resolution graphics mode divides the screen into ________ columns and ________ rows.
2. There are ________ possible colors for any high-resolution pixel.
3. The high-resolution graphics mode is activated by the statement ________.
4. An alternate way of creating different colors is to ________ portions of the graphics display by using the ________ statement.
5. The distance from the center of a circle to any point on the curve is called the ________ of a circle.

ANSWERS: 1. 640,200. 2. two. 3. SCREEN 2. 4. shade, LINE. 5. radius.

SOUND ON THE PC

Sound can be produced on the IBM PC with three different commands: BEEP, SOUND, and PLAY. The easiest and most used of the three is the BEEP command.

BEEP

The BEEP command does exactly what it says. When executed, it produces a tone with the frequency and length already set. BEEP is most commonly used in applications programs when it is necessary to call attention to error messages or user input. Its format is as follows:

Line# BEEP

Figure 17–14 shows how this command can be used to indicate user input.

SOUND

The SOUND command allows the user to change the frequency and length of the tone. Its format is as follows:

SOUND frequency, duration

Changing the frequency will produce a beep at a higher or lower tone. The frequency can be set to any number between 37 and 32767 Hertz (cycles per second). The duration of the sound is how long the sound is to last. The number specified is actually the number of clock ticks, which can range between 0 and 65535. There are approximately 18.2 clock ticks per second. With the ability to change frequency and duration, a large variety of interesting sounds can be created. The program in Figure 17–15 produces a series of increasingly higher-pitched tones and a siren.

PLAY

The PLAY command allows the user to program music. The sounds produced are sophisticated, yet the program is not difficult to use. Some background in music is helpful, but even beginners can create music easily.

Figure 17–14 PROGRAM USING THE BEEP COMMAND

```
10 CLS
20 PRINT "PRESS Y FOR BEEP"
30 PRINT "PRESS N TO END PROGRAM"
40 INPUT "BEEP?",A$
50 IF A$ = "N" THEN 99
60      BEEP
70      GOTO 40
99 END
```

```
10 REM *** TONES ***
20 FOR I = 300 TO 1200 STEP 100
30       SOUND I,8
40       FOR T = 1 TO 500
50       NEXT T
60 NEXT I
70 FOR T = 1 TO 600
80 NEXT T
90 REM *** SIREN ***
100 FOR I = 1 TO 3
110       FOR F = 450 TO 1200
120             SOUND F,.1
130       NEXT F
140       FOR F = 1200 TO 450 STEP -1
150             SOUND F,.1
160       NEXT F
170 NEXT I
999 END
```

Figure 17–15 PROGRAM USING THE SOUND COMMAND

The format for the PLAY command is as follows:

Line# PLAY string

A string is a series of letters, numbers, and symbols that represent coded music. Some combinations of letters and numbers are referred to as commands, and they will be explained and described shortly.

Figure 17–16 gives two examples of what coded music strings might be like for the PC. Although they look difficult to code, actually they are quite simple. Following is an overview of how to code music on the PC.

Octave. The octave is specified with the letter O followed by the octave number. Each octave goes from C to B. There are seven octaves, numbered 0 to 6, with Octave 3 starting at middle C. For example, O3 means that all notes will come from the third octave until another octave is specified.

If no octave is specified, the notes are assumed to come from the fourth octave. Octaves 1 through 4 are shown in Figure 17–17.

Notes. Just as always, notes are specified with the letters A through G, and each octave starts with C. A sharp is indicated by the note followed by a # or +; a flat is indicated by the note followed by a −. For a #, +, or − to be put after a note, the note must correspond to a black key on the piano. For example, the notes B# and F− would be invalid; the notes C and B should be used instead.

Length. The length is set in the same way as the octave. It is coded by the letter L followed by a number that indicates the length of all following notes until another length is specified. The length of the note may range from 1

Figure 17–16 CODED MUSIC STRINGS

to 64. For example, L1 is a whole note, L2 is a half note, L4 is a quarter note, and so on to L64.

The length of a single note can also be specified. Instead of the letter L being typed a number is simply placed immediately after the letter of the note to indicate its length. For example, A4B2 means a quarter note A and a half note B.

Pause (Rest). A pause, or rest, note is indicated with the letter P. P1 is a whole note rest, P2 is a half note rest, and so on. A dot, or period, after a note causes the note to be played as a dotted note. That is, its length is multiplied by 3/2. For an example, see Figure 17–18.

Tempo. The speed at which the music is played is the tempo. Setting tempo is much like setting length. The user sets the number of quarter notes per minute, between 32 and 255. For example, the command T60 sets the tempo at 60 quarter notes per minute. That tempo will remain until another T command is given.

Style. The IBM PC allows three styles of music to be played: staccato, legato, and normal. *Staccato* is indicated by the characters MS; each note plays three-quarters of the time specified by the L (length) parameter. *Legato* is indicated by the characters ML; each note plays seven-eighths of the time specified by the L parameter. *Normal* is indicated by the characters MN; each note plays the full period set by the L parameter. As with the other settings, the style chosen will remain in effect until the user changes it.

Repeat String. Almost all musical compositions have a section that is repeated. Instead of recoding the same piece of music each time it is to be played, the IBM PC has a special way of handling repetitions. First, the user must assign to a string variable the string of coded music to be repeated:

```
100 LET M$ = "L4CEL2G"
```

Figure 17–17 OCTAVES 1 THROUGH 4

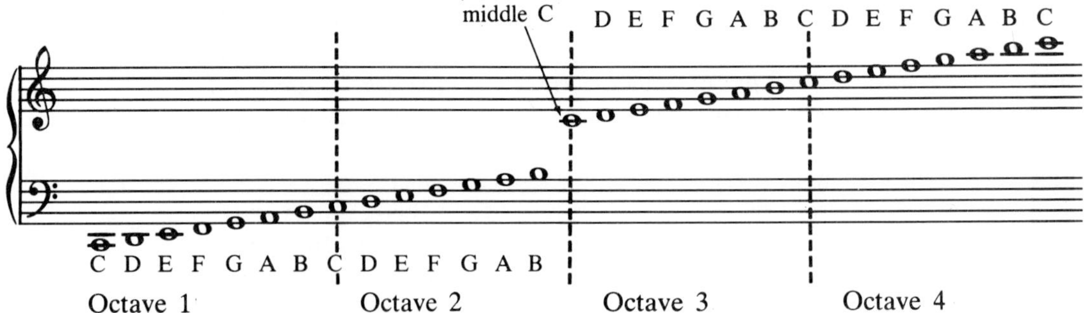

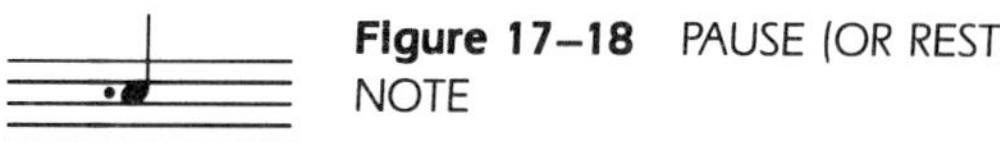

Figure 17–18 PAUSE (OR REST) NOTE

Then, to include this string with the string in the PLAY command, the user types in the letter X followed by the variable name and a semicolon. Thus, if M$ is defined as indicated here, the following two statements are equivalent:

```
200 PLAY "O3L4CEL2GL4CEL2GL4GFED"
200 PLAY "O3XM$;XM$;L4GFED"
```

LEARNING CHECK

1. The three commands on the IBM PC that will produce sound are ________, ________, and ________.
2. The frequency and length of the tone cannot be changed with the ______ command.
3. Music can be programmed by using the ________ command.
4. If no octave is specified all notes come from the ________ octave.
5. A sharp is indicated by following a note with a ________ or a ________.

ANSWERS:

1. BEEP, SOUND, PLAY. 2. BEEP. 3. PLAY. 4. third. 5. number sign(#), plus sign(+).

SUMMARY POINTS

- The IBM PC and PCjr have three display modes: text, medium-resolution graphics, and high-resolution graphics.
- The SCREEN command is used to select the desired display mode.
- The text mode divides the screen into twenty-five rows and eighty columns.
- The LOCATE statement moves the cursor to a specified character position.
- The medium-resolution graphics mode divides the screen into 320 pixels across and 200 down.
- The medium-resolution graphics mode has sixteen possible background colors (0 through 15) and two palettes (0 through 1), each having three foreground colors (0 through 2).
- The PSET statement is used to illuminate a specified pixel.
- The PRESET statement returns a specified pixel to the background color.
- The LINE statement draws a straight line from one pixel to another.
- The high-resolution graphics mode divides the screen into 640 pixels across and 200 down.

- The high-resolution graphics mode has only two possible colors: white (1) and black (0).
- The CIRCLE statement will draw a circle of a specified radius, centered at a specified pixel.
- Sounds can be produced using the BEEP, SOUND, and PLAY commands.

REVIEW QUESTIONS

1. Write the statement that will position the cursor at Row 11 and Column 20.

2. Which display mode allows for the sharpest detail?

3. How many background colors are there in the medium-resolution graphics mode? What are their numbers?

4. Which command is used to program musical compositions?

5. Write the statement that will light up the pixel at Column 80 and Row 40 in the color green, assuming Palette 0 is active.

6. What single statement will draw a line from pixel 10,20 to pixel 40,80 in Color 1 of the active palette?

7. What single statement will draw a 50 × 40 rectangle whose top-left corner is at 2,30 and whose color is Color 2 of the active palette?

8. What statement will draw a circle of radius 60 with its center at 100,100, in Color 1?

SAMPLE PROGRAMS

1. The following program produces a graph of the function $f(x) = 199 - \sqrt{X}$. The high-resolution graphics mode will be used so the interval of the graph will be large. The x-axis must lie at the bottom of the screen, and the y-axis must lie on the left edge. Therefore, the dimensions of the graph will be 99 × 200. Also, because the behavior of the graph in the first quadrant is to be plotted, the *Y*-values will be determined by the formula Y = 199 − SQR(X).

```
10 REM *** PROGRAM PLOTTER ***
20 KEY OFF
30 CLS
40 SCREEN 2
50 REM *** DRAW X-AXIS AT THE BOTTOM OF THE SCREEN ***
60 LINE (0,199)-(600,199),1
70 REM *** DRAW Y-AXIS AT LEFT EDGE OF THE SCREEN ***
80 LINE (0,199)-(0,0),1
90 REM *** PLOT POINTS OF FUNCTION F(X) = X - 1
100 FOR X = 0 TO 600
110     PSET(X,199-SQR(X)),1
120 NEXT X
998 GOTO 998
999 END
```

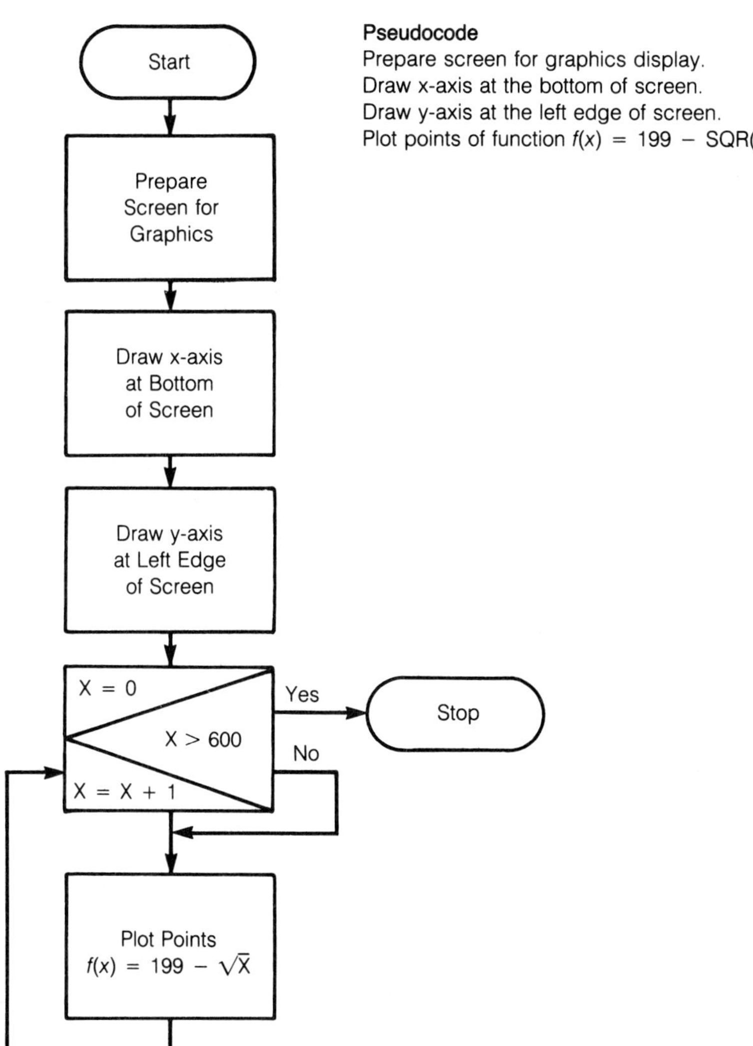

Pseudocode
Prepare screen for graphics display.
Draw x-axis at the bottom of screen.
Draw y-axis at the left edge of screen.
Plot points of function $f(x) = 199 - \text{SQR(X)}$.

2. Following is a program that creates a rectangle in the middle of the screen and then enlarges it to twice its original size. Notice how inside the FOR/NEXT loop the coordinates of the upper-left corner are decreased in value and the coordinates of the lower-right corner are increased. Lines 140 and 150 draw the rectangle at a certain size and then erase it so the next bigger rectangle can be drawn when the loop is reentered.

```
10 REM *** PROGRAM SIZE CHANGER ***
20 KEY OFF
30 CLS
40 SCREEN 2
50 REM *** BEGIN DRAWING SQUARES ***
60 LET X1 = 350
70 LET Y1 = 90
80 LET X2 = X1 + 30
90 LET Y2 = Y2 + 30
100 FOR X1 = X1 TO (X1-100) STEP -5
110     LET X2 = X2 + 5
120     LET Y1 = Y1 - 3
130     LET Y2 = Y2 + 3
140     LINE (X1,Y1)-(X2,Y2),1,B
145     LINE (X1,Y1)-(X2,Y2),0,B
150 NEXT X1
160 LINE (X1,Y1)-(X2,Y2),1,B
998 GOTO 998
999 END
```

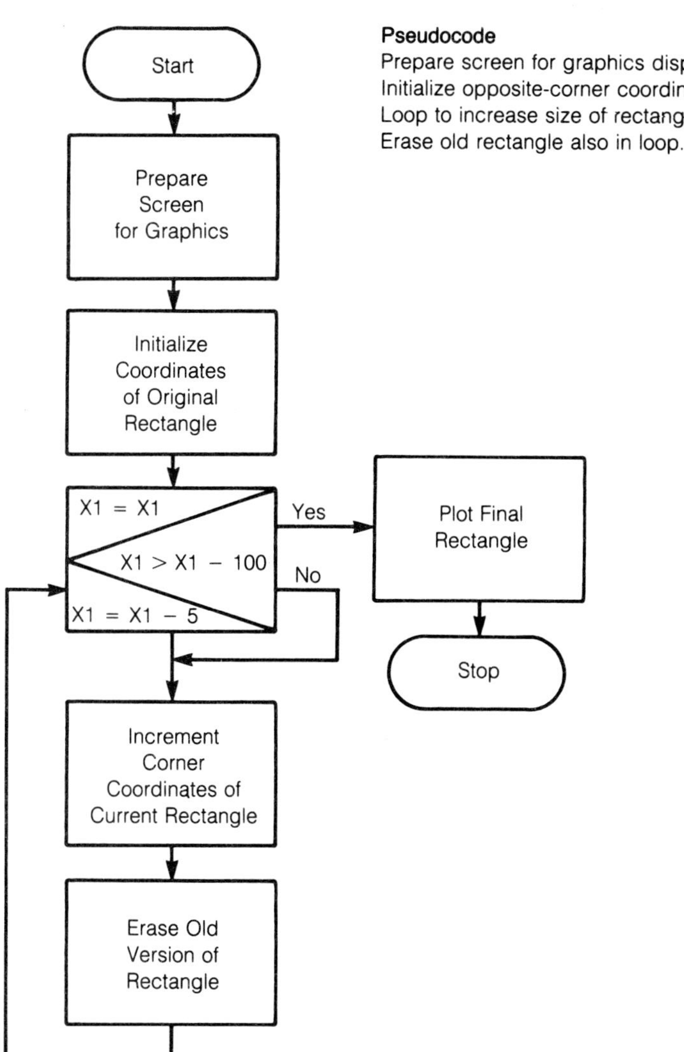

Pseudocode
Prepare screen for graphics display.
Initialize opposite-corner coordinates.
Loop to increase size of rectangle.
Erase old rectangle also in loop.

PROGRAMMING EXERCISES

1. Write small BASICA programs that produce the following graphics displays with the LINE statement:

a. A straight line that connects pixels 10,40 and 100,90.
b. A rectangle with corners at 30,50; 150,50; 150,100; 30,100.
c. A 50 × 100 black rectangle, whose upper-left corner is at pixel 100,20.
d. The rectangle described in part b, colored in with Color 2.
e. On a blue screen, the rectangle described in part c, filled in with the color green.

2. Write small BASICA programs that produce the following graphics displays with the CIRCLE statement:

a. A circle with radius 64 and center at pixel 100,71.
b. A circle with radius 25 and center at pixel 100,100 in Color 1.

3. Write a small BASICA program that causes the computer to do the following:

a. BEEP twenty-five times with a pause between each beep.
b. Allow the user to enter a certain frequency parameter and hear the resulting sound for one second.
c. Use the PLAY command to program the following four measures of Beethoven's Ninth Symphony:

GLOSSARY

Abacus One of the earliest known calculating devices on which rows of beads on wires are used to perform mathematical operations.
Access mechanism The device that positions the read/write head of a direct-access storage device over a particular track.
Accumulator A register that gathers results of computations.
Address register A register that holds the address of a location containing a data item called for by an instruction.
Aiken, Howard Harvard University professor who designed the Mark I, the first automatic calculator.
American Standard Code for Information Interchange (ASCII) A standard seven-bit binary code used for information interchange among data processing systems, and associated equipment.
Analog computer A computer that measures continuous physical or electrical conditions.
Analytical engine An invention by Charles Babbage that incorporated several ideas used in computers today such as memory and punched cards.
Analytical graphics Charts and graphics used for financial analysis and other types of numerical comparison.
APL A Programming Language; a terminal-oriented, symbolic programming language especially suitable for interactive problem-solving; can be used in execution or definition modes.
Application program A sequence of instructions written to solve a specific problem.
Arithmetic/Logic Unit (ALU) The section of the CPU that performs mathematical computations and logic operations.
Array An ordered set of data items, such as a table.
Artificial Intelligence (AI) The ability of computers to reason and think like humans; an area of study that seeks to develop techniques to use computers to solve problems that appear to require imagination, intuition, or intelligence.
Assembler program A language translator program used to convert assembly language into machine language.
Assembly language A symbolic programming language that uses convenient abbreviations (mnemonics) rather than groupings of 0s and 1s; intermediate-level language in terms of user orientation.
Automatic calculator A device that used electromagnetic relays and mechanical counters to handle numbers.
Automatic pagination Enables the word processor to automatically number the pages of the printed copy.
Auxiliary storage Storage outside the computer; also known as external or secondary storage; it supplements primary storage but operates at slower speeds.

Babbage, Charles The father of computers; designed the difference engine and the analytical engine.
Bar graph A graph that uses horizontal or vertical bars to visually represent values.
Bar-code reader A device that reads a bar code by means of reflected light, such as a scanner that reads the Universal Product Code on supermarket products.
BASIC Beginner's All-Purpose Symbolic Instruction Code; a programming language commonly used for interactive problem solving, often used by people who are not professional programmers.
Batch processing Processing in which an entire program is executed at once, with no interruption; all instructions and data are submitted at one time.
Binary digit See Bit.
Binary number system The number system that uses the digits 1 and 0 and has a base of 2.
Binary representation The use of binary numbers to represent data.

Biochips Minute computer chips assembled from organic molecules or genetically engineered proteins.
Bit Short for BInary digiT; a digit position in a binary number; the smallest unit of information that can be represented by binary notation.
Bit cells Storage locations in semiconductors.
Block movement A word-processing feature that allows the user to define a block of text and then perform a specific operation on the entire block. Common block operations include block move, block copy, block save, and block delete.
Branch Program logic pattern that allows the computer to bypass (branch around) instructions and, therefore, alter the normal flow of execution.
Bubble memory A recently developed memory device in which data is represented by magnetized spots (or bubbles) that rest on a thin film of semiconductor material.
Byte A string of bits that represents one character.

Cartridge tape A mass storage medium that uses high-density tapes.
Cell A storage location within a spreadsheet.
Central Processing Unit (CPU) The "brain" of the computer; it interprets and executes instructions and communicates with input/output devices and storage devices; composed of three sections—arithmetic/logic unit (ALU), control unit and often the primary storage unit.
Chain printer A line-at-a-time impact printer with its character set assembled on a chain that moves horizontally past all print positions; it prints when a print hammer (one for each column of the paper) presses the paper against an inked ribbon that in turn presses against the appropriate characters on the aligned print chain.
Character A letter, number, or symbol.
Character enhancement Underlining, boldfacing, subscripting, and superscripting.
Check digit An additional bit determined by performance of some calculation on the code; used to catch input errors.
COBOL COmmon Business-Oriented Language; a business programming language.
Coding The process of expressing a problem solution in a programming language.
Compiler A language translator program used for high-level languages, such as FORTRAN or COBOL; translates source-program statements into machine-executable code.
Computer A general-purpose machine with applications limited by the creativity of the humans who use it; its capabilities are derived from its memory and the speed and accuracy with which it can process data.
Computer literacy Knowledge of how to use computers and understanding of their societal implications.
Computer Output Microfilm (COM) Miniature photographic images of output produced on microfilm rather than on paper.
Computer-Aided Design (CAD) The use of the computer to help design, draft, and analyze a product; uses computer graphics on a video terminal.
Computer-Aided Manufacturing (CAM) The use of the computer to simulate the steps in the manufacturing process.
Computer-Assisted Instruction (CAI) Direct interaction between a student and computer acting as instructor.
Computer-assisted diagnosis Use of computers to evaluate medical data to show variations from normal.
Conditional transfer statement A statement that transfers program control only if a specified condition is true.
Connect time The actual time a customer is using a commercial data base.
Control character A coded character that does not print but is part of the command sequence in a word processor.
Control program A set of instructions usually part of an operating system, that helps control the operations and management of a computer system.
Control unit The section of the CPU that directs the sequence of operations by electrical signals and governs the actions of the various units that make up the computer.
Coordinate The location of a cell within a spreadsheet.
Coordinates On a graphics display screen the intersection of a row and a column; also the location of a cell within an electronic spreadsheet.
Counter A value used to control how many times a loop will be executed.
Cursor The marker on the display screen indicating where the next character can be displayed.

Daisy wheel printer A character-at-a-time impact printer with removable daisy wheels (print wheels); produces letter-quality type.
Data Raw, unorganized facts.
Data base A grouping of independent files into one integrated whole that can be accessed through one central point; a data base is designed to meet the information needs of a wide variety of users within an organization.
Data base package A data management software package that consolidates data files into an integrated whole, allowing access to more than one data file at a time.
Data communications The electronic transmission of data from one location to another.
Debugging The process of removing any type of error or malfunction from a computer's hardware or software.
Decrement Decrease a value. Generally used when referring to loop variables.
Dedicated computer A computer that has a specific function determined by its hardware.
Dedicated system Computers equipped to handle only one function, such as word processing.

Default settings Values used by an application when not instructed to use any other.
Deletion A word-processing feature in which a character, word, sentence, or larger block of text may be removed from the existing text.
Difference engine A machine developed by Charles Babbage in 1822 to compute logarithm tables.
Digital computer The type of computer that operates on binary digits and relies on counting for its operations; commonly used in business and education applications.
Direct access Retrieval in which stored data can be found in any order, at random; common of magnetic disks.
Direct mode The communication mode in which commands are executed as soon as they are entered.
Disk drive Machine used to rotate magnetic disks during data transmission.
Disk Operating System (DOS) A portion of the operating system that resides on disk and manages disk operations and input/output to peripheral devices not controlled by the OS.
Disk pack A stack of magnetic disks mounted on a center shaft.
Distributed processing A system in which several microcomputers are linked together by cables to form a network. The data processing resources are located at various geographical locations to permit faster response to the users.
Document-oriented work processor Word processor that operates on a text file as one long document.
Dot graph A graph that uses points to visually represent values.
Dot matrix printer A character-at-a-time printer that consists of a metal cylinder with rows of characters engraved across its surface; one line of print is produced with each rotation of the drum.
Double-precision variable A variable used to represent a number with a decimal point and eight or more digits.
Downtime The time when a computer is not working.
Drum printer A line-at-a-time printer that consists of a metal cylinder with rows of characters engraved across its surface; one line of print is produced with each rotation of the drum.
Dummy value A value used to indicate to the computer that the end of the data has been reached.

EDVAC Electronic Discrete Variable Automatic Computer; an early-stored-program computer; performed arithmetic and logic operations without human intervention by using stored programs.
Electronic bulletin board A type of remote network run by other microcomputer users; can be accessed by using a telecommunications system.
Electronic Data Processing (EDP) Data processing performed by electronic devices such as computers rather than by manual or mechanical means.
Electronic mail Messages sent at high speed by telecommunication facilities and placed in a special computer storage area where they can be read.
Electronic spreadsheet A large computerized grid divided into rows and columns; uses computer storage and computational capabilities for financial analysis.
Electrostatic printer A nonimpact printer that forms an image of a character on special paper using a dot matrix of charged wires or pins. When the paper is moved through a solution containing ink particles of an opposite charge from the pattern, the particles of ink adhere to each charged pattern on the paper.
Electrothermal printer A nonimpact printer that uses heat in the print element to create characters on heat-sensitive paper.
ENIAC Electronic Numerical Integrator and Calculator; the first electronic computer put to large-scale practical use.
Erasable Programmable Read-Only Memory (EPROM) Memory that can be erased and reprogrammed when submitted to a special process.
Execution The computer's carrying out of the instructions in a program.
Expert system Simulation and/or modeling computer systems that use the same information a human expert would to make decisions.
Exponential notation The representation of a real number in base 10.
Extended Binary Coded Decimal Interchange Code (EBCDIC) An eight-bit binary code used to represent numbers and characters.
External storage See Auxiliary storage.

Field A meaningful item of data.
File A collection of related records.
File handler A data management software package designed to access only one data file at a time.
Firmware Software programs put in hardware form.
First-generation computers Computers developed in the period 1951–1958; used vacuum tubes; faster than earlier mechanical devices, but very slow compared to today's computer.
Floppy disk Also called diskette or flexible disk; low-cost, random access data storage device made of plastic.
Flowchart A graphic representation of the processing performed in a program; also called block diagram or logic diagram.
Footer A word-processing feature that allows a piece of text to be stored separately from the text and printed at the bottom of each page.
Foreground pixel Any pixel point that is not the same color as the background pixels.
Format See Initialize.
Formula A mathematical equation used in a spreadsheet.

FORTRAN FORmula TRANslator; a programming language used primarily in performing mathematical or scientific operations.

Four-bit Binary Coded Decimal (BCD) A four-bit binary digit computer code used to represent decimal numbers.

Fourth-generation computers Computers developed in the period 1971-present, the era of large-scale integrated circuits and microprocessors.

General-purpose register A register that can be used as an accumulator or an address register.

Global search and replace A word-processing feature that enables a search and replace operation to be carried out throughout the entire document without user intervention.

Graphic display device A special visual display terminal used to display graphic images.

Graphics dot A rectangle that appears on the screen at a specified coordinate.

Graphics set The complete set of graphics images available in a software package.

Graphics tablet A small tablet that is sensitive to pressure. When you press on the surface of the tablet, the position of that pressure is transmitted to the computer and the corresponding location on the display screen is illuminated; most graphics tablets permit only two-dimensional drawings.

Hard copy Printed output on paper, microfilm, or slides.

Hard wired Describes memory devices that cannot be changed or deleted by other stored-program instructions; programmed by the manufacturer.

Hardware The physical devices that make up a computer system.

Hardware diagnostic tools Programs that help identify problems with the computer hardware.

Header A piece of text to be stored separately from the text and printed at the top of each page.

Hierarchy of operations The order in which mathematical operations are performed.

High-level language English-like language coding scheme that is procedure-, problem-, and user-oriented.

Hollerith code A method of data representation of numbers, letters, and special characters by the placement of holes in eighty-column punched cards.

Hollerith, Herman An American who designed a machine to read data from punched cards; used the machine to process U.S. census data in 1890.

Impact printer A printer that physically presses the print elements together with the ribbon and paper to make the impression.

Increment Increase a value. Generally used when referring to loop variables.

Incremental spacing A method in which the printer inserts spaces between words and letters to produce justified margins; also called microspacing.

Indirect mode The communication mode in which program statements are stored in main memory and not executed until the RUN command is given.

Infinite loop A loop that never stops executing.

Information Data that has been processed so that it is meaningful.

Initialize (or **format**) Prepare a disk so that programs can be saved on it.

Ink jet printer A nonimpact printer that uses a stream of charged ink to form characters.

Input Data submitted to the computer for processing.

Insertion A word-processing feature in which a character, word, sentence, or larger block of text is added to the existing text.

Instruction register A register where each instruction is stored until decoded by the control unit.

Instruction set The basic set of instructions built into a computer that tells it what to do.

Integer A number with no decimal portion, a whole number such as 104.

Integer variable A variable used to represent a whole number between −32768 and +32768 and having no decimal point.

Integrated circuits Electronic circuits etched on a small silicon chip less than one-eighth-inch square; permits much faster processing than with transistors at a greatly reduced price.

Intelligent terminal A terminal that can be programmed to perform functions such as editing of data, data conversion, and controlling of other terminals.

Interactive program A program that allows the user to enter data during execution.

Internal storage See Primary storage unit.

Interpreter A language translator program used to translate the source program into machine language—one instruction at a time.

Jacquard, Joseph A Frenchman who used punched cards to alter weaving loom settings without human intervention.

Joystick A piece of equipment to control the cursor or object movement on the CRT screen.

Justification A feature for making lines of text even at the margins.

Key-to-disk system Several keying devices connected to a minicomputer and a disk drive.

Key-to-diskette system A keyboard display screen and a flexible disk drive.

Label Information used for describing some aspect of a spreadsheet.

Language translator program A program that translates programs written in English-like programming languages into machine language instructions of 0s and 1s.

Large-Scale Integration (LSI) The process of packing thousands of electronic circuits onto a single silicon chip.

Laser printer A type of nonimpact printer that combines laser beams and electrophotographic technology to form images on paper.

Leibnitz, Gottfried von A German mathematician who developed a device that added, subtracted, multiplied, divided and calculated square roots.

Librarian program Software that maintains a directory of programs in auxiliary storage and contains appropriate procedures for additions or deletions.

Light pen A stylus that is connected to the computer by a wire; it tells the computer the x,y coordinates of the spot on the visual display screen where the pen is pointing (x being the horizontal axis and y being the vertical axis). It is most often used to create graphics and to point to menu options.

Line editor The type of editor that allows the user to edit only one line at a time.

Line number Number at the beginning of a line that is used to show the order in which program lines are stored in main memory.

Local Area Network (LAN) A system that links microcomputers in adjacent offices and buildings for intercompany communication.

Logic error An error caused by an incorrect solution to a programming problem; often this is caused by a step being left out or misplaced. Also known as a bug.

Logo An educational, problem-oriented programming language that is easy for children to learn yet is powerful enough to be used for complicated programming tasks.

Loop A program logic pattern in which the computer repeatedly executes a series of instructions as long as specified conditions are met.

Looping Executing a part of a program as many times as needed.

Machine language A language based on 0s and 1s that is the only set of instructions a computer can execute directly.

Machine-oriented language A program language that achieves maximum efficiency and speed in the computer; examples are machine language and assembly language.

Magnetic core A type of computer memory; doughnut-shaped rings strung on wires and magnetized to represent either an "on" or "off" condition when electrical current is passed through the wires.

Magnetic disk A storage medium consisting of a platter made of metal or flexible plastic and coated with a magnetic recording material upon which data is stored in the form of magnetized spots.

Magnetic drum A cylinder with a magnetic outer surface on which data can be stored by the magnetizing of specific positions.

Magnetic tape A storage medium consisting of a narrow strip of material upon which spots are magnetized to represent data.

Magnetic-Ink Character Recognition (MICR) A process that allows magnetized characters to be read by a magnetic-ink character reader.

Mainframe A large central computer system; mainframes are very sophisticated and are used in many applications. Also, the central processing unit (CPU) of a computer system.

Management Information System (MIS) A system that extends computer use beyond routine reporting into the area of management decision making.

Mantissa The decimal part of a number written in exponential notation.

Mark I The first automatic calculator; used electromagnetic relays and mechanical counters instead of mechanical gears to perform arithmetic operations.

Mass storage device A device that allows relatively fast access to large amounts of data at a low cost.

Mechanical calculator A calculator in which the numbers are manipulated through a series of gears.

Memory The part of the computer that provides the ability to store data.

Memory-only word processor Word processor that cannot exchange text between internal memory and disk during the editing process.

Menu-driven A program that provides the user with "menus" listing options that can be selected.

Merging Combining two arrays into one, usually in a particular order.

Microcomputer A very small, low-priced computer popularly used in homes, schools, and businesses; sometimes a single-function computer.

Microprocessor The central processing unit of a microcomputer; fits on a small silicon chip.

Microprogram A sequence of instructions wired into read-only memory; used to tailor a system to meet the user's processing requirements.

Microspacing See Incremental spacing.

Minicomputer A computer with the components of a full-size system but with a smaller memory; the second smallest type of computer.

Mnemonics Symbolic names (memory aids); used to represent machine operations in symbolic languages such as assembly language and high-level programming languages.

Model A numeric representation of a real-world situation.

Modeling Computer construction of models, or prototypes, on the viedeo screen.

Modem An inexpensive piece of electronic equipment that lets the computer use telephone lines to send information to other computers and receive information from them.
Mouse A desk-top input device that controls cursor movement, allowing the user to bypass the keyboard; must be used with special software.
Multiple conditional transfer statement A statement that allows for program control to transfer to various specified lines.

Nanosecond One-billionth of a second.
Nested loop A loop that is situated inside another loop.
Nonimpact printer A printer that uses heat, laser technology, or photographic techniques to make impressions; the print element never touches the paper.
Numeric variable A variable used to represent a number.

Object program A sequence of machine executable instructions converted from source-program statements by a language-translator program.
Office automation The integration of computer and communication technology with traditional manual procedures in the office.
On-line processing Processing that allows the user to interact with the computer during program execution; permits direct communication between the user and the computer.
On-line service A company that sells access to information in its data bases and other services to computer users over a communication network.
One-dimensional array An array that has only one column.
Online In direct communication with the computer.
Operating system A collection of programs designed to permit a computer system to manage itself.
Optical-Character Recognition (OCR) A capability of devices with scanners to read numbers, letters, and other characters and convert the optical images into appropriate electrical signals for a computer.
Optical-Mark Recognition (OMR) A capability of devices with a scanner to convert marks on a page into computer data by reading the position of the marks; also known as mark sensing.
Output The information that comes from the computer as a result of processing.
Overstrike To type directly over an existing character, replacing it with a new character.

Page-oriented word processor Word processor that operates on a text file as a series of pages.
Parity bit A bit used to detect incorrect transmission of data; it conducts internal checks to determine whether the correct number of bits are present.
Pascal A programming language named after French mathematician Blaise Pascal; developed to teach programming techniques to students; it is rapidly expanding its original intentions because it is powerful and highly structured; used for batch and interactive processing.
Pascal, Blaise A French mathematician credited with developing the first mechanical calculator in 1642.
Peripherals Auxiliary computer equipment such as printers, disk drives, and storage devices.
PILOT Programmed Inquiry, Learning, Or Teaching; an easy-to-learn problem-oriented programming language used mostly for designing computer-aided instruction (CAI) programs.
Pixel The smallest graphic point addressable by a computer; pixels are turned on or off to form the characters and graphic images on a computer screen.
PL/1 Programming Language One; a general-purpose programming language used in both business and scientific applications.
Plotter A special printer used to print graphic images such as charts, graphs, and pictures.
Point-Of-Sale (POS) terminal A terminal that serves as a cash register but can also send sales and inventory data to a central computer.
Primary storage unit The section of the CPU or main computer that holds instructions, data, and intermediate and final results during processing; also known as internal storage, main memory or main storage.
Print formatting The function of a word processor that communicates with the printer to tell it how to print the text on paper.
Print preview A word-processing feature that allows the user to view a general representation on the screen of how the document will look when printed.
Print wheel printer A line-at-a-time impact printer that has one print wheel for each print position on a line; the print wheels rotate until an entire line is in the appropriate print position, then a hammer presses the paper against the print wheels.
Print zones Vertical zones into which the print or display area is divided.
Printer-keyboard An impact printer similar to an office typewriter but instructions for printing come from the CPU; a keyboard allows the user to communicate with the system.
Problem-oriented language A programming language designed to solve specific kinds of problems allowing the user to focus on desired results rather than the individual steps needed to get those results; RPG is an example of this type of language.
Procedure-oriented language A programming language designed to solve processing requirements with a minimal amount of programming effort.
Processing The producing of output or information from

the input or data; can include the steps of classifying, sorting, calculating, summarizing, and storing.
Processing program A routine, usually part of the operating system, used to simplify program preparation and execution.
Program A series of step-by-step instructions that provides a problem solution and tells the computer exactly what to do.
Programmable Read-Only Memory (PROM) Read-only memory that can be programmed by the manufacturer or the user to meet the user's unique needs; once programmed, it maintains the same characteristics as ROM.
Programmer The person who writes the step-by-step instructions that tell the computer what to do.
Prompt A statement that tells the user that data should be entered at this point.
Proper program A program using the structured programming approach, with only one entrance and one exit.
Pseudocode A brief set of instructions written in sentence form, in the same sequence as the program statements.

Random-Access Memory (RAM) Memory that stores programs or data and can be written to or read from very quickly.
Read-Only Memory (ROM) Memory containing items that cannot be deleted or changed by stored-program instructions because they are "hard-wired" into the circuitry.
Real number A number with a decimal portion.
Real-time system A system that receives data, processes it, and provides output immediately.
Record A collection of data items, or fields, that relates to a single unit.
Register An internal computer component used for temporary storage of an instruction or data; can accept, hold, and transfer instructions or data very quickly.
Relational symbol A symbol used to compare one value or variable with another.
Remote terminal A terminal that is placed at a location distant from the central computer.
Resolution The number of pixels on the display screen. These determine the clarity of the image; the more pixels on a screen the higher the resolution, or quality, of the image.
Robotics The science dealing with the construction, capabilities, and applications of robots.
RPG Report Program Generator; a problem-oriented programming language designed to produce business reports; requires little programming skills.

Scaling factor A method of showing an entire graph on the display screen that otherwise would be too large to display.
Screen editor The type of editor that allows the user to edit an entire screen at a time.
Screen formatting A function of a word processor that controls how the text will appear on the screen.
Scrolling Moving a line or lines of text onto or off the screen.
Search and find A word-processing feature that searches for, and places the cursor at, a specific string of characters.
Search and replace A word-processing feature that searches for a specified character string and replaces it with the specified replacement string.
Searching Locating a particular value; often used when attempting to find a given value in an array.
Second-generation computers Computers developed in the period 1959–1964; used transistors; smaller, faster, and had larger storage capacity than first-generation computers; first computers to use English-like programming languages.
Secondary storage See Auxiliary storage.
Selection A program logic pattern in which the computer makes a choice between two paths.
Semiconductor A transistor used as a type of primary storage medium; it stores data in bit cells located on silicon chips.
Sequential access Retrieval in which stored records must be read, one after another, in a fixed sequence, until the needed data is located; common of magnetic tapes.
Service bureau A computer facility that provides data processing services to users who do not have their own computer system.
Simple sequence A program logic pattern in which one statement, or instruction, after another is executed in the sequence in which it is stored.
Simulation When the computer duplicates the conditions likely to occur when certain variables are changed in a given situation; also computer graphics that create a model of an object on the display screen so changes can be made without building an actual model.
Single-precision variable A variable used to represent a number with a decimal point and seven or fewer digits.
Soft copy Output displayed on a CRT screen; not a permanent record, as hard copy is.
Software Programs used to direct the computer in solving problems and overseeing operations.
Sort To arrange data elements into some order to facilitate processing or printing.
Source program A sequence of instructions written by the programmer in either assembly language or a high-level language.
Source-data automation The process that allows data to be collected in computer-readable form at the source or collection point of that data.
Spatial digitizer An input device that can graphically reconstruct a three-dimensional object on the computer display screen.
Special effects commands Commands that affect the way in which output is displayed on the screen.

Spreadsheet A ledger or table used in a business environment for financial calculations and for the recording of transactions.
Spreadsheet analysis A mental process of evaluating information contained with an electronic spreadsheet; also called what-if analysis.
Spreadsheet program A set of computer instructions that generates and operates an electronic spreadsheet.
Status line A message line above or below the text area on a display screen that gives format and system information.
Storage register A register that holds information coming from or going to the primary storage unit.
Stored-program computer A computer that stores instructions in memory in electronic form in order to process data at its own speed without human intervention.
Stored-program concept The idea of storing instructions in computer memory in electronic form so the computer can process data at its own speed without human intervention.
String variable A variable used to represent one or more characters.
Structured programming A top-down modular approach to programming that emphasizes dividing a program into logical sections in order to reduce testing time, increase programmer productivity, and bring clarity to programming.
Subscript A value used to indicate the position of a data item in an array.
Subscripted variables Variable names that include a subscript.
Supercomputer Also called a maxicomputer; the fastest, most powerful computer system available; performs at least 10 million instructions per second.
Superscript A character that prints above the usual text baseline.
Supervisor program Also called a monitor or an executive; the major part of the operating system, it coordinates the activities of the system's other parts.
Symbolic languages Languages that use symbols to represent instructions; must be translated into machine language before being executed by the computer.
Syntax The rules of computer grammar that must be followed in writing program instructions
Syntax errors Errors that violate the rules of a programming language.
System analysis A detailed, step-by-step investigation of a system aimed at determining what must be done and how best to do it.
System analyst A specialist who evaluates the goals, priorities, organization, and needs of a business to develop an efficient method for conducting operations.
System program A sequence of instructions written to coordinate the operation of computer circuitry and to help the computer run quickly and efficiently.
System residence device An auxiliary storage device (disk, tape, or drum) in which operating system programs are stored and from which they are loaded into main storage.

Tape cassette A sequential storage medium using high-density digital recording tape to record data in small computer systems.
Tape drive A device used to read from or write to magnetic tape.
Telecommunications The combined use of communications facilities, such as telephone lines, and a computer.
Telecommuting A way to use computer hookups between offices and homes to allow employees to work at home.
Teleconferencing A way to hold cross-country conferences by image-producing means.
Terminal A device through which data can exit or enter a computer.
Terminal value The value that is used to signify the end of a loop when reached by a loop.
Text buffer An area set aside in memory to temporarily hold text.
Text editing The function of a word processor that allows the user to enter and edit text.
Text window The four lines at the bottom of a graphics screen that can be used for text.
Third-generation computer Computers developed in the period 1965–1971; featured integrated circuits, reduced size, lower costs, and increased speed and reliability.
Time-sharing company A computer facility that rents computer time to users who have purchased input/output devices, which they link to the computer with some type of communication lines.
Touch screen A computer screen that can detect the point at which it is touched by the user; it allows the user to bypass the keyboard.
Touch-tone terminal A remote terminal that uses telephone lines to pass data from a special keyboard to the computer.
Track One of a series of concentric circles on the surface of a magnetic disk.
Transistor A type of electronic circuitry that controls current flow without the use of a vacuum; smaller, faster, and more reliable than vacuum tubes.
Two-dimensional array An array with both rows and columns.

Unconditional transfer statement A statement that always transfers control to another part of the program.
UNIVAC I UNIVersal Automatic Computer; the first commercial electronic computer; became available in 1951.
Universal Product Code (UPC) A code that uses ten pairs of vertical bars to represent the identities of the manufacturer and the item; commonly used on most grocery items.

Update To alter a data field within a record to reflect accurate information.
User-friendly Describes software or hardware that is easy for people to use and understand.
Utility program A subsystem of the operating system that can perform specialized, repeatedly used functions such as sorting, merging, and transferring data from one input/output device to another.

Value A single piece of numeric information used in the calculations of a spreadsheet.
Variable A symbolic name to which a value may be assigned.
Very-Large-Scale Integration (VLSI) Integrated circuits on a silicon chip, packed even more densely than with LSI.
Virtual representation An approach to screen formatting that allows the user to see on screen exactly how the printed output will look.
Visual display terminal A television-like screen used to display soft-copy output; sometimes called a CRT (cathode ray tube).
Voice mail Messages spoken into a telephone, converted into digital form, stored in memory until recalled, and then reconverted into voice form.
Voice-recognition system A system in which the user can "train" the computer to understand his or her voice and vocabulary. The user must follow only the patterns the computer is programmed to recognize.

Window The portion of an electronic spreadsheet that can be seen on the computer display screen.
Word processing The act of composing and manipulating text.
Word processor A program or set of programs designed to allow you to enter, manipulate, format, print, store, and retrieve text.
Word-processing system A system that allows text material to be entered, corrected, added or deleted, and printed.
Word wrap The word-processing feature in which a word is automatically moved to the beginning of the next line if it goes past the right margin.

Xerographic printer A nonimpact printer that uses printing methods similar to those used in common xerographic copying machines.

INDEX

puter, Inc., **Fig. 4–9** Courtesy of Sperry Corporation, **Fig. 4–10** Courtesy of International Business Machines Corporation, **Fig. 4–11** Courtesy of Cray Research, Inc., **Fig. 4–12** Courtesy of Nestar Systems, **Fig. 5–1** Courtesy of Tomy Corporation, and Courtesy of Atari Incorporated, **Fig. 5–2** Courtesy of Zenith Data Systems, **Fig. 5–3** Courtesy of AT&T Bell Laboratories, **Fig. 5–4** Courtesy of Mouse Systems Corporation, **Fig. 5–5** Photo courtesy of RB Robot Corporation, Golden, Colorado, **Fig. 5–6** Phot courtesy of Strand Century, **Fig. 5–7** Courtesy of New England Digital Corporation, **Fig. 5–8** Courtesy of Executive Producer—Robert Abel; Director/Designer—Randy Roberts; Technical Director—Ann Kerbel/Michael Wahrman; Technical Supervisor—Bill Kovacs; Editor—Rick Ross, **Fig. 5–9** Courtesy of Hewlett-Packard Company, **Fig. 5–11** Courtesy of the New York Yankees, **Fig. 5–12** Courtesy of MGM/UA and CompuPro, **Fig. 5–13** Photo courtesy of CPT Corporation, **Fig. 5–14** Courtesy of AT&T Bell Laboratories, **Fig. 5–15** Courtesy of Digital Equipment Corporation, **Fig. 5–16** Courtesy of The Source, a subsidiary of The Reader's Digest Assn., Inc., **Fig. 5–17** Courtesy of Optronics International, Inc., **Fig. 5–18** Photo courtesy of Form & Substance, Inc., **Fig. 5–19** Courtesy of The Mt. Sinai Medical Center, Cleveland, Ohio, **Fig. 5–20** Courtesy of The University of Utah, **Fig. 5–21** Courtesy of Hewlett-Packard Company, and Courtesy of Polaroid Corporation, **Fig. 5–22** Courtesy of Chrysler Corporation, **Fig. 5–23** Courtesy of Cincinnati Milacron, **Fig. 5–24** U.S. Army Photo by Sp4 Fred Sutter, **Fig. 5–25** Courtesy of International Business Machines Corporation, **Fig. 6–1** Courtesy of Federal Bureau of Investigation, **Fig. 6–2** Courtesy of International Business Machines Corporation, Fig. 9–3 Courtesy of MINDSET Corporation, Courtesy of Matt Rothan, Columbus College of Art & Design, Computer Graphics, and Courtesy of Evan & Sutherland Computer Corporation.